Education for Rural Development

edited by
Manzoor Ahmed
Philip H. Coombs

Prepared by the International Council
for Educational Development under
Sponsorship of the World Bank and
the United Nations Children's Fund

The Praeger Special Studies program—
utilizing the most modern and efficient book
production techniques and a selective
worldwide distribution network—makes
available to the academic, government, and
business communities significant, timely
research in U.S. and international economic, social, and political development.

Education for Rural Development

Case Studies for Planners

PRAEGER SPECIAL STUDIES IN INTERNATIONAL POLITICS AND GOVERNMENT

Praeger Publishers New York London

Library of Congress Cataloging in Publication Data

Main entry under title:

Education for rural development.

    (Praeger special studies in international economics
and development)
    Includes index.
    1. Education, Rural—Case studies. 2. Under-
developed areas—Education—Case studies. I. Ahmed,
Manzoor, 1940-   II. Coombs, Philip Hall, 1915-
III. International Council for Educational Development.
LC5146.E388   370.19'346   75-944
ISBN 0-275-07380-7

PRAEGER PUBLISHERS
200 Park Avenue, New York, N.Y. 10017, U.S.A.

Published in the United States of America in 1975
by Praeger Publishers, Inc.

789   038   98765432

Printed in the United States of America

The seventeen case studies included in this volume
provided the central core of empirical evidence for two
international analytical studies of education for rural
development commissioned by the World Bank and the United
Nations Children's Fund (UNICEF) and carried out by the
International Council for Educational Development (ICED)
between 1971 and 1974.

The UNICEF-sponsored study focused on the basic
learning needs of rural children and youth, and on ways
of improving the environment and upbringing of vulnerable
infants and young children through the education of their
elders. The study sponsored by the World Bank, using a
similar conceptual and analytical framework, focused on
the learning needs of a generally older rural clientele--
mainly small farmers, rural artisans and craftsmen, and
small entrepreneurs--and on educational means for improving
their economic productivity and employment possibilities.
Both studies paid particular attention to the poorest
categories of rural families and rural areas.

The findings and recommendations of the above studies,
addressed to policymakers, planners, and other practi-
tioners, are contained in three ICED reports: 1) New Paths
to Learning for Rural Children and Youth, a first report
to UNICEF, published by ICED (1973); 2) Attacking Rural
Poverty: How Nonformal Education Can Help, ICED's final
report to the World Bank, published for the Bank by Johns
Hopkins University Press, Baltimore, Maryland (1974); and
3) New Educational Strategies to Serve Rural Children and
Youth, a final report to UNICEF (forthcoming 1975).

Roughly half of the case studies were prepared by
well-qualified analysts in the countries concerned; the
others were prepared by ICED staff members with the close
involvement of individuals and institutions in the
countries. The principal authors and contributors are
listed at the end of this Preface. To them we especially
want to express ICED's warm gratitude. We also ask their
forgiveness if our editorial pencils seem at times to have
been unduly harsh, but we were obliged by limitations of
space to reduce some of the original manuscripts by half
or more.

Many other individuals and organizations also made
valuable contributions to these case studies and to the
three general reports listed above. Unfortunately there
is not space here to thank each one by name, but a few
exceptions must be made.

ICED is most grateful to the World Bank and UNICEF
for providing the rewarding opportunity to conduct these

v

studies. These sponsoring organizations not only gave
the main impetus and financial support for the studies
but their staffs made important substantive and intellectual contributions. Our gratitude extends also to the
Ford Foundation, a silent partner whose general financial
support to ICED was drawn upon to broaden and deepen the
two overall studies, including enlarging the number of
case studies, and whose experienced staff members were a
rich source of useful information and ideas.

While the support of the above three organizations
was indispensable, it should be made clear that they hold
no responsibility for--and do not necessarily concur in--
what is said in this publication. That responsibility
rests solely with the ICED, the editors, and the individual authors.

We also want to thank the other international and
bilateral organizations that cooperated in the ICED
studies, in particular the United Nations Educational,
Scientific and Cultural Organization (UNESCO) and its
affiliate the International Institute for Educational
Planning (IIEP), the International Labour Office (ILO),
the Food and Agricultural Organization (FAO), the World
Health Organization (WHO), the United Nations Development
Program (UNDP), and the bilateral aid agencies of France,
Sweden, the United Kingdom and the United States. Officials and experts of these organizations helped ICED in a
variety of ways: by identifying noteworthy programs and
giving other useful leads, by providing documentation and
expert counsel, by reviewing draft reports and making
useful criticisms and suggestions, and in the case of ILO
and FAO, by releasing personnel to work temporarily with
ICED.

In addition to those listed as the authors and the
major contributors, our special thanks go to the following individuals and institutions for their help on
particular case studies in this volume: Monseñor José
Joaquín Salcedo, Director General, and Dr. Hernando Bernal-
Alarcón, Director of Planning, of Acción Cultural Popular
in Colombia; the Ministry of Education of Cuba; the
Ministry of Youth and Community Development and the Ministry
of Education of the Government of Jamaica; Sir Philip
Sherlock of Jamaica, Secretary General of the Association
of Caribbean Universities and Research Institutes; the
Ministry of National Education of Mali; the Marga Insti-
tute in Colombo, Sri Lanka; the Divisions of Adult Educa-
tion and Vocational Promotion of Thailand's Ministry of
Education; the Institut d'Étude du Développement
Économique et Social, University of Paris; the Project
Manager and staff of the Program on Agricultural Credit
and Cooperatives (PACCA) in Afghanistan; Drs. Gonzalo
Sánchez and Jaime Orozco of Colombia's National Appren-
ticeship Service (SENA); the Commissioner for Small-Scale
Industry, Government of India; the Central Educational
Research Institute of the Republic of Korea; the Rockefeller

Foundation and the Director and staff of the International
Rice Research Institute in Los Baños, the Philippines;
and the Commissioner of Cooperative Development, the
Secretary General of the Cooperative Union of Tanganyika,
and the Director and staff of the Cooperative College in
Tanzania.

To complete the record it should be noted that the
strictures of time and space prevented the final write-up
and inclusion here of five other case studies that figure
prominently in ICED's analytical reports. They are: a
study of the Chilalo Agricultural Development Unit (CADU)
in Ethiopia, by Sven Grabe; a study of rural training
centers in Senegal, by Sven Grabe and Pierre Furter
(Professor at the University of Geneva); a study of the
Comilla Project in Bangladesh, by Manzoor Ahmed; a study
of Plan Puebla in Mexico by Paul Martin and others; and
a study of rural nonformal education programs in the
state of Pernambuco in Northeast Brazil, by Francisco X.
Swett, assisted by Pierre Furter and several faculty
members of the Federal University of Pernambuco in Recife.
We are most grateful to the national authorities and to
the officials and experts of specific programs in the
above countries for their very generous and useful
assistance in carrying out these studies.

These acknowledgements would not be complete without
an expression of my personal appreciation to past and
present ICED colleagues whose hard work made this volume
possible. My co-editor and present deputy, Manzoor Ahmed
from Bangladesh, has been with ICED from the start of the
World Bank and UNICEF studies in 1971; he was principal
author of several of the case studies, a co-author of all
three general analytical reports, and has done the lion's
share of the work of preparing this volume for publication.
Sven Grabe could be with ICED for only one year (on leave
from his important post in ILO) as deputy director of the
World Bank study, but during that time his work was pro-
lific and he taught us much. Roy Prosser came to ICED
with a rich background of educational and rural development experience in East Africa and Jamaica; he served two
years as deputy director of the UNICEF study, had a major
hand in preparing several of the case studies and final
analytical reports, and recently joined the staff of the
World Bank. Barbara Baird Israel served as principal
editorial consultant on this volume; Ellen G. Helfer,
Suzanne Knox, and Fessenden Wilder assisted in the editing;
Ellen G. Helfer also prepared the index; and Debra S. Hyde
and Frances L. O'Dell patiently typed the numerous drafts
and the final "camera-ready" copy.

Philip H. Coombs
Vice Chairman and
January 1975   Director of Educational
Essex, Connecticut, USA   Strategy Studies, ICED

vii

Manzoor Ahmed is Associate Director of Educational Strategy Studies at ICED.

Stephan F. Brumberg, former ICED staff member, is now Assistant Professor of Education at Brooklyn College, City University of New York.

Philip H. Coombs is Vice Chairman and Director of Educational Strategy Studies at ICED.

Isabelle Deblé is a senior researcher at l'Institut d'Étude du Développement Économique et Social, University of Paris.

John C. de Wilde, now retired, served for many years as an economist for the World Bank.

Victor P. Diejomaoh is Lecturer in Economics at the University of Lagos, Nigeria.

Clifford Gilpin, a former ICED Research Intern, is on the staff of the Education Department of the World Bank.

Shirley Gordon is on the faculty of the University of the West Indies, Kingston, Jamaica, and a consultant to the Jamaican Ministry of Education.

Sven Grabe, heads the Studies and Reports Section, Vocational Training Branch, International Labour Office, Geneva.

B.E. Kipkorir is Professor of History at the University of Nairobi, Kenya.

Michel Lefèbvre and Yvonne Lefèbvre are staff members of l'Institut d'Étude du Développement Économique et Social.

Marvin Leiner is Associate Professor of Education at Queens College, City University of New York.

A.H. Lubis is on the faculty of the Teachers Training Institute (IKIP), Jombang, Indonesia.

Fakoney Ly is the Director of Literacy and Basic Education, Ministry of National Education, Bamako, Mali.

Hyun Ki Paik is former Director of the Central Educational Research Institute, Republic of Korea.

R.C. Prosser, a former ICED staff member, is now an educational expert on the World Bank's staff.

Lê Thi Nam Trân is a member of the staff of l'Institut d'Étude du Développement Économique et Social, University of Paris.

Kasama Varavarn, was on the staff of the Functional Literacy and Family Life Project, Bangkok, Thailand, and is currently a graduate student at Harvard University.

Kowit Vorapipatana is the Chief of the Division of Adult Education, Ministry of Education, Bangkok, Thailand.

G.H.F. Welikala, retired from government service, is now associated with the Marga Institute (Sri Lanka Centre for Development Studies), Colombo, Sri Lanka.

E.L. Wijemanne, is the Director of Education (Planning), Ministry of Education, Colombo, Sri Lanka.

S.J. Woodhouse served with UNICEF in Jakarta, Indonesia, and is presently with UNICEF in Rangoon, Burma.

CONTENTS

PART II: PROGRAMS FOR EMPLOYMENT-RELATED EDUCATION

LISTS OF TABLES AND FIGURES

xxi

ACPO	Acción Cultural Popular
ADC	Agricultural Development Corporation
ANIM	National Agency of Information of Mali
APC	(Philippine) Agricultural Productivity Commission
ARD	Accelerated Rural Development Program
ASK	Agricultural Society of Kenya
BATC	Business Apprenticeship Training Centre
BGDE	Body for Guidance and Development of Education
BLEO(I)	Block-level Extension Officer for Industries
BPP	Office of Educational Development
BSC	Behavioral Science Center
CAR	Centre d'Animation Rurale
CAST	College of Arts, Science and Technology
CCPA	Comités Culturel et de Plein Air
CCU	Correspondence Course Unit
CEC	Cooperative Education Centre
CERI	Central Education Research Institute
CFAF	Communauté Financière Africaine Francs
CFJA	Centre de Formation de Jeunes Agriculteurs
CIMMYT	International Center for Maize and Wheat Improvement
CNC	Consejo Nacional de Cultura
COMPAC	Comprehensive Rural Development Package Program
COP	Centre á Orientation Pratique
CPE	Certificate of Primary Education
CUSO	Canadian Universities Service Overseas
CUT	Cooperative Union of Tanganiyika
DEF	Diplome d'Études Fondamentales
EACE	East African Certificate of Education
EC	Extension Centre
FAO	Food and Agriculture Organization
FED	European Development Fund
FEEM	Federación de Estudiantes de la Enseñanza Media
GCE-A	General Certificate of Education, Advanced Level
GCE-O	General Certificate of Education, Ordinary Level
GIIC	Gujerat Industrial Investment Corporation
IBRD	International Bank for Reconstruction and Development
ICA	Instituto Colombiano Agropecuario

ICAIC	Instituto Cubano de Arte e Industria Cinematograficas
ICED	International Council for Educational Development
IDC	Industrial Development Centre
IEDES	L'Institut d'Étude du Développement Économique et Social
ILO	International Labour Office
INADES	Institut Africain pour le Développement Économique et Social
INAFLA	National Institute for Functional Literacy and Applied Linguistics
INCORA	Instituto Colombiano Reforma Agraria
INDER	Instituto Nacional de Deportes, Educación, Física, y Recreación
INRA	Instituto Nacional de Reforma Agraria
IPEG	Teacher Training Institute for General Education
IPN	National Education Institute
IPR	Rural Polytechnic Institute
IRRI	International Rice Research Institute
ITC	Industrial Training Center
JSC	Jamaican Certificate of Education
JYC	Jamaica Youth Council
KNCSS	Kenya National Council of Social Services
LIVE	Loan for Improvement of Vocational Education
MINCIN	Ministerio del Comercio Interior
MINSAP	Ministerio de Salud Pública
MINTRANS	Ministerio de Transporte
MTTS	Mobile Trade Training School
MTTU	Mobile Trade Training Unit
NACF	National Agricultural Cooperative Federation
NCCK	National Christian Council of Kenya
NITB	National Industrial Training Board
NVO	National Volunteers Organization
NYS	National Youth Service
ORD	Office of Rural Development
PACCA	Program of Agricultural Credit and Cooperation in Afghanistan
PCC	Partido Comunista de Cuba
PLK	Pusat Latihan Kerja
PLPM	Pusat Latihan Pendidikan Masjarakat
PMD	Pembangunan Masjarakat Desa
PORD	Provincial Office of Rural Development
PPP-R	Promoción Profesional Popular-Rural

RDO	Regional Development Organization
REC	Rural Education Center
RIP	Rural Industries Projects
SCAER	Society for Farm Credit and Rural Equipment
SENA	Servicio Nacional de Aprendizaje
SIC	Small Industry Credit Scheme
SIDA	Swedish International Development Authority
SIET	Small Industries Extension Training Institute
SISI	Small Industries Service Institute
SNTEC	Sindicato Nacional de Trabajadores de la Educación y Cultura
SNU	Seoul National University
SRDP	Special Rural Development Projects
SSIDO	Small-Scale Industrial Development Organization
TANU	Tanzanian African National Union
UJC	Union de Jóvenes Comunistas
UNDP	United Nations Development Program
UNESCO	United Nations Educational, Scientific, and Cultural Organization
UNICEF	United Nations Children's Fund
UNIDO	United Nations Industrial Development Organization
U.S. AID	United States Agency for International Development
USOM	United States Operation Mission
VED	Vocational Education Department
VIC	Vocational Improvement Centres
VOK	Voice of Kenya
VP	Village Polytechnic
VPD	Vocational Promotion Division
VSO	(British) Voluntary Service Overseas
YCTC	Youth Community Training Centre
YDA	Youth Development Agency
YFC	Young Farmers Clubs
YMCA	Young Men's Christian Association
YWCA	Young Women's Christian Association
ZAFs	Zones of Functional Literacy
ZERs	Zones of Rural Expansion

This collection of cases requires no lengthy introduction; each case study speaks for itself. Different
readers, by using the chapter headings and subheadings
as guides, can find their own way to whatever interests
them most. Those interested in comparative analysis will
find much grist in the way of issues and problems that
surface repeatedly in the various cases despite their
many differences. There should be something of interest
for a very wide audience: educators, economists, sociologists, political scientists, and agriculturalists;
specialists in public health, nutrition, family planning,
skill training, literacy, development planning, educational
technologies, and costs and finance; and those interested
in indigenous learning systems, school reform, and all
aspects of basic education.

It may be helpful if we explain briefly the purpose
these case studies were meant to serve, the basic analytical concepts that shaped them, their major similarities
and differences, and the diversity of rural clienteles
and educational objectives addressed by the programs
examined.

The cases may serve a variety of purposes for
readers of this volume, but their prime function for ICED
was to provide a body of empirical evidence rooted in
samples of real life experience to undergird its broader
analytical studies for the World Bank and UNICEF (see
Preface) that were aimed primarily at assisting policymakers, planners, and program managers. The central task
of these studies was, first, to assess the potentialities
of various types of nonformal education (taken in conjunction with other forms of education and other development
factors) for meeting the basic learning needs of children,
youth, and adults in the poorer rural areas of the developing world and; second, to recommend practical steps
that developing countries and external assistance agencies
might take to exploit these potentialities more fully.

In constructing an analytical framework for these
purposes, ICED adopted from the outset a comprehensive
view of rural development that embraces all the main
dimensions of personal and economic development and of
family and community life improvement. This broad view
equates rural development with the fundamental transformation of rural societies--socially, economically, and
politically. Seen in this perspective, the sharp distinctions made in the past between social and economic development, and between different development "sectors"
(usually handled by separate ministries and agencies) are
forced to give way to a more integrated view of rural

development. The case studies, it was hoped, would
demonstrate how educational inputs dovetail with other
essential components of rural development, and why it is
therefore important to plan and operate the various
elements of this complex process as harmoniously as
possible.

A similarly broad and functional view of education
itself was adopted--a view that equates education not
simply with "schooling" but with learning, regardless of
where or how the learning takes place. Seen in this
perspective, education is obviously a life-long process,
spanning the years from earliest infancy through old age
and taking many different forms, only one of which is
formal schooling. Most of what any individual learns
throughout life clearly is acquired through informal
education--that is, through daily experiences and inter-
actions with that particular person's social and economic
environment.

But informal education usually requires supplementing
by organized educational activities designed to meet
certain important learning needs not readily satisfied by
informal education. This applies especially today to
transitional rural societies where all members of the
population, according to their particular roles, need to
acquire many new kinds of knowledge and skills not yet
available in their local informal learning environment.
Organized educational activities have existed all through
history, even in the most primitive of societies (where
various institutional provisions evolved for passing on
basic beliefs, skills, and customs from one generation to
the next). Most such organized learning activities--as
they exist today in actively changing and developing
societies--fall into two general categories, formal education and nonformal education.

Formal education refers to the hierarchically-struc-
tured and chronologically-graded modern "educational
system" that stretches from primary school through the
university. In the poorer and least developed agrarian
countries--as the cases of Mali and Upper Volta demon-
strate--the rural primary schools (not to mention the
secondary schools and post-secondary institutions) serve
and benefit only a tiny minority of the total child and
youth population, often fewer than 10 percent. The
situation in the rural areas of some of the relatively
richer developing countries is not much different.
Moreover, apart from the shortage of primary schools and
their inefficiency (in terms of high drop-out and repeater rates and low levels of student achievement), the
formal schools at best are equipped to take care of only
part of the essential learning needs of rural children,
youth, and adults--mainly literacy and numeracy. Thus
it is left to nonformal education (and informal education)
to meet the other essential learning needs, as well as to

cater to the many millions who have been bypassed by the formal schools.

Nonformal education as defined here refers to the motley assortment of organized and semi-organized educational activities operating outside the regular structure and routines of the formal system, aimed at serving a great variety of learning needs of different subgroups in the population, both young and old. Some nonformal programs cater to the same learning needs as the schools and in effect are substitutes for formal schooling. Examples are the "second chance" program in Thailand, the radio-correspondence "school equivalency" program in Kenya, the Rural Education Centers in Upper Volta, portions of ACPO's program in Colombia, and functional literacy programs in such countries as Mali and Thailand.

But most nonformal education programs covered by the case studies are directed at serving important learning needs and benefiting clienteles not generally catered to by the formal schools. These learning needs relate, for example, to health, nutrition, family planning, and other requisites for improving family life; to developing good personal character traits and positive attitudes; to increasing economic productivity, family incomes, and employment opportunities; and to strengthening local institutions of self-help and self-government and broadening participation in them. Most of the programs are aimed at benefiting particular subgroups in the local population--such as small farmers, craftsmen, and entrepreneurs; older girls and women; infants and young children (through the education of their elders); unemployed out-of-school youth; members and leaders of community organizations such as cooperatives, farmer societies, and local councils. But several multipurpose programs--such as the Sarvodaya Movement in Sri Lanka--seek to serve all members of the family and community and a broad spectrum of learning needs.

The extreme diversity of nonformal education programs--not only in their target audiences and learning objectives but in their forms and structures and educational technologies and methods, precludes fitting them neatly into a refined classification system. The following list, without pretending to provide such a classification, illustrates the diversity of programs contained in the case studies.

Learning Objectives	Major Clienteles	Programs
1. General education (literacy, numeracy, change-motivation, development-orientation)	Rural youths and adults	ACPO in Colombia; Functional Literacy Programs in Mali and Thailand; Sarvodaya in Sri Lanka

Learning Objectives	Major Clienteles	Programs
2. General education plus occupational orientation and training (including elements of both farming and nonfarm occupations)	Early dropouts from formal schools, primary school leavers, youths in formal institutions	Cuba's Schools-in-the-Countryside; Jombang Project in Indonesia; Youth Camps and Youth Centres in Jamaica; Village Polytechnics, National Youth Service, and Youth Centres in Kenya; COPs in Mali; Diyagala Boys' Town in Sri Lanka; prevocational courses in Sri Lanka secondary schools; Rural Education Centres in Upper Volta
3. Improvement of family life (health, nutrition, home economics, family planning, etc.)	Rural adults, women and girls	ACPO in Colombia; Women's Organizations in Kenya, Mali, and Sri Lanka; literacy and family life program in Thailand; Sarvodaya Movement in Sri Lanka
4. Training in farming and allied sideline production	Youths and adults in rural families, rural out-of-school youths	PACCA in Afghanistan, SENA-PPP-R in Colombia, ORD programs in Korea, Jombang Project in Indonesia
5. Training in rural nonfarm skills	School leavers and other adolescents, rural adults employed in nonfarm occupations	SENA-PPP-R in Colombia; mobile skill training and cottage industries programs in Sri Lanka; Rural Industries Projects in India; Vocational Improvement Centres in Nigeria; Mobile Trade Training Schools in Thailand
6. Training for small entrepreneurship and management	Workers and owners of nonfarm enterprises, unemployed educated adults	Rural Industries Project and Entrepreneurship Training Programs in India; Vocational Improvement Centers in Nigeria

Learning Objectives	Major Clienteles	Programs
7. Training for village level leaders, animateurs, and extension workers	Extension officers; new recruits for animation and extension work; village youth and women leaders; cooperative officers; unemployed educated youth	CARs in Mali; Sarvodaya in Sri Lanka; National Youth Services in Sri Lanka; ORD and 4-H Programs in South Korea; IRRI Extension Training Program in Philippines; Tanzania's Cooperative Education Program

The impression should not be left that nonformal education is meant only for poor and unschooled people or for rural areas. Actually, nonformal education exists most extensively and in greatest variety in the highly industrialized countries. Among other functions it constitutes a principal means by which the most highly educated experts--medical doctors, scientists, engineers, and other professionals--keep pace with the fast moving frontiers of their respective fields. Nonformal education is also extensively used by secondary school and college graduates to enrich the cultural and general intellectual dimensions of their lives.

Nonformal and formal education, contrary to the impression sometimes conveyed by their protagonists, are not competitors. They should be seen as mutually reinforcing partners. Both are essential, in many different forms, to flesh out a comprehensive and coherent "lifelong learning system" that can serve all members of a population in response to their diverse and changing needs.

The case studies in this volume indicate the differences between formal and nonformal education, but they also warn against pressing this dichotomy too far. Some of the programs, as will be seen, fall into a grey area between the two modes and are best described as hybrids. Some of these hybrids--such as Cuba's "Schools-in-the-Countryside," Kenya's Village Polytechnics, Upper Volta's Rural Learning Centers, and Thailand's "second chance" school equivalency program for adolescents--are especially creative and innovative and point the way toward new solutions to difficult educational problems confronting the developing countries.

All of these case studies help to illuminate the meaning of "basic education"--a tired and ambiguous term, yet one that is now making a comeback in international discussions and must be reckoned with. One popular view defines basic education as four to six years of primary schooling, or its nonformal equivalent.

But this narrow and mechanistic institutional definition
makes little substantive sense for it tells nothing about
the real needs of learners or how well they are being met.
In New Paths to Learning ICED therefore adopted a broader
and more functional view that equated basic education for
rural children and youth with six categories of minimum
essential learning needs. These are needs that must be
satisfied in the course of growing up if young people are
to take command of their own lives and make the most of
their opportunities as determined by their particular
socioeconomic circumstances. They include in particular:
1) the acquisition of constructive attitudes, character
traits and values conducive to effective personal development and to contributing to community and national
development; 2) a functional grasp of literacy and
numeracy; 3) a scientific outlook and rudimentary understanding of one's natural and social environment;
4) basic knowledge and skills for rearing a family and
managing a household; 5) functional skills and knowledge
for earning a living; and 6) the knowledge and skills
requisite to effective civic participation.
     These essential learning needs obviously differ in
detail from place to place, group to group, and from one
time to another for the same person or group as conditions
change. But the categories listed above offer a useful
starting point for identifying in more detail the learning needs of any particular group in a particular situation. Most of the nonformal education programs cited in
the case studies are addressed to one or more of these
essential needs, not only for children and youth but for
adults as well.
     The two way grouping of the case studies under the
rubrics "Basic General Education" (Part I) and "Employment-related Education" (Part II) requires explanation.
The division is largely a matter of convenience but there
are in fact some significant differences between the two
sets of cases. The case studies in Part II were prepared
primarily for ICED's World Bank study and therefore focus
mainly on various kinds of occupational skill training,
both agricultural and nonagricultural. Also, most of
these case studies deal in substantial detail with only
one or two specific programs. By contrast, the case
studies in Part I, are geared primarily to the aims of
ICED's UNICEF study. Most of them are broader in scope,
covering a greater number and diversity of educational
programs aimed at a wider variety of basic educational
objectives and clienteles. Attention is given by this
group of cases to the needs of infants, children, and
adolescents; to the strengths and weaknesses of formal
schooling; to literacy and school equivalency programs
and to some radical alternatives to conventional school
models; to the learning needs of girls and women, and to
programs of health, nutrition, family planning, home
economics, and the like, tied to improving the quality of

rural family and community life. Some of them also include prevocational and more specific occupational skill
training for young people and to this extent are related
to programs dealt with in Part II.

The idea behind these case studies was not to evaluate
their overall success or failure but rather to discover
the particular factors--both inside the programs and in
their environment--that strongly conditioned their performance and effectiveness, whether for better or worse.
Not surprisingly, many of the same important factors,
both favorable and unfavorable, turned up repeatedly in
a variety of situations. These are obviously the factors
that educational planners in all countries need to keep
in view.

It should also be said that ICED was not looking
for "successful models" that could be recommended for
wholesale copying by other countries. Actually this
propensity to copy emerged as one of the major causes of
poor effectiveness in many programs. On the other hand,
one point of interest in the case studies was whether
certain pilot projects or small innovative programs that
were clearly yielding effective results on a limited
scale could be successfully replicated in the same country
on a larger scale. The answer was usually traceable to
how they were conceived and planned in the first place.

Finally, it should be noted that these case studies
reach well beyond the purely educational aspects of the
programs in question to take account of their general
milieu. Thus one gets from some of these studies--
especially those prepared by indigenous researchers and
observers who know their own society well, a variety of
fresh insights into the complex interplay of dynamic
political, social, economic, and cultural forces that
profoundly influence the success of any educational
effort. And one also acquires a humble appreciation of
why it often takes more time and effort than most experts
have generally assumed to be necessary to bring about
basic social and economic change and educational progress
in transitional societies.

PROGRAMS FOR BASIC
GENERAL EDUCATION

1

COLOMBIA: A MULTIMEDIA
RURAL EDUCATION PROGRAM
Stephan F. Brumberg

A major question for all who are concerned with nonformal education for rural development is to what extent various mass media--radio, films, mass printed materials, and the like--can be combined and harnessed for broadening and enriching various educational programs in rural areas. The Acción Cultural Popular (ACPO) program in Colombia has gone further than almost any other rural education program throughout the developing world in making combined use of various media to serve a wide assortment of educational objectives. At the same time, it demonstrates that no single medium by itself constitutes a viable teaching-learning system but, combined with others and with human elements at the learning scene, these media can become potent tools of learning-- provided always that they are appropriately programmed.

This case study, completed in spring 1972, involved the cooperation of a number of people from the ACPO organization itself, from elsewhere in Colombia, from the Food and Agriculture Organization (FAO) as well as the ICED. Dr. Eduardo Ramos, of the Instituto Colombiano Agropecuario, served as the study team leader, and sociologists Fernando Isaacs, of the Fundación Colombiana de Desarrollo and Rosa Esther Buitrago, served as team members. Dr. José Castañon-Pasquel, agricultural extension expert of the FAO in Colombia, served as adviser to the study team and helped to facilitate the work while in Colombia. Dr. Jack Lyle, communications expert at the School of Journalism, University of California at Los Angeles, joined the study team in Colombia and contributed much to the report. Full responsibility for the interpretations presented in this report, however, rest with the author and the ICED.

INTRODUCTION

Acción Cultural Popular (ACPO), begun in 1947, is a private, nonprofit educational service directed at the rural population of Colombia.

ACPO has adopted extensive mass media techniques to
carry its program to all rural Colombians. It owns the
largest and most powerful radio network in Colombia (500
kilowatts of radio transmitting power). ACPO also produces high-volume low-cost printed matter in the form of
a textbook series with supplementary reading materials,
and the largest circulating weekly newspaper in the
country. It produces phonograph records, and, most
recently, has experimented with tape cassettes. As a
complement to the mass media employed, ACPO has developed
an extensive network of local workers (predominantly
volunteer) and two institutes for the training of rural
personnel. Finally, it has encouraged written correspondence as feedback from the rural population to the
central ACPO organization.

In this case study, we shall approach ACPO as a
learning system. After examining its basic orientation
and prime educational objectives, we shall focus on the
means employed to attain the objectives, especially the
use of mass media. We shall then turn to an examination
of the impact of the ACPO learning system in the rural
areas of Colombia, using data collected by an ICED study
team, by other researchers who have studied the ACPO
programs, and the findings of ACPO staff. In a following section, we shall look at the costs and the benefits
of ACPO activities. The chapter will conclude with a
critique of the ACPO program, aimed at identifying the
major lessons of the ACPO experience in rural education
over the past 24 years and how these lessons may usefully
be applied in other developing societies.

The programs of ACPO are founded on the belief that
the rural population can be brought into the mainstream
of society--and particularly that the campesino (rural
inhabitant) can, with education and training, play an
active role in his own development and can move from
being the "marginal man" to an integrated position in
the society as a whole.

About half of Colombia's total population of 20
million live in rural areas. In large part due to the
mountainous terrain, land communications are still difficult in Colombia, and many campesinos are physically
isolated from urban centers.

Per capita income in Colombia as a whole is low
(US$289 in 1968); in rural areas it is considerably less,
and most rural dwellers are extremely poor. In 1960
approximately 45 percent of the cultivated and pasture
lands were held by 1 percent of the people, and 65 percent of the rural population were on 5.5 percent of the
land.[1] The Colombian Land Reform Agency (Instituto
Colombiano de la Reforma Agraria, INCORA) founded in
1961, is working toward the goal of more equitable land
distribution, but the distribution of landholdings in
Colombia is substantially the same today as in 1960.

Many farm families live on "subfamily" farms (farms whose produce cannot support a family at subsistence levels). These as well as landless agricultural workers find full-time employment on large estates or seasonal employment as migrant laborers for the coffee, cotton, and rice harvests.[2] Others seek to supplement their meagre farm income by off-season migration to towns and cities in search of unskilled jobs.

In large part due to low rural incomes and population pressures on the land, Colombia has experienced considerable rural to urban migration. Over half the population is classified as urban and this proportion continues to rise. The country's major cities are growing extremely rapidly (6 to 7 percent a year) with concomitant high unemployment, poor housing facilities for many, and overburdened public services.

Rural Colombia lags far behind urban areas in education. The average length of schooling of the rural population in 1964 was only 1.7 years compared to 5.1 years for urban dwellers.[3] In part, these figures are due to selective migration: the better-educated rural inhabitants have a greater tendency to migrate to cities than those with little or no education. But the low average level of schooling also reflects the abysmal condition of rural schools. Few rural schools provided a full five-year primary course and, as of 1964, 64 percent provided only one or two years of schooling under poorly trained and often unqualified teachers. Only 3 percent of those who enter rural primary schools complete the five-year course compared to 46 percent of urban children.[4]

Further primary and secondary education are virtually nonexistent in rural areas. Most children must commute or move to towns if they wish to continue their education beyond the first few years of primary school.

In the 1964 census, in rural areas the level of reported illiteracy (of those over 15 years of age) was 41.3 percent; in urban areas the illiteracy rate was 15 percent.

ACPO: AN OVERVIEW

ACPO began in 1947 with the founding of the radio station that has since become Colombia's largest radio network, Radio Sutatenza. The station, founded by Monseñor José Joaquín Salcedo (who is still director of ACPO), was conceived as the prime vehicle through which a basic educational program (including structured courses) could be directed to the rural population. This educational program is now a wide-ranging multimedia effort encompassing a newspaper, textbooks, book series, and recordings, as well as radio.

Objectives

    The objectives of ACPO are, in general, the creation
of a

        . . . new type of Latin American man, capable
        of making rational decisions based on a
        Christian ideology and of contributing to
        the establishment of a different social
        order based on the idea of human dignity.[5]

ACPO maintains that the major problem of underdevelopment
is not the lack of material things, but in the inability
of the campesinos, individually and collectively, to
overcome their backwardness and to conquer cultural
obstacles related to such traditional attitudes as a high
degree of conformity, fatalism, and dependency. The
campesinos are thus trapped by outmoded attitudes and
this entrapment is reinforced by external conditions in
the world around them.
    In the view of ACPO, if the attitudes of the mass of
the rural peasantry can be altered to fit overall development objectives, one of the major barriers to social and
economic development will be removed. In ACPO's terms,
this "development from below" is a necessary precondition
for national development. One may deduce from ACPO's
stated position that development from above, from a central government or oligarchy, is counterproductive in
that it reinforces the dependence, fatalism, and pater-
nalism which serve at present as a brake on development.
    ACPO has stated as its objectives:[6]

    1. motivation of campesinos for development
    2. human promotion: creation of the "whole"
        man, understood in terms of physical well-
        being, intellect, spiritual and creative
        senses, and capacity to fulfill social roles
    3. integration of the campesino into society
        through an attempt "to diminish social
        distances and seek to ensure that all
        citizens have access to the opportunities
        and services that society has to offer and
        participate in them."[7]
    4. organization and development of the community:
        creation of the feeling of solidarity,
        especially through promoting participation
        in local organizations
    5. productivity: a) to promote increased pro-
        duction by means of new agricultural tech-
        nologies; b) to stimulate sale of agricultural
        products; c) to encourage capital creation
        through the promotion of savings, investments,

the use of credit and improved utilization
of available technical resources; and d) to
encourage a sense of the value of work
6. spirituality of development (creation of an
authentic humanism): a) to help the campesino
to realize his God-given ability to become an
agent of personal and societal development,
b) to create a critical consciousness of
his world, and c) to promote the "renewal"
program of the Roman Catholic Church, which,
among other things, has assigned greater
importance to the leadership roles of the
laity

The attainment of these six basic objectives is
sought through the provision of what ACPO has termed
"fundamental integral education" (FIE). Fundamental
integral education is composed of five basic content
areas which, according to ACPO, cover the knowledge
required for the growth and development of the campesino:
1) health, 2) literacy, 3) mathematics, 4) economy and
work, and 5) spirituality. Such education is considered
fundamental in that it strives to impart to the campesinos
basic knowledge directly relevant to their real life
situation, which will foster new development attitudes.
It is integral in that it attempts to cover all aspects
of life--social, psychological, moral, physical and
intellectual.
ACPO's ideological orientation is central to the
formulation of organizational objectives and the design
and implementation of its programs. The very name of
the organization signifies a commitment to the masses of
campesinos--to bring "culture" to these masses and to
activate them through the provision of "culture." The
program is firmly grounded in the belief that the unschooled masses can be brought to realize their full
human potential by means of proper education. Thus
enlightened, the campesino can actively improve his
living conditions on his own and in concert with his
neighbors. The mission of ACPO broadly defined, therefore, is to transform rural man by motivating and educating him.
Although ACPO does not discount the need for new and
improved physical inputs into the impoverished rural
milieu, for credit and marketing facilities, and for
technical assistance, it has defined its role in terms of
motivation and education.

The Institution, its personnel, its patrimony,
its organization, and its methods must be
directed only and exclusively to [the fundamental integral education of the people].

And this also signifies that ACPO is not,
nor can it be an agency of social assistance, nor a builder of houses . . .
nor become involved in other social work.[8]

Organization

ACPO is administered from central headquarters in
Bogotá. It has been directed since its founding by
Monseñor Salcedo and has experienced continuity and
stability of personnel at all levels in the organization.
The institution is organized into three major
divisions: cultural, administration, and radio transmission management. Backing up these three divisions
are the financial office and the board of directors of
ACPO. The radio division is responsible for the technical aspects of the radio network and also includes
production of noneducational programming. The division
of administration is concerned with the personnel of
ACPO; it controls Editorial Andes, ACPO's wholly owned
publishing house, a profit corporation which produces
ACPO's printed materials; and is generally responsible
for administrative matters pertaining to the operation
of ACPO.
The Cultural Division is the most important in terms
of this study. It is responsible for the educational
radio programs (including program content and supervision of radio teachers), the weekly newspaper of ACPO,
editorial responsibility for the production of ACPO's
textbook series (cartillas) and special campesino book
series, the operation of the two campesino training institutes created by ACPO to train field personnel, and
coordination of the educational activities of the three
regional centers of ACPO in Cali, Medellín, and Barranquilla.
The organizational structure of ACPO, in simplified
form, may be seen on Figure 1.1.
ACPO employs approximately 200 full-time staff in
Bogotá and the regional offices and institutes, with an
additional 130 employed in the Editorial Andes. However,
in addition to permanent staff, about 200 field workers
(local and regional leaders) can be counted as part of
the ACPO organization although they receive small stipends
rather than salaries. ACPO also relies upon many unpaid
volunteers. Many of the parishes in Colombia have paro-
chial representatives and more than 20,000 campesinos
serve as unpaid auxiliaries in ACPO's radio school.
The three regional organizations at Cali, Medellín,
and Barranquilla include transmission centers for Radio
Sutatenza.

FIGURE 1.1

Acción Cultural Popular Simplified Organizational Chart

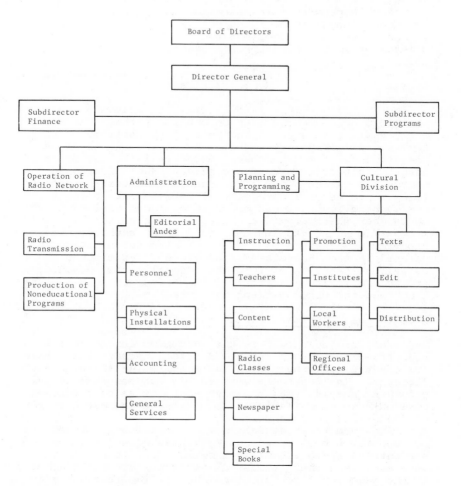

Source: ACPO, Mensaje de la Dirección General a los Colaboradores de la Institución (Bogotá: Editorial Andes, 1971).

ACPO AS A DELIVERY SYSTEM

ACPO's program is carried to its rural audience
through multiple reinforcing channels. These can be
grouped into three major modes of communication: radio,
printed matter, and personal contacts.

Radio Sutatenza

ACPO owns and operates Colombia's largest radio network, Radio Sutatenza. The name of the network is taken
from the small municipality in the Department of Boyacá
where the first station was founded in 1947. By means of
long- and short-wave transmissions, Radio Sutatenza
covers the entire geographic area of Colombia. Its focus
to date has been primarily rural Colombia, although it is
now seeking to cultivate an urban audience during the
hours when there are fewer rural listeners.

Radio Sutatenza has a 19-hour broadcast day. Its
programming consists of 6 hours of structured courses
offered in the "Escuelas Radiofonicas" (radio schools),
as well as programs of informal education (for example,
programs offering practical advice on agriculture and the
home, general entertainment, and news).

Escuelas Radiofonicas (Radio Schools)

The "radio school" is the seed from which the entire
ACPO organization has grown. Started in 1947 with a handful of students, there were 303 schools in 1950 with 3,636
students. In 1965 there were 28,535 schools with 240,915
students, and in 1968, the last year for which comprehensive data were available (as of 1971), there were 169,696
students in 22,212 schools.

The term radio schools may be misleading. These are
not special school buildings with classrooms filled with
students; a radio school is a small group of individuals
(the average number is less than eight), often all members
of the same family or close neighbors, who meet daily in
one of the student's homes to listen to the radio class.

The "school" is administered by an auxiliar immediato
(immediate auxiliary)--a member of the local community who
usually has slightly more formal education than his
neighbors (or other family members) and who volunteers
to organize a radio school. It becomes his duty to help
promote enrollment, organize a regular meeting site,
obtain a radio for the class, see that the students
attend regularly and on time, tune the radio into the
proper station, assist the students during the radio
class (upon instruction from the radio teacher),

encourage discussion after class, and ensure that a set
of textbooks is available for the class as well as a
blackboard and chalk (if possible) and pencils and paper.
He must send in enrollment statistics to the regional
ACPO office and attend regular meetings (in theory, these
are weekly meetings) of auxiliaries, lideres (local ACPO
staff), and parish priests in the municipal center.

  Course Content. Three courses of study are offered
by ACPO: basic, progressive, and complementary (see
Table 1.1). The Basic Course is literacy instruction in
the four fundamental operations of arithmetic. The class,
30 minutes long, is aired six days a week with equal time
allotted to literacy and arithmetic. The complete course
lasts for 90 lessons and is completed in one semester.
The aim of the Basic Course is to provide campesinos with
the reading and number skills required to follow the
Progressive Course.

  The Progressive Course requires, on the average, two
years to complete and constitutes the core programming of
ACPO; it accounts for 60 percent of all enrollment. This
course seeks to impart fundamental integral education
(see Table 1.1). Its one-hour daily broadcast (repeated
three times) is broken down into several time blocks.
A specific subject matter is assigned to each block--one
of the five basic content areas (health, literacy, mathematics, economy and work, and spirituality); subsidiary
subjects (these include geography, history, civics,
community education, home economics, and human relations);
or special campaigns.

  Although one objective of the course is to impart
factual knowledge relevant to the campesinos' needs, the
greatest emphasis is placed on motivation to overcome
inertia among campesinos and encourage them to participate actively in developmental tasks, and in so doing
put their new learning to immediate and practical use.

  A student can begin the Progressive Course any time
during the school year since program content is segmental
and not sequential. This is not true, however, for the
Basic Course which follows a sequential pattern.

  The Complementary Course, ACPO's newest offering,
began in 1970 in response to audience requests (via
written correspondence). This three-year course is still
in an experimental stage. It is aimed at preparing
primary school dropouts for the primary school leaving
exam. Unlike the Basic and Progressive Courses, the
enrolled students do not take an ACPO final test. Rather
they sit for the government primary school leavers test
(at the end of primary 5) along with formal school
students at the end of the school year. (Although the
Complementary Course is not conceived of as following
sequentially upon the Progressive Course, a number of
those enrolled in the Complementary Course are simultaneously enrolled (or have completed) the Progressive
Course.)

TABLE 1.1

Radio Courses of ACPO

Course	Duration	Target Audience	Content	Emphasis	Objective	(approx.) No. Students	(approx.) % Distribution of Students
Basic	1/2 yr.	Illiterates (primarily adults)	Literacy and arithmetic	Reading, writing, and calculating skills	Literacy (reading and numbers)	42,500	25%
Progressive	2 yrs.	Literates with incomplete primary education (farm families)	Health, literacy, arithmetic, economy and work, spirituality	F.I.E.*	Motivation for developmental actions	102,000	60%
Complementary	3 yrs.	Literates with incomplete primary education (presumed to be adolescents and young adults)	Primary school curriculum	Systematic knowledge	Preparation for primary school leaving exam	25,500	15%
						170,000	100%

*Fundamental integral education

Source: Information supplied by ACPO to ICED in 1971.

Students in the Complementary Course tend to follow the radio classes individually, not in groups. A printed supplement to the radio classes is included monthly in the ACPO newspaper, El Campesino. These supplements will be discussed in greater detail below.

Preparation of Course Materials. The program content for each course year is planned well in advance of the year's first program. The preparation of the pedagogical input (with the exception of religious instruction content) is the responsibility of a staff of 12 teachers who are well qualified in both teacher training and subject matter specialization. This same teaching team was largely responsible for the preparation of the textbook series as well. The radio classes are prepared anew each year, thus permitting revision and updating of material.

All radio lessons are prerecorded, a procedure with several advantages: errors can be edited out before broadcasting; a quality check can be maintained on content and presentation prior to presentation; program continuity is ensured from day to day despite absences of teachers or other staff; and more efficient utilization of teachers' time, studio facilities, and technical staff is possible. Moreover, since radio classes are taped, a class can be repeated several times a day. As shown in Table 1.2 a student may listen to a class at various times of the day on either long- or short-wave radio. (Because of the difficulties presented to long-wave signals in some of the mountain and rural areas, short-wave transmission is also provided on three frequencies with transmission powers of 50, 25, and 10 kilowatts. This short-wave system is said to blanket the country and functions as a backup transmission system.)

Although any radio can receive ACPO broadcasts, ACPO sells special radio receivers to participants in their courses. At present, some 25,000 receivers are sold annually. The sets are sold at a small profit to ACPO (about 7 pesos per set). The present model, a four-tube transistorized Sanyo with free long-wave tuning and fixed frequency short-wave tuning, sells for 460 to 480 pesos, which is lower than the general market price for comparable sets, although cheaper radios are available. The key advantage of the ACPO receiver is that fixed frequency short-wave tuning ensures good reception of ACPO broadcasts.

With normal use and care the sets last 10 years or longer. Repair of sets is facilitated through the regional representatives of ACPO and the affiliated stores. Broken sets can be exchanged at regional offices until repairs are made so that the student does not have to miss lessons.

TABLE 1.2

Air Time of Formal Radio Classes, Mon.-Sat.
Transmissions A, 1971 and B, 1969[a]

| | | Type of Course | |
	Basic	Progressive	Complementary[b]
Trans- mission A (1971)	7:30-8:00 p.m. 6:30-7:00 a.m.(R)	3:00-4:00 p.m. 6:00-7:00 p.m.(R)	9:00-10:00 p.m. 11:00-12:00 a.m.(R)
Trans- mission B (1969)	1:30-2:00 p.m. 3:30-4:00 p.m.(R) 5:30-6:00 p.m.(R) 5:30-6:00 a.m.(R) 7:30-8:00 a.m.(R) 9:30-10:00a.m.(R) 11:30-12:00a.m.(R)	2:00-3:00 p.m. 4:00-5:00 p.m.(R) 8:00-9:00 a.m.(R) 10:00-11:00a.m.(R) 12:00- 1:00p.m.(R)	9:00-10:00 p.m.[c]

[a]Radio Sutatenza broadcasts two sets of programs--transmission A and transmission B. The A or regular program includes 6 hours of classes and the balance (13 hours) in general programming (Table 1.3). It is the program transmitted over the long-wave network and backed up by a 50 Kw.short-wave transmitter.

Transmission B, which is entirely short-wave (two frequencies), devotes half its air time to formal classes (with repetitions of the same lessons several times a day) and fills out the rest of its air time with general programs from transmission A (live and taped) (Table 1.3). While all programs of Transmission B originate in Bogotá, about a third of the air time on Transmission A originates in the regional stations for broadcast to their respective audiences.

[b]The complementary classes are broadcast only Monday-Friday.

[c]In 1969 the complementary class was not part of an organized program. The complete course was organized in 1970.

Note: (R) = Repetition. A class is initially broadcast in the afternoon and/or evening and repeated the following morning.

Source: ACPO, Programación, (Bogota: Editorial Andes, 1969).

Other Programming of Radio Sutatenza

Classes of the radio school account for one-third of air time on the long-wave stations. An additional quarter of air time is for programs that are educational in nature but not structured into classes as in the case of the radio school programs. The most important of these, "Buenos Días," is an hour and a half network show carried daily from 4:00 to 5:30 a.m. It has the largest audience of Radio Sutatenza's programs and is directed toward farm families. The show includes news items of interest to rural audiences, motivational messages, practical home and agricultural advice, weather, and the time, interspersed with music.

General entertainment, which accounts for 30.7 percent of air time, is intended to provide "cultural uplift" to the listening audience. These programs compete with commercial radio for listeners, and the more cultural programs (such as classical music) do not find a ready audience in most rural households.

One of the most popular forms of entertainment is the music request program. A considerable volume of mail is received and the possible mention of one's name on the air is a strong stimulus for listening.

Although most programming is directed to rural areas, programs aired from 12:00 noon until 2:00 p.m. and from 8:00 to 11:00 p.m. tend to focus on an urban audience. During these hours the farmer is presumably in his fields or in bed and the time can thus be freed for a more urban-oriented audience. It is hoped that increased advertising revenues will be realized by developing an urban listening audience.

The final category of programming is the news, taking up more than 10 percent of air time (not including the short news bulletins of "Buenos Días"). ACPO sees the news broadcasts as a means of breaking down the sense of isolation of the rural masses, who are not only physically separated from the national society, but also isolated from contemporary currents of public opinion. In ACPO's view, "news is offered as an information service which will extend to the rural milieu the possibilities of information which are enjoyed by citizens in urban areas."[9]

The objectives of the news program are to: 1) create an interest in national events among campesinos and how they affect and are affected by them, 2) create consciousness of national unity, 3) create currents of opinion, and 4) motivate the masses to present themselves in a unified and organized manner and in so doing take their rightful place among all sectors in national policy debates.[10]

The distribution of air time by type of program is shown in Table 1.3, using both transmissions A and B.

TABLE 1.3

Distribution of Weekday Radio Programs by Type, by
Transmissions A, 1971 and B, 1969

Type of Program	Transmission A Air time (Mins.)	%	Transmission B Air time (Mins.)	%
Formal courses	360	31.6	570	50.0
Informal education	310	27.2	315	27.6
General entertainment	350	30.7	145	12.7
News	120	10.5	110	9.7
	1,140	100.0	1,140	100.0

Source: Information supplied by ACPO to ICED.

More than 31 percent of air time is devoted to formal
classes, 27 percent to other educational programs, and
the remainder to general entertainment and news.
     Regional Programming. The three regional stations
at Cali, Medellin, and Barranquilla are required to carry
the various school programs as scheduled on the network
from Bogotá. Beyond that they are relatively free to cut
from the network and substitute locally produced programs.
As shown in Table 1.4, on weekdays about 6 of the 19 hours
are filled with local programs. However, the percentage
is considerably higher on Saturday and Sunday.

TABLE 1.4

Local vs. Bogotá Origin of Weekday Programming
Transmission A, 1971

Origination	Regional Broadcast Stations Barranquilla min.	%	Cali min.	%	Medellin min.	%
Local	365	32.0	335	29.4	395	34.6
Bogotá						
Formal courses	360	31.6	360	31.6	360	31.6
Informal and general	315	27.6	345	30.2	285	25.0
News	100	8.8	100	8.8	100	8.8
	1,140	100.0	1,140	100.0	1,140	100.0

Source: Information supplied by ACPO to ICED.

In addition to broadcasting network news (100 minutes per day), each of the regional stations produces its own regional newscasts totaling at least 20 minutes a day. The national and regional news programs are among the most popular of Radio Sutatenza's programs and have served as one of the few sources of national information available to Colombia's rural inhabitants.

Much programming is built around music, particularly music that is typical and popular within the regions covered by the individual transmitter, although concert music is also broadcast.

Audience

Although Radio Sutatenza's formal courses attract adolescents and children in particular, most programs are directed to the farm family as a unit. In 1968, for example, nearly half of enrolled students were under 15 years of age.

Programs generally do not have a male-female bias. The agricultural programs, among others, take into account the important role of women in the farm enterprises. Some programs, however, are specifically geared to women, such as "Female Themes."

Most programs are for an audience with limited or no formal schooling; particular attention is given, therefore, to using simple language on the air so that content will be comprehensible. The formal courses of the Escuelas Radiofonicas are directed toward those with either no education or with some primary education. The urban-directed programs, however, do assume more formal education on the part of their listeners.

The intended audience is composed of agricultural workers--including landowners and agricultural laborers without land. The formal courses include little special-ized information for nonfarm rural occupations. Its general content is, however, applicable to all rural inhabi-tants.

Audience studies were undertaken by ACPO in 1969.[11] Because of the nature of Radio Sutatenza's audience, listener research is difficult. It seems worthwhile, therefore, to briefly outline these studies.

The first coincided with the expansion of the net-work's tranmission power and a change in the programming. Listeners were asked to write in and tell how good their reception was and to provide some information on their living conditions. To stimulate response, a raffle was conducted. More than 97,000 persons wrote in. Later a sample was drawn from these 97,000 for a mail survey on audience response to the news programs of Radio Sutatenza; 400 replies were obtained.

In the period May to July 1969, teams of lideres and staff from the Sutatenza Institute toured the country promoting the program. Upon completion of their work,

they were interviewed to obtain their perception of
audience reaction and information on the reception they
found in various areas.

In another study in 1969 lideres were used as inter-
viewers. The sample was proportionate to the geographic
distribution of population. In all, 781 interviews were
obtained, 566 with regular Radio Sutatenza listeners.

The latter studies provided generally consistent
results on estimation of program success. The four most
popular programs were:

Buenos Días	(Good Day)
Uds. Hacen el Programa	(You Make the Program)
Temas Femeninos	(Female Themes)
Charlas Con la Familia	(Talks with the Family)

The next rank of programs were:

El Maestro Agricola	(The Agricultural Teacher)
Viajemos por America Latina	(Let us travel in Latin America)
Misterios de la Naturaleza	(Mysteries of Nature)
Ronda Infantil	(Children's Round)
La Juventud	(Youth)
Trampas de Lenguaje	(Language Traps)

Of the 781 persons interviewed, 449 were students in
the Sutatenza courses: 111 in the Basic Course and 260
in the Progressive Course (78 did not specify the course).[12]
For the students the daily lessons took priority over all
other programs. "El Correo de Radio Sutatenza" (The Mail-
bag) and "Con Los Lideres" (With the Leaders) also had
considerable audiences.

The news program was found to be one of the most
popular broadcasts of Radio Sutatenza and had the greatest audience for the 7 a.m. and 7 p.m. presentations.
From the results it was concluded that the news program
served four purposes: 1) creation of interest in national
affairs; 2) creation of national identity and consciousness; 3) creation of public opinion; and 4) motivation of
organization for public action.

Of the 400 respondents in this study only 16 percent
said they preferred the news on other stations. Of those
preferring Sutatenza's news, 67 percent said they particularly liked the simplicity of language, 37 percent
cited completeness, and 33 percent mentioned the good
elocution of the announcer. Greatest interest was expressed in national news and most of the respondents indicated
they wanted commentary on the news.

For a subsequent study, <u>Enquesta Sobre Radiodifusion
Entre Los Campesinos</u> (Investigation of Radio-diffusion

Among Campesinos), 157 lideres were asked to evaluate
programs of both Radio Sutatenza and its competitors.
The programs winning highest approval from the lideres
were the practical programs dealing with aspects of farming and family life. The cultural programs such as the
radio novelas and, particularly, broadcasts of concert
music not only had few listeners, but were criticized as
of little use or interest.

Broadcasting Facilities

The Bogotá station facility is housed in ACPO's central headquarters, the Edificio Cardenal Luque in central
Bogotá. The installation is among the best in Latin
America and compares favorably with the best large-city
radio stations in the United States.

The principal studios and offices occupy one full
floor of the building. On another floor is a large
storeroom containing the library of several thousand disc
and tape recordings. Two additional studios are located
on the ground floor, each with an individual control room.
Adjacent to the regular production studios are suites of
offices for persons responsible for writing, performing,
and producing the various programs broadcast from Bogotá.
Other offices on the same floor house the chief engineer
and his staff. Equipment is of the highest professional
caliber.

The Barranquilla installation is typical of the
regional stations. Radio Sutatenza/Barranquilla occupies
a house that has been converted for its use. The ground
floor contains six offices accommodating the administrative staff, providing one office for the three announcers
and a two-room suite used by the local coordinator of
the Escuelas Radiofonicas. In the basement are three
studios, well-soundproofed and air-conditioned. Another
basement room houses the station's record library.

At present Radio Sutatenza has at its disposal 500
kilowatts of long-wave transmitting power: 250 kw. at
Bogotá central, 120 kw. in Cali, 120 kw. in Barranquilla/
Magangué and 10 kw. in Medellín. Its capacity will be
increased by 90 kw. when a new 100 kw. transmitter goes
into service this June in Medellín. (All of the transmission sites except for Magangué have backup transmitters of lesser capacity to ensure that the stations
remain on the air in the event of failures.) With its
considerable transmitting capacity Radio Sutatenza is
able to cover most of the land area of Colombia as well
as parts of adjacent countries.

Short-wave transmission is also provided on three
frequencies with transmitting powers of 50, 25, and 10
kilowatts. The largest of the three serves as a backup
transmitter to transmission A and the others to broadcast transmission B.

Interconnection of the long-wave transmitters into
a national network was completed in 1969 through installation of a chain of five FM repeater transmitters.
Paralleling the FM network is a radiophone system which
provides two-way communication between network installations.

Publishing Activities

ACPO produces three major printed components as
adjuncts to its radio programs: the cartillas (textbooks)
for the Basic and Progressive Courses, El Campesino, its
weekly newspaper, and the Biblioteca del Campesino, a
special book series. The total output of ACPO educational
materials consists of approximately 600,000 cartillas and
300,000 books annually, plus 70,000 copies of El Campesino
each week.

ACPO's educational materials are printed by Editorial
Andes, which ACPO owns. One of the five largest printing
firms in Colombia, Editorial Andes employs approximately
130 persons. Commercial work constitutes about 75 percent of the Editorial Andes plant's traffic, and the
profit from such work, which is undisclosed, goes into
the general ACPO budget.

The plant is well equipped to do almost any kind of
printing job, from calendars and labels to comic books
and financial reports. Its equipment, much of it donated,
includes both letter-press and offset equipment and an
extensive photo-engraving department capable of doing
fine quality color separation.[13]

Cartillas

The use of visual materials as a complement to the
radio classes was introduced shortly after Radio Sutatenza went on the air. Initially, posters were prepared
for the radio classes. In 1951, the first textbook,
prepared by the Ministry of Education, was employed in
conjunction with the radio classes. In 1954 ACPO, with
technical assistance from the United Nations Educational,
Scientific, and Cultural Organization (UNESCO), prepared
its own cartilla for radio instruction in literacy and
numbers. In 1960 ACPO revised and expanded this cartilla
into five basic texts: literacy, arithmetic, health,
agriculture, and spirituality. These texts, in conjunction with the radio classes, formed the two-year curriculum in fundamental integral education.

The cartillas were revised in the late 1960s. In
the new format there was a single cartilla for the Basic
Course, focusing on literacy and arithmetic, and five
for the Progressive Course: "Nuestro Bienestar" (health);

"Hablemos Bien" (language improvement); "Cuentas Claras" (arithmetic); "Suelo Productivo" (agriculture), and "Comunidad Cristiana" (religion). The basic text is 112 pages in length; the texts in the Progressive series range from 112 to 160 pages.

In preparing the new cartillas, which were published in 1971, there was much consultation among the members of the pedagogical staff, the staff of the campesino institutes, the sociology staff, and subject matter experts. Some testing was made of the materials, primarily to determine comprehension and campesino responsiveness to the illustrations. A preliminary revision was prepared in black and white editions before publishing the final editions in color.

The instructional matter in the basic text includes 50 pages devoted to literacy and 54 pages to arithmetic. The literacy portion is devoted to teaching the reading and writing of Spanish. It is not a language-teaching course, but rather a course to help persons who know the spoken language gain access to it through its printed/written form.

At present, it is impossible to provide a set of textbooks to each student. Often one "school" must share a set. This is a serious drawback which can be remedied if production and distribution is increased. Another problem of the series, however, cannot be so easily remedied. The books have few built-in exercises that would allow the students to practise and reinforce their learning. There are some exercises in the arithmetic section of the Basic text as well as in the Progressive Course arithmetic book, but virtually no exercises in the other books.

Another criticism which has been made of the Progressive series relates to the organization and presentation of content. At present, material (radio classes and textbook) is presented segmentally and not sequentially. The ICED team was advised that ACPO is looking at the possibility of using programmed instructional methods in their courses. For the immediate future, however, the new textbooks will continue to be used. It should be added that segmental programming allows students to enter the course at any point and complete the course in two years.

El Campesino

In 1958, ACPO opened a third channel of communications as a complement to its radio programs and textbooks by founding El Campesino. This weekly newspaper was the first publication in Colombia devoted to a rural audience and still has the largest rural circulation. It provides a continuation and extension of the subject matter covered in a given week by the Escuelas Radiofonicas. In addition,

the paper seeks to build pride among the campesinos by
giving them a paper that espouses their cause.

The newspaper, which began with an edition of twenty
pages in tabloid format and a press run of 30,000 copies,
has been printed in standard newspaper size format since
1960. Seventy thousand copies are sold each week. There
are plans to increase circulation substantially, provided
financing is available and production and distribution
problems can be solved. (Several years ago a campaign
was mounted to stimulate sales, and circulation passed
100,000. However, this could not be maintained under
normal operating conditions, and the circulation appears
to be relatively stable at 70,000 copies.)

El Campesino is not a "news" paper. Because of the
immense difficulties of maintaining distribution to its
rural and frequently remote readership, the papers are
printed six days prior to distribution. Preparation of
the content begins a week prior to printing so that there
is a time lag of almost two weeks in preparation. Further,
El Campesino is considered an integral part of the overall ACPO effort and the main thrust of its content is to
support that effort.

Each edition consists of three sections: information,
recreation, and knowledge. The first and largest section
(eight pages) is information, and is the last section to
be prepared. It contains general news and information
primarily concerning the agricultural sector, together
with news about various ACPO and Escuela Radiofonica
groups. There is also an editorial page with the editorial and leading articles of this section coordinated
with the campaigns of ACPO (discussed later). By the
first of each year, themes are set for each week's edition
corresponding to the campaigns to be conducted by ACPO.
This list is published along with El Campesino's rate
card and is used by the business office to attract advertising from agencies or companies that might have an
interest or concern for specific topics.

The recreation section, four pages in length, contains color comic strips, games and puzzles, jokes and
stories, and directions for home activities and sports.

The four-page knowledge section is a direct extension
of the radio classes, containing articles that are coordinated with content themes of the various instructional
courses presented that week. The articles in this section
are prepared by the Radio Sutatenza teaching staff.

Each month El Campesino carries an educational supplement which serves as the text for the Complementary
Course. The supplements are eight full-sized newspaper
pages in length. However, when cut, they form a 32-page
booklet. This allows all students in the Complementary
Course to have their own printed material at the nominal
40 centavo price of the newspaper. The supplements are
well illustrated with drawings, maps, and charts, and are

printed in both black and red ink for better visual appearance and to add emphasis to key material.

The newspaper's editorial staff consists of an editorial director and two assistants, an artist and a photographer. With the exception of the knowledge section, they are responsible for the entire content of the paper. They draw heavily upon outside resources, particularly for the technical articles on the theme subjects of the week. Their sources include various government ministries, agricultural, educational, and research institutes and agencies. All copy, however, is rewritten by the editorial staff. Their major effort is to adjust the vocabulary and style so that the content can be easily read and understood by the campesinos.

The three professionals on the staff have had training in journalism or communications. The editorial director has been with the paper since its beginning. Although the salaries paid are comparable to those of other leading Colombian papers, the director states that he has had difficulty retaining his assistants. Most ambitious journalists want to work on metropolitan dailies and they feel that El Campesino, because of the nature of its audience and its simple style, lacks prestige. The director himself takes pride in the mission of the newspaper, stating that they are trying to create a "campesino journalism" for which there is no precedent.

Although El Campesino seeks advertising the amount carried each week is rather small—usually less than one full page in a 16-page edition. Most advertising is of an institutional nature. The business director for ACPO states that El Campesino suffers from the same problem as the radio stations. Despite the size of the audience, the readership is not of interest to the businesses that do the most newspaper advertising.

The newspaper is distributed through a network of 17 regional ACPO offices and 1,200 distributors or vendors. The single copy price of the paper to the reader is 40 centavos (about U.S. two cents). However, there is a discount schedule for the distributors which ranges from 27 to 31 centavos per copy. The selling agents can contract and pay for their papers through the agricultural credit bank.

The total actual cost per copy is 1.33 pesos. The income per copy is 29 centavos from the sale price and 21 centavos from advertising, a total of 50 centavos, which means the ACPO subsidy per copy amounts to 83 centavos. According to the business manager, the main cost burden is distribution. This is greatly inflated by the cost of getting relatively few copies to many isolated locations. Since 80 percent of circulation is in rural areas, it appears unlikely that distribution costs can be significantly lowered.

From information gathered through surveys and informal evidence from other sources, it appears that El
Campesino has built a loyal audience that goes far beyond
the actual purchasers of individual copies: sales are
not necessarily to the same individuals from week to week
and there is a considerable passing along of copies and
information read in the paper.

Biblioteca del Campesino (Campesino Library)

Just as El Campesino is intended to provide a newspaper designed and written specifically for the campesinos, the Biblioteca del Campesino (Campesino Library)
is designed to provide books appropriate to a rural
audience. In both cases, there is a recognition of the
fact that, in order to retain their literacy skills, the
students need reading material that is written at a level
they can comprehend, is easily and cheaply available, and
is of interest.

The book series is seen as perhaps the final extension of the Escuelas Radiofonicas structure. The books
are written under commission of ACPO to provide further
reinforcement and expansion of the subject matter covered
in the other instructional elements. Originally ACPO intended to publish 100 titles. To date, only 16 titles
have been issued and it appears that there are no additional ones now in preparation.

Some of the books have been written by members of
the pedagogical staff and some by outside experts. There
have been difficulties, however, in achieving the desired
combination of specialized subject matter and a text
written and illustrated at a level appropriate to the
campesinos. It appears that the inability or unwillingness of experts to try to explicate their subject in
simple language has meant that work done by outsiders
has had to be edited, which some authors have resisted.
This difficulty is cited as one of the reasons for the
slow growth of the Biblioteca series.

Sales of existing titles, however, have been impressive and the series still has high priority within ACPO.
In 1970 alone, 686,000 copies were distributed (101,000
were a single book, "Mother and Child"). The plan is to
edit and distribute five million books in this series
over the next five years.

The cost of producing these books averages 1.49
pesos, although it is not clear whether or not this takes
into account considerable amortization of the original
typesetting and make-up. The books, which have a retail
price of 2 pesos (U.S. 10 cents) are sold primarily
through individual dealers. If dealers buy in quantities
of 50 copies or more, the cost to them is 1.50 pesos. If
most of the books are sold by ACPO at discount through
dealers, it would appear that the book series just about
breaks even.

Personal Contact

Radio messages and printed information are reinforced by personal contacts between ACPO and the campesinos. By means of local staff working in municipalities throughout the country, local volunteers, and the collaboration of parish priests, ACPO has carried its program on a personal level to large numbers of rural Colombians. In this section, we shall briefly review the local organizations of ACPO, the training institutes run by ACPO to develop local staff, and the vehicles of campaigns and correspondence-- all of which ACPO uses to strengthen ties with its audience.

Local Parish Organizations

ACPO has developed a network of local parish organizations throughout the country to promote and strengthen its mass media educational programs. Initially, the key figure in the success of such local organizations was the parish priest. "When he [the priest] wishes, there is an organization; when not, none exists."[14] However, since 1965 greater emphasis has been placed on lay leadership at the local level, though in collaboration with the local priest.

The parish priest, who is nominally the director of the local radiophonic schools, is assisted by a lay leader known as the representante parroquial (parish representative). He is in charge of local administration: collecting statistics, calling meetings of auxiliaries, visiting schools, and providing teaching materials. Under the representative are the auxiliares immediatos, those who are in direct control of the schools and whose functions were described above. These individuals are all volunteers and receive no salary from ACPO.

In communities where there is considerable ACPO activity, a lider local (local leader) is assigned by ACPO. Such an individual is provided with a five-month training course at one of the two Campesino Institutes of ACPO and is selected by ACPO and his own parish to attend such a course. His or her duties are to assist the local parish organization in promoting the schools, improve their functioning, and take part in ACPO campaigns. The local leaders generally serve in the field for one to two years and receive a small stipend for this work. They are expected to continue with their normal work activities while serving as leaders.

Local leaders with good performance records may be selected by ACPO to attend a regional leader course at one of the institutes. This course (divided into five months at an institute, five months in the field, and five months back at the institute) prepares the regional leaders to administer ACPO efforts at the regional level. At present,

the country is divided into 20 regions, with each
regional center composed of a regional secretary, a
regional leader, and several local leaders. In 1971,
there were approximately 200 regional and local leaders
working in Colombia.

As in the case of local leaders, the post of regional
leader is not considered a full-time career position.
He serves in this capacity for several years and receives
a "scholarship" in lieu of salary. By keeping job
appointments of short duration, ACPO has encouraged considerable turnover in local personnel. In part, this
results from a shortage of funds to create a career
service. But the resultant turnover is also considered
desirable; it increases the number of campesinos who can
benefit from the work experience and increases the total
pool of local leadership which ACPO hopes to encourage
and develop.

Outside the organizational structure outlined above
is the dirigente campesino (literally "leader of the
campesino"). These are young adults who have been
selected by their parish to attend the first level
course at one of the institutes. Upon completion of this
four-month course, they return to their local communities
and are expected to promote the activities of ACPO. Many
become auxiliaries, some parish representatives. It is
from this group of dirigentes that the local leaders are
usually selected. ACPO sees this group as serving the
functions of opinion leaders and innovators within the
local communities. At present, approximately 640 dirigentes are graduated from the Campesino Institutes each
year.

Campesino Institutes

To provide a staff for its local organizations, ACPO
founded its first Campesino Institute in 1954 in the town
of Sutatenza. Initially it was only for men, but later
a women's program was begun. In 1962, a second institute
(for men only) was begun in Caldas, Antioquia. As shown
in Table 1.5 more than 6,300 dirigentes were graduated
from these centers by 1968. In addition these institutes
graduated 590 local leaders between 1962 and 1968 and 94
regional leaders (1965-1968).

Table 1.6 presents an overview of the institutes.
In all three courses, the major educational content is
"fundamental integral education." The institutes, however, also offer technical training in such fields as
agriculture, rural construction, health, and home economics.
In the local and regional leader courses there is also
training in administration and organization of radio
schools and in the techniques of radio instruction. In
all courses there is considerable emphasis on inculcating
in students ACPO's mistique: to motivate and dedicate

TABLE 1.5

Number of Dirigentes Trained
in Campesino Institutes
1954-1968

	Male	Female	Total
1968	402	240	642
1967	259	211	470
1966	269	212	481
1965	219	287	506
1964	39	130	169
1963	154	131	285
1962	179	138	317
1954-1961	1,631	1,802	3,433
TOTAL	3,152	3,151	6,303

Source: Information prepared for ICED team by ACPO, 1971.

one's efforts to the cultural, economic, and spiritual
development of rural Colombia.

The institutes, both set in rural communities, are
staffed in part by members of Catholic religious orders
and in part by lay teachers, a few of whom have progressed through the ACPO ranks from dirigente to leader
to institute teacher. Such teachers serve as success
models to the students and also help ground the educational programs firmly in the realities of rural Colombia.

Upon interviewing students in the leaders' courses
at the Sutatenza Institute, the ICED study team found
that, while generally satisfied with the basic educational instruction, students felt courses were too short
and did not provide them with sufficient technical expertise to be of assistance to farmers. However, ACPO
views its local personnel more as motivators and administrators rather than technical assistance experts, a
role filled, in their view, by other rural service
agencies.

Campaigns

In order to reinforce learning and demonstrate its
practical utility, ACPO continually mounts campaigns.
By means of the campaigns, "the notions and content
learned from the radio are translated into concrete realities of improvement. In addition, they serve as a ther-
mometer which measures the degree to which radio teaching
has achieved results."[15] The local organizations are
responsible for the promotion and organization of these

campaigns. The campaign subjects may be grouped under
five headings: 1) defense of the soil, 2) nutrition,
3) living accommodations, 4) recreation, and 5) participation in community organizations. Campaign themes for
the entire year are selected prior to the beginning of a
calendar year. They are publicized by radio and newspapers and a new campaign may be mounted as often as
every week. The campaign of the week is usually related
to the subject matter covered in that week's radio classes.
In addition, a special radio class is devoted to the
campaign theme. Concurrently that week's newspaper
carries articles related to the theme and illustrations
where appropriate. The local ACPO staff, having been
previously alerted to the week's campaign, tries to
motivate the local residents to participate.

If the week's campaign relates to constructing floors
in houses, the radio class on health might include information on the health benefits of having floors, and the
mathematics class might deal with area measurements. The
class devoted to campaigns would deal with some of the
technical aspects of floor construction and the newspapers
would carry illustrations of the procedures to be followed.
The local ACPO workers (local leaders, auxiliaries, and
dirigentes) would try to promote floor building, provide
what technical assistance they can, and inform prospective
participants on how and where to secure the required
building materials. Floors which are in fact constructed
are counted by the local staff and reported to regional
leaders.

TABLE 1.6

Entry Requirements, Length of Training, and
Enrollment at Campesino Institute

Course	Prior Training Requirements	Length of Training	Average Number Enrolled per Year
Dirigente	Literacy	4 mos.	640
Local leaders	Dirigente course	5 mos.	90
Regional leaders	Local leaders course	10 mos.	25

Source: Table prepared by ICED based on ACPO statistics.

In 1968 (the last year for which figures are available) it was reported that over 100,000 trees were planted as part of the "defense of the soil" campaign, more than 11,000 fruit orchards begun as part of the nutrition campaign, and 4,600 floors constructed in the "living accommodations" campaign.

Personal contact with the campesino is also maintained through correspondence. The radio network and its local stations all receive a considerable volume of mail, some of which is answered on the air and the remainder in writing. ACPO's Cultural Division, which runs the formal radio classes, maintains a permanent staff devoted to answering the radio school correspondence. El Campesino also receives letters from its readers, some of which are published in the newspaper and the rest answered directly.

Integration of the Teaching Elements

The full power of ACPO's delivery system derives not only from the multiple delivery channels it employs--radio (the courses and informal educational programs plus entertainment and news), the textbook series, El Campesino, special book series, local staff, campaigns, and correspondence--but from how these several elements complement and reinforce one another.

The key example of internal integration is the radio schools. A given class brings together the radio course, the appropriate textbook, the physical equipment (radio, blackboard and chalk, paper and pencils) and the auxiliar immediato. The radio lesson provides a quasi-personal stimulus to the students. The radio teacher covers specific textbook material, explains and expands the content, asks and answers questions, and directs performance of exercises. The auxiliary sees that students are ready for the broadcast and to follow the program text material. He also assists in performance and checks responses. The weekly newspaper reinforces the content of the materials presented via radio and textbook and also serves to reinforce the reading ability of students. The special book series goes a step further in amplifying techniques and knowledge. It is important to note that the same teaching staff is responsible for radio class production, editing of textbooks and special book series, and writing of the newspaper's knowledge section.

ACPO's campaigns serve as another integrating element within the organization. The five campaign themes are treated each week as part of the Progressive Course. Promotion of projects and instruction in specific knowledge and techniques required to undertake these projects are offered on the radio and are coordinated

with the weekly theme of El Campesino. The actual work
required to realize a campaign's objective--latrine
building, piped water projects, organizing neighborhood
meetings, and so forth--is coordinated and directed by
local ACPO staff who are backed-up by their regional
offices, the Institutes, and ACPO central.

Another example of internal program coordination is
the overall programming of the radio network. Even though
most air time is devoted to other than formal class presentation, most program content seeks to reinforce and
expand upon the formal class instruction.

ACPO has thus built a full range of communication
channels, including both physical production (radio transmission and printing house) and program content production
and, to a considerable extent, has coordinated the messages
sent out over these channels. Each element or medium, however, makes a different contribution to given educational
objectives. Table 1.7 shows the relative importance of
each medium in providing content that meets the five
objectives of "fundamental integral education."

Feedback, Evaluation, and Research

A program as complex and extensive as ACPO's requires
considerable feedback to gauge whether its objectives are
being realized.

Through a system of statistical reporting, examinations, correspondence, and special research projects,
ACPO has tried to monitor results and, in turn, adjust
programs to meet the needs and interests of the target
audience. However, because this audience is remote and
widely dispersed, the monitoring of results has been
extremely difficult.

Statistics on enrollment, number of schools, and
student characteristics are collected by the local ACPO
organizations and forwarded to regional offices and
ultimately to Bogotá. Unfortunately, the capacity of
local organizations to collect and tabulate data is uneven. Thus the aggregate figures compiled at ACPO headquarters may be inaccurate. They do, however, serve as
useful rough quantitative measures. The same local
organizations report on campaign activities, but because
of poor returns from a large number of municipalities in
which ACPO is known to be active, the accuracy of these
figures may be questioned.

Examinations are given for both the Basic and
Progressive Courses; these consist of a few very general
questions appearing in the weekly newspaper. The examination is administered in class groups and subsequently
marked by the class auxiliary. ACPO sees these examinations more as a motivational tool (to encourage those

TABLE 1.7

Relevance of Media Employed in the
Delivery of Information According
to Educational Objectives

Medium	Health	Literacy	Arithmetic	Economic	Spirituality
Radio **Programming:**					
Courses	A	B	B	A	A
Informal	C	X	X	B	B
General	X	X	X	X	C
News	C	X	X	C	C
Textbooks	A	A	A	A	A
Book Series	B	B	X	B	B
Newspaper **Sections:**					
Information	C	B	X	C	C
Recreation	C	B	X	C	C
Knowledge	B	B	B	B	B
Supplements	B	B	B	B	B
Correspondence	C	C	X	C	C
Recordings	C	X	X	C	C
Campaigns	B	X	C	B	B
Local personnel (personal contact)	C	B	B	B	B

Key: A Highly relevant
      B Relevant
      C Minor relevance
      X Little or no relevance

Source: Table prepared by ICED in collaboration with H. Bernal,
Director of Planning and Programming for ACPO.

who pass by giving them a certificate and exhort them to
continue their good work, and encourage those who fail
by praising them for learning at least part of the material and exhorting them to keep studying and try again)
than as a rigorous test of learning.

ACPO does make use of correspondence in a most
imaginative way--making it an effective feedback mechanism. Letters to the radio school (approximately 6,000
per month) are recorded and tabulated by area of the
country and topic. The selection of radio program content can then be determined in view of the kinds of
information requests received from listeners. All correspondence is answered, either directly or over the air,
and the staff of letter writers draws upon the technical
expertise in their department or requests information from
various government ministries and research agencies to
help them frame replies.

Finally, sales of newspapers and books are another
form of feedback, indicating the degree to which these
publications find acceptance among their rural audience.

At present, ACPO's Department of Planning and Programming (in the Cultural Division) carries on field research
as part of its many activities. In general, however, ACPO
has suffered from a lack of field research--because of
lack of means rather than lack of qualified personnel.
There appears to have been no major internal evaluation
until the "Cruzada Cultural Campesina" of 1964. In the
"Cruzada," 21 persons in seven groups spent four months
canvassing 104 localities. The teams included primarily
the staff from the Institutes and some lideres. Interviewing focused on alumni of the Institutes and the parish
clergy. The results provided considerable (and frequently
qualitative) data on the operation of, and attitudes
toward, the school program in these communities, reception
of signal, response to various campaigns, as well as
tracing what became of Institute alumni. The study
generated suggestions for modification in almost all
elements of the ACPO program.

From 1964 on, ACPO's Department of Sociology and its
expanded entity, Planning and Programming, have issued
reports on a series of "studies." Some of these have
been more think-pieces than actual research (which is not
to demean their importance). In 1970, two working papers
were published outlining several studies. These have
been discussed above with regard to ACPO's audience.
There has also been a series of external studies and
"evaluations" of ACPO which will be reviewed below in
the section on ACPO's impact.

On the whole, there has been no organized program of
continuing internal research and there has been no real
testing of program content. Pedagogical techniques and
materials have been developed largely by relying primarily upon outside advice, tradition, and professional

insight. Although some efforts have been made to pretest instructional materials, there has been no effort to validate methods and program content by controlled testing.

Two major research programs are planned for 1972. One will be a 10 percent sample of new registrations in courses to provide, for the first time, a detailed analysis of the current class. Computer time has been offered by a large local corporation which will make it possible to computerize work of this kind. The other study will involve a national sample and will be designed to find out what use is being made by whom of the different ACPO media programs.

In the view of the Director of Planning and Programming, additional research that focuses on the life of the campesino is needed so that the program plan and content can be adapted to it. One possibility as a research technique would be to send the program's pedagogical cadre out into the field to obtain personal observations. They would live with the campesinos, participate in their life, and would keep diaries to note what interests the community, what the actual daily schedule from season to season is, what local resources there are. Such research would be qualitative. The cadre would then gather at a planning seminar to share and discuss their observations prior to beginning work on programming. The content and program schedule could then be adapted to what has been learned.

Coordination and Decentralization

ACPO has agreements of cooperation with several national agencies with rural activities. It has an agreement with the National Apprenticeship Service (Servicio Nacional de Aprendizaje, SENA) to provide air time for SENA to promote its programs. In turn, ACPO regularly calls upon SENA for technical assistance and information in producing its own programs and can ask SENA to train some of ACPO's own personnel in specific job skills.

ACPO has also worked with the Coffee Growers Federation to supply radios and organize radio schools in coffee-growing areas. It also works through the Agricultural Credit Bank to finance local sale of radios to campesinos and newspapers to local sellers.

Through its radio programs and newspaper, it actively encourages its listeners to participate in local organizations, such as the Association of Lenders (those who receive bank credits) and local neighborhood organizations such as those sponsored by Acción Comunal. This agency attempts to promote local organizations (juntas comunales) and, in general, promotes self-help community agencies. In the late 1950s ACPO promoted similar local organizations and was one of the initial promoters of Acción Comunal, which now has responsibility for this field.

ACPO also uses its radio and press facilities to inform campesinos of the rural services provided by government and private organizations, such as Acción Comunal, the agricultural extension service of the Colombian Agricultural Institute, and the Land Reform Agency. Interestingly, many of the former ACPO local staff now are connected with these rural service agencies, either as members of sponsored organizations or as employees.

In some of the more remote areas of Colombia, ACPO is virtually the only service agency, thus foreclosing attempts at local coordination. Even where other agencies are represented, however, cooperation at the local level is not always smooth, particularly as ACPO is often viewed by government as a private instititution which is aligned with the Catholic Church--even though it is legally an autonomous institution not directly within the church establishment. One of the most conspicuous points of incomplete coordination would appear to be between ACPO schools and the formal school system. It is possible, however, that ACPO's new Complementary Course, which prepares dropouts for the primary school leaving exam, will improve this linkage.

One issue that has become crucial in ACPO's multi-faceted program is that of centralized versus local organization. As noted above, the three regional stations have considerable autonomy in developing radio programming, but the courses given in the escuelas radiofonicas are produced and transmitted from central headquarters. The two Campesino Institutes enjoy a degree of autonomy, although policy is formulated at central headquarters. Since the instructional content of the institutes is largely determined by the textbooks and radio lessons, the central organization again exerts influence on these institutes.

Some studies of ACPO, especially that of Musto,[16] have been severely critical of the centralized nature of the organization and its program. This criticism is also heard within the ranks of ACPO itself, particularly as one moves from central headquarters to the regional stations and offices.

From a strictly structural point of view, the centralization of ACPO, and especially its radio network, is one of its most admirable aspects. First, it has yielded considerable economic savings without sacrificing continuity of the local operations. Good airline connections within Colombia make it feasible for the program to centralize technical staff and the great bulk (90 percent) of the storehousing of parts. Without these transportation advantages, however, a program would have to balance such economic savings against the possible

loss of impact of the program due to prolonged disruption
of local operations.

The real dilemma of the centralization/localization
argument is in the realm of content. The arguments for
decentralization are to permit the adaptation of programs
and lessons to the local accent, idioms, living conditions,
and so on. Originally, Radio Sutatenza was to have less
powerful, localized stations. This plan was not feasible
because of the competition for frequency allocations.
Thus, although there is considerable programming in the
three regional stations, such programs end up serving
the large regional audience rather than being specifically
directed to local centers.

For the instructional program, which depends heavily
on volunteer and minimally trained persons at the local
level, the question of decentralization is a vexing one.
To adapt the basic materials--the cartillas and the radio
lessons--to specific local audiences would greatly increase the operational cost.

In addition to this economic argument against localization of materials, another counterargument is that one
purpose of ACPO and Sutatenza is to work for the creation
of national identity. Local characteristics (at least in
their extreme) are one of the stumbling-blocks to achieving this. Since the differences between regions--in
accents and traditional regional jealousies (some of
which have intensely strong historical and political roots)
--have created problems, it may be well to have at least
some programs and instruction which give impetus to
creating better internal understanding without destroying
the valuable aspects of regional differences.

Perhaps the best area for effecting decentralization
would be in the training program for the auxiliaries and
leaders and in strengthening the preparation of these
persons. As their personal competence rises, they could
be depended upon to take more initiative and provide the
localization and adaptation of the uniform materials
provided by the textbooks and radio.

IMPACT OF ACPO

It is extremely difficult to gauge the impact of
ACPO's programs in rural Colombia, partly because of its
extensive and isolated audience and partly because of the
scope of ACPO's programs.

As we have seen, ACPO's messages are carried throughout the country by means of its multiple delivery channels.
Thus rural dwellers could be affected by ACPO's radio
programs, newspaper, books, or contact with local personnel, or all four as integrated in the radio schools.

Quantitatively, we can gauge ACPO's impact in terms of the numbers of individuals who are reached by various media. In this regard, we shall examine statistics gathered by ACPO. We shall also draw upon studies that have sought to determine psychological and behavioral changes in campesinos that can be attributed to ACPO's influence. Finally, we shall present the findings of the ICED study team which examined the impact of ACPO on rural living conditions in two areas of Colombia.

Reach of the Media

Tables 1.8-1.10 present radio school statistics for the years 1960-1968. The number of schools grew from approximately 14,500 in 1960 to a high of 28,500 in 1965, and declined to 22,200 in 1968. The number of auxiliaries each year is approximately equal to the number of schools, with almost an equal number of males and females. The number of students increased from 110,000 in 1960 to 1965's peak of 234,200, declining to 167,400 in 1968.

TABLE 1.8

Number of Radio Schools and Auxiliaries
1960-1968

| | Radio Schools | | Auxiliaries | |
	Total	Rural	Total	Female
1968	22,212	22,145	22,212	11,539
1967	22,781	22,663	22,781	11,847
1966	22,129	21,912	22,129	9,574
1965	28,535	28,264	28,535	13,250
1964	26,101	25,838	26,101	11,616
1963	24,059	23,509	24,101	12,906
1962	22,148	21,914	22,617	10,855
1961	15,924	15,689	17,226	8,229
1960	14,504	14,194	15,614	7,240

Source: Statistics prepared by ACPO for ICED.

With approximately 9 million rural inhabitants in 1968, enrollments represent only about 1.9 percent of the rural population. However, if we discount: 1) those too young for school (approximately 3 million below seven years of age), 2) rural youth presently enrolled in government schools (approximately 700,000), 3) those considered too old to substantially benefit from schooling

TABLE 1.9

Radio School Students[a] by Age
1960-68

	Less than 15 yrs.	More than 15 yrs.	Total
1968	82,429	85,022	167,451
1967	79,895	96,756	176,651
1966	89,193	106,032	195,225
1965	110,225	123,945	234,170
1964	95,253	136,484	231,737
1963	*99,896	*121,100	*220,996
1962	*102,283	*107,833	*210,116
1961	*54,275	*71,237	*125,512
1960	*49,030	*61,075	*110,105

[a]Does not include students in urban areas, who constituted about 2 percent of total enrollment.

*More or less than 14 years--not 15 years.

Source: Statistics prepared by ACPO for ICED.

(approximately 1 million over the age of 60), and 4) those who have already completed both the Basic and Progressive Courses (approximately 290,000), ACPO may have reached roughly 4.5 percent of its potential rural audience in 1968, through its organized radio schools (assuming that children and adolescents are part of that audience).

According to ACPO statistics, the audience is predominantly rural. Only 67 of 22,212 schools are located in urban areas and only a small fraction of students are urban dwellers, whereas rural coverage is extensive, with schools located in every department of the country and in a majority of the municipalities.

Table 1.10 shows the literacy level of students enrolled in the ACPO schools. Approximately 45 percent of ACPO's students are illiterate when they enroll. Interestingly, this is about the same level of illiteracy (41.3 percent) recorded for rural Colombians over the age of 15, according to the 1964 census. For the literacy variable, therefore, ACPO's students approximate the general rural experience of Colombia.

Table 1.11 presents examination results of the Basic Course which provides literacy instruction. As we have explained above, given the weakness of the examination instrument and the procedures followed, it is impossible

TABLE 1.10

Literacy of Rural Radio School Participants Shown by Sex*

1960-1968

	MEN			% of Male Illiterate at Enrollment	WOMEN			% of Female Illiterate at Enrollment
	Literate at Enrollment	Illiterate at Enrollment	Total		Literate at Enrollment	Illiterate at Enrollment	Total	
1968	48,919	40,449	89,368	45.26	43,257	34,826	78,083	44.60
1967	50,355	40,894	91,249	44.81	46,711	38,691	85,402	45.30
1966	54,426	45,135	99,561	45.33	49,175	46,489	95,664	48.59
1965	60,085	58,960	119,045	49.52	59,020	56,105	115,125	48.73
1964	62,433	56,286	118,719	47.41	58,612	54,406	113,018	48.13
1963	56,994	52,054	109,048	47.73	57,035	54,913	111,948	49.05
1962	55,231	52,437	107,668	48.70	53,712	48,736	102,448	47.57
1961	37,169	32,228	69,397	46.44	30,172	25,943	56,115	46.23
1960	35,405	27,211	62,616	43.45	26,463	21,026	47,489	44.27

*Excludes urban students

Source: Statistics prepared by ACPO for ICED.

to use these statistics to prove that literacy has been
gained by these students because of the ACPO course. The
data suggest that literacy can be attained through these
courses, and other independent observers have reported
that ACPO has been successful in forming new literates.[17]
The ICED study team findings also tend to corroborate this
position, but more detailed research is needed to yield
proof of the teaching effectiveness of the literacy course.

TABLE 1.11

Results of Literacy Instruction in
the Radio School Basic Course*
1960-68

	Illiterates Enrolled		Illiterates Who Took Exam		Illiterates Learning to Read & Write in Course		Exam Pass Rate
	Total #	Female #	Total #	Female #	Total #	Female #	%
1968	75,275	34,826	27,509	13,640	20,186	10,174	73.38
1967	79,550	38,691	33,856	16,013	28,645	13,827	84.61
1966	91,624	46,489	43,341	21,385	40,429	18,977	93.28
1965	115,065	56,105	52,838	26,505	44,698	22,566	84.59
1964	110,692	54,406	53,701	25,903	28,945	13,021	53.90
1963	106,967	54,913	55,240	24,975	30,637	12,598	55.46
1962	101,173	48,736	50,236	20,434	28,064	11,860	55.70
1961	58,171	25,943	41,865	20,582	26,592	13,366	63.57
1960	61,868	26,463	43,748	19,060	30,747	12,150	82.11

*Excludes urban students

Source: Statistics prepared by ACPO for ICED

    Likewise, examination results for the Progressive
Course (Table 1.12) can be interpreted as suggestive,
not definitive, measures of the course's effectiveness.
Not everyone enrolled in a school program takes the year-
end exam: some students may drop out, others may not
feel prepared and, in the case of the Progressive Course,
it usually takes two years to complete the course.
    The radio network reaches many individuals who are
not ACPO students. In 1969, all the stations in the network broadcast 33,462 hours, most of which was composed
of nonradio class programming. To date, it has proved
impossible to judge the size of the listening audience.
However, in the audience survey conducted in 1969, over
97,000 letters were received by Radio Sutatenza from its

TABLE 1.12

Examination Results in the Progressive Course*

	Students Enrolled in Progressive Course		Students Who Took Exam		No. Who Passed Exam		Percent Who Passed
	Total	Female	Total	Female	Total	Female	
1968	92,176	43,257	19,916	10,748	15,163	8,309	76.13
1967	97,066	46,711	24,855	14,260	18,611	10,251	74.79
1966	103,601	49,175	56,938	27,996	34,787	16,341	61.09
1965	119,105	59,020	65,422	32,284	44,986	21,216	68.76
1964	121,045	58,612	66,415	31,295	52,829	23,305	79.54
1963	114,029	57,035	64,101	31,121	50,485	24,478	78.76
1962	108,943	53,712	57,679	25,776	46,161	21,455	80.20
1961	67,341	30,172	50,478	21,078	43,113	16,772	85.41

*Excludes urban students

Source: Statistics prepared by ACPO for ICED

listeners. Since many more individuals listen than tend to write, we can judge the size of the audience to be substantial.

El Campesino is read by many who are not enrolled in radio schools, although there is no way of determining what proportion of the 70,000 weekly copies are sold to nonstudents. Nor do we know the number of readers per copy, although it has been estimated at 10 persons.

The sale of books in the campesino book series is another measure of "contact" with the rural population. In 1969, over 100,000 books in the series were sold and over 650,000 between 1964 and 1969.

Finally, even though campaign projects tend to be underreported, data on campaigns are suggestive of the impact of ACPO's programs in the field. (See Table 1.13.)

Research Findings

While it is impossible to sum up the above statistics and arrive at a judgment as to the total impact of ACPO in rural Colombia, various researchers have attempted to gauge certain aspects of ACPO's impact.

In a study of radio schools in 1967 in two Departments (Condinamarca and Boyacá), Hernando Bernal-Alarcón, who later became director of planning and programming of ACPO, found that the radio school programs of ACPO were a factor in the adaptation of innovations.[18]

Families participating tended to adopt more innovations
than nonparticipating families. His results were qualified, however: they were held valid only for the area
covered in the survey (the Departments of Condinamarca
and Boyacá), and it was found that certain of the items
were not true innovations. He concluded that "the media
systematically employed by ACPO appear to produce both
reinforcement effects and creative effects."19
    Bernal's second major conclusion, however, points
out the varying degree of influence of ACPO among different population subgroups. He found that landowners (with
smallholdings and generally functioning at the subsistence level) were more likely to adopt the innovations
promoted by the radio schools than the landless. In
addition, it appeared that very few landless peasants
participated in the radio school movement.
    Whether or not Bernal's results can be generalized
is problematical, as he himself points out:

TABLE 1.13

Rural Improvement Campaign Projects Realized
in the Period 1954-1968

Category	No. of Projects Realized
Household improvements	93,440
New houses	39,271
Piped water	32,257
Latrines	50,457
Flower gardens	85,702
Trees planted	4,469,106
Vegetable gardens	108,058
Compost heaps	136,509
Vaccination of animals	99,977
Stables	29,078
Pig sties	37,507
Chicken coops	44,241
Bee hives	24,481
Spraying crops with insecticides	88,606
Neighborhood boards formed	18,397
Bridges constructed	6,635
Improvements to rural roads	37,348
Sports fields constructed	14,279
Musical groups formed	10,306
Rural theatre groups organized	14,121

    Source: ACPO, Los Campesinos Trabajan por el Desarrollo
(Bogotá: Editorial Andes, 1971).

As has been observed by Primrose (1965), Torres
(1960) and Ferrer (1958), the degree of effectiveness (of the radio schools) varies from
place to place due to the intervention of such
factors as the interest of the local priest in
the radio schools, the intervention of other
agencies, and the cultural values of each
group, etc.[20]

Sister V. M. Primrose, author of another examination
of the radio school's impact, addressed her study directly
to the regional variation in impact.[21] Her study was
conducted in three socioculturally distinct areas of
Colombia. She found that while regional responses varied
to ACPO's educational program, the radio schools were
likely   1) to change and improve the living conditions
of campesinos, 2) to communicate basic knowledge to participants, and 3) to increase the level of literacy.
She felt, however, that the effectiveness of ACPO's
educational efforts could be improved through changes
in the pedagogical practices, especially through simpli-
fying didactic materials.

Stefan Musto, in a study that sought to analyze the
impact on the lives of rural Colombians,[22] found that
radio school students scored higher on a) modernity of
attitudes, b) innovativeness, c) integration (into
society), and d) income, than did those who were just
listeners of Radio Sutatenza, who in turn scored higher
than those not influenced by ACPO.

Musto found that the students tended to be considerably better informed concerning facts and current events
and generally more progressive in their attitudes and
orientations than those not influenced by ACPO.

Although crude income measures were used, it was
found that a larger proportion of the ACPO students earned
above the median income than in the other two groups.[23]

As Musto points out, the superiority of ACPO students
on various scales need not be causally related to ACPO
influence. Such a link apparently exists where ACPO
students are better informed and more innovative, in a
quantitative sense, than the control group, and were more
apt to adopt innovations that ACPO had promoted. Musto
concluded that even though ACPO was not the only organization working to promote rural improvement, it was the
most successful in promoting innovations at least in a
quantitative sense.

As shown in Table 1.14, ACPO's influence extends
beyond its students and listeners.

This again demonstrates that the campaigns of
the institution exercises an undoubted impact,
not only among the students of the radiophonic
schools and the listeners to Radio Sutatenza,

but also among those who are not influenced by
the other elements of action of ACPO.[24]

TABLE 1.14

Relative Importance of Different Influences with
Respect to the Totality of Innovations Adopted

Factors of Influence	Students	Listeners	Not Influenced
	%	%	%
ACPO	54.0	25.5	15.0
Other development organizations	9.0	13.5	20.0
Imitation (of neighbors and so on)	33.0	53.5	58.7
Other factors (such as priest, and so on)	4.0	7.5	6.3
TOTAL	100.0	100.0	100.0

Source: S. Musto, Los Medios de Comunicacion Social al
servicio del   Desarrollo Rural (Bogota: Editorial Andes, 1971),p.17.

Musto appends certain limitations to his findings
which corroborate the findings of Bernal and Primrose.
First of all, the superior position of ACPO students is
relative. While more progressive than their compatriots
in their own region, they may not score as high (relatively) in other regions of the country.[25] Secondly, the
students' superiority cannot be attributed exclusively to
the influence of ACPO. Radio Sutatenza is especially
well received among small landholders who, even before
they are influenced by ACPO, are more innovative, more
integrated, and better off economically than their landless neighbors.

As a general conclusion Musto states that

. . . the results of the investigation clearly
confirm that the institution has undeniably
achieved improvements at the level of subsistence economy. Such effects can, in the long-
run, contribute to the success of other
programs, public and private, that will be
carried out to promote rural development.[26]

It is not surprising that ACPO has an uneven impact
among regions of the country and groups within the rural
population. One would suspect that, in regions that
exhibit more progressive tendencies and among individuals

with a more progressive or innovative outlook, there would
be a greater tendency to "volunteer" and "participate" in
ACPO programs. Based on available research it would
appear that ACPO does serve to reinforce (and perhaps
extend through imitation) the progressive elements in
rural Colombia. Whether or not its influence is strong
or pervasive enough to expand and mobilize progressive
forces in rural Colombia to bring about a sustained
development effort cannot yet be determined.

ICED Study Team's Findings

     The ICED study team conducted interviews in two
areas of Colombia in an attempt to determine ACPO's
influence at the level of the farm family and to observe
the functioning of the local ACPO organization. It was
especially concerned with determining the degree to which
ACPO students adopted innovations promoted by the institutions and the degree to which the local ACPO organization influenced the institution's impact in a given
community.
     The study team was composed of a team leader (the
Director of Programming and Evaluation, Office of the
Colombian Agricultural Institute) and two field investigators. All three are sociologists by profession. The
two field investigators spent 12 days (at the end of
November-beginning of December, 1971) in the field conducting personal interviews with campesinos (using a
formal questionnaire). They also spent two days at the
ACPO Campesino Institute in Sutatenza informally interviewing students and staff. Personnel at ACPO Bogotá
were also interviewed.
     At the end of the one-month study a seminar was held
with the team members, ACPO officials, and outside parties
to discuss the study's findings. The author served as
coordinator of the study and provided administrative
support to the team.
     Interviews were conducted in the municipalities of
Onzaga and Mesopotamia, which are fairly distinct
socially and culturally. Onzaga, a municipality of
approximately 11,000 (1971), is located in a cold and
extremely mountainous region in the northeastern part
of the Department of Santander. It has poor road communications with urban centers. Mesopotamia, with an
estimated 1971 population of 6,000, is located in a low
mountain region in the center of the Department of
Antioquia. It is located within a short distance of the
main road to Medellín, three hours away.
     It was known that ACPO was quite active in Onzaga
and much less so in Mesopotamia (although several years
ago ACPO efforts in this area were considerably greater).

Given the limited time available for field work, it was hoped that in selecting two contrasting communities it would be possible to suggest (but not attempt to prove statistically) the amount of impact made by ACPO in rural communities with and without a strong ACPO presence.

As may be seen in Table 1.15, the samples in both locations were drawn from graduates of radio schools, students in these schools, and "beneficiaries" of ACPO programs who were not in schools--that is, listeners to the radio programs and readers of the newspaper. Samples were also drawn from those not benefiting from ACPO programs: those who neither listened to Radio Sutatenza nor read El Campesino. In all 211 interviews were conducted and all but 7 interviewees were either farmers (nearly all smallholders or renters of parcels) or members of a farm family. Most questions related to farm family practices and any adult member of the family could answer for the entire family.

TABLE 1.15

ICED Study of ACPO: Sample Distribution

	Onzaga		Mesopotamia		Totals	
	No.	%	No.	%	No.	%
Graduates of radio schools	36	27.3	2	2.5	38	18.0
Students in radio schools	40	30.3	24	30.4	64	30.3
Beneficiaries[a]						
(not students)	30	22.7	34	43.0	64	30.3
Not beneficiaries[b]	26	19.7	19	24.1	45	21.4
TOTALS	132	100.0	79	100.0	211	100.0

[a]Nonstudents who listened to Radio Sutatenza or read El Campesino

[b]Those who neither listened to Radio Sutatenza nor read El Campesino

Source: ICED Study Team Report

Tables 1.16-1.20 summarize some of the major findings of the study. In general those interviewed in Onzaga were more progressive in terms of adopting the practices recommended by ACPO and in terms of the total number of new practices adopted compared to the Mesopotamia sample. A larger proportion had increased their farm production over the past three years in Onzaga (56.8 percent) as compared with those smallholder farmers in Mesopotamia

TABLE 1.16

Effect of ACPO on Agricultural Production

	Percentage of Interviewees who Claimed Increased Agricultural Production				Agency whose Influence was Related to the Increase		
	Yes	No.	n.a.[a]	Total Number Inter- viewed	R.S.[b] No.	Other than R.S. No.	R.S. Influence as % of Total Influence
	%	%	%				
Onzaga	56.8	41.7	1.5	132	61	14	81.3
Mesopotamia	34.2	53.2	12.6	79	6	21	22.2
TOTAL	48.3	46.0	5.7	211	67	35	65.7

[a]n.a. = not ascertained
[b]R.S. = Radio Sutatenza

Source: ICED Study Team Report

34.2 percent) and were most likely to cite ACPO as the
agent which was most influential in bringing about such
increases (Table 1.16).
     In terms of household improvements (Table 1.17) ACPO
exerted a considerable influence on Onzaga where proportionately more improvements were made than in Mesopotamia.
The strength of ACPO influence in the health field is suggested by the data in Table 1.18. Nearly all families with
children in the Onzaga şample had had their children vaccinated in part due to the influence of ACPO. In Mesopotamia, the proportion of vaccinated children was lower, as
was ACPO's influence. ACPO also exerted a stronger influence
on Onzaga eating habits than on Mesopotamia (Table 1.19).
     One of ACPO's major campaign rubrics is the promo-
tion of community organizations and participation of the
campesinos in such organizations. Table 1.20 would suggest that ACPO has succeeded in this undertaking in
Onzaga. In this community about 87 percent of those interviewed participated in one or more community organizations (and 55 percent in more than one), while in Mesopotamia over three-quarters did not participate in any
community organization (of those who participated no one
was in more than one organization). It should be noted,
however, that there appears to be a greater tendency
toward group participation in the area of Onzaga compared
to Mesopotamia, and ACPO may serve to reinforce such
participatory behavior in Onzaga rather than initiate it.

TABLE 1.17

Selected Household Improvements Undertaken by Campesinos

Improvement	Onzaga		Mesopotamia	
	No.	% Sample Dist.	No.	% Sample Dist.
1. Install fences				
Yes	89	67.4	7	8.9
No	29	22.0	72	91.1
n.a.	14	10.6	-	-
TOTAL	132	100.0	79	100.0
Influencing agent (where stated)				
ACPO	44	49.4	0	-
Other	45	50.6	7	100.0
2. Enlarge house				
Yes	102	77.3	31	39.2
No	27	20.5	48	60.8
n.a.	3	2.2	-	-
TOTAL	132	100.0	79	100.0
Influencing agent (where stated)				
ACPO	73	70.9	3	9.7
Other	29	29.1	28	90.3
3. Build latrines				
Yes	45	34.1	9	11.4
No	85	64.4	70	88.6
n.a.	2	1.5	-	-
TOTAL	132	100.0	79	100.0
Influencing agent (where stated)				
ACPO	30	66.7	4	44.4
Other	15	33.3	5	55.6

Note: n.a. = no answer or not applicable

Source: ICED Study Team Report

Some of the differences noted in the study can probably be traced to differing sociocultural characteristics of the two communities. Also, some of the practices adopted may reflect the influence of other rural development agencies functioning in these areas. But it appears from the data that ACPO has exerted considerable influence in Onzaga and considerably less in Mesopotamia.

In large part the differing degree of ACPO influence is related to the strength of the local ACPO organization in each community. In Onzaga the local organization is

strong. Over 670 radio schools are in operation there,
compared to only 43 in Mesopotamia (none of which were
found to be operating in November 1971 by the ICED field
researcher). Mesopotamia, however, had as many as 180
radio schools in 1965 (a year in which there had been a
major effort to promote ACPO activities in Antioquia).
In Onzaga the local priest is active in the radio school
movement while the local priest in Mesopotamia (who had
newly arrived at the time of this study) is not. In
Onzaga the priest and parish representatives are assisted
by 16 active and former ACPO lideres, and the schools
appear to have been adequately supplied with teaching
materials (textbooks, paper, pencils, and so on). In
Mesopotamia, however, there is an elderly ACPO parish
representative who appears to be the only ACPO worker
in the community.

TABLE 1.18

Adoption of the Practice of Child Vaccination

	Onzaga		Mesopotamia	
Vaccinate Children	No.	% Dist.	No.	% Dist.
Yes	107	81.1	46	58.2
No	5	3.8	25	31.7
Not applicable	20	15.1	8	10.1
TOTAL	132	100.0	79	100.0
Influencing agent (where stated)				
ACPO	35	32.7	7	15.2
Others	72	67.3	39	84.8

Source: ICED Study Team Report

A further problem in Mesopotamia is the poor reception of Radio Sutatenza. The transmitter for Antioquia
is of limited power (and is in the process of being replaced) and the poor signal discourages many from listening to the broadcasts. In addition, most of the ACPO
radios in Mesopotamia are not in working order (foreclosing the use of the shortwave band) and, due to the
almost nonexistent local organization and apparent lack
of interest or means on the parts of campesinos, they
are not being repaired.
     Even with the limited ACPO presence in Mesopotamia,
ACPO is one of the few development agencies known by the

TABLE 1.19

Adoption of Improved Nutritional Practices

Nutritional Item	Onzaga No.	%	Mesopotamia No.	%
1. Eat beans				
Yes	105	79.5	33	41.8
No	27	20.5	45	57.0
n.a.	-	-	1	1.2
TOTAL	132	100.0	79	100.0
Influencing agent (where stated)				
ACPO	94	89.5	8	24.2
Others	11	10.5	25	75.8
2. Drink milk				
Yes	116	87.9	62	78.5
No	16	12.1	16	20.3
n.a.	-	-	1	1.2
TOTAL	132	100.0	79	100.0
Influencing agent (where stated)				
ACPO	80	69.0	5	8.1
Others	36	31.0	32	51.6
n.a.	-	-	25	40.3

Note: n.a. = no answer

Source: ICED Study Team Report

population and is held in high regard. ACPO's news-paper is well received (Table 1.21) and sells about 100 copies a week (compared to five copies of national daily papers sold in the community each day). Even though ACPO's impact is not as great as in Onzaga, many of the innovations and new practices promoted by ACPO are adopted by the residents of Mesopotamia.

In both areas it was found that little use was made of the Campesino book series, and few campesinos corres-ponded with ACPO.

The study team also found that there was little coordination between the local ACPO organization and other rural development agencies. In Mesopotamia such coord-ination was effectively ruled out because of the limited ACPO official presence and the fact that there was only one other agency functioning in the community--Acción Comunal. But in Onzaga, where many agencies were active, little cooperation was noted. There was, however,

indirect collaboration: ACPO had promoted student participation in a considerable number of organizations and
programs sponsored by these agencies.

Another element of impact the study attempted to
include was ACPO's role in forming new literates.
Approximately 17 percent of the sample claimed to have
gained literacy through ACPO radio schools (Table 1.22).
Interestingly, a larger proportion of the sample in
Mesopotamia than in Onzaga named ACPO as their teaching
source.

TABLE 1.20

Participation of Local Organizations

Participation	Onzaga		Mesopotamia	
	No.	%	No.	%
1. Participate in more than one organization	73	55.3	–	–
2. Participate in one organization	40	30.3	19	24.1
3. No participation	17	12.9	60	75.9
4. n.a.	2	1.5	–	–
TOTAL	132	100.0	79	100.0

Note: n.a. = no answer

Source: ICED Study Team Report

In order to test the level of literacy among those
sampled and at the same time probe the "readability" of
El Campesino, a short reading comprehension test was
administered as part of the interview (Table 1.23). The
interviewees were given a short passage from the newspaper to read aloud and then were asked several questions
based on the passage. Well over half the sample was able
to read with fair to good comprehension (based on inter-
viewer's judgment), with the proportion higher in Onzaga
than in Mesopotamia.

Table 1.24 shows the results of the reading comprehension test among those who claimed to have gained
literacy through ACPO teaching. The results, quite
similar in both communities, are not as good as for the
sample as a whole if judged in terms of the proportion
who score "good." But if "good" and "fair" are grouped,
better than four out of five in this group could read
and understand the content of El Campesino. This would
suggest that the literacy teaching of ACPO has achieved
a degree of success.

TABLE 1.21

Interviewees Who Claimed to Read
El Campesino

Read El Campesino	Onzaga		Mesopotamia	
	No.	%	No.	%
Yes	100	75.8	51	64.6
No.	31	23.5	25	31.6
n.a.	1	0.7	3	3.8
TOTAL	132	100.0	79	100.0

Source: ICED Study Team Report

TABLE 1.22

Stated Source from which Literacy Acquired[a]

Source	Onzaga		Mesopotamia		Total	
	No.	%	No.	%	No.	%
Public school	62	47.0	52	65.8	114	54.0
Radiophonic school	17	12.9	18	22.8	35	16.6
Other	21	15.9	9	11.4	30	14.2
n.a.[b]	32	24.2	–	–	32	15.2
TOTAL	132	100.0	79	100.0	211	100.0

[a]If public school and radiophonic school was indicated,
the individual was classified under public school.

[b]n.a. = no answer. The majority of such individuals are
illiterate.

Source: ICED Study Team Report

The studies of various researchers and that of the
ICED team tend to corroborate one another and strongly
suggest that ACPO has had an impact on rural Colombia,
especially in those areas where the local ACPO organization is functioning effectively. Such impact as can be
measured includes the various projects and innovations
promoted by radio and newspapers and reinforced by
campaigns. It also appears that the formation of new
literates is another area where ACPO has had impact.
Finally, as tentatively measured by Musto and suggested

by the ICED study team findings, ACPO appears to be
successful in fomenting new development attitudes among
a number of campesinos--this, of course, being the prime
objective of the institution.

TABLE 1.23

Results of ICED Study Team Reading
Comprehension Test

Level of Comprehension	Onzaga		Mesopotamia	
	No.	%	No.	%
Good	60	45.5	20	25.3
Fair	41	31.1	27	34.2
Deficient	20	15.1	23	29.1
None	11	8.3	9	11.4
TOTAL	132	100.0	79	100.0

Source: ICED Study Team Report

TABLE 1.24

Reading Comprehension of Those Claiming the
Radiophonic Schools as the Source
of Literacy Instruction*

Level of Comprehension	Onzaga		Mesopotamia		Total	
	No.	%	No.	%	No.	%
Good	5	21.7	4	22.2	9	22.0
Fair	15	65.2	11	61.1	26	63.4
Deficient	3	13.0	3	16.7	6	14.6
None	-	-	-	-	-	-
TOTAL	23	100.0	18	100.0	41	100.0

*Includes 6 persons in Onzaga who had attended one year of
primary school but reported they had learned to read from the
radiophonic schools.

Source: ICED Study Team Report

COSTS AND FINANCING

ACPO is clearly a major educational undertaking as can be seen from the current estimated operating budget for 1972 (Table 1.25). It is also growing rapidly. In 1967 the cost of operating ACPO was 26.7 million pesos compared to approximately 86 million pesos in 1972 (approximately US$4.3 million). This reflects an increase in broadcast operations (most of the new transmitting equipment as well as the regional broadcast centers were

TABLE 1.25

Anticipated Operating Expenses of ACPO, 1972

Category	Anticipated Expenses (Pesos)	% Dist. of Expenditures	% Devoted to Nonformal and Informal Educ.
1. Radio system program production and creative staff	12,000,000	(14.0)	60
2. Cultural Division-- teaching department, promotion (including institutes) and text-book department (excluding cost of printing)	14,000,000	(16.3)	100
3. Operation of publishing house (including commercial work), cartillas, books, and so on (excluding newspaper)	20,000,000	(23.3)	40
4. Newspaper	7,000,000	(8.1)	100
5. Regional activities-- including regional stations and local staff	15,000,000	(17.4)	30
6. Administration-- physical maintenance, maintenance of transmitters, administrative personnel, interest, and so on	18,000,000	(20.9)	61
Total	86,000,000	(100.0)	61

Note: All expenditure figures are approximations

Source: Information supplied to ICED study team by ACPO.

established after 1968), an increase in the number of local personnel in the field, increased publishing activity, expanded regional activities, and considerable inflation of the Colombian peso.[27]

In Table 1.25 we have sought to segregate educational expenditures (the structured courses and the informal educational activities) from commercial operations based on information provided by ACPO. Approximately 61 percent of all recurrent costs, or nearly 52.5 million pesos, are for educational efforts.

To put this figure into perspective, we should note that the 1970 Ministry of Education budget was nearly 2,000 million pesos (with over 626 million assigned to primary education) and the Agricultural Division budget of SENA for its rural training activities was more than 95 million pesos in 1971.

Table 1.26 presents the distribution of estimated ACPO income for 1972 by source. It must be noted that these figures are estimates and are dependent upon the publishing house's generating a substantial surplus and the radio network's earning considerably more revenue than in past years. As previously noted, Radio Sutatenza is attempting to build up its urban radio audience, in part through inclusion of more general entertainment aimed at this audience during appropriate hours (mid-day and evening), to attract more commercial advertising. Its attempt to self-finance nearly 74 percent of its expenditures, however, may fall short of its goal. This shortfall would have to be balanced either by reduced program activity or increased donations.

Apart from government funds of about 10 million pesos annually,[28] ACPO receives private contributions, many from Catholic Church-related agencies. It has also received some foreign government support in the form of long-term low-interest loans and has received gifts of capital equipment from foreign donors.

The capital investment figures for ACPO are not available and are difficult to calculate. Much of the equipment used by the organization has been donated and imported items have been exempt from duties (as ACPO is classified as a nonprofit educational organization).

ACPO had an endowment fund of approximately 67 million pesos in 1967. This has been invested and yields income to the organization which is applied against recurrent costs. The net worth of ACPO, however, was greater than 67 million pesos in 1967 as this figure did not include the value of fixed capital assets. The value of such assets (which includes a high-rise office building in downtown Bogotá, transmission facilities, printing house and equipment, and so on) is considerable but we do not know their actual worth.

TABLE 1.26

ACPO Estimated Income by Source, 1972
(000 Pesos)

Source of Income	Amount	% Self-Financing
A. Self-Generated		
1. Radio network	12,000	100.0
2. Cultural Division	---	0.0
3. Publishing house	30,000	150.0
4. Newspaper	2,000	28.6
5. Regional activities	7,500	50.0
6. Administration	13,000[a]	72.2
Subtotal self-generated	63,500	73.8[b]
B. Outside Funds		
7. Public funds	10,000	0.0
8. Contributions	11,500	0.0
Subtotal outside funds	21,500	0.0
TOTAL	86,000	73.8

[a]Includes among other things income from investments, rents received from the Edificio Cardinal Luque and long-term loans. Includes receipts from commercial work performed by phonograph record plant.

[b]Total expenses extimated at 86 million pesos.

Source: Information supplied by ACPO to ICED.

The most significant aspect of ACPO financing is its ability to generate income and thus self-finance much of its own activities. The printing house takes on commercial work; the radio and newspaper carry advertising; the phonograph record plant; which is little utilized for educational purposes, does pressings for commercial labels; the radio studios are used to record commercial advertisements; and the ACPO auditorium is rented out to the local symphony orchestra. In addition, ACPO uses only part of its headquarters building and rents out over half of the floor space to other enterprises. It also receives income from investments (the money for which comes from its endowment funds). Finally ACPO realizes income from the sale of its newspaper, its special book series, and radios.

It does not appear that ACPO's commercial activities have been undertaken at the expense of its educational program. Rather the commercial activities have allowed ACPO to utilize more fully its installed capacity (capacity in excess of that portion required to produce its educational programs) and to purchase more modern and

diversified plant and equipment than would be warranted
for solely educational purposes. This more complete and
sophisticated capacity, however, can be usefully employed
for educational ends as well as commercial undertakings.

The organizational objective of self-financing a
substantial portion of expenses appears to have had an
interesting effect upon the institution. It has resulted
in a greater awareness of program budgeting and planning.
There also seems to be a greater cost consciousness than
would normally be found in an educational organization and
considerable pressure exerted to reduce program costs
wherever possible. Maintenance of equipment and inventory
control, which were noted above, are examples of attention
to costs and the general business-like attitude found
within the organization.

Unfortunately we are not in the position to weigh
the benefits of ACPO's program against program costs.
ACPO does make an impact in rural Colombia, but there is
insufficient data available to quantify and qualify this
impact nationwide. Nor do we know with any degree of
certainty what costs are incurred by campesinos as they
seek to adopt the innovations promoted by ACPO. It is
impossible to quantify the value of "literacy," one of
ACPO's prime educational objectives. Finally, the
attitudinal changes among campesinos which ACPO seeks to
effect are difficult, if not impossible, to measure, and
exceedingly difficult to value. Given the objectives of
the program, most of which are not primarily economic,
and their long-term nature, a cost-benefit judgment is
difficult to make. That the program has survived and
grown for 24 years strongly suggests, however, that benefits are being realized by campesinos. The sale of
publications, enrollment in radio schools, radio-listener
correspondence, number of volunteer workers, and volume
of campaign projects realized indicate acceptance over
many years and, indirectly, that campesinos view ACPO's
efforts as beneficial.

MAJOR LESSONS OF ACPO'S EXPERIENCE

The preceding sections of this paper have described
and analyzed the evolution of ACPO's educational program.
In this concluding section, we shall try to extract the
major lessons of ACPO's 24 years of experience in the
field of mass nonformal education in rural Colombia.

1. ACPO has demonstrated that the mass media can
be effectively utilized to reach a sizable rural population which is both widely dispersed and isolated. It was
found, however, that one medium, namely radio, was not in
itself a sufficient teaching vehicle. Printed matter in
the form of textbooks, newspapers, and special readers
were required in order to reinforce the radio messages.

2.   The multiple media must be employed in a coordinated manner. The same message delivered by the various
communications channels, picks up additional audience in
the process and more importantly reinforces the given
message, increasing the probability that it is accurately
perceived.
3.   Mass media were found to be insufficient even
when several communications channels were employed.
Personal contacts were needed to motivate the learners,
reinforce the messages, organize the distribution of
materials,and particularize the learning.
4.   To ensure coordination and reinforcement of
messages disseminated through various media channels,
complemented by field personnel, it would appear that
a single entity must control the production and transmission of the messages and the training and administration of field personnel.
5.   While mass media educational efforts can make an
impact among rural dwellers, the ACPO experience clearly
demonstrates that such impact can be greatly increased
if a local organization is present to motivate the
campesinos, organize them, and provide reinforcement.
6.   ACPO has demonstrated that it is possible to
mobilize local human resources to volunteer their time
and effort in a mass educational program. Such volunteers (auxiliares) can perform limited and specific
functions with minimal training. They function best when
their duties are limited and sharply defined and when
they are backed up by a local organization that includes
individuals with more extensive training.
7.   Getting individuals to volunteer apparently
requires a strong motivational and inspirational message.
Potential volunteers must believe that their efforts will
be of value to themselves and their community. The
possibility that such volunteers may be selected for
special training at one of ACPO's institutes and that
further promotion may be anticipated may encourage individuals to volunteer.
8.   The influence of the local priest appears to
have a significant effect on ACPO programs. His active
participation has tended to result in the program's
success at the local level whereas his lack of participation or active opposition has usually meant less acceptance for the programs in that locality. Over the years
ACPO has sought to increase lay control of local activities, thereby reducing reliance upon participation of
the local priest. With this aim, the local lideres
course and later a program for regional leaders were
mounted. Such leaders not only serve in an administra-
tive/motivational capacity, but also are seen as crucial
to the adaptation and localization of instruction.
9.   Reliance on the local priest and appeals to the
religious loyalties of the campesino may be seen in a

more positive light. A mass education program must gain
the support and approval of the local power structure if
it is to be effective within given communities. In
Colombia, the local priest figures very prominently in
this power structure; in other countries a similar power
position may be held by a local chief or mayor, and he
too would have to be won over to the objectives of the
educational program. ACPO (even as it seeks to reduce
reliance on the priesthood) has sought to involve the
local priest in the programs, has held special courses
for them, and has attempted to present their role as
complementary to, rather than in conflict with, that of
the priest.

10.   ACPO has not sought to supplant existing religious loyalties and beliefs. Rather it has attempted to
expand upon and, in some cases, reinterpret prevailing
beliefs in the direction of what it has called the "authentic Christian humanism." In the case of ACPO, which has
church ties, ideological conflict may not have presented
serious problems. But it appears clear that prevailing
beliefs and loyalties must be taken into account in any
mass educational efforts.

11.   ACPO's policy of training rural young adults to
serve as local staff for one- to two-year periods and of
using local volunteers has resulted in a considerable
spin-off of trained and experienced people who, according
to ACPO, generally remain in their rural communities.
They provide a much needed leadership pool, serving as
both indigenous organizers and local opinion leaders.

12.   In a mass education program that seeks to treat
the "whole man," a clear ideological stance is important.
It lends cohesion to the program, serves to establish
clear objectives, and lends authenticity to spiritual
and motivational messages. ACPO has fostered a developmental mystique among its workers and its audience, and
evidence suggests that this has resulted in greater dedication among staff within the organization and a considerable degree of voluntary action on the part of campesinos.

13.   The educational content of a mass media program
needs to be practical and motivational, applicable and
applied. The content of fundamental integral education
is based on ACPO's diagnosis of campesino real-life needs
and does not duplicate the formal school curriculum.
(The departure from this position in the content of the
Complementary Course is questioned by the author on these
very grounds.)

14.   The movement within ACPO is seemingly away from
imparting information or "knowledge" and toward more
accent on motivation and attitude formation. This appears
to be an attempt to overcome rural inertia and to help
campesinos understand that they can be active agents in
their own and their communities' development.

15. Action campaigns appear to be an excellent means of demonstrating that learning can be applied and can result in an improved standard of living. The success of campaigns, both as ends in themselves and as didactic devices, depends in large part on the presence and involvement of local personnel.

16. A mass media educational program coupling radio, printed materials, and local staff appears to be effective in teaching campesinos to read and write. But perhaps more importantly ACPO has provided considerable reading matter appropriate to campesino reading levels which serves to reinforce and maintain the literacy levels of campesinos.

17. The success of an educational program based on mass media depends upon a professional staff of high calibre. Such staff must not only produce and transmit educational programs, but also serve as a back-up staff to local level personnel with whom they must maintain close contact. The technical staff also must be competent to ensure that radio transmitters stay on the air, that programs are technically perfect, and that the newspaper and other publications meet their deadlines.

18. Mass media educational programs require effective feedback mechanisms to ensure that the right messages are being broadcast, that they are being accurately perceived, that a loyal listening audience is being built up, and that the learning offered is put into practice. ACPO has successfully used correspondence as a feedback mechanism in order to adjust its program content. In general, however, it has not effectively monitored its program and cannot accurately gauge its impact in rural areas. Full use has not been made of local personnel as a potentially rich feedback channel.

19. Related to the problem of feedback is the need of the campesinos to communicate their needs, interests, and desires to the agencies concerned with rural development. These include ACPO and the various agencies of the central government. At present the campesinos have little voice in the development of ACPO's programs, nor has ACPO systematically solicited their views. This is now recognized by ACPO, which plans to involve campesinos more directly in the selection of content and editorial position of El Campesino, making the newspaper more a voice of the campesino than the voice of ACPO.

20. ACPO rightly sees its educational efforts as one complementary input into the total rural development effort. It must, therefore, coordinate its activities with those of other rural development agencies. On one level, ACPO has succeeded in informing campesinos of the availability of given services and has encouraged campesino utilization of such services and participation in local activities. At the national level it has concluded agreements with several prominent rural development

agencies. At the local level, however, its own organization does not always achieve effective coordination with
other services.

    21. One of the benefits which may be expected of a
national mass media program employing radio and newspapers is the development of a national consciousness
and sense of national identity on the part of hitherto
isolated campesinos.

    22. ACPO has demonstrated that the mass media
components of its educational program can be commercial-
ized, which has enabled it to self-finance a substantial
portion of its activities. This can be done without
jeopardizing the institution's educational program. It
even has certain benefits in that it encourages efficiency
and a generally professional attitude among the staff.
The danger is that the institution may try to increase
business at the expense of the educational program.
ACPO's attempt to cultivate an urban radio audience in
order to attract more advertising, for example, may
deflect its attention from the prime target group,
which is rural.

    23. It is difficult to design a program that
attracts all subgroups in a rural audience. ACPO draws
most of its audience from among small landholders. It
has little apparent impact among landless farm workers
and the technical information offered in its radio programs (most of such information deals with farm practice)
is in general not of direct practical value to nonfarm
rural dwellers.

    24. It is to ACPO's credit that it has been able
to expand and adapt over time. It seems to have profited
from research (internally and externally conducted) and
has adjusted its program to meet the criticisms that it
has deemed legitimate. Since ACPO objectives are long-
term it must remain flexible and adjust itself to rapidly
changing circumstances.

    In large part, ACPO demonstrates the effectiveness
of a mass media-based educational program as a major
complement in rural development efforts. The lessons
arising out of ACPO's experience in Colombia should
serve as useful guides in planning for human resource
development in rural areas, though it must be recognized
that ACPO has features that may not be readily transfer-
able to other countries.

NOTES

1. International Labour Office, Towards Full Employment: A Programme for Colombia (Geneva, 1970).

2. The leading cash crop is coffee, which accounts for approximately 70 percent of export earnings. There is also considerable cotton growing and cattle raising as well as staple crop production (wheat, maize, potatoes, and yams).

3. Dragoslav Avramovic, Economic Growth of Colombia: Problems and Prospects, World Bank Country Economic Report (Baltimore and London: The Johns Hopkins University Press, 1972), p. 408.

4. Ibid.

5. Stefan A. Musto, Los Medios de Comunicación Social al servicio del Desarrollo Rural (Bogotá: Editorial Andes, 1971), p. 15.

6. Acción Cultural Popular (ACPO), Programación (Bogotá: Editorial Andes, 1969), pp. 15-20.

7. Ibid., p. 16.

8. ACPO, Que es y que no es ACPO [What ACPO Is and Is Not] (Bogotá: Editorial Andes, 1971), p. 3.

9. ACPO, Programación (Bogotá: Editorial Andes, 1969), p. 59.

10. Ibid.

11. ACPO, La Audienca Campesina de Radio Sutatenza(The Campesino Audience of Radio Sutatenza) (Bogotá: Editorial Andes, 1969).

12. The Complementary Course did not exist at the time of this survey.

13. The cartillas are produced on a new offset press which can run signatures of 32 book pages at the rate of 25,000 copies an hour. Production on this press is coupled with a Singer/Freiden phototype setting installation (Justotext 70) with four consoles and two processing units. El Campesino and the books for the Biblioteca series are printed on a Goss rotary letterpress unit which can produce 24 8-column newspaper pages at the rate of 20,000 copies an hour. Covers for the books are printed on Heidelberg job presses. Four linotype machines are maintained for setting letterpress type.

14. ACPO, "Cruzada Cultural Campesina," mimeographed, Documento de Trabajo no. 1 (Bogotá, 1964), p. 10.

15. Ibid., p. 32.

16. Stefan A. Musto, op. cit.

17. Sister V. M. Primrose, "A Study of the Effectiveness of the Educational Program of the Radiophonic Schools of Sutatenza on the Life of Colombian Peasant Farmers" (Ph.D. diss., St. Louis University, 1965).

18. The innovations accounted for in this study, all of which were promoted by ACPO through its radio programs, newspapers, and organized campaigns, were: compost heaps, cheese production, cheese consumption, barn construction, defense against erosion, construction of new rooms, wall painting, floor improvement, bamboo-pipes aqueduct construction, and participation in cooperatives. Hernando Bernal-Alarcón, "Effectiveness of the Radio Schools of 'Acción Cultural Popular' of Colombia in the Adaptation of Innovations" (M.S. thesis, University of Wisconsin, 1967).

19.   Ibid., p. 50.

20.   Ibid., p. 80.

21.   Sister V. M. Primrose, op. cit.

22.   Stefan A.Musto, op. cit.

23.   The testing instrument did not, however, permit adequate measurement of income for purposes of statistical ranking. The differences among students, listeners, and those not influenced, while statistically significant, were not considerable according to Musto. Ibid., p. 173.

24.   Ibid.

25.   Ibid., p. 188.

26.   Ibid.

27.   The peso inflated by better than 25 percent between the end of 1968 and end of 1971.

28.   The Colombian Government's contribution has been fairly constant at this level over the past few years. Such public funds have, however, declined as a proportion of total income from 18.1 percent (1967) to an anticipated 11.6 percent (1972).

CUBA: COMBINING FORMAL
SCHOOLING WITH
PRACTICAL EXPERIENCE
Marvin Leiner

This case study focuses on two interesting educational initiatives in Cuba--schools to the countryside and schools in the countryside--which represent an attempt to combine formal schooling with work and production experience in rural areas. The study is based on information gathered by Professor Marvin Leiner of the Queens College of the City University of New York on his visits to Cuba between 1968 and 1971, on the reports of other scholars, and on available documentation from Cuba. A field mission to observe the operation of the countryside schools was contemplated in 1972, but was not possible to arrange for various reasons. As a consequence, it has not been possible to provide as much solid evidence as would be desirable on how the innovative countryside schools, especially the more recently initiated schools in the countryside program, have actually worked out.

BACKGROUND AND SETTING

Although it is not the intent of this study to analyze the genesis of the 1959 revolution in Cuba and the extent of its progress, certain characteristics of Cuban society before and after the revolution provide background to an examination of the Cuban countryside programs.

In the 1950s Cuba was one of the most culturally homogeneous of nations. All but several thousand Cubans spoke Spanish. Cuba did not suffer from the separatism and strife of language differences, the land disputes, or the severe tribal and religious differences that beset other countries in Asia, Latin America, and Africa. There was and is no overpopulation problem in Cuba, and the geography and climate present a land without extreme conditions or barriers.

There was a large black minority population in Cuba; the 1953 census classified 26.9 percent of the population

as black or "mixed race." However, it has been pointed
out that:

> . . . because racial relations were of the Latin
> rather than the Anglo-Saxon variety, mulattoes--
> like Batista--could be found in top political
> and upper-middle economic positions, if not in
> the front ranks of high society. There was,
> however, widespread social and economic dis-
> crimination based on custom and personal pre-
> judice, and the man of dark skin was in general
> greatly disadvantaged in pre-revolutionary Cuba.
> But this racial cleavage was not so complete as
> to constitute an enduring impediment to mobili-
> zation and cultural transformation after Castro
> came to power.[1]

Cuba's economic and social condition in the 1950s
before the revolution placed it among the top seven
countries in Latin America in gross national product per
capita, radios and television sets per thousand, and phy-
sicians per thousand.[2] However one notes upon further
examination of the data that large percentages of material goods, such as TV sets and radios, and of services
such as those supplied by doctors, were available mainly
to the rich and middle class in the large cities of
Havana and Santiago. Vast inequalities existed. A 1956
study of rural Cuba states that sixty percent of the
island's rural families lived in dwellings with earth
floors and roofs of palm leaves; two-thirds lived in
houses without water closets or latrines; only one of
every 14 families had electricity.[3]

The rural areas also were the most neglected in
educational opportunities. Forty-three percent of the
rural adult population could not read and write. Lowry
Nelson summarizes rural education in prerevolutionary
Cuba:

> The conclusion appears warranted that little if
> any progress has been made since 1907 in provid-
> ing school opportunities for the nation's child-
> ren. The impetus to education provided in the
> early years of the Republic has barely been
> maintained. Rural children, especially, are the
> victims of poor schools or the absence of any
> schools at all. Conditions vary throughout the
> island, getting relatively worse as the distance
> from Havana increases. This situation is not
> due to the opposition to education among the
> rural people. On the contrary, the author is
> convinced that the campesinos are anxious for
> better educational facilities for their children
> . . . .[4]

After the 1959 revolution, the new government attacked the problems of medical care, housing, land distribution, public health, and illiteracy through a variety of programs and reforms. The history of these specific programs and the efforts to provide for Cuba's independence and growth has been documented, reported, and discussed in the growing literature on the Cuban Revolution.[5]

The Cuban revolutionary government sought to achieve the following four main objectives:

1. to expand and utilize fully the society's productive capacities and to transform the Cuban economy, stagnant for the half century prior to the revolution, into a rapidly growing system capable of insuring increasing abundance for all

2. to eliminate economic, political, and cultural dependence on the United States; to achieve national sovereignty within the framework of cooperation and mutual economic benefit among socialist countries

3. to replace the rigid class structure of capitalist Cuba with a classless and egalitarian society; to eliminate sexism and racism; to end the city's economic, cultural, and political domination over the countryside

4. to transform work into a challenging and creative activity for a new socialist man, motivated by social consciousness and the desire for self-expression[6]

In order to accomplish the above objectives, from the start the revolutionary government has given education major priority in its developmental strategy. As a consequence of this emphasis, the focus, aims, and practices of the educational structure have been completely reworked from pre-1959 Cuba. In his analysis of the relationship between the Cuban economy and the development of Cuban education, Samuel Bowles states that "the boundaries between school and society are never distinct: in revolutionary Cuba they have been blurred beyond recognition. Revolution and education are inseparable facets of social transformation."[7]

The following data collected in 1971 on the growth of the number of schools, teachers, and enrollment of students go far to document the Cuban policy of heavy investment and commitment to a variety of educational fronts:

In the decade from 1959 to 1969 the number of schools in Cuba increased almost 500 percent-- from 7,783 to 42,460. By 1971 the number of primary-school pupils doubled--from 717,417

to 1,664,634. By 1971 the teaching force (primary schools) increased more than three-fold--
from 17,355 to 60,592.

Prior to the Revolution there were 2,580 teachers
employed on the secondary level. By 1971 the number of teachers had grown to 15,273. The student
enrollment on the secondary level increased from
63,526 to 186,667, or nearly three times.

The number of students in industrial-technological
schools more than quadrupled in the decade from
1959 to 1969--from 6,259 to 29,975. Agricultural
schools increased from zero to 37 institutions
with 2,335 teachers and 36,812 students. In
higher education the number of faculty members
had grown from 1,053 before the Revolution to
4,645 by 1971. Student enrollment increased
from 25,599 to 45,247 in the same period.

In Worker-Farmer, or adult education schools, a
total of 365,720 persons had completed sixth
grade by 1969 and 57,844 had completed secondary schools. In the area of special education
only one public school existed before the Revolution. In 1971 there were 129 schools with an
enrollment of 7,880 students and 1,401 teachers.

One could cite additional data to indicate the
tremendous growth in enrollment and number of
schools in such specific areas as fishing,
sports, arts, etc. One-quarter of Cuba's population goes to school: two million of eight
million people are in a program of free, universal education from nursery school through
university.[8]

Figure 2.1 presents the reorganization of the
national educational system of Cuba to accommodate the
quantitative and organizational changes since 1959.

The tremendous importance of education in the
development of Cuba has been repeatedly emphasized by
the Cuban leadership. Fidel Castro has articulated the
view that people who want to build a socialist society
must recognize that a nation cannot develop its resources
without economic development and a revolution in education.

Dr. Max Figueroa of the Ministry of Education was
asked by the author in an interview in 1971 whether the
objectives of Cuban education had changed after 12 years
of experience. His response emphasized the goal of
developing a "new man"--a new consciousness--and the
importance of education for all age levels from the
very young to older citizens:

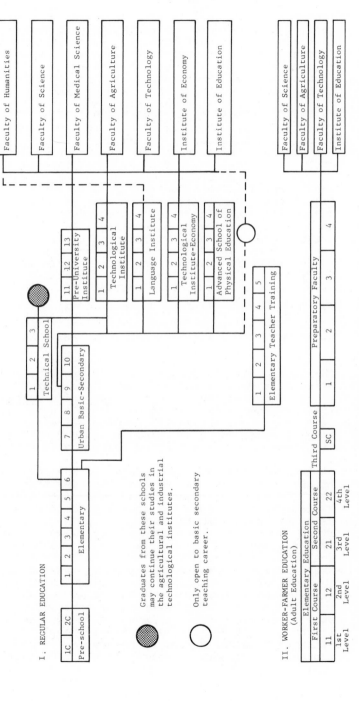

FIGURE 2.1

Structure of the National Education System
1970-1971

I. REGULAR EDUCATION

Graduates from these schools
may continue their studies in
the agricultural and industrial
technological institutes.

Only open to basic secondary
teaching career.

II. WORKER-FARMER EDUCATION
(Adult Education)

Source: Cuba, Ministry of Education, Report to the XXXIII International Conference on Public Instruction, OIE and UNESCO
(Havana, 1971).

65

There has been, for example, quantitative progress, extraordinary quantitiative progress at
the primary and adult education levels. But
of course these are two very different things,
because the primary level involves the formation of the new generation, while the problem
at the adult level is the struggle against
cultural underdevelopment, since the imper-
ialists left this country with a very low
cultural level. Our struggle in this respect
began with the Literacy Campaign in 1961 and
has continued since then with our programs of
adult education. . . . Thus we might say that
at this point we are broadening, enriching,
and learning in relation to our educational
objectives. We are struggling against underdevelopment and all of the backwardness left
here by our stage of a neo-colony. And we
are concerned not only with the material but
also with the spiritual needs of our people.
I don't know if that answers your question:
the formation of a new man and a powerful
development of his social conscience; that's
the fundamental thing.[9]

NONFORMAL EDUCATION IN REVOLUTIONARY CUBA

The Cuban idea of education is not restricted to the
formal school structure and programs under that structure;
Cubans have endorsed the concept of educación permanente,
which features the view that formal schooling is only one
aspect of education. Educación permanente refers to the
entire population, young and old, in and out of formal
schooling, and is explained by Dr. Figueroa in these terms:

It is life-long education. Now, in what way is
it different? In that in the countries that
have not made their revolution none of this is
systematized, whereas the socialist countries
all give great importance to what we may call
extra-school education. Here, for example, our
organizations and other organizations such as
the Union of Pioneers and the Young Communists
Organization cooperate in extending, amplifying
the work of the school in satisfying the cultural needs of our people. In the recent reorganization of the Ministry, for example, a
special department was created as the Office
(Dirección) of Political and Extra-School Activities. In other words, we now have an organization that concerns itself not only with what

our people learn in school, but what they acquire
through the radio, the cinema, through television. Our National Student Games (Juegós
Deportivos Escolares), Technical-Scientific
Interest Circles (Groups), the Cultural-Artistic
Activities--all of these activities in which the
student participates outside of his school hours
strengthen the educational work of the school
and are to receive still greater attention in
the future. As you know, the recent First
National Cultural-Educational Congress here
placed special importance on still greater
attention to this kind of social education,
which encourages the student to view his society
as a single unit, as a united organism. So this
is our concept of permanent education.[10]

Later in this chapter, a description of the transformation of the "school to the countryside" to the
"school in the countryside" will reflect the importance
the Cubans have given to nonformal schooling. Very often
the vehicle or channel for nonformal education program
is a mass organization such as the Federation of Cuban
Women (FMC), the Committee for Defense of the Revolution
(CDR), or the Union of Communist Youth (UJC). Below are
some of the different nonformal educational opportunities
available to Cuban adults or children.

1. Federation of Cuban Women. The FMC, made up of
more than a million women, sponsors a variety of programs.
One of its major responsibilities is the sponsorship and
supervision of day care programs for working parents.
There are more than 50,000 children enrolled in approximately 400 centers throughout Cuba. The FMC and its
sub-unit, the Institute of Infancy, have established
these centers, trained staff, and carried out the programs. Adult education and parent meetings during lunch
hour or in the evenings are included in most day care
programs.[11]
2. Círculo de Interés (Interest Circles). Established in most secondary schools, these interest groups
attempt to go beyond "extracurricular" activities found
in other countries. Most interest circles are related
to productive activities in the community, for example,
groups for electricity, agriculture, mechanics, soil,
food chemistry, animal sciences, meteorology, oceano-
graphy, and construction. Cooperating agencies, such as
hospitals, factories, and laboratories, work with the
interest circles on intervisitations, advice, and leadership. Cuban educators see these circles as important
connections between curriculum and ultimate vocational
choice. They feel that national economic interests
indicate the development, for example, of a fishing
industry or other technical, scientific, industrial, or

agricultural activities. These groups are seen as vital
components in "guidance" to students about options available in their changing society. According to Bowles:

> By tying the educational experience more closely
> to the economy, the círculos de interés perform
> a very important function. A society which has
> foregone the use of wage incentives needs an
> alternative means of encouraging young people
> to enter particular occupations. Thus the
> círculos de interés provide a means of inform-
> ing young people about the content of various
> occupations, while at the same time stimulating
> interest in careers that are likely to make a
> major contribution to national development.[12]

3. Peer Group Teaching. This use of students to
teach others is part of the process of group and individual study activities. The monitor program is an
arrangement in which each class selects monitors to
assist other students in need of help. For instance,
the author visited a 9th grade science class of 15- and
16-year old boys and girls, in which no adults were
present. A member of the school student council determined what difficulties several of the students were
encountering and appointed volunteers (although they
were not formally designated as monitors) to assist those
in need of help after school, either in the building or
at home. Here the students accepted responsibility for
helping each other learn. The nonformal arrangement to
meet later was left to the peer couple, that is, the
peer "teacher" and the peer "student."
4. The Padrino System. As a further stimulus to
parental and wider community involvement in the schools,
the Cubans established the padrino system. Borrowed
from Eastern Europe socialist countries, it is a cooperative arrangement between neighboring institutions and the
schools. Padrino organizations, usually factories, agree
to adopt a school in order to offer special services and
assistance on a voluntary basis, for example, help with
repairs, transportation, and arrangements for such
special occasions as collective birthday parties.
On a strictly pragmatic basis, Cuban padrinos provide a variety of important services and repairs that
would be difficult for a school to obtain, considering
the current shortage of skilled labor and materials.
Moreover, as a function of revolutionary education,
padrinos serve to tie the school to the factory, providing children with practical, visual confirmation of the
workers and peasants as revolutionary altruists. Ultimately, it is hoped that by seeing padrinos help maintain the school, the children will develop a profound
respect for work.

The padrino also reflects the revolutionary concern with education and the central position it holds. The Cubans take every opportunity to remind the people that education of their children should be given top priority, even at the expense of work in the factories.

Many padrinos invite the children into their factories, give the youngsters guided tours, offer them candy, and give them the opportunity of working together in the fields on agricultural labor brigades. Padrinos go as far as visiting families to discover why children are not attending class. They encourage parents to send their children to school and day care centers and explain the importance of education, discipline, and caring.[13]

5. Special Youth Programs. The author observed during his Cuban visits the activities and the agricultural work in two special youth programs, the Centennial Youth Column and the Seguidores de Camilo y Ché.[14] In both programs there was an intense effort to provide educational programs in the recreation rooms of the dormitories or outdoor improvised class setting and other places for students who had dropped out or did not attend formal schools before. These students needed to acquire basic skills. Classes met several times a week and were part of the ongoing program of the youth groups whose primary purpose was not the pursuit of formal education but voluntary labor to help Cuba in its agricultural turnpike approach.[15] Fidel Castro and other leaders see these nonformal programs as important means of reaching young people who have not been absorbed by the regular school programs. Castro views compulsory military service and the Centennial Youth Column as key ways to achieve discipline and overcome the negative effect of sexism. He stated that the Centennial Youth Column and compulsory military service are the "two key factors that have instilled discipline . . . in the mass of males who could not be won over and forged by the formal educational system . . . who didn't study or work and hadn't learned a skill or a trade."[16]

Dr. José Aguilera Maceiras, Vice Minister of Education, suggested that the less formal workshop movement and youth column programs are new ways outside the formal programs that are attempting to solve the dropout problem and the problems of young people who have not succeeded in being attracted to or adjusted to the regular school program.

There are a number of students, especially between the ages of 13 and 16, and the problem of these students is that many of them were 'sub-schooled'; they had a very low level of schooling. Then it was not possible to reincorporate them to the regular system of learning. There were 13-year old boys in second

grade; well, this is a real problem. With this
vision of things, a movement has been formed
called Youth Movement, based mainly on the so-
called Workshop Schools. In other words, these
boys between the ages of 12 and 16 who have
abandoned their studies and who have a low academic level do not go back to the regular educational system. Instead, a number of programs of
another type are being created specifically for
youths, on the basis of the combination of work
and study. These workshop-schools are established always in connection with a productive
or service enterprise. The students are sometimes boarders, sometimes semi-boarders, and
other times 'day' students (non-boarding). They
have a regular session during the day devoted to
raising their general cultural level, general
learning; and they have another session during
the day in which they are learning some elementary trades under the guidance of technicians
or qualified workers at the enterprises. In
this way, these students who were practically on
the streets with nothing to do (since they were
not of working age nor of draft age) are reincor-
porated to learning. Upon reaching working age
they have raised on the one hand their academic
(scholastic) level and on the other hand have
acquired a training or qualification even if
elementary, in a specified field of work. This
permits them to incorporate themselves into production and be useful. In addition, this student, now working, can continue his studies by
means of adult education courses; he can attend
secondary (education) courses or he can go to a
'worker's-peasant's' preparatory school, and if
his will to study is strong enough, he may some
day enter the university to pursue university
studies.

There is another type of school called Youth
Classrooms or Youth Schools--generally non-
boarding--which are not work-shop schools
proper but which have a more or less similar
organization in which the student receives
general instruction but also participates part
of the time in production, as in the plans, for
example, for the school in the countryside.

And there are also the so-called Columns and
Pre-Columns, such as the Centenario de Camagüey
Column, the Sea Column, or the Textile Column.
These are also groups of youths who have a program of work and study similar to that of the
workshop-schools, and then also work (participate) in production. The ones in the column

are older; they spend more time working and
less time studying.   Those under 16 spend equal
periods at work and at study, in one specific
direction.   For example, the Sea Column is made
up of boys who are training for work in our
fleet.   Well, then, part of the time they receive general instruction; part of the time
receive practical training on the fleet's ships.

Those in the Camagüey Agricultural and Cattle-Raising Column devote themselves to activities in agriculture and cattle raising, but
they also have a system of schools.   Thus, this
is all part of the movement which is being
developed to rescue the students who have
abandoned the school system.   We are even analyzing the question of offering these programs
to students with a marked academic retardation,
i.e., to place them in programs with greater
possibility--because sometimes a student of 15,
who is say on a third or fourth grade level,
really doesn't get much out of the regular
program.   We then prefer to take him out of
there and to a youth classroom or to a workshop program.[17]

6.   The Literacy Campaign of 1961.   An important
experience in Cuba's educational history that has provided impulse for other nonformal programs was the
historic, massive, unprecedented attack on illiteracy
in Cuba in 1961.   The campaign was comparable to a
national war effort. Two hundred and fifty thousand
young people and adults volunteered at the urging of
revolutionary government leadership to go throughout
the island, including the most rural areas, to "fight"
illiteracy.   "Death to illiteracy will be the number-
one goal of 1961" was the call of the first Congress of
the Municipal Councils of Education in October 1960.
Schools were closed during the campaign and most of the
105,000 full-time volunteers were recruited from adolescent students.   The "alphabetizers" worked singly or in
small groups under the supervision of thousands of volunteer teachers.   After eight months of intensive effort,
the illiteracy rate in Cuba dropped to 3.9 percent
from 25 percent before the campaign.[18]

However, the campaign not only had literacy results;
it also played an important "ripple effect" in both formal and nonformal Cuban educational programs.   In a 1970
report the author observed:

Many of the 106,000 brigadistas, or student
alphabetizers, who participated in the 1961
effort, now play a key role in Cuba's education.
The 15-year old who went to the rural hut
of a campesino in 1961 is now that 24-year old

principal in Las Villas; the 14-year old who
was an alphabetizer in Pinar del Rio is now a
teacher trainer. In conversations with these
'battle veterans,' they spoke about their life
with poor, uneducated families in distant isolated mountain settings, with the pride of
bringing the rewards of the Revolution to its
origin.
        These young veterans and more experienced
educators are working on several new programs
introduced by the Castro government.[19]

        These "new programs" include the escuela al campo
(schools to the countryside) and escuela en el campo
(schools in the countryside), programs discussed in the
following sections.

SCHOOLS TO THE COUNTRYSIDE

        The school to the countryside program began with an
experimental plan in the spring of 1966 and was introduced into the secondary school programs that fall. However, the roots of the plan go back to the early revolutionary, nonformal educational activities. The emphasis
on connecting study and work was apparent in 1961, when
literacy teachers of the Conrado Benitez Brigade worked
with campesinos in the fields; in 1962, when the "alphabetizers" in the Oriente Mountains worked in the coffee
harvest; and in 1963, when scholarship students worked
at agricultural and industrial tasks.
        On May 25, 1964, the Ministry of Education issued
Resolution 392, which stated the principles of "poly-
technization" and stressed student involvement in "productive work." The resolution also established that,
"students go to cooperatives, state farms, or other
areas and remain in these picking coffee or other harvests, or other types of agricultural work. The period
of time will fluctuate between two and seven weeks."[20]
        In April and May 1966 the first large-scale country-
side experimental program was introduced when some 20,000
junior high school students participated in the program,
working together with teachers and agricultural workers
in Camagüey Province. In addition to agricultural work,
the program included cultural, recreational, and sports
activities. According to José Aguilera Maceiras, the
Camagüey experience provided:

        a concrete way to put into practice the Marxist
        principle of educating the new generations
        through work and for work, of forming for the
        new society a new man for whom work would be an

eternal and natural condition of human life, as
Karl Marx foresaw, and of utilizing work as the
main element of training, since, as Fidel said,
work must be the best teacher of youth.[21]

The Camagüey experience was unique in Cuban educational plans because, for the first time, working in the
country was incorporated into a school program that dealt
with large numbers of students. The leadership in the
Ministry of Education (MINED) concentrated on the Camagüey project, not only to facilitate the effort but (again
in the words of Maceiras) to "study it, evaluate it, and
derive the necessary experience to implement it in all
junior high and senior high school education."
   In 1966-67 the school to the countryside plan, was
systematically incorporated into the school program; that
is, at fixed times of the year junior high school and
secondary school students throughout Cuba went to the
countryside for 45 days. During that academic year,
140,000 secondary education students were involved. The
following year the number increased to 160,000.[22]
   Cuban educators were convinced that the school to
the countryside program was an important step in the educational and revolutionary transformation of Cuba. G.
Jorge García Galló wrote:

   Its development and consequences have as much
   vital importance for Cuban education . . . as
   that of the great literacy campaign carried out
   in 1961, since its adequate application will become the main link that will allow us to pull
   the whole educational chain, transforming in
   this way the structure, the contents, the technique, and the spirit of learning.[23]

A Ministry of Education report to UNESCO cites the
benefits to be gained from the school to the countryside
plan:

1. The plan, by means of its various activities,
    and basically through productive work, is a
    powerful instrument for the moral and ideo-
    logical training of our youth.
2. It contributes to the development of a real
    agricultural consciousness in accordance with
    the reality of the economic development of
    our nation.
3. Although this plan was not conceived for
    economic but rather educational purposes,
    it helps to solve production problems.
4. The plan, with its problems of living to-
    gether in the camps, initiates the students,
    in a concrete form, into organizational

practices and self-government on the basis
of group cooperation and work, and it also
helps to develop collective tendencies and
weed out individualist ones.[24]

The Plan in Practice

The Cubans were faced with the formidable task of
"bridging the gap between theory and practice" (to use a
favorite Cuban expression). The introduction of the plan
in every junior high and secondary school throughout the
island meant the mobilization of thousands of students
and teachers; safety and health were paramount concerns
as the entire school population moved to the countryside
camps for 45 days.

Although the Ministry of Education had the coordinating or catalytic role, other government agencies were
involved on a national and local level. These agencies
were separate organizations from the educational administration of the country, yet worked carefully with the
school to the countryside plan "from its preparatory
stage to the students' return."[25] The agencies involved,
in addition to MINED, were the following:

INRA: Instituto Nacional de Reforma Agraria
         (National Institute for Agrarian Reform)
MINCIN: Ministerio del Comercio Interior (Ministry
         of Internal Commerce)
MINSAP: Ministerio de Salud Pública (Ministry of
         Public Health)
MINTRANS: Ministerio de Transporte (Ministry of
         Transportation)
INDER: Instituto Nacional de Deportes, Educación
         Física, y Recreación (National Institute
         of Sports, Physical Education and Recreation)
ICAIC: Instituto Cubano de Arte e Industria Cinema-
         tograficas (Cuban Institute of Cinema Art
         and Industry)
CNC: Consejo Nacional de Cultura (National Council
         of Culture)
UJC: Union de Jóvenes Comunistas (Union of Commun-
         ist Youth)
FEEM: Federación de Estudiantes de la Enseñanza
         Media (Federation of Students of Intermed-
         iate Education)
SNTEC: Sindicato Nacional de Trabajadores de la
         Educación y Cultura (National Syndicate of
         Workers in Education and Culture)
PCC: Partido Comunista de Cuba (Communist Party of
         Cuba)[26]

The provincial and regional commissions of the MINED, together with the individual school councils, have the following organizational responsibilities:

1. propagandizing the plan and its goals and activities, holding meetings with the students and their parents, especially with the youngest (seventh-grade) group so that they will realize the importance of the plan and the benefits it imparts to both the children's education and the country's economy
2. visiting camp sites and, with the help of teachers', students', and parents' commissions, creating the proper sanitary conditions in the camps, familiarizing themselves with the type of work to be carried out, where it will be carried out, and other details, and reporting all this to the students and the parents with the purpose of orienting them to the importance of what they must do
3. vaccinating the students and participating personnel prior to departure in order to prevent epidemics
4. organizing and coordinating transportation and safety, including meetings with drivers and the assignment of at least one professor to each bus
5. orienting students as to what clothes, etc., are provided
6. making sure the right quantity of supplies are in the camps on time so that students are fed well from the first day
7. informing the students before they leave about the rules of the camp, how to carry them out, and to which squadron or brigade each student is assigned, so that when they reach the work area they know what to do
8. coordinating the system of students' communications with their families
9. assuring continued health care
10. program planning, in a general sense, including cultural, sports, recreative, and scholastic activities as well as civil defense.[27]

Organization of Camps

Visits to camps (<u>campamentos</u>) in different parts of Cuba and in-depth interviews with leaders, teachers, students, and parents led to the following understanding of camp organization.

The administrative head of the camp is the director of the school or his designate. He is also a member

of an administrative camp council, which includes representatives of the PCC, UJC, FEEM, SNTEC, a representative of the state farm, and other workers who have
specific camp responsibilities, such as supplies and
production.

Although there were variations in organizational
patterns from camp to camp, there were certain common
trends. The leadership in every campamento included a
secretary general who had the major leadership responsibility, supervised the whole campamento, and chaired the
meetings of the buro, or student council. The buro was
composed of student leaders called responsables. At the
Carlos Marx camp, for example, there was one responsable
for each of the following: education, political work,
sports and culture, emulación and production, círculo des
interés (interest circles), and discipline.

The education responsable coordinated all educational
activities, including the class problems of attendance
and teacher coverage. He or she was also responsible for
any educational activity related to the camp. The sports
and culture responsable coordinated all sports and recreational activities, including combos, trios, songfests,
and movie programs. For the last activity he worked with
the movie industry, ICAIC. He was also responsible for
the problem of materials, that is, finding sports equipment and enough chess boards and pieces for a match. The
political responsable coordinated discussions on national
and international issues, distributed whatever materials
were available on economic and socialist issues, and
helped to organize intercamp meetings, that is, meetings
with small groups from other campamentos. The production responsable coordinated agricultural production and
recorded on a mural the production of each week. He sent
a report daily to the Puesto Mando, the headquarters in
the province, which sent all the processed campamento
reports to the central provincial headquarters.

Círculos de Interés on different topics were organized. Usually the topics were related to agriculture;
for example, a técnico would talk to the students about
the relationship of their specific tasks to Cuban agriculture. After the economic or social introduction, the
students dealt with specific questions and were taught
the reasons for specific agricultural techniques; for
example, why they treated seedlings in a certain way.
The interest circles were not compulsory, but many students voluntarily signed up.

In 1968-1969 emphasis on educational practice shifted
away from formal classes. Teachers active in the first
program said that postevaluation sessions by students and
teachers alike were critical of expecting youngsters to
follow a heavy academic load while they were in the
country for 45 days. Although emphasis on study is tied
to the Cuban educator's concern about achieving or

learning--with the key criterion a high percentage of
grade promotion--the "reality," according to Miguel
Dehesa, Director of one of the campos, is that the school
to the countryside cannot carry on a regular school program because of the limited time and work schedule.

> Not all who are included in the group must
> study. Only those students who are behind in
> one or two courses must attend. And this is
> not in order to study or learn any new mater-
> ial, but simply to brush up on their studies
> once or twice a week. Last night, for example,
> those who have history went to class; tonight,
> those who have mathematics; tomorrow, Spanish.
> In other words, the subjects they are behind in
> are the ones they must work on here. This is
> not meant to make them worry about their studies,
> but just to keep up the necessary spirit so that
> when they return to school they can get off to a
> good start, and not have lost all that was gain-
> ed during the last semester.[28]

The day in the camp generally starts at 5:30 a.m. and
ends at 10:00 p.m. after two work sessions, one from 7:00
to 11:45 a.m. and the other from 2:00 to 5:15 p.m. Between 8:00 and 10:00 p.m. there are cultural or recreational activities. This 1971 schedule, currently in
operation in the escuela al campo programs, is different
from the earlier schedules in 1966, 1967, or even 1968.
The earlier schedules made a strong effort to include
daytime academic sessions, that is, to continue studies
without interruption.
The schedule of a typical day as recorded by a student at Amaded Roldén Camp provides an illustration:

> 6:00 to 6:30   "De Pie" (Reveille)
> 7:00   Breakfast
> 7:15   Matutino (morning exercises)--this
> took place in front of the camp; every day a
> different brigade had its turn. The National
> Hymn was sung; there were gymnastic exercises;
> the instruction [schedule] and the schedule for
> baths by year and brigade were made known; the
> problems of internal lodging [housing], produc-
> tion, discipline, and organization for the pre-
> vious day were discussed; the type of work to
> be carried out was made known; the newspaper
> was read or Ché's diary; and finally, each bri-
> gade would say its slogan and leave for work.
> In general, the tasks carried out in the country-
> side were: weeding, planting, grafting, pruning,
> fertilizing, lining up of bags, and throwing
> [stretching out] strings.

8:00 to 12:30   Work
10:30   Recess--snacks were distributed,
and we rested. Of course, this was all organized
by brigade.
1:00   Lunch. All the brigades lined up
in front of the dining room.
1:30 to 2:00   Rest period. During this period
many girls wrote; some brigades met [to discuss]
a deficiency, or because one of the comrades had
been outstanding during the day, etc.
2:00 to 6:30   Work
4:30   Recess
6:30 to 6:40   Report to the comrades [in charge]
of general production for the lodging. This was
done individually by brigade and in an organized
fashion; the number of members constituting the
brigade was made known, those out ill, and the
number or quantity or amount of work done.
7:00 to 8:00   Bath
8:10   Dinner
8:40   "Círculo"[circle], entertainment, meeting for brigade analysis, etc.
10:00   The camp had to be silent until the
next day when another working day awaited us.
Wednesday: Interest circles (groups) on citrus
fruits held by the person in charge of the nursery.
In the beginning three comrades incorporated themselves to this group out of each brigade; later
on, because of the interest of our members, we
achieved full membership.
Thursdays: Red Brigade; it was voluntary. We
understood that its members were those comrades
who were more ready and willing to undertake any
task.
Fridays: Political circle. This was one of the
most serious endeavors in the camp, as we needed
everyone's full attention to achieve our objective. For materials, we would [use and] discuss
Fidel's speeches, Ché's diary, the problems of
the society, Cuba before the war, etc.

Self-Government

A fundamental aim of the school to the countryside
program is to encourage self-government; the young people
should be able to "run" the camp, lead themselves, and
participate in both planning and executive programs.
    In camps that the author visited, the students were,
in effect, running the camp. This self-government,
according to one camp director, did not simply "happen."
For example, at the Amadeo Roldán camps, the girls'
campamento responded much sooner to their own student

leadership than did the boys'. Although student leaders were effectively handling the day-to-day work routines and problems in the Rosita camp, students still turned to adults and teachers at the beginning at the boys' campamento.

One of the student leaders explained the self-government and leadership development as follows:

> Autogobierno (self-government) was not introduced in all the camps as quickly as in ours because to launch this it was essential that certain difficulties of unity between the leaders and students--of discipline, etc.--be eliminated. Once self-government had been introduced, those in charge would be the ones with a good attitude [of leadership], as agreed to by the mass of students. We needed leaders responsible for lodging, production, instruction, and discipline, and another responsible for the ideological, political, and cultural level. In this plan the students responsible for brigades had a role that was extremely important, since their contact with the students was more direct, and they carried the entire responsibility for the development of our camp.[29]

Thus, the basic organizational unit of the camps was the brigade. Students and leaders at camps stated that the spirit of collective living and self-government was developed through the brigade unit. Recognition or reward was not given to individuals who excelled or did well; rather, the brigade was honored for production or for whatever criteria were being used. Thus, logically, the individual in the brigade looked at his collective work or life, examined why they did not accomplish goals, and discussed how to correct errors. "Everyone is responsible for each other."[30]

Recognition and reward for brigade work was through the system of moral stimulus and emulation of excellence, as opposed to the use of material incentives. This was done by announcing vanguardia status for the best brigades. At the Carlos Marx Campamento, vanguardia honor was decided at a weekly meeting of all the brigade heads. One such meeting that the author attended began at 9 p.m. and lasted until 1 a.m. The meeting took place in a small, empty room, and the brigade leaders sat on the floor, leaning their backs against the walls. At the buro head's request, the production responsable of the buro gave the production statistics for each brigade, and each brigade leader then reported on his group and discussed different aspects of brigade life. The brigade leader offered his own analysis of the group's work and the discipline for that week. After questions and

discussion, the group then voted on the brigade's performance (exelente, muy bueno, bueno, regular). After
the analysis of each brigade was completed, the vanguardia
brigade for the week was chosen.

During the discussion of "discipline," the brigade
leaders dealt with specific problems, attitudes, and in-
terpersonal relationships that influenced brigade efforts.
Very often there was an attempt made to determine whether
a situation reflected a brigade attitude or whether it was
a "specific case," that is, whether the infraction was
peculiar only to an individual. The "discipline" evaluation often led to the hottest discussion of the meeting.

Under the self-government concept, students are responsible for solving a wide range of problems. The
author's notes from a buro meeting provide illustrations
of the range of campamento problems dealt with by these
young people.

1. Safety. A boy fell from one of the trucks and
was slightly hurt. The buro members who reported this
said that the real problem was the overcrowding on the
trucks and not what the boy might have done to cause the
accident. There was danger that others would be hurt
unless something was done to alleviate overcrowding.

2. Cultural activities. Some of the students had
visited a girls' camp for songfest. It was suggested
that the girls from the camp be invited for a return
visit. The buro secretary noted that a transportation
problem again existed, since it was difficult to arrange
intercamp visits when so few vehicles were available.

3. Failing students. The education responsable
inquired, "What else can we do to help students who are
failing in subjects back in school? Attendance at classes
is a problem. Some students sign up but say 'present'
and then take off. They don't see that conciencia is
not just tied to production but to study and attendance
at classes." One leader suggested that the content of
the classes may be the problem. Another responded that
they were not following the school plans that had been
discussed in Havana, to which a third buro member replied:
"Yes, but we're here now. We can't look back to Havana
plans. You're not considering the tiredness of your
friends when you're planning in Havana. We have to talk
about what makes sense here."

4. Cleanliness and beautification. The problems of
trash and the best approach to the clean-up job was discussed. An argument developed as to the "responsibility
for clean-up." According to the discussion, this responsibility could be given to an assigned brigade, a volunteer brigade, the young communists, or the members of the
buro.

5. Visuals and displays. "Can't we let everyone
know what's happening with our production effort without

reciting production figures?" This question led to a
variety of suggestions for bulletin board displays. One
student said, "What about visuals about that part of our
life other than production, such as sports, our political
work, or our class work?"

6. <u>Problems in selecting vanguardia</u>. The buro discussed the system of selecting the vanguardia brigade and
whether it was fair. For example, in one case five of
the 20 boys in a brigade were not working, so the whole
brigade could be punished by not being selected as vanguardia. The education responsable suggested, "Maybe the
five should be separated out. The 15 are doing the work
of the five." But another buro member responded: "You
can't do that. How are you going to have lazy students
develop conciencia if you separate them out? It's like a
teacher. It's easy for a teacher to say, 'I have 30
students. I'll throw out the five difficult ones.' A
good teacher does not do that. We have to find the ways
to help the five."

7. <u>Favoritism</u>. The discussion of lateness and the
kitchen led to another point about food--the problem of
a kitchen staff member who was favoring one or two students by giving them extra food. "One of us should talk
to her. Our parents and the people of Cuba have sacri-
ficed so that we can have the food we have, and it should
be evenly distributed. It's not right that because she
likes someone she then favors that person."

The sports responsable then said, "I don't think we
should continue to individually tell students about the
decisions that we've made, such as the one that we're
talking about now. Instead of hearing it from one or
another person, it is important that it not be whispered
as if it's a secret around the camp. Instead, everyone
should hear about the decision at the same time. I'm
talking about the fact that nobody should accept favors
from anyone in responsibility and no one in responsibility
should give favors. This should be announced to the whole
camp at a total camp meeting."

8. <u>Production norms</u>. "Brigade VI has been reaching
its norms but it seems that they are not working to capa-
city--there are problems of discipline and attitude."
Brigade VI leader, Jefe, was questioned about problems in
the brigade. He said, "Our brigade has been hoeing for
two days straight, and the brigade members don't think
that the work allocation is fair. Other brigades seem
to be doing easier tasks."

The buro secretary replied, "There is no personal
spite involved. The other brigades are going to get that
assignment for two days also. If this wasn't clear, it's
our fault for not stating that this unpleasant task was
going to be rotated. A revolutionary brigade should be
able to handle the less pleasant tasks as well as the
easier tasks. We are sorry for not making it clear to
all the brigades."

Community Involvement

The campamento leadership encouraged the students to "serve" the community and learn from it. Community-related activities carried out during the school to the countryside period include socioeconomic studies of the area, research on historical events happening there, and visits to interesting geographic places. These activities are directed by the teacher and monitors of history, geography, and Spanish. Students also work to improve the schools of the surrounding area; they set up recreation areas for neighbors. They help to raise the cultural level of the local campesinos and farm workers.[31]

At one campamento, several students spoke about their house-to-house visits to campesinos to talk to peasants about the role of the CDR (Committee for the Defense of the Revolution). There was no CDR in the area, and when one was finally formed, the students felt that this development was related to their house-to-house canvassing efforts.

At another campamento, the senior high school students helped the elementary school children celebrate the birthday of José Martí. They led songs, helped with the food, and organized the play after the party.

At Carlos Marx Escuela al Campo, 17-year old Raul Acosta was teaching in a one-room schoolhouse not far from the camp. When a young school teacher had to leave to give birth to her baby (she was in the eighth month), the community asked the camp to provide a teacher, so Raul volunteered.

The students at the Amadeo Roldán Camp were invited by the local town leadership to a school festival. They drew upon their musical talent and performed, and one student buro leader said they had once again "broadened the ties of friendship between us and the rural schools." The three farm families whose land bordered the camp were always invited to the evening program. Throughout the interviews with students and leadership, the author found a great emphasis on conscious efforts to establish friendly relations with the rural countryside.

Conciencia and Emulación

Cuban students and teachers kept referring to the term conciencia when asked about their reasons for being in the campo and their work. Joseph Kahl, a Cornell University sociologist who has visited Cuba several times, defined conciencia as an "amalgum of consciousness, conscience, conscientiousness, and commitment." And, he added, it is "perhaps the most repeated word in the Cuban language of the revolution."[32]

Two student leaders responded to the following question about the escuela al campo program: "If Cuba develops such technical knowledge that our labor in the fields is not crucial to the country's economic needs, do you think the campo program would be necessary?" Carlos' answer was that they were there not only because of the necessity of their labor, "we are here also to develop conciencia. We are here to develop a spirit, a consciousness, an attitude toward work. And this agricultural work is necessary because it forms this conciencia."

When asked, "What does this mean, to form conciencia," his response was:

> One has to look at what life was like under capitalism before the revolution. Thousands of people died so that we could have the society we have now--not to have corruption, not to have the misery of the previous regime. And now we're in the midst of a process to develop. The students are here because of the success of the revolution, because of the people who died to construct this society, because of sacrifice. Right now people are sacrificing so that we can be here: they are on rations--food is being shared. This is all evidence of the fact that a conciencia exists and that it is continually being formed.

The other student leader, Omar, came into the conversation and said,

> If we were to define conciencia, it simply means understanding of the revolution. Conciencia is giving without asking for anything in return. Conciencia is working collectively. Conciencia means you don't have to chase anyone to work. Conciencia is measured by this voluntary spirit. If one has to compel someone to do something for the revolution then this means there is no level of conciencia.

Asked about the concept of emulación, they replied that it is working for your own benefit in some sort of spirit of competition. Emulación is a spirit of helping others, and it is a way to get ourselves to sacrifice to help the society. By working for vanguardia, which is a part of the emulación process, you are working because of a certain stimulus.

Another buro member explained that there are stages of development in the growth of the country. "For the first stage we may need material incentive. The next stage uses a moral incentive. And I think there will be a future stage where you won't need any incentive. Vanguardia is a level of development." The author asked,

"Doesn't a man or a woman need to be recognized for his or
her work, so that he or she can be inspired to continue?"
Omar answered that ultimately man will not need a stimulus
to work. He will not have to receive an honor or recognition, for he will be contributing to society, either
material or moral, because he wants to.

Political Work

Political work in schools to the countryside took
two forms. First, students were doing political work in
their everyday conversations on an individual basis. When
you spoke to a person, when you discussed aspects of the
revolution, when you discussed issues and goals and working and living, you were doing "political work." Second,
there were the organized political activities, such as
political circles (círculo de interés) or going to meetings with peasants. At these political circles the students read documents and discussed speeches on national
and international questions of a political, social, and
economic nature. While political circles were organized
encounters, the ongoing personal contact was not planned
or organized in any way--it was just part of daily living.
At one camp, the author observed, students were
divided into several groups, each group having about 30
students and one student leader. One particular student
leader was reading parts of Fidel Castro's recent speech
on the Cuban cattle industry. The leader would stop from
time to time and raise questions such as, "Why is the
cattle industry important to the development of our
country?" Sometimes other students would read excerpts
from Fidel's speeches. One student was reading about the
artificial insemination system used, when the leader
asked questions such as, "What is sperm? Why are Cubans
using the artificial insemination system?" One student
said, "Read to us about Rosafe" (a famous Cuban cow used
in the artificial insemination program). It was explained
that the sperm from model bulls, in the sense of strength
and health, was used to fertilize Cuban cows in the hope
of producing offspring that would both produce more milk
and be able to withstand the climate. The students were
involved in the discussion and were apparently interested
in the content and the dynamic style of the leader.
The same topic with a different leader resulted in
a very different kind of discussion. The students were
seated under a tree about a hundred feet from the first
group, but they were not interacting at all with each
other or with the student leader. The leader would read
paragraph after paragraph, and the students seemed bored.
There was an occasional question raised by a student or
the leader. In this group there was minimal participation.

Agricultural Production

The school to the countryside was cited by the Cubans not only as a pedagogical-social-political instrument to achieve the goals of their society, but also as an economic necessity.[33]

The production aspect of life varied among camps. At some, the young people worked the land on which they lived. At other camps, the dormitories and kitchen were at the campsite, but trucks transported the youngsters to the fields. Since sugarcane cutting was considered the most difficult agricultural work, it was reserved for eleventh grade students and older.

The specific agricultural tasks at schools to the countryside depended upon the school's location. In Oriente, for example, coffee was often heavily emphasized; in Havana, it was work with citrus fruit plants at different stages of the development of the citrus fruit industry.

The students of Perez Senior High School (Sancti Spíritus, Las Villas) worked at the Banao agricultural project. "The work includes picking coffee in the Escambray Mountains, harvesting fruits and vegetables, and seeding tobacco fields."[34] Production in 1971 at the Banao Project was 132,743 root and other vegetables, an increase of 35,242 over 1970, which was attributed to the school to the countryside student effort.[35] For example, one center reported that on February 14, 1969, "100 comrades planted 18,335 posturas [seedlings] and 92 comrades weeded 32,977 posturas."[36]

The following is the report on the work done in one week in Reunion Afuera by tenth grade male students of the Carlos Marx School camp as prepared by the student Responsable for production:[37]

Type of Work	Work Accomplished
Pulling plants (citrus fruit seedlings)	796,910 (7 days)
Weeding	1,500 rows
Lining up of bags	216,890 bags
Filling bags	4,000 bags
Irrigation (12 men)	1,728 hours
Planting of seedlings	93,735 plants
Pruning	28,440 plants

Loading and unloading trucks	
Goal of plants to unload	3,000,040 plants
Plants pulled out (7 days)	796,910 plants
Plants still to be pulled out	2,703,130 plants
Daily goal per man	500 plants
Per capita achieved	620 daily
Over goal	24%

Young people interviewed by the author at the camps
were often quite knowledgeable about the agricultural
process in which they were involved and could answer questions in detail about the process. For example, they would
explain that by grafting valencia oranges with agrio
oranges, the resulting orange would have the sweet taste
of the valencia quality and the resistance and strength
of the agrio. "The new orange plant and fruit would thus
be able to fight off disease and taste delicious." This
knowledge and skill was gained at "interest circle" meetings with técnicos who explained, demonstrated, and answered questions about the work.

What are the benefits of the productive efforts of
the al campo students? It is difficult to obtain total
data that would evaluate the students' economic contributions. Goals of production for agricultural crops,
such as vegetables, fruits, coffee, and sugar often include estimates of the labor contributions of al campo
students.[38] Evidence indicates, however, that the productivity of a teenager who does not work regularly at the
job is not comparable to that of an experienced farm
worker. The director of the Camagüey escuela al campo
program said,

> The work norms are more or less 50 per cent
> of the productivity of a regular worker. Given
> the condition of age and knowledge of the stu-
> dent, in general it is a good average . . .;
> but the children often achieve the norm, repeat
> it, and thus come close to the production level
> of the regular workers.[39]

In the author's visits to al campo programs he observed the active student participation and pride in
achieving norms set by regional agricultural leadership
for specific farms and regions within the province.
Students and teachers were involved in organization and
all phases of production and were proud of achievements
in the various areas of agricultural development.

However, there were problems of organization and
wasted time and effort. For example, in one youth program the students had worked hard picking fruit, then the
fruit rotted because trucks assigned to pick up the fruit
were late. Fidel Castro and trade union leaders have
criticized the poor interagency organization and inefficient use of volunteer labor.[40]

SCHOOLS IN THE COUNTRYSIDE

Results achieved from the schools to the countryside
program prompted Cuban educators to consider the possibility of moving to a higher level of revolutionary

pedagogy, an escuela en el campo (schools in the countryside) plan for junior high school students. The new program would not only combine the Cuban emphasis on universal
educational opportunity but would provide an opportunity
for secondary school students to support their own schools.
This was crucial because, as Fidel Castro admitted in his
analysis to the Education Congress of April 1971, "our
educational plan is way above our real economic possibilities."[41] Thus, the en el campo program "would provide an
institution that was simultaneously educational and self-
financing."[42]

The first escuela en el campo--Ceiba I--was opened in
the province of Havana on January 7, 1971. By January
1973, 51 schools were open and functioning. The goal for
1975 is 300 such schools and 1,000 by 1980, when all
junior high education will take place in the countryside
schools.[43]

That Cuban commitment included heavy expenditures
and involvement of parents, students, teachers, and
leadership was apparent both from statements of officials
and from 1971 interviews with construction workers, pupils,
and teachers. Fidel Castro has emphasized the theoretical
basis for the programs while discussing the goals and
practices during opening ceremony exercises in junior
high schools in every province. Speaking of the goals
of the escuela en el campo, Castro states:

> This school responds to conceptions concern-
> ing pedagogy; this school responds to realities;
> this school responds to necessities. It responds
> to pedagogical concepts in accordance with the
> most profound principles of Marxist thought,
> which conceives of education, the formation
> of man, as linked to productive work, to crea-
> tive work, according to the traditional concepts
> of our fatherland, and in agreement with the
> conception of Martí, who also imagined this type
> of school. And this type of school responds to
> the real possibility of forming man: the real
> possibility of combining education, study, and
> work.[44]

Castro has emphasized that the new schools must
balance educational and agricultural work. Schools must
be wary of becoming "agricultural specialty institutions";
that is, although productive activities are undertaken,
they are always in addition to intellectual work. At the
same time, Cubans are urged to avoid a "narrow, intel-
lectualist, practicist approach."[45]

The schools in the countryside are tied to Cuban
efforts toward combining universalization of education
and participation in the developmental process. Cuban
leadership sees the en el campo program as a program
that evolved to meet the needs of a developing country,

while at the same time it is consistent with Marxism-
Leninism. In response to the author's question seeking
clarification of the term "revolutionary pedagogy," Max
Figueroa responded:

> We found a great contradiction between our
> shortage of manpower for our agricultural de-
> velopment on the one hand and the low scholastic
> level of our adult population on the other. How
> could we get the necessary labor force without
> interfering with our educational program? Here,
> for example, the productive work of our students
> is a form of revolutionary pedagogy.
> Productive work is a part of the formative
> process in all socialist countries, but the form
> in which it has developed here is, probably, a
> national form, as are, perhaps, also those forms
> which other countries adopt. We consider that
> productive work is an essential part of the
> formative process at the level of secondary
> school, and when the students are, at the same
> time, contributing decisively to the agricul-
> tural development of the country with their
> production, then the contradiction is eliminated.
> The development of our schools in the country-
> side is a contribution above all to other coun-
> tries on the road to development--that is, to
> countries in revolution--because the countries
> that haven't yet made their revolution are all
> countries that are still underdeveloped. They
> are underdeveloped and maintain capitalist
> regimes. Once they make their revolution,
> they enter immediately upon the road to develop-
> ment.[46]

The school in the countryside is seen as the succes-
sor in educational theory and practice to the school to
the countryside, and it seeks to achieve the same purposes. The educational objectives seem to be clearer
and the results more direct and obtainable with the latter system, but neither one replaces the other--rather,
they complement each other. And as long as the school
in the countryside program is not universalized, the
other program will be applicable and in use.[47]
Gallo summarizes the en el campo goals, showing
that they stem from guidelines derived from Marxism-
Leninism and Cuban revolutionary leadership. The principles governing the program include: 1) channeling
education toward concrete objectives such as participation of youngsters, while studying, in social production,
contributing to the elimination of the differences between the city and countryside and between brain work and
physical work; 2) establishing close links between the
school and life; 3) training the new generations for work

and in work; 4) educating for the collectivity doing away with narrow individualism typical of bourgeois and petty-bourgeois mentality; and 5) combining conscious but firm discipline with the most strict respect for the personality of the student.[48]

Organization

Each of the schools in the countryside follows a similar organization and plant pattern.[49] Each school is equipped to handle 500 students--250 boys and 250 girls--from seventh through ninth grades.

The schools are under the responsibility of the following:

1. a director
2. an Administrative Council that includes the director, the subdirector in charge of academics, the chief of production, the manager responsible for economics and services, the secretary, and the head of the Labor Education Department
3. the Central Council, consisting of the Administrative Council, the political agencies, the organization of the masses, and representatives from parents
4. the Technical Council, composed of the person in charge of each subject area and headed by the director of the en el campo school
5. the faculty, which is made up of 37 teachers who usually cover the following areas:[50]

Subject Area	Number of Teachers
Mathematics	5
Spanish	4
Geography	6
History	4
English	3
Physics	3
Chemistry	1
Biology	4
Labor Education	4
Physical Education	3

The student body of each school is divided into halves. In the morning, half the students work the school farmlands and the other half attend six periods of classes. In the afternoon, the procedure is reversed; that is, the group that worked in the fields in the morning attend afternoon classes, and the students who

attended morning classes work in the fields. Students are
expected to study three nights a week and may use the
other two nights for recreational activities. They may
leave the school during the weekend.

The school program at Ceiba I, the first school in
the countryside built in Cuba, is as follows:

6:00	Reveille
6:15 to 7:00 a.m.	Breakfast
7:00 to 7:30 a.m.	Morning exercises
7:30 to 11:00 a.m.	Agricultural work for eighth and tenth grades
12:00 to 1:00 p.m.	Lunch
1:00 to 2:00 p.m.	Rest
2:00 to 5:30 p.m.	Agricultural work for seventh and ninth grades
7:00 to 8:00 p.m.	Dinner
8:30 to 10:00 p.m.	Study and recreation Study on Mond., Wed., Fri.; Recreation on Tues., Thurs.
10:00 p.m.	To bed
10:30 p.m.	Silence

Below the program schedule was posted a quotation from
Martí: "Schools we should not say, but rather workshops;
and the pen should be wielded in the afternoon at the
schools, but in the morning,the hoe."[51]

The escuela en el campo program has provided Cuba's
educational planners with the opportunity to provide the
"material base" for physical development through sports
activities. Urban schools in crowded city streets could
not provide the space for students to play, practice, and
develop a variety of sports skills. In discussing the en
el campo program, Fidel Castro states: "One of the problems faced by our schools in the cities is that they are
completely devoid of sports fields. Here we have them
. . . ."[52] The en el campo schools were seen as a means
of offering "broad possibilities for children to participate intensively in sports."[53] The escuela en el campo's
strong accent on sports reflects the Cuban special emphasis
on sports in both formal and nonformal programs.[54]
According to a leader in the Ministry of Education, "Study,
defense, work, and sports are the four pillars of communist education."[55]

Educational Plant

The first en el campo schools, built in 1971, were
composed of four three-floor buildings. One building is
used for academic activities and has classrooms for
Spanish, English, mathematics, geography, and history;
four laboratory areas (two for biology, one for physics,

and another for chemistry); a workshop for labor education;
a classroom workshop for technical drawing; and a library
facility. In another building, the second and third floors
provide the male students' living quarters. The main floor
contains teacher and other staff quarters, recreation and
conference rooms, and a little theater. In the third
building, the second and third floors are used for the
female students' quarters. The first floor contains the
infirmary, the barber shop, conference and recreation
rooms, and a little theater. In addition, another single
story building includes the dining room, kitchen, refri-
geration unit, and three storage rooms.

In 1972 several changes were made for economic reasons
in the design and construction of the en el campo prefabricated plant. At the "symbolic" inauguration of 44 new
schools on September 25, 1972, Castro explained the changes
in plant design:

> As you can see, the design of this school is
> different from the first ones, saving materials
> and labor. Two of the buildings that the first
> schools had have been changed--that is, this
> school doesn't have three-story buildings as the
> others did. It has one building like those, but
> the other two are combined in one building, which
> is longer and taller than the others had been and
> which links up with the other building through a
> lower and upper staircase, making it easier for
> the students to move around . . . . The beauty
> hasn't been affected--quite the contrary, now
> it is taller. It can be seen from farther away
> and we suppose it will be cooler on the fourth
> floor.[56]

All Year Use of Facilities

The new en el campo facilities are part of a concept that sees the school as a facility that serves the
total family. During the summer student vacation, the
escuela en el campo is still an active, busy center,
because the parents and relatives of the children vacation at the school on a rotating basis. Each week 200
to 250 people sleep in the dormitories and eat in the
dining room. During the day they use the sports fields,
swimming pool, and game rooms (ping pong, chess, and so
on). The vacation plan arranges for daily trips to parks,
museums, historical sites, and beaches. Bus transportation is provided for all guests. At night there are
"cultural events," including music, drama, entertainment
by the guests themselves, and student and professional
groups. The relatives pay no fees for the vacation, but
they do contribute two hours daily to the school's
agricultural plan.

At the end of the vacation week, an evaluation assembly is held with the guests and staff. At this time the guests discuss which activities and programs they thought were worthwhile and what should be done to improve the vacation plan.

In July 1971 Fidel Castro described the logic and purpose of the nonformal en el campo summer vacation plan:

> We feel that the participation of the parents in the vacation plans will result in having better care taken of the school. And, since the school is surrounded by crops, what would we do if everyone went home at vacation time, and nobody was left at the school? A lot of interests are served by the vacation plan: the interests of the school, the interests of the workers, their interest in a vacation, and the interest of the economy as such. All this in one. What work will they do? The same kind of work that students do every day. What will they do after their work stint in the morning? A bath, lunch, a rest, and then a program of sports and recreational activities for the rest of the afternoon. . . . Just as we build these schools . . . we are also going to use them as magnificent vacation camps for our workers, for the parents of the young people who are going to study in these schools. And parents won't be the only ones who are able to rest there--the younger brothers and sisters of the junior high school students will also vacation at the school they will later attend as students. What can be viewed as the dream of a child? Where is he going to study? The place where he spent his vacation one day, the place which was so aggreeable and pleasant.[57]

Costs and Resources

A goal of the new en el campo program is to make the countryside schools a part of the strategy of economic and educational development. This includes the concept that these schools must be self-financing. This goal has been repeatedly stated by Castro at the openings of the first junior high schools in the countryside.

> . . . if we didn't combine our program for education with our program for economic development, we would never be able to put through these plans for building 100, 300, and even 1,000 schools of this kind. This is why these schools are being built in areas where the students can participate in the economic development of our country.[58]

Financial estimates of Cuban school expenditures are not easy to find, since financial statements--which would include money estimates--are not available. However, careful reading of several speeches by leadership, examination of juceplan reports, personal interviews, and recent analyses have led to the following observations.

First, Cuban estimates of current student production input in the en el campo program indicate that the 1,000,000 students anticipated in the program in 1980 (there were 80,000 students in the program in 1973) will be able to meet the total costs of education.

It is evident that no poor country could educate everybody unless everybody participates in productive activities. Otherwise, many would be unable to study, and only a few could receive an education. The participation of the young people in our production plan will also make it possible for the country to do whatever it finds necessary in the field of education.

Today, the cost of education is approximately 500 million pesos. By 1980 the value of production turned out by the 1,000,000 students will surpass the cost of education, even though the cost may be over 1,000,000 pesos.[59]

Some of the production forecasting at specific schools indicates that each school farm has a high yield potential. In each school in the countryside there are 500 cultivated hectares (40 caballerias) under the care of students, teachers, and some workers. Each of these hectares could yield 2 million pesos a year.

With the conditions of our climate, 500 well-attended hectares of citrus fruit technically should produce enough to underwrite all the costs of this school--more than enough. Thus, building schools of this type does not constitute a luxury.

We could cite a statistic. We believe that the production of 500 hectares of citrus fruit, with a high yield, would be equivalent to 2 million pesos a year . . . 1,500 schools with this level of productivity would be fabulous. Of course, one must not think that all products are as highly productive, but this is an example.[60]

In an interview in 1971, Vice Minister Maceiras made the following observations about the actual economic benefits of the en el campo program:

Work productivity is very high, because one cannot forget the fact that these youngsters have a certain degree of schooling, and that

the work they do, therefore, benefits by their
level of schooling. Generally, they can develop
a work rate that is about that of a seasoned
agricultural worker for this type of crop. In
other words, the product of the labor of these
young students in a short time can contribute
to repaying the investment involved in each
school-farm, because these are costly centers.
I am not absolutely certain, but I think that
between installations and maintenance they run
to some 650,000 or 700,000 pesos; thus, such
schools are a major investment. But this investment is more than repaid with the students'
labor, since they produce much more than what
the school costs, so that in time, their labor
not only pays for the school itself, but it
counters the expenses incurred in their education, such as room and board, clothing, etc.,
and even leaves an excess for the establishment
of more schools of this type.[61]

Maceiras' answer briefly mentions the issue of capital investment costs and recurrent costs. Gillette[62]
has attempted to calculate whether the escuela en el
campos are self-financing. He used total cost estimates
of 237.7 million pesos for the total annual budget
(1968/69) and 1 million pesos approximation for each
school. These figures do not reflect the 1973 data (see
the previous statement by Fidel Castro of an estimate of
500 million pesos for the total 1972 budget and Maceiras'
above reference to 700,000 pesos per school in 1971).

However, Gillette calculated student's work hours
per year at 630 hours (3 hours per day, 5 days per week,
42 weeks per year). He then assumed a 5 percent loss
for sickness, examinations, and so forth, and concluded
with an estimate of 600 productive hours per year. Based
on a minimum wage scale, the resultant productive effort
was worth 123,000 pesos per school year, which more than
offset the total annual recurrent expenditure on the
school (96,552 pesos).[63] Student production not only
paid for current expenditures, but the productivity would
return the capital investment in schools in less than 35
years. (Gillette's figure of 35 years must be lowered,
because his million pesos per school estimate, as we have
seen, was 300,000 pesos high.)

Available data appear to indicate that the Cubans
are achieving their goal of self-financing of recurrent
expenditures and, within a generation and a half, students'work will reimburse the capital investment in the
school.

COMMENTARY ON CAMPO PROGRAMS

In the following pages commentaries are offered on some of the significant aspects of both the al campo and the en el campo programs. Because the latter program is still at an initial stage, having been in existence only for a short time, and because the author has not had much opportunity to observe first-hand the operation of these institutions, the remarks below are based more on the author's impression of the al campo program--although, it should be remembered, that the basic goals and rationale of the two are the same.

Developing a Collective Consciousness

One goal emphasized by Cubans, and even more diffi-cult to evaluate than economic goals, is the development of a collective consciousness. This is a goal of both the al campo and en el campo programs. Cubans are aware of the paucity of research data on the accomplishment of their more intangible goals, and they hope to gather more data in the future. Dr. Guillermo Arias (head of the psychology unit of the Ministry of Education in 1971) emphasized the need for research to answer questions about the effectiveness of the campo programs. Arias admitted that there has been little or no research done on the countryside program. At the 1971 Congress of Edu-cation and Culture, teacher representatives also urged that the Ministry of Education study and appraise their program.[64]

In an effort to determine whether "collective atti-tudes" were being developed in the al campo program, the author asked the tenth-graders in one escuela al campo to respond to a questionnaire. The students were requested to respond anonymously without the presence of any faculty members. One of the questions asked was, "Discuss what you think your life will be like when you are 30 years old." This open-ended question was asked in order to ascertain how students viewed their future life and whether their aspirations were centered on or directed toward personal "self" goals and concerns, or toward societal commitments and collective goals. The responses of the 92 students in the class are summarized below:

Tenth Grade Student Aspirations at Age 30

Total No.	Personal		Social-Political and Personal		Social-Political	
	No.	Percent	No.	Percent	No.	Percent
92	26	28	34	38	32	34

Responses in which students referred only to personal aspirations with no reference to their role in the social order--are listed in column 1 under the category, personal aspirations. These responses included: "have a wife, children," "be at home with my wife; playing guitar," "honest, comfortable life," and "live for education of my children."

Those students who responded with life and work aspirations that only referred to social-political goals are listed in column 3. They wrote such responses as "be useful to society," "help the revolution and defend the principles of Communism," "work to serve others," "lead a life for the benefit of all," "in the service of the revolution," and "concerned with justice for all."

Those who combined personal and social-political aspirations are listed in column 2. These responses included: "marriage and children and work for the revolution," "wife and children and dedicate work to others," "to have a family and contribute to the development of my country," "marry and teach children to help the country and the revolution," and "work, children and be a good revolutionary."

It is interesting to note that for 72 percent of the students, a vision of their life at 30 included working and living for societal or collective consideration, whether those of Cuba or of other people. In describing their young adult life, 28 percent did not mention these goals.

Although this exercise does not provide a basis for drawing general conclusions, it appears that the new forms of secondary schooling do help advance changes in the consciousness of young people.

Providing Role and Behavior Models

The al campo and en el campo programs provided opportunities for teachers and students to offer "models" in behavior roles. These models were more difficult for the students to obtain in a normal academic setting. Recent psychological experiments on the importance of modeling in human development suggest that the Cuban emphasis on "models" is supported by empirical data.[65]

In the campo, formal leadership status is often bypassed for student leadership, although the student leaders' talents may not have been tapped in the usual school atmosphere. In addition, the efforts to fight elitist tendencies in leadership appear to be more successful in the campo. In the countryside, teachers and administrators relate to students in a setting in which their academic book expertise and knowledge are not the needed functional skills and abilities, and they have the opportunity to do physical work side by side with students. Dehesa thought that the political-social models in the campo were crucial to the fulfillment of Cuban educational goals. Furthermore, these goals are often difficult, if not impossible, to achieve outside the campo.

Dehesa was asked these questions: "Are you accomplishing your goals? Are you helping to change attitudes among these young people? If so, how do you measure these changes?" His reply was:

> Although we cannot offer documentation for it, we can certainly cite experiences which demonstrate that there have been enormous changes in the students. I will focus on the specific group of students that we have here with us now. This first year in Carlos Marx was something very special. Many of the students are beyond school age and many of them have problems. They have had difficulties in other schools and we have come to know about them here in the campos. Why is it that we have discovered them here when they have gone unnoticed elsewhere? It is because we have dedicated ourselves to them here with greater concern, and so have been able to give them the attention we could not give them there. . . . Besides all this, there is the political work, which is fundamental. We believe that it is fundamental in any school whatsoever, but it is even more basic in the escuela al campo . . . They do not hear me, for example, saying to them, 'We're going to work now. It is necessary to do.' Instead, they see this work spring from compañeros who say to them, 'Let's go, compañeros, we've got work to do.' They see that it is necessary to do it for this, that, and the other reason. Regardless of our wishes to the contrary, a system of hierarchy still exists in their minds, and they see us as authority, mainly because of the position we represent. They do not see any functional authority in us, but rather an established one, because this is the type of authority we have in the school. And if, for instance, we stand before them and say, 'We must do this now,' they immediately recognize the established authority rather than the functional.
>
> But these compañeros work with them and work at the same rhythm. In fact, they are the compañeros who work the most. And so, when this compañero, who has arisen from among them from the mass of students--whether he be head of a brigade, member of the juventud [vanguard youth], or participant in the comite de base de la juventud [grassroots committee of youth]-- says to them, 'Let's go; let's get to work,'

they go, and they work, for he wields an authority that no one has given to him, but which he
has earned through his attitude and work.

Elsewhere the teachers work and then they go
home. Not here. Here they work and they stay.
They live together with the students. They
participate in the same way. We always put this
most important political work in first place--
and we hold that one cannot go to an escuela al
campo without having set up an organización
juvenil (youth organization) that is sufficiently
responsible. . . . We must not demand what we
are not capable of doing ourselves. And so,
this is the second most important concern in
the escuela al campo. First and foremost is the
political work which should be done mainly by the
juventud working with the youngsters. Second, the
teacher's attitude is an important factor.[66]

Participation in Development

Another benefit of the campo programs is the opportunity provided to students and teachers to actually have
the responsibility and experience of participation in the
economic development of Cuba. One of the goals of Cuban
society is to improve the conditions of the masses of the
people through improved agricultural productivity. Thus,
junior high and senior high school students do not "learn"
in classrooms about Cuban factories and farms and the
productive efforts of these institutions. By actual involvement in production, students are becoming aware of
the problems that Cuba faces in coming up from "backward
development." At the same time, they do not suffer the
problem of alienation from the productive process. Each
is contributing to his country's economic development
through his involvement and production.

The teachers, too, are involved in this process, and
guidelines were set up to prevent them from imposing their
views on the students at different levels of the participatory process in the campo programs. The teachers
do not merely talk about "linking learning and practice."
The conditions at the campo programs provide them with
opportunities to draw on agricultural work for specific
academic lessons in the humanities or sciences. By living
with the youth, the teachers are able to establish a
personal relationship with students in a nonformal setting and thus learn their problems, work habits, and
aspirations. The teachers' supportive and guidance role
is emphasized as the authoritarian nature of the classroom is broken down by teachers and students working and
studying toward common goals. This leadership model becomes a possibility in the nonformal Cuban educational
structure of the campo programs.

Social Equality

The campo programs play an important role in contributing to the achievements of additional goals of Cuban society, including the breakdown of the class structure and other forms of social inequality. These programs demonstrate the following directions in Cuban education:

1. opportunities for blacks to attend secondary school and to aspire to advanced education
2. mixing of children from various backgrounds: working class, white collar, professionals, administrators
3. new opportunities for rural students as <u>all</u> the new escuelas en el campo are in rural areas
4. involvement of young women students in en el campo programs--most of the opportunities offered in the en el campo programs for young women students to contribute to the economy on an egalitarian basis and to secure advanced education were not available before to the masses of Cuban girls and women [67]

Bowles discusses the fact that the very structure of the campo programs equalizes and "inverts" the hierarchical school structure:

This radical transformation [to educational equality] has been best implemented by and reflected in the new forms of schooling. . . . Students generally learn lessons from what they do, and what their teachers do, as well as from what they read and study. In a society in which the manual work is, to a great extent, shared by all, the conventional class distinctions become blurred. And the school activities themselves-- students and teachers working side by side with the <u>campesinos</u>, workers attending school--contribute greatly to the obliteration of the class lines based on manual versus nonmanual work distinctions. Moreover, in the <u>Escuela al Campo</u> program, the leadership of the camp often goes to those who work well, not to the monitors or others who excel in intellectual tasks. The occasional inversion of the hierarchy of the school system itself teaches an additional lesson for equality.[68]

Academic Benefits

As has been noted previously in this report, the al campo program seriously modified its earlier ambitious academic programs for the students during their 45 days in the countryside. The present al campo program offers evening classes to those students who need help in specific subject areas, but these review efforts to not attempt to continue the all-year program for all of the students.

The en el campo schools have completely different academic goals from the al campo programs. Escuela en el campo offers a junior high school academic program alongside the "work" part of the program.

The integration of formal and nonformal programs in the escuela en el campo aims not only at maintaining academic performance by students but also at improving the academic quality of secondary education.

The academic subjects offered are the same subjects taught in the junior high schools throughout Cuba. However, the curriculum is "adjusted" to the agricultural work needs, so that students are additionally offered classes on the operation and maintenance of agricultural machinery. These courses--meaningful in the en campo program--are not available in the regular junior high schools.

A staff of 100 serves the 500 students at each campo. This includes teachers, kitchen workers, custodial staff, agricultural workers, and mechanics. Classes are organized heterogeneously: thirty-five to forty pupils per class with mixed sex and a wide range of academic abilities. There is no ability grouping. Three evenings per week are set aside for "study nights" and may be used for study, tutoring, or individual study.

What are the results? The Cubans place emphasis on the percentage of promotion (on a grade, school, and regional level) as the key criterion for measuring the success of a school. The bases for determining promotion are achievement tests. Available Cuban data emphasize the improved "quality" (as measured by higher grade promotion percentages) of education in en el campo schools. Fidel Castro has pointed out pedagogical results of the countryside programs.

From the pedagogical point of view, the results have been very good. The school with the highest promotion rates in the country was a junior high school in the countryside, that Ceiba-I school, with a 94 percent promotion rate before the repeat exams. The Ceiba-III school also obtained a 94 percent promotion rate, though it did not have any tenth grade students, which is why Ceiba-I took first place. But, anyway, that school made a great effort to reach a 94 percent

promotion rate before the repeat exams. With
the second exams, both schools should raise their
promotion figures even more.

There were several junior high schools in the
countryside in Havana province. The promotion
rate of the Havana schools was 94 percent after
the repeat exam; the traditional nonboarding
schools had a promotion rate of 82 percent.
Junior high schools in the countryside did 12
percentage points better than the traditional
schools in promotion, with a promotion rate 14.6
percent higher.

The quality of these schools is being clearly
demonstrated in spite of the fact that they are a
new phenomenon. We will have to start getting
our experience together.[69]

Reports, interviews with teachers and students, and
published articles reflect Cuban pride in the high passing and promotion percentages of students in en el campo
schools--usually in the 90 to 99 percentage range. The
factors that seem to account for this improved percentage
of promotion are:

1. The boarding school nature of the program. The
study aspect of their lives is not only emphasized, but
time and help are available for individual assistance.
The evening study hours are used for students who need
additional help, and teachers and monitors are available.
The nonboarding school student who is having difficulty
with the new Cuban modern mathematics secondary program
returns to a home environment where parents usually cannot help because they do not have a command of the subject
or because they do not have the time or patience. The
student in the en el campo program faces none of these
problems. On the contrary, he has peers and adults who
can and want to help.

2. The relationship between student and teacher
benefits from the nonformal aspects of the en el campo
program. One twenty-five year old teacher of the Heroes
of Varsovia Junior High School in the Countryside explained:

> The high test scores are the result, among
> other things, of more studying and complete
> identification between the students and their
> teachers, who wind up being not only their
> teachers, but also their work comrades and
> close friends. All this makes for an atmos-
> phere of well-being and happiness.[70]

3. The utilization of students to teach students.
The shortage of teachers has not prevented the Cubans
from continuing their expansion of the en el campo program.

This is possible because monitors--advanced students--
have been utilized to teach and tutor when teachers are
not available. Although the Cubans developed this educational strategy out of necessity, recent research studies
have shown that there is much to be gained from peers
teaching peers.[71]

4. The introduction of new plants, equipment and
materials--including spacious classrooms, laboratory facilities, audiovisual equipment, Cuban-made textbooks,
and sports and recreational facilities--facilitate the
learning process. During the past five years the Secondary Education Department of the Ministry of Education has
introduced a range of new textbooks in almost every curriculum area, books written by Cuban teachers for the Cuban
course of study. This qualitative and quantitative change
is a departure from the earlier phase of the production of
Cuban educational materials when foreign textbooks were
translated and reproduced to fill the vacuum in materials
during the increase in school registration. Now, secondary education teachers work on new texts and use Cuban
contextual references, visuals, and graphics to supplement the texts. There is also junior high school student
and teacher input, that is, texts are "tested" in mimeographed form and criticisms are incorporated into the
manuscript before the texts are published.

Although these new facilities and materials and
board and clothing are available free to the students,
the self-financing character of the schools provides a
positive psychological or "morale" factor. Students and
teachers are not only proud of the plant and equipment
but quick to point out that it is their labor that is
paying for these modern facilities and aids. The "our
sweat is making this possible" attitude indicates that
the Cubans consider these schools to be their own creation
and not something handed to them by an anonymous bene-
factor, whether a private or government agency or political
leader.

5. Although the schools are boarding schools, parent
involvement is emphasized. First, the extended family--
parents, grandparents, and siblings--use the school for
vacation. As was noted earlier, the free summer vacation
at the school includes the maintenance of the self-financing aspect of the program. The student concept of "our
school" is thus extended to the rest of the family. In
addition, parent representation on the administrative
council and parent meetings provide a vehicle for their
involvement in student achievement and progress. However,
the geographic separation of the urban parent population
from the site of the school presents a serious problem
for parents who want to maintain close contact with their
child and his school faculty.

6. Improvement of student and teacher attendance.
Teacher absenteeism and poor student attendance were
serious problems before the revolution.   Since the

revolution there has been an emphasis on teachers' professional responsibility and parents' and students'
responsibility for excellent attendance and punctuality.
Attendance of students has gone from 60 percent prerevolu-
tion to 90 percent since the revolution.[72] The en el
campo program with its boarding school nature encourages
every child and teacher to be in school every day unless
he or she is ill.

Problem of the Quality of Teaching
and Teacher Shortage

A major problem that the author observed during
visits to classrooms in Cuba was the problem of the
quality of the teaching-learning situation within each
classroom. Many teachers viewed their role as one of
"telling"--of simply presenting content to the students.
Also, teachers were found to follow the "blue-book syndrome"; the students were busy filling blue-covered note-
books with notes from the lectures of the teacher. These
notes were later memorized for the testing program.
Interviews with Cuban educational leadership and
published reports indicate that the quality of the teaching is a major concern. In discussing the principal
problems and contradictions related to the school to the
countryside, Gallo states:

> Will the so-called 'combination' (conferences,
> books, blackboard--with the help of illustrations,
> drawings, sketches) still prevail in the technique
> of learning as a principal source of knowledge, or
> will new techniques be introduced--accepted theo-
> retically up to now, but not in common use--
> founded upon the exposition, discussion, and
> analysis of problems? Will the professor still
> continue to be the fundamental object of knowledge
> for the student, or will the student be taken to
> life, so that, oriented by the professor, he may
> question and investigate on his own all that which
> the opportunity of social productive work offers
> him?[73]

Gallo strongly suggests that the "vicious practice of
verbal exposition of content and the passive memorization
of the same must be eradicated."

> Without completely doing away with the method
> of oral and systematic exposition of the informa-
> tive content of the lesson by the professor,
> complemented by the use of books, research, writ-
> ten exercises, and laboratory or workshop practices,

we must move toward a utilization of pedagogic
techniques that are geared toward a greater
participation by the student himself in the
learning process.[74]

The question of improving the quality of teaching
becomes more serious when one notes that the predicted
increase of new schools and student population will cause
a deficit of 18,000 teachers by 1976. In September 1973
approximately 80,000 new secondary education students
will enter the Cuban schools (teacher training, poly-
technical, monitor, technological, and junior high schools),
and starting in 1974 there will be enough secondary schools
built to handle at least 100,000 more students every
year.[75] Castro suggests that the only way to provide
enough teachers for this greatly increased student body
is to go to the tenth grade young people in the junior
high school and ask for volunteers to enter the teacher-
training programs. After the tenth grade they would start
their teacher-training in the junior high schools, a practice that is consistent with Cuban efforts in all professional areas (medicine, engineering, and so on) to conduct
training in the field.

> We have to start a movement among our junior
> high school graduates this year. There are
> 20,000 tenth graders in the country, and a move-
> ment for training these tenth graders to teach
> in the junior high schools in the countryside
> must be developed by the student organizations
> and the U.J.C. [Union of Communist Youth]. They
> will teach under the supervision of teachers with
> more experience and should enroll in the Pedago-
> gical Institute. Thus, a tenth grade graduate
> would be able to go to a junior high school and
> work under the supervision of experienced teach-
> ers and get his pedagogical training right there
> in the school. We must start a movement among
> those young people, getting them to combine
> teaching junior high with studying pedagogy.
> At present there simply is not any other formula
> except to go to our tenth graders and recruit at
> least 2,000 of them this year and at least 5,000
> next year, and so on.[76]

Cuban leadership chose not to wait until they had
fully trained staff before expanding the en el campo
programs. The decision on the junior high school level
to draw upon recent graduates of the program to solve
the teacher shortage is consistent with the strategy of
not waiting for ideal conditions before proceeding with
radical change. There were no data available to this
researcher on how this emergency teacher-training plan
is functioning.

An important advantage of the Cuban educational structure is the strong commitment to inservice training. The
Cubans have adopted and incorporated into their basic
structure the idea and the practice that a teacher must
continually improve her pedagogical and content skills.
Abel Prieto Morales, who has served in a variety of top
leadership positions in the Ministry of Education since
the revolution, states:

> Our country suffered not only from an under-
> developed economy but from underdeveloped
> pedagogy as well--these elements which enter
> into the question of the quality of teaching.
> We have imposed on ourselves the task of improv-
> ing the quality of education, not only by im-
> proving the school program, but by improving
> the teacher. You can have   beautiful programs
> but they may just remain on paper, unfulfilled.[77]

All junior high teachers spend one month a year (July)
on inservice training, which includes pedagogy, psychology,
and subject content study. In addition to this month of
concentration, there are school level, grade level, and
subject area meetings of teachers during the academic
year. There are also conferences of staff from different
en el campo programs to evaluate the existing programs,
share experiences, and make recommendations for constructive changes in the program.

Conclusions

Although the escuela en el campo program is still in
its early stages--with 1980 as the target date for the
operation of all junior high schools in the program--the
experience suggests a number of lessons for other developing countries.
First, the institution of a radical change in secondary school programming, such as the escuela en el campo,
has a chance to succeed if it is strongly supported by
the leadership of the nation, the Ministry of Education,
and the classroom teachers in the field. The excerpts
in this report from Fidel Castro, the Prime Minister, and
the Ministry of Education leadership, and students and
teachers exemplify the national commitment, priority,
and support that the program has received in Cuba.
Second, the encouragement and moral support by the
leadership of the nation must be backed by a serious
investment of the resources of the country. The investment in the escuela en el campo program reflects the
overall value and emphasis on education in Cuba. Cuba
has devoted about one-fifth of her total productive

capacity to education, "a figure unsurpassed among the major nations in the world, rich or poor."[78] More than adequate resources have been allocated to each school in the program: a new physical plant with sport facilities, laboratories, and so forth, in a boarding school setting that includes food, lodging, clothing, and a full-time staff.

Third, Cuba's strategy to invest in education for development is tempered by the reality that a developing country follows an economically disastrous course if it permits investment in education to disrupt the economy. The self-financing characteristic of the escuela en el campo schools and the economic contribution of the escuela al campo program of the other secondary schools is an alternative that other developing countries with an agri- cultural economy may well consider as they weigh the problems of possibly being overburdened by educational costs that produce only delayed benefits to the nation.

Fourth, the escuela en el campo experience demon- strates that the planning and introduction of a major program benefit from national experience with nonformal programs. The escuela en el campo programs were built upon the Cuban experience for five years with the escuela al campo. Also, the experience with other nonformal pro- grams, especially the Literacy Campaign, provided another basis for action--the willingness to take bold steps in educational policy, steps that did not pursue formal, traditional school approaches.

Fifth, with respect to staff recruitment and planning, in order to solve the teacher crisis (shortage), the en el campo programs are drawing upon motivated and able young people who are products of the same en campo program. The cycle of providing education and then using the newly educated to enable the program to expand to meet the regis- tration bulge is a critically important step. The teacher training approach of "learn and teach" at the same time, which uses the en campo school as a teacher-training center, is an approach that merits careful consideration by developing nations facing similar shortages in personnel.

Sixth, the en el campo program provides a vivid example of the active role students can play in a secondary- level program. Students actively participate in and lead academic activities (monitor programs during the day, individual and group study in the evening). They also organize and are responsible for productive farm work, recreational programming, and boarding and living arrange- ments.

Seventh, nonformal programs outside the classroom have enabled Cuban students to explore relationships be- tween adults and students that are not adult-centered and authoritarian. Student-shared leadership with a genuine involvement in decisionmaking and real responsibility are integral parts of the nonformal activities.

The formal classroom structure, however, has not reflected the democratic approach of the nonformal activities. Exams and grades remain a key source of motivation and the teacher-dominated classroom, with the teacher talking and students listening passively, is the basic methodological approach. Classroom habits of longstanding are considerably more difficult to change.

The en el campo program is an important example of the integration of nonformal activities into a formal, national educational program. In the escuela en el campo nonformal activities (interest circles, agricultural work, and so forth) have been incorporated on a mass basis in a regular junior high school program. Although this concept of integrating formal and nonformal activities is not new, the mass national application of this concept is a major contribution to contemporary educational theory and practice.[79]

Finally, the en el campo program serves as an example of the viable merger of the educational process with societal goals. The emphasis on collective consciousness, on active and real participation in the economic development of the society, and on the development and living exemplification of social and political attitudes and awareness, function to link the education of youth to the emergence of the "new man" who, it is hoped, will perpetuate and safeguard the national goals and the societal aspirations.

NOTES

1. Richard R. Fagen, The Transformation of Political Culture in Cuba (Stanford: Stanford University Press, 1969), pp. 21-22.

2. Ibid., p. 23.

3. James O'Connor, The Origins of Socialism in Cuba (Ithaca: Cornell University Press, 1970), p. 58.

4. Lowry Nelson, Rural Cuba (New York: Octagon Books, 1950), pp. 236-239.

5. See Dudley Seers, ed. Cuba: The Economic and Social Revolution (Chapel Hill: University of North Carolina Press, 1964); Fagen, op. cit.; O'Connor, op. cit.; Ramon Eduardo Ruiz, Cuba: The Making of a Revolution (Amherst: The University of Massachusetts Press, 1968); Rolando E. Bonachea and Netson P. Valdes, Cuba in Revolution (New York: Doubleday and Co., 1972); Irving Louis Horowitz, ed. Cuban Communism (New Brunswick, N.J.: Transaction Books, 1972); Carmelo Mesa-Lago, ed. Revolutionary Change in Cuba (Pittsburgh: University of Pittsburgh Press, 1971).

6. Samuel Bowles, "Cuban Education and the Revolutionary Ideology," Harvard Educational Review 41, no. 4 (Nov. 1971): 474.

7. Ibid., p. 472.

8. Marvin Leiner, "Major Developments in Cuban Education," Warner Modular Publications, module 264 (1973), pp. 1-2.

9. Interview with Dr. Max Figueroa Araujo, General Director, Center of Education and Development, Ministry of Education, 1971.

10. Ibid.

11. Marvin Leiner, Children are the Revolution: Day Care in Cuba (New York: Viking Press, 1974), pp. 50-117.

12. Bowles, op. cit., p. 489.

13. Leiner, Children are the Revolution, op. cit., pp. 245-249.

14. The Centennial Youth Column and the Seguidores de Camilo y Ché (Followers of Camilo and Ché) are volunteer youth groups of young men and women who work and live together (a commitment of several years) to help wherever the economy needs them (for example, in agriculture and construction).

15. See David Barkin, "Cuban Agriculture, a Strategy of Economic Development," in Cuban Communism, Horowitz, op. cit, pp. 123-158, for a discussion of Cuba's "agricultural turnpike" strategy of development.

16. Felix Santie, "La precolumna Juvenil del Centario: Expresion del sistema paralelo dentro del marco de la educacion permanente en nuestro pais"   (Paper presented at the Interidsciplinary Seminar on Continuing Education, Havana, Cuba, December 1970), p. 22, and Fidel Castro, "Speech to the Second Congress of the Young Communist League," Granma Weekly Review, 4 April 1972, pp. 1-8, both cited in Rolland G. Paulston, "Cuban Rural Education: A Strategy for Rural Development," in The World Year Book of Education 1974, edited by Philip Foster and James R. Sheffield (London: Evans Brothers, Ltd., 1973), pp. 249-250.

17. Interview with Dr. José Aguilera Maceiras, Vice Minister of General and Special Education, Ministry of Education, 1971.

18. See Fagen, op. cit., pp. 33-68 and Cuba, Ministry of Education, Methods and Means Utilized in Cuba to Eliminate Illiteracy (Havana, 1965).

19. M. Leiner, "Cuba's Schools: Ten Years Later," Saturday Review, 17 October 1970, p. 69.

20. José Aguilera Maceiras, "El plan 'La escuela al campo,' un logro de la educación en Cuba," Educación, Año 1, no. 3 (Oct.- Nov. 1971), p. 9.

21. Ibid., p. 11.

22. Cuba, Ministry of Education, Report to the XXXI International Conference on Public Instruction, OIE and UNESCO (Havana, 1968), p. 53.

23. Gaspar Jorge García Galló, "La escuela al campo," Educación en Cuba, Año 1, no. 1 (January-February 1967), p. 8.

24. Cuba, Ministry of Education, op. cit., pp. 54-55.

25. J. Maceiras, op. cit., p. 11.

26. Ibid.

27. Ibid., pp. 12-13.

28. Interview with Miguel Dehesa, Director of the Escuela al Campo, Carlos Marx Pre-Universitaria, 1969.

29. Interview with Nefertiti Tellería Gonzalez, student leader, escuela al campo, 1969.

30. Interview with Christina Rodriguez, director, escuela al campo, Amadeo Roldán.

31. See Maceiras, op. cit., p. 13.

32. Joseph Kahl, "The Moral Economy of a Revolutionary Society," Transactions (April 1969), p. 32.

33. Interview with Dehesa, 1969; also see Cuba, Ministry of Education, Report to the XXXI International Conference, op. cit., and Cuba, Ministry of Education, Consejo Nacional de Education, La Escuela al Campo (Havana, 1967).

34. Lino Oramas, "Sancti Spíritus High School Students at Work in Banao," Granma Weekly Review, 20 February 1972, p. 2

35. Ibid.

36. "Report on Production at the Escuela el Campo," mimeographed (Amadeo Roldán, 1969).

37. "Report on Emulación at the Escuela el Campo," mimeographed (Carlos Marx Senior High School, 1969).

38. L. Oramas, op. cit.

39. Elio E. Constantin, "En Camagüey: La Escuela al Campo, un orgullo legitimo," Granma Weekly Review, 17 February 1971, p. 2.

40. F. Castro, "Speech in Celebration of the 17th Anniversary of the Attack on the Moncada," Granma Weekly Review, 2 August 1970, pp. 2-5, and "Discurso en la Plenaria Provincial de la CTC," Granma Revista Seminal, 10 September 1970, pp. 2-4; and Carmelo Mesa-Lago, The Labor Force, Employment, Unemployment and Underemployment in Cuba, 1899-1970 (London: Sage Publications, 1972), p. 63.

41. F. Castro, "Address Delivered at the Inauguration of the First National Congress School," Granma Weekly Review, 2 May 1971, p. 7.

42. Arthur Gillette, Cuba's Educational Revolution, Fabian Research Series 302 (London: Fabian Society, 1972), p. 26.

43. Daura Olema, "Escuela en el Campo," Cuba Internacional, Año 5, no. 41 (January 1973), p. 37.

44. F. Castro, "La Escuela en el Campo," Educación, Año 1, no. 1 (April-June 1971), p. 13

45. Ibid., p. 17.

46. Interview with Max Figueroa Araujo, 1971.

47. G. J. G. Gallo, "The School Goes to the Countryside and the School in the Countryside," Granma Weekly Review, 17 October 1971, p. 9.

48. Ibid.

49. This summary is based on the author's 1971 visit to the Ceiba I school in the countryside and interviews with teachers, students, parents, and educational leadership; on a review of Cuban educational reports (published and unpublished); and published articles in Educación, Cuba, Cuba International, Bohemia, and Granma Weekly Review.

50. F. Castro, "Escuela en el campo," op. cit., p. 13. Also, interview with the faculty secretary at Ceiba I, 1971.

51. Ceiba I bulletin board, 1971.

52. F. Castro, "Address Delivered at the Inauguration of the First National Congress School," op. cit., p. 7.

53. Maceiras interview, 1971.

54. See F. Castro, Granma Weekly Review, 2 May 1971. Also interviews with Aguilera Maceiras (1969, 1971), Abel Pristo Morales (1969, 1971), and Max Figueroa Araujo (1971), emphasize sports as crucial to Cuba's educational programs.

55. Figueroa interview, 1971.

56. F. Castro, "Address Delivered at the Ceremony Inaugurating Forty-Four Junior High Schools in the Countryside," Granma Weekly Review, 1 October 1972, p. 3.

57. _____. "Speech Delivered at the Inauguration of a Junior High School in the Countryside in the Isle of Pines," Granma Weekly Review, 29 June 1971, p. 2.

58. _____. "Address Delivered at the Inauguration of the Comandante Pinares Junior High School in the Countryside," Granma Weekly Review, 1 October 1972, p. 3.

59. _____. "Address Delivered at the Ceremony Inaugurating Forty-Four Junior High Schools in the Countryside," op. cit., p. 2.

60. Ibid., pp. 38-39.

61. Maceiras interview, 1971.

62. Gillette, op. cit., pp. 32-33.

63. Ibid., p. 33.

64. Arias interview, 1971.

65. Urie Bronfenbrenner, Two Worlds of Childhood: U.S. and U.S.S.R. (New York: Russell Sage Foundation, 1970) pp. 124-135; also see Albert Bandura and Frederick J. McDonald, "The Influence of Social Reinforcement and the Behavior of Models in Shaping Children's Moral Judgments," Journal of Abnormal and Social Psychology, 2 (1965): 689-705.

66. Dehesa interview, 1969.

67. Elizabeth Sutherland, The Youngest Revolution: A Personal Report on Cuba (New York: Dial Press, 1969); Susan Kaufman Purcell, "Modernizing Women for a Modern Society: The Cuban Case" (Paper delivered at the Latin American Studies Association, Austin, Texas, December 3-4, 1971).

68. Bowles, op. cit., p. 494.

69. F. Castro, "Address Delivered at the Ceremony Inaugurating Forty-Four Junior High Schools in the Countryside," op. cit., p. 3.

70. Joaquin Oramas, "Hereos de Varsovia Junior High School: A New School for the New Man," Granma Weekly Review, 6 May 1973, p. 8.

71. Alan Gartner, Mary Conway Kohler, and Frank Riessman, Children Teach Children: Learning by Teaching (New York: Harper and Row, 1971).

72. Abel Pietro Morales, "Algunos logros de la Educacion en Cuba," Educacion en Cuba, Año 1, no. 1 (1967): 68-69.

73. Gallo, "La Escuela al Campo," op. cit., pp. 19-20.

74. Ibid.

75. F. Castro, "Address Delivered at 2nd Congress, U.J.C. [Young Communist League], Granma Weekly Review, 16 April 1972, p.6.

76. Ibid.

77. Abel Prieto Morales interview, 1969.

78. Bowles, op. cit., p. 486.

79. Gillette, op. cit. Also see Arthur Gillette, Participation of Youth in Local and National Development: Patterns and Issues (New York: United Nations, n.d.).

3

INDONESIA: A COMPREHENSIVE
LOGICALLY INITIATED
YOUTH PROGRAM

Prepared by the Editors
on the Basis of Materials
from S. J. Woodhouse
and A. H. Lubis

*This case study in Indonesia was prepared at the ICED with
extensive assistance from A. H. Lubis of IKIP (Teachers' Training
Institute), Jombang, and S. J. Woodhouse, a member of UNICEF's staff
in Indonesia. Several visits to the project have left little doubt
as to its dynamism, uniqueness, and general value. At the same time,
because of the highly variegated, local, and pragmatic character of
the project, it has been exceptionally difficult to secure systematic data on such matters as costs and finance, the number of participants in various activities, and follow-up of the participants.
This summary report presents what could be gathered up to late 1972
on the project.*

BACKGROUND

The multifaceted youth education program in the
Jombang district in the province of East Java in Indonesia
illustrates how a locally initiated, locally managed
effort can mobilize personnel and resources to serve a
wide range of learning objectives and local development
goals by combining educational activities with small
economic projects.

Nestled in the heart of Java, the district of Jombang
shares many common features of the most populous island of
the Indonesia archipelago. The island's population density
in 1971 was 530 per square kilometer, and the population
growth rate is about 3 percent annually. The population
under 19 constituted 54 percent of the total.

Though the country as a whole is rich in natural
resources and has large tracts of undeveloped lands, the
agriculture sector still generates 55 percent of national
income and provides the livelihood for 75 percent of the
people. The island of Java is even more heavily agrarian
than the rest of the country.

Despite brisk economic development efforts and a high annual rate of growth in GNP (6 to 7 percent since 1968), Indonesia is one of the poorest lands in the world, with a little over US$60 per capita income in 1971. In addition to general poverty, there is serious economic and social disparity: a small urban population enjoys a disproportionate share of the economic gains, while most of the people engaged in subsistence farming, rural handicrafts, and rural and urban services continue to live in abject poverty without a rapid enough change in their condition.

The district or kabupaten (literally, "regency") of Jombang comprises the third tier from the top in the highly centralized governmental hierarchy of Indonesia. Between the national government headed by the President and the district government headed by a district administrator (the Bupati), lies the provincial government under a governor. Both the governor and the Bupati are appointed by the central government and are responsible for overall administration of their respective territories according to policies and instructions of the central government. The Bupati, if he is so inclined, can exercise considerable de facto authority over development efforts in the district by guiding and coordinating the activities of district-level officials of different national ministries and by enlisting the support of the community. The Jombang Kabupaten itself is administratively divided into 17 subdistricts (Kecamatan) and 306 villages; both types of divisions are headed by a government-appointed official, the camat and the lurah , or village-head, respectively.

Educational Opportunities

The responsibility for formal education for all of Indonesia is centered in the national Ministry of Education and Culture, which includes an Office of Educational Development (BPP) entrusted with the task of overall educational planning. In addition, the Ministries of Religious Affairs and Agriculture also run formal institutions. About 80 percent of the children in the primary school age-group (6-12 years) are estimated to remain enrolled for the first two years of primary school, but less than half of them finish six years of primary education. The overall literacy rate for the population is estimated at about 40 percent.

Organized educational provisions for Indonesia's young people outside the formal school system, including dropouts, are sporadic, uncoordinated, and limited. The total effort is unlikely to have affected even 5 percent of the country's children and youth. There is, however, growing recognition in the government of the need for broadening educational opportunities for youths and adults,

particularly in the rural areas, and of the important
role of nonformal education in this effort.

In 1972 the Ministry of Education and Culture ran a
network of over 100 community education centers (PLPM or
Pusat Latihan Pendidikan Masjarakat) which offer short
training courses for villagers in subjects related to
rural occupations, community improvement, and family life
improvement. The villagers, individually or through community contributions, are expected to defray their own
expenses while in training, whereas the training staff is
paid by the government.

The Department of Manpower and Internal Affairs runs
two types of short courses: the PLK (Pusat Latihan Kerja),
for practical vocational training in rural areas; and the
PMD (Pembangunan Masjarakat Desa), for training village
leaders in social organization. Courses are also given
for women on family life, home skills, and other subjects
by the many women's groups in the country.

A nationwide youth organization, Pramuka, has become
the source of some nonformal educational opportunities
for children and youths, and in Jombang the Pramuka has
been used as the umbrella organization for sponsoring
various educational projects.

The nationwide membership of Pramuka in 1972 was
estimated to be 12 million boys and girls between the
ages of seven and 25--75 percent of whom were from rural
areas. About 30 percent were said to be from the out-of-
school population.[1] The nature and educational significance of the Pramuka activities depend largely on the
local organization and leadership of the movement. In
the country as a whole the Pramuka educational activities
are extremely uneven in quality and content.

JOMBANG YOUTH PROJECT

Regency of Jombang

The kabupaten of Jombang situated west of the town
of Surabaya in the province of East Java is not very
different from the other 36 regencies in the crowded
province on the island of Java. The census of 1971 reported about 812,000 people as residents in an area of
1,160 square kilometers in the regency--giving an average density of 700 people per square kilometer compared
to 539 for the whole island. The majority of the people
in the district, however, live in the fertile alluvial
areas in the center and north of the regency, the area
to the south being hilly and the soil less fertile.

The economy of the district is entirely based on
agriculture and agriculture-related activities. Some
80 percent of the total working population are engaged

in agriculture, though about 70 percent of these workers
have second jobs or sources of income in trading, small
manufacturing, and daily wage-labor. The most important
crop is rice, which takes up about two-thirds of the farmland and is primarily cultivated during the wet season.
Other crops are coconut, corn, soybean, and tobacco. Animal husbandry and fish culture have been of relatively
minor commercial importance, though buffaloes, chickens,
and goats are frequently raised for household consumption.
      The general economic condition of the people of
Jombang has been on the decline over the years. The
fertile alluvial land once produced sufficient rice for
the people of the district; in addition a commercial
sugarcane crop supported a bustling sugar industry providing cash and off-farm employment for the people of
Jombang. Two major elements combined to destroy this
economic balance. The population of the district has
doubled over the past quarter century, while the area of
cultivable land has remained about the same. At the same
time the progressive silting of the riverbeds and
deposits of sand on farmland have almost totally killed
the sugarcane crop and the sugar mills, in addition to
creating a serious flood problem and reducing the productivity of the rice fields. (Of the original 11 sugar
mills, only two survived in 1972 and even these were in
danger of closing down.)
      The increasing pressure of population and decline in
economic opportunities have created a serious employment
problem in the district. It is, of course, impossible to
calculate precisely the number in the work force and the
extent of unemployment and underemployment in a semi-
subsistence rural economy. What follows here, therefore,
is a very rough picture of the general employment situation constructed by a group of trainees from the local
Secondary Teachers Training College (IKIP) through
village-by-village interviews.
      Assuming that all people over the age of 15 were
willing to be employed in gainful economic activities
the work force in Jombang district in 1972 consisted of
458,000 men and women. Of this number, 146,000 or 32
percent were classified as "permanently unemployed" and
another 137,000 or 30 percent were "seasonal workers."
[No clear definitions of these categories were available.
However, given the nature of agrarian economies, it is
presumed that those categorized as "permanently unemployed"
did not engage in any cash-earning jobs and the "seasonal
workers" earned cash-incomes only a part of the year,
though both groups, which included women, engaged in
non-wage-earning but productive activities, in their own
households. The net economic value of these household
activities probably would not be very high.] The work
force in the district has been found to be distributed
in the following proportions among the broad groups

listed below. The percentages in parentheses are for
women in each group out of the total female population.

	Percent
Merchants and traders	5.0 (5.0)
Village administrators and public servants	6.5 (2.2)
Farmers	26.5 (30.8)
Seasonal workers	30.0 (15.0)
Unemployed	32.0 (47.0)
	100.0 (100.0)

Assuming that most of the seasonal workers are employed
in agriculture and the unemployed look for work in agriculture, then well over 80 percent of the labor force
can be described as dependent on agriculture for employment.

Women, obviously, play a very prominent role in the
economy of the district. Proportions of women employed
as merchants and traders is the same as that of men and
a larger proportion of women are engaged in farming.
Traditionally women in Java do most of the rice planting,
harvesting, and transporting to market, while men are
expected to dig and plough the soil, repair and build
irrigation canals, and work on crops other than rice. The
preponderance of males as seasonal workers is due to the
fact that much seasonal work such as road building and
construction is considered unsuitable for women.

The age structure of population in the regency is
typical of Java. In 1971 about 54 percent or 429,500
people in Jombang were under the age of 19. The usual
school age population of 6 to 19 years numbered 278,000.
About 148,000, or 53 percent, of this population were
following formal instruction in an educational institution. In Jombang there were 294 primary schools under
the Department of Education and Culture with some 72,000
pupils and 238 religious primary schools with 58,000
pupils.

We do not have enough information to characterize
and describe adequately the 130,000 young people who are
estimated to be out-of-school in the district. A head
count of all 6-14 year old youngsters in one village in
the district revealed that 20 percent of this group had
never gone to school.[2] Government sources also indicate
that about one-third of students in first grade drop out
by the end of the third grade.[3] Applying these proportions to Jombang, we can come to the approximation that
at least 56,000 of the 130,000 (that is, 20 percent of
the total youth population of 278,000) have never had
the opportunity to attend a school. Another 25,000
(that is, one-third of those out-of-school people who
have gone to school at some stage) have had only three
years or less of primary education and most probably
are illiterate.

The older of the out-of-school youths would be certainly looking for employment. But given the general
condition of the employment market with a high proportion
of adult unemployment and underemployment, it is unlikely
that a large number of the young job-seekers would find
gainful and satisfying employment.

Origin of Jombang Project

The political upheaval of 1965 was felt quite
strongly in Jombang, where rival groups fought with each
other, the administration broke down, economic activities
came to a halt,and an atmosphere of tension and suspicion
prevailed. The new regime in Jakarta appointed in 1966
the Chief of Police of Jombang as the Bupati in order to
restore a semblance of order and peace in the district.
The new Bupati turned out to be a man of vision,
organizational ability, and sensitivity to community
needs. He proceeded immediately to diagnose the most
urgent problems of Jombang and to devise ways of doing
something about these problems with the means and resources
available to the people.
Among many problems of the district, one of the most
serious was relating to the young people of Jombang. What
could be done for the youth of Jombang, particularly those
who were not enrolled in any educational institution?
What opportunities could be provided them to prepare for
a reasonably satisfying and productive life? What training, assistance, and guidance could be given to them? Or
would they be left to themselves--some to crowd the slums
and alleys of Surabaya and Jakarta ; others to live an
equally miserable life of hunger, disease, poverty, and
frustration in their villages; and yet others to adopt
the path of delinquency, crime, and violence? Even for
those who went to school and stayed there for some years,
how relevant was the school to the realities they faced?
What kind of a life could they expect after school? What
training and assistance did they need after they dropped
out from school or completed a certain level?
These questions of course had no quick answers and
were deeply rooted in the overall social, economic, and
political situation of the district and the country. It
was, however, clear that an attack on the problem of
youth education would have to combine provisions for
relevant education and skill training with actions to
create new economic opportunities; that it would have to
be planned on a relatively long-range basis recognizing
the need for sustained and painstaking efforts for a long
time; and that its success would depend on the mobilization of human and physical resources as well as initiatives and support of the people in the district in addition
to what assistance might be available from outside.

The people of Jombang faced another major problem which demanded immediate action and the handling of which had a bearing on what could be done later in respect to youth education. Sand deposits on the river bed and flooding had threatened the livelihood of a large number of people in Jombang. Bupati Ismail used all his ingenuity and authority to raise the necessary funds and to engage the Department of Public Works and Power to dredge the Konto River. At the same time the Kasseman dam in the neighboring Kediri district, which controls the flow of water to Jombang, was repaired.

Earlier, right at the time of the inauguration of the new Bupati, a danger arose of breaches on the embankment of the Brantas river--the longest river on the island of Java--by rapidly rising floodwater. The Bupati then bypassed many bureaucratic hurdles and took it upon himself to find a loan of Rp900,000 and to organize a 24-hour watch and repair operation for several days to safeguard the embankments. As a result 4,500 hectares of standing crop, the sugar mills, and the iodine factory were saved and the people escaped a disastrous flood.

The emergency measure on the Brantas embankment and the dredging of the Konto were, apart from yielding substantial economic benefit to the people, of great significance for other reasons. These proved the bona fides of the regency administration and the Bupati to the people, who had come to regard the governmental machinery as ineffective, untrustworthy, and unconcerned about people's welfare. These experiences also demonstrated to the people, the officials, and the Bupati that when people organized themselves and the needed support came from the administration some successes could be achieved.

The Bupati was a great believer in maintaining the line of communication wide open between the people and the officials. It was his belief that the way to get the support and participation of people in development programs was to encourage a continuous dialogue between the people and the officials, to keep the people informed of government actions and plans, and to keep himself and his staff fully aware of the needs and problems of the people. Several specific measures were taken to keep the line of communication with the people open:

1. The Bupati made himself very easily accessible to all segments of the population; anyone could visit him freely on any matter. He constantly invited people from different parts of the district and listened to their ideas on various problems. He frequently traveled to all parts of the district.

2. The administrative staff of the district including the subdistrict heads and village heads were required to visit frequently with village people, inquire about their problems, and find out their opinion on various matters.

3. A number of people regarded as "opinion leaders" were briefed on government actions, programs, and policies with the expectation that the information would spread through them to others in the community. Social occasions and institutions as well as the folk-art media such as dance dramas and songs were used for disseminating information.[4]

The new district administration also made a deliberate effort to revive and utilize the Javanese tradition of gotong royong, or mutual self-help. It is a system whereby families in the village come together to help a family when an occasion demands such help. For instance, all the villagers would feel obligated to contribute their labor to build a new house for a family that needed a new house. There would be no expectation of any compensation except that every villager knew he would in turn receive similar help when he needed it. In the traditional Javanese villages where money did not play an important role in acquiring services and goods, and each family was largely a self-sufficient economic unit, gotong royong was the means of getting accomplished those tasks which were beyond the physical means and abilities of individual families. The spirit of gotong royong was considered an asset that could be utilized for development projects which required cooperative action by the community.

In this generally propitious setting, the Bupati proceeded to plan and implement a long-range and multifaceted program to broaden and improve the educational opportunities for the children and youths of Jombang, combining and linking the educational efforts with economic development and community improvement activities.

Comprehensive Educational Approach

The educational changes initiated and new opportunities created in Jombang since 1967 constituted, at least in concept, an effort to build a comprehensive educational program which would be relevant, practical, and feasible for the young people in Jombang.

The program could be described as comprehensive, because it attempted in principle to serve the entire youth population including those who were enrolled in formal schools and those who were not in the formal system. Even more important, the program aimed at serving a much broader range of educational needs than the formal schools. In fact, the program could be viewed as a realistic approach to the task of meeting the minimum essential learning needs for rural children and youths in the district.[5]

The main elements in the overall strategy that was followed in unfolding the program beginning in 1967 were as follows:

1. New educational opportunities had to be created for the large number of young people who were not enrolled in schools. This group included those who had never been to school, those who had dropped out early gaining little from school experience, and those who had completed a stage of formal education but needed further training and assistance before they could find gainful employment and assume adult social roles. This group consisted of a wide age-spread ranging from children of six or seven to young adults of over twenty years. It included both boys and girls who, of course, had disparate ambitions, aptitudes, and backgrounds, and differed in their ability and willingness to take advantage of educational opportunities offered. Appropriate educational experiences had to be devised for this melange of a clientele. These experiences had to be closely linked to what economic opportunities existed either in the district or outside; or the educational activity itself had to be a part of the process of creating new economic opportunities. Moreover, to provide a well-rounded educational experience, attention had to be given to such aspects as health, family life, community improvement, civic responsibilities, and cultural heritage.

2. The curricula and teaching methods of the formal schools had to be reformed. If the schools continued to be purely academic and largely irrelevant to the rural and agrarian life of the people of Jombang, they would continue to produce early dropouts and others not much better equipped to face the world outside the school. The school experience had to be made more practical and meaningful to the students by introducing useful skills in the curriculum and by bringing it closer to the realities of rural life. Schools had to become in a true sense institutions of the community, helping and enriching the community and in turn drawing support and inspiration from the community. The learning experience had to, at least in part, consist of participation of students and teachers in the process of uplifting the community. Unless the formal system changed and improved substantially along this line, the out-of-school educational activities would largely become a remedial program for those who came out of schools instead of the two types of activities being complementary to each other.

3. The personnel who would be associated with the new educational activities in schools and outside, either on a regular basis or in part-time and indirect capacities, had to be trained and oriented to the new approaches and methods. These people had to understand and be convinced of the significance of the new activities, had to

unlearn and shed some of their old attitudes and methods,
and in turn would have to contribute in designing and
implementing the new activities. Some of these people,
particularly those whose primary responsibility would be
education, such as the teachers and headmasters, could be
trained in inservice training courses, supplemented by
various other means. Others, who would not be professional educators, but would play important educational
roles especially in out-of-school nonformal activities
(such as officials of the departments of agriculture
and health, cooperative managers, and village heads),
had to be given an orientation and understanding of the
new educational approach through various means such as
seminars, meetings, supervision, explanatory instructions and directives, mutual sharing of experiences, and,
of course, through on-the-job learning from their participation in the planning, guiding, implementing, and
evaluating the educational activities.

4. For the new multifaceted educational approach to
have a significant impact and to survive, a large-scale
mobilization had to be undertaken of all resources in
the district that could be put to use in the educational
program. Such resources included a) the personnel of
the government service agencies in the district; b) staff
of the formal educational system; c) people with leadership ability, specialized knowledge and skills, and
special experience in the community; d) physical facilities of the formal educational institutions, private and
public industrial establishments and other economic enterprises, and other public and social institutions; and
finally, e) the enthusiasm, initiatives, and willingness
to contribute of the district people for a better future
of the younger generation.

All of these resources, in addition to what was
available from national and provincial governments and
through the usual education budget, had to be used in
order to launch and operate a wide assortment of educational activities that were needed in the district.

Within the framework of the strategy outlined above,
a large number of specific activities--some on a one-time
and ad hoc basis and others on a more regular basis--were
initiated during the years between 1967 and 1973. Areas
of learning included:

1. Agriculture: participation in various stages
    of growing specific crops; animal husbandry
    involving chickens, goats, and cows; fishery
    including fish-breeding, processing, and
    preserving
2. Nonagriculture skills: making metal farm tools,
    fishing equipment, carpenters' tools, roofing
    tiles; woodwork; simple building construction;

small-scale irrigation; road-building; repair
of radios and bicycles; and maintenance of
tractors
3. Health and family welfare: preventive health
practices, first-aid, family planning concepts,
and basic tenets of happy family life
4. Cultural education: appreciation and playing of
gamelan and angklung (bamboo orchestra), appreciation of the folk cultural heritage including
the Javanese comedy show Ludruk, participation
in sports
5. Literacy training: mostly compensatory courses
in literacy and arithmetic for dropouts, organized in the local primary schools or community
centers

Other educational activities include courses in the
cooperative management of rice mills for youths selected
to run their own cooperative rice mills; orientation
courses for primary school teachers, headmasters, and
village heads; training courses for village youths for
programs of antimalarial spraying and poultry innocula-
tion. Specific information about the different training
activities and the numbers of youths served by these was
unavailable, mainly because of the ad hoc nature of many
of the training activities and their diffuse content,
methods, and sponsorship. A sample listing will illustrate the range of activities and numbers of participants:

1. general agricultural training in Malang agricultural training center for 60 young people,
including those who had left school early as
well as some who had completed the secondary
school
2. training in animal husbandry and poultry raising for 30 young people who had dropped out
from the secondary school
3. a course lasting six months for 255 youths in
inland fishery with the cooperation of the
Inland Fisheries Department and the Community
Education Centers
4. training in operating and managing rice-hulling
machines for 155 members of the Wira Karya
Tarune Bumi Pramuka Troop
5. training in cooperative organization and management for 160 youths who have left the secondary
school
6. inservice training in management and administration for 40 cooperative managers
7. inservice training on primary school curriculum
reform for 400 primary teachers and headmasters
8. orientation about primary school reforms for 54
heads of villages where the new reforms would be
tried

9.   a special course in mathematics teaching for
     300 religious primary school teachers

The main institutional facilities used for the
educational activities are the Ngoro Pramuka Training
Center and two community education centers (Pusat Latihan
Pendidikan Masjarakat or PLPM). The Ngoro Center, run
by the Pramuka, has three full-time staff members who
teach a variety of courses of different lengths and
organize others with part-time help from the community.
In addition it has a regular three-month skill training
program for 100 youths at a time, in which half of the
training time is spent in practical experience in the
community. This procedure permits the center, with its
residential facility for 50, to alternate a group of 50
between the center and the village. The PLPM centers
under the Department of Community Education of the
Ministry of Education also have five or six instructor-
organizers who arrange courses of varying duration in
such subjects as bicycle repair, chicken raising, family
life, pests and plant diseases, woodwork, pottery, sewing, irrigation and road building, and literacy.
      The distinguishing feature of the training activi-
ties in Jombang is that they do not end with just training. The Pramuka and the respective government agencies
continue to maintain contact with the youths and provide
assistance in utilizing the skills in profit-making enterprises. Such enterprises include growing cabbage and
potatoes; raising chickens, ducks, and other animals;
growing fish; running shops for small repairs, for making
farm tools, and carpentry; making tiles and bricks; and
running cooperative rice-hulling mills. The educational
program thus comprises a vertically integrated process
with several steps: identifying the educational need,
designing a training experience, carrying out the training, combining it with practical and productive experience, and continuing assistance in production, raising
capital, marketing, and so on, to ensure utilization of
acquired skills.

Organization

The operation of the multifaceted educational program obviously required some central coordination of the
numerous activities and mutual cooperation among all
government agencies, in addition to the sharing of a
common purpose and an atmosphere of mutual support between the government personnel and the people of Jombang.
A reversal was needed of the customary bureaucratic style
of each department,carving out its own respective jurisdiction, zealously guarding its own territory, and operating independently even when the tasks of different

departments were clearly complementary. Not infrequently,
different departments of the government even worked at
cross-purposes, confusing the people who were to be served
by these activities and reducing the effectiveness of the
total government operation.

The key to coordination among various activities,
cooperation among government agencies, and the evolution
of a rationale and a framework of common purpose for all
the activities as far as the education program was concerned, it appears, was the energetic leadership and
commitment to education of the Bupati as the chief administrator of the regency. The institutional form this
spirit of cooperation and coordination took was known as
the Body for Guidance and Development of Education (BGDE).
This body was established by the Bupati by the Regency
Decree No. 18 of 1969. This body is headed by the Bupati
himself and is composed of personnel from all the government agencies at the Regency level which have direct or
indirect roles in the educational program. The body has
four committees under it with specific areas of responsibility regarding the operation of the educational program
--planning, execution, supervision and investigation, and
logistics. The chairman of these committees respectively
are: the Chief Headmaster of the primary schools, the
Rector of the Secondary Teachers Training Institute,
the Chief of Pramuka in Jombang, and the Head of the
Primary Teachers Training College. The activities of
these committees, which draw membership from the rank of
the professional educators as well as from the administrative and technical personnel of different government
agencies in the district, are guided by two groups known
as the Ideological and Intellectual Support Team and the
Administrative and Materials Support Team. The former
consists of professional educators from institutions at
all levels and others with education and extension
functions, while the latter is composed of the heads of
all government agencies in the regency. (See Figure 3.1.)
The direction of these teams as well as the overall coordination function of the BGDE bears the imprint of the
Bupati's authority and style of operation.

All ideas and plans regarding the educational program
are either initiated in the BGDE or brought before it for
deliberation. The plans and policies of the program are
approved by the Body. Directing the implementation of
the program and securing the cooperation of government
personnel and private citizens are also the responsibilities of BGDE.

Specific tasks in the educational program are assigned
to appropriate groups and individuals by the Body on the
basis of special competence and interests of these people.
The curriculum reforms in primary schools, for instance,
were entrusted with the staff of the primary teachers'
college, the regency education office, the Domestic Science

FIGURE 3.1

Organization Chart - Body for Guidance and Development of Education (BGDE) in Jombang

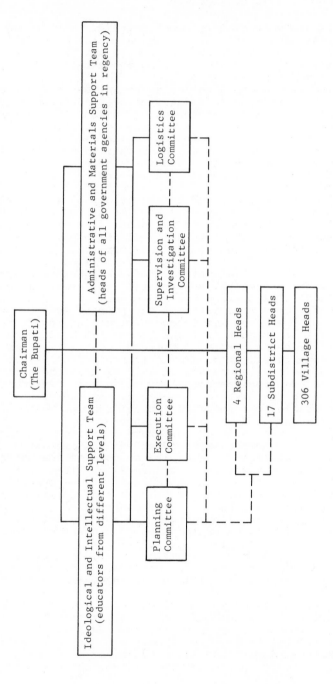

High School, and the Junior High School. The reforms in
the high school program were made the responsibility of
the staff in the Secondary Teachers College, the Senior
High School, and the Technical High School. Similarly,
the design of the training courses under the Pramuka
auspices was directed by the Bupati himself with assistance from the teachers' colleges as well as all other
members of BGDE as and when their specialized knowledge
and experience were needed for particular courses or
activities.

The BGDE, ostensibly an educational body, in fact,
served as a regional planning and development unit. The
educational program went so far beyond the confines of
the conventional Ministry of Education territory, and was
so closely linked with the activities of virtually all
government services and many private enterprises, that
no BGDE action or decision could be "purely" educational
without any ramifications for activities in other spheres.
The fact that the chief administrator of the area was
deeply interested in and sensitive to educational issues
and the BGDE included within its fold the representatives
of all government agencies certainly helped to give it
the character of a planning and development unit of the
area.

The BGDE also proved to be the mechanism for drawing
all kinds of personnel resources into the educational
program. The committee structures of the Body made use
of talents from the Regency bureaucracy as well as from
the education profession. The diversity and flexibility
of educational activities initiated by the Body and its
pragmatic approach to methodology permitted the use of
all specialized knowledge and experience for educational
purposes. Teaching was undertaken by whoever was most
capable and willing to teach in villages--government
technical officials, their wives, or skilled villagers
themselves. The spirit of gotong royong apparently
also played a role in getting the villagers' services
to teach their neighbors once the need for the teaching
was established. For example, a village-head might report
to the camat that there was a demand for furniture-makers
in his village. The camat would recruit some willing
furniture-maker from the district to start an on-the-job
training project on furniture-making and carpentry and
the village-head would find young men from his village to
join the project.

Resources and Costs

Detailed information on the resources and costs of
the program was unavailable. The main resource items
and the total financial cost are shown below.

<u>Budgetary resources</u>: The bulk of the funds came from the Cooperative Department allocation for out-of-school training and allocation from the provincial government. Other supplementary sources were the Pramuka budget for the district and allocations from the Department of Transmigration (resettlement in Southern Sumatra) and the Department of Community Education (PLPM).

<u>Nonbudgetary resources</u>: These include the contribution of time and services by government personnel other than the staff of the program itself, voluntary service by community people, use of facilities of formal institutions and other establishments.

Thus far on the average it seems that the government department officials at Kabupaten level spend three hours a week teaching at the Ngoro Training Center and BGDE meetings, while at Kecamatan level six hours a week is spent on actual teaching of Pramuka out-of-schoolers. The government services most often involved include the Departments of Agriculture, Inland Fisheries, Health, Religion, and Transmigration and Cooperatives.

In addition, on a very ad hoc basis skilled members of the community give time to teaching such things as furniture-making to dropouts. The spirit of gotong royong and the village as a social entity of great importance engenders a spirit of sharing knowledge and resources within the village as needs arise and are identified by the village chief. Likewise all tools and other equipment, although owned by individual families, are available to any village member for the good of the community. It is unheard of for a family to deliberately withhold needed tools from the community.

<u>Self-financing</u>: These include funds generated from the sale of services and commodities in projects, share of profit from cooperative projects, and fees and prices paid by trainees.

The total direct financial cost (almost wholly recurring costs) of the program during 1967-1972 was reported as Rp10,879,440 or about US$27,000.

A potentially valuable resource not at present utilized is radio. Bupati Ismail agreed that in theory radio could be useful to follow up upgrading and other courses at the village level, but because radio is provincial-based, no progress has as yet been made at Kabupaten level in tapping the resources.

Also, better use could be made of current resources. The department officials, especially those working at Kecamatan level, could give much more time to the program if they were given more salary to enable them to retire from their second jobs. (These jobs, incidentally, seldom make use of their special skills; for example, a fertilizer expert may operate a small food stall during the afternoon hours.)

IMPACT AND SIGNIFICANCE OF JOMBANG PROJECT

Like most educational programs, particularly those that are locally initiated and operated on shoestring resources, Jombang has not been very conscious about the importance of systematic evaluation of its activities and maintenance of records on what happens to its clientele. However, its major achievements, problems, and significance are probably sufficiently visible.

It is clear that so far only a small fraction of the total youth clientele in Jombang has been effectively served by the program. Due to lack of follow-up evaluation, it would be very difficult to say whether or to what extent the program has significantly altered the life prospects of any sizable number of young people, though certainly the participants in the program have gained varying degrees of usable skills.

Pramuka, the organizational umbrella for youth education and economic projects, does not appear to have permeated effectively into the countryside. Though a majority of out-of-school youths in the district are claimed to be members of the Pramuka (itself an important achievement), not all local units of the organization are effective instruments for the new educational approach. Moreover, the most disadvantaged of the rural youths—in economic and educational senses—are those who do not belong to Pramuka groups.

An opinion sampling of 232 out-of-school youths who have dropped out from various stages of education gives clues to various reasons for their not being members of the Pramuka. The reasons mentioned include: need for the youth's service at home, distance of Pramuka group location, inactivity of local Pramuka, Pramuka training not particularly useful, unfamiliarity with or lack of information about Pramuka. (See Table 3.1.) It appears from the sample of opinions that the need for the service of the youths in their households is probably the most important reason for nonparticipation in Pramuka. For the younger children an important deterrent was the distance of the Pramuka group from their homes. Distance became less of a disincentive for older youths. A substantial number of youths considered the Pramuka training activities not sufficiently useful for them to invest their time in them.

Responses were also sought from 58 parents regarding reasons for nonparticipation of their children in Pramuka. The most frequently-mentioned response by the parents was that the children needed to help their parents at home. Other responses in order of frequency of mention were distance of the Pramuka group, irrelevance of the training activity, lack of information about Pramuka, and inactivity of local Pramuka.[6] (See Table 3.1.)

TABLE 3.1

Reasons Mentioned by Out-of-School Youths and
Parents for Nonparticipation in Pramuka

Reasons Mentioned (%)	Dropout from Primary School (%)	Dropout from Junior High School (%)	Dropout from Senior High School (%)	Dropout from Postsecondary Institution (%)	Parents (%)
Help needed at home or preoccupied otherwise	10	15	52	26	50
Pramuka group located too far	50	52	18	10	25
Local Pramuka group inactive	25	7	13	27	2
Pramuka activities not too useful or relevant	0	27	17	27	18
Unfamiliar with Pramuka activities or insufficient information about these	15	0	1	10	5
TOTAL	100%=58	100%=58	100%=58	100%=58	100%=58

Source: Sample survey in four kecamatans of Jombang districts
by A. Halim Lubis.

What stands out from the simple and limited inquiry
described above is that the Pramuka activities are not
dispersed widely enough at least for the younger children,
that there are questions about the quality and relevance
of the Pramuka activities, and that a large number of
youths do not join Pramuka because their help is needed
at home.

Even if a large number of out-of-school youths belonged to the Pramuka, the effectiveness of its educational role would depend on how intensively the Pramuka network
was used for educational activities, to what extent Pramuka
programs reflected the purposes of the educational program,
and to what extent Pramuka members benefited from the

educational activities. Out of 294 primary schools (with
72,000 students) and 238 religious schools (with 58,000
students) in Jombang, only 54 primary schools have been
affected to some extent by 1972 by the curriculum reform
efforts under the project. In a number of secondary
schools, practical skill training under Pramuka auspices
has been introduced, but number of schools and students
involved was not available. The number of young people
in formal schools affected by educational changes,
apparently, is small.

The most serious problem in all rural occupational
and skill learning programs--how to set up the learners in
successful enterprises--remains a problem in Jombang even
though the educational approach of the program is particularly mindful of this difficulty. Identifying economic
and occupational opportunities when the overall economy
of the area is not dynamic enough, ensuring mastery of
technical skills as well as proficiency in entrepreneurship,
avoiding competition with already established tradesmen,
making new skills more than marginally productive and
profitable, and preventing youths from being lured to the
city after training--these are but some of the many difficult tasks that affect the success of the program.

The local origin and the dynamic leadership and support of the Bupati have lent the program a special
strength. But at the same time it is deprived of the
strength and resources of programs that have a national
base in terms of organizational and administrative support
and resource provisions. The program would have a firmer
foundation and assurance of continuity if its local roots
could be nurtured by a national commitment and thrust toward rural development and by decentralized development
planning.

Undoubtedly the program has found a viable organizational means and has established a structure for mobilizing
personnel and resources at the local level and putting them
to use in a coherent manner. It has also developed an
approach that can combine education and the creation of
economic opportunities for learners, can adapt educational
activities to individual and community needs, and can make
the educational activities an essential ingredient of a
socioeconomic development effort in the area.

One important measure of the value of an educational
program is how it is perceived by the participants of the
program and by the community. According to a small sample
survey, an overwhelming majority of trainees found the
educational activities in some way valuable in satisfying
their own career ambitions. Similarly, an overwhelming
majority from the community said they approved of what
the program was trying to achieve.

The Jombang program has by 1973 attracted nationwide
attention and the Bupati who initiated the program has
been promoted to the provincial government level with

responsibility to extend the Jombang approach to other districts of the province. The tests of the program's real significance will be whether it can survive the departure of its originator and whether it can take hold in other districts.

NOTES

1. Ministry of Education and Culture estimates.

2. Survey by IKIP trainees in Johowinong village in Jombang District.

3. Indonesia, Ministry of Education and Culture, Educational Statistics (Jakarta, March 1972).

4. A popular form of folk entertainment is ludruk, a comedy show that originated in Jombang but now enjoyed by all Javanese. The heads of the ludruk groups were given special briefings by the Bupati on the development activities and problems of the district.

5. A general formulation of the concept of the minimum essential learning needs is given in Philip H. Coombs, Roy C. Prosser, and Manzoor Ahmed, New Paths to Learning for Rural Children and Youth (New York: International Council for Educational Development, 1973), Chapter 2.

6. Interviews by A. Halim Lubis in four areas in Jombang District.

4

JAMAICA: RESIDENTIAL
CAMPS AND OTHER PROGRAMS
FOR OUT-OF-SCHOOL YOUTH
R. C. Prosser

This case study draws heavily on an initial report prepared for ICED by Dr. Shirley Gordon of the Jamaica Ministry of Education under an arrangement with the Association of Caribbean Universities and Research Institutes. The completion of Dr. Gordon's work in 1972 coincided with a general election and a change of government ending ten years of Jamaican Labour Party rule. Since then the new government formed by Dr. Manley's People's National Party has introduced sweeping policy changes that have affected many aspects of Jamaican life including education. Although the case study focuses primarily on the situation prevailing before Dr. Manley's government came to power, an effort has been made to reflect some of the more significant changes initiated since that time.

INTRODUCTION

The focus of this study is on Jamaican efforts to spread basic learning more widely among rural children and youth. The purpose is not to make prescriptive judgments or specific suggestions to the Jamaican authorities, but rather to make a helpful contribution to the broader process of identifying approaches and lessons that will have value in developing countries making similar efforts.

Jamaica was selected for a case study for several reasons. Although it is relatively wealthy among developing countries and has a broad coverage of schools, the island faces problems, shared by many other developing countries, of making education relevant to the young and of maintaining educational standards at a time of severe youth unemployment and widespread rural exodus and decline. It also has a multiplicity of nonformal programs. Most of these have been devised either to follow up or to remedy the defects of the formal school system; taken together with the formal educational effort they comprise a variegated pattern of learning opportunities that can

offer useful lessons to other countries. Finally, Jamaica
has developed an interesting prototype program of residential basic learning centers--the youth camps. This
approach has recently been modified to suit special
Jamaican needs; nevertheless, it has valuable lessons for
other countries searching for ways to increase learning
opportunities for the most deprived of their young people.

The study is divided into five parts. The first part
sketches a broad background of salient influences and
features of Jamaican life that bear on the attitudes and
motivations of young people. This sketch is based on
Jamaican account of these influences and the writer's own
subjective impressions. The second part of the study
reviews that operations of the formal school system: whom
it reaches and what it teaches--or, more importantly, the
converse, whom it does not reach and what it does not
teach. The third part is an overview of the spectrum of
nonformal programs--the extent to which they help fill
the gap in meeting the learning needs of young people,
their organization and interrelation, their costs, and,
within the limitation of Jamaican resources, their
strengths, weaknesses, and capabilities for expansion.
The fourth part examines one of the important nonformal
programs--the youth camp system--describing its origins
and evolution, administration and costs, problems and
potential. The final part reviews briefly the strategy
for providing basic learning in rural areas and points up
the lessons, both positive and negative, of Jamaican
experience that may be helpful to other countries moving
along a similar path.

General Background

Two hundred miles from the Florida coastline of the
United States and some one hundred miles from Cuba, the
small lush tropical island of Jamaica rises mountainously
from the Caribbean Sea. Home for two million people, it
stretches a hundred and fifty miles east to west and at
its greatest breadth about fifty miles north to south.

Jamaica was one of the oldest of the British colonial
possessions, having been wrested from Spain in 1655. The
early British planters were attracted by the potential
for growing sugar and producing rum cheaply by slave
labor. Prosperous under the overall sovereignty of Great
Britain, the planters had a great measure of responsibility
for managing island affairs for two hundred years. In
1833, however, the abolition of slavery dealt a deadly
blow to the plantation system, and the resulting economic
decline and unrest led in 1866 to direct colonial rule
that continued until 1944. In 1962 the island became
independent, although it remained a constitutional monarchy
within the British Commonwealth.

After their emancipation in the mid-1800s many of the
freed slaves, rejecting overtures to work as hired plantation hands, took to the hills of the interior where they
carved out smallholdings and lived precariously as subsistence peasant farmers. Their descendants still form
the bulk of the agricultural smallholders, the largest
and poorest segment of the population.

The place of the negro slaves on the plantations was
taken for a time by immigrant indentured laborers from
India and China who later moved on to monopolize trade
and shopkeeping. Whether white, black, yellow, or brown,
all Jamaicans share a common immigrant heritage.

Major Cultural Influences

From the entangled influences that affect attitudes
and behavior of young Jamaicans, the vast majority of
whom are black, it is useful to stress a few strands of
major significance.

First, an important influence is the legacy of
slavery. This traumatic experience has done much to shape
the prevailing loose family structure. Unusual parental
roles characterize much of the Caribbean and contrast
sharply with conventional practice in other parts of the
world. The impossibility for slaves to marry legally or
to have a conventional family life has, to a marked extent, determined the prevailing pattern of "fatherless"
families. As a result of transient unions or casual
liaisons, many women are left with offspring by different
fathers.[1] In the absence of adult male support, girls
are brought up from an early age to expect and to assume
the burdens of bringing up children alone and working
to provide for the family.

However, while young girls are forced by circumstances
to assume heavy responsibilities, the same is not true of
boys, who grow up without the influence of a father and
often with little male supervision of any kind. Within
the family the main guidance comes from the women, and
convention demands little contribution from the male
as a family breadwinner. This pervasive characteristic
perpetuates itself and is only slowly undergoing change.

A second influence which heavily conditions Jamaican
life is the prevailing "plantation system,"[2] under which
one- or two-crop plantations, or large managerial estates,
dominate farming--the largest, if not the most prosperous,
occupation in the land. As in many developing countries,
there has been a natural trend for the young to attempt
to move away from the drudgery of the land and the stigma
of an unforgotten slave status for preferable occupations
elsewhere. Ironically, hopes of escape and new employment have not been realized for most, while the plantations
remain short of labor. Furthermore, the emphasis of the

opulent plantations on large-scale farming and export
crops--mostly bananas and sugar--has been to the detriment
of small-scale, often poverty-stricken, peasant holdings
occupying the less fertile areas of low productivity.
Perhaps the most pernicious, if least tangible, effect of
the plantation system is the way in which it colors general
attitudes, again particularly among the young, and creates
a "plantation mentality." This is manifested in the hierarchical social structure, distribution of job functions,
rigid lines of authority, and lack of social mobility in
the plantation. Those who remain within the system are
divided between the few "born to rule" and the many who
"know their place"; those who break away from the system
become, for better or worse, more aggressive in shrugging
off a heritage of subservience.

A third major influence on Jamaican attitudes and
behavior patterns is that of the long and close association
with Great Britain and, more recently, the wide contacts
with North America. Endowed by the mother country with the
unity of the English language, unencumbered by problems
implicit in multilingual countries, Jamaicans maintained
close ties with the home country for nearly three hundred
years. White Jamaicans created for themselves a variation
of middle and upper class British life. Children of the
elite were educated in Britain. Even black Jamaicans
traveled abroad and established themselves easily in
Britain. Codes of conduct and Victorian morality were
transferred across the seas and their outward forms at
least were there to be copied by the mass of Jamaican
folk not of British extraction. British expatriate
missionaries and school teachers taught a way of life in
the rural areas as effectively by personal example as by
precept in the schools and churches.

Another cultural and economic force that has become
dominant more recently, comes from the North American
continent. On the one hand, it sets styles and modes of
living in a social and cultural interchange--in part
through a flow of visitors, in part through the mass media,
in part through thousands of emigrants to North America
who have kept in close contact with their stay-at-home
friends and relatives and abetted their rising expectations
for higher standards of living and consumption. The
symbols of North American culture--pop music, western
movies and canned television programs, hamburgers, hot
dogs, and milk shakes--are part of the evolving Jamaican
way of life. On the other hand, North America provides
export markets (bauxite is the largest item sold in the
United States), capital for development projects, hundreds
of thousands of tourists to expand one of Jamaica's most
rapidly growing industries[3], and jobs for migrating
Jamaicans. Although large numbers of Jamaicans settled in
Britain in the immediate postwar years, most have gone
to Canada and the United States in recent years. More
than half of the emigrants are young people between 20

and 40 years of age.[4] At present an average of 15,000
laborers move seasonally every year into the United States
to work in the fields.[5] Curiously, plantation labor is
acceptable outside Jamaica where it is less socially
conspicuous and, of course, better paid.

The onslaught of alien culture, not unexpectedly, has
brought forth a strong reaction. Older Jamaicans try
vainly to preserve the more genteel traditions of their
British-type culture. Others look back still further to
a longstanding and ingrained force in Jamaican life, that
of its Africanness or blackness. The search into African
antecedents for an identity of their own is a distinctive
influence[6] on Jamaican life. This search manifests itself
in its extreme form in the Rustafarian Movement, which
seeks to trace black Jamaican roots in ancient Ethiopia
and to revive African values. Another manifestation is
the sympathy shown by some young Jamaicans for the Black
Power movement.

However, blackness still equates to poverty and
economic deprivation, and, although this relationship is
in a process of change, the historical legacy still leaves
the white, Chinese, Syrian, and Jewish Jamaican minorities
in a strongly dominant position.

Enunciation of these somewhat intangible influences
is cursory and impressionistic, and their impact cannot be
measured. However, they are important for an understanding
of the environment within which young Jamaicans are growing up. These cultural and historical influences, of
course, interact with the more concrete realities of the
various demographic, economic, and employment factors to
shape the prospects and guide the choices regarding livelihood and education for young Jamaicans.

Economic Factors

Population and Employment

The population of Jamaica is almost two million, with
a density of nearly 450 per square mile, comparable to
that of the United Kingdom, but approximately ten times
that of Kenya and the United States. The net annual
population growth, however, has been kept far below the
natural rate of increase by fairly substantial emigration.
In recent years, there has been a significant reduction
in the birth rate, brought about by vigorous birth control
policies, which between 1960 and 1970 fell by nearly one-
fifth. In 1970 a rate of natural increase of 2.7 percent
was achieved, and emigration further reduced growth to
around 1.5 percent, underlining Jamaica's great reliance
on emigration as a means of softening the worst effects
of population growth.

A population projection for 20 years with age breakdowns made in 1970 reflects a continuation of the impact
of both the lowering birth rate and of emigration. (See
Table 4.1.)

TABLE 4.1

Projection of Population Growth in Different Age-Groups, 1970-1990

Age Group	1970	1975	1990
4-5	119,360	118,500	134,120
6-11	335,280	342,840	379,440
12-14	156,840	164,340	176,880
15-18	167,120	201,200	216,080
19-23	167,300	207,180	264,980
TOTAL POPULATION	1,861,000	2,045,900	2,671,800

Source: Jamaica, National Physical Plan for Jamaica 1970-1990
(Kingston, 1970).

The Jamaican economy has been expanding in recent
years.[7] At current prices, the gross domestic product has
been growing at an average rate of around 6.5 percent for
the period between 1950 and 1968. However, the rate of
growth is slowing down: from 1965 to 1968 it had decreased
to under 4 percent. The average annual per capita income
grew from J$98 in 1950 to J$431 in 1970. But as in the
case of the gross domestic product, the annual rate of
growth has been declining.

Some important trends emerge from the changing composition of the gross national product. First is the declining importance of agriculture. Between 1966 and 1970,
the contribution of agriculture to GNP declined from 11
percent to just over 8 percent and is recorded as sixth
in the list of major sector contributors. Mining, virtually
nonexistent in 1950, achieved first place in 1970 with a
contribution of almost 17 percent, largely because of the
development of bauxite-allumina, of which Jamaica is one
of the world's largest producers, although the industry
is predominantly foreign-owned. Another feature is the
massive growth in the tourist industry. After bauxite-
allumina, tourism has replaced sugar as the second largest
foreign exchange earner.

Although total national income is increasing, there
are no data available on the way it is distributed. It is

safe, however, to conclude that income distribution is
exceedingly skewed.

Reliable and accurate data on the nature and extent of
unemployment are not available, but a constant topic for
worried discussion among Jamaicans in all walks of life is
its current high level. An official estimate of total
unemployment based on a labor survey completed in 1969
concludes that 17 percent of the labor force is unemployed
and that unemployment is most marked among the younger age
groups, with 40 percent for the cohort 14 to 19 years.[8]
High as it seems, this could well be an underestimate since,
for instance, a surveyee had only to be employed for eight
hours during the week of the labor survey to qualify for
inclusion among the employed. If a comparison were made
between the 1969 figures for employment with the population
figures from the preliminary results of the 1970 census,
one would arrive at an unemployment ratio for the same
cohort of over 60 percent, and this would include as employed those working only a minimum of eight hours a week.

The 1969 survey is revealing on the size of incomes
of those employed. Nearly 60 percent of the male cohort
14 to 24 years had incomes of less than J$10 per week,
while a further 16 percent received between J$10 and J$20
per week; 6 percent were recorded as having no income;
10 percent were not reported at all. Females of the same
cohort were even worse off--70 percent received less than
J$10 per week, and 12 percent were recorded as having no
income.

There has been no occupational census since 1960,
but informed opinion claims that there has been little
significant change since then. In 1960 about 60 percent
of the employed group of 15 to 24 years were classified
as being in manual and service occupations, most as farm
laborers, self-employed cultivators, general laborers,
garden boys, or factory hands. The remaining 40 percent
were classified primarily as craftsmen and technical
workers. On the female side for the same age-group, 70
percent of those employed were recorded as in manual and
service occupations, with 60 percent of these as domestic
servants. The remaining major occupations for young
women include dressmaking, farm laboring, factory work,
and teaching.[9]

The problem of unemployment cannot be separated from
high emigration, decline in agriculture, and growth of
capital intensive industry. Emigration has helped to keep
unemployment at a reduced level, and it is estimated that
over the past 10 years some 75 percent of the total addition to the labor force has left the country. This has
not been wholly advantageous, however, because a dispro-
portionately large number of those who have emigrated
have been the best qualified and most skilled. For example,
in 1967 and 1968 the numbers of professional and technical
people who emigrated almost equalled the numbers of new
entrants to those professions. It is not unreasonable to

suppose that, had they remained, they could have helped
stimulate employment enterprise. As it is, there now
exists a shortage of personnel with managerial, professional, and technical skills, and a consequent dramatic
increase in salaries and wage rates for those who have
remained.

Emigration overseas is paralleled by migration within
Jamaica: a rapid "high quality" rural exodus is in progress. Kingston and its environs are growing at a rate of
just under 3 percent per annum; a third of the total
population is now centered there, and the urban complex
is now responsible for two-thirds of the island's manufacturing. In 1967, for instance, some 20 percent of the
migrants from the countryside to the town were those who
had completed secondary or higher level formal education.[10]

Rural Sector

In sharp contrast to the growth in manufacturing and
mining, agricultural development has lagged behind. Operating under antiquated methods, exploitative land tenure,
and social prejudice, farms suffer an acute labor shortage
at the low wage rates they can afford to pay. Although
agriculture still employs some 40 percent of the labor
force, total land under cultivation is diminishing, the
less competitive farms have closed, and Jamaica has been
forced to import certain foodstuffs she might otherwise
produce herself. An exception to a generally disappointing
picture was the creation of two Land Authorities, Christiana
and Yallahs Valley, which with some success have helped
to settle new peasant farmers. In general, however, rural
development has been fraught with abortive efforts, fragmented ministerial and departmental jurisdictions, strongly
vested urban interests, and the absence of a strongly
committed, broadly-based, national policy for rural development. A new government since 1972 is showing more vigor
in tackling the problems, but it is too early to assess
the results.

What then are the prospects for young Jamaicans growing up? Reality for most young Jamaicans reaching adulthood consists of a harsh and limited choice. Where there
is a parental smallholding, one option is to come to terms
fatalistically with its futureless drudgery. Another is
to accept the almost irreversible choice of toiling on one
of the large farming estates. Another, perhaps more
attractive, is that of, as the Jamaicans say it, shuffling
idly in the town in the vain hope that some rewarding
employment will turn up. A lucky few, usually the better
connected, will find an industrial job. Still fewer, with
schooling or trade training to buttress them, will find
well paid posts or choose to follow a well-trodden path
overseas. It is clear that for the vast majority of young
people this range of options will change much too slowly
without massive and radical societal and economic changes.

In such circumstances, the role of both formal and nonformal education is severely circumscribed. Where the public insistence on creating new national goals and developmental programs to meet them is strong enough, education can very likely be harnessed as one means for their success. Where the insistence and determination are weak or vacillating, education alone can aim at little more than an attempt to help the young meet life as it exists and make the best of it. Manifestly, educational goals must include equipping the young with the basic tools and knowledge that they need for a more satisfying vocational, family, and civic life. At the same time, the goals must include the overcoming of prejudices and attitudes that impede the development of valuable personal qualities--self-confidence, self-discipline and initiative --so that young people can learn to recognize and have the courage to grasp new opportunities for themselves. Equally as vital, they must learn from the maelstrom of national life which expectations are realistically capable of fulfillment and which are not.

In the following sections, with these learning requirements as a frame of reference, the major educational programs are described and examined beginning with the largest one--the formal school system.

GENERAL FORMAL EDUCATION

The main focus of this study is Jamaican out-of-school education, but the tasks and clienteles of programs in this category are determined to a large extent by the effectiveness of the school system.

One of the aims of Jamaican schooling is to provide six years of learning to all children between the ages of six and eleven years. At the end of the six years in primary school, youngsters take the Common Entrance Examination, which gains them admission to the three-year course of first cycle secondary education. After the first cycle secondary course, pupils sit for the Jamaican Certificate of Education (JSC), an examination designed to select students of about fifteen years of age for entrance to teacher training colleges, the Jamaican School of Agriculture, the Schools of Nursing, and to some of the courses of CAST (College of Arts, Science, and Technology). Those who remain within the secondary school system take a two-year second cycle senior secondary course which culminates in the examination for the General Certificate of Education, Ordinary Level (GCE-O). This is a British school-leaving qualification conducted by either the University of London or Cambridge in the U.K. Success in the examination is a major goal for pupils remaining in the formal school system, since the result is publicly recognized

and has become a minimum achievement necessary for access
to desirable white-collar jobs. It may also be added that
this external qualification facilitates finding worthwhile
jobs abroad. Following the second cycle, it is possible
for successful students to remain at school for a further
two years and complete the General Certificate of Education,
Advanced Level (GCE-A). Success in this makes it possible
to enter the University of the West Indies or other universities outside Jamaica.

While the formal schools concentrate on a highly
academic curriculum and preparation for the university,
most of the youngsters at age 15--around 90 percent-- leave
school and begin to seek a living for themselves. Official
figures suggest that around 10 percent of children never
go to school at all and that of the 90 percent that do go
only 60 percent or so attend with any regularity. Some
80 percent of primary graduates proceed to first cycle
secondary schooling and of these about 60 percent attend
with regularity. At age 15 most children who have not
already dropped out will leave school, with 10 percent
continuing in higher levels of formal full-time schooling.[11]

What are the schools achieving? One criterion is
literacy. Here the evidence suggests that, at age 15, about
half of all youngsters are insufficiently trained to be
considered as fully literate, with little facility in
reading, writing, or, for that matter, simple arithmetic.[12]
It is quite possible and not unusual for young people to
proceed through primary school and still emerge largely
illiterate at the end.

This assertion is borne out by the results of a recent
test given in 1972 to primary school leavers seeking
admittance to high schools. They showed that 90 percent
of the candidates were scoring below the passing mark in
English and over 80 percent were below the passing mark
in arithmetic.[13] The continuation of poor performances
after junior secondary school can be seen from the equally
bad results from tests given to grade 9 candidates for
entry to technical schools. In arithmetic over 85 percent
were below the passing mark, and in English 91 percent were
below. The results at higher levels are little better,
in spite of additional years of training at school. Too
many candidates still achieve passes in only two or three
subjects of the five to eight that they take for the
GCE-O level.

The 50 percent illiteracy rate for the 15-year-old
group could well prove to be conservative. The accounting
here makes allowance only for those who attend school
infrequently and not for dropouts or repeaters at the
various educational levels.

What this means in absolute numerical terms is that
around 53,000 youngsters reach age 15 each year and that
of this number about 26,000 will be illiterate, that 21,000
will be somewhere between a basic literacy and a proficiency

level allowing them to enter senior secondary schooling,
and that about 5,000 will go on to higher levels of education. The 53,000 will become 57,000 by 1985, even with
the continuation of a high emigration rate. Should there
be no change in the quality of schooling, the total number
of illiterates will continue to grow both absolutely and
relatively.

One inescapable result of this dearth of achievement
is the enormous and widespread debilitating effect that
the sense of academic failure has on the young Jamaican
on the threshold of adult life. It is difficult to escape
the conclusion that at present the formal school system is
simply not doing efficiently the job it has set for itself.

A basic question, however, is this: how relevant in
fact are the goals of the formal system to the basic
learning needs of young Jamaicans? In the circumstances
of modern Jamaica, one might presume that, by age 15, a
young Jamaican should ideally have acquired the following:
a mastery of the three "Rs"; the rudiments of an occupational skill or a combination of skills; an appreciation
of the nature and needs of the labor market; an understanding of the way the country is organized and run; and
an appreciation of the basic rules of good health and
family life. He or she also should probably be equipped
with an ability to reason and to set realistic goals
capable of being achieved, and have developed an imagination capable of perceiving practical solutions to everyday
problems.

The acquisition of such qualities is an ongoing life-
long process, and the burden of responsibility cannot be
placed solely on the school. Yet if the school does not
play a major role, how can these objectives be achieved?
The family can often make a contribution, but in general
not much can be expected. In fact, far too often, family,
social, and local community life make wholly negative
contributions.

Both human and capital resources are scarce. Jamaica
in 1970 was expending about 3 percent of its GNP on
schooling, or about 13 percent of the government's national
budget. Cost for schooling is increasing: in 1970 expenditure per head on primary schooling was about J$44; for
junior secondary schooling, around J$75.[14] While it may
be possible to pour more resources into the formal schools
to improve them and increase their numbers, especially as
the economy and the public revenue grow, the picture that
clearly emerges of the existing condition is of a system
that is not accomplishing its objectives very well.

OVERVIEW OF NONFORMAL EDUCATION FOR CHILDREN AND YOUTH

The need to provide out-of-school educational and
training opportunities for young people who are not at

school, who have never been to school, or who have had
incomplete formal schooling has not gone unappreciated in
Jamaica. Indeed, whereas in 1966 out-of-school education
accounted for 9 percent of the total government expenditure
on education, in 1971 it accounted for 21 percent.[15] Many
organizations have responded individually and variously
to this need. Some have concerned themselves with remedial
education programs that offer the young a chance to re-
capture opportunities that they missed by not being able
to attend primary and secondary schools. Others have
been more concerned with the development of vocational
skills that complement academic learning. Still others
have concentrated on spreading basic knowledge and skills
in such areas as housecraft, family life, and citizenship.
       The nature and extent of the responses have often
depended on the perception of the role of education in
furthering the aims or interests of the sponsoring organization, because only a few of the organizations have
education per se as their major objective. Furthermore,
the spread and strength of each program has depended
heavily on the proportion of its resources that each organization is prepared to expend in education and training.
       From the list of activities organized somewhere on
the island the young Jamaican today theoretically has a
choice among literacy classes, trade and vocational training, farmer training and membership in young farmers'
clubs, family life education, home craft, civic and citizenship education, sports, leadership training, and various
cultural and recreational activities. Taken together they
make up a formidable coverage of the academic, vocational,
spiritual, moral, and physical educational needs of boys,
girls, young men, and young women. Despite the breadth
and variety of the programs they do not really measure up
to the demands of the situation, as will be seen in the
following review of the more significant programs.

                 Remedial and Continuing Education

       Refreshingly, since not many ministries of education
conventionally take responsibility for those who are "out-
of-school," the Jamaican Ministry of Education provides
a second chance for young people not at school to take
school courses extramurally. At the basic schooling
level, the Ministry has deferred to other organizations
to assume the responsibility of teaching literacy and has
concentrated on the running of evening classes that prepare
young people predominantly for the Jamaican Certificate of
Education--normally taken at the end of the ninth year of
full-time education. These classes, attached to junior
secondary or other schools throughout the country, are
supplemented by a correspondence course serviced by a

special department of the Ministry and cater to some 8,500 students.

The certificate in question is granted on the basis of passes on at least five subjects, including English, mathematics, and civics, together with two optional subjects chosen from geography, history, biology, health science, and general science. Usually most candidates take five subjects at one time. However, in 1971 there were over 5,000 students who registered for more than five, including 200 who sat for over 10 subjects.

The result of this effort, in terms of subjects passed, is discouraging. The unexceptional results in 1971 show that of the 44,000 or so candidates who sat for the examination, 19,000 passed nothing at all. Another 22,000 passed only one to four subjects and so did not qualify for the certificate. Just under 3,000, or 6 percent, of the students passed five or more subjects, but this accomplishment does not guarantee the cherished certificate because not all passes are necessarily in the "right" subjects.[16]

This extraordinarily high failure rate of at least 94 percent is no doubt accounted for by a lack of supervised learning (only about a fifth of examination enrollers can possibly be participants in the correspondence program), weak teaching when there is any, lack of guidance, and unsatisfactory facilities.

There are a number of important features that are revealed by the program. First and foremost is the enormous demand for the certificate. Second is the extremely high failure rate that contributes enormously to the exacerbation of a widespread "failure" complex already created by the formal system. Third, implicit in the failure rate, is the wastage of both resources and the strong potential for learning. There is, of course, the basic question of the relevance and value of the JSC course itself. Apparently, however, a large number of youngsters find it attractive enough in the existing structure of employment and rewards to participate in the program.

In parallel with the formal system are other programs of remedial and continuing formal out-of-school education that are not under the auspices of the Ministry of Education. A much smaller number of candidates than those for the JSC present themselves annually as private students for the U.K. ordinary level examinations. A small number of students also attend evening classes at the university and eventually attain a degree. Some of these students get help through commercial correspondence courses, private schools in the urban areas, and other classes, such as those offered under the university extramural program. There is, however, minimal personal guidance and supervision for participants outside the metropolitan area in these higher educational courses.

Literacy Programs

Literacy classes are a component of the educational programs of many voluntary organizations, but the agency specially charged by the government with the responsibility for eradicating illiteracy was until 1972 the Literacy Section of the Social Development Commission, which received its funds through the Ministry of Youth and Community Development.

The Literacy Section both organized its own classes and serviced those of other organizations, arranging short training courses for literacy teachers and for the production of literacy teaching materials. The literacy courses were based on four specially prepared books, progress being reported in terms of the number of illiterates completing each book. These basic books were supplemented by other work books and periodicals for further reading practice. Most classes adopted conventional teaching methods and, although every effort was made to use materials interesting to an adult audience, the approach cannot be termed "functional" in the true UNESCO sense. Since 1967, radio and television programs were produced by the Section to supplement regular classes.

The classes run by the Literacy Section were normally held in community centers of the Social Development Commission. Other important literacy-sponsoring bodies include the Sugar Industry Labour Welfare Board, the Jamaican Federation of Women, the YMCA, the Youth Development Agency, and some of the churches.

A recent report showed that in 1971 there was a total of 291 classes in progress with an enrollment of 5,879 youths and adults. Those under 21 years made up 47 percent of the total enrollment, with slightly more females than males. Of these classes 32 were making use of TV, 107 of radio, and 152 were conventional classes with straight face-to-face teaching. A sample survey concluded that attendance in classes without media was better than in those using TV and radio. This could probably be explained by the fact that the majority of radio and TV sets were out of order.[17] The evidence is that literacy classes suffer from erratic attendance and a high dropout rate. In 1971 only about 10 percent of the students completed the full course.

Worth stressing here is the degree of shame attached to the state of illiteracy. Too often illiterates will not attend classes for fear of publicly exposing their deficiency, and cases are not infrequently found of illiterates traveling regularly to classes outside their home area even though there are local classes nearer at hand.

Although the Jamaican literacy program can justifiably claim merit for its pioneering work in the use of

mass media, it has unhappily been inadequate when measured
against quantitative needs. The evidence suggests that
the few who embarked on a literacy course actually completed it and that those few who did enroll were but a
minute fraction of the total population in need of the
training.

The literacy program, until 1972, was essentially
an "adult" program, and no special provision was made
for younger adolescents. Nevertheless, about half of
those who attended were between fifteen years and their
early twenties. About 3,000 young persons participated
annually, of which only a small fraction gained any degree
of literacy proficiency.

Vocational Training by Ministry of Labour

The most significant program for the vocational preparation and training of young Jamaicans is organized
through the Ministry of Labour and National Insurance.
The present structure dates from plans drawn up in 1966,
which were put into operation in 1968. Overall charge for
the program is vested in a National Industrial Training
Board, specially set up for the purpose, consisting of
representatives from various government ministries concerned with training and from employing bodies in private
industry and commerce. Intended as an independent statutory board with executive powers, the NITB still awaits
a charter, and in practice its role remains largely advisory. However, it acts as a forum in which the demand
and supply of different kinds of skills can be discussed,
and it helps in deciding the location and development of
vocational training institutions.

The main thrust of vocational training is through an
expanding pattern of nonresidential Industrial Training
Centers (ITCs). In 1972 there were 14 centers catering
to some 1,000 young people and 10 additional centers,
almost ready to open their doors to 1,275 more. About
25 percent of the centers are in the Kingston area; the
remainder, in small towns scattered throughout the island.

Each center offers full-time day courses to about
100 students. Candidates for the courses have to be 17
years of age and familiar with the basics of a skill.
They will often have been in paid employment and have a
basic education sufficient to allow them to benefit fully
from the skill training. Attempts have recently been
made to standardize entry at the grade 9 schooling level,
that is, at the completion of first cycle secondary education. A few centers run evening courses and Saturday
courses for those working and unable to attend on weekdays.

Courses of a year's duration are not intended to
give a complete vocational training, but rather to give

a sound basic training in each skill offered. About 20
different kinds of skills are taught, as well as English,
mathematics, and general subjects. Courses include welding and auto mechanics, which are generally oversub-
scribed, and various electrical courses and carpentry and
building, which are the least popular because they offer
the lowest remuneration in the work market. At the end
of each course, theoretical and practical tests are given,
and successful candidates acquire a proficiency grading at
one of three levels. The testing is supervised by a panel
representing both industry and the Ministry.

An analysis of the achievements of the ITCs for the
three years, 1968 to 1971, shows that 1,980 candidates
attended courses, 1,486 completed them, and 714 gained
certificates. There was a dropout rate of about 25 percent, and for those who completed the courses there was
just over a 50 percent failure rate. Highest dropout
rates were in carpentry, building, and construction
courses, which do not require a high level of skill attainment to qualify for employment.[18] The NITB advances a
number of causes for the high dropout and failure rates.
Most trainees come from poor families and lack means of
subsistence while they are taking courses. Another cause
is the lack of self-discipline of trainees necessary to
sustained learning. In some skill fields, the knowledge
that there is no job outlet at the end of the course
becomes a disincentive. Another cause recognized by the
NITB is the inexperience of instructors. A final reason
for failure is attributed to the duration of the training
courses, found to be much too short for some of the trades.

The network of ITCs is backed by an embryonic Vocational Training Development Institute. This institute
is responsible for course development and staff training,
while simultaneously running courses for senior employees
in industry and foreman level workers. The ITCs were
originally staffed directly from schools and industry,
and few of the instructors had any formal teacher training.
The situation is being corrected by part-time courses
for existing instructors, organized in Kingston and in
the rural areas by a small traveling staff training team.
New staff attend a six-month preservice training course
in Kingston, which includes skill upgrading, general
industrial knowledge, and pedagogy.

The program is helped financially and with personnel
by a strong ILO team, the World Bank, and the bauxite
companies. The costs of the vocational training program
have been mounting rapidly. Total government expenditure
on the program has risen sharply in the four years between 1967/68 and 1971/72. Total annual recurrent costs
have grown from J$70,000 to J$700,000 in the period, and
capital costs from J$7,000 to J$1,500,000. A simple
calculation based on the recurrent expenditures in the
years 1968 to 1971 and the numbers of trainees completing

courses produces a rough per capita (recurrent) expenditure
for completers of just under J$1,000 per annum. If only
those who gain a certificate are counted, the cost is
doubled.

In relation to the need of young people the program
is small. Confined to those who are at least 17 years,
the courses offer nothing to the 15 and 16 year-olds.
Those who are selected normally have had nine years of
full-time education; those who are educationally less
privileged gain nothing. Even within its own terms of
reference, the intended 2,000 a year enrollment can
cater to only a small percentage of the age-group--probably
no more than 3 percent--and this 3 percent is likely to
be those who already have or have had some kind of paid
employment. By 1972 the program had made little contribution to the training needs of young girls. Only one
ITC, in West Kingston, takes in girls for training in
addition to males.

Although the program is small, also expensive, in
relation to need, it represents the major skill training
effort in the country. In spite of many problems the
program is well planned and executed. Attention is paid
to relating course skills to employment needs as a joint
venture of both government and industry. An attempt has
been made to coordinate the various interests involved in
skill training. A resource support unit is being developed
to help with course development and staff training and
retraining. The major problem to be solved is the recruiting and keeping of good quality instructors.

Other vocational training programs, though of local
importance, are small in comparison to that of the Ministry
of Labour. The Boys' Town organization operates a training center in Kingston, recruiting primary school leavers.
Operation Friendship runs a center, also in Kingston,
which mounts various skill courses lasting a year. The
bauxite companies have their own training schemes for
staff, usually at a higher educational level. The Ministry
of Education has two Technical Institutes and a Trade
Training Centre, which cater to around 700 junior secondary
leavers. Courses last from one to two years and are at
preapprenticeship level. The courses include both academic
and skill training. Finally, there are the vocational
training programs of the Youth Development Agency and the
Social Development Commission, to be discussed in a later
section.

Young Farmer Training: 4-H Clubs

To offer an orientation of farming to the younger
generation, the most important means chosen is the 4-H
Clubs, a youth agricultural movement first successfully

developed in the United States and then exported with
varying degrees of adaptation to many other parts of the
world. In its original form the 4-H Movement is a voluntary effort that brings young people together into clubs,
primarily to stimulate and develop interest in farming
and to encourage social and recreational activities. In
Jamaica the movement is heavily supported by the government. Maintaining an identity separate from the Ministry
of Agriculture, the 4-H Board of Management is appointed
in consultation with the Ministry, which has a special
section of its organization assigned to 4-H work. The
Ministry employs a full-time supervisory staff working at
field level in the parishes, and the staff is backstopped
by a headquarters administrative and training staff in
Kingston and 11 small 4-H Training Centres established
with the help of the Ministry of Agriculture.

Official statistics for 1970 record a total membership of nearly 25,000 young people between the ages of 10
and 21 years in 454 junior clubs and 110 senior clubs.
Girls predominate in the clubs, making up 60 percent of
the membership. Most clubs are based on schools as extracurricular adjuncts.

Club educational activities, beside agriculture and
farming, include home economics, citizenship and leadership training. The day-to-day running of the club and
its management through elected committee members is one
of the important ways in which character training and
the development of leadership qualities take place. The
4-H training centers are used for short specialist agricultural courses and for courses in club management and
leadership. Members of senior clubs may also attend
courses at the farmer training centers of the Ministry
of Agriculture. Small youth settlement schemes have in
the past drawn on 4-H support, and two-thirds of the
settlers in a dairy scheme were 4-H members at one time.

The movement is financed primarily by annual government contributions, but financial and material support
from private organizations, both local and foreign, have
been important in the development of the organization.
In 1969/70, 4-H received J$155,000 from the central govern-
ment, a rough annual per capita cost to government of
J$6, assuming that all members are active. The benefits
are less easy to assess, but it has been reliably estimated
that 80 to 90 percent of the total membership is built
up through the schools with a "captive" audience. In
spite of being organized through schools, membership is
small compared with the size of the well over half a
million cohort to which it relates. Effective membership
is made up primarily of those youngsters in the formal
school system who can afford to participate and appreciate
the value of such extracurricular activities and also
those "landed" children who have a marked interest in
farming.

One is forced to conclude that the 4-H movement offers little to the most educationally deprived. It is doubtful whether this kind of youth association can be really effective in circumstances marked so significantly by shortage of land, stock, and equipment, and where incomes for all grades of farm workers are so far below those of equivalent grades in trade, industry, and commerce. At best the movement may sustain an interest in farming for those who might otherwise lose interest, thus checking the trek away from the land. There is, however, no sign of any change in the predominant, strongly entrenched, widespread antipathy against farming.

Apart from the work of 4-H in young farmer training, there is no other major program in this area. The Ministry of Education has a residential vocational school which trains for agriculture. The school accepts boys, between 15 and 17 years, and most of them move off, either to the Jamaican School of Agriculture for further training preliminary to an agricultural career, or directly into jobs on the large commercial estates.

Training for Girls and Young Women

Almost all organizations working with youth groups offer a form of homecraft training. The Jamaican Federation of Women has home economics groups in practically all of its 400 branches. Classes in home economics are regularly held in all 114 community centers of the Social Development Commission and the 50 centers of the Sugar Industry Labour Welfare Board. The bulk of 4-H work with the female members is in homemaking.

There are no exact figures for participation rates of girls and young women involved in this statistically large number of programs. But, to give some indication of participation, the Social Development Commission claims an enrollment figure of around 2,500 girls and women with an active attendance of around 1,800, or about 70 percent.

Another important training focus for young women is in the field of handicrafts. The work carried on in community development centers producing and marketing handicrafts is a continuation of a movement that began in the late 1930s. The recent development of tourism has stimulated the demand for native handicrafts, and the transmission of handicraft skills is regarded as respectable spare-time work for women through community groups and at home. The number of women trained in crafts through the Social Development Commission was nearly 2,000 in 1970-71. The chief skills taught include needlework, straw work, dyeing, garment making, and the production of soft toys. The average enrollment and attendance of producers at all centers is around 2,000; of trainees, about 1,300. The scheme has a target for each worker to earn J$12 per month from her work at the center. This amount, however, is too low even as a supplement to family income and probably does not induce a great deal of enthusiasm for the scheme.

Experiments have recently begun to train girls for more remunerative employment. Both the Social Development Commission and the Sugar Industry Labour Welfare Board have small schemes operating to train girls as household help. The first output of about 500 graduates has found immediate well-paid work in North America, in the Bahamas, and in hotels and canteens in Jamaica.

In the growing hotel industry there are varied openings for young women. This is one of the few prevocational training areas where both young men and young women are trained together. The most sophisticated training is given at the Casa Monte Training School, run by the Ministry of Industry and Tourism. The Sugar Industry Labour Welfare Board also has a training center for hotel workers in western Jamaica. Other programs include training in nursing, carried out by the Sugar Industry Labour Welfare Board, and a school leaver training project centered mainly in the Kingston area and organized by the YWCA. This project consists of homecraft, typing, bookbinding, hairdressing, and childcare elements.

All these programs are small and sporadic. The majority of programs for girls presume a continuation of their traditional role as nonearning members of poor households and the transfer of this role for some girls to the paid employment field through domestic service. For the 160,000 girls and young women who make up the 15-23 year female cohort, there is negligible opportunity to learn a paying vocational skill that offers a chance to move away from the traditional subsistence existence. One viable alternative to the traditional way of acquiring status is that of childbearing. There are few better reasons for remaining at home, and there are no more assured means of support than that of a common law marriage.

Youth Organizations for Social and Leisure Activities

Almost all the major North Atlantic conventional, voluntary-type youth organizations have their counterparts in Jamaica: secular youth clubs, church clubs, Boy Scouts, Girl Guides, YMCA, YWCA, Boys' Town, Girls' Town, Boys' Brigade, Girls' Brigade, and so on. By far the largest of these are the secular clubs, supported by government funds provided through the Youth Development Agency (YDA) of the Social Development Commission. Official statistics in 1972 placed the membership of those clubs at around 35,000. Since they are a related part of the Youth

Development Agency camp program, they are discussed more fully later in this study.

In comparison with the YDA program, the other voluntary youth bodies are small. The largest group, the Boy Scouts, states that its membership is just over 5,000; the YWCA claims 500 members. It is not possible to give a meaningful figure for the total membership of all these organizations, since a youth may belong to more than one of them. At best, however, the total number of youths affected cannot be more than 15,000, or about 3 percent of the 10-20 year age group. Those affected are generally in the urban areas; effect on rural youngsters who have the most need is at best transient.

Most voluntary youth clubs are centered on church or school. They receive small annual subventions from the government, sometimes funds from overseas sources, and derive income from membership fees and local donations. Adult voluntary helpers are sources of senior leadership, but it is difficult to generalize on the degree to which responsibility devolves on the young people themselves. Most activities include sports and dancing as well as educational activities, and few clubs omit from their list of aims the development of leadership qualities and character building. Youths leaning toward radical and extremist views claim that such clubs perpetuate the cloying respectability of undesirable middle class virtues.

Policymaking and Coordination

Although there is no one body in Jamaica that takes a complete overview of the variegated needs and programs for young people, there are a number that have the potential for doing this. The Ministry of Youth and Community Development has responsibility for certain activities and programs that are delegated to a statutory body, the Social Development Commission. The Ministry has remained primarily a channel through which funds are disbursed to the Commission and to voluntary bodies.

The new government has recently blueprinted and set up a new National Youth Service with implications for both formal and nonformal education. The main goals of the new approach are to integrate youth more closely into the mainstream of national life and to help create circumstances by which young Jamaicans can help each other to spread learning opportunities more widely.

Beginning in 1975, for instance, all young people leaving school (junior secondary and above) will spend one to two years in community service. This enterprise has already begun on a voluntary basis with over a thousand participants, and service recruits after appropriate training are being assigned to "developmental" activities that include help in youth centers and schools.

Two other organizations that have a potential for coordinating activity are the Jamaica Youth Council (JYC) and the National Volunteers' Organisation.

The Jamaica Youth Council was set up in 1967 with government approval as a standing committee of the Council of Voluntary Social Services. Consisting of three representatives from each of about 24 voluntary organizations, all of which are engaged in some form of youth work and set up to coordinate voluntary youth work, the JYC embarked on an independent life of its own in becoming yet another "providing" body. The reasons for this are complex. The pitfalls awaiting a young organization which attempts positive coordinatory action but has little power to maintain effective liaison with major government programs cannot be overestimated. For whatever the reasons the main focus of the JYC has not been coordination, but rather the organization of field work camps, part-time youth staff training, and the construction with volunteer help of a small field training center in eastern Jamaica.

The National Volunteers' Organisation (NVO), like the JYC, was set up by the Ministry of Youth and Community Development and intended to be a statutory body, although the necessary government legislation had yet to be passed in 1972. The function of the NVO was originally to identify areas of need, find and organize sources of volunteer help, and, acting as clearinghouse, bring the two together. The NVO, however, has preferred to develop an operational identity of its own--concern with small urban work projects among the elderly, although it was expected that youth would be a major source of volunteer help.

A third body worth mentioning in this respect is the National Council of Jamaican Organisations (NACJO). This was established in 1969 by a group of representatives from business, education, church, and welfare organizations, bringing together leadership elements at all levels to improve collaboration and avoid duplication in programs of an educational and social nature bearing on national problems. Made up of fifty organizations in 1972, its main achievements to date have not been addressed to coordination, but rather to the development of Citizens' Colleges in the Kingston area, and to drawing up plans for a training center for small businessmen. The program of the colleges, still embryonic, includes literacy, basic education, and prevocational training.

Finally may be mentioned recent attempts at coordination made by organizations involved in adult education, but in 1972 they still awaited government approval before becoming operational.

The purpose of describing these various attempts to establish effective overall policymaking, strategy-building, and coordination is to stress the point that the real question is not so much what to do, but rather how to do it. A number of organizations expressly established

for this purpose have somehow shied away from their basic
responsibilities. The efforts of the new government to
institute a National Youth Service, integrate youth activities, and give an enhanced role to the Social Development Commission may be helpful. However, many problems
remain. There is still a need for machinery that effectively coordinates the work of the Ministries of Youth,
Education, Agriculture, Labour, and Health with each other
and with the many voluntary bodies, all of which share
responsibility for the total youth effort.

YOUTH CAMPS AND ROLE OF THE
YOUTH DEVELOPMENT AGENCY

The youth camp program has been for many years of
central importance in the Jamaican strategy for the education and training of the most deprived young people. Well
known internationally, it has attracted international
financing and support and has been used as a model by
other countries. However, the program has not been without its critics both inside and outside Jamaica. Recently,
as part of its overhaul of national youth policy and programs emphasizing out-of-school youth education and training, the new government has reviewed and radically revised
the role of the camps. The following account of the youth
camp program dwells largely on the way it operated prior
to 1973, with an indication of the new directions the
program is taking as a result of the government's new
policy.

Evolution of the Camp Program

Early in the 1950s, concerned about the growing number of unemployable youngsters, the Ministry of Education
undertook two experimental projects to meet this emerging
problem. The first was the creation of a new Youth Corps,
based on a system of largely self-help residential youth
camps that could provide education and training for youngsters. The second was the Ministry's support of local
nonresidential youth clubs throughout the island, supervised by a new cadre of paid full-time government youth
organizers and a new parent Youth Club Council to provide
a national focus and forum for the program.
Soon after their inception, however, the responsibility for these activities was transferred to the Ministry
of Housing and Welfare, because these were considered
welfare activities rather than educational. In 1963,
following a change of government, responsibility was
again transferred when "welfare" as a ministerial portfolio joined "development" in a ministerial reshuffle.

Between 1955 and 1963 two youth camps were established as part of the new Youth Corps, and seven youth organizers were appointed on the basis of one organizer for every two of the fourteen parishes (the smallest unit of local government administration) to oversee the two hundred clubs located at that time mainly in Kingston and Western Jamaica.

With the leadership of a vigorous Minister of Development and Welfare, plans were laid in 1963 for expanding the number of existing camps and for strengthening field staff. Additionally, plans were laid for the construction of youth center buildings to provide permanent facilities for the clubs which normally held their meetings and activities on a temporary basis in any convenient building.

The Minister took a fresh look at the two youth organizations--the Corps and the Council--which had developed independently of each other, and decided that the two should be amalgamated and integrated more closely with other social development activities being supported by government. In 1965, therefore, the Youth Development Agency was formed as an arm of the Social Development Commission[19]--the other arms being the Social Development Agency with community development, community center, and literacy programs; the Craft Development Agency with programs for the development of local handicrafts; and the Sports Development Agency. Each agency within the Commission, however, maintained its independence and developed its programs autonomously. Even within the Youth Development Agency, until 1972 the old Youth Crops structure of youth camps remained separate from the clubs and centers, with one having little effect on the other. It is noteworthy too that the largest youth program, that of the 4-H Clubs, kept a completely separate identity under the Ministry of Agriculture.

The original purpose of the camp was to remove unemployed young men, ages 15 to 19 years, from the labor market and to expose them to a year (later 18 months) of disciplined life in a camp where they would develop skills and gain experience that would fit them for more effective participation in community life. Over the years greater emphasis has been placed on the teaching of trades and the improvement of academic standards, but the general preparation for community life has remained a basic goal.

The archetype camp was to be the creation of a group of youngsters with the guidance of adult leadership. Government helped provide a minimum of land and supplies, and the youths were responsible for building the camp. The earliest camps were located on the theory that the farther away from towns they were the better for the enhancement of the spirit of adventure and for the development of personal ruggedness. The camps were kept as simple as possible: semipermanent army barrack-like sleeping quarters, cook house, mess hall, classrooms, and

workshops. Basic foodstuffs, clothing, and equipment
were supplied, but as far as possible the camp aimed at
being self-supporting. Campers made their own clothes,
made their own furniture, and maintained the camp in good
order. Campers were to discipline themselves and look
after their own welfare under the benevolent supervision
of adult staff. Staff were to live in camp and provide
practical instruction that included farming as an integral
part of a productive process designed to meet camp needs;
skill training linked to the building, construction,
repair and equipping of camp; literacy and basic education;
cooking, nutrition, the principles of good health and
hygiene, civic, citizenship, and moral training.[20]

Staff and campers together organized their evening
social activities, physical training, and games. Spiritual
development and moral guidance were supervised by the staff
and a regular feature included the short daily morning
and evening church services and full services on Sunday.

Location and Clientele

The first youth camp, Cobbla Camp, was opened in 1956
in a most rural part of central Jamaica in the bounds of
the Christiana Land Authority.[21] Chestervale was established a few years later high in the Blue Mountains in
the Yallahs Valley Land Authority. By 1970 Kenilworth
camp was opened in western Jamaica and Lluidas Vale, in
St. Catherine, central Jamaica. A fifth camp, the first
for girls, was opened in 1971 on the north coast in the
parish of St. Mary. The first two camps were constructed
in simple style reminiscent of semipermanent army barracks.
Chestervale, the second camp, was able to use a run-down
"Great House" as a nucleus for its buildings. The three
later camps are more lavish. Lluidas Vale makes use of
a housing estate built by the Ministry of Housing but
never occupied; Kenilworth rivals the north coast tourist
hotels in permanence and design; and Cape Clear, situated
in a restored Great House, recaptures the elegance of its
original construction.

The camps in 1972 catered to about 1,700 unemployed
youths between the ages of 15 and 19 years. Individual
camp capacities in 1971 ranged from 50 to 640. (See Table
4.2.) Courses lasted eighteen months, with a third of
the campers entering or leaving the camp every six months.
The average age for campers was 17 years and the large
numbers of candidates presenting themselves for selection
made it possible to give preference to the older age-
groups rather than to the younger.

Recruitment of campers was carried out largely by
the individual camp directors, aided by local dignitaries
at convenient temporary recruitment centers. Because

TABLE 4.2

Enrollment in Youth Camps

	Camper Capacity (1971)	Educational Level of Campers (mid-1971 intake)		
		Illiterate	Other	Not Known
Cobbla	640	38	447	?
Chestervale	360	170	143	19
Lluidas Vale	250	58	139	53
Kenilworth	400	201	122	77
Cape Clear	50	3	42	5
TOTALS	1,700	470	893	154

Note: Lluidas Vale, Kenilworth and Cape Clear were still incomplete. The educational level of campers for Cobbla are estimated on the basis of class attendance not on testing.

Source: Jamaica, Youth Development Agency, Annual Report (Kingston, 1972).

there were no stringent recruitment regulations to be enforced, much depended on the inclinations and personal interests of the camp directors. It was generally accepted that camps should recruit at least 10 percent of their intake from among the most educationally deprived, but with no immutable ruling on educational entry requirements. Cobbla and Lluidas Vale, for instance, tried to keep their recruitment of illiterates to a minimum, while Chestervale usually recruited a substantial proportion of these. A lack of clear policy reflected the dichotomy of views on the prime purpose of the youth camp. Some, for a variety of reasons, felt it preferable to take the best educated applicants; others held to the initial camp principle that there was a moral obligation to provide for the most deprived. Educational attainment of recruits varied greatly from intake to intake and from year to year. In recent years only a bare majority of campers have been literate, and only a minute fraction have entered with an educational level equivalent to a junior secondary schooling. The majority of campers were recruited from the rural areas, and there were many more applications than places available.

Campers paid no fees and received a small amount of pocket money, some of which they saved, being encouraged to practice thrift. Campers provided their own clothes, which they were expected to keep in good repair; working overalls that were issued were usually made in camp.

Instructional Organization and Content

Camps operated on an imaginative system of discipline and welfare that combined practical camp management with learning through the exercise of responsibility. The raw recruit's first introduction to camp life was through the Round. The Round was a basic organizational unit, and every camper belonged to the same one throughout his stay. Each intake was divided equally among the Rounds, so that at any one time each Round consisted of one-third recruits, one-third intermediates, and one-third seniors. The Round was further subdivided into subgroups descending to a basic cell of ten campers. At each organizational level there was a cadre of elected leaders and prefects pyramiding to the head of the Round. The Round and cell system provided opportunity for the campers to learn by regulating their own discipline and welfare, and it facilitated camp administration. In this way, it was argued, campers learned to wield responsibility and to understand by practice the essentials of sound decision making and team work.

Each Round was under the supervision of a Round director, a full-time member of the teaching staff, though he may have had no actual teaching duties. The efficient operation of the system naturally depended on him, since the delicacy and tact with which he manipulated his authority determined the degree to which true responsibility was delegated and learned by the campers.

The more formalized education and training that was provided in the camp is best described by subject category: agriculture, vocational training, general education, and extracurricular activities.

Agricultural Instruction

The inculcation of a healthy affection for the land and a recognition of the economic possibilities that derive from farming were considered of such importance that agriculture as an activity took up much of the recruit's day for the first six months of the period at camp. This was a tradition firmly entrenched in the camp program when the first camps were established and which has only just been abandoned under the new governmental policy. With the importance of farming in mind, together with the intention of making the camp as self-sufficient as possible in foodstuffs, the camps had been established with large land acreages: Cobbla with 321 acres, Chestervale 91 acres, Kenilworth 266 acres, Lluidas Vale 260 acres, and Cape Clear 51 acres. Not all these acreages, however, were suitable for farming.

Prior to 1972 the program of agricultural training operated under severe constraints. The strong Jamaican

prejudice against farming in general has already been
described. Most recruits entered camp with a strong
aversion to farming, usually with no intention of becoming
farmers. Agricultural staff and equipment were in short
supply. The shortages allied to the way training was
conceived meant that for the first six months the campers
acted like unpaid farm labor, resenting what they were
doing and seeing little result for their effort. Working
under such conditions, the few staff were severely
strained as they went through the motions of teaching and
producing, and it is to their credit that a fraction of
campers remained in agriculture for the full eighteen
months. There is no clear evidence that camp farms made
net profits; indeed, observation suggests they did not.
There is every reason to suppose that the state of the
farms and the training methods they employed tended to
reenforce the prejudices against agriculture.

Vocational Skill Training

Vocational skill training is what most campers came
for, and a variety of courses were offered, including
carpentry, construction and building, electrical maintenance, mechanics, tailoring, welding, plumbing, metal
work, barbering, and cooking. Courses were also arranged
in clerical work for the few campers who had a sufficiently
high educational standard. Most popular courses were
naturally those leading to the most highly paid jobs,
which included industrial and mechanical crafts. About
three-quarters of the campers, however, usually found
themselves in building construction or "service" type
courses, expedients that reflected availability of equipment and staff and the maintenance needs of the camp.
As with agriculture, learning combined with production was the basic instructional method, although it was
implemented in vocational skill training with considerably
more success. Campers in on-the-job training made clothes,
repaired shoes, gave haircuts, cooked food, made and
repaired furniture and equipment, supported building
projects, repaired engines, installed and repaired
drainage and electrical circuits. The skill training took
place during the second and final six months of the stay
in camp. The intention was not to produce a semiskilled
craftsman, but rather to provide a minimum preparation
that could lead to employment and higher level training
elsewhere.
Although constraints on nonfarm skill training were
not as severe as those on agricultural, they were serious
enough. There was no initial camper prejudice to overcome.
However, morale often underwent change when most campers
found that the desired training in motor mechanics or
welding was not available and that building or barbering
had to be accepted as an alternative. The program

suffered from a serious staff shortage, a high turnover
rate, and a paucity of workshop space and equipment. The
preponderance of poorly educated campers meant that a
year's training was usually too short to achieve the camps'
modest goals.

Nevertheless, successes were claimed by the YDA.
It has asserted that most campers who passed through a
trade course eventually found employment, although there
has been no official follow-up of campers. In spite of
operating difficulties, ways of combining production and
training have been successfully demonstrated, and there
was always a queue of would-be campers awaiting the opportunities offered.

Since 1972 camps have begun to specialize in certain
types of skill training, and one camp now concentrates on
farming. The compulsory six months' farm laboring chore
has been abolished.

General Education

Complementing the agricultural and vocational training
is a program of general education. Until 1972 this
comprised literacy teaching, basic formal education, physical education, civics, and citizenship. The general education program was intended to improve upon the low formal
educational level of campers and additionally to provide
basic knowledge essential for responsible adulthood.
General education as conceived in camp was a basic necessity
for intellectual and physical development, for successful
skill training, and for meeting the important socializing
needs of the youthful camper. Yet, after agriculture, this
effort turned out to be the least satisfactory part of the
system. General education seemed to lack clear policy,
goals, and most of the means for success. The growing
preoccupation with skill training, agricultural production,
and camp chores gradually squeezed general education into
a smaller and smaller segment of the timetable. Classes
for literacy and formal subjects suffered from chronic
staff shortages, lack of classroom space, and inadequate
teaching materials. At any given time over half of all
campers were not functionally literate, and it is not
surprising that most of these left camp after eighteen
months still illiterate. The following figures give an
indication of the situation in December 1971 and they
are not untypical[22]:

	No. of Campers	No. Receiving General Education	No. of Weekly Class-Hours
Cobbla	600	321	40
Chestervale	360	190	6.40
Kenilworth	380	45	6
Lluidas Vale	220	30	2

The weaknesses of the general education program was appreciated by camp management. Consideration was given to making it more functional and to relating its content more closely to everyday camp life and in particular to the needs of skill training. Since 1972 only literate recruits have been enrolled in the camps, and special literacy training is provided for before entry in the new nonresidential Community Training Centres.

Extracurricular activities were considered an important element of camp life. Most camps had a 4-H Club, a Boy Scout troop, a Boys Brigade Company, a youth club, and a choir. Physical education and games featured in the daily program, and camp teams entered local and national competitions. Evening and weekend social events included current affairs, lectures, debates, cultural activities, music, and dances, although the effectiveness of such extracurricular activities depended largely on the commitment of camp staff as well as on the initiative of the campers.

An important feature of life in the earlier camps was the services provided by the camp for the local community. However, in recent years community service has declined and become almost nonexistent, because of the pressure on camp time of the internal programs and the difficulty of properly identifying community projects. Since 1972 renewed emphasis has been placed on community services, and ways are being sought to involve camps in local development.

Post-camp Follow-up

Post-camp life was considered almost as important as that which took place in the camps. To take care of follow-up the YDA had a small welfare section in its headquarters with responsibility for helping in the recruitment of campers, for taking care of welfare problems of campers that could not be solved in camp, and for helping with placement of campers in jobs after they left camp. Up to 1972, however, only two welfare officers serviced these functions, and little more than token services have been maintained. Little is known of the fate of campers after their departure. Recently steps have been taken to strengthen the section, to fill staff vacancies, and to develop a more systematic relationship with potential employing organizations.

It is evident, then, that an effort was made to provide in eighteen months a fairly comprehensive preparation for adulthood. Causes of failure lay not so much in weakness of concept, as in its practical application. Solutions to problems of staffing and of financing could only be found externally. However, before examining these constraints, it is necessary to look briefly at the other YDA program, the nonresidential youth center and clubs that have been closely bound up with the camp program.

Youth Centers and Youth Clubs

The evolution of the YDA centers and clubs--separate from the camps--has already been described. Until 1972 the two programs were administered and managed as distinct operations. Clubs were formed on the voluntary initiative of a group of local youths--boys and girls--between the ages of 11 and 21 years. They held their meetings in any suitable accommodation and organized themselves under the guidance of a voluntary adult leader approved by the YDA. The ebb and flow of membership reflected the enthusiasm of leaders and members.

The number of clubs was estimated in 1971 as between 400 and 500, with a total membership varying from 25,000 to 35,000.[23] Clubs were scattered throughout the island and a typical program offered a variety of social and recreational activities, sports being particularly important. Joint social activities and competitions organized between clubs culminated in parish and national events during an annually held Youth Week.

Clubs recognized or sponsored by the YDA qualified for a small YDA grant toward the cost of equipment, the cost of summer camps (a feature of the national program), and the cost of participation in special international events. The YDA assisted the clubs through its 14 youth centers and the help given by the 45 YDA youth organizers posted throughout the island. The aim was to provide three organizers for each parish: one male and one female for general club supervision and one to run the youth center.

Youth centers provided a permanent base for the clubs and consisted of a sports field with equipment, a meeting hall with a stage, offices, changing rooms, a store, and facilities for light refreshments. They were located in the parish urban centers, five of which are in Kingston. The success of the youth centers depended on the enthusiasm and initiative of the organizers, and they varied enormously in their state of maintenance and in the programs they offered. During 1970-71 efforts were made to introduce and expand a rudimentary vocational training program that included commercial subjects, sewing, cooking, and cosmetology, taught to about 150 participants as a daytime activity for a few hours each week.

The new government program introduced in 1972 has placed a new emphasis on nonresidential education and training in the centers. These--along with youth camps--have now been redesignated Youth Community Training Centres. The basic YCTC program is designed to include six months

of general education followed by a year of combined occupational training and community service.

Organization and Management: Youth Development Agency

The YDA headquarter organization up to 1972 consisted
in essence of a staff of director, deputy director, and
an assistant director for centers and clubs. Also in the
headquarters were units responsible for welfare and employment, for general administration, and staff officers for
agriculture and vocational training. Camp administration
was in the immediate charge of the YDA deputy director,
although camp directors had free access to the YDA director.
Camps were administered by a camp director and a
deputy. Assistant directors were assigned as Round
directors or for general education duties or for vocational
training. Subordinate to the assistant directors on the
vocational side were instructors and project officers.
The camp administrative channel continued from Round
director down to the camper through the structure earlier
described. The camp director was additionally supported
by a small clerical and accounting staff, a camp-mother
who also carried out the functions of a nurse, and chef-
cook instructors responsible for both camp feeding and
teaching.
For centers and clubs, the administrative line was
vertical from the headquarters assistant director to the
field senior organizers and, through them, to their subordinate organizers and club officers.
Coordination took the form of periodic headquarter
staff meetings and other meetings to include camp directors
and senior club organizers. In practice camp directors
and senior youth club organizers enjoyed a large measure
of responsibility for the development of local programs.
Externally the YDA had a formal relationship with the
Social Development Commission and with the Ministry of
Youth and Community Development. In practice, apart from
control exercised in the appointment of staff, the Social
Development Commission had little impact on the YDA.
For important YDA policy decisions and major developments,
discussions were usually held directly with political
heads in the Ministry of Youth and Community Development.
Channels of communication with other ministries or
organizations involved with youth work in Kingston and
in the field were very informal and rarely for any purpose
other than the token exchange of information. There was
little interagency collaboration of any significance.
Exceptions to this, however, included collaboration with
the Ministry of Labour for trade testing and, to a small
extent, staff training; with the Literacy Section for

literacy testing; and with the Ministry of Labour for
identifying employment opportunities for camp graduates.

Staff assigned to camps worked under severe constraints.
Prepared to work long and often inconvenient hours under
conditions unlike those pertaining to a formal school or
a conventional training center, staff members had to be
resourceful, imaginative, sympathetic, and firm. Unused
to self-discipline and communal life, campers (often
failures in the formal school system) required special
management if they were to profit from the experience and
not be frustrated by unfulfilled hopes. Although in the
earlier years staff salaries were higher than those of
equivalent grades in other services such as teaching, in
recent years they fell dramatically behind, making it
increasingly difficult to recruit and hold good staff.
Terms of service and fringe benefits were less attractive
than those for equivalent grades in government, and chances
of promotion were negligible. Although staff were expected
to live in camp, there was no provision for families
except those of camp directors. Finally, an islandwide
shortage of well-educated and skilled staff of all kinds
added to the difficulty of finding quality personnel.
Camps were often forced to appoint inadequately trained
candidates, some of whom were recipients of political
patronage.

In 1972 the staff-camper ratio fluctuated from 1:20
to 1:30,[24] said to be inadequate if allowance is made for
sickness, authorized absences, and assumption of duties
not associated with vocational training and camp maintenance. Detailed records are inadequate, but in 1972 official YDA reports referred to a 50 percent annual turnover
of assistant directors and a 20 percent annual turnover
of instructors and project officers. The same report
showed vacancies in 12 percent of headquarter posts, 24
percent of assistant director posts, and 31 percent of
posts for organizers of the center and clubs program.[25]
Lower in the scale, deficiencies in staffing were particularly pronounced in general education and agriculture,
and the somewhat better staffing in skill training offered
little ground for complacency. Classes in welding,
mechanics, and woodworking often had over 50 campers for
one instructor, a situation that, taken into consideration
shortages in workshop space, tools, and other equipment,
shed doubt on the effectiveness of the instruction.

There was really no systematic staff training and no
staff organization charged with this responsibility. The
Social Development Commission had a small training unit
that was intended to service all the agencies, but in
practice (and for historical reasons) it was concerned
mainly with community development training. Recently
steps have been taken to include some of the skill training staff in courses organized by the Ministry of Labour,
while a few senior staff have attended courses run at the
university or overseas. The new government has set up a

Resource Development Unit in the Social Development
Commission to backstop all its agency programs with research and training. There is also a small youth work
training center at Braco on the north coast, used for the
training of youths in leadership subjects and for staff
seminars.

Costs, Resources, and Effectiveness

The most important inputs to the YDA came from government and international aid sources. The total contribution
from government sources amounted to J$1,718,000 in 1971/72,
which included J$730,000 on capital account and J$988,000
on recurrent account. This compares with a total vote
allocation from government of J$362,000 for the year
1965/66.

For 1972/73 estimates of expenditure prepared by the
YDA reached a total of J$3,081,000, of which capital
account claimed J$1,293,000 and the recurrent account
J$1,788,000. A simple calculation based on the recurrent
expenditure for 1971/72 for the camps showed a camper per
capita annual recurrent cost of J$435,[26] and this did not
take into account depreciation, contributions from camper
production, and foreign inputs of staffing and equipment.
It compared with a per capita cost of J$300 for the year
1965/66. Camp farm production was not valued systematically, but indications are that this had been declining.
For instance, the net income from the farm at Chestervale
reached J$3,000 at current prices in both 1965/66 and
1970/71.

The high figures for capital expenditure were a
reflection of the expansion program for the camps. Kenilworth, Lluidas Vale, and Cape Clear were still under construction in 1972, and there were plans for the improvement
and expansion of Chestervale and Cobbla. The capital
account estimates for 1972/73 also took into account the
building of two new camps and the Braco Training Centre.

The construction costs of new camps built in the
more expensive style of Kenilworth, and certainly more
elaborately than the first two camps, were quoted in 1972
as J$400,000 for a boys' camp with a capacity of 600
campers (considered the optimum size), and J$300,000 for
a girls' camp of 300 campers.[27] These cost estimates did
not include the cost of land, but did include the contribution made by the campers to their construction. It is
not surprising, perhaps, that one of the first acts of
the new government was to freeze plans for camp expansion.

International aid organizations have been and still
are a major source of support for the YDA program. Until
1972 bilateral volunteer youth aid agencies provided
volunteer help for the camps. Expatriate youth volunteer
teachers and instructors usually stayed for one or two

years and were then replaced by new volunteers. The
agencies that have helped in this way have included the
U.S. Peace Corps, Canadian Universities Service Overseas
(CUSO), the West German Volunteer program, and the British
Voluntary Service Overseas (VSO). Since 1972 bilateral
programs have been superseded by a UN volunteer program
in agreement with UNDP, which provides for 20 international
volunteers on two-year assignments to help primarily with
vocational training. In 1972 eleven volunteers of the
twenty were in post, although as part of the agreement
their Jamaican counterparts had yet to be appointed.
These new personnel should have ameliorated the staffing
difficulties in the camps.

A more important and comprehensive UN initiative,
of which the UN volunteer program was one small part,
was a major project which began operations early in 1971,
organized through the UNDP and ILO. This project, based
on surveys carried out by ILO and UNESCO during 1970,
was designed to expand and strengthen the youth camp
program. A team of twelve international experts and
associate experts, aided by short term consultants, were
assembled from ILO, UN, UNESCO, UNICEF, and FAO to support
the project.[28]

The cost of the first phase of the UNDP project
amounted to almost US$1,000,000, three-quarters of this
attributable to the cost of experts and administration,
with US$256,000 for equipment to be used in the camps.
The first phase ended in 1973, and the total cost to
UNDP represents an annual per capita expenditure of about
US$200 for each camper during the period of the project.

In 1972 the cost of the YDA center and club activities represented about 15 percent of the total YDA budget
from government sources, and 30 percent of the total YDA
recurrent costs. The capital cost of a center was estimated at around J$40,000, while the inescapable recurrent
costs for the centers and clubs were estimated at J$300,000
per annum, which on the basis of 15 centers each with a
club complex allowed J$20,000 per annum for each.[29]

The effectiveness of the YDA program to 1972 is
impossible to quantify. One group of objectives clustered
around the personal development of the camper. These
include good character development, the development of
leadership qualities, a sense of civic and community
responsibility, self-discipline, and attitudes to facilitate their continuing intellectual and technical development. No studies exist on the progress of campers after
they left, nor was the stage of development of individual
campers known before joining.

More useful comment can be made on such tangible
objectives of the camp system as those of providing trade
training to enable ex-campers to obtain employment,
literacy skills and formal schooling equivalency, and
encouragement and knowledge for a farming career. It is

generally believed that most campers did find paid employment after leaving camp, although there are no data to
substantiate this. Neither is it known what kind of
employment they gained nor how well they performed. It is
reasonable to suppose that employers in need of unskilled
or semiskilled labor gave consideration to campers with
the recommendation of youth camp experience. What is not
known, however, is how important the general recommendation
was in comparison with the specific trade qualifications.
If employers simply wanted a good character slip, there
may have been other effective but cheaper ways of achieving this. However, if, as is officially alleged, most
campers did get employment, then this must be considered
a positive benefit of the program.

As for the teaching of literacy and general education,
there is every reason to believe that the camps were less
effective, and that as youngsters could proceed through
primary and junior secondary schooling and emerge after
nine years still not functionally literate, so they could
spend a further eighteen months in camps and still emerge
illiterate. In addition, the real possibility existed
that a failure complex acquired in school might well be
reenforced in the camps.

Achievements were weakest in farming. Youngsters
entered camp heavily prejudiced against farming, and it
is likely that most left camp even more prejudiced. It
remains to be seen how effective the new approaches to
literacy and agricultural training work out through the
new Youth Community Training Centre program.

The Camp Experience: Commentary

The preceding account is intended to provide a few
of the significant lessons that emerge from Jamaican
Youth Camp experience, and the commentary that follows
focuses primarily on the camp system viewed from within.

Pouring Quarts into a Pint Bottle

The youth camp system was perceived as a major thrust
for providing nonformal learning opportunities for disadvantaged youth. Yet its quantitative impact in relation
to needs was small.

The camps in 1972 had places for 1,800 youths representing a coverage of less than 2 percent of the illiterate and unemployed in the eligible age-group of 15-19
years. Plans for camp expansion envisaged an ambitious
doubling of places between 1972 and 1974, which would
meet at best only 4 percent of the target group, girls
being barely catered to at all. Recognizing the quantitative limitations of the camp approach, the new govern-

ment has rightly placed greater priority on nonresidential training, and on the education and training of girls through revamped coeducational clubs, centers, and camps, all classified as YCTCs.

A major constraint on a greater rate of expansion has been the costs of the program. Both capital and recurrent per capita costs were very high in comparison with those of primary schools: camps were at least ten times more expensive, in no small part because of the residential nature of the camp system.

One conclusion is clear. By 1972 the camp system provided no realistic strategy to meet the massive needs of the target cohort. Indeed, the important general question is raised of how far an educational program with high residential costs can ever be considered as a viable strategy for carrying the front line teaching load of a massive and expanding educational effort. The lesson is not that residence need be deliberately avoided, but rather how to use this facility to such advantage that the benefits can be maximized and felt by a larger clientele.

Courses might, for instance, be shortened to permit a larger clientele. Camps might be utilized as the apex of a system of youth training, selecting their clientele from nonresidential institutions like the centers and clubs. They could be used for staff training, the production of teaching materials, and the development of teaching methods, as well as in a direct teaching role. Possibilities for improvement are many, but there are no ready answers.

Evolution and Obsolescence

The evolution of the camp system has demonstrated an interesting lesson on the dangers of extending a program devised initially to meet a given set of circumstances that have changed their nature.

The initiators of the system in the mid-1950s did not view their new departure as either a long-term or large-scale program. The prevailing opinion was that a strong and expanding formal school system would soon provide a full and adequate preparation for all young folk. The camps therefore were designed to fill a temporary role and pick up what was confidently expected to be a rapidly decreasing number of youngsters who had missed their schooling through no fault of their own.[30]

Ten years later, when this premise proved to be unrealistic, a hurried groping for a feasible alternative to the school led to the decision to expand the camp system without considering its appropriateness in the light of the magnitude of needs or alternative ways of meeting them.

The evolution of the camp system has also shown how easily debilitating rigidities can set in. For instance,

the 18-month period of camp residence was treated as
immutable. That all campers should spend their first
six months laboring on the farm was viewed as sacrosanct.
However illogical it appears now, all trades had equity
in time allocation (barbering, for instance, was allocated
as much time as auto mechanics) and those aiming at the
JSC stayed at camp as long as illiterates. A conclusion
that has emerged is that a program devised to meet one
set of circumstances must be continuously reviewed to
take into account changing circumstances. It is evident
that there is a need to ensure management renewal to ensure
vital flexibility, adaptation, evaluation, and the introduction of new ideas.

Getting Right Political Backing

    Although the camps originated in a powerful Ministry
of Education, their rapid transfer to "social welfare"
where they remained reflects the prevalent view of most
government bureaucracies that such activities are primarily "social."
    The rubric "social welfare" would matter little, if
it were not associated with deleterious consequences,
especially in government budget allocation and planning.
The common interpretation that social activities are
economically unproductive usually results in "social"
ministries having a weak political clout, and their programs being more frequently hamstrung for finance and
staffing than their counterparts in economic or "production" ministries. In its infancy and after being transferred from the Ministry of Education, the new camp program rapidly lost status, salaries and staffing fell behind, and serious planning was abandoned. And so were
created many of the serious problems the camp management
found impossible to overcome.
    A lesson from this is to ensure that such programs
gain and keep the political and governmental support from
their inception and so safeguard a sufficient resource
allocation for their continuing viability.

Replicating Programs: Staffing and Expansion

    For the first ten years the camp system consisted of
only two camps in which staff quality and conditions of
work were good. Plans for expansion were based on the
assumption that sufficient staff of a similar high calibre
could be found and kept and that there would be a flow
of dedicated "welfare" staff agreeable to being paid less
than the market rate. That these assumptions proved to be
invalid underscores the fact that programs cannot be
expanded without giving due consideration to the supply
and flow of good quality staff and the price that must
be paid to get them and to keep them.

A further problem that had to be faced was how to keep capital costs down using cheap and simple buildings and equipment. The camps started out being relatively cheap constructions of prefabricated materials, capable of being built largely through the campers' own efforts. Later camps became more and more lavish and expensive. The latest, Kenilworth, cost well over J$400,000, and facilities in the newer camps, besides being very expensive, gradually ceased to reflect the actual home living conditions of rural youths. The experience demonstrated that the more elaborate and expensive physical facilities became, the more inappropriate was the learning environment and the less possible and likely it was to replicate and maintain them.

Specifying Target Clienteles

The camp program has been bedeviled by a characteristic common to many nonformal programs that initially set out to meet the needs of the poorest and most educationally deprived. This is the constant urge to gain the professional recognition accorded to those teaching at the higher levels by upgrading entrance requirements and so being assured of a better-educated clientele. Furthermore, it is certain that the most educationally deprived are the most difficult to provide for.

The struggle to upgrade entrance requirements seemed particularly important, especially in the late 1960s, in the field of vocational training, partly to meet higher trade and professional standards, and partly to ensure future employability. The dilemma persisted: was it better to hold fast to original purpose and perhaps fail, or to succeed with more competent candidates? The trend was to avoid the difficult cases with poorer educational and economic backgrounds; to select the older "good" boys whose credentials promised future employment rather than their juniors who had begun, as Jamaican idiom has it, to "shuffle" and get into mischief.

The lesson to be drawn is less a value judgment on the merits of one target group over another than a need to identify the group clearly, so that it can be adequately provided with the kind of learning it needs.

Defining Aims and Means

From its inception the camp system has aimed at something more than providing remedial training. An emphasis on character training distinguished the camps from conventional training centers and other kinds of remedial formal education; it constituted the basic case for an extended period of residence in which "indirect" influence could play a part. However, character training raised certain definitional problems; not all Jamaicans subscribed to its qualitative goals. Detractors claimed that "good" character in camp terms meant subservience to authority, unwarranted conformity, and the unhealthy acceptance of a drab future. The fact that employers preferred camp graduates to "open market" employees and pointed to their better sense of discipline as a fruit of special effort, ironically, lent support to such criticism, specially because the employers' preference meant discrimination against those who did not find a place in the camp.

Perhaps a more telling criticism was that camp life was unnatural, that with the possible exception of the camp director's household, it bore little resemblance to stable family life. Furthermore, taking boys away from their rural home areas for a lengthy period loosened important bonds and encouraged the movement from country to town.

CONCLUDING COMMENTS

It is apparent in the first place that the totality of the expanding nonformal educational effort had insufficient impact on the learning needs of the out-of-school youth population. The Ministry of Education's efforts at providing out-of-school continuation courses was not a particularly successful effort to remedy a problem that was partially a creation of its own school system. However, even if more could have been done to equip youngsters with such merit badges as the JSC, it is doubtful that this alone would have been directly beneficial, since such qualifications opened few doors to employment. In relation to the number of youngsters in need of functional literacy, the government's effort in its literacy program was not enough, touching less than 0.3 percent of the 15-23 year age-group. The Ministry of Labour's vocational training program reached only 3 percent of the target 17-21 year age-group. The 4-H program barely touched rural youth, reaching perhaps 6 percent of the 11-20 year age-group--more as an extracurricular activity than as a preparation for an occupation. Youth camps catered to less than 2 percent of the 15-19 year-olds, and youth clubs to less than 3 percent of their target cohort between 11 and 20 years of age. Given the constraints under which these programs operated, their efforts, even in a limited sphere, were often commendable. Nevertheless, recognition of the constraints should not blind one to the fact that in relation to needs their impact was not strong enough.

Second, it is clear that most of the programs were heavily weighted in favor of those who were already at an educational, economic, and social advantage. The

Ministry of Education's continuation program favored the literate who had completed a primary education. The vocational training program, demanding at least a JSC, was available only to those of 17 years or over. The 4-H movement was built largely around the school, and the most effective and regular participants were those youngsters most secure in the school system. The scouts, guides, and kindred youth movements, similarly based on the school, had few participants coming from the most deprived group. While it is commendable to round off the education and training of those who have had the benefit of formal schooling, the fact remains that for those who had the most need there was the least provision.

Third, too little was provided for the benefit of girls and young women and such provision was focused mainly on better subsistence livelihood for women and their contribution to an improved household.

Finally, given the constraints imposed by the Jamaican economy (and in consideration of what cost data exist), few of the programs permit rapid and large-scale expansion. The vocational training program of the Ministry of Labour had in 1972 a high annual per capita cost of US$1,000 that demanded substantially increased allocations if it were to expand to any appreciable size. High as the costs were, however, the cost-effectiveness of this program was almost certainly better than, for instance, the difficult to quantify but more dubiously effective 4-H, literacy, and camp programs.

This study has been based largely on the nature and spread of nonformal education in Jamaica prior to 1972. Since 1972 the newly formed Jamaican government has attempted to view general educational development and the youth programs in a fresh perspective as a part of a new national development effort. Some of the major changes, in the process of being realized now, are briefly reported below.

The new government has abolished school fees and restructured the original six-year primary cycle into a compulsory one lasting nine years. The school leaving age has been raised from 15 years to 17 years, and a new emphasis is being placed on prevocational training in the schools. A new two-year course above the basic nine years focuses predominantly on the preparation of young people for their emergence into working life. The new grade 10 has already begun, while grade 11 begins in 1974. One of the major problems still to be overcome is how to provide sufficient teachers of good quality. As part of the effort to remedy this shortage, young men and women recruited to the new National Youth Service (to be made a compulsory service from 1975) will assist by teaching in the schools.

The government has also announced its intention to eradicate illiteracy in Jamaica within four years; to

give bite to this resolution a National Literacy Board
has been established under the direct control of the Prime
Minister's Office. It is reported that in 1973 there were
around 30,000 students in 3,000 classes taught by 10,000
volunteer teachers from the National Youth Service.

To help integrate youth more fully into national
development and to strengthen youth and other programs,
a National Youth Service organization has been set up to
be administered through the Social Development Commission.
This organization will conduct the mandatory one- or two-
year full-time community service after leaving school
(junior secondary and above), beginning in 1975. The
embryonic service has already begun on a voluntary basis
with over a thousand participants. After appropriate
training, service recruits are assigned to one of various
"developmental" activities, of which school teaching is
among the most important.

Pledged to expand rapidly the educational and vocational opportunities for young people, especially the
unemployed, the government has placed an emphasis on the
widespread development of the new youth community training
centers (YCTCs), as explained earlier.

Some important organizational changes have also been
made in the YDA program. First, this has been decentralized
to regions with a new cadre of Senior Regional Officers
responsible for coordinating and developing the various
youth programs at subnational levels. Second, a new
Resource Development Unit has been established within
the Social Development Commission to assist in staff training, in the development of teaching materials, and in
operations research, both for the youth program and other
programs organized by the Commission. The National Youth
Service is helping to provide instruction for the YCTCs,
and assistance from UN agencies is now being redirected
into staff training and the development of materials.
Both staff training and the development of teaching
materials remain major hurdles to be overcome.

Finally, embodying these new departures, a new overall
national strategy has been formulated, first, to make a
concerted effort to integrate youth more completely into
the mainstream of national life; and second, to create the
circumstances under which young Jamaicans can, by their
own efforts and in partnership with the government, contribute to a wider, more significant spread of the learning opportunities that will enable them to acquire attitudes, knowledge, and skills leading to a satisfying
adulthood. How effectively the new strategy and plans
will be implemented and what impact these will have on
improving learning opportunities and, ultimately, the
life prospects of young Jamaicans are yet to be seen.

NOTES

1. See Shirley Gordon, "Out-of-School Education for Youth Groups," unpublished ICED working paper (Essex, Conn., 1972), p. 32.

2. For a full discussion of the effects of plantations on the Third World, see George L. Beckford, Persistent Poverty: Underdevelopment in Plantation Economics of the Third World (New York and London: Oxford University Press, 1972).

3. See Jamaica, Central Planning Unit, Economic Survey Jamaica 1970 (Kingston, 1970), p. 84. Between 1969 and 1970 accommodation for visitors increased 25 percent to provide nearly 14,000 beds for some 400,000 visitors.

4. Ibid., p. 49.

5. Ibid.

6. For an interesting discussion of this phenomenon, see R.M. Nettleford, Mirror Mirror--Identity Race and Protest in Jamaica (London: Collins, 1970).

7. For a valuable survey of Jamaican economic problems see Owen Jefferson, The Post-War Economic Development of Jamaica (Kingston, Jamaica: University of the West Indies, Institute of Social and Economic Research, 1972).

8. Jamaica, Dept. of Statistics, Labour Force Survey (Kingston, 1969).

9. Jamaica, Dept. of Statistics, Census of Jamaica (Kingston, 1960).

10. For a discussion of urban-rural growth see James W. Trowbridge, Urbanization in Jamaica: An International Urbanization Survey Report to the Ford Foundation (New York: The Ford Foundation, 1972).

11. Projections of the Central Planning Unit, Kingston.

12. It is officially admitted that 10 percent of the children of primary school age did not go to school at all. Of the 90 percent who go to primary school, only 60 percent attend with any regularity. The ineffectiveness of schooling for a large proportion of the primary intake is borne out by an examination of achievements of primary school leavers. A recent test given to youths at the end of grade 6 (final year of primary schooling) showed that 55 percent had not reached a grade 4 standard. A grade 4 standard may be equated to a minimum standard of literacy. Adding together those who do not go to school at all and those who leave after first cycle secondary school still largely illiterate, the proportion of illiterates for the age group in the 15-year-old cohort cannot be less than a half.

13. See Gordon, op. cit., p. 9.

14. Official per capita figures are not available. These figures are calculated by a simple division of recurrent budget for primary and junior secondary education by the enrollment figures.

15. "Report of the Working Party on Adult Education in Jamaica" (Paper prepared for the Third International UNESCO Conference on Adult Education, Tokyo, July 1972).

16. Ministry of Education records.

17. Jamaica, Ministry of Youth and Community Development, Report of the Literacy Evaluation and Planning Committee (Kingston, June 1971).

18.   National Industrial Training Board records.

19.   The Social Development Commission was created in 1965 as a statutory board to assume the functions of the Social Welfare Commission and the responsibilities of youth activities, crafts, and sports.

20.   See, for instance, Fred Milson, "Youth Programmes in Jamaica," mimeographed (Kingston: Youth Development Agency, 1969), and "Youth Camps," mimeographed (Kingston: Youth Development Agency, 1968).

21.   Land Authorities were established in peasant farming settlement areas to provide a structure for their development.   It was expected that campers would help with service to the peasant communities and in their early years this was a feature of the camp program.

22.   Youth Development Agency records, 1971/72.

23.   Ibid.

24.   Ibid.

25.   Jamaica, Youth Development Agency, "Report of the YDA Retreat 1972," mimeographed (Kingston, January 1972), p. 5.

26.   This is calculated by a simple division of the recurrent expenditure ascribed directly to the camps with a 40 percent addition for HQ costs, since total recurrent costs of the YDA also include an element for the center and club program.

27.   Jamaica, Youth Development Agency, op. cit., p. 4.

28.   In addition to the Project Manager and assistant, experts and associate experts covered in 1972 the following specialties: vocational training, youth employment promotion, out-of-school education and methods, girls' training, youth policies and programs, agriculture, home economics, horticulture, labor-market analysis, and reporting systems.

29.   Jamaica, Youth Development Agency, op. cit.

30.   It is worth digressing here to note that the numbers and plight of the out-of-schoolers were considerably worsened by a decision to expand and strengthen junior secondary education and to introduce automatic promotion of pupils in school.   This had the effect of drawing off the best teachers and resources from the primary schools and weakening the base of the school system to the extent that young people could pass through the schools and emerge illiterate at the end.

KENYA: DEVELOPMENT
AND COORDINATION OF
NONFORMAL PROGRAMS
B. E. Kipkorir

Kenya is of special interest to the ICED study, first, because it has given birth to a number of innovative nonformal education schemes which, while small in coverage, provide useful clues for other countries; second, because of the substantial role played in Kenya by voluntary organizations in creating prototype nonformal programs, some of which the government has later undertaken to expand; and third, because of the several efforts made in Kenya to coordinate fragmented nonformal education programs. The case study was prepared in late 1973 by Dr. B.E. Kipkorir of the University of Nairobi, on the basis of a design worked out with ICED.

INTRODUCTION

Straddling the equator on the east coast of Africa, Kenya is a country of more than 12 million people with an area of more than 583,000 square kilometers. The overall density of population is 20 persons per square kilometer. This figure is deceptive, however, as less than one-third of the country is arable. Indeed the rest consists of dry savannah with the northeastern region (almost half the land surface) virtually semidesert. A real constraint on agricultural development is thus the scarcity of good agricultural land. Estimated availability of such land in terms of high potential land equivalents per person varied in 1969 from 0.3 to 7.3 hectares. The bulk of the population is concentrated on the one-third of the land that is arable. In districts such as Kakamega and Kiambu, the density of population is very high, rising in places to more than 1,000 persons per square kilometer.

The bulk of the land is held by 1.2 million small-holders. About 20 percent of these were able to make use of modern agricultural techniques and services to operate on a commercial basis and substantially improved their

earnings during the decade 1960-70. These farms also
regularly employ hired farm laborers. The remainder of the
rural farming households operates mostly on a subsistence
basis; most of them live in poverty, although it is not
generally as severe as in some other African countries.
     There is a tendency among the youths of Kenya to
leave the land and to seek employment in the urban areas.
Apart from the inclination of school leavers to seek wage
employment outside the rural areas, there is a new economic trend: the agricultural sector is unable to employ and
hold what might be regarded as its proportion of the working population. The main reason for this is that agricultural technology has failed to keep pace with the growing
demands of the society. The adoption of innovations, such
as hybrid maize, has been slow; farm incomes have, therefore, not risen as fast as the cost of living, nor have
they satisfied the aspirations of the rural population.
     Although agricultural products such as coffee, sisal,
and tea continue to figure prominently in the Kenyan
economy, tourism is now the biggest source of foreign
exchange. In addition, the secondary industry infrastructure that Kenya has built up since independence has enabled
it to trade most competitively in Eastern Africa, so that
today Uganda, for example, is almost wholly dependent on
Kenya for its external trade. This has been achieved at
the expense of agriculture by the transfer of resources
in the form of agricultural taxes to support infant industries.
     Because of the increasing importance of industry,
employment has become a national concern and worry. An
equally important concern is the distribution of income.
Although the economy of the country as a whole has demonstrated remarkable dynamism with average annual growth
rates of 7 percent in recent years, internal inequalities
and economic disparities between individuals and communities are increasing at a high rate.
     The country is divided into seven provinces, each
headed by a Provincial Commissioner who is the personal
representative in the province of the President. The
Provincial Commissioner is in charge of overall security
and development in his province. However, the central
government is made up of ministries and departments, each
of which is responsible at every level for either security
or development in its sphere. Quite often, therefore,
there are ambiguity and conflict in the roles of the two
structures. But somehow, in a truly Kenyan fashion, the
system has worked and promises to continue to work. The
provincial administration has been in the forefront of
all local projects that politicians, civic leaders, or
churchmen may have initiated. The central government
ministries have "serviced" as many of these projects as
funds have allowed. There has been no conflict. In education, self-help has been particularly significant.

In Kenya, education accounts for more than 30 percent of the nation's recurrent expenditure. The government, therefore, on the basis of the financial allocations alone, can reasonably be assumed to take education very seriously. This study will focus attention on the evolving educational system now generally referred to as "nonformal education." In order to place nonformal education in its proper perspective, it is necessary to discuss education as a whole in the context of national development. In Kenya, however, there can be no question that education is generally identified rather too closely with formal schooling. To most people education means the school and classroom. It follows, therefore, that education is a matter of hierarchical structures and well-defined systems. But if we accept the premise that education is a lifelong process of learning, then there are clearly three main types of it--formal education, nonformal education, and informal education.[1]

By formal education we mean that branch of education that is associated with schooling and classroom and with children and youths from birth to approximately 30 years of age. This includes playgroup schools, kindergarten or nursery schools, primary and secondary schools, colleges and universities. By nonformal education we mean any organized instructional program for any age-group outside the institutional framework of the formal system. Nonformal education is thus viewed as being complementary to formal education--the two being mutually reinforcing rather than competitive. Informal education consists of all learning that an individual acquires in ordinary life from birth to death outside any organized instructional system. It is practical education--education that a person acquires of necessity in the course of his daily life.

In this study, we are principally concerned with organized education; that is, the formal and nonformal. We discuss the formal educational system first, in order to place the nonformal system in its proper perspective.

KENYA'S FORMAL EDUCATION SYSTEM

What are the objectives that Kenyans enunciate for their formal education system? Various government reports have addressed themselves to this question of objectives of education. The Ominde Commission of Inquiry into education (1964)--incidentally, the first such commission to look at Kenyan education as a whole and not in segments--laid the foundation for later surveys. The Commission noted the following as among the objectives of education:

> Education . . . must foster a sense of nationhood and promote national unity. Every young person coming out of our schools must be made to realize that he has a valuable part to play in the national life.

> Education must be regarded, and used, as
> an instrument for the conscious change of atti-
> tudes and relationships, preparing children for
> those changes of outlook required by modern
> methods of productive organization. At the same
> time education must foster respect for human
> personality.[2]

The current National Development Plan echoes the Ominde
Report in many respects. It argues that the government is
aiming at three goals in education planning:

> The first and most important of these is to
> produce sufficient numbers of people with skills,
> knowledge and expertise required to support an
> independent modern economy at a high rate of
> growth. The second is the rapid achievement of
> universal primary education. There is, finally,
> the social objective of all educational systems;
> that is, the inculcation of those cultural values
> which not only contribute to the enrichment of
> people's lives, but which are essential for the
> maintenance of a cohesive and productive society.[3]

Clearly it appears to be the Kenyan interpretation
that education must be a tool in national integration and
national development. For most Kenyan parents, however,
formal education is a means to formal or wage employment.
Even though educated parents send their children to school
as a matter of course, they expect them to secure paid
white-collar employment on completing their schooling.
Given the normal interplay of social and economic background in relation to education, the children of the elite
perform in the formal system better and have a better
chance of realizing their goal of modern sector paid employment than those from homes not previously exposed to
education. Formal education, therefore, has become a
means of perpetuating and accentuating social stratifica-
tion.

Formal Structure:
Primary, Secondary, University Level

The primary school in Kenya, consisting of Standards
1 to 7, takes in pupils of the age-group 6-13 years.
However, 45 percent of the age-group do not at present
go to school. Of those who do not attend schools, 60
percent are female. The unschooled are not evenly distributed throughout the country. The Central Province
(consisting of the purely Kikuyu districts of Kiambu,
Murang'a, Nyeri, Nyandarua, and Kirinyaga) boasts an

enrollment of more than 82 percent of the age-group, far
ahead of all other rural provinces. At the bottom of the
ladder is the North Eastern Province with a total enrollment of 6 percent. This disparity is shown in Table 5.1,
which compares the percentages of total national population
and of total school enrollment in each province.

TABLE 5.1

Distribution of Education Services by Province

Province	Percentage of Total Population, 1969	Percentage of School Enrollment 1970	
		Primary	Secondary
Rift Valley	20.4	14.7	12.1
Nyanza	19.4	16.1	13.1
Eastern	17.4	20.1	13.6
Central	15.3	24.9	22.9
Western	12.3	13.1	10.1
Coast	8.6	6.3	9.3
Nairobi	4.4	4.4	18.7
North Eastern	2.2	0.3	0.2
TOTAL	100.0	100.0	100.0

Source: Kenya, Ministry of Education.

     The performance of students in primary school deter-
mines in the first instance whether a child may go on to
the next stage of formal education. Inevitably, a large
proportion of primary school children repeats Standard 7
in order to be better prepared for the Certificate of
Primary Education (CPE) examination. Sometimes children
repeat even Standards 6 or 5. Over one-third of Standard
7 students repeat grades, and only about a quarter of
the successful primary school leavers go to secondary
schools. (Table 5.2.)
     Given the statistical realities of primary and
secondary enrollment, the primary school for the majority
of pupils is terminal formal education. But the primary
school content and teaching methods, dominated by the CPE
examination--a computerized multiple-choice test made up
of three papers (English, mathematics, and general knowledge)--are almost inseparably tied to the task of preparation for secondary schools. Although there are no statistics relating to follow-up of the small percentage who
can continue their education in state-run or maintained
schools, the CPE is essentially a secondary school selection test, in which the performance of repeaters (and

TABLE 5.2

Distribution of Students after CPE Examination

Student Placement After CPE	1966		1967		1968		1969	
	No.	%	No.	%	No.	%	No.	%
Secondary Aided Form I[a]	14,067	10.6	15,169	11.0	17,900	11.2	20,198	12.8
Secondary Unaided Form 1	17,738	13.3	20,455	14.8	21,936	13.7	20,845	13.3
Teacher training	1,344	1.0	1,463	1.1	1,310	0.8	1,381	0.9
Mombasa Technical Inst.	110	0.1	110	0.1				
Vocational schools[b]	415	0.3	537	0.4	999	0.6	967	0.6
Trade schools[b]	215	0.2	253	0.2				
Repeaters (estimated)	46,565	35.0	48,473	35.0	55,881	35.0	55,034	35.0
Not continuing schooling	52,588	39.5	52,035	37.6	61,633	38.6	58,815	37.4
CPE Candidates	133,042	100.0	138,495	100.0	159,659	100.0	157,240	100.0

[a]Technical schools intake included in the number for Aided Form I.
[b]Vocational and trade schools merged in 1968.
Source: Kenya Ministry of Education, Statistical Branch.

therefore older children) is better than that of first-
sitters or younger candidates.[4] A test of accumulated
learning rather than of the acquisition of skills, it is
nevertheless grossly inefficient at identifying the most
intelligent youths. In fact, it has been argued that to
a large extent the CPE tests the teachers rather than the
pupils.[5] It is unlikely, however, that reform only of
the examination will remove its most definitive characteristic: that of dividing, virtually once and for all, the
primary school leavers into sheep and goats.

In the years immediately after independence, the
secondary school level of education was given much attention by the government. In order to alleviate the shortage
of well-qualified secondary school leavers for public
and private sector jobs in the newly independent country,
the government launched as many new classes at Form I as
it could afford.[6] Altogether, the growth in secondary

schools was phenomenal--from a total of 151 in 1963 to
809 in 1971.

For many children, secondary school is the single
target of their aspirations, because it is from secondary
school that other viable openings in life (teacher training, employment in commerce, recruitment into the armed
forces, and so on) become real possibilities. At the
moment secondary school means the traditional Form I-IV
unit for most children; Sixth Form School (Forms V-VI),
introduced in 1961, is still very much geared to entrance
to the university. However, there is evidence to suggest
that employers, operating from a market inundated with
Form IV leavers with good grades in the East African
Certificate of Education (EACE) examination, are beginning
to look for sixth form leavers first. Some employers, in
fact, prefer sixth form candidates to university graduates
for jobs. They argue that, although they do not possess
the degree, they are more amenable to on-the-job learning.

The big problem of the Kenya educational system is
Form I, because there are far too many qualifiers at
Standard 7 for far too few places in secondary schools.
In 1971 there were 173,150 primary school leavers and in
spite of the phenomenal growth of secondary schools, there
was room for only one-third of the total at most. In the
fully maintained and assisted schools there is room for
only one-sixth of the Standard 7 leavers. Although the
Ministry of Education talks in terms of plans that will
ensure Form I training for all primary school leavers,
the situation remains desperate.

Besides the general secondary schools, there exists
two types of vocational institutions at the secondary
level--trade schools and technical schools. The secondary
trade school (for example, Kabete, Eldoret, and Sigalagala)
places emphasis on workshop experience and craftsmanship.
The secondary technical school "is a school which, while
giving some introductory experience of workshop technology,
is in reality much more concerned with the subjects basic
to higher technological studies, notably mathematics,
chemistry, physics and biology."[7] The main purpose of the
workshop experience at the technical school is to improve
manual dexterity and create a feeling for material and
for productive techniques in engineering. The trade school,
then, is vocational, but at a lower level, while the technical school is prevocational, preparing its students for
higher professional training either at the Kenya Polytechnic or the university. The total enrollment in these
schools, however, does not amount to even 1 percent of the
primary school leavers.

At the apex of the vocational education system is the
Kenya Polytechnic and, more recently, the Mombasa Polytechnic. The Kenya Polytechnic provides courses of instruction for apprentices and trainees in industry and commerce
which, when linked with practical inservice training, are

expected to produce skilled and competent personnel. It
offers a number of professional courses leading to such
qualifications as those of the City and Guilds of London
Institute, Royal Society of Arts, and Association of
Certified and Corporate Accountants. It also provides
courses at the secondary school level. Basically, however,
the Kenya Polytechnic is concerned with improving the
quality of working manpower, and hence the majority of
its courses are offered on a part-time basis (sandwich,
block-release, day-release, or evening classes). The
Kenya Polytechnic is being taken as a model for several
currently projected colleges and institutes of science
and technology.

Higher education is more directly concerned with the
provision of high-level manpower than any other educational
effort. The University of Nairobi and its predecessor,
the University of East Africa, have always recognized this
connection. There was even a government attempt at bond-
ing state-sponsored students for direct recruitment to
predetermined public occupations, but it was later discontinued. On the assumption that the private sector of
the economy is as crucial as the public sector, it is
presumably realistic to operate an open employment market
even at the university graduate level, notwithstanding the
enormous sums of public funds (computed at ₤1,000 per
annum) expended in producing a single university graduate.
However, insofar as the Kenyan economy is still largely
in foreign hands and likely to persist there, and because
of the declared need for development in rural areas (where
90 percent of Kenyans live), it would seem that the
laissez faire attitude adopted to date is not working very
well. Indeed, there is no indication that the buoyant
Kenyan economy is being Kenyanized very rapidly. This
is in contrast to the public service which, notwithstanding
its over 3,000 expatriate "advisers" and "technical assistants," is almost wholly Kenyanized as far as regular
personnel is concerned.

                    School Leavers and Dropouts:
                 The Basis of Nonformal Education

The rationale for Kenya's nonformal education is
largely to be found in the thousands of youths who fail
in the formal educational system. A child fails in one
of two ways: he may be unable to complete a school unit,
primary or secondary school, or he may complete it but
fail to secure a place either at a higher formal educational stage or in wage employment. In either case, the
aspirations that a youth has normally developed in his
brief, formal educational experience will be shattered.
It is largely in response to this disappointment that
nonformal educational schemes have been formulated.

The schemes under discussion in this study are concerned largely with primary school leavers and dropouts. The dimension of the problem of leavers is recognized to be gigantic but precise numbers have been unavailable for a variety of reasons. Although the primary school in Kenya theoretically involves children in the 6-13 age-group, in fact there are many primary school "children" over 20 years of age, and 20 percent of Standard 7 pupils are over 15. The repeater syndrome, less common at the secondary school stage, is large in primary schools. It is caused in large part by the determination of parents and their children that the latter should obtain the necessary grades on the Certificate of Primary Education examination in order to be placed in secondary school. It is also known that teachers encourage some of their students to repeat Standard 7, or even lower classes, to the same end. For these and other reasons primary school statistics tend to be inaccurate; the figures of the harambee, or unaided schools, are the most inaccurate.

The dropout factor is also substantial, but again one that is difficult to quantify. A number of general observations may be made. There are more dropouts among the poorer districts than in the richer. Inability to pay school fees is an obvious reason; but also important is the fact that pastoral families are more likely to maintain a casual attitude to formal schooling than others. There are large numbers of dropouts during the not infrequent famines, although many return later to classes and repeat them. In 1971, among 1.5 million primary students, dropout between Standards 1 and 6 was estimated to number 46,000 and the number discontinuing school after leaving Standard 7 was computed at 54,000.

By way of summary, it may be said that, despite Kenya's avowed intention of providing universal primary education and despite great progress made in expanding formal educational facilities since independence, the fact remains that close to half of the school age children of the nation never go to school at all. Of those enrolled, probably 10 percent are mere literal registrants. Well over a third of the primary school children are doomed as failures, being functionally illiterate and without any practical knowledge and skill. There is a marked imbalance between boys and girls in the Kenyan schools, and this means that the entire population suffers from underprovision of education for women. There is also a glaring imbalance between the various Kenyan regions.

There are other dimensions to consider. Although there is a considerable visible agricultural commercial growth (small scale and petty trade) in the rural areas, in overall terms it is growth and development in the urban areas that dominate Kenya's postindependence development. It is estimated that national income from the rural sector

is between one-seventh and one-eighth of income in the
modern nonagricultural sector and that this disparity is
constantly widening.[8] This means that the modern nonagricultural sector of the economy is going to attract more
and more Kenyan youths, especially those who are beneficiaries of any segment of the formal educational system.
Without substantial investment in agriculture and in
rural areas there is less and less to be earned in that
sector.

It is clear that the solution of the problem of education and employment for Kenyan youth cannot lie in expanding the formal system of education in the foreseeable
future. The sheer cost of providing universal primary
education places too great a burden on the limited resources of Kenya and would deal a crippling blow to other
necessary forms of social and economic development. It is
also agreed that the present educational system is unsuitable for reasons that we have seen. However, the
system is so rooted and entrenched in people's minds and
in the nation as a whole, that recommendations for a
radical or revolutionary change are more likely to find
themselves shelved in public libraries as interesting
but "impractical" proposals.

The nonformal educational schemes discussed in succeeding pages also do not offer clear directions for the
future because they are but a shadow of the formal educational system of Kenya. In many ways they seek to emulate
the formal system. In any case, youths who perform well
in the nonformal system try at the earliest opportunity
to secure a "permanent" placing in the modern nonagricultural sector of the economy and not, as intended, in the
rural areas.

Kenya's nonformal educational programs for rural
children and youth may be grouped into three main categories:

1. Supplementary Programs. These are designed to
    supplement the formal education system. Some
    are aimed at character building and the forma-
    tion of appropriate attitudes; others develop
    particular skills that may or may not be relevant
    to the needs of Kenyan youth. Many of them are
    the local branches of international organizations
    and are aimed at the school-going population.
    The following fall into this category:

        Young Farmers Clubs
        4-K Clubs
        Y.W.C.A.
        Y.M.C.A.
        Boy Scouts
        Girl Guides
        St. John's Ambulance
        Kenya Red Cross Society

> Outward Bound Trust
> Kenya Voluntary Development Association
> World Assembly of Youth

2. Follow-up Programs. These attempt to provide primary school leavers and dropouts from the formal system with some form of training and education that will equip them with skills for employment or self-employment, preferably in the rural areas. They include the following:

> Village Polytechnics
> National Youth Service
> Correspondence Courses
> Christian Industrial Training Centres

3. Alternatives to Formal Education. These are for the unschooled who are not covered by other educational programs. They are basically in the form of literacy classes and are run by various organizations such as the following:

> Youth Clubs/Centres
> Farmers and Rural Training Centres
> Maendeleo ya Wanawake (Progress for Women)
> Community Development Divison of the Ministry of Co-operatives and Social Services

Major features of the three categories of nonformal education activities are described in the following pages, making special reference to some of the programs--the Young Farmers Clubs, the 4-K Clubs, the Village Polytechnics, the National Youth Service and the Youth Clubs/Centres.

PROGRAMS SUPPLEMENTING FORMAL SCHOOLS

The programs included under this category are the entire range of extracurricular activities provided by schools, voluntary organizations, and government for the purpose of enriching youths' education and making them better citizens. At one end of the spectrum are the Boy Scout and Girl Guide movements, which engage youths of different age levels in various activities. At the other end of the spectrum are the Young Farmers Clubs. Each of these may be said to advance the same "philosophy": that to be a responsible citizen one must have a useful contribution to make to society, and that contribution can only be made through self-discipline, training, and

dedication. All these programs are designed to stress the
behavioral aspects of youths' growth and development. The
instructional programs are not in themselves adequate to
made a youth stand on his own, nor are they available,
except in rare circumstances, outside a formal educational
institution. Two such programs are described here.

Young Farmers Clubs (YFC)

The Young Farmers Clubs (and the 4-K Clubs described
later) attempt to provide agricultural knowledge and experience primarily to Kenyan youths who go to a formal
school. These clubs are modeled on experience and practice in other countries--particularly those of the 4-H
movement in the United States and the Young Farmers Clubs
in the United Kingdom. In 1949, Thomas Hughes-Rice, an
Agricultural Officer, convened a conference in Nyeri
District that attracted over 200 local youth delegates
and resulted in the formation of four Young Farmers Clubs
before the end of one year with membership in each ranging
from 60 to 120. By 1951, with the cooperation of other
Agricultural Officers, the clubs numbered 25 in Nyeri.

By 1953 the movement attracted the support of the
Commissioner for Community Development and a special five-
week course for 25 YFC leaders was organized at the Jeanes
School. It was believed that YFCs encouraged youths to
take up agriculture after leaving school instead of drift-
ing to the towns. The clubs, it was hoped, would also
provide government officials valuable contact with young
men, and through this contact an agriculturally informed
public would be created.[9]

By 1955 there were 39 clubs with 4,122 members in
Central Province. Clubs were also organized in Nyanza
Province, and the movement made reasonable progress until
independence, particularly remarkable in view of the fact
that no officer in any department was specifically assigned
to the program.

Since independence the largest YFC membership has
been in the secondary schools. As of 1972 there were 160
clubs with a membership of over 6,000. The aim was to
open a branch in every secondary school. In addition the
organization is looking forward to participation by the
Teacher's Training and Agricultural Colleges, which have
been made eligible for membership as well.

How, in fact, do the YFCs operate as educational
units and to what end? The Agricultural Society of Kenya
(ASK), a professional organization of agricultural experts,
organizes visits by YFCs to "modern farms" that have shown
themselves to be of a high standard and profitability.
Visits are also arranged to research stations and to industries allied to agriculture. Whenever and wherever the

ASK stages agricultural shows, parties of YFC members are taken round in order to impress upon them the virtues of agricultural production. Each club is an affiliate of ASK, which is responsible for the organizational details: formats for the conduct of meetings, internal organization, bookkeeping, and activity plans. There is, therefore, considerable uniformity throughout the YFC movement. All the clubs regard the local (district) or national agricultural show as the high point of their year's activity.

It appears that YFCs have failed to develop their own programs and have remained dependent on the ASK, whose handouts on pig-rearing, cattle-keeping, the growing of crops, and so on are used as inflexible directions, rather than as guidelines. The general impression is that there are many leisure talks by important people, safaris to urban centers to see movies, dances, and general social intercourse. Very little is actually being done by club members about the real job of an agricultural club, which is, to determine the proper use of the land and to learn the lessons of the shamba.

4-K Clubs

Closely related to the Young Farmers Clubs are the voluntary 4-K Clubs. In theory, the 4-K Clubs are not meant to be located in schools and thus may not technically be viewed as supplementary to formal education. Indeed the administrators of the clubs' program have in mind the promotion of agricultural education of youths in their homes as the primary objective. Nevertheless 4-K Clubs seem to thrive best when associated with (primary) schools. The term "4-K" refers to the Swahili words kuungana (unity), kufanya (work), kusaidia (assistance), and Kenya.

Aims of the Kenya 4-K program, geared to the pressing needs of rural Kenya, are the following:

1. to teach rural boys and girls better farm and home practices that will contribute toward better nutrition, health, and a higher standard of living
2. to teach youth to appreciate the dignity of labor and have respect for agriculture as a profession
3. to help youth to produce food for their families and for sale
4. to develop leadership among the membership and to prepare young people to be better citizens of the future by teaching them democratic practices and principles

From its inception the 4-K program has made a special effort to bring about changes in the habits of adult

farmers. To help accomplish this the leaders have emphasized a community-based rather than school-based organization. The expectation is that when a farmer observes
his son or daughter using an improved practice on the farm,
he is more likely to relate it to his own situation than
if he observed it at a school.

The 4-K Clubs, then, may be regarded as the extension
of the YFC idea into the rural household. Part of the
Kenya Rural Youth Program, it was started by the Ministry
of Agriculture and Animal Husbandry in 1963. By 1966, 899
clubs with 24,995 members had been formed. In 1972, there
were more than 1,000 clubs in 26 (out of 41) districts with
an estimated total membership of 26,000. The clubs were
led by 1,400 voluntary workers.

A club usually has from 26 to 32 members. Members are
organized into two age-groups, 8-16 years and 16-22 years.
While it is explicitly stated that the 4-K Clubs are for
farm youth, the majority of clubs seem to be attached to
a school or Youth Centre. A club is guided by an extension
officer who is a regular employee of the Ministry of Agriculture. He is assisted by adult volunteer leaders from
the community.

How effective is it as a movement? In a survey of its
effectiveness carried out in 1967 the conclusion was
reached that the introduction of 4-K Clubs into a school
improves the knowledge of good agricultural practices among
its members and also among the children in the school.
The survey also states that extension officers have tended
to be technical experts who concentrate on the largely
technical problems of particular aspects of agricultural
production and have not been well qualified to advise
farmers on the most appropriate policies from the stand-
point of farm business as a whole.

Generally the only men trained in rural extension work
in each district tend to be the District Agricultural
Officers. These people are so bogged down with paper-work
and serve such large areas that it is impossible for them
to pay attention to local activities. Their divisional
lieutenants, the Assistant Agricultural Officers, the
majority of whom hold diplomas, are equally overwhelmed
by distances to travel and administrative work. On-the-
ground extension work, therefore, is left to the local
Agricultural Assistants and Agricultural Instructors,
most of whose knowledge of agricultural extension is
minimal, largely limited to the use of fertilizers and
insecticides and to planting in straight lines. The
consequence is that there is no effective communication
between these local personnel and the 4-K Clubs, whose
youthful members recognize clearly the limitations of
these supposed experts.

If it were asked how many members of YFCs and 4-K
Clubs continue being interested in agriculture after
formal schooling, the answer would be "negligible." In

other words this whole exercise in nonformal education is
a stopgap operation during school days that keeps the kids
busy. There is no evidence that their engagement with
agriculture, apart from encouraging a few students to go
to Egerton and Embu (training institutions for extension
workers) for formal agricultural training, leaves any
permanent stamp on the youth. YFCs and 4-K Clubs are
comparable to physical education exercises in school:
good while they last, but to be put aside once school is
over.

FOLLOW-UP PROGRAMS FOR SCHOOL LEAVERS

By far the most impressive programs of nonformal
education are those which cater to the school leavers.
Kenyan leaders have overreached themselves in expressing
concern for this category of youth. Because the great
majority of the leavers of primary and secondary schools
do not find formal employment (the formal educational
system is still geared largely to turning out white-collar
job seekers) the planners of nonformal education are
generally interested in devising programs that give the
school leaver practical know-how leading to paid employment.
There are several programs which may be included in
this category. The oldest of them include government and
commercial vocational and inservice training. The extra-
mural (adult education) programs of the University and all
but a few adult literacy classes and public lectures fall
into this category. The government-run National Youth
Service (NYS) might well fall into this category too, but
because the NYS originally took in a larger proportion of
illiterates or semiliterates and still does so, we shall
discuss the program later among the alternatives to the
formal school system. The most novel of the follow-up
programs is undoubtedly the Village Polytechnic (VP) program.

The Village Polytechnic

Of the many problems to which the National Christian
Council of Kenya (NCCK) has addressed itself, the plight
of the school leavers is probably the most important. This
was for good reason because the Christian Council had
earlier persuaded the government to change its eight-year
primary school system into one of seven years, a change
that was in part responsible for aggravating the primary
school leaver problem. In 1966 a working party of the
Council considered the problem of future education, training, and employment of primary school leavers, and published

its recommendations in the famous document <u>After School-What?</u>[10] The concept of the Village Polytechnic as a solution to the problem of employment and education for primary school leavers was outlined in this document and the program was initiated with the establishment in 1966, under NCCK sponsorship, of the first VP in Nambale in Busia District. Three more--Mucii wa Urata in the Mwea-Tebere Scheme, Ndere, and Maseno Depot--were established by 1968.

There were three important components in the organization of the VP movement. First, of course, was the NCCK as the initiator of the project, which continued to provide the movement with the necessary propulsion and training as well as funds. If a local authority or the local church or other body was to be associated with a given VP by providing some of the funds, it became the "sponsor." Sponsors tended to be churches, and in the VPs that have been established since 1967 church support, the second component, has been the key to success. The third component of the VP movement was the local committee, or Management Committee, consisting of the local leaders at a given center, village, or location, who employed the staff to man the VP.

A striking feature of the organization is the by-passing of the Kenya Provincial Administrative System. The VP movement has so far been "administered directly"; that is, there has been direct communication between the rural committee and the VP committee in Nairobi. Because the number involved has so far been small, this has not created any problems. The NCCK, however, has not got the staff and means to cope with VPs on a large scale and the coordination function has been gradually transferred to the Ministry of Co-operatives and Social Services.

The VP movement began at the same time that the Kenyans were directing their energies to rural development through the self-help, or harambee, movement. In a sense also, it coincided with the official Special Rural Development Projects (SRDP), which followed the Kericho Conference on Education, Employment, and Rural Development. The NCCK may thus be credited with spearheading policy for the solution of a national problem.

The setting up of a VP requires considerable local self-help momentum, because the essence of the VP concept is local community control. Local leaders must therefore see their local problems in relation to national development. They must also define their own problems in terms of tasks that village people themselves can undertake, such as the construction of bakeries, the making of bricks, the building of stone houses, and the establishing of a blacksmithery.

Parallel to the meeting of local needs is the task of finding employment for unemployed primary school educated youth. In attempting to solve both problems in one move, emphasis is placed on building intradependent communities. In seminars organized for the VP managers, the central theme of self-reliance is illustrated by a money game, which shows how the VP can create the products and services that will keep the money within the local area.

Expansion of VPs

The VPs are being gradually taken over by the Youth Development Division of the Department of Social Services, and Youth Centres (described later) are being converted to VPs. In 1971/72, 40 VPs were aided by the Department of Social Services, and this number rose to 60 in 1972/73, with the projected figure for 1973/74 being 75. It is proposed that there will be 250 VPs in 1977/78. Table 5.3 shows the distribution of existing VPs and the number of available places. The regional disparity that was apparent in the allocation of places in the formal education system appears again in the case of VPs, with Central Province being the most favored and, considering the size of its population, Rift Valley falling far behind. At the moment (1973), VPs cater to 0.5 percent of the total 16-19 age-group, or 2 percent of the primary school leavers.

Curriculum

There is a distinction between the curricular objectives of the initiators of the VP movement and the subjects now taught. Originally, agriculture was intended to be an important, if not the dominant, element of the curriculum. It was argued that since the VP would be in areas where subsistence agriculture was the mode of life, the VP was to be the place for imparting elementary knowledge and techniques for small-scale farming. The hope was to enable the youths to assist their parents to farm their smallholdings scientifically and more profitably. However, quite early in the program the curriculum took a more technical turn and by 1970 the following subjects were offered in 14 of the VPs covered in a survey.

Subjects	Number of VPs Teaching the Subject
Craft/Skill	
Carpentry	12
Masonry	7
Tailoring (male)	2
Tailoring/dressmaking (female)	2
Domestic science, including baking and some dressmaking (female)	5
Typing (male and female)	1
Sign writing	1
Tractor driving (special course, three months)	1

Subjects	Number of VPs Teaching the Subject
Craft/Skill	
Poultry keeping (special course, three months)	1
Tin smithery (bicycle repairing, option in the evening)	1
Agriculture	
Agriculture (male)	10
Animal husbandry	1
Academic Subjects	
English	11
Mathematics	10
Technical training	3
Science	1
Hygiene (female)	2
Civics	5
Religious knowledge	7
Swahili	1
Recreational	8

In addition, at two of the VPs some on-the-job learning took place. At Karima quarrying was taught. At Soy the following were taught: rabbit keeping, masonry, agriculture-vegetable growing, poultry keeping, tin smithing, baking, well-digging, bookkeeping, carpentry, beehive making, and quarrying.

The curricula have not varied much in the last two years. Perhaps the most important ingredient of VP curricula is on-the-job training, in which trainees are encouraged to determine the needs of the community and then to design and construct things that meet the need-- if possible with local materials. Newly acquired business training is useful in marketing items made by the trainees, either through cooperatives formed for the purpose or possibly exhibitions, such as the agricultural shows held in most districts of the country. Unlike the formal school the VP has to translate its training into tangible results; technical skills alone do not create jobs. For this reason elementary business management has become an important part of the training.

Of course, the effectiveness of the curriculum, in the last analysis, depends heavily on the availability of an able and imaginative director. For example, the success of the VP at Soy (in the Rift Valley Province) is in large part due to the perceptive and adaptable director, formerly a farm manager, who had acquired skills in a number of trades.

Costs

One of the chief attractions of the VPs has undoubtedly been their low running costs. Of course, the more

TABLE 5.3

Government-Approved Village Polytechnics, Nov. 1973

District	Number	Total Enrollment	Percentage of Total Enrollment and Population*
CENTRAL			
Kiambu	4	281	
Muranga	3	365	
Nyandarua	2	65	
Kirinyaga	2	232	
Nyeri	4	226	
		1,169	30.5 (15.3)
COAST			
Taita	4	220	
Mombasa	1	107	
Kilifi	2	74	
Kwale	3	99	
Tana River	1	37	
		537	14.0 (8.6)
EASTERN			
Embu	1	89	
Machakos	2	194	
Kitui	2	94	
Meru	3	203	
Isiolo	1	20	
		600	15.6 (17.4)
NORTH EASTERN			
Garissa	1	15	
Wajir	1	40	
Mandera	1	30	
		85	2.2 (2.2)
NYANZA			
Siaya	3	200	
Kisumu	2 (one new)	72	
S. Nyanza	3	211	
Kisii	3	105	
		588	15.3 (19.4)
RIFT VALLEY			
Kajiado	1	26	
Narok	1	30	
Kericho	1	74	
Nandi	1	19	
Elgeyo Marakwet	1	69	
Baringo	1	30	
Laikipia	1	20	
W. Pokot	1	38	
Turkana	1	12	
		318	8.2 (20.4)

(continued)

TABLE 5.3 continued

District	Number	Total Enrollment	Percentage of Total Enrollment and Population*
WESTERN			
Kakamega	4	290	
Busia	3	162	
Bungoma	2	87	
		539	14.1 (12.3)
GRAND TOTAL	67	3,836	100.0

*Percentages of national population in the provinces are shown in parenthesis. These do not add up to 100 percent, because population of Nairobi is excluded.
    Source: The Kenya Village Polytechnic Programme.

moderately a VP is equipped and the larger the number of trainees, the more economical is the operation. Because a great deal of self-help goes into the total effort and recurrent expenditures are often confused or combined, with capital costs (for example, the employment of trainees in the construction of VP buildings), it is difficult to come out with a clear picture. Estimate of costs made in 1969 are helpful. In that year cost per annum per student varied from K Sh220 to K Sh1,026 (the mean given was K Sh624). Actual costs of running a polytechnic ranged from K Sh3,012 per annum to K Sh45,409 (Mucii wa Urata). Rough estimates of running an average VP have been re-constructed as follows:

Staff cost: director, @ K Sh600 per month:	K Sh7,200
instructors @ K Sh375 per month:	K Sh4,500
Maintenance and improvement of build-ings (cost of equipment only)	K Sh800
Depreciation and replacement tools (K Sh20 per student)	K Sh600
Equipment, less cost of sales, K Sh20 per student	K Sh600
Books, manuals, and so forth, K Sh20 per student	K Sh600
Travel, stationery, and so forth	K Sh1,500
TOTAL	K Sh14,800
Cost per student per annum (30 students)	K Sh493

The most expensive item of recurrent expenditure, namely salaries of managers and instructors, is relatively small compared with those of formal institutions or even

other nonformal establishments. A VP needs on the average
something like three instructors, one of whom acts as the
director. The charges paid to them range in honoraria
from K Sh30 to 60 a month or in actual wages from K Sh100
to 400.

The VP movement has received funds from various
sources. The NCCK has been the channel for some international and local aid (for example, the World Council of
Churches and the Motor Mart Trust). In addition local
authorities, local churches (through collections), self-
help units, and fees have constituted the other sources
of income. Efforts have been made to find more income
through the sale of items made by VPs.

Each Polytechnic has its own pattern. Much depends
on its contracts, the initiative of its organizers, and
the interest generated among local organizations supporting the VP. While the early VPs (for example, Nambale)
received grants of K Sh10,000, more recently a tendency
has been for grants from outside sources to be less frequent and smaller. In the years to come the biggest
sources of financial support for the VPs will be central
government grants and self-help collections. It is possible that revenue from contracts and sales of work produced by the VPs will also constitute an important proportion of VP finances.

Observations on the VP

To a large extent the laissez faire political approach
to economic questions that has characterized the Kenyan
government's stand in many matters has favored the VP
movement in its early period of development. Government
finance has not been necessary; its participation has
been on a voluntary basis. The government has now recognized the potential of the VP movement and is consequently
prepared to play a more active role in expansion of the
program. In any case neither the NCCK nor the church
organizations that have so far shouldered the burden of
the VP movement are in a position to implement the 1966
Working Party's resolution to the fullest possible extent.
Although there is no guarantee that the government will be
more capable, potentially it is the best organization for
the task.

A real danger for the VP movement lies in the movement's acting as a shadow system of education, playing an
ancillary role to the formal system. By attracting
"failures" and the children of the poor, the VP movement
has encouraged trainees to "fall in line" as soon as
possible with those who have succeeded in the formal
system and are employed in urban areas. Those charged
with VP management have shown a tendency toward formali-
zing their system, which in turn has suggested the need
for certification, whose magic the VPs (whose stand on

certification is in marked contrast to that of National
Youth Service) cannot and, in fact, do not dispel.

Furthermore, it may be argued that the VPs and similar
efforts designed to cater to those who have failed in
the formal system are meant for the members of a new class.
Kenya society is fast becoming stratified. Already in
existence is a fairly definable elite--the professional
class, large-scale farmers, and businessmen. The rest
are the smallholders--the great majority of Kenyans--and
a small number of semiskilled and unskilled workers. It
is unlikely that the children of the elite will find their
way into the VP. Their parents are in a position to
place them in state-run (high or low cost) secondary
schools. Thus the VP movement may be said to be designed
to meet the needs of the children of a new lower class.

Such a description,[11] however, should not ignore
the constructive role of the movement. When large numbers
of primary school leavers and dropouts are thrown on the
employment market without hope of achieving satisfaction,
the VP acts as a means of siphoning off this threat. In
providing local youths with some form of vocational training, it also transforms many from being semieducated,
unskilled unemployable individuals into semiskilled employable citizens. But in a wider sense it casts doubt
on the national educational policies as a whole and the
formal system in particular, which "writes off" as being
unemployable or unsuitable for further studies those
youths who fail a given examination or do not pass at a
particular level. In either case the youth is transformed
from being a "neutral" individual to a "negative" one.

Comparisons between the formal system of education
and the VP movement suggest themselves at every hand.
David Court has attempted to distinguish the various
features of the VP and the formal school.[12]

Dimension	Formal School	VP
Catchment areas	National	Local
Recruitment criteria	Formal qualifica-tions	Interest
Location	Centralized; institu-tional	Dispersed
Objectives of Training	Short-term, graduation to next level; long-term, wage employment	Self-employ-ment and family im-provement
Curriculum	Standardized and group oriented	Individual-ized
Medium of instruc-tion	English	Vernacular and Swahili
Standards	National certified	Self and local de-mands

Dimension	Formal School	VP
Form of instruction	Classroom teaching	On-the-job learning
Leadership	Hierarchical-authoritarian	Participatory
Time period	Chronological sequence of predetermined periods	Time necessary to master skill in question

Whereas formal education is wasteful, VP training has shown possibilities of greater economy. Where the formal system has regarded education and schooling as synonymous, VP has insisted that education is a commodity useful to both the individual and his community. Where the formal approach is elitist, the VP movement, by holding that everybody can be useful, maintains a traditional (precolonial) egalitarian structure of society.

The National Youth Service

Objectives

The 1966/1970 Development Plan outlined the objectives of the National Youth Service (NYS) as follows:

1. to put the unemployed youth into an environment that will inculcate good citizenship and provide an opportunity to contribute to the social and economic development of the country
2. to promote national unity by bringing together young persons from all parts of Kenya for training and work in a project of national importance
3. to help alleviate unemployment hardships among young persons, by providing employment, education and training to prepare them for future productive employment after completion of their service
4. to contribute to the economy of the country by helping to conserve, rehabilitate and develop Kenya's natural resources

The NYS began as a voluntary work and educational program for Kenyan citizens between the ages of 16 and 30; it was classified as a Disciplined Force under the Kenya Constitution and the National Youth Service Act of 1965. The planners of NYS decided at the very beginning that only under military discipline could a large number of men and women, living mostly in camps, and yet hardly paid for their work, be banded together effectively. In

the view of the Director, youth service projects in many
other countries had failed because their officers did not
employ the technique of military discipline.

What the NYS planners set out to do is well expressed
in the words of President Kenyatta:

> The young people who enlist in the Service
> will be dedicating two years of their lives to
> their country, without thought of personal re-
> ward other than the knowledge that the work
> they accomplish will be of positive and tangible
> contribution to the rapid economic, political
> and social development of Kenya.
> The NYS is a challenge. Those who join
> must be prepared to work hard and accept dis-
> cipline. There is no room in the Service for
> tribalism, parochialism or racial antagonism
> and those who enlist must do so in a spirit of
> brotherhood determined to show that youth from
> all parts of Kenya can work and live together
> in amity.[13]

The origins of NYS go to the nationalist agitation
during the closing years of colonialism. In the first
year of independence, the members of the youth wings of
the country's political parties became an embarrassingly
vocal community, as virtually all were unemployed, often
unhoused, and poor. The NYS was established, therefore,
with the immediate goal of alleviating the frustration of
the youthful freedom-fighters. In its long-term planning
the NYS set out to provide a pool of trained manpower to
undertake a variety of duties, including support of the
Armed Forces and Civil Service when called upon.

NYS Training Program

As noted earlier the NYS enlistment is for two years.
Trainees are recruited in batches, called companies, of
100 people. The standard timetable[14] calls for two
months of basic training (drill), followed by six months
of project farm work and six months of centralized full-
time education. Each of these segments totals a full
nine months of training before the final four months are
given over to "general duties." This apparently rigid
scheduling of the training period is misleading, because
the NYS does not take the view that work and education
can be separated into watertight compartments. The project work is held to be an education in good work habits,
although much of it is conducted in the field. As each
company progresses, its numbers dwindle, members continually being withdrawn to undertake specialist courses, such
as agricultural training, storekeeping, accounts and
clerical work, and health inspection duties.

The service men and women, for the most part, are primary school leavers. There are, however, illiterates among the recruits and some with several years of secondary schooling. The NYS undertakes to improve whatever formal education level the recruit had reached on joining the service. Thus, those who are illiterate leave the service after two years able to read and write, having mastered the 3Rs. The NYS does not set tests that correspond to the formal school tests, but conducts aptitude tests to dtermine how service men and women should be placed in the various work projects. In classroom instruction Swahili is written, English is spoken. Among the subjects taught are civics, health science, agriculture, and general science, in addition to English and mathematics.

The NYS maintains an educational center at Gilgil, and service men and women therefore keep getting in and out of Gilgil during their overall two years' enlistment. The NYS also maintains a vocational training center at Mombasa that is geared to the Ministry of Labour Trade Test System. The center at Mombasa takes 300 to 400 service men at a time and trains them in masonry, carpentry, motor vehicle mechanics, fitting and turning, electronics, and plumbing. One-third of the group leaves after each fourth month of the year, having sat for the government Grade 3 Trade Test. Those who show exceptional competence are sent to the NYS Central Workshop in Nairobi for the Grade 2 Trade Test.

It is estimated that 80 to 90 percent of the service men pass the Grade 3 Trade Test of the Labour Ministry on the first attempt. It is also of note that girls perform well and successfully take such trades as fitting and turning, which had never before been entered by women. Virtually all those who pass the Trade Test and have good recommendations are in great demand by industry.

Other types of training offered are in agriculture, plant operating, office work, and storekeeping. In agriculture, service men who show particular aptitude are sponsored in a six months' course at one of the Ministry of Agriculture Farmers' Training Centres. They then go back to one of the NYS farms for further practical experience in a supervisory role. They may then qualify for a special certificate that will enable them either to gain employment on private farms or to go on to advanced training with the government Agriculture or Veterinary Departments. This is one of the areas that causes the NYS some concern. Virtually all the service men are poor, and their poverty is one of the reasons why they were recruited into the service in the first instance. Consequently, they do not have the capital to enable them to go out in self-employment, as they do not have land on which to practice and apply their newly acquired skills. They are more likely to be exploited by farmers who appreciate their qualifications, but are unwilling to give

them monetary recognition. On the other hand, the service
man who qualifies through the Trade Test System is readily
a marketable commodity.

NYS teachers are qualified, approved, and employed by
the Teachers' Service Commission. In addition, there are
uniformed cadets who act as instructors, especially at
Mombasa. A severe shortage of qualified technical instructors in the country has affected the NYS from time to time.
Indeed, although Kenyan counterpart instructors are being
trained, the majority of the instructors for the vocational
training center at Mombasa has been provided by the World
Peace Organization for Rehabilitation and Training of
Geneva, under a contract financed by the U.S. Agency for
International Development (AID).

NYS Projects

The most striking feature of the NYS is its construction projects. To get an idea of the heavy capitalization
involved, a few statistics are necessary. The NYS value
their current (1972) assets at Ł9 million. They operate
a fleet of 568 vehicles and machines, ranging from small
cars to the largest bulldozers available, valued at
Ł2,629,000. In 1972 they had a tactical staff of 233, made
up of 9 professional engineers, 216 technicians, and 8
others. In addition NYS occupies property and buildings
valued at a fairly high sum.

NYS property and equipment have been acquired with
assistance from a number of sources, particularly the
Kenya government and U.S. AID. The major part of NYS heavy
equipment was given by U.S. AID between 1964 and 1969. The
total value of equipment given amounted to Ł524,449. In
addition, U.S. AID contributed to the NYS running expenses.
The total cost of all these amounted to Ł714,397 bringing
the total U.S. AID gift to NYS for 1964-1969 to Ł1,238,836.

Well furnished with equipment from foreign grants, and
with recurrent expenditure taken care of by the government,
the NYS has played a prominent role in the implementation
of the national development projects. The following is a
list of the projects which have been undertaken or are
being undertaken by the NYS:

1. Road Building: NYS first built the access roads
    in one of the national parks. It then undertook
    a 335-mile road access to Aberdare Mountains; it
    then moved on to complete a Ł500,000 road project
    serving the Seven Forks Hydro-electric works.
    Currently it is constructing a 300-mile access
    road through the semiarid northern Kenya to link
    the country with Ethiopia (to be completed in
    1974). The NYS has built other small roads and
    bridges.

2. <u>Bush Clearing and Tree Planting</u>: NYS has cleared 146 acres of dense bush near Lake Victoria, both to combat tsetse fly infestation and to open up new areas of land for settlement. It has also planted thousands of trees (1,000 trees were planted at Kinangop settlement land).

3. <u>General Earth Work</u>: This includes construction of air strips in remoter areas of the country.

4. <u>Agricultural Research</u>: The NYS has carried out experiments in growing tobacco and mulberry trees (for silk). It has also built fish ponds.

Assessment of NYS

NYS is the most expensive nonformal education organization in Kenya. The ILO Mission found that the cost of keeping a service man for a year was ₤241 4s. This compares with ₤13 for keeping a student in a rural primary school for a year; ₤60, in a government secondary aided school; ₤100, in a government secondary technical and vocational school; ₤100, in the Kenya Polytechnic; and ₤882, in the University of Nairobi.

The NYS, of course, is more than an educational institution. It trains its service men to improve themselves and at the same time makes them perform productive tasks; on the other hand, an ILO evaluation team found the cost of NYS Development Projects slightly higher than would be the cost for the same tasks if performed by private firms.

From the time of its establishment until 1972 a total of 17,481 service men had been through the NYS mill; the number still in service in 1972 was 3,730. Although there are contradictory assessments of the proportions of trainees in wage employment, the ILO team assumed that 65 percent of ex-service men were "not known to be employed." The Director of the NYS informed the writer that 6,040, or approximately 34 percent of all ex-service men had been directly placed by the NYS by the middle of 1972. However, the question arises: should NYS be seen as an expensive training organization or should it also be judged as an organization performing national development tasks? What is clear is that the NYS cannot be regarded as the means of solving Kenya's unemployment problem. Its efforts, impressive as they are, pale to insignificance when one takes into consideration the large number of primary school leavers and the rural youths in the country who are not provided for.

Institute of Adult Studies,
University of Nairobi

The Institute of Adult Studies is divided into three major divisions with provision for a possible fourth

division, an adult education training unit. The entire
organization is headed by a director. The three existing
divisions are Extra-Mural Division, Correspondence Course
Unit, and the Adult Studies Centre.

Extra-Mural Division

The smallest of the three departments or divisions
of the Institute, the Extra-Mural Division concerned
itself during its first years of operation with providing
secondary school-level courses for adults as well as
courses of general interest (for example, politics and
economics) to the working public. English was the most
popular of the formal subjects; accounting and bookkeeping,
among the nonschool subjects.

In offering school subjects, the Extra-Mural Division
made use of all available local high-level manpower. The
majority of its tutors--taken from the county or Municipal
Hall, private companies, and government offices--were
graduates or people of university level, professionally
qualified as lawyers or accountants. The division has thus
made use of the limited resources of university material
available in a given locality. The courses, however, are
available only in the urban areas.

In addition to its "formal" evening classes, the
Extra-Mural Division conducts weekend seminars on topics
pertaining to national development at selected centers
outside Nairobi. More recently, the division has been
exploring the possibilities of using the mass media,
especially radio and television, for educational purposes.
In 1972 the Extra-Mural Division also organized a pilot
training program for teachers of adult literacy classes.

Correspondence Course Unit[15]

The Correspondence Course Unit (CCU), a second division of the Institute, is a more recent development.
Begun in 1966, priority was given in its early years to
courses that prepare adults, particularly school teachers,
for upgrading purposes. It was noted that of the 37,923
teachers employed in Kenya's primary schools 10,438 were
not professionally qualified. The CCU therefore sought
to assist in upgrading the primary teachers. At the same
time the CCU conducted inservice training courses for
unqualified teachers in collaboration with the Kenya
Institute of Education.

In 1968, 90 percent of registered CCU students were
teachers, and the small remainder were clerks, farmers,
members of armed forces, cooperative staff, and housewives.
The curriculum, geared to the junior secondary education
system and worked out by the Ministry of Education, includes English, Swahili, history, geography, mathematics,
biology, and physical science. The instructional program
is comprised of the following:

1. a correspondence study guide, text books, and other teaching materials, such as maps, mathematical instrument sets, and science experiment kits
2. supplementary radio broadcasts covering the material in one or more lessons of the study guide
3. evaluation of students' lessons by qualified secondary and university teachers
4. occasional face-to-face teaching during residential courses (at the Adult Studies Centre, Kikuyu)

The CCU broadcasts are regularly listened to by many registered students. A survey conducted in 1969 by the Voice of Kenya (VOK), the state radio service, revealed that there were a minimum of 318,000 and a maximum of 817,000 adult listeners who had their radios tuned in when the CCU broadcasts were on the air. Since the broadcast reaches an audience wider than registered correspondent students, CCU has modified its radio lessons to cater to a larger public.

The average pass rate for CCU candidates is considerably higher than that of school or private candidates. In 1970, when the government-aided schools averaged 47 percent, unaided schools 20 percent, and the private candidates 13 percent, the CCU achieved a pass rate of 51 percent. It should be noted, however, that most of CCU students were school teachers attempting to improve their professional status.

The cost of this program is absorbed by the taxpayer through grants to the University, although students meet some part of the expenses through small fees. The cost of running the unit in one year is said to be Ŀ85,000. Of this amount about Ŀ30,000 comes from fees charged to students; the rest is a government grant through the University. Radio transmission facilities are made available free of charge by the Voice of Kenya. The number of students registered is approximately 4,000 (actual number in 1971 was 3,300).

Adult Studies Centre

The last of the three divisions of the Institute of Adult Studies is the Adult Study Centre at Kikuyu. It was originally set up by a liberal multiracial political organization called the Capricorn Africa Society to be a center for youths of all races. From the very beginning it was closely associated with the then University College, now the University of Nairobi, and in 1966 became fully integrated with the university through the Institute of Adult Studies.

The center conducts residential courses from time to time for 60 or so people in the public service, such as local authority councillors and government executive

officers. It has a residential teaching staff of 9 or 10
members, all of whom enjoy full status as university
lecturers.

ALTERNATIVE PROGRAMS FOR THE UNSCHOOLED

Considering the large proportion of Kenyans who
never see a formal classroom, almost any alternative at
all of nonformal education is inevitably of the greatest
consequence. Therefore, although they are limited in
scope, passing mention should be made of the literacy
classes of the NYS and also of the educational programs
of the armed forces and various commercial firms. Furthermore, although the full potential of the mass media as
educational instruments has not yet been fully grasped
and much broadcasting time on the centrally controlled
national radio is devoted to entertainment and commercials,
the fact that there are a million radios for a population
of 12 million means that virtually every village community
in Kenya is at the receiving end of national educational
propaganda--such as it is.
      Of the major programs offered as alternatives to for-
mal schooling, the most important are the youth centers
and clubs and the adult literacy classes.

Youth Centres and Clubs

Youth Centres were not originally conceived of as
educational programs, but rather as stopgap measures
designed to meet a crisis. Such, for example, was the
origin of the Starehe Boys' Centre in Nairobi (it has
since evolved into a formal school) that was established
in the dying years of the Mau Mau emergency for orphaned
and destitute children in the Central Province. The
first actual Youth Centre was set up in 1957 in the Nyere
District, the unashamed object of which was the prevention
of juvenile delinquency and vagrancy; another purpose was
to contribute to the effort to halt the rural-urban traffic.
It may then be said that the modern youth centers emerged
as a result of a negative response to the challenge of
social development. As time went on, it became clear
that delinquency and vagrancy were not forestalled simply
by recreational activities in a sophisticated boy scout
association. So emerged the idea that the Youth Centre
should become an educational establishment.
      Soon after independence a national Youth Council was
given the responsibility of directing youth centers. It
became the policy of that Council to provide such courses
of training as would lead youths to employment in such

vocations as masonry, carpentry, tin smithery, and domestic science. It soon became apparent, for instance, that the domestic science taught at the centers was totally irrelevant to the needs of most rural communities; therefore baking and all the modern cooking that used to feature prominently in the curriculum of young women at youth centers were dropped in favor of commercial courses, such as typing and bookkeeping, knitting, and tailoring. Over a period of time, the centers became almost indistinguishable from the Village Polytechnic devised in 1966 by the Christian Council of Kenya.

To see in some detail what was offered at a typical center we might consider the example of Kiptere in Kericho District. The local community depends on its single crop, tea, grown in smallholdings by farmers using small implements (such as jembes, watering cans, pails, and wheelbarrows) obtainable only at a distant town. The center was initiated by a local craftsman called Arap Rono. Under his direction the Kiptere Youth Centre was established, and a number of youths were taught how to make some of the needed tools. Those who completed the instruction set out to establish cooperative ventures for themselves. The idea caught the imagination of planners and Arap Rono has continued to work in behalf of the effort, first for the county council, later for the central government.

The government became involved in youth centers in a more tangible way with the introduction of a grants-in-aid scheme by the Ministry of Co-operatives and Social Services. The scheme provided for the employment by the government of an average of three instructors per grant-aided center. This included the manager of the center (who was expected to be a fully trained instructor) and two instructors who had passed at least the Grade 2 of the Trade Test of the Ministry of Labour. Only in the remoter areas of Kenya does the Ministry employ instructors with less than these qualifications. Some 40 centers were started in the 1971/72 fiscal year and 60 were operating in 1972/73. They are expected to cost the government a total of Ł200,000 per year.

The Youth Centres have not been supported financially by the Ministry of Co-operatives and Social Services and local authorities alone. The Ministry has until now given its support through the Kenya Association of Youth Centres, which in turn received funds from the Dulverton Trust, the Save the Children Fund, and other funds both known and anonymous. The funds derived from all these sources have assisted in the purchase of equipment; local authorities have on the whole been expected to employ staff. A difficulty that has arisen from this has been the employment by some local authorities of unqualified staff. In fact some local authorities have not paid full wages to staff but offered honoraria only. Thus quite often when

there has been no qualified staff, some of the centers
run by local authorities have had to close.

The Kenya Association of Youth Centres has played a
more practical role in providing training courses for
instructors. After 1953, training was offered at the
Jeanes School (now renamed the Kenya Institute of Education), but since 1963 most of the training has been given
at the Government Training Centre at Maseno. The training
offered has not been adequate because the Centre has been
fully occupied with other courses and there have been
inadequate funds to meet the running expenses of the
course.

The differences between youth centers and VPs have
increasingly narrowed. At one time the VP tended to
take in CPE leavers only, while the centers took in CPE
leavers, primary school dropouts, and illiterate youths
as well--much as the NYS does. The VPs' tendency to
discriminate made the centers appear to be inferior.
Furthermore, the VPs were better equipped and more attractive as a means of alternative education to primary school
leavers of higher aspirations than those of the average
youth. The recent (1973) position of the youth centers is
that they have become lumped together under the now rapidly
expanding village polytechnic program. Wherever the youth
centers have been established they have continued to serve
the local community but primarily by offering the VP type
of curriculum. As a result some uniformity of educational
opportunities has been introduced. At the same time, however, there has been a major departure from the original
conception of the role of Youth Centres: they started
as places offering an alternative educational opportunity
to unschooled youth; they now have joined the scramble
for taking on the training of the already schooled.

Programs of the Adult Education Division

The Adult Education Division in the Ministry of Cooperatives and Social Services began its life in 1966 as
a tiny unit of the Ministry of Labour and Social Services.
After a number of transfers during which, for a time, it
was part of the giant Ministry of Education, it eventually
found a permanent home in the new Ministry of Co-operatives
and Social Services. It has grown rapidly. Headed by a
Senior Education Officer, it had a staff of 85 in 1970,
not counting three Provincial Adult Education Officers,
one School Inspector, and an Adult Education Officer in
each of the districts.

At first the Division was concerned largely with
adult literacy; now it has many more programs, although
adult literacy continues to be its most important concern.
A policy statement issued in 1972 stated that the program

is geared towards "national development and the general improvement of the living conditions of the people." Attempt is made to meet this objective by taking the following steps:

1. organization and development of the National Literacy Campaign as a functional literacy and numeracy program throughout the country, using the development programs of other institutions as guides
2. organization of vocational and technical training programs, plus a variety of other courses, seminars, lectures, and public meetings on subjects of national and cultural importance
3. organization and development of formal education programs to take adults, on a part-time basis, through to CPE and other public examinations, while plans are being made to introduce adult-oriented and recognized CPE equivalents more relevant to adult needs
4. research, curriculum development, and inservice training
5. coordination of district training centers with a view to developing them into multipurpose training centers
6. support of programs related to community education organized through community development, social welfare, youth development, and cultural activities of the Ministry of Co-operatives and Social Services
7. support of similar educational programs of voluntary agencies, local authorities, and other public bodies[16]

Literacy Program

The most important exercise undertaken by the Division is the National Literacy Campaign, the primary objective of which is the achievement of universal literacy, or the elimination of "the enemy number one."[17]

Accompanied by considerable publicity and propaganda, the campaign initially proposed that illiteracy be eliminated among the wage earners beginning with those in the public service. Later it proposed expansion of the campaign to the whole country and organization of classes at the village level. The aim of the planners was "functional literacy," conceived as a component of economic and social development projects.

There are three types of classes: self-help classes (client initiated and organized), voluntary agencies' classes, and government-sponsored classes. In 1969, out of a total of 62,000 people enrolled in literacy courses, 30 percent were in government-sponsored classes (about two-

thirds were women and about one-fifth were youths) and
the remaining 70 percent were in either community development or voluntary agency "self-help classes." An official
estimate for 1973 places total enrollments at around
100,000. In 1972 Adult Literacy Certificates were introduced for the first time. While large numbers have passed
through the adult literacy classes, it is apparent that
illiteracy is not really being wiped out. There is a
need, therefore, to conduct research to determine whether
adults once literate remain so. The Division as of now is
in no position to ascertain this.

The government-sponsored literacy classes are designed
as the first step toward eventually earning a full primary
equivalency certificate (which is an important motivating
factor for many participants in literacy courses). In
practice, however, only a small proportion--some 4,000 in
1970--go on to the follow-up primary school equivalency
program, run by the Department of Adult Education of
the Ministry of Education, and most of these live in
cities or larger towns. The complete "adult" part-time
primary course (including literacy) is contracted into
four years of part-time study, as against seven full-time
years in the schools. Earlier the adult curriculum was
essentially a carbon copy of the regular school curriculum,
but in 1970 the Ministry of Education agreed to recognize
a primary leaver equivalency certificate based on a considerably revised adult-oriented curriculum--including, for
instance, agriculture, home economics, and civics.

In addition to these there are opportunities (again
predominantly in the cities and rural townships) for out-
of-schoolers to continue with secondary education, particularly in a program offered by the University's Institute
of Adult Studies. The first two years of this course may
be taken by correspondence, the remainder by self-instruc-
tion supported by extramural classes. Again, however, the
numbers involved are fairly small.

Theoretically, these literacy programs and the subsequent equivalency courses, taken together, would appear
to provide a full-scale alternative to the formal school
system. But in practice it does not function in this
manner, for it was not designed to be an alternative route
to a secondary certification that would allow schoolage
children to bypass formal schooling altogether. By regulation these various programs are restricted to persons who
are 15 years old and above.

There are two major comments to be made on all literacy programs. First, it is wrong to maintain that they
are or should be exclusively for adults. It is known that
a fifth of the total enrollment in the classes is made up
of youths. In the poorly developed areas of the country,
literacy classes present an important opportunity for
youths who may otherwise never learn to read or write.
Second, there is far too little reading material available

to the newly literate. Newspaper distribution in the
country is governed by commercial interests, and in most
parts of rural Kenya papers are not a regular feature.
In addition the papers are in English and Swahili, and
newly literate tribesmen in the country cannot be expected
to read them unless they also learn a second language
while learning to read and write in their own. Finally,
the papers are sold at what amounts to prohibitive prices
for rural people.

Indeed, it would appear that apart from traders and
progressive farmers whose interests demand that they know
how to read, write, and add, the only form of functional
literacy in rural Kenya tends to be allied to religious
organizations. Most Christians are literate, perhaps
because a legacy of schooling has been nourished by the
church. Illiterate elders who become converted to
Christianity soon acquire literacy for the purpose of
enjoying the scriptures. This is one form of literacy
that is functional. There must be lessons to be learned
from this that can help other programs.

Other Adult Programs

So far we have been discussing programs that are, in
terms of content, related to formal education and are,
therefore, more youth-oriented. There are other equally
important programs that technically fall outside our
three-fold classification. These are adult programs that
are concerned directly with "better living" or personal
improvement. Some are of immediately professional or
material value to the individual; others have intangible
returns. At the very least, we should list a few.

Adult literacy is of course the most basic of these
programs. There are also Farmers and Rural Training
Centres spread over strategic places in Kenya. Recently
established are a couple of Large-Scale Farmers Training
Centres to help the new African large-scale farm owners.
There are numerous Homecraft Training Centres, and the
giant Maendeleo ya Wanawake Movement that organizes women
in numerous ways.

In the private and public employment sector, there
are a variety of inservice training programs whose value
is obvious enough. Also, as noted earlier, increasingly
important as an educational organ are radio and television.
The extent to which these media can be used for educational purposes will depend on how planners and policymakers address themselves to the question.

HARMONIZING NONFORMAL PROGRAMS

The great variety of nonformal education activities
and of sponsoring organizations that have proliferated

in Kenya pose coordinatory problems at both local and
national levels.

First, it must be stated that no one ministry or
national body is yet in a position effectively to take
cognizance of all the formal and nonformal endeavors and
to plan for their integrated and harmonious development.
While this function could be performed, for instance, by
the Ministry of Finance and Planning, it is too far from
a consensus in its thinking and too short in competent
staff to assume such a task at this time. Thus individual formal and nonformal programs still develop along
quite separate and often parallel paths.

Second, the perspective and foresight that permit
education--informal, formal, and nonformal--to be counted
among the many components leading to the development of
rural areas are still only slowly emerging. In the
various district programs comprising the Special Rural
Development Program, for instance, formal education was
allocated no role, although individual nonformal programs
like Village Polytechnics and district training centers
were taken into account and included in some of the local
development plans.

Managers and administrators of nonformal programs with
similar interests and similar educational problems or
clienteles have with varying degrees of success created
"umbrella" organizations to facilitate liaison and coordination. These include the Board of Adult Education, The
National Christian Council of Kenya, The National Council
of Social Services, and the Youth Council of Kenya, also
known as the Standing Conference on Youth.

Board of Adult Education

The Board of Adult Education was set up by an act of
Parliament in 1966 to advise the Minister (for the time
being responsible for adult education) on any matter
relating to adult education. Its membership was made
sufficiently representative of government, voluntary
agencies, and key educational establishments (for example,
the University), in order to give it the best expertise
and authority.

Although the Board is an independent body, it is
financed through the Ministry of Co-operatives and Social
Services, which currently holds the government's portfolio
for "adult education." The chairman of the Board is the
Assistant Minister for Education, an arrangement that
allows maximum liaison with the Ministry of Education.
The Board is large and meets two or three times a year,
delegating its specialized business to an executive
committee or to one of the specialist standing committees
set up to deal with different kinds of educational pro-

grams (such as, school equivalency, fundamental education, and skill training) and interdisciplinary committees dealing with such matters as research and training, finance and planning, and teaching materials and publications.

In addition to this central committee structure, in most districts there are also committees of the Board that consist of local bodies, both government and nongovernment, operating programs such as farmer training, literacy, cooperatives, women's education, and skill training. There can therefore be a flow of information between headquarters and field on the progress of these programs. The Board and its committees are serviced by a small permanent secretariat consisting of an Executive Secretary, an Assistant Secretary, and other clerical staff.

Over the past five years the Board, though not without its problems, has had considerable success in helping establish a broad conceptual understanding of the nature and potential of nonformal education as an agent of development. It has carried out operational research projects that are vital for future planning; for example, on the present financing of adult education, and the spread of the variety of rural training centers. It has formulated interagency plans for the development of integrated multipurpose training centers. It has reviewed and reported on the broad field of literacy training and school equivalency. And it has taken a lead in helping establish professional training to backstop the nonformal field.

Its potential remains to be fully exploited. Recent organizational changes (for instance, the one replacing the system of institutional representation with one based on named individuals) expose the difficulty of attaining adequate and continuous attendance and participation by member organizations. It remains to be seen whether this weakens the Board's effectiveness in relation to its constituent organizations. There are also plans for the Board itself to set up and administer an instructional and training center, which, it has been suggested, poses a threat to conventional jurisdictions of some of the operational organizations that attempt to perform the functions planned for this new center.

Both the National Council for Social Services and the NCCK are represented on the Board. Youth work, however, overtly at least, remains outside the Board's jurisdiction, a situation no doubt reflecting a fundamental weakness in concept and nomenclature, since many of the "adult" programs (for instance, literacy) are as important to adolescents and youths as to adults.

National Christian Council of Kenya

The NCCK traces its origins to 1913 when a group of
Protestant missionaries in Kenya, inspired by the contemporary ecumenical spirit, met at Kikuyu with a view to
formulating a common approach to their work. Attempts
at a united church failed, but the spirit of coordination
persisted and resulted in the founding of the Alliance
High School in Kikuyu in 1926 as Kenya's first secondary
school. In 1943, the Council then known as the Christian
Council of Kenya, was born. Among the issues the Council
addressed itself to then were the rehabilitation of
soldiers returning from the Second World War, and the
development of Christian education. During the Mau Mau
years (1952-60) the Council played a prominent role in
the rehabilitation of detainees, by tackling the social
problems of "villagization" and generally moderating both
government and settler opinion in the tense and racially
charged atmosphere. In the early 1960s, following unprecedented floods (which were preceded by an equally
severe drought) the Council moved into the sphere of famine
relief, especially among the Maasai and the Turkana--two
of the most severely hit pastoral tribes. This led the
Council to devise comprehensive agricultural and nutrition
projects. In this way, it may be seen how the Council
gradually moved into the sphere of nonformal education.

With the admission after independence into the fold
of a number of churches founded in Kenya by people other
than western missionaries, the Council changed its name
by prefixing the designation "National" to the "Christian
Council of Kenya."

NCCK consists of 18 churches developed with missionaries' support, 4 churches independently founded in Kenya,
6 mission societies with their own legal status, 10 other
local Christian organizations, and 2 probationary member
churches.

NCCK regards itself as playing the role of stimulating and initiating development programs. Wherever possible, it seeks to fit its programs into the government's
development plan. Often it has provoked government
interest and generated shifts in government's approach
and emphasis. Classic instances of the NCCK role are
publication of the influential document, After School,
What? in 1966, initial instigation of the VP, and encouragement of the government's massive expansion of the
VPs and the youth programs.

In attacking matters of this kind, NCCK is thoroughly
methodical, whenever there is a serious national problem,
such as a famine or unemployment, NCCK sets up a working
committee to analyze it and to make recommendations. It
makes use of the best expert advice available in the
country. The report of the working committee is then

discussed by the NCCK, which might adopt it for implementation or might recommend it to the government or to
its members. In this way, NCCK has played a most significant role in the formulation and implementation of
policies in education, famine relief, and rural development.

One of NCCK's most important units is the Conference
Center at Limuru, 15 miles north of Nairobi. The center
has a director and four resident tutors but can call on
at least 12 other tutors on a part-time basis. The job
of the conference center is to organize discussions and
workshops on any of the problems that NCCK has adopted
as its concern.

Other Coordinating Bodies

The Kenya National Council of Social Services (KNCSS)
was established in 1964 as a nonprofit limited company.
It consists of representatives from member organizations,
government ministries, and others. Its primary objective
is the promotion and coordination of social services in
Kenya. It has no legal powers to enforce any of its
recommendations and herein may lie its strength. It has
successfully brought under its umbrella the former youths'
and women's councils, by initiating a system of "standing"
conferences/committees (of which there were seven in
1970). The KNCSS is in a position to participate in many
spheres of public welfare.

The KNCSS has a full-time director and supportive
staff who are responsible to a managing executive committee
that is representative of a wide cross section of inter--
ested parties, both governmental and voluntary. Within
its limitations, the Council has discharged its responsibilities admirably, and it has done so, largely by bringing together for an exchange of ideas and experiences the
various organizations represented in it. Through seminars,
research, training programs, and so forth, it has provided
guidance in the advancement of social welfare in Kenya.

Of all the coordinating organizations in the sphere
of nonformal education, potentially the most important is
the Youth Council of Kenya. The Council had as its affi-
liates in 1972 over 30 organizations ranging from Dr.
Barnado's Homes to the Kenya UN Student Association.

At the moment, the Youth Council is concerned largely
with the purely spiritual and physical needs of the youth.
If it were to address itself to other equally compelling
educational needs of youth, it could find itself dramatically at the center of the total educational effort in
Kenya.

In late 1973 plans were in hand to formulate a comprehensive youth policy and to devise the coordinating

machinery for all youth activity with special emphasis on nonformal education. This is in part a reflection of the pioneering and thorough work of the NCCK and the KNCSS, both of which organizations, through their enquiries, research, and other activities, have demonstrated to the government that Kenya essentially has no firm youth policy.

CONCLUDING REMARKS

Review of nonformal education in Kenya leads to a number of general observations. First, Kenya has a rich variety of nonformal programs, but most are designed for those who are already schooled--even if partially or poorly so. Second, nonformal education in Kenya is a poor sister of formal education. Indeed, it can be argued that the present nonformal education programs are mere shadows of the formal education system of the country. Third, there is little or no central coordination of nonformal educational activities in the country.

The programs, separately or collectively, do not go very far in meeting the learning needs of rural out-of-school children and youths. The three significant programs for youths--the Youth Centres, the Village Polytechnics, and the National Youth Service--together serve only about six to seven thousand youngsters at a time. Of this number a large majority has completed at least seven years of primary education. In fact, concern for the primary school leavers has been the overriding influence in the determination of objectives and content of the programs. About two-thirds of all rural children and youths who do not go to primary school or drop out before completing it remain largely ignored by the nonformal education programs.

Even when the main concern is preparing primary school leavers for an occupation, the programs generally have not found a viable approach insofar as a livelihood on the land or in the informal economic milieu of the rural society is concerned. The programs have been more effective in teaching specific skills or making the youths generally better equipped for employment in the urban sector. There is also an increasing tendency for the nonformal programs, partially in response to parental expectations, to take on the features of formal institutions in content, method, and goal. The overall socioeconomic structure and the system of incentives reinforce this tendency. Thus, the youth center tends to become a substitute primary school and the VP an ill-equipped vocational school.

The multiple mechanisms for coordination of nonformal education have not caused adoption of a comprehensive view of the learning needs of children and youths or a

nationwide integrated effort to meet these needs. Nor
has there been sufficient progress in making the educational activities integral components of the process of
planning and implementing the special district rural development programs. It is true that the siting of certain
institutions has been influenced by the locations of the
rural development projects. But educational activities
have tended to be more peripheral than central, a situation reflecting partly the production-oriented bias of the
program in question and partly the indifferent progress
in its implementation.

    Positive elements in the Kenya situation, as already
noted, are that a number of innovative nonformal educational programs for rural youths are in operation, a
number of government and voluntary organizational structures exist, and there is a special emphasis on integrated
rural development which could provide a favorable context
for more effective nonformal educational efforts. All
these elements constitute a potential base for building a
comprehensive and relevant educational program for rural
youths.

NOTES

    1.   Philip H. Coombs, Roy C. Prosser, and Manzoor Ahmed, New
Paths to Learning for Rural Children and Youth (New York: International Council for Educational Development, 1973), Chapter 2.
    2.   Kenya Education Commission Report [The Ominde Report] (Nairobi,
1964), part 1, p. 25.
    3.   Kenya, Development Plan 1970-74 (Nairobi: Government Printer,
1969), p. 450.
    4.   International Labour Office (ILO), Employment, Incomes
and Equality: A Strategy for Increasing Productive Employment in Kenya
(Geneva, 1972), p. 517.
    5.   Ibid.
    6.   Kenya, Ministry of Education, Ministry of Education Triennial
Survey, 1964-66 (Nairobi: Government Printer, 1967), pp. 5-6.
    7.   The Ominde Report, op. cit., pp. 75-76.
    8.   Kenya, Report of the Commission of Inquiry, Public Service
Structure and Renumeration Commission [The Ndegwa Commission Report]
(Nairobi: Government Printer, 1971), pp. 43-44.
    9.   J.J. Corry, "History of Agricultural Education in Kenya"
(Ph.D. thesis, University of Wisconsin, 1970), pp. 154-156.
    10. After School, What?--A Report on the Further Education,
Training and Employment of Primary School Leavers, prepared by a
Joint Working Party of the Youth Department of the Christian Council
of Kenya and the Christian Churches' Educational Association (Nairobi,
March 1966).
    11. David Court, "Dilemmas of Development: The Village Polytech-
nic Movement as a Shadow System of Education in Kenya," mimeographed
(Nairobi: University of Nairobi, Institute for Development Studies,
1972).

12. Ibid.

13. Excerpt taken from speech given to NYS participants.

14. G.W. Griffin, "The Education and Training of Young People for National Development through National Youth Organizations," mimeographed (Nairobi: National Youth Service, 1969).

15. I am greatly indebted to Mr. P.E. Kinyajui, Assistant Director (CCU) of the Institute of Adult Studies for information on this section. Most of the facts which follow are contained in his "The Development of Radio/Correspondence Education in Kenya" (Paper delivered at the Ninth Commonwealth Broadcasting Conference, Nairobi, 17-27 October, 1972).

16. Kenya, Ministry of Co-operatives and Social Services, Department of Social Services, "Policy for the Division of Adult Education," mimeographed (Nairobi, January 21, 1973).

17. M. Mwandia, "Literacy and Adult Education," mimeographed (Nairobi, April 12, 1966).

6

MALI:
EDUCATIONAL OPTIONS
IN A POOR COUNTRY
Fakoney Ly

Mali was chosen for a case study primarily because, as one of the world's poorest nations with no realistic prospect of making conventional primary education available to more than half its children even by the end of this century, its educational leaders have been especially open to unconventional ideas. The study was prepared in late 1973 by Mr. Fakoney Ly of the Ministry of Education in his personal capacity on the basis of a design supplied by ICED. The present text is a translated and edited version from the original French.

INTRODUCTION

Mali is one of the poorest West African countries lying in the drought-ridden Sudano-Sahelian belt of Francophone Africa. Faced with severe difficulties in providing basic schooling for its young, the Malian government since independence has been particularly receptive to ideas that might lead to a massive expansion of basic learning opportunities. These have crystalized in attempts to "ruralize" the still embryonic primary school system and to develop a variety of nonformal, experimental out-of-school programs. Mali's nonformal programs for young people include the Centers for Functional Literacy; Rural Animation Centers (Centres d'Animation Rurale, CARs); Vocational Training Centers (Centres d'Orientation Pratique, COPs); sports and recreational programs; nonformal scientific educational programs--the "science circles"; and programs designed especially for women and girls. Mali is also using the press and radio as educational media to supplement these activities and programs in rural areas.

The purpose of this study is to examine the nature and the extent of the educational needs of Mali's rural young people, with particular emphasis on those who do

not attend school; to examine to what extent formal primary education can and does meet these needs; and to
evaluate the contribution--actual and potential--of various
nonformal programs to the training of young out-of-schoolers (taking into account the organization and costs of
these programs).

Situated between the 10th and 25th parallels in the
heart of West Africa, the Republic of Mali covers 1,204,000
square kilometers. The country has three major geographic
areas: the Saharan, which includes a number of oases; the
Sahelian, the area of animal husbandry; and the Sudanese,
the agricultural savanna. Two great rivers, the Senegal
and the Niger, flow through Mali. The country has no
natural frontier. The closest and most accessible ports
to Bamako, the capital, are Dakar (1,230 kilometers) and
Abidjan (1,200 kilometers).

Administratively, Mali is divided into six regions
(Kayes, Bamako, Sikasso, Segou, Mopti, and Gao), 42
cercles, 280 arrondissements, and nearly 10,000 villages.

The per capita income amounts to less than US$80.
The Malian economy is essentially agricultural and pastoral; agriculture accounted for 67,300 million Malian francs
out of a GNP in 1970 of 134,900 million. (MF1,000=
US$2.17.)

Most (94 percent) of Mali's 5 million people live in
rural areas, and over half are under 20 years of age. The
average population density is four persons per square
kilometer. The various population groups are the Bambaras,
Peuls, Songhai, Tuaregs, Dogons, Miniankas, Senoufous,
Sarakoles, Bobos, Bozos, Somonos, Khassankes, and Malinkes.
Nearly all of the rural young are illiterate and are underemployed or unemployed.

Although the national educational system receives
28.2 percent of the national budget, and 60 percent of
educational expenses are devoted to primary education,
only 22.7 percent of the school age population are affected, and only 17.5 percent among the rural young.
Moreover, most children never reach the secondary level
at all. Fifty percent of the young enrolled in the first
year of primary education leave school before the fourth
year.

Because of the size of the Republic of Mali and the
great number of ethnic groups, the problems of the rural
young are here illustrated by examining a particular
region, Segou, and the Bambaras who make up its largest
population group (44.6 percent).

Segou, a relatively fertile region of 56,187 square
kilometers, has a population of 759,000 (13.5 inhabitants
per square kilometer), of which 683,000 or 90 percent are
dependent on agriculture, animal husbandry, and fishing.
The major crops raised are cotton, rice, groundnuts,
millet, corn, cassava, and sweet potatoes. Animal husbandry is centered in Macina and in the area of the Niger

district. Fishing takes place all along the Niger. The
area also contains several industrial units: the textile
combine at Segou, the sugar refinery at Dougabougou, the
steam-generating station at Markala, and the cotton gin
at Segou. The work force constitutes about 50 percent of
the rural population, including children.

Bambara society is based on the family unit. The
Bambara extended family includes the head of the family--
the oldest male member--and his household, his brothers
and their households, his widowed sisters, aunts, and
their children. The head of the family is considered a
living ancestor and enjoys undisputed authority: he is
the arbitrator of any disputes between family members; he
manages community property; he pays the family's taxes
and all the expenses of the young people's wedding ceremonies; and under his authority divisions of labor and
responsibility are created. On questions of general in-
terest--such as which fields to cultivate in cotton, millet, or groundnuts and which to let lie fallow or, sometimes, which to lend out--he consults a family council
composed of the various heads of household.

The extended family cultivates land collectively.
The produce is put in storehouses kept under the authority
of the family head. In addition each individual family
may cultivate a plot of land for its own needs. The
members of the extended family work first in the family
fields, and then for themselves, usually in the afternoons
and on Friday.

The Bambara father is obliged to feed and educate
his children until they are married. The mother nurses
her children, gives them basic care and their early education, particularly training the girls in the performance
of household tasks. After weaning, boys fall under the
special authority of the father. However, in a general
way, the education and training of children is a group
responsibility, extending from the older youths to the
very old.

Both girls and boys play an important role in the
economic life of the family. From the age of 7 or 8 the
young boy is initiated into work in the fields under the
supervision of his father. The young Bambara participates
in family tasks in accordance with the principle of "learning by doing," or "developing while producing." From the
age of 8 to 14 the Bambara boy accompanies his elders to
the fields to protect the crops against birds and animals.
He carries the food. And, if the father owns a cart, it
is the child's task to drive the team while work is going
on. Young Bambaras also tend herds of sheep and goats,
look for termites to feed the chickens, and cut grass for
the horses and donkeys. The girls carry water, help their
mothers do household tasks, and take care of the babies
while the mother is working. Parents appreciate their
children's part in the family's work, which to a degree
explains their reluctance to send children to school.

From the age of 15 the young Bambara begins to play
a more adult role in production. The young work their
own plots (jonforo), raising mainly groundnuts, vegetables,
and cotton. They sell these products and use the money,
which belongs to them, for clothing or incidental purchases. During the off-season most young people leave the
village for the city where they work for three or four
months. The money they make helps pay the family taxes
or goes to personal use for bicycles, radios, or similar
purchases.

The ton--a most important element in Bambara society--
is an association of mutual assistance which includes a
large number if not all the village young over 15. The
activities of the tons include the maintenance of roads
and wooden bridges and the construction of literacy centers
and youth centers. This group also polices the village,
keeps animals from straying, fights brushfires, and so on.
The ton lends its services to farmers in, for example,
weeding and harvesting rice and threshing millet. If the
farmer who receives the service is himself a member of the
ton he feeds the group and pays them in tobacco and cola.
If he is not a member of the group, he pays a sum of money
in addition to furnishing food.

Generally the ton is made up of two-thirds men and
one-third women; the number of members varies from 50 to
200. The maximum age of the members of the ton is 25.
The leader is a tonkuntigi (the head of the ton) who is
assisted by the tonjeli (the father, or honorary president
of the ton). The latter serves as a liaison between the
young and the elders. The officers of the ton are sometimes elected but more often appointed.

In addition to their economic functions, the tons
sponsor cultural, artistic, and recreational activities.
The koteba is one such activity--an entertaining and
educational performance made up of narrative, song, and
dance, and treating every rural endeavor (hunting, fishing,
harvest) and anything that threatens the moral standards
of the community (infidelity, theft, and so on). Artistic
evenings, put on after the harvest or during religious
feasts and marriage ceremonies, are occasions that offer
the young an opportunity to acquire cultural traditions.
The tons might be an ideal instrument to encourage new
ideas and to help in an integral program of village development, and they appear to be eager to expand their
activities, but thus far their efforts have remained
embryonic.

In sum, traditional Bambara society possesses a
well-knit social framework and a comprehensive learning
system perpetuating the Bambara heritage. Embedded within
this cohesive societal framework, however, lies the dilemma
facing all societies in a state of change: What can usefully be harnessed from the past to strengthen the future?
What must be obliterated and how fast must this be done
to ensure a viable future? For although the traditional

learning system transmits a vital body of knowledge and skills, important gaps are left. Modern Malian life requires literacy skills and knowledge of the French language, of basic methodologies of a cash-based agricultural economy, of health and hygiene, of ways of dealing with government, and of the responsibilities of national citizenship. New modes of learning are needed to fit these modern requirements.

FORMAL EDUCATION SYSTEM

Though 28 percent of the government national budget is spent on formal education (more than half of this on primary alone), most children in Mali get no formal schooling at all. In 1970/71, of the age-group 8-20 years, barely over 1 in 10 were in schools of any kind, while of the age-group 8-14 years, less than 2 in 10 were in primary school. (See Table 6.1). Of those few who attend primary school, half do not complete four years. In the country as a whole, though there are great regional variations, primary school classes average 43 children, and for every two boys there is only one girl. French is the language of instruction for primary schooling and beyond, and the curriculum of the primary school allocates 50 percent of school time to learning the French language.

TABLE 6.1

School Enrollment in Age-Group 8 to 20 Shown by
Educational Level, 1970/71

	Student Population, Aged 8 to 20 Years		
	Total	Number of Girls	Girls as Percentages of Total
Primary education	207,400	69,150	33%
First cycle	180,000	63,000	35%
Second cycle	27,000	6,150	23%
Secondary education	3,350	400	12%
Normal school	840	170	20%
Technical and vocational	2,100	500	24%
Higher education	160	15	9%
Total number of students	213,850	70,235	33%

Source: Adjusted estimates based on data from Mali, Ministry of Education, Annuaire de Statistiques Scolaires du Mali, 1970/71 (Bamako, n.d.).

Since 1962 a major effort to expand the number of primary school places has resulted in a trebling from 65,000 to more than 200,000 in 1970. (However, the rate of expansion slowed down dramatically from an average annual increase of 18.1 percent in 1960-65 to 6.5 percent in 1965-70.) The goal was to assure to every Malian, from the age of six, the opportunity for at least nine years of education in two cycles. The reform foresaw a need for 10,000 classes and an equal number of teachers in order to achieve 100 percent schooling within 10 years. However, given the present rate of expansion in school places, and the current annual rate of population increase (2.8 percent), by the year 2000 only half of all children will have places in primary schools. Even this modest goal, however, is of doubtful economic feasibility.

The texts relating to the reform of 1962 defined the aims of primary education along two lines:

1. to prepare them [the children] to understand thoroughly their civic and vocational duties within the framework of the nation's free institutions

2. to enable them . . . to continue their studies through the elementary and intermediate levels of general secondary education or of technical and vocational training that would enable us to establish degree equivalencies with other modern states

The first point suggests an orientation of primary school toward the vocational and civic training of children, the majority of whom are destined for jobs as farmers and artisans--training that would be useful to the majority of school children and oriented toward the actual needs of Mali's job ranks. The second point suggests, on the contrary, that school is preparation for continued studies and that education will be geared in such a way that children who pass the exam for the diploma of basic education (diplome d'études fondamentales, DEF) will have the required body of knowledge to go directly on to secondary education. That body of knowledge has been defined not on the basis of Mali's actual needs but in conformity with the educational systems of modern states abroad in order to obtain diploma equivalencies.

Primary education has thus far tended in the second direction. Despite the "reform," schools went on functioning as they had in the past and standards for exams remained the same. More efforts were made to open new classrooms than to apply the new direction in education. Yet, by 1972, a decade after the reform when school attendance was to have risen to 100 percent of the school age population, the rate of school attendance was calculated as 22.7 percent.

Among the reasons for the wide divergence between
goals and actual achievements was the high growth rate of
population. The forecast of 1962 was for 656,000 children
of school age in 1972. Yet by 1970 there were 1,311,100
in the 7 to 15 year old age-group alone. At present, each
new year brings a group of about 140,000 children into
the "education market." However, of every 1,000 students
entering school, 500 do not reach the fourth year; 133
pass the certificate marking the end of the first cycle
of studies; and 15 succeed in the DEF. This is a far cry
from a primary education made up of two cycles that the
State would assure "in principle to every citizen from
the age of six."

From the point of view of financial yield, too, a
good part of the 28.2 percent of the national budget spent
for education is wasted. Students who do not reach the
fourth year probably lapse into illiteracy, after spending
from one to five years in school at a cost of 12,000 Malian
francs each year. (See Table 6.2.) The high number of
repeaters (in the neighborhood of 30 percent) has also
decreased the return on the educational dollar, since 30
percent of the education budget is spent for labor that
has to be done again. The considerable number of students
who cannot keep up with their schoolwork suggests that
the education is irrelevant and too difficult for the
majority of children. It takes place in a foreign language and deals with subjects that have no relation to
the knowledge that the students have acquired in their
native milieux.

TABLE 6.2

State Expenditures and Cost per Student in Primary and Secondary
Education Shown by Type of Expenditure, 1971

	Expenditures (in '000s Malian francs)	Cost per Student (in '000s Malian francs)
First cycle primary		
Personnel	2,158,967	10.7
Materials	168,754	.8
Total	2,327,721	11.5
Second cycle primary		
Personnel	1,161,354	48.8
Materials	101,354	4.3
Total	1,262,708	53.1
Secondary education		
Personnel	195,100	56.0
Materials	243,600	64.0
Total	438,700	120.0

Source: Mali, Ministry of Education.

Certain schools in rural areas have difficulty in recruiting students. Twenty-three percent of the classes of the first cycle in the region of Kayes have fewer than 20 students, as do 20 percent in the region of Gao. Because school is considered foreign, the farmer who sends his child to school considers him lost to the family farm, destined to take a job in the city that, it is hoped, will profit the family. It is understandable that a farmer would choose this path for one child only and that recruitment in these schools suffers--and especially recruitment of girls.

Current Directions in "Ruralization" of Schools

The experiences of the past years and the current difficulties have influenced many educators who support a greater degree of adapting education to the realities of rural life. The question of the use of national languages in the schools is also of increasing interest to educators at every level. Current directions regarding reform of primary education affirm the necessity for change, define ruralization of the schools, reflect recognition of the need for special training or retraining for teachers, and emphasize the need for mental reconditioning of students and parents. For example, the Director General of Primary Education and Literacy, in notes on the ruralization of primary education prepared in December 1969, stated the need for

> . . . tremendous effort to instill a new mentality in our students. What we must have is a true mystique of the land. It is necessary and of high priority to renew the value of manual labor, craftsmanship, and the cultivation of the land.
> Students . . . who are not accepted in the classes of the ninth year . . . should be welcomed by the state farms already in existence. A model farm could be created in each region, and the students could specialize in such different areas as agriculture, fishing, and handicrafts.
> . . . it is not too late to introduce boldly a significant agricultural program into the curricula (first and second cycles). Consequently, there will be changes in schedule, and teachers will be required to undergo special training or take refresher courses in order to teach elementary agriculture, manual labor and domestic arts.

By 1972, however, only 30 experimental schools had opened and achievements appear to be limited to the introduction of practical agriculture from the third grade onward.

Following the Lomé Conference (of West African
countries to consider educational strategies for rural
children, youth, and women held in 1972) the first steps
were taken to try out a new approach of building education
into crop development operations. The former Ministry of
National Education has been split into two. One ministry
now has a portfolio for basic education, youth, and
sports, combining primary and fundamental education (including functional literacy). The other has jurisdiction
over secondary and higher education.

A number of serious obstacles are impeding the progress of the reforms. There are difficulties in overcoming the entrenched conventional academic approach to
schooling, which is heavily reinforced by the examination
system. There are problems in recruiting, training, and
holding teachers. Rapid increases in school enrollment
in Mali created an increased need for both male and
female teachers, resulting in a shortage of teachers in
the first cycle of primary education. Under these circumstances, the Ministry of National Education could not
afford to remove teachers for a year's reorientation and
training in teaching agriculture or home economics. Their
presence was indispensable to the functioning of primary
education.

Attempts to mesh the training of children in year-
round practical farming with the other components of the
school syllabi have raised further problems. In addition
there have been serious logistical difficulties: a
shortage of resources and equipment for the schools;
problems of feeding the children at school (being partly
overcome by a system of school <u>cantines</u>); and problems of
adequate water supply.

As far as the ruralization of primary education is
concerned and, in a more general manner, with regard to
educational reform, Mali is still at a stage of exploration and experimentation, the results of which will
determine the orientation of the eventual reform of education, how it is applied, how far it extends, and what
means should be used to implement it.

Recent Initiatives

In support of the reform efforts, a number of new
initiatives have been taken by the government and external assistance has been sought. For example, a project
is under way for a preinvestment study for the reform
of the first cycle of primary education. The National
Institute for Functional Literacy and Applied Linguistics
plans to create a division that would explore the use
of the functional literacy experiment in formal education. A program of teacher reorientation was presented

and accepted by UNICEF and UNESCO with regard to financing
and technical support.   UNICEF currently gives aid to the
30 existing ruralized pilot schools.   In areas where school
ruralization is linked to the work of community development, aid could also probably be obtained from community
development organizations.

At the second primary cycle, a project with World
Bank support, foresees the opening of a number of centers
to be built and equipped by the year 1977-78.   This project will include: the construction and equipping of
34 multipurpose laboratories of practical skills, 28 technology workshops, and 17 workshops devoted to practical
skills in domestic science; the retraining of 60 specialized teachers; the training of 11 administrators to manage
the centers and of 30 technicians for the technology workshops; and the supplying of teaching materials for the
first three years of activity.

Whether all of these moves will result in effective
reform of primary education in Mali is uncertain.   As
O. Le Brun in his report on "Strategies of Development"
(presented at the UNESCO Round Table of Specialists on
Out-of-School Education Programmes in Sub-Saharan Africa,
Dakar, 7-12 February 1972) pointed out,

> In some countries truly innovative projects have
> been launched, but in the end they have been
> absorbed by the conventional system because of
> the resistance to change from within (the people
> responsible for promoting change are, themselves,
> products of the school system) and from without
> (parents think diplomas have magical powers).[1]

NONFORMAL EDUCATION: PROMOTING LITERACY

Mali's attempts to reform its formal education system
have been paralleled by the establishment of a wide variety
of educational programs outside the school system.   These
programs bear witness to Mali's willingness to experiment
and to try to find educational modes that will more effectively mesh with the needs and circumstances of its rural
population, as well as with the nation's need for greater
development of its material and human resources.

The programs described in the following sections are
but a sampling of nonformal education in Mali.   They are
those most relevant to the needs of youth.   It should be
noted, however, that Mali has other nonformal education
programs for adults in such fields as cooperative education, health and sanitation, family planning, and the like.

Functional Literacy Program

More than 85 percent of the adult population of Mali is illiterate and in some areas this proportion reaches 95 percent. The functional literacy program is aimed at combatting this widespread illiteracy. The program is being carried out, for the most part, in the context of a variety of projects to improve the rural economy as a whole. These projects--called "development operations"-- are intensive efforts to spread modern agriculture and to improve the production and marketing systems for certain major crops, such as cotton and rice.

Operation Cotton operates in the cercles of Segou, San, and Tominian, with a population estimated at 395,000 (1968), in 15 zones of rural expansion (ZERs). Operation Cotton affects, in addition, the regions of Sikasso and Bamako with a farming population of 1,500,000. In the Segou region alone, there are 416 Centers for Functional Literacy connected with Operation Cotton. (See Table 6.3.)

Operation Rice in the Segou region, with financing from the European Development Fund (FED), is aiming for a projected increase in production from 18,500 tons to 90,000 tons by increase of cultivated areas, land development, a credit system, a drive to publicize the program, and a campaign for functional literacy to affect 20,000 young rice producers. It is the first development operation to have integrated campaigns for functional literacy and community development (23 Functional Literacy Centers opened in 1972, and another 80 were to have opened in 1973).

TABLE 6.3

Number of Functional Literacy Centers in Operation,
Animators, and Enrollments
March 1973

Regional Administrations	Total Number of Centers	Number of Animators	Students		
			Men	Women	Total
Kita	205	352	3,952	426	4,378
Koulikoro	144	199	1,861	70	1,921
Bamako	66	218	3,412	60	3,472
Diofla	213	301	5,670	33	5,703
Koutiala	481	604	10,364	245	10,609
Segou	493	846	15,431	203	15,634
Mopti	7	11	87	42	129
Total	1,609	2,531	40,777	1,079	41,846

Source: Mali, Ministry of Education.

Objectives and Structure

In the early 1960s Mali had a national literacy service, which drew heavily on the methodologies of the primary school, including teaching in French and in classroom situations. By the mid-sixties, however, Mali became one of the first countries to participate in UNESCO's large-scale experimental literacy program--a new functional, selective, and intensive approach to literacy.

A "Plan of Operation" signed on February 11, 1967, between the UNDP, UNESCO, and the Government of Mali, describes the program of functional literacy. Its purpose was twofold. It was to contribute to the development of key sectors of the Malian economy by increasing productivity, by training 100,000 farmers in cotton, rice, and groundnut production, 1,000 workers for state projects, and 4,000 housekeepers. Secondly, the program was to help determine the best techniques and methods of teaching literacy in order to obtain lasting results that would be beneficial to economic and social development.

A national center for functional literacy includes an administration section which deals with personnel, materials, and finance; an evaluation section responsible for contributing to preliminary research and for assessing the results of the functional literacy program; and a production section, which is responsible for teaching materials, language editing, preparation of appropriate materials including teaching posters, photographs, films, exhibits, radio scripts and broadcasts, as well as the printing and distribution of these materials.

The seven district centers of functional literacy-- Kita (groundnuts); Bamako (industry and cotton); Koulikoro (groundnuts); Diofla (cotton); Segou (cotton and rice); Koutiala (cotton); Mopti (rice)--are charged with the organization and control of the program. They direct and coordinate the activities of the heads of the 45 zones of functional literacy (ZAF).

A ZAF includes one or two administrative arrondissements and has between 25 and 50 literacy centers. The head of the ZAF is a paid agent responsible for every aspect of functional literacy in his ZAF. He receives two months' training at the national center and in the regions with the development operations. He canvasses the villages to ascertain the level of production, the presence of literates willing to act as unpaid animators, and the degree of support of the village authorities for the opening of a literacy center. He is also responsible for training animators and supporting them in the implementation of their programs.

The basic village literacy center is constructed and furnished by the villagers. The local committee on literacy includes the head of the village (president), two village councillors, one representative from the

young people, one from the women, and the animator of
the center. This committee is expected to mobilize
village support for having a literacy center and for its
construction, to organize the courses, and to furnish
kerosene for the lamps (since most classes are held in
the evening).

The one or two animators are generally literate
farmers (recruited from the farmers of the village concerned) who volunteer to give free courses in functional
literacy. They receive a one-week indoctrination
followed by frequent reviews and guidance through the
radio. Former participants are often recruited as animators; they continue their education by training their
unlettered fellow-villagers.

By early 1973, 2,302 centers had been opened, of
which 1,609 were functioning (see Table 6.3). Of the
total of 41,846 students (from 15 to 35 years old) 40,777
were men and 1,079 were women.

The recruitment of students is made on the basis of
application. The literacy centers are open to everyone;
priority is given to the cultivators of groundnuts, cotton,
and rice, and to applicants between the ages of 15 and
35 who speak Bambara or Peul.

About a fifth of the centers are closed permanently;
others are closed temporarily during the months of January,
February, and sometimes March, for the farmers to transport their products to the markets. It is also the time
when the young country people leave for the cities to
earn some money.

Content and Methods of Training

The first step in establishing a literacy program is
a study in depth of production problems undertaken by the
literacy team (editors, training specialists, audiovisual
staff, and evaluators) and representatives of the village
collectives, agricultural overseers, and farmers (including those who will become animators).

Production problems are inventoried and classified
in order of importance and urgency, and form the basis
upon which the training program is built. Teaching
materials are produced in segments corresponding to one
"school" week. Each training theme is represented by a
poster showing a drawing or photograph. The poster is
designed to facilitate the discussion of a particular
problem and its solution. The "poster question" serves
as a guideline to the editing team who prepare a paper
on associated professional, technical, or scientific
training; a paper on socioeconomic training; and related
information on reading, writing, and business arithmetic.
This same group prepares material for the animator,
including a teaching guide, a time schedule, a guide to
"How to form the letters of the Bambara alphabet," infor-

mation on socioeconomic questions, phonetic tables of the
letters of the Bambara alphabet, and tables of arithmetic
terms in Bambara. The implementation of the plan is entrusted to the animator, who is introduced to the problems
and made familiar with the techniques required to solve
it.

A meeting with the students takes place at the
literacy center or in the fields. The animator leads
the group in analysis and discussion of the poster illus-
trating the problem and connects it to the socioeconomic
context. The intellectualization of the problem and its
solutions are attacked through applied arithmetic and
reading and writing presented in the course of the same
sequence or during the preceding ones.

The real conditions of the farmers' lives are incorporated into every aspect of the teaching and are linked
to a total view of production methods. The total effort
is designed to cause the students to reflect and think
about the problems of their milieu and the utilization
of reading, mathematics, and modern farming techniques
as tools for their solution.

The literacy program is based on use of the languages
already spoken by the mass of the people. The problem of
the transcription and utilization of the national languages
for the teaching of reading, writing, and arithmetic to
the adults of rural communities has been a longstanding
preoccupation of the government. Linguistic researchers
with the literacy service have undertaken a vast program,
which includes the regularization of a transcription
system common to the four languages spoken in Mali and
neighboring states and the establishment of rules of
spelling, a collection of words most commonly used, and
simple rules of grammar for each of the four languages--
Bambara, Peul, Songhoy, and Tomasheq. Because of this
research the National Center for Functional Literacy has
been able to prepare materials in 15 socioprofessional
fields and progressions in Bambara of 15 to 20 sequences
for the study of reading, writing, and applied arithmetic.

Costs and Assessment of Results

The total cost of the program for the three years,
1971 to 1973, was MF431,721,500. The sources of funds
are shown below.

Financing	1971	1972	1973	Total
Malian				
Budget	60,618,000	55,924,000	52,203,000	168,745,000
UNDP	117,616,500	66,750,000		184,366,500
FAC		24,583,000	29,167,000	53,750,000
FED			24,860,000	24,860,000
Totals	178,234,500	147,257,000	106,230,000	431,721,500

The Malian budget covers the expenses of personnel, materiel, and operation. Outside aid is for costs of operation and equipment.

A study dated March 1972 estimated that the average cost of training a farmer through functional literacy was 9,874 Malian francs. This cost did not include contributions of the people toward construction of the center, the unpaid work of the animators, and expenses for propaganda and upkeep. Since the time of this estimate, a new formula for more intensive training extending over two periods of three months (in contrast to the earlier system of two nine-month periods) has been adopted. The average cost of training under this new formula is expected to be reduced to about MF3,900.

The functional literacy program has demonstrated that many farmers are aware of their problems and are enthusiastic about creating committees for promoting literacy, constructing and equipping the centers, providing unpaid animators, following the courses regularly, and subscribing to Kibaru, a lively monthly newspaper produced in cooperation with the Ministry of Information. The methodology of functional literacy, involving selectivity, direct application, a flexible approach, and above all the use of the native languages, is apparently responsible for the good results thus far.

As yet no authoritative evaluation of the functional literacy program has been made, though there are some early signs of achievements. The Ministry of Production, impressed with the work so far, has decided to insert a literacy component into all relevant agricultural projects under its supervision. In 1973 the government created the National Institute of Functional Literacy and Applied Linguistics (INAFLA) which will assist in overcoming the language problems. INAFLA is under the authority of the Ministry of Higher and Secondary Education and Scientific Research. This new arrangement should not only reinforce functional literacy, but also enable the other modes of education to profit by the experience gained in functional literacy. The government is paying close attention to the effects of using local vernaculars in place of French in the functional literacy program, as achievements could affect teaching in primary schools, where French is now the classroom language.

Role of Press and Radio in Promoting Literacy

Kibaru, the first rural newspaper issued in Mali in the Bambara language, was started in March 1972 with the collaboration of the United Nations Educational, Scientific and Cultural Organization (UNESCO). A four-page monthly publication, its purpose is basically to furnish reading matter for the 60,000 new literates (resulting

from the introduction of the functional literacy program);
to give them practical advice on agricultural, sanitary,
and social problems; to inform them of events concerning
their localities, the country, and the outside world; and
to serve as a link between the city and the country.

Kibaru is under the authority of the Ministry of
Information and published under the management of the
National Agency of Information of Mali (ANIM). An interministerial commission on the rural press has been
appointed which includes representatives from all ministry
departments, as well as from the operations of agricultural
development (groundnuts, cotton, rice, and Haute-Vallée).

An editorial committee entrusted with the make-up
of the newspaper is made up of delegates from Information,
Education, Health, and Social Welfare. The permanent
staff consists of the director of publication who is at
the same time director of the ANIM, the editor-in-chief,
the editorial secretary, a stenographic secretary, and
a transcriber. There are 45 correspondents and reporters
spread throughout the zones of functional literacy. They
are technicians in agriculture or literacy and are in
permanent contact with the peasants. Articles are prepared in part by the journal's management, and in part at
the National Center of Literacy. The printing is done by
Editions Imprimeries of Mali.

The administrative service undertakes distribution
either through the channel of the Office of Telecommunications or by private means in the distribution sectors.
About 50 percent of the copies are distributed through
the local centers of functional literacy. The rest are
taken care of by subscription, individual sale, and
distribution by means of diverse organizations.

Kibaru's articles concern farm problems having to do
with crops, cattle raising, hunting, and fishing; contain
news of meetings, fairs, visits of important people;
current events (drought, eclipse of the sun); information
on farming techniques, matters of hygiene and health,
problems of women and children, civic matters, the
literacy centers, social problems, as well as articles
for amusement (fiction, oral tradition, games, contests,
humor, and comic strips).

The price of the newspaper is fixed at 20 Malian
francs, to fit the limited means of the rural masses.
The approximate expenses for one regular issue are for
costs of composition, including expenses for personnel
(MF140,000); printing, including expenses for paper,
material, labor (MF80,000), and distribution (MF8,000).

Special issues of six or eight pages have appeared
many times but are generally too expensive to produce
regularly.

The help given by the functional literacy service
and by the Ministry of Information in the matter of
personnel or occasional gifts (paper, printing, and so
on) have enabled the newspaper to balance its budget.

Radio is used in conjunction with the functional literacy program. During the first phase of this colla-boration, a program of twenty themes was prepared to explain the utility, duration, and responsibilities of functional literacy and to approach the problems, both socioeconomic and sanitary, of the rural milieu. The second phase of educational radio began in March 1970 and dealt primarily with the instruction of animators in the functional literacy centers.

Among the important programs is "Learn in Order to Produce," started in January 1969. This 15-minute 5-day-a-week broadcast gives general information on the func-tioning and life of the literacy centers, helps in the training of animators, attempts to create a healthy competition among the centers by periodic reporting and interviews conducted by a group from the National Center for Functional Literacy, and conducts a continuing and fruitful dialogue between the listeners and those respon-sible for functional literacy.

The functional literacy service has created 90 centers for collective listening and discussion. The reports from these centers are sent to the National Center for Functional Literacy and reinforce the dialogue between the producers of groundnuts and cotton on the one side and the literacy and agriculture operations on the other.

The animation rurale section of the radio unit produces a 15-minute daily broadcast which treats all the socioeconomic problems of the rural milieu. Its purpose is to spread information about the latest methods and techniques of farming. This group works in close collabora-tion with the development operations in cotton, groundnuts, Haute-Vallée, and the services of cattle-raising, waters and forests. This program is presented in the local languages. "Housekeeping Put to Music" is a daily 30-minute program which presents women's interests in the form of discussion given in local languages.

With the construction of the new broadcasting building, which will include two studios for taping and three announcing cubicles, it is hoped that there will be an expansion of educational programs. In addition there are plans for strengthening the center at Kati, renovating broadcasting apparatus, and extending the campaign for listeners by the establishment of new centers for collective listening.

NONFORMAL EDUCATION: FOSTERING COMMUNITY AND INDIVIDUAL
WELFARE

This section deals with a sampling of "activity" programs for young people to help in their physical, moral, and cultural development, and to expand their

contribution to the community. The programs discussed
are the Comités Culturel et de Plein Air, the Pioneer
movement, science circles, the women's movement and
community development. These programs are nationwide and,
in many cases, the degree of local participation--as well
as of local impact--is impossible to estimate.

Comités Culturels et de Plein Air (CCPA)

The CCPA is designed to include all young people
in one educational organization which will foster their
civic, moral, and practical training. Membership in the
CCPA, open to young people of all philosophic and
religious convictions, is free and voluntary.
The national youth service to which the CCPA is
associated is directed by the Inspector General of Youth
and Sports assisted by the Adjutant General Inspector.
At the head of each branch of activity there is a sports
director, a director of arts and culture, and a director
of supervised activities. In each of the six regions,
there is a regional director of youth. CCPAs have been
created at the regional, cercle, arrondissement, village,
and quarter levels. Each CCPA is administered by a
coordinating animator, a general secretary, a general
treasurer, and a keeper of materiel.
The CCPA conducts activities in three fields:
Sports activities. There are about 72 athletic clubs,
19 in Segou, 18 in Mopti, 16 in Bamako, 12 in Kayes, and
7 in Gao.
Supervised and outdoor activities. These activities (including those of the Pioneers) are youth exchanges
(study trips in different parts of the country), youth
workshops (construction of homes for the young, schools,
and dispensaries), centers for popular education and
youth homes. Gao has 13 centers; Segou has 5; Bamako,
Kayes, and Mopti have 4 centers each; and Sikasso has 1.
Artistic and cultural activities. These include
music, singing and dancing, cultural exhibits, lecture
clubs, and reading rooms. At present there are about 22
orchestras and 72 folklore troupes. The government has
organized artistic and cultural "biennials" which offer
regional groups an opportunity to compete in folklore
troupes, orchestras, theatrical troupes, choruses, and
ballet. At these competitions there are also art
exhibits. The biennials are preceded by intercercle and
interregional contests.
The following projects were formulated at the time
of preparation of the five-year plan (1974-78), which has
not yet been implemented. Therefore, they give an idea
of the future direction and magnitude of the program.

In the area of sports:
  upkeep and improvement of the <u>Stade Omnisport</u> in
    Mamadou and in Oeuzzin Couli<u>baly at Bamako</u>
  establishment of village sport centers which would
    include a football field and handball and volley-
    ball courts; lecture, class, and show rooms,
    a swimming pool, and lodging facilities
  sports equipment for the five primary schools at
    Bamako
  for each main regional center a basketball and
    volleyball court, a running track, a sand pit
    for jumping, an area for weight throwing
In the area of the arts and culture:
  construction and equipment of a national theater
    of 5,000 seats at Bamako
  grants for artistic training and instrumental music
In the area of supervised activities:
  upkeep and renovation of the equipment of the youth
    sports and culture clubs, and of the Pioneer
    buildings
  provision of each regional management with camping
    material and other resources

The estimated cost for these projects will exceed MF13,000
million in the course of five years.
  The regional CCPAs derive their funds from the organization of artistic events (theater, concerts), athletic
events, dances, film showings, and subsidies. For example,
in 1972, the regional CCPA of Segou received a subsidy of
MF1,500,000 from the governor for its preparations for
the biennial arts festival.
  The CCPA puts a mobile cinema at the disposal of the
local CCPAs; film showings are organized at the village
level and may bring the local CCPAs as much as MF60,000
a week. The CCPA in the city of Segou has an arts
company which took in nearly MF250,000 in 1972; its
various athletic events have netted nearly 300,000 Malian
francs. This, however, is an urban CCPA; rural CCPAs
show smaller profits.
  It is impossible to generalize about the effectiveness of this committee structure; it varies locally with
the vitality and strength of village and district initiative. Outside of periods of intense activity (such as
preparation for a biennial art exposition) the CCPA has
some difficulties in bringing all of the young together,
in part because the lack of material prevents the youth
clubs and centers from running and from undertaking more
activities. These problems in turn have caused some
negative attitudes toward the CCPA.
  The CCPA has potential, however, as a central and
local multipurpose organizing body. For instance, it is
currently playing a role in the development of an experimental "science circle" program, which aims at encoura-

ging scientific thinking through the study of the environment. This program is discussed later in this chapter.

Pioneer Movement

The Pioneer movement (Mouvement National des
Pionniers) embraces all extra- and post-curricular activities in a program to complement and reinforce the training of the family and school. Its aim is to provide a
setting for civic, moral, and practical training. Like
the CCPA, it is open to all. Statistics on membership
are unavailable.

The Pioneer movement is under the management of the
supervised activities bureau of the Inspector General of
Youth and Sports. It admits young people from 8 to 18
years. The movement has three divisions: minimes, under
8 years old; cadets, 8 to 18 years; guides or cadres,
16 to 18 years. Membership in the movement is allowed
only with the consent of the parents.

The program for the minimes includes an introduction
to understanding the spirit of the movement, learning
about the motto and the flag, learning dances, skits, and
songs, performing manual activities, playing team and
individual games, having campfires, and so forth. The
cadet program covers further knowledge of the spirit of
the movement, planting and upkeep of trees, protection
of animals, discussion of books and scholarly heritage,
manual activities, sports, learning about plants, use of
a compass and chronometer, decoration, learning how to
help a comrade in danger, and so forth. The guides learn
discipline and respect for the laws, development of self-
control and the sense of observation through games; they
learn about trees, camping and its techniques, topo-
graphy, seamanship, broadcasting, self-expression, and
theater.

The activities of the Pioneers take place in popular
education centers, youth houses, and the homes for young
people. A center for popular education generally consists
of a large hall used for lectures, theatricals, and
cinema; an office; and a store. The equipment of these
community education centers includes tables, chairs,
closets, shelves, and educative and sports materials,
such as musical instruments, a radio, a tape recorder,
a phonograph, records, newspapers, magazines, and games.
This equipment is far from complete everywhere and needs
to be repaired often. The movement has suffered from a
shortage of funds and its activities are now more limited
and sporadic.

Science Circles

Since March 1971, the Science Circles, an institution of extension courses in scientific education, have been operating under the direction of the Inspector General of Youth. Their aim is to introduce young people to the uses of science and scientific thinking. The circles are designed to coordinate various educative projects with school and the family and to contribute to the integration of school and village life.

The science circles operate in close association with the CCPA, the Pioneer movement, the CARs and the ruralized schools. The cadres of the science circles are generally teachers, youth animators, agricultural agents, or students of the 8th or 9th year. The training of the cadres takes place on the regional level. The steps that led to the establishment of the science circles began in 1966 with the introduction of scientific training for animators and teachers. Related programs continued in 1968, 1971, 1972 and 1973, with the aid of consultants and experts from UNESCO.

For students, the activities of the science circles are based on the program of the local school. At a rural school the program might cover germination, biological cycle of plants, the influence of climate, and meteorological study. These studies take place outside of school hours and are organized either by the instructor or by the youth animators. The job of these cadres is basically to arouse and keep the interest of the young.

For those out of school a certain number of "technical priority sequences" are established which correspond to the study program of the local development operation. A typical action program is participation in the sanitation plan of the city of Bamako. The aim of this program is to interest the young in participating in the solution of a problem in sanitation and to unify the different aspects of this study. The group proceeded by doing an analysis of public routes, a study of ways to arouse the population, and received training in problems of hygiene and health. Scientific extension education proceeds through three phases:

1. Through observation of the locality, the young people, working in groups, make an inventory of scientific phenomena which appear as so many "mysteries" in their daily lives.
2. With the aid of specialists, they analyze and synthesize scientific facts in order to apply their knowledge to their own experience.
3. In the third phase they apply their new knowledge in practical ways using appropriate equipment, doing research and case studies, and collecting valuable data.

For 1975 and 1976 US$25,000 will be available for·
the purpose of supporting and equipping the science circles
of the regional districts and of the Teacher Training
Institute for General Education (IPEG). There were in
1973 six circles in this embryonic program.

Women's Movement

During the first years following independence, local
women's associations were formed which were later consolidated at regional and national levels (L'Union National des
Femmes du Mali). Their purpose was to enable women to
take a more active part in the economic, social, cultural,
and political life of the country. Social centers were
also set up specifically to educate women for their roles
as wives and mothers.

In principle, the women's movement includes all the
women of Mali. By 1971 there were 58 social centers used
for the activities of the women's movement. Most of these
centers are in cities such as Bamako and in other major
population centers.

The activities undertaken by the women's associations
are political and economic as well as social and cultural.
They hold meetings to discuss questions regarding women,
children, or the whole community--such questions as the
launching of a literacy campaign for women, ways to
encourage attendance at the social centers, the creation
of day nurseries, and problems of education for the young.
They also participate in meetings dealing with community
problems, engage in public health activities, and organize
educational cultural activities (dances, film showings,
lectures on health and other topics). Thus far the
movement seems concentrated in urban centers, with little
impact in rural areas. These various activities are undertaken with resources from subsidies, grants, and receipts
from various activities such as presenting concerts.

In each region a bureau of five women--president,
vice president, secretary, treasurer, and assistant
treasurer--direct the activities of the groups. There
is a parallel organization at the city, village, and
quarter levels, with the secretary and treasurer chosen
from among literate women. There are separate working
committees at each level to handle 1) liaison with national
and international women's organizations, 2) liaison with
the animation groups, 3) marriage counseling, 4) women's
cooperatives, and 5) organization of lectures.

The social centers from which the women's movement
operates have been infused with a new community development orientation since the second Seminar on Public Health
and Welfare (1966), which advocated social service to
promote a better life for the whole community, with the

active, voluntary participation of all residents. In some areas community development centers will replace the former social centers; meanwhile the community development method is being introduced into all the social centers.

Among the projects envisaged are the creation of a center for the training of the blind, and the creation of community day nurseries (with a target schedule of five per year in Bamako, and one per region during the period 1974-1978). Each new center of community development is planned to be staffed by a trained director (male or female), a social assistant, two social aides, and two (male) agents of community development, in addition to any specialized personnel needed at particular centers. The program is run by the Division of Social Affairs, under the jurisdiction of the Ministry of Public Health and Social Welfare.

One of the aims of the community development movement is to foster collaboration between the technical and administrative services involved in the overall economic and social development of the nation. In line with this goal, the Office of the Ministry of Public Health and Social Welfare hosted an interministerial meeting (August 30, 1972) including the Ministry of National Education, Youth and Sports, and the Ministry of Production. They recommended the creation of a permanent interministerial committee with representation from the three ministries. This committee would work out a policy of community development acceptable to all the services, implement an annual work plan, and encourage collaboration between the different services at the national, regional, and local levels.

The principal expenses of the community development centers are for buildings, teaching materials, sponsoring activities in the centers, and training volunteer animatrices. Five community development centers planned for the area of the Segou rice project will be constructed by the FED at a cost of about MF30 million. A 12-bed lying-in home was built at Sanakoroba with help from the local people, the government, and a grant from Oxfam. UNICEF gave financial aid for the training of animatrices at the Sanakoroba center. A woman counselor in social welfare from the United Nations participated in the planning of the community development program in the two centers at Sanakoroba and Hamdallaye.

NONFORMAL EDUCATION FOR TRAINING IN AGRICULTURE

This section deals with two of Mali's foremost efforts to provide agricultural training for its rural young people. The Centres d'Animation Rurale (CAR), which provide residential training for young adults, are one of

the main nonformal educational programs for rural development. The nonresidential Centres à Orientation Pratique
(COP), an experimental program, are designed to provide
an educational program to follow up primary education for
school leavers between 14 and 17 years.

Centres d'Animation Rurale

        Since the independence of Mali, a number of training
systems for young farmers have been assisted through a
national youth service (la service civique, a paramilitary
youth organization) and the seasonal farm schools. The
fusion of the functions of these kinds of organizations
resulted in the creation of the Centres d'Animation Rurale
(CARs), under the jurisdiction of the Ministry of Production.
        The CARs provide a residential training program in
agriculture, for a period of two years, for young rural
illiterates between 18 and 21 years. The goal is to
create an enlightened peasantry through training designed
to make young farmers aware of the possibility of bettering
their standard of living through the application of modern
methods of cultivation, cattle raising, and management.
        The trainees are expected to act as rural animators
upon completion of their training--that is, they will
return to their villages and, by their example and through
disseminating what they have learned, influence others to
adopt better production methods.
        Of the 98 CARs in existence by 1972, 48 were operative.
Their total enrollment was 1,150 students, with an average
group of 20 to 25 young people per center. Preference
is given to illiterate men. However, two special centers
have been set aside for young married couples, and more
mixed centers may be established.[2] The plan is to open
10 centers in 1974, 20 in 1976, and 10 more in 1978,
bringing the total number of CARs in operation to 88 by
1978.
        Each CAR is staffed by an instructor of agriculture
and a military noncommissioned officer. The agricultural
instructor is recruited at the level of 8th or 9th school
year and goes through three years of training in one of
the centers of farming apprenticeship. His training consists of general education oriented toward agriculture,
technical theory, practical technique, and periods of
practice in the farm country.
        The training schedule is modified to suit local condi-
tions, depending on climate, jobs, and ongoing educational
programs. Emphasis is given to the highest profit-earning
jobs or projects, to areas where there is evident deficiency, or to those which will bring a sure and rapid
increase in returns. The syllabus includes technical,

social, and economic studies related to agriculture (including study of the principal crop in the region, agronomic research, soil conservation, and horticulture); animal husbandry; farm-related skills, including construction; social and economic conditions of production; and other topics related to rural life, such as cooperative organizations, sanitary education, civic instruction, and quasi-military instruction.

The training also includes literacy courses given by the monitor (functional literacy in working zones; conventional literacy courses in other centers). Daily activities of work and study and of service and leisure in common are organized by the monitor. A humanist outlook is emphasized. In the two new "family" centers the syllabus for young wives includes rural home economics, farming, small animal rearing, handicrafts, and nutrition.

Originally the intention was that, after training, young graduates would be provided with the basic tools and equipment to start them off on their farms in the home village, but difficulties in getting repayments and shortages of funds have precluded offering this service for the past four years. The lack of follow-up services to former trainees has constituted one of the major weaknesses in the whole program.

The question of financing the construction of new centers in the years to come will not arise, since there are already 98 centers in existence, only 48 of which are functioning. By 1978, 88 should be in operation. The anticipated expenses for opening new centers will be for the financing of agricultural material, and the upkeep of the trainees during the first year's training. FED has assured aid for the financing of these expenses. For the period 1974-1977, the estimated total is MF139,530,000.

Each student receives a monthly stipend of MF500. The wages of the agricultural monitor are MF250,000 a year. The service budget of the CARs for the year 1973 breaks down as follows:

Personnel	MF66,998,940
Materiel	MF32,480,000
Total	MF99,478,940

It is difficult to estimate the precise cost per pupil in the CAR training program, especially because the amortization of the expenses for construction of the CARs will be divided among the different organizations utilizing the buildings when they are not occupied by a CAR. In the opinion of CAR officials, moreover, the actual cost of a trainee is much lower than the budget figure because the activities of the personnel cover all the farmers in the villages near the CAR rather than just the trainees. It is estimated, however, that the cost is about MF100,000 per student.

Centres à Orientation Pratique (COPs)

Organized by the Ministry of National Education, the COPs aim at giving "young people, after their first basic cycle, instruction which prepares them for the occupation of farmer and encourages their integration into the milieu of their orientation." For boys and girls between 14 and 17 years, the training program lasts two years, in two annual sessions from May to February. The centers are nonresidential, and the normal quota of students in a COP is 40 students.

The training and instruction are oriented toward farming and cattle raising in addition to general studies and handicrafts. For boys, 60 percent of the schedule is related to the dominant agricultural activity of the region, 20 percent to handicrafts, and 20 percent to study of the area, functional arithmetic, French, history, civic instruction, sanitary education, domestic economy, and so forth. For girls, 50 percent of the schedule relates to the rural household economy, 30 percent to agriculture, and 20 percent to general training. Practical projects have an important place in these programs. Each COP takes charge of improving a plot of land of approximately four hectares. School canteens ensure the feeding of those who cannot get their meals outside.

The prerequisites for establishment of a COP include: the existence in an area (with a radius of six kms.) of sufficient potential students, the existence of a rural development program, accessibility for pupils in all seasons, land of reasonable quality, and the availability of water. Four teachers are required: two agriculturists, one craftsman, and one teacher for general education.

The original plan foresaw the opening of 10 centers in 1973, 10 more by the end of 1974, and 10 in each of the following years. Studies were made in the regions of Segou and Mopti and also in the zone set aside for the groundnut operation. Yet only eight COPs have been opened in the Sikasso region since May 1972.[3] A year later, seven of them were functioning with a <u>total</u> enrollment of about 100 boys. Three girls had been recruited but it was thought advisable to send them to a private COP opened in Sanzana in 1970 by the Catholic Mission of Sikasso.

A training center at Kouodimini (region of Segou) was constructed in June 1973. Containing four classrooms, a workshop, and places for the office and lodging of the center's director, this center is to serve as a training place for COP teachers. Forty students from 70 applicants have been accepted for this center's first year. Care was exercised in choosing candidates from families not too distant from the center.

Initially a sum of 150,000 Malian francs was alloted to each center for the operation of a school canteen and a sum of 10,000 Malian francs for occasional small expenses. The total bill for the equipment of a COP has been estimated to be 5 million Malian francs.[4] The cost of construction of a COP is an estimated 10 million Malian francs. Personnel expenditures average 600,000 Malian francs per teacher. The expenses of the school canteen, estimated on the basis of an attendance of 80 students for nine months at a daily expense of 250 Malian francs per pupil, total 2,700,000 Malian francs. Based on these figures, the cost of training one student during his stay at COP can be estimated at about 150,000 Malian francs. In addition, the cost of the follow-up equipment needed to enable "graduates" to practice their skills ranges from 30,000 Malian francs for a harrow or plow to 70,000 Malian francs for a pair of working oxen.

Recruitment of young people to COPs has been a serious problem. Some parents see no point in a two-year training course that simply returns the youngster to the village; others cannot spare their youngsters for lengthy periods. Since the schools are nonresidential, students who live too far away tend to drop out. Since the existing COPs are the products of the local population they reflect the available assets rather than the actual needs of the localities. There has also been difficulty in recruiting and training staff willing and able to work in the rural areas.

Moreover, there has been insufficient action in inspiring motivation, particularly because of the lack of precise information about the material to be supplied to students upon finishing training at the COP. An agreement is made with the students' parents whereby the student is assured of the assignment of a parcel of land on which to put in practice techniques learned at the center. In reality, however, the young people coming out of the COP have no control over the working of the family farm and cannot, in the traditional milieu, impose their points of view. This reality circumscribes their ability to secure loans for the purchase of animals or equipment since no guarantee can be made. At an August 1972 seminar on the Problems of Training and Animation in Rural Areas, it was recognized that, "A policy of farm training for young people would not have a real impact on agricultural development, except insofar as the young agriculturists have the equipment indispensable to the demands of their occupation." Yet the question of how to finance equipment of the "graduates" was not solved, and it has been recommended that a solution be found before a possible premature extension of the number of COPs.

Concerning the need for follow-up services to COP graduates, it has been suggested that the cooperative organization within the village could borrow money and purchase animals for collective use, since young people

have difficulty obtaining loans through the Society for
Farm Credit and Rural Equipment (SCAER) because SCAER
does not make loans in the absence of insurance on livestock.   The Agriculture and the Waters and Forest Services
can help in determining the type of equipment to give.
     The Seminar on the Problems of Training and Animation
in the Rural Areas recommended that the rural development
operations apply themselves to keeping up the training of
these young people from the COP". . . in the form of
continued contacts, periodic studies and meetings."   And
the Social Service Department proposed a training program
for parents, parallel to that of the young in the COP, in
order to prepare families to receive these young people
after they leave the COP.

A NOTE ON COORDINATION

     For coordination and cooperation in educational
efforts at the national level, the establishment of a
permanent committee on education and training in rural
areas was recommended by the seminar on the Problems of
Training and Animation in Rural Areas (August 1972).
This seminar included participants from the Ministry of
Education (primary education; National Education Institute [IPN]; COP; IPEG; Rural Polytechnic Institute [IPR]
of Katibougou; functional literacy; secondary education
and higher education); the Ministry of Production (development operations, rural animation, institute of rural
economy, and cattle raising); social welfare; finance and
business; cooperation; administration; SCAER; private
education; and others.
     Other measures already taken are:

    1. creation of an interministerial commission for
        the rural press to include the various interested
        ministries and representatives of the development
        operations
    2. creation of an interministerial committee com-
        posed of permanent members appointed by the
        ministries of Education, Youth, and Sports, Pro-
        duction, and Public Health and Social Welfare
        at an interministerial meeting held to discuss
        community development
    3. integration of the functional literacy agency
        with Operation Rice at Segou
    4. the creation of various commissions with repre-
        sentatives from all the ministries, services,
        and operations interested in the preparation of
        the five-year plan (1974-1978)
    5. the creation of INAFLA, to study the pedagogical
        approaches used in functional literacy which could
        facilitate the reorganization of primary education

6.   coordination of seminars held on family planning, sex education, and other topics, bringing together representatives of concerned organizations

At the regional level, the governor is charged with the economic and social promotion of the region and in this role supervises and coordinates the activities of the various services and development operations. Meetings are regularly held at this level, bringing together the directors of the various activities of the region to define priorities and orientation. The governor takes field trips accompanied by the heads of the principal services, to gain an understanding of the problems and to develop means for practical coordination of different operations.

The commandant of the cercle coordinates and supervises activities of the local services. He organizes periodic meetings of the chiefs of the service, in which each one contributes information concerning his activity in the cercle. At the cercle level there are also seminars of the parents' associations to examine school and youth problems, and seminars of the women's associations.

The head of the arrondissement, in direct contact with the beneficiaries of the projects, exercises constant supervision of these activities and arbitrates any differences that may arise either among the agents of the different services or between the agents and the population.

The procedures cited above engender exchange of information about the activities, means, needs, and problems of the different services. On the basis of this reciprocity, numerous relationships develop between the various projects, either within the staffs which offer special services, or among those who coordinate the operations in progress.

Field-level coordination of programs is most often achieved by integration of the different educational programs. Thus, for example: the staff of the development operations are more and more involved in the activities of functional literacy, the rural press, and SCAER. The proposed community development centers and the CARs are expected to capitalize on this cooperation among the cadres.

CONCLUDING REMARKS

The different educational programs described in the previous sections were begun at various times and based on divergent theories. Some of them are solidly established and have fashioned a real educational philosophy; others are much more recent and are still in an experi-

mental phase. Certain of them benefit by large funds,
others lack the means to implement their goals. Given
these diverse conditions, problems of imbalance have
inevitably arisen; problems that may be solved gradually
with increased cooperation and a better division of
available funds.

One of the primary issues that remains to be resolved
is the inequality of opportunities for the education of
rural young people compared with those of the young city
dwellers. As noted earlier, the rural areas include 93.5
percent of the entire population and 86.5 percent of the
group aged 8-20 years. Nevertheless, rural Mali has only
63.5 percent of the attendance at primary schools. In
pastoral areas of the rural zone young people are even
more disadvantaged. These areas contain 22 percent of
the whole population, but only 12.8 percent of school
students. The rural sector thus enjoys very little benefit from the school system. Moreover, most of those who
do attend school and pass their examinations will go into
nonagricultural occupations; this same unfortunate situation will obtain for those who leave school after seven
or eight years of study.

Despite the numerous nonformal programs, the disparity
between urban and rural opportunities continues. Many
nonformal programs were developed in the urban milieu
(such as the old type of social centers before the community development formula was introduced), the children's
day school, and the Pioneer movement. Likewise, the CCPA
and the local women's association seem to have more
intensive programs in urban areas than in the rural areas.

Moreover, certain training programs oriented toward
the rural area affect a very small number of young people
relative to the needs. The COPs and the CARs, for example,
with their small budgets, risk never reaching more than a
minuscule fraction of the rural population, unless they
succeed in financing themselves. At present the Functional
Literacy program reaches only about 3 percent of some
1,700,000 rural illiterates of the 15-40 year old group.
And the rural press, one of the aims of which is to forge
contact between the urban and rural areas, obviously
reaches only the literates.

On the other hand, radio has had real and effective
influence in rural areas, as has the health education
effort, through its showing of films, though this program
is still not very extensive because of the lack of funds.
Another active influence in rural areas is the indoctrination effort initiated by the Department for the Populari-
zation of Agriculture in the development operations,
which reaches more than half of the rural population,
and some farmers in every village.

The problem of inequality is not only an urban-rural
one, but has to be faced within the rural world itself,
between those zones intensively staffed by the develop-

ment operations and the others. On the whole, already the most favored zones (in terms of natural endowment and infrastructure) have been chosen for intensive development operations. For reasons of efficiency, the zones with development operations have the most intensive educational programs (in functional literacy and community development, the rural press, and skill training). These same zones also benefit more than others in opportunities for obtaining aid (credit guaranteed by the development operations, provision of material, selected seed, fertilizer, and insecticides).

Another problem is the cultural dichotomy between the schooled and the unschooled. As it now operates, the formal education system tends to separate the educated from the rest of the population (especially in the rural area). This is because programs are oriented toward foreign educational models (equivalency of diplomas) rather than toward the actual situations that the majority of educated young people will have to face. Also the prospects of a comfortable life for those who succeed in their studies are greater: a life devoted to intellectual tasks is not only more remunerative but also considered less tiring than one devoted to manual work in the rural areas. The villager has understood this very well—a child is sent to school so that he may have a chance to leave his original milieu.

The cultural dichotomy is reinforced as well by the general atmosphere of the school (the buildings, school equipment and furnishings, discipline; the separation from the family for the greater part of the day; the initiation into a different view of the world) and above all, by the use of a language other than that used by the rest of the population.

Among the solutions now being sought to overcome this cultural dichotomy are the efforts toward the ruralization of education; the adaptation of the educational system to the sociocultural needs of the sector; and research stemming from the functional literacy experiment that may indicate innovative directions for the reform of conventional education.

NOTES

1. O. Le Brun, "Strategies of Development: Economic Background in Educational Programmes for Youth," in Action-Training for Development: An Alternative Education for Youth?, comp. by the UNESCO Regional Office for Education in Africa (Dakar, Senegal, 1972), p. 49.

2. At the seminar on "Problems of Training and Animation in Rural Areas," in August 1972, it was noted: "In view of the encouraging results obtained by the CARs in accepting young farm couples,

the seminar hopes that this formula will be made as general as possible."

    3. Two in each cercle of Koutiala and Sikasso, one each in Kacholo, Bougouni, Kolondyeba, Yorosso.

    4. Estimates made by a subcommittee of the seminar on "Problems of Training and Animation in Rural Areas."

7

SRI LANKA:
NONFORMAL EDUCATION
FOR RURAL YOUTH
The Marga Institute

Sri Lanka was chosen for a case study in part because it depicts the educational and youth problems of a developing country that has made unusual progress toward meeting the goal of universal primary education and toward providing secondary education to a large fraction of the age-group. The case study was prepared by E. L. Wijemanne, Director of Education (Planning) in the Sri Lanka Ministry of Education, and G. H. F. Welikala, under the auspices of the Marga Institute (Sri Lanka Centre for Development Studies) and was completed in early 1973. The present chapter is a condensed and edited version of the full case study report, which has been published by the Marga Institute under the title Nonformal Education in Sri Lanka *(Colombo, 1974).*

GENERAL BACKGROUND

Lying to the southeast of India and separated from that subcontinent by a narrow strip of shallow sea, the Palk Strait, the island of Sri Lanka extends 270 miles from north to south, 140 miles from east to west, comprising an area of about 25,000 square miles, or 16.2 million acres. A mountainous section in the south central part, from which numerous rivers radiate, is surrounded, first by an upland belt, and then by a flat coastal plain that broadens, particularly in the north, to vast tracts covering more than half the length of the country. Oceanic effects and the hills, some as high as 7,000 feet, tend to moderate the high equatorial temperatures. Although the island is divided into two climatic zones, the Wet Zone in the southeast and the Dry Zone largely in the northeast, no part of the country is completely free of monsoon-borne rainfall.

Of Sri Lanka's 16.2 million acres, 4.8 million are devoted to agricultural use, coconut and paddy predominating

(tea and rubber to a lesser degree); of the 9 million
acres under shifting cultivation and forest, about 3.5-4.0
million acres can be developed for productive use; and of
the rest nearly 2 million acres are covered by towns and
villages, parks and reserves, roads, reservoirs, and
streams. The major rivers, notably the Mahaweli and
Samanalawewa, are considered adequate to the task of
providing necessary irrigation and hydroelectric power.
Properly exploited, the forests of both climatic zones
can meet the demands for timber; coastal and offshore
resources of fish offer scope for the expansion of the
fishing industry. Although Sri Lanka is relatively poor
in minerals, there are apparently appreciable resources
of iron ore on which a steel industry of moderate size is
contemplated; the exploration of promising petroleum
deposits is in progress; and, in spite of unstable markets
and costly production, Sri Lanka remains the world's
leading producer of high-grade graphite.

The population of Sri Lanka nearly doubled during
the 25 years from 1946 to 1971 when it was 12.75 million.[1]
This upsurge is attributable to the expansion of free
government health services and success in controlling
epidemic diseases, particularly malaria. This high rate
of population increase meant that a relatively large,
economically nonactive segment of the population became
dependent on the economically active segment. It also
meant that the total work force increased rapidly from
2.5 million in 1946 to 4.1 million in 1970.

At the same time the modern sector of the economy,
both in manufacturing and plantation agriculture, was
expanding much too slowly to absorb the growing numbers
of workers. The government had embarked on a major agricultural program, under the provisions of which new
agricultural settlements were provided with irrigation and
the peasant smallholdings expanded. But this program,
generating some employment, was unable to meet the total
need for work, and both urban and rural sectors began to
accumulate a large mass of young unemployed persons. A
large proportion of the work force has continued over the
years to be engaged in agriculture--53.8 percent in 1946,
declining only slightly to 51.6 percent in 1970,[2] and the
contribution of agriculture to the gross domestic product
has remained constant at about 35 percent.

In 1970 over 80 percent of the unemployed were between the ages of 15 and 24, and of this age-group
approximately 22 percent had completed only primary
education (grades 1-5), 46.8 percent had reached middle
school (grades 6-8), and another 23.9 percent had passed
General Certificate of Education, Ordinary Level (GCE(O)).
If one relates the unemployment data to the data relating
to the levels of educational attainment, it would appear
that those with higher attainment have less chance of
findings jobs or are unwilling to accept available jobs.

The high level of unemployment described above reflects conditions in the economy in which there is a growing imbalance between population and resources, of which
agricultural land is the most important. About two-thirds
of Sri Lanka's population live on one-third of the land.
This one-third, the Wet Zone, is exploited quite intensively under a dual structure of holdings in which peasant
smallholdings, producing rice and other food crops for
home consumption, exist side by side with large-scale
plantations that are operated commercially, thanks to
foreign capital and some imported labor, and are the main-
stay of Sri Lanka's "export economy."

In sharp contrast is the situation in the Dry Zone,
which is sparsely populated and where only 16 percent of
the land area has been brought into effective use. Further exploitation of the land, however, would depend on
large-scale intervention of the state in the form of heavy
capital outlays to construct major irrigation systems and
other infrastructures for agriculture.

In 1971 the government decided to undertake a program
on land reform, involving the imposition of land ceilings
of individual holdings and the releasing of 400,000 to
500,000 acres for redistribution. The government has also
attempted to build a system of cooperative enterprises for
which unemployed young persons would be selected. This
appears to be most advantageous in land given over to
coconut cultivation, because such land is more amenable
to diversified cultivation. Levels of employment on the
new farms, of course, vary with the crops and additional
employment does not necessarily follow transfer of ownership. It is certain that the success of land reform and
cooperatives in generating additional employment and
increased productivity will depend on the underpinnings
of a well-organized package of services including appropriate forms of education.

Although the structure of holdings in both the Wet
Zone and Dry Zone reflects a general situation of scarcity
of usable land, much of the high land adjacent to villages
remains very poorly exploited. Accustomed primarily to
low paddy cultivation, the peasant sector has been unable
to evolve a satisfactory technology for the efficient and
economical use of the high land, which is admirably suited
to the cultivation of chillies, onions, vegetables, and so
on. Recently, however, a ban on the imports of such products has provided favorable price incentives. With
necessary institutional support, better use of the
high land may be the source of additional employment and
income to the villages.

While the rate of unemployment in the urban sector is
higher than that of the rural sector in Sri Lanka, the gap
is not so wide as to suggest a significant difference in
the quality and intensity of the unemployment situation in
the urban sector. This phenomenon is the result of social

and economic policies aimed at maintaining a relatively
satisfactory rural-urban balance and preventing a dis-
orderly migration of rural masses to the city. Any significant shift in the balance is not expected during the
next ten years or so under current development strategies.

In view of the foregoing and the fact that growth in
the manufacturing sector, relying heavily on expansion
and dispersion of agro-based industries, will not generate
much employment anyway, it is clear that the main burden of
employment creation will fall on the agricultural sector.
Some encouragement lies in the proposed development of two
major river basins, which together with a number of smaller
agricultural settlements is expected to yield an additional
250,000 acres and to provide employment in the cultivation
of a wide range of crops. It is also clear that the occupations in agriculture and rural industry will have to
match the aspirations of the new job seekers--in both the
incomes they will yield and in the quality and character
of the work. Much will depend on the capacity of the
learning system and the value system to form the needed
skills and the right attitudes to work.

FORMAL EDUCATION AND PREVOCATIONAL STUDIES

Traditional Learning System

An understanding of the role of formal and nonformal
education in present day education of Sri Lanka is elusive
without some knowledge of the institutions and modes of
learning that formed the total educational system of the
traditional village society. Although this system has
been often described in roseate terms by its protagonists
and presented as an idealized model that did not always
resemble reality, the model serves as a framework within
which the role of nonformal education can be evaluated.[3]
The village community, existing in Sri Lanka before
the impact of western commercial civilization, was an
organic traditional society in which Buddhism provided
the basis for both the value system and the operation of
the agrarian economy, supported by ancillary crafts and
kindred occupations. The society was organized in hierarchical occupation-based castes. Within such a system an
individual's training in a given skill, introduction to
an occupation or craft, education into the value system,
and acceptance of the normative patterns of behavior in
the society were indivisible elements of a single learning system. The various institutions in that society--
the formal educational institution attached to the temple
(the Pirivena school), the temple itself, the workplace
or workshop, and the family--combined to provide the

requisite basic education of the individuals. Crucial
situations in the life of individual or community were
ritualized, and through the rituals the discipline of
religion, myth, and folklore were affirmed.

In short, the educational components implicit in
acquiring occupational skills, codes of behavior, value
systems, and religious disciplines were part and parcel
of the social organization. Formal, informal, and nonformal processes merged into one another in such a manner
that no sharp separation obtained in the passage from
childhood and apprenticeship roles to the roles of adult
responsibility. While providing for the integration of
the young into adult society, the master craftsmen, religious teachers, and other leaders also set standards and
imparted skills as a continuing process of adult learning.
Although vast social and economic changes took place
during the period of occupation of Ceylon by the Western
powers, it was essentially against this technologically
simple and economically static background of learning
that any new system of formal education would have to
operate.

Spread of Modern Education

The beginning of the modern formal education on a
mass scale dates back to 1944 when a universal free education system was introduced, permitting all segments of
the population access to formal education. Up to that
time formal education at the secondary and higher levels
had been the monopoly of an English-educated minority,
responding to the need of a foreign imperial government
for a flow of native employees for their commercial or
governmental administrative tasks.

The expansion and conversion of the old elite system
of education into a mass system, without any fundamental
change in the curriculum or in the objectives of education,
was not without serious implication. Because secondary and
higher education had always been demonstrated as the one
means of achieving upward social mobility, secure employment, high income, and improvement of status generally,
it was inevitable that the same expectations would motivate the rapidly increasing group to whom secondary and
higher education were being made available free of charge.

Two developments occurred with the implementation of
the new system that are relevant to our discussion. First,
the economy simply did not expand fast enough to receive
more than a fraction of the newly educated generation, and
the 1960s ended with widespread frustration and a massive
backlog of unemployed educated youth. Second, the academic
curriculum was frequently not related to the occupational
needs of the economy and the employment opportunities that

students could expect to have. Furthermore, the modes of
instruction tended to neglect many fundamental and time-
tested aspects of instruction, related to the development
of values, the formation of character and personality, the
acquisition of social skills to participate in community
action, norms of behavior, and so on--which, as noted
above, were part of the learning system of the traditional
society.

The process of change and development generated a
further educational demand that could not be met by the
formal system or by any part of the traditional system
that was available. This was the demand of the nation to
raise the level of technology in the agrarian economy and
to transform and modernize the rural sector. Involved in
this process was the transfer of know-how to the subsistence farmers to enable them to improve their methods of
production, raise their income levels, and achieve a
higher quality of living. Involved also was a knowledge
and understanding of the essential scientific facts pertaining to such things as nutrition and sanitation and
the acquisition of managerial and organizational skills
to cope with greater production and a monetized economy.
There had to be a basic understanding of the workings of
the society in which the individual lived and some elementary appreciation of the social and economic significance
of these activities. This would include a familiarity
with topics ranging from government administration and
its functions to taxes and public expenditures insofar
as they are relevant.

To summarize, the efforts at nonformal education and
the curricular changes in the formal education system
which are described in this study must be considered in
the context of at least three significant developments.
First, there was the rapid expansion of the modern school
system which, controlling the most significant phase of
the individual's life, confined itself to imparting formal instruction in selected subjects and fell far short
of forming a comprehensive learning system. Second, those
elements which went to make up the comprehensive learning
system in the traditional society became increasingly
inadequate under the weight of social and economic changes.
Third, the goals of development called for a new and
different educational effort to transform the nonmodern
sector, raise its level of technology, transfer modern
knowledge and know-how to that sector, inculcate scientific attitudes, and improve its managerial capability:
in short, a new effort to educate the whole community
for development.

Various reforms have been attempted in recent years
by the government in order to reorient formal schooling
to the more practical needs of the people and the development of the country. The main features of the latest
educational reforms instituted in 1972 were the following:

1. age of admission to school raised from 5 to
    6 years
2. four segments in the previous school system
    reduced to three--primary school (grades 1
    to 5), junior secondary school (grades 6 to
    9, and senior secondary school (grades 10
    and 11)
3. at junior secondary level, common comprehen-
    sive curriculum prescribed which leads to a
    new public examination for the National Certi-
    ficate of General Education
4. introduction in curriculum at junior secondary
    level of "prevocational studies"

Prevocational Studies

Content and Objectives

The term "Prevocational Studies," as used by the
Ministry of Education of Sri Lanka, refers to one area
of the secondary school instructional program, the content
of which is related to specific vocations in such a way
that students have opportunities of learning about vocations without necessarily acquiring professional skills
in them. Where the skills are relatively simple, students
should of course acquire a degree of proficiency in them
through school courses. Where the skills are complex,
demanding a level of maturity not ordinarily attainable
by novitiates, an opportunity is provided for the acquisition of some component skills that are consonant with
their stage of development.

Associated with each vocation there is not only a
specific set of manual skills, but also a body of theory
and knowledge. Accordingly, every prevocational study
includes instruction in certain areas which have not
received sufficient attention in the past. For example,
a prevocational study of brick making should concern
itself with such matters as the raw materials, the process of manufacture, and the criteria by which a good
brick should be judged. It would also include such
questions as these: What is involved in the marketing
of bricks? Who are the users? For what purposes are
bricks used? And so on. Prevocational studies in agriculture should include discussion of managerial and
organizational decisions faced by the farmer; should
emphasize production, not in vacuo, but under existing
conditions in the community; should explore areas of
possible improvement attainable with initiative, cooperation, and effort. The course should be based on the
premise that scientific agriculture is not merely the
development of the high-yielding varieties of paddy or

the development of particular methods of cultivation, but
is also the application of the scientific knowledge to
make wise decisions in the day-to-day running of the farm.
The school agricultural program should not be divorced
from the problems of production. To do so would develop
the belief that scientific agriculture is uneconomical
and that, indeed, it is not a propitious vocational option.
In short, prevocational studies are concerned with manual
skills and with cognitive studies that are inextricably
associated with them.

Although organization of Prevocational Studies in
general varies in different schools, it is intended that
students completing the four-year prevocational studies
program will have the following knowledge, skills, and
attitudes:

1. execute selected manual skills related to
   vocations with an appropriate degree of proficiency
2. comprehend appropriate aspects of selected
   vocations
3. acquire knowledge of major vocations practised
   in the community
4. develop the awareness that knowledge gained in
   other studies, such as mathematics and science,
   can be applied in studying about vocations
5. develop a feeling of confidence and pride in
   their ability to participate in the production
   of marketable goods or services

Prevocational Program in Operation

All students in grade 6 in 1972 embarked upon the
common curriculum in which Prevocational Studies was made
an important component. This curriculum was designed to
extend to grade 7 in 1973, grade 8 in 1974, and grade 9
in 1975. In the 5,500 schools with these grades, seven
periods a week (out of 40 periods) are allotted to this
subject in the following manner:

Prevocational Studies I--Three periods a week. Not
unlike earlier practical arts courses, this part of
the course is devoted to instruction in woodwork,
metal work, weaving, ceramics, light miscellaneous
crafts, agriculture, home science, and also commerce.
Prevocational Studies II--Three periods a week. The
really new entrant in the curriculum, this part pre-
supposes the selection by a school of one or more
vocations in its locality that can be studied to
advantage by its students. Syllabi prepared locally
and approved by the Ministry of Education's Curriculum Department range from cloth printing, poultry

keeping, fisheries, and fruit cultivation to motor
mechanism, electrical wiring, and concrete grill work.
Country's Natural Resources--One-half period a week.
This brief part is concerned with the natural
resources of the country from an economic point of
view, with particular reference to the resources
available in the school district.
Elementary Geometrical Drawing--One-half period a
week. This part has been introduced in the belief
that skills acquired in it will be indispensable
to any citizen as science and technology advance.

Evaluation of a student's prevocational studies
accomplishment is difficult because manual skills do not
lend themselves to common written examinations. Furthermore, each prevocational study is likely to have a strong
local bias which could vary from school to school.
Nevertheless Prevocational Studies will be tested for the
National Certificate of General Education at the end of
grade 9 beginning in 1975. The final grade of each
candidate will be an appropriate composite of the written
examination and the marks earned in grade 9.
The role of the school principal in organizing
Prevocational Studies in his school is of first importance.
After soliciting the aid of teachers and others in the
community, he selects the studies to be taught for which
facilities and manpower are readily available and appoints
a committee to assist him in the development of curricular materials. The committee, in pursuing its curricular responsibilities, outlines workable teaching
sequences and methods of instruction for each level of
instruction and serves as a clearinghouse of information
in a search for helpful resource materials and knowledgeable personnel in both the public and private sectors.
The community itself, often encompassing more than one
school, is similarly important in identifying specialists,
buildings, and work sites and providing instruction and
equipment appropriate to the vocations selected.
Organization above the community level is in the
charge of the Circuit Education Officer, the Regional
Staff, and ultimately, the Ministry. The Circuit Education Officer is primarily responsible for effective
liaison, not only among circuit schools, but also between
them and those government officers who may be instrumental
in providing circuit schools with special facilities. He
sees to it that circuit schools receive equitable treatment, and he organizes inservice teacher training. The
Regional Staff clarifies and interprets broad ministerial
policy and briefs departments other than the Ministry of
Education on the prevocational enterprise. It helps
schools to market goods they have difficulty in selling
and to cooperate in their procurement problems; it assists
in formulating evaluative procedures and advises on

financial matters. The Ministry is responsible for basic
policies, allocation of resources, and general administrative support and supervision. More specifically it is
responsible for the preparation and dissemination of
vocational publications, the release of progress reports
sent in by schools, and the conduct of national examinations.

Commentary

It is too early to judge the effectiveness of a program that is still in the process of getting off the
ground. Nevertheless, one or two comments may be ventured
at this time. It is clear that if the new prevocational
studies are able to demonstrate their relevance and practical application to actual life and work situations of
young people, they will have a definite value; but if
they are confined to these objectives, they may serve
only as another method of improving the pedagogical
effectiveness of formal education. On the other hand, if
they are to contribute to correcting the imbalance between education and the existing work opportunities, they
must ultimately motivate students to take up the occupations toward which these courses lead.

Such an objective is beset with numerous difficulties.
For example, many of the occupations for which prevocational training is provided are currently pursued by
persons of comparatively low educational attainment at
a low level of technology and income and will not prove
attractive to school leavers. Although it is not expected
that students would take to these occupations at their
present technology and income level, the new program of
studies may enable students to identify the potential for
employment and livelihood at a higher level of both productivity and income than   currently obtains. Because
there is little point in studying traditional occupations
that offer no opportunity for upgrading and higher productivity, it is essential that the selected studies be
strongly linked to those occupations with unquestioned
potential for modernization and improvement. The selection of prevocational studies in the curriculum must in
effect be part of the total development program envisaged
for the country at large. Clearly there has not been
sufficient relationship between broad educational policy
and specific programs or between the school itself and
the community whose future it proposes to serve.

Other roadblocks lie ahead. It will be difficult to
insinuate new and relatively uncharted prevocational
training into a curriculum, the teachers of which have
long been accustomed to conventional guides, texts, and
teaching aids associated with traditional academic subjects.
New structures relative to content and conduct of prevocational training are emerging, but it will be quite some

time before the rank and file of teachers will handle the
new subject with the same confidence felt in teaching
conventional subjects. It will be difficult to introduce
this unconventional new entrant into the curriculum,
because, even in rural areas, its organizational inflexi-
bilities (timetable, classes, grades, and large numbers)
set serious limits on the extent to which students can
participate in real live vocational situations. Also it
will be troublesome to examine students and evaluate their
achievement in the several prevocational studies. Because
traditional paper and pencil tests do not assess a student's pride in his work nor his real ability to execute
a manual skill, he must be observed and compared critically when engaged in specific tasks, tested orally in
certain studies, and asked to present his actual "produc-
tions" or finished articles for scrutiny. Evaluative
criteria in these areas are incomplete. Furthermore,
whether the examination is considered to be a necessary
evil or not, if a subject is left out of the public
examinations, it is unlikely to merit the attention it
deserves from either students or teachers.

There is finally the inescapable matter of costs,
difficult to compute but assuredly heavy for a country
whose current expenditure on education is at about the
highest level it can afford. Implementation of prevocational studies, involving broad varieties of equipment
(particularly in the scientific subjects), must not be
such as to constitute a continuing heavy liability on
the national exchequer. The provision of useful but un-
essential equipment by import has to be ruled out. Self-
reliance in the communities themselves, not dependence
on an inexhaustible state supply, must be the watchword.
The expedient of marketing goods produced in vocational
studies may offset some expenditure or provide replacement of what is depleted or worn out, but harder decisions will have to determine whether, for example, local
plants can adequately supply schools' equipment needs or
whether more sophisticated materials are required. In
the last analysis, available funds and resources will
have to be matched against the needs, and the best in
compromises reached.

We turn in the following sections to the major nonformal education programs for rural children and youth in
Sri Lanka. The more significant of the diverse nationwide and local activities, both under government and
voluntary auspices, are discussed under the following
headings: agricultural programs and settlement schemes
for rural youth, women's training, skill training programs,
and rural development and employment generation programs.
Within these categories, special attention is given to
Sri Lanka Mahila Samili (Sri Lanka Women's Association),
the Diyagala Boys' Town, and the Sarvodaya Shramadana
movement, because these have certain distinctive features
that make them specially interesting.

AGRICULTURAL PROGRAMS AND SETTLEMENT SCHEMES

There are several government departments and voluntary organizations which conduct training programs directly
related to the agricultural sector. The government departments involved one way or another are the Departments of
Agriculture, Agrarian Services, Co-operative Development,
Forestry, Irrigation, and Rural Development, as well as
the Office of the Land Commissioner and the River Valleys
Development Board. Two training programs, significant in
terms of clientele and objectives, are the Young Farmers
Clubs and the Practical Farm Schools, both run by the
Department of Agriculture. A third program of youth
settlement schemes is under the Land Commissioner's jurisdiction. Voluntary organizations such as the Lanka Mahila
Samiti, the Sarvodaya Shramadana organization, and several
church organizations offer agricultural training as an
element in their own broader programs. Such programs are
described in later sections of this study.

Young Farmers Clubs and Farmer Training

The work of the Department of Agriculture in respect
of youth training is centered on developing effective and
active Young Farmers Clubs, responsibility for which is
vested in the "range" Agricultural Instructors and Food
Production Officers under the supervision of the District
Agricultural Extension Officers. The objective of the
Young Farmers Clubs is to orient rural youths toward
modern farming techniques, to teach them principles of
farm management and marketing, and to foster a "community
approach" to agricultural development. Membership in
these clubs, some 3,000 in number, consists of about
100,000 boys and girls, 15-25 years of age, who have left
school. Although a 1968 survey indicated that less than
half of these clubs were functioning effectively, gains
have been made since then in strengthening the movement
generally and in making individual clubs self-reliant by
promoting and developing leadership at the village level.
The approach is not to attempt a simultaneous development
of youth clubs all over the island (which led to a diffusion and waste of effort in the past) but to concentrate
on selected areas. The program will be expanded as the
knowledge and skills of organizing and managing youth
clubs develop.

The main weakness of the Young Farmers Clubs program
is that its resources and personnel are too meagre to meet
its broad goals. The extension personnel do not have the
time and training to give adequate guidance to the youth
program. Because of these problems, in 1973 five specially

trained district-level officials were appointed to work
exclusively with youth clubs in five districts, and a
policy of selective and phased improvement of club activities was adopted.

The Practical Farm Schools were established from
1942 onwards to give training in practical agriculture
to young men and women on their own lands or on land
alienated to them by the government. By 1958 there were
19 such schools, but the single year of training proved
to be inadequate preparation for realization of basic
objectives, and even those trainees who had land of their
own sought government employment upon completion of the
course--thus defeating a main purpose of the program. In
1965, staffed by the Department of Agriculture, 14 of the
Practical Farm Schools were diverted to the six-months'
training courses of secondary school teachers in the
Department of Education, but it is expected that these
schools will gradually be released from this responsibility.

The most recent proposal as of 1973 is that five
Practical Farm Schools now run by the Department of Agriculture be maintained for general agricultural training,
with emphasis on practical aspects for men and women who
desire to practice farming on their own or who wish to
seek employment in the public or private sectors at the
junior technical level. The present output from the
schools is 250 students per year.

In addition to the Practical Farm Schools, a two-
year course in agricultural science and home economics
is offered by the School of Agriculture (Kundasale).
Students with only the GCE(0) certificate with passes in
specified subjects are admitted to this school. The
present output of the School of Agriculture is 150 students. Any increase in this number will depend on a
careful examination of the employment opportunities that
will arise in succeeding years.

The Department of Agriculture also provides formal
one-day courses in farmer training in different parts of
the island. The single objective of each course is to
isolate one or two practical problems of immediate concern to the farmers of the given localities and to educate
them in solving them. Class instruction is accompanied by
field demonstrations. Seventy-one thousand farmers have
participated in this popular utilitarian program in the
years 1970 and 1971.

Akin to the one-day courses are the one-day visits of
farmers to the important research stations of the Department, so that there may be closer links between research
and extension and a better appreciation by both farmers
and research officers of their mutual problems. Both the
Department of Agriculture and the Department of Agrarian
Services provide training for those who will instruct
others; they range from two-day fixed curriculum courses
to discussions and seminars on such topics as crop

insurance, rural credit, the guaranteed price scheme, and agricultural extension. Inservice training is typified by the Department of Agriculture Inservice Training Institute at Peradeniya, which provides a two-week course of training for new recruits in the grades of Agricultural Instructor and Food Production Overseer.

Youth Settlement

The settlement of unemployed educated youth on newly opened land was started in 1965 by the Land Commissioner's Department, with a target of 15,000 youths to be actively engaged in self-employment in agriculture, horticulture, and animal husbandry over a five-year period. The program gained in intensity in the first two years, but then fell off when multiplication of separate facilities deferred to consolidation and expansion of existing schemes. By the middle of 1972, there were 2,783 youths resettled on 41 settlement schemes, covering a total of 11,285 acres of shifting cultivation and forest land (see Table 7.1). The original proposal that each scheme be operated on the basis of a communal farm was virtually abandoned in favor of having each youth work his own portion of land and market its produce independently of the others.

TABLE 7.1

Acreage and Number of Youths in 41 Settlement Schemes
June 1972

Type of Scheme (Cropwise)	No. of Schemes	Acreage		No. of Youth Actively Engaged	
		Home-stead	Culti-vable	Potential	Resident
Subsidiary food crops and/or paddy	21	1,354	4,585	1,770	1,474
Paddy only	1	33	72	19	19
Tea or tea and cinnamon	5	199	1,046	398	350
Cinnamon only	2	75	217	150	103
Coconut and paddy	2	49	912	167	153
Fruits	3	300	1,950	650	514
Vegetables and mixed farming	6	165	320	220	159
Animal husbandry	1	6	2	12	11
TOTAL	41	2,181	9,104	3,386	2,783

Source: Sri Lanka, Department of the Land Commissioner, "Youth Settlement Scheme Progress Report, April-June 1972," mimeographed (Colombo, 1972).

Costs in the early stages of the schemes were high: the average cost of resettling one youth ranged from Rs10,400 to Rs17,500 during the first three years of the program. It was reported by the Land Commissioner's Office in 1972 that in 25 of the schemes average income per settler ranged from Rs250 to Rs500 per month. It was also reported that 40-50 percent of the settlers, all of whom were originally bachelors, soon became even more settled as husbands and fathers of families.[4]

Two of the more successful Youth Settlement Schemes are the Muthu Iyan Kaddu and Ihala Hewessa Schemes. Their initial stages were reasonably well planned and managed; their leadership, particularly as motivating forces of youth, exceptional. The crops selected were capable of yielding incomes not inconsistent with those earned in any other sector to which youth normally aspired. The methods of cultivation, the management and organization of the farm, and the marketing of produce all made demands on the skill, enterprise, and education of the young colonists. These schemes, approximating the prototype of scientific high-income intensive agriculture, suggest a closer, if brief, examination.

Muthu Iyan Kaddu Scheme. Between March 1967 and June 1970, 300 youths at the Muthu Iyan Kaddu Youth Settlement Scheme were allotted 900 acres of land--or two acres apiece of cultivable land and one acre of homestead. For a subsistence allowance of Rs2 per day, plus World Food Programme food rations and financial assistance to erect a temporary hut and purchase initial supplies, each youth was expected to cultivate one acre of chillies and one acre of a subsidiary crop, with the object of realizing an annual net income of Rs3000. In actual fact, 21 youths, in cultivating a full three acres, realized incomes over Rs15,000; 26 youths, in cultivating two acres, realized incomes between Rs10,000 and Rs15,000. The average income of Rs6,117 (498 acres) was more than twice the target figure.

Most of the youth in this scheme came from farming families who owned no land but had a long tradition of intensive cultivation on small extents of leased out lands. Most of the 102 youths who earned less than Rs3,000 were the somewhat unimaginative sons of subsistence farmers who had passed on little or no incentive to their progeny. Nevertheless the success stories of the industrious youths have not been without influence on the others. The number of applicants for an expanded scheme in 1973, many of whom were satisfied with only two acres and no government aid at all, was vastly in excess of the number to be accommodated.

Ihala Hewessa Scheme. After a slow beginning, much hard work, and initial disappointment, 600 youths at the Ihala Hewessa Scheme were allotted 2,000 acres (of a government allocation of 3,500 acres), and were trained

under an incentive system that has gradually replaced the
original collective or communal farm system. In addition
to their field work and agricultural practices, youths
lived in dormitories and worked together in groups of
25 and received an initial all-round training that included
such tasks as domestic chores and a manual clearing of the
jungle. Later they split up into groups of five, each
settler receiving three and a half acres of land, of which
three were for the cultivation of passion fruit (primarily)
and pineapples,[5] and one-half an acre for homestead. Soon
dormitories were converted to recreation halls, as the
youths set up their own households and gained experience
and confidence to run their plots separately. Average
income has been Rs300 per month. However, more than half
have received Rs500 or more per month, and a number of
original trainees, without any money of their own at the
start, have become owners of property worth Rs20,000 to
Rs25,000.

Commentary on Agricultural Programs

Signal progress is being made in a broad variety of
agricultural programs. However, there has been a lack of
relatedness and coordination among the several programs.
Each has been functioning in an almost water-tight compart-
ment without sufficient relation to other government programs or to others sponsored privately. Such autonomy
tends to confuse rather than help the people for whom the
broad effort is intended. If the central purpose of
developing the rural and agricultural sectors is the common objective of all, these programs must be more effectively coordinated. But even more important is the
question of whether or not farming as an occupation is
being made sufficiently attractive to young people of
both sexes. Denied the type of employment for which
formal education has done so much to prepare them, are
they sufficiently rewarded and satisfied in the vocations
toward which the agricultural training leads? It appears
that training can fulfill its basic objective of providing
useful skills, only when it is accompanied by necessary
incentives in keeping with youthful aspirations.

Despite the relative successes of the youth settlement movement, its expansion and development has been
painfully slow when compared to the magnitude of the
problems it seeks to alleviate. Settlement schemes are
costly, but part of their costliness lies in the decision
preponderantly to cultivate permanent crops rather than
cash crops that mature sooner and, in so doing, hasten
income. Some schemes have been unsuitably located--with
water supplies inadequate or other vital needs unavailable nearby. Other schemes have suffered from inadequate

planning and insufficient cost-benefit analyses. Resident
leaders of the projects, though professionally competent,
are often without adequate training in extension methods
and, worse still, are deficient in handling youth. The
youth who have employment aspirations appropriate to their
level of education and have given up their previous social,
economic, and cultural environment have often found the
advice to go back to the land paradoxical. Other leaders
have failed properly to project an image of the youth in
his new environment, much less helped him to achieve it.
No sociological and economic studies have been made on the
most appropriate patterns of land ownership and the means
for production, collection, and distribution of the produce in the settlement; communication has been faulty in
clarifying types of problems that settlers would be unlikely to foresee or anticipate from their previous training or predisposition. No attempt has been made to help
the youth develop a pattern of social organization within
their settlement or in relation to their neighbors beyond.
The importance of delegating responsibility to the youth
for discussion and decision-making in the day-to-day
activities in the settlement and of developing leadership
among them has not been sufficiently recognized.

WOMEN'S TRAINING

While most nonformal educational programs do not
specifically bar girls and women, female participation
in most is limited. The activities of the Lanka Mahila
Samiti (National Women's Association) are, of course,
aimed exclusively at women. Also described in this section is the Department of Small Industries training
program in handloom weaving and other cottage crafts,
because almost all the participants are rural women.

Lanka Mahila Samiti

The most important program for rural women is operated by the Lanka Mahila Samiti with beginnings in 1930,
when the new universal suffrage emboldened a small group
of dedicated women to make up a Central Board of Women's
Institutes and to form a few Mahila Samitis in villages
not far from Colombo. By 1955 there were Mahila Samitis
in 850 villages scattered over many parts of the island
with a membership of 55,000. Further spread of the movement brought the estimated membership to more than 200,000
women in at least 2,300 Samitis.
    The objectives of the Lanka Mahila Samiti are to help
establish Mahila Samitis in Sri Lanka villages and through

them to further women's educational, sanitary, social,
and economic progress, and to carry out through them a
vigorous propaganda for the uplift of island women everywhere; to act as a central organization of the Samitis
formed and to further their interests in every way; and
to appoint Provincial Committees in the promotion of:
social intercourse irrespective of caste and creed, agricultural pursuits, homecraft and mothercraft, cottage
industries, cooperative enterprise and mutual help, thrift,
social hygiene, and interest in local institutions, such
as hospitals and welfare centers.

In support of these objectives, village Samitis function democratically with office-bearers elected annually,
and the planning and implementation of training and village
development projects placed under the guidance of the
trained Sevikas (paid workers) and trained Sweecha Sevikas
(voluntary workers). Field staff members of such government departments as Health, Agriculture, and Small Industries are often invited to some of the regularly scheduled
village meetings and discussions--these contacts serving
as a means of informal education of village women and of
making them better and more efficient mothers and housewives. As a further consequence of these contacts, village women have organized a wide range of activities for
their own betterment--such as constructing compost pits;
promoting the use of boiled drinking water; improving the
village well; organizing adult literacy, sewing, and crafts
classes; kitchen gardens, fruit canning, and so on.

Formation of a local Mahila Samiti is initiated upon
request signed by at least 10 village women; it becomes
reality soon after the parent organization sends its
trained personnel to the village to explain objectives.
Membership is confined to women in the age-group 15-50
years, with young married and unmarried women under age
25 predominating. At least 20 of the membership then
petition the parent organization for a nominee of theirs,
unmarried and in the age-group 18-30 years, to undergo a
course of training at the Training Institute run by the
central organization. Although exceptions to the general
rule have been made, the nominee should have reached the
GCE(O) level in formal education. The nominee returns to
her village to function as a Sweecha Sevika after completing three and a half months of intensive training at the
Training Institute.

The Training Institute, established (1948) and financed by the Association, is well equipped for its
purpose under the leadership of a resident warden, four
handicraft instructresses and staff. Three courses
are conducted each year with 30-35 trainees in each
course. Course content includes such larger topics as
health, agriculture, thrift, cooperation, and family planning, conducted by officials of the appropriate government
departments, and both theoretical and practical aspects of

such specific topics as agricultural handicrafts, embroidery and needlework, pillow lace work, and creche work. Each trainee must make with her own handiwork certain household artifacts; and training in public speaking enables her later on to explain and illustrate the type of articles Samiti members can themselves produce. During the final two weeks the trainees practice organization of a village Samiti, conduct simulated meetings, programming, and so forth.

The Training Institute provides more advanced courses of shorter duration for office-bearers of village Samitis, who pay Rs15 apiece for needed equipment, materials, and educational tours. Refresher courses are available for Grama and Parikshana Sevikas (paid supervisory personnel), many of whom have been chosen and appointed from among particularly effective Sweecha Sevikas. At the headquarters of the Association in Colombo, classes and demonstrations in cookery, preserving, batik work, and pillow lace-making are conducted for young women under 25 years of age.

Finally, the Lanka Mahila Samiti maintains 25 Model Centres[6] throughout the island, where the following activities are organized: 1) agriculture,   2) needlework and sewing,   3) food preservation and canning, and 4) creche work, that is, early training, largely through play, of small children and infants. The creche is in the charge of a Sevika trained by the parent organization; she in turn has a voluntary assistant. In addition to training through play, singing, personal hygiene, obedience to parents and elders, and religion are taught. Not included in the model center effort are 45 creches run by the Lanka Mahila Samiti (with grants of Rs10 per infant per month by the Department of Social Services), 8 creches financed by their own resources, and 5 village Samiti creches, maintained by local resources. The average daily attendance at a creche is about 30 infants.[7]

Administration of the Lanka Mahila Samiti organization is basically in the hands of the policymaking Central Board of 27 members--elected officials and representatives of government departments whose programs are germane to Samiti activity. The Board's Executive Committee of seven members attends to such matters as finance, correspondence, and general supervision of staff and village Samiti activities. Since the aim is to decentralize the work of the Association, the responsibility for day-to-day supervision and promotion is delegated to District Committees for each of the 22 Revenue Districts, membership in which consists of the district Parikshana and Grama Sevikas (supervisors and village workers) and a few others involved in nearby Samiti or Association work. There are also 55 Mahila Samiti Unions, each of which has representatives from all the village Samitis within its area.[8] At Union meetings, held in rotation in the area, progress

reports of member Samitis are submitted, government programs explained, and ideas exchanged, all in support of
furthering the Samitis' goals.

In addition to the permanent headquarters personnel,
ranging from 7 to 14 people, this islandwide program is
staffed in the field by 25 trained volunteer Regional
Organizers (and 25 understudies), 15 Grama Sevikas, 25
Parikshana Sevikas, and 58 Creche Sevikas. Most of the
funds for the operation of the Samiti come from the government (Departments of Rural Development and Health) or as
allocations from the Department of Social Services for
running the creches. Less than 10 percent of income is
from donations, finance campaigns, affiliation fees,
subscriptions, special shows, interest on deposits, and
so on.

Training in Handloom Weaving

No study of women's educational programs can be made
without some reference to the influence, training, and work
of the Department of Small Industries in its promotion of
rural industries--in particular that of handloom weaving
organized through the Handloom Weavers' Cooperative Societies and private handloom weaving enterprises. Annually,
10,000 out-of-school youth, 90 percent of whom are female,
are enrolled in these training opportunities for eventual
employment in an industry giving gainful employment to no
less than 250,000 people. Educational level for the training programs ranges from grade 6 to the GCE(0) level;
on-the-job training is of six months' duration in all
aspects of the industry. Each trainee is paid on a piece-
rate basis according to his or her output. Often for
reasons beyond his or her control the average weaver
realizes only Rs60 per month, working an eight-hour day;
however, an efficient weaver can earn as much as Rs200
per month.[9] About 40 percent of the workers operate on
looms belonging to the Cooperative Societies; the remaining 60 percent are employed in private workshops. About
100,000 handlooms were registered in the country in 1973.
As electricity is becoming available in rural areas,
powerloom weaving has been introduced and more than 50
training centers have been opened.

Other rural industries under the auspices of this
department are many and varied. The Department operates
52 carpentry training centers and provides financial
assistance for more than 75 centers for training in assor-
ted rural crafts, such as making ivory, brass, silver,
lacquer, and rattan products; wood carving; and mask making.
These centers enroll a total of about 1,000 trainees. When
young men and women complete their training at government
or assisted workshops and centers, many continue to work

at these units as paid workers and trainers of new trainees, while others seek employment in private enterprises or set up their own businesses.

Commentary on Women's Programs

The efforts of the Mahila Samiti have undisputed potential for effective work among infants, children, and female rural youth and adults. It also has a corps of dedicated leaders and workers. However, it remains handicapped by several constraints. First, the trained permanent staff is inadequate to cope with a program of this breadth. Second, the great bulk of their financial resources is in the form of government grants that, often for political reasons, are subject to change if not outright withdrawal. If the Association is to continue and develop its programs in the future, it is imperative that it proceed to do so with its own fund-raising campaigns, both locally and abroad, with minimum dependence on government support. Such a task is feasible if it is carefully planned and calculated to fire the imagination, sympathy, and enthusiasm of its potential supporters.

Because of political factors again, the effort of the Small Industries Department has been largely one of social service; the economic aspects of various programs have often received secondary emphasis. Constraints arising from barter trade agreements and ineffective coordination between the handloom industry and the growing powerloom industry have prevented expansion of employment opportunities that otherwise would be in the realm of possibility. Inasmuch as the Five Year Plan of the government calls for enormously increased output from cottage industries by 1976[10] and the employment of an extra 40,000 men and women, it is clear that, in addition to an efficient training program for imparting craft skills, there is pressing need for (among other things) well-organized servicing agencies for the provision of raw materials, improved techniques and tools of production, marketing research findings on consumer preferences (both local and foreign), and appropriate collection, distribution, and marketing facilities.

SKILL TRAINING PROGRAMS

There is a variety of skill training programs in Sri Lanka, some under the auspices of the government, others under private management. The efforts in the formal school system to give students an introduction to vocational skills and the activities of the Department of

Small Industries have **already been** described. Two other
significant government programs, the Mobile Skill Training Centres and an apprenticeship scheme under the auspices of the Department of Labour, are reviewed in this
section. Among the private ventures, Diyagala Boys' Town
is given special attention because it is one of a number
of small church-organized programs which offer relatively
low-cost, efficient, and highly "employable" skill training.

Two Government Skill Programs

The Vocational Training Branch of the Department of
Labour has established two permanent centers in Colombo
and 105 mobile centers throughout the island. The purpose is to provide training at craftsman level in manual
and machine skills, together with an understanding of
tools and material to be used, sensitivity about accuracy
and finish, and an ability to understand drawings and
written instructions. There is also provision for unskilled persons already in employment to follow an intensive course to equip them with basic skills. The trainees,
generally with 10 years of formal education, are in the age-
group of 18 to 30 years and are recruited from those registered at the Employment Exchanges.

At least 26 different courses ranging from cooking,
gardening, and barbering to taxidermy, tractor mechanics,
and sheet metal work are taught in the mobile centers.
The duration of the courses varies from six to nine months.
About 1000 trainees are enrolled in the mobile centers at
one time. Of more than 12,000 youth who have passed
through the courses, about 7,000 are reported to be
employed. The Employment Exchanges do not have information about the others, although it is presumed that they
found self-employment or employment under contractors
without informing the Exchanges.[11]

The National Apprenticeship Act of 1971 provided for
the establishment of the National Apprenticeship Board
(and an Apprenticeship Fund) to formulate, implement, and
supervise a scheme of training for apprentices in 16
defined trades and to set up certain guidelines and
standards for each, such as numbers to be trained, hours
and conditions of work, allowances and entitlements during
training, and evaluative criteria leading to the award of
certificates upon completion of training. The 16 defined
trades at the craftsman level to which trainees are apprenticed range from four types of fitter, carpenter, molder,
and plumber to blacksmith, welder, automobile mechanic,
and electrician.

At its inception there were 800 trainees with GCE(O)
level formal education apprenticed to various firms. In

1972 there were 600 young men receiving apprentice training at 50 private firms, plus a number of firms in the
public sector. All apprentices are paid an allowance of
Rs100 per month.

The Board also sponsors a one-year practical training program at the Katubedda Technical College and the
Hardy Institute at Ampirai. This course makes provision
for the training of 400-500 students per year at these two
institutions. These young men receive an allowance of
Rs5.35 per day.

Diyagala Boys' Town

Diyagala Boys' Town is described by its sponsors as
a vocational training institute in industries, agriculture, and farming for the manufacture of carpentry goods,
wooden structures for buildings, for production of screws,
nails, manufacture of goods out of metal, and electricity
and electric installations. Set up under the Sri Lanka
Technical Institute Project by the Brothers of Christian
Schools (Ceylon) Trust, it started in 1963 with an enrollment of 24 boys, some of whom were resident while others
commuted from their homes. By 1971 over 600 boys had
completed the course, all of whom found gainful employment as mechanics, welders, fitters, drivers, electricians,
and farmers. About 100 of them became self-employed; 16
grouped together in small units and started cooperative
ventures.

Admissions to Boys' Town are restricted to the age-
group 16-20 years. Although no minimum educational requirement is insisted on, boys in general have had an
education ranging from grade 6 to GCE(0). Almost all
boys are from the working or peasant classes with very
low family incomes or no income at all. No fees are
charged--each boy earns his board and lodging while in
residence. The annual intake is 75 boys; the applications for admission far exceed the number that can be
admitted. The duration of training is four years. The
dropout rate is about 10-15 per year, especially during
the first year of enrollment, but even these, it is
claimed, learn some useful skills.

Training is provided in three areas:

> Agriculture: general estate work covering
> coconut, rubber, and rice
> cultivation; mixed farming;
> and animal husbandry (poultry,
> piggery, dairy, sheep, goats,
> and rabbitry)
>
> Technology: machine shop work, welding,
> smithy, carpentry, electricity,

	electronics, foundry, metal work, motor mechanism, tinkering, metal sheeting, plumbing, garage work, and maintenance of pumps and motors
Trades:	masonry, brick-laying, cooking, bakery, tailoring, hairdressing, gardening, driving, tractor operation, vegetable farming, meat processing, fisheries, painting, music, and art

A certificate is awarded on successful completion of basic training (theory and practice of both bench work and agriculture) in the first two years. Private firms often engage some of these boys as third- or fourth-year apprentices. They continue to remain in the register of Boys' Town and return to it, as to their home, after each day's work. Those working at a distance return once or twice a month. A final certificate is awarded on successful completion of training in the third and fourth years--during which a boy specializes in one branch of technology or agriculture. It is compulsory for every boy to do farm work throughout his course. Capable boys may learn a trade or trades (for example, welding, carpentry, poultry) while undergoing major training in agriculture or technology.

Much importance is attached to a regular schedule, which starts normally at 5:45 a.m. and continues until 9:00 p.m. or later if there is a cinema or camp fire. Lectures, instruction, and practical work are conducted between 9 and 12:30 in the morning and between 1:30 and 3:30 in the afternoon. Before and after these sessions (for an hour or so) boys are engaged in farm work, bakery, playground activity, road and building maintenance, and so on. Before dinner at 8:00 p.m. there are games and sports and religious services. Not only are skills acquired for eventual gainful employment, but regularity and discipline are expected to breed self-reliance and confidence and ultimately civic consciousness and social responsibility.

Organization and Management

Diyagala Boys' Town functions on a democratic basis with responsibility and leadership vested in the boys themselves. The boys are divided into two Houses and each House elects a House Master (usually a young staff member) and a House Captain (usually a senior boy). They also elect a House Secretary (a boy), whose main function is to keep the House accounts, and other officers for special duties. Each House meets every Saturday in plenary session, in which boys may express their views on any of the activities; next day the House officials select topics commented on at the plenary session and submit them to the Administrative Body (described below).

Each House is given the full responsibility to run Boys' Town every other week. For this purpose, the House has to make available an Officer-in-charge, an Assistant Officer-in-charge, Duty Officers, Safety Officers for supervision, a Gate-keeper, the "Police," a night supervisor, and an officer for each section of activity on the premises. Every evening this group prepared a "Report for the Day." If the report includes anything of a serious nature, it is forwarded to the Director of the Institute, who decides whether it should be referred to the Tribunal.

The Tribunal is composed of a Chief Justice (a young teacher), a jury of five (a staff member and two boys elected from each House) together with a Prosecutor and a Defence Lawyer. Depending on the nature of the offence, the Tribunal may hear a case in public or in camera. Findings and recommendation of the Tribunal are forwarded to the Director, who may approve the recommendation or make alternative suggestions. Often the "offender" admits his fault and agrees voluntarily to perform an additional task in lieu of any punishment the Tribunal might recommend.

For every sphere of activity in Boys' Town (technology, agriculture, farms, lights, water, food, entertainment, sports, and so on) a group of five boys is organized into a Corporation. One of the group is elected Chairman and the other four assist him. For instance, in the Food Department the Chairman is assisted by one boy to obtain the food, another to store it, a third to prepare it, and a fourth to distribute it. Each Corporation (there are 18 Corporations in Boys' Town) is in the charge of a staff member, who is responsible for the supervision, guidance, and assessment of the output of each boy in that group.

In order to inculcate thrift, team spirit, and a sense of achievement in the boys, a point system has been introduced under the provisions of which boys are awarded points (usually 50 points per hour) for regular work, extra points for additional work, and bonus points for those House members who at the end of a month have, in one way or another, scored higher than those in the other House. At the end of each month points are converted into rupees and cents at the rate of one cent per point. Of the amount earned, which averages about Rs80, roughly half is deducted to meet the cost of board and lodging, and more if special approved expenses or obligations have been incurred. At the end of the four-year training period, a boy has an average of Rs600 to his credit--the amount varies from about Rs400 to as much as Rs1,500, depending on the boy's efficiency and thrift.

The Administrative Body comprises the Director, two of his staff members, the House officials (two House

Masters and two House Captains), and the 18 Chairmen
of the Corporations. This body meets about once a month
to ensure that Boys' Town is functioning efficiently and
that boys are making the best use of their facilities.
The Director enunciates policy after discussion with his
several staff members. They in turn implement policy
through constant contact and communication with House and
Corporation officials. Staff members function as teachers, instructors, and guides to the boys. In order to
perform their tasks well, staff members must be resident
within Boys' Town. Their training is provided, first,
within Boys' Town itself, then in private industrial and
engineering firms in Sri Lanka and in institutions abroad.
       The Director and staff maintain contact with the
alumni of Boys' Town and, wherever possible, assist some
of them (in the form of interest-free loans) in establishing themselves in agriculture, mixed farming, or a
trade.
       Two extension programs are in the process of develop-
ment. The first is at Nuwara Eliya in the mountains and
is described as the "highland extension program." This is
a nine-acre farm on which mixed farming along with cultivation of seed potatoes and vegetables is carried on.
Expansion of this farm is contemplated. The other program
is at Ekala, the "lowland extension program," about eight
miles from Boys' Town, where the emphasis is on the cultivation of rice. These two centers are primarily for the
training of local boys, but Boys' Town members also do
some of their practical work here. Furthermore, some
extension projects are aimed at reaching teachers, village leaders, and cooperative leaders, as well as groups
of young farmers who may come from considerably farther
afield. Also serving as an extension center is Diyagala
Boys' Town itself at which training is given to persons
desirous of starting similar projects elsewhere.

Resources and Costs

       The development of Diyagala Boys' Town has been
financed by individuals and organizations, both local and
foreign. The net assets in land, buildings, machinery,
equipment, and so forth, have been estimated at over
Rs5,000,000. But the running costs are met from three
main sources:

   1. the income generated within Boys' Town, from
       the industrial and engineering workshops,
       and the agricultural and livestock farms
   2. the grant paid by the Department of Social
       Services at the rate of Rs35 per month for
       each handicapped or orphan boy placed at
       the institution by this department
   3. the grant paid by the Department of Probation

and Child Care Services at the rate of
Rs35 per month for each delinquent boy
referred to the institution by this
department

Management of Boys' Town takes advantage of many
economies. While the food requirements are largely met
from Boys' Town's own produce, the surplus is sold outside. On-the-job trainees in the engineering workshop
earn further income in undertaking numerous repair jobs
for various firms on a contract basis. The cost per boy
for board, lodging, and instruction is set at Rs1,200 per
year. The religious Brothers on the staff receive no
salaries; a large part of the lay staff are retired persons or volunteer instructors for whom only an allowance
is paid. In short, wages and allowances amount only to
Rs3,500 per month.

Expansion of the program is contemplated in order
to increase enrollment in the same institution and to
start similar projects in other parts of the country.
Enrollment of 280 to 300 in the existing facilities can
be raised if additional funds can be found for meeting
the running costs. Another need felt by the Boy's Town
managers is that of a revolving fund that can be used to
assist boys in establishing themselves on their own after
completing their training.

Other Programs

More than passing mention should be made of at least
two youth skill projects that are much smaller than Diyagala Boys' Town, but not dissimilar to it. One is the
Yahapath Endera Farm, a vocational center for girls, set
up in 1960 by the Good Shepherd Congregation and currently
located on roughly half of a 200-acre estate at Hanwella.
(The other half is a coconut and rubber plantation, proceeds from which meet part of maintenance costs.) Another
is Navajeevanam, a small project for boys that was started
in 1959 on a ten-acre extent of land within a Government
Resettlement Plan by an Anglican priest of the Church of
Sri Lanka. Fees at both institutions are nominal for
those who can afford fees at all. The religious sisters
who run Yahapath Endera Farm get no salary; only three of
the eight active workers at Navajeevanam receive wages.
Admissions--without regard for religion, caste, or race--
are for roughly the same age-groups, children who have
reached the GCE(O) level of formal education. Enrollment
at Yahapath Endera is 60 (with 30 entering each year),
plus four or five religious sisters in training and eight
girls living in cottages and following specialized training in the cultivation and preservation of fruit;

enrollment at Navajeevanam is 75-80, including 30 or so
underprivileged children who attend nearby primary or
secondary schools. However, each of these residential
schemes has special characteristics of its own.

Yahapath Endera Farm. Yahapath Endera Farm at its
original location provided training in agriculture,
largely as therapy for 25 girls in the 16-25 age-group
who were orphans or had other social handicaps. By 1972
it became a two-year training opportunity for girls, ages
17-25, who had chosen agriculture and or animal husbandry
as a vocation and a few others who needed intensive work
in crash courses in one or two aspects of the total training. Boys are occasionally in evidence. In 1972 at
least four boys were undergoing the same basic training
as the girls. In August 1972, a symposium was held on
the Farm for 50 unemployed boys from 10 surrounding
villages on Agricultural Cooperation.

The learning process is based on lectures, demonstrations, and practical experience. The main vocational
emphasis is on poultry-keeping, dairy farming, pig-rearing,
and agriculture. Attention is also given to such subjects
as personality development, English, nutrition and food,
food preservation, needlework, child care, first aid,
household management, laundry, and physical training.
The inclusion of personality development as a subject
reflects a strong interest in sociopsychological attributes of trainees, covering such topics as "Understanding
Self," "Moral Values," "Social Relationships," and (for
Roman Catholics only) "Situational Catechesis." Music,
dancing, art, swimming, and weaving are offered as
optional subjects.

From 1965 to 1971 a total of 175 girls completed
training, and continual alumni contact has established
that almost all of these girls are in some sort of employment that is appropriate to the training received. Plans
for expansion include establishment of a revolving fund
to assist "graduates" in setting themselves up in farming
ventures.

This institution, the property of the Good Shepherd
Congregation, is self-supporting, thanks to income derived
from the coconut and rubber plantation and from student
enterprises in farming and livestock. Capital development
has been financed by grants from Roman Catholic organizations outside the country. Fiscal efficiency is in no
small part due to careful planning, budgeting, and the
self-sacrifice of the staff.

Navajeevanam. Navajeevanam (the new life), located
on 180 acres of land outside Colombo, was designed as a
home for underprivileged and mentally handicapped youth,
18 to 30 years of age, to whom values and attitudes would
be taught in consonance with new skills leading to productive economic ventures in their own and in the nation's
interest. It offers facilities for the training of

apprentice farmers, tractor drivers, carpenters, masons,
as well as housing of the homeless and the accommodation
of children attending state schools in the neighborhood.

The training combines shop work and study facilities
in addition to the education provided in the state schools.
This "family" of 75 people or so is a microcosm of the
religious and ethnic composition of Sri Lanka: Hindus,
Buddhists, Muslims, and Christians, as well as Tamils,
Sinhalese, and Burghers drawn from the length and breadth
of the island.

Much of the activity, while not exactly an imitation
of Diyagala Boys' Town, is nevertheless reminiscent of it
in the importance of the daily routine, the practice of
earning one's board and lodging by honest labor, and the
crediting of earnings in the bank against future need.
The three hostels (Senior, Junior, and Workers) recall the
Houses of Boys' Town; the Panchayat (Council of Five) is
not unlike the Tribunal; and the Director has duties much
like those of the Director of Boys' Town.

This is a relatively small project which has implications out of proportion to its size as a model for self-
supporting work and study facility for underprivileged
youth. It has grown under dedicated leadership, with very
little financial outlay, into a haven for the underprivileged. It survives in large part on income realized
through the agricultural, livestock, and industrial activity within the settlement, supplemented by donations and
boarding fees. With additional investments to develop
the 180 acres, the institution has the potential of becoming fully self-supporting and of expanding the program
to accommodate more children from depressed and deprived
homes.

Commentary on Skill Programs

The mobile centers and the apprenticeship program
are designed to give training in industrial skills for
employment in the urban areas. They also serve clienteles with relatively high formal education. The impact
of these programs, whatever their effectiveness in their
own sphere, is very limited in respect to rural youth,
especially those with limited education.

Diyagala Boys' Town and the other church-sponsored
programs, insofar as they combine a variety of skills
including farming in their training and are less rigid
about formal education prerequisites, obviously have a
greater potential for serving rural youths with limited
formal education.

The Boys' Town, representing a genre of private and
church-sponsored nonformal programs of education in Sri
Lanka contains some important, if not unique, characteristics. Chief among them is the challenge laid down by

the authorities to the young trainees to help themselves.
They are allowed to feel intimately the satisfaction that
their own initiative and labors have produced. While the
capital development has been and continues to be financed
by local and foreign aid, the working and maintenance costs
are borne mainly by the productivity of the boys themselves.

The boys earn enough during their period of training
to pay for their board and lodging and even have a substantial saving to their credit at the end of their training.
All the boys have been able to obtain gainful employment
or to set themselves up in gainful self-employment.

The training is of a comprehensive character, imparting to the youth a sense of honesty, loyalty, discipline,
self-reliance, and mutual cooperation, as well as a variety
of technical skills--a combination of attributes that
should enable him to earn a decent income and to be an efficient, productive, and useful citizen of Sri Lanka. His
active participation in the varied activities of Boys' Town,
including its actual administration, is a fine example of
how leadership and a sense of responsibility are developed.

The question remains, however, whether this and other
similar programs truly represent a viable approach in the
long range and on a national basis to occupational learning
for rural youth. The answer cannot be definitive at this
time. Manifestly there are obvious problems of duplicat-
ing the leadership and dedication of members of a religious
order. Furthermore, it is known that although the trainees
find the employment they seek, most of them find it in
cities instead of in rural areas. It may be that the rural
areas cannot absorb new skills unless appropriate national
policies and actions for rural development create the
right conditions.

RURAL DEVELOPMENT AND YOUTH DEVELOPMENT

A number of programs with broad objectives in community development, economic improvement, and employment
generation that also include educational elements are considered in this section.

Divisional and District Development Activity

The Ministry of Planning and Employment established
the Regional Development Division in 1971, entrusting it
with the task of organizing, financing, and guiding Divi-
sional- and District-level groups of community representatives and government officials for planning and implementing development activities. The Division is an administrative unit lower than the District. Rs35 million was
appropriated for the program in its first year.

The Divisional Development Council (there are 600 in number) is comprised of 25-30 people, in large part representatives of local cooperative societies, village councils, rural development societies, and also including representatives of such ministries as Agriculture, Small Industries, Education, as well as the Member of Parliament representing the electorate within which the Council falls. Each Council meets monthly and recommends to the District Development Committee projects, which, if approved and funded, it directs and monitors by coordinating popular effort and government services.

A District Development Committee, assisted by a planning unit in the Ministry of Planning, evaluates Council requests and recommendations. Final approval of projects, based on feasibility and appropriateness in terms of national development, is the responsibility of the Ministry of Planning, which also apportions the necessary funding.

Although adults contribute chiefly to Council and Committee discussion, the youth are involved in the "grass roots" aspects of each program. The majority of persons actively participating in these projects are in the 18-35 age-group. This youthful involvement means potential mastery of new skills in which satisfactory and rewarding employment is more likely. The expectation is that involvement in rural development activities will change the aspirations of young people from white-collar employment to blue-collar rural oriented occupations. A fair proportion of girls is involved, notably in garment manufacture, cottage crafts, sand mining, and agriculture. At the end of the first year 646 projects in agricultural production, animal husbandry, and small industries had been approved for funding, and 275 projects were already operational. It is estimated that the approved projects would create about 12,000 jobs. The five-year target was 30,000 jobs.[12]

It is premature to assess the success of this program, or indeed any of the programs so recently established. An observation or two, however, are not amiss. The Regional Development Division of the Ministry of Planning maintains that most of the agricultural projects have already proved to be viable and that the youth are happily settled down in their new patterns of activity. While most of these projects, in the short term, are likely to prove successful insofar as employment is generated and the output favorably marketed, the possibility of excessive production and marketing problems cannot be ignored. The expansion of poultry farming is a case in point. It was found at one stage that there was a surplus of eggs in the market, and the new production could only depress prices and even force the small farmer out of business.

One palpable shortcoming lies in the extension services. Although the numbers of people involved in

extension work may be regarded as adequate and the level
of their expertise in their fields of specialization
acceptable, the extension workers generally lack basic
knowledge and training in human relations and the awareness necessary to develop a cohesive social organization
among the youth. The importance of this knowledge cannot
be overestimated in a program designed to redirect people
toward new forms of development activities and new
aspirations. In the absence of an effective extension
support, projects that otherwise appear to be feasible are
likely to end in failure.

Rural Development Societies

The Ministry of Public Administration, Local Government, Home Affairs and Justice established the Department
of Rural Development in 1947, when Sri Lanka emerged as a
politically independent state, for the purpose of effecting a closer liaison and coordination between government
officials and villagers and to harness the enthusiasm and
voluntary cooperation of the latter for their own village
improvement. The result has been the formation of more
than 8,000 Rural Development Societies, of which 1,500
have a membership exclusively for women. It is estimated
that one-third of these are active; another third partially
active; the rest, inactive.
The Rural Development Society is a voluntary organization, functioning in a village or group of villages, meeting from time to time and responding to present needs--
basically on the principle of self-help, but nevertheless
drawing upon technical and financial assistance of the
Department, when such assistance is available. The value
of self-help contributions in 1971/72 was roughly the
same as government expenditure. In that year Rural Development Societies completed 861 public utility projects
and constructed 138 miles of road. The total value of
self-help contributions, as reported by the Department,
was Rs1,327,308; the total government expenditure was
Rs1,481,408. Primary concerns of the Societies have been
construction and building projects, irrigation and transplanting, and the organization of rural industries. The
women's Societies undertake vegetable production, hygiene
and sanitation drives, and since 1972 they have maintained
147 needlework centers in which field staff members of the
Department and local staff members conduct courses of a
year's duration. Over 4,000 young girls benefited from
these activities in the first year.[13]
The Rural Development Department has in 1972 initiated
a pilot project to develop 500 villages on an intensive
scale. To be chosen, each village must be accessible, have
a relatively active Rural Development Society, and be

unencumbered by any major social, economic, or political
problems. Approximately three such villages in each
electorate send ten young men and women in the 18-35 age-
group to a Divisional Training Centre (see below) for
two weeks' training in general development problems. On
their return priority needs are discussed in a Society
seminar, a three-year program is outlined, and an annual
program implemented--usually by an Implementation Committee selected by consensus. By late 1972, 300 village
plans had been prepared.

The Department runs ten Training Centres with residential facilities for 30-35 trainees at each Centre. In
1971/72, 3,500 young people underwent at government expense the standard two weeks' course in conducting village
surveys, programming, and implementation. The senior
Rural Development Officer put in charge of each Centre is
assisted by a panel of lecturers from related government
departments. Besides his administrative duties, he is
charged with organizing the development programs of the
four nearby demonstration villages, which are attached to
his Centre. Furthermore, he attends the deliberations of
each Rural Development Society, when its three-year program is under discussion.

In addition to personnel working at policy levels,
the Rural Development Program is supported in the field
by the following full-time paid staff:

> 22 Supervisors of Rural Development (one for each
> District)
> 11 Inspectors of Work (one for two Districts)
> 12 Needlework Supervisors (one for approximately two
> Districts)
> 145 Rural Development Officers (one for each Division
> and one for each Training Centre)
> 147 Needlework and Home Economics Demonstrators
> (one for each Needlework Centre)
> 400 Community Development Workers (these are trained
> young volunteers from the villages who are paid an
> allowance of Rs30 per month)

Also under the auspices of the Rural Development
Department and besides programs undertaken for the better-
ment of themselves and the village, the people undertake
programs of shramadana (voluntary labor). A shade of
difference is drawn between these two. In the former,
people contribute their self-help and mutual help to
achieve better conditions of living for themselves and
their village. In the latter, people of one or more
villages get together to implement a project that will
not necessarily benefit either the participants or their
respective villages. The projects, sometimes in an entirely different village, range from varied agricultural
activities and the construction of roads, irrigation
channels, and public buildings to setting up a burial

ground or building a house for a destitute and homeless
person.

The islandwide rural development movement provides
opportunities to youth of both sexes to play an active
role in social and economic change, to become familiar
with rural needs and problems and assist in the cooperative resolution of them, and to participate jointly
through self-help and mutual help in improved family and
community living. These benefits appear to accrue in
greater measure in the relatively more developed regions
of rural Sri Lanka, where educational levels are relatively high, economic activity is diversified, and the
traditional structure of the extended family is more
resolutely in the process of change. In the more remote
rural areas, where traditional patterns persist and the
elders almost congenitally resist change, opportunities
for equitable participation and decisionmaking seem to
be somewhat limited.

Although this movement was started 25 years ago, its
impact on youth has been slow--in large part because
resources, both in personnel and finances, have been
limited or spread too thinly. The pilot project of 500
villages covering 2.5 percent of all the villages on the
island, is an attempt to overcome this deficiency.

Another problem is posed by the political tradition
that causes every newly elected government to be suspi-
cious of the loyalties of village level organizations and
leads to lukewarm support to the village societies, or
even denial of it, without due regard to their effectiveness. The net result is disappointment, frustration, and
loss of momentum.

National Youth Service Council

The National Youth Service Council, established in
1969 by an Act of Parliament, functioning under the direct
supervision of the Prime Minister, and "subject to the
general or specific direction and control of the Government," is the national level policymaking, planning, and
coordinating body on youth services in Sri Lanka. In
principle, the Council aims to coordinate existing agencies within the context of national objectives, and to
extend its support and surveillance wherever required by
young people of both sexes, 14-25 years of age, whether
in school or out, employed or unemployed. Basic in the
National Youth Service programs are 1) involvement of
youth in activities beneficial to themselves and the
nation, 2) training and education to equip them for
competent and responsible adulthood, and 3) integration
of youth into the mainstream of economic activities.

In support of these general goals, the specific
responsibilities given to the Secretariat of the Council

include establishing a Central Institute of Training and
Research to conduct research and training in respect of
youth leadership and youth programs; working with the
Ministry of Planning and Employment to promulgate strategies for youth employment and to raise capital for
investments creating employment for youth; undertaking
sports, cultural, and other youth welfare activities; and
promoting for youths vocational training that has promise
in the light of national economic trends.

In practice, the implementation of the program has
been most active and conspicuous in the area of national
service, and this has been accomplished through two components that function concurrently: residential training
schemes, and the involvement of youth in national development schemes.

Residential Training. In an attempt to foster a
sense of both dignity and discipline in labor, as well as
an awareness of socioeconomic problems and a spirit of
national consciousness, two types of residential work-cum-
training organizations have been set up for young people,
16-18 years of age, who have completed their secondary
education and are ready for employment or tertiary education:

1. work camps, accommodating 100-200 trainees
2. agricultural farms or estates, accommodating
    200 or more trainees

The training in camp or farm over a three months' period
comprises equal amounts of manual work and classroom study
on weekdays, religious and cultural activities on Sundays
and full moon days. Classroom training covers such subjects as "The Individual and Society," "Governmental
Mechanisms," "Social Welfare," "Sri Lanka in Relation to
the World," and "Appreciation of our Culture"--with modifications and adjustments according to the sex and educational attainments of each group. An incentive system,
that of the National Service Credit Card, under the terms
of which a young person earns one credit for each five
days of service, is intended to give him some preference
in gaining employment or admission to an institution of
higher education.

Youth in National Development. Without the trappings
of actual recruitment and enrollment, the Youth in National
Development program, running concurrently with residential
training, motivates, encourages, and ultimately "invites"
young people between 17 and 25 years of age voluntarily to
participate in national development schemes and work projects directed toward social welfare, social rehabilitation,
and general economic development. There is no contractual
obligation here beyond one's innate duty to himself and
the nation he serves. Credits and cash bonuses are earned,
as in Residential Training. More often than not the youth
lives at home, participates in nearby projects, and is a

direct beneficiary of them when completed. Projects, many
of which are short-term, producing quick and visible
results, are generally in support of agricultural production (minor irrigation and kindred works), community
development (road or playground construction), and the
construction or strengthening of community buildings and
rural installations. The size of the work project determines the number of participants, but general manage-
ability and other factors seem to require not less than
50, nor more than 150 volunteers, on each job. A sense
of responsibility and devotion to the state is encouraged
within the discipline of a relatively demanding timetable.
The participants are expected to develop skills and
abilities that are currently in demand and are likely to
be in demand in the future.

In the course of the first year, the work of the
National Youth Service Council progressed according to
plan: more than 40,000 youth enrolled in about 200 work
centers--with 27,000 reporting for work on any given day;
furthermore, it realized Rs2.9 million worth of development for an expenditure of Rs2.2 million, mostly in
bonuses paid to the youth. However, the general elections
intervened in May 1970, and the new government, distrust-
ful of the loyalties of the young participants under the
original scheme, suspended the work of the old Council
and ultimately appointed a new one, which, in turn 27
months later, inaugurated a new program much like the old
program. One difference under reorganization--not without
possible implications--is that there is no longer assurance that those who earn credits will in fact be given
priorities in employment or school opportunities.

Conceivably the task assigned to the Council is too
large for its capacity and resources. Massive youth
mobilization schemes, as they are envisaged and proposed
here, must necessarily involve short-term and long-term
planning and coordinating strategies guided by a competent and trained staff. Such a staff does not now exist,
and the Council, preoccupied with the details of certain
programs of mobilization and training, has not yet assumed
its mandated role of overall policymaker and coordinator
of all youth programs--whether governmental or nongovernmental, industrial or agricultural, urban or rural, skill-
oriented or those geared primarily to leadership and civic
consciousness. Nor has there been any progress in establishing a central training and research institute.

Lanka Jatika Sarvodaya Shramadana Sangamaya

Origin and Objective

Founded in 1958, Lanka Jatika Sarvodaya Shramadana Sangamaya (translated as "the national harnessing of the goodness of all, for the awakening of all in Sri Lanka") offers a community development approach to education that is permeated with spiritual and ethical objectives. A government-approved charity, incorporated by an Act of Parliament, it has gained considerable international recognition, partly because of its contribution to national development and the philosophical content of its program.

Membership in the main statutory association may be obtained by anyone over 16 years of age who accepts the principles, objectives, and rules of the association. There are six categories of membership: Youth (or Student), Ordinary, Donor, Life, Honorary, and International.

Management of the Sarvodaya movement is in the hands of an Executive Council of 35 members, 20 of whom, mainly younger persons over 25 years of age, are elected annually by the membership; the remaining 15 are the Council of Elders, honorary or life members of the organization, who function in an advisory capacity. The movement is especially interested in involving youth in its activities, and counts on youth to have an important part in Executive Council decisionmaking.

The general principles governing the activities of this organization must be grasped before its general objectives can be set down. Truth, nonviolence, and self-denial are the initial watchwords. Truth presumably is self-explanatory. The principle of nonviolence looks back to the teachings of the great religious teachers and looks forward to the total nonviolent revolution "in all matters, social, moral, political and economic," so that justice and equality shall prevail and all exploitation of man by man shall be eliminated. Self-denial begins with simplicity of living by the reduction of one's everyday needs; it also means the exercise of unselfish cooperation and love, leading to self-reliant and self-supportive harmonious communities in a social order untainted by political (in the sense of narrow partisan politics) motivations and the hatred and greed associated with private ownership and selfish competition.

Concepts drawn from the Buddhist tradition that are emphasized in the movement are as follows: 1) metta (loving kindness)--to convey the idea of respect for life and preservation of nature and the improvement of the quality of the human being in order to have a better society; 2) karuna (compassionate action)--finding the cause of the sufferings of people and helping them to remove that cause; 3) muditha (sympathetic joy)--the

experience of detached joy on the fruition of an objective such as a development or welfare program; 4) upekkha
(equanimity)--the ability to develop a balanced personality; 5) dana (sharing)--as opposed to the profit motive;
6) priya vachana (noninjurious speech)--to help to integrate the community; 7) artha charya (constructive acti-
vity--as opposed to antisocial activity; 8) samanathmatha
(equality)--equality in association in decisionmaking
implementation, sharing of benefits, customs, ceremonies,
and so on.

Sarvodaya activities are divided into five evolution-
ary phases. The first is shramadana, or participation in
voluntary labor for self-help. The second is gramodaya,
or the group-awakening aspect. The third is grama
swarajya, or the community decisionmaking and self-rule
stage, which is achieved through the "haulas" (functional
groups), leadership, and the acquisition of skills. The
fourth phase is deshodaya, or the national awakening
stage, in which there will be nonviolent transformation
of the means of production from private ownership to
people's (not state) ownership and management, and the
emergence of a party-less participatory people's demo-
cracy. The fifth and final stage is vishodaya, or world
awakening stage, when a world brotherhood, free from war
and exploitation, will be established. Rich and poor
nations will be linked, even as rich and poor villages
are linked, and science and spirituality will progress
side by side.

Progress along these phases calls for education of
all members of the community for acquiring various skills
as well as for understanding of the socioeconomic and
other problems of the country; enlistment and mobilization of all resources, whether human or material for
the welfare of all; and voluntary exercise of hand,
heart, mind, and spirit in village development and community welfare projects.

Organization at Village Level

Sarvodaya has established its movement in close to
400 villages (of a total of 22,000 villages) in Sri
Lanka, concentrating on some of the poorest areas.
Within the broad frame of community development, specific
objectives vary according to the age-group and sex of the
villagers. With a well-established program in a village,
there would be, in total, seven groups or categories
covering all persons in the community:

1. The Singithi Hamuwa--infants up to about seven
   years old, divided into two groups: a) those
   below the age of three and a half, who are
   closely associated with the Mau Haula (see below),
   and b) children from three and a half to seven

years, who attend a preschool center, where they
spend at least three hours a day under the guidance of a trained preschool helper. Sixty villages now have these preschool groups, which were
first organized in 1971. Objectives of these
groups are the development of the sociability
of the child as well as his physical, mental,
and psychological well-being.

2. The Singithi Haula--children from the ages of 7
    to 14, most of whom are attending school. In
    relying on the primary schools to meet the
    basic needs of literacy and numeracy, Sarvodaya
    makes every effort to assure school attendance
    of the needy children by giving them clothes
    and books. Among its more organized activities
    are helping children in school subjects in which
    they are weak, planning educational tours and
    exhibitions, holding religious classes, conduct-
    ing programs for the physically and mentally
    handicapped, organizing children's farms and
    assisting home gardening projects, promoting
    social and cultural activities and recreational
    games. These groups, the largest and most in-
    fluential of all the haulas, were first formed
    in 1968; in 1972 there were 160 with an enroll-
    ment of more than 30,000. These groups place
    great emphasis on historical and traditional
    values, human rights, and world brotherhood,
    regardless of differences in race, class, creed,
    and color. They also emphasize the importance
    of a good diet, personal cleanliness, and the
    virtues of a well-balanced life.

3. Yovun Haula--young people, 15 to 30 years old, of
    both sexes, whose activities include vocational
    training and the acquisition of skills by involve-
    ment in rural industries and other economic
    ventures, and general guidance by involvement in
    such enterprises as services for children, library
    work, adult education, and attendance at the
    Sarvodaya training institute at headquarters.
    Strongest of all haulas in motivating other
    groups in development planning and implementation,
    the Yovun Haulas, started in 1969, claim a pro-
    visional enrollment of 12,000 in 120 groups in
    1972. Objectives undergirding the activities
    are to develop personality, leadership, and unity
    among the youth; to provide appropriate educa-
    tional and vocational training leading to employ-
    ment; and to instruct young people in an aware-
    ness of "their rights through education, training,
    employment, and participation in the organizational
    life of the community."

4. Govi Haula--farmers, organized for education in
   social and economic principles. Started in
   1969, there are 42 such formations in 1972
   with an enrollment of 5,800 members. Objectives
   include unity among rice farmers in particular
   and all farmers in general, awareness of rights
   and freedom of participation in agricultural
   policymaking assistance in increasing farmer
   income, and restoration of traditional ceremonies
   and observances that have given meaning to life.

5. Mau Haula--mothers had only two groups with 16
   members when first organized in 1972. Objectives stress assistance to mothers in developing
   a sense of importance in their task of ensuring
   family welfare and a sense of their own importance in participating (as equals of men) in
   village, national, and world development efforts.

6. Samadun Haula--elders (teachers, craftsmen,
   laborers, government servants working in the
   area) who do not belong to other groups. These
   have not yet been organized. Objectives of
   these groups are to ensure that no one in the
   village is left out of the community's organizational life and that each one contributes to the
   common purpose.

7. a) Gramodaya Mandalaya--the village awakening
   council, originally an ad hoc body of particularly enthusiastic Sarvodaya workers, but intended
   as a nonstatutory voluntary body of workers
   elected from the several haulas. Council responsibility includes initiation of development
   projects and programs through Shramadana camps,
   selection of suitable persons for training at
   the Sarvodaya Institute and other field training
   camps, assistance in village socioeconomic
   surveys, organization of the productive capacity
   of the village for maximum productivity, insurance of equitable wages and wage scales, and
   regulation and development of the village's
   cultural life. Although they do not yet function at maximum capacity, 260 villages of the
   400-odd villages subscribing to the Sarvodaya
   movement have already set up these awakening
   councils.
   b) Grama Swarajya Mandalaya--a council for
   village self-government, emerging as a natural
   development from the Gramodaya Mandalaya. Three
   self-governing councils have been activated. A
   successful case in point is the village of
   Uruwela, a relatively backward community, whose
   Swarajya Mandalaya has organized in five years
   no less than 13 subgroups (for example, communications and roads; sanitation, health, and

medical care; functional literacy; irrigation;
savings and credit; children's and adults'
libraries) and brought into being a school,
community hall, temple, dispensary, sanitary
toilets for every home, sufficient community
wells, an industrial workshop, burial ground,
cooperative stores, and a road frontage to
every house.

In a demonstration of village unity all seven haulas
meet once a week or so in a Gami Pawul Hamuwa (the village
family gathering), which is either a cultural or cere-
monial occasion or a functional foregathering to render
special assistance to the needy, to promote some village
activity of common benefit, or perhaps to make generally
known decisive actions taken by individual haulas.

Because most of the activities undertaken through
the Sarvodaya movement fall into the category of community
development, most of the programs and projects come
within the orbit of central government or local government authority. The cooperation of government authority
is generally sought to ensure maintenance of the projects;
where the cooperation of the government, usually through
its extension services, has been readily forthcoming,
the movement has been able to achieve maximum results.

Because the Sarvodaya movement insists on lofty
principles designed to create an entirely new social
order in which hate, acquisitiveness, avarice, and competition are replaced by love, respect, and sharing, the
rate at which these principles can actually be diffused--
among both the peasantry and the intelligentsia--in the
face of major social, economic, and political obstacles
will be a determining factor for the movement's success.
Its development activities, dramatic and effective in
individual places, are still confined to only about 2
percent of the total population. Expansion must of necessity be slow. Furthermore, the movement is not really
geared to an extensive program of employment creation
and increased productivity, and these, it must be
remembered, are the two basic problems facing the country.
The impact of Sarvodaya could be considerably enhanced
were it able to relate more closely to other development
programs within the context of a widely supported govern-
ment-backed strategy for rural development. It is not
clear that the institutional framework of Sarvodaya and
the commitment of the rural participants in its activities
are as strong as the principles that guide the ambitious
effort.

CONCLUDING REMARKS

Unlike most developing countries, Sri Lanka has no major nonformal education program for basic literacy. The extensive formal education system has most of the children in the primary age-group attending school. But the widespread availability of formal education has by no means eliminated the need for diverse nonformal education programs, even for those rural youths who have acquired substantial formal education.

Despite the diversity of nonformal programs and wide-ranging government and voluntary initiatives, the total number of children, youths, and women in rural areas served by nonformal programs amounts to a small fraction of the population. Many programs, particularly those of voluntary agencies concentrating on character and attitude-formation and recreation, benefit mostly those who are enrolled in formal institutions. The skill training programs for rural youths are also small--especially the private programs.

The diverse initiatives to provide opportunities for training in occupational skills are reflected in the pre-vocational school program, the mobile training centers, the rural crafts centers, and the private training programs. While these activities are meeting important needs and in some instances are achieving a high degree of efficiency, they still do not constitute a comprehensive program with an overall strategy for employment-related learning in rural areas.

The prevocational program in the middle schools, if successfully implemented. will broaden and enrich the educational experience of students, will offer them an opportunity to discover and improve their manual dexterity, and will possibly instill in them positive attitudes toward manual skills. However, various difficulties in implementing the program are well recognized by its operators. In any event, it cannot be viewed as a substitute for occupational training or a means of employment generation.

A viable approach to training in agricultural occupations for the large number of rural youths who will live on the land is yet to be found. The settlement scheme, a qualified success at best, is too expensive and its expansion is limited by the scarcity of easily reclaimable land. The Young Farmers Clubs, like their counterparts in many countries, serve mostly as social and recreational outlets for youths. The small church-sponsored training programs for young farmers have proved more effective mainly because they select the most motivated learners, provide intensive practical training, and gear the training to specific employment opportunities. It is doubtful if these programs can be successfully expanded and, even if they could be, it is by no means

certain that there would be sufficient economic opportunities for a large number of these trainees. Appropriate
policy measures in respect of agricultural prices, supply
of inputs and credit, and land reform, which would make
smallholding farming sufficiently rewarding will be
needed to induce youths to choose willingly an agricultural
occupation and to make agricultural training programs for
them effective.

    In the field of rural crafts and cottage industries,
the commendable program run by the Small Industries Department makes it possible for a sizable rural population to
earn a livelihood through small-scale handloom and powerloom weaving enterprises, and for many others to supplement their earnings through craftsmanship and cottage
industries. The realization of the full economic potential of rural crafts and small industries will again
depend on a comprehensive program linking training with
the provision of other necessary services such as design,
quality control, marketing, and management assistance.
It will depend also on the extent to which the government adopts certain facilitative measures in respect of
credit, prices, supply of raw materials, and so forth.

    Of the three interesting government programs described
above which combine elements of skill training and charac-
ter- and attitude-formation with the goals of alleviating
rural unemployment and harnessing youths for national
development projects, two are too recent to offer definitive lessons. The other has apparently been hamstrung
by internal political rivalries and has failed to attract
enough budgetary resources and administrative support to
make any substantial impact. The three programs could,
in principle, constitute three important elements of a
concerted thrust in rural development. The Divisional
Councils and District Committees could serve as the
local planning and implementing agency, the Rural Development Societies could become the vehicle for mass participation in the process, and the Youth Service Council
could function as the mechanism for mobilizing and harnessing the energies of the youth population for rural
development, while providing a learning experience. In
practice, this organizational design may or may not be
the right one for Sri Lanka, but for the existing
separate efforts to have any significant impact in rural
areas and on the life prospects of rural children and
youths, a more comprehensive approach, undergirded by a
greater political determination and resource commitment,
will be needed. The self-help and moral reawakening
approach of the Sarvodaya movement may also be able to
play an important role in such a broad-visioned strategy.

NOTES

1. The population, in 1971, consisted of various ethnic groups: Sinhalese (70 percent), Ceylon Tamils (11 percent), Indian Tamils (9.5 percent), Indian Moors, Burghers and Eurasians, and Malays. Sri Lanka, Department of Census and Statistics, Census of 1971 (Colombo, 1972).

2. Of the agricultural work force about 45 percent is in the plantation sector, another 36 percent in the cultivation of paddy and other food crops, and a substantial portion is self-employed in the domestic agricultural sector. Sri Lanka, Department of Census and Statistics,"Preliminary Report of the Socio-Economic Survey of Ceylon 1969-70," mimeographed (Colombo, n.d.).

3. For instance, Ananda Cumaraswamy discusses the structure of the traditional society and the status of craftsmen in Mediaeval Sinhalese Art, 2nd ed. (Broad Compden,England: Essex House Press, 1908).

4. A study assessing the costs and benefits of 40 schemes in Sri Lanka is included in International Labour Office, Youth Training and Employment Schemes in Developing Countries: A Suggested Cost-Benefit Analysis (Geneva, 1972), pp. 77-109. Another discussion of the schemes is found in R. K. Srivastava and S. Selvaratnam, "Youth Employment in Ceylon--Problems and Prospects," Marga 1, no. 4 (1972): 48-51.

5. In addition to the highly successful fruit cultivation projects, a livestock farm is run (under Ministry of Planning sponsorship) on a collective basis by 28 youths with incomes in excess of Rs1,000 per month.

6. One of these (the 25th Model Centre), the gift of the Asia Foundation, with some of its equipment given by NOVIB, CARE, and UNESCO, is a mobile unit.

7. The Sri Lanka Women's Association [Lanka Manila Samiti], Forty-First Annual Report, 1970/71 (Colombo, 1971).

8. A Union covers an area of one or two Divisional Revenue Officers' divisions, which is only part of a Revenue District. These Unions exist in at least 20 districts of the island.

9. Better performance in the private workshops than in the Cooperative Societies accounts for extra yarn allocations, and, therefore, for higher incomes.

10. The Plan proposes to double small-scale industry output, with particular emphasis on handloom textiles, wood products, light engineering, rubber products, and mining and quarrying products. It provides for an increase in handloom textiles from 40 million yards to 90 million yards (1970-76) and powerloom production from 15 million to 50 million yards. Sri Lanka, Ministry of Planning and Employment, The Five Year Plan, 1972-1976 (Colombo, November 1971), pp. 73-78.

11. Sri Lanka, Department of Labor, Administration Report 1969-70 (Colombo, n.d.).

12. Sri Lanka, Ministry of Planning and Employment, Regional Development Division, "Progress Report up to 25th August 1972," mimeographed (Colombo, 1972).

13. Sri Lanka, Rural Development Department, Administration Report of the Director of Rural Development for 1970/71 (Colombo, n.d.).

8

THAILAND: AN INNOVATIVE APPROACH TO FUNCTIONAL LITERACY

Adult Education Division
Thailand Ministry
of Education

The report on the functional literacy and family life education program and the upper primary and secondary equivalency program, presented here in an abridged form, was prepared by the Division of Adult Education in the Department of General Education of the Thailand Ministry of Education as a contribution to the ICED/UNICEF study of nonformal education for rural children and youth. The report, completed in fall 1972, was prepared under the direction of Dr. Kowit Vorapipatana, head of the Division of Adult Education and Kasama Voravarn of the Division. The description of the program and other background and contextual information presented in the chapter do not reflect developments following the governmental change in 1973.

GENERAL BACKGROUND

Geography and Government

The Kingdom of Thailand covers an area of 518,000 square kilometers in the center of Indochina, bordered by Burma, Laos, Cambodia, and Malyasia. Topographically it can be divided into four areas: the northern highlands, the northeastern plateau, the low-lying central plains, and the southern peninsula.

The country is divided into 71 provinces, which further subdivide into 540 districts (amphoe), 5,238 boroughs (tambon), and 46,669 villages (muban). At the provincial level, the administration is under a governor, who is a civil servant appointed by the Ministry of Interior. With assistance from a Provincial Board, consisting of officers from other ministries, the governor is responsible for the implementation of law and policies of the national government in the province.

Similarly, at the district level a district officer, appointed by the Ministry of Interior, is in charge of

the administration and welfare of the district, with the
assistance of officers from other ministries. At the
borough and village levels, the inhabitants elect their
own village headmen. The village headmen are paid by the
government and are under the direct supervision of the
governor and the district officers.

In 1932 the government system of Thailand changed
from an absolute monarchy to a constitutional monarchy
with a centralized government. The King now exercises
legislative power through the Parliament, executive power
through the Cabinet, and judicial power through the courts.
Since its introduction in 1932 the constitutional system
in Thailand has evolved slowly, interrupted by several
coup d'états leading to periods of military regimes.

Demographic Factors

The population in 1970 was estimated at 37 million
with a density of approximately 70 per square kilometer.
Ninety-five percent of the population are Thai-speaking
Buddhists; the chief minority groups are Malays, Hill
Tribes, and Chinese. Fifteen percent of the population
live in the urban areas with 10 percent, or 3.6 million,
in the metropolitan city of Bangkok-Thonburi alone. Urban
population is growing, as a steady influx of rural people
into the cities has continued. The age structure of the
population is relatively young with 45 percent of the
population under 15 years of age and 64 percent under
25 years of age. A high birth rate and a sharp drop in
the mortality rate have caused the population to grow by
3.2 percent every year. This rapid rate of population
growth has grave implications for the Thai government's
ability to meet basic human needs in the future.

According to 1972 official statistics, the government
has succeeded in educating only 36 percent of children in
the seven-year compulsory primary program. If the present
rate of population growth continues, the number of school
age children will double in 14 years. This means that the
government will have to invest a virtually prohibitive
proportion of the national budget to achieve universal
compulsory education, and at the same time, maintain its
present quality. Higher levels of education, which require more investment and more qualified staffs, present
even more intractable problems.

The prospect of proper health care in the country is
no less alarming, despite the government's efforts to
improve public health services. The ratio between doctors
and the population is 1 to 7,000. At the present rate of
growth at least 1,000 doctors will have to be produced
annually in order to achieve a 1 to 3,000 ratio within the
next twenty years. However, the number of new doctors

produced annually is only 300. To maintain the present
ratio of hospital beds, an additional 4,000 beds must be
installed each year, while the present government budget
will provide only 1,000 beds per year. In short, the
government will have to invest large amounts of capital
for medical personnel and facilities simply to maintain
the present inadequate health service.

Food production is another problem with many Thais
suffering from protein starvation and malnutrition. The
increase in population and a lack of general education
have brought about considerable land devastation, de-
forestation, and water pollution, which led to the aban-
donment of many rice-growing areas. Rapid population
growth will aggravate another long-standing problem--the
gradual decrease of cultivable land for each Thai farmer
when it is apparent that the need for rice will grow each
year. If new agricultural practices fail to increase
rice yield, Thailand will have to import the food that
has been one of her main exports and a major source of her
revenue. Furthermore, since 78 percent of the Thai labor
force is engaged in agriculture, the decreasing land of
farmers, together with growing use of machinery to increase
agricultural production, will lead to serious unemployment
in the rural areas and an even greater rate of influx of
unskilled labor into the cities. Apart from providing
additional jobs, the government will have to consider construction of more low-cost housing and public facilities,
such as schools, hospitals,and recreational areas.

These are but a few obvious consequences of rapid
population growth in Thailand. The failure of the government adequately to cope with them could bring about
serious social and political repercussions. Therefore the
government has decided in the Third National Social and
Economic Development Plan to try to reduce the present rate
of population growth to 2.5 percent by 1976. Nonformal
education programs for the out-of-school population should
help to develop an awareness of population problems, and
also, it is hoped, to solve some of them.

Economy and Employment

Thailand's economy is based heavily on agriculture,
which accounts for 30 percent of the GDP. In recent years
the government has attempted to increase yields through
modernization and to promote cultivation of new crops,
but at the same time it has encouraged the growth of
commerce and manufacturing. As a result, agriculture's
contribution to the GDP has declined, while that of
commerce and manufacturing has increased. In 1970 manufacturing accounted for 17 percent of the GDP. Per
capita GNP in 1970 was US$180 at current prices. The

annual growth rate averaged 9 percent between 1966 and
1969, but fell to 6 percent in 1970, rising slightly to
6.5 percent in 1971.

Thailand's labor force in 1970 was estimated to be
17.8 million, or 45 percent of the population. Of the
total labor force, 78 percent are engaged in agriculture
(most of whom cultivate rice), 12.4 percent in commerce
and services, 4.5 percent in manufacturing, and the remainder in transport, communication, and other activities.
Although a very small percentage of the labor force is
officially recorded as unemployed,   there is considerable
underemployment in the rural areas, especially during the
dry season.

The educational attainment of employed persons in
municipal areas as shown in Table 8.1 is still quite low:
only 15 percent have completed secondary and preuniversity
education, approximately 55 percent have a primary education, and almost 20 percent have no education at all. The
educational level of workers in rural areas is even lower.
To improve agricultural practices and to foster new developments in commerce and industry, a skilled labor force
must be developed and utilized to its full potential.
During the Third National Social and Economic Developmental Plan, the government aims to improve the quality
of human resources through education and training courses
and to create more employment opportunities, particularly
in the rural areas.

TABLE 8.1

Educational Level of Labor Force in Municipal Areas, 1968-69

Level of Education	All Municipal Areas	
	Number	Percent
No education	336,987	19.3
Preschool and primary	978,074	55.9
Secondary and preuniversity	264,198	15.1
Vocational and technical	54,112	3.1
University	41,837	2.3
Short voactional course	8,194	0.5
Teacher training	32,735	1.9
Others	27,778	1.6
Unknown	5,986	0.3
TOTAL	1,749,901	100.0

Source: Thailand, Office of the Prime Minister, National
Statistics Office.

FORMAL GENERAL EDUCATION

Historical Background

Before the establishment of a western educational system in Thailand, there already existed a tradition of Thai education that catered to both the masses and the elite through the Buddhist temples, which served as learning institutions for young men. Boys were sent to the local temples at age nine to serve the priests, who in turn taught them reading, writing, occupational skills, and even the art of self-defense. When these boys reached the age of twenty, some became ordained as monks to receive further religious training, while others entered informal apprenticeships with local craftsmen and the elders in the village. The girls, on the other hand, were rarely allowed to learn to read and write, but were prepared for roles as wives and mothers at home.

Outside of the temple, and with the exception of the children of the royal families and the noblemen who had a more literary type of education at home with special tutors, education was informal or nonformal in nature. Learning took place within the everyday environment of the children, often unconsciously, and was of immediate use. This form of education in which parents prepared their children from their own experience was adequate for a slowly changing society in which the future role of each member was well-defined and relatively unchangeable.

In the early nineteenth century, however, the threat of western imperialism forced Thailand to initiate modernization of various aspects of her national life. The educational system had to be reformed to train Thais for the great changes of the future. In 1870, King Chulalongkorn founded the first western-type school for the children of his family and noblemen, and this marked the beginning of modern Thai education.

But the King also attempted to provide education for the masses. Apart from encouraging missionaries and members of the royal families to open schools, he also sought to utilize the existing Buddhist monasteries as learning institutions for people in the rural areas. In 1884 the abbots of the provincial monasteries were asked to formalize their educational programs that hitherto had operated informally. Later, in 1891, the government offered to pay the salary of the teachers as well as provide the textbooks for one school in each province. The great change in the education system came in 1960, however, when a large expansion of primary schools was undertaken and the objectives of education were redefined to emphasize educating the people according to their individual needs and capacities.

Formal education in Thailand is now under the administration of three main ministries. The Office of the
Prime Minister is in charge of the overall planning,
policy formation, research and evaluation, budgeting, and
staff administration, as well as the implementation of
higher learning; the Ministry of Interior has responsibility for the administration of primary schools; and the
Ministry of Education remains in charge of curriculum
development, experimentation and research, supervision,
and school standardization, as well as the planning and
the administration of secondary and vocational education.

Primary and Secondary Education

According to the 1960 plan, primary (pratom) education consists of four years of lower elementary education
and three of upper elementary education for children from
7-13 years of age, although older children who repeat are
also included. The present policy is to extend compulsory
education from four years to seven years of primary education, as soon as funds and qualified personnel are available.

The enrollment in the four-year program of lower
primary education in 1972 was 4,981,162, or approximately
118 percent in the relevant age-group. (The enrollment
is over 100 percent because of repetitions of grades and
enrollment of those who are outside the age-group.)
Although the recently established (1960) upper primary
level has been growing at a very impressive rate (125
percent during 1960-71), it still accounts for only 39
percent of the population in the appropriate age-group.
Forty-nine percent in the relevant age-group are expected
to be enrolled in upper primary education by 1976.

Secondary (mawsaw) education consists of three years
of lower secondary levels and two years of upper secondary
levels for youths from 14-19 years of age. The policy
of the government towards secondary education has emphasized improved educational quality rather than increased
enrollment. As a result the enrollment has been increasing at a slow rate; in 1970 the total number of secondary
students accounted for only 14 percent of the population
in the relevant age-group.

During the five-year period of 1972-76, the enrollment in secondary education is planned to rise at an
average rate of 10.7 percent. It is also planned to
devote greater efforts to produce better prepared students
for higher learning and more qualified manpower for employment. An increase in the number of public schools
is also envisaged to decrease the demand for private
schooling, which offers low quality instruction at very
high fees.

Although the modern educational system stemmed from the need to train personnel for civil service, other functions of education have long been recognized. As early as 1919, for example, Chao Phrya Dhamsakdimontri explained his educational policy to educational officers:

The first job of the Ministry was to train people for civil service work. Later, His Majesty's objective of education was to provide education for all citizens, both men and women, so that they would gain knowledge, to the maximum of their individual abilities. Education for all . . . should not include only general education, it should include specialized subjects like agriculture, handicrafts and commerce.[1]

Since the majority of the Thai population, particularly those who live in the rural areas, receive only primary education, it is particularly important that the primary curriculum serve the dual purpose of providing children with learning tools and knowledge that will enable them to function effectively in society and at the same time prepare them for further education in the formal school system. In practice, however, attempts to include more practical subjects--from embroidery and dressmaking to carpentry--have always failed. The existing primary curriculum continues the attempt to integrate the two objectives of education, with grades 1-4 spending almost one-fourth of their time on a practical, or vocational, subject, and grades 5-7 over a third of their time.

There are several reasons why attempts to include more practical subjects in the primary curriculum have not been successful. Often the subjects are not suited to the training of the children, particularly those from rural areas. Aree Sanhachawee has offered several plausible explanations:

First, the parents' understanding of education as a stepping stone to prestigious jobs has not changed. The ones who sent their children to school prefer to have them pursue the more academic subjects.

Second, the teachers' concept of education is still academically oriented. Many of them use the class hours allotted to practical subjects to teach the more academic subjects.

Third, the teachers are trained to teach in the academic areas and do not feel competent to teach practical subjects which require specialized training.

Fourth, partly because the teachers' performance is often evaluated by the number of the students who pass the examination, a large

number of teachers concentrate on preparing the
students for the examination.[2]

The secondary schools share the primary schools' problems in curriculum development, but they have an even
more urgent need to provide training for employment as well
as for general education, since enrollment in secondary
schools has been expanding far beyond the number than can
be absorbed into higher learning institutions. For this
reason a diversified curriculum (known as Comprehensive
School Type 1 and Type 2) was introduced into secondary
education in 1966 to train students in specialized fields
of their interest, rather than to prepare them solely
for further formal education.

According to official reports, there were approximately
185,000 teachers working in primary schools all over the
country, but they were concentrated largely in the urban
areas. In spite of special compensatory inducements
offered by the government, the tremendous teacher shortage
in rural areas, particularly in remote districts, is caused
by such factors as limited opportunities for further education or outside employment, difficult living conditions,
and limited social activities. In view of the sharp increase of school age children expected within the next
few years, the government has attempted to produce more
teachers by doubling the number of graduates from teachers'
colleges between 1968 to 1970. By 1976 at least 45,000
teachers are expected to be available for primary school
posts. But unless drastic measures are taken to solve the
problem of unequal distribution of teachers, the shortage
of teachers will continue to hinder primary education in
the rural areas.

Problems of numbers and distribution are matched by
those of finding teachers of adequate qualifications. The
majority of the teachers in the rural areas have received
lower certificate training only. It is hoped that increased enrollment in teachers' colleges, together with
inservice training for teachers, will do much to rectify
this deficiency. In the secondary schools in 1971 there
were 25,100 teachers working in academic and comprehensive
schools all over the country. The ratio between students
and teacher is around 24:1 in public schools and slightly
lower in private schools. Over one-third have bachelors'
degrees or better, and over one-half a higher certificate
or equivalent. But in order to upgrade the standard of
teaching and to establish more comprehensive schools,
more trained teachers and supervisors will be required.

At the lower elementary level no actual tuition fees
are charged, although parents are expected to pay from
80 to 300 baht for each child. Because these small additional costs are often beyond the capacities of a large
number of parents, the government in some instances supplies
children with books and uniforms. At the upper elementary

level, a maximum tuition fee of only 40 baht per year can
be collected. As a result, the costs of operation of
public elementary schools have come to be mainly the
central government's responsibility. Since most of the
recurrent costs are for the teachers' salaries, the cost
per head in elementary schools varies according to teacher
and student ratios and the qualifications of the teachers.
In 1971, for example, the cost per head for the schools
under the Ministry of Education was 610 baht, while the
cost per head in the local authority school was 440 baht.
Exclusive of capital costs, the cost of educating one
child through a four-year lower primary program ranges
from 2,440 baht in the schools under the Ministry of Education to 1,740 baht in local authority schools, and from
1,830 baht to 1,320 baht through a three-year upper primary
program.

The government finances the bulk of the cost for
secondary education as well, spending approximately 3,300
baht to educate one child through a three-year lower
secondary program and 2,200 baht for a two-year upper
secondary program. These estimates do not count the
capital cost per child, which differs according to the
facilities required and is higher in the comprehensive
schools. In general the average capital cost is 800 baht
per place.

Problems and Future Plans

Ever since the establishment of the first modern
school in 1870, primary education has undergone continual
improvement. Universal education up to pratom 4 has been
achieved, and provision for increase in enrollment in
upper elementary education has been highly satisfactory.
Efforts in teacher training, supervision, and curriculum
development have done much to standardize the quality of
education. Secondary schools have made similar strides
forward, but in a sense, as we have seen, they are victims
of their own success. There also remain several problems
that are of particular significance to our study on how
nonformal education can be employed to complement formal
education.

The reversion to illiteracy of primary school graduates
presents a crucial problem. A study conducted by the
Department of Elementary and Adult Education in 1968
found that approximately 33 percent of primary school
graduates reverted to virtual illiteracy a few years after
leaving schools, largely because of insufficient training
and follow-up.[3] This problem is of grave importance,
since it implies that approximately 33 percent of the total
cost of educating elementary school students is wasted.

The rapid increase of population and rising educational aspirations will cause a lowering of standards in the formal primary schools, unless large additional resources can be found and used effectively. Many secondary school students will have to rely on expensive and inadequate private schooling, unless the government can establish more secondary schools or provide viable alternatives to them. The need for alternatives of successful employment-oriented curricula in rural areas is crucial. At present the government is trying to improve the standard of secondary schools in many of the rural areas.

Ways must be found to attract qualified teachers to work in the remote rural areas. At the same time, existing teachers' training programs will have to be reexamined and improved in order to produce the best qualified teachers. Training qualified teachers for the comprehensive secondary schools must be intensified, because, as noted above, the number of secondary students exceeds the quota that can be absorbed into the higher learning institutions.

Curricula will have to be studied with care, so that they will respond to the needs of the learners as well as the needs of the nation; in the case of secondary schools, they must provide alternatives for those not going on to higher education.

Poverty, poor health, irregular attendance, low quality in teaching, and insufficient instructional materials have contributed to high wastage rates in elementary education (see Tables 8.2 and 8.3) which raise the educational cost considerably.[4] In order to reduce the wastage rate, the government plans to provide inservice

TABLE 8.2

Repeater Rates in Primary Education

Year	Primary Grades						
	1	2	3	4	5	6	7
1965/66	23.0	12.2	9.5	1.0	3.1	3.8	–
1966/67	23.2*	13.2	10.6	3.2	3.0	7.0	11.8
1967/68	23.0*	10.7	8.5	–	3.0	2.6	–
1968/69	23.0	12.2*	7.4*	–	3.0*	3.3*	3.5*
1969/70	23.0	12.0*	8.0*	–	3.0*	3.5*	3.5*
1970/71	23.0	12.0	8.0	–	3.0	3.5	3.5

*The repeater rates for Primary 1 from 1967 and for Primary 2-7 from 1969 are estimated.

Source: Thailand, Ministry of Education, Educational Planning Division, Statistics for Educational Planning (Bangkok, 1969), p. 47.

TABLE 8.3

Dropout Rates in Primary Education

Year	Primary Grades				
	1/2	2/3	3/4	5/6	6/7
1965/66	5.0	2.9	3.5	12.0	5.6
1966/67	5.8	2.6	4.1	10.0*	7.0*
1967/68	5.0*	3.0*	4.0*	10.0*	7.0*
1968/69	5.0*	3.0*	4.0*	10.0*	7.0*
1970/71	5.0*	3.0*	4.0*	10.0*	7.0*

*Estimated rates.
Source: Thailand, Ministry of Education, Educational Planning Division, Statistics for Educational Planning (Bangkok, 1969), p. 48.

training for teachers, reconsider the rigid examinations, and take steps to improve general living conditions in rural areas.

Although wastage rates in secondary education (see Tables 8.4 and 8.5) are low in comparison with those in primary education, poor teaching quality, lack of motivation among students, and opportunistic attitudes of the private institutions, particularly in the upper secondary level, contribute to substantial wastage. The government policy now is to reduce this wastage and improve the overall standard of secondary education rather than to expand enrollment.

During the five years of the Third National Social and Economic Developmental Plan (1972-1976), 53 percent of the total educational budget is planned to be allocated to primary education. Even then only 49 percent of the population in the relevant age-group will be enrolled. In order to achieve 100 percent enrollment up to pratom 7 and at the same time to improve the quality of education, the government will have to spend an even larger proportion of the national budget, which does not appear to be probable. Furthermore, secondary education will require an even greater proportion of the total educational budget (allocation at present is 19.8 percent of the total educational budget during the Third Plan) in order to increase enrollment and to improve the quality of education through the development of diversified curricula and the establishment of expensive schools. Formal education cannot afford to carry this heavy load in the future.

It is apparent from the above that, although the formal system of education is relatively successful in

preparing students for higher education, it is not equally
successful in training the school leavers for employment
and social obligations. Nor can it be with the available
financial and personnel resources. It is clear that alternatives must be explored for making better use of the
formal institutions and initiating effective programs to
serve the out-of-school population.

OVERVIEW OF NONFORMAL EDUCATION

        Until 1940 education for the out-of-school population
received little attention from the government. The first
breakthrough came after 1938 when the first national
census found 68.8 percent of the population over the age
of 10 illiterate. In order to remedy this situation, the
government established the Adult Education Division under
the Ministry of Education in 1940 to plan and implement
educational programs for the out-of-school population.
        In those days, however, adult education was charged
solely with eradicating illiteracy and fostering responsible
citizenship. The programs, therefore, were mainly literacy
classes using curricula adapted from the formal elementary
schools.
        Increased contacts with the western countries after
the Second World War led to the rapid influx of new ideas
into Thai society, some of which was alien to traditional
Thai beliefs and way of life. The conflict between old
and new and between the need to change and the desire to
adhere to accustomed patterns was and still is felt in
every segment of society. The limitations of the formal

TABLE 8.4

Repeater Rates in Secondary Education

Year	Secondary Grades				
	1	2	3	4	5
1965/66	7.0	5.7	2.4	27	21
1966/67	10.0	12.6	8.2	28	10
1967/68	8.1	9.8	8.2	30	10
1968/69	11.8	9.5	9.2	24	8
1969/70*	10.0	9.0	8.0	23	10
1970/71*	10.0	9.0	8.0	22	10

*Estimated
        Source: Thailand, Ministry of Education, Educational Planning
Division, Statistics for Educational Planning (Bangkok, 1969), p. 49.

TABLE 8.5

Dropout Rates in Secondary Education

		Grades			
Year	Primary 7/ Secondary 1	Secondary 1/2	Secondary 2/3	Secondary 4/5 Public School	Secondary 4/5 Private School
1965/66	14.6	2.5	2.9	19	32
1966/67	16.2	8.9	1.9	18	18
1967/68	15.0*	2.6	1.9	13	16
1968/69	15.0*	3.0*	2.0	13	15
1969/70	15.0*	3.0*	2.0*	13*	15*
1970/71	15.0*	3.0*	2.0*	12*	15*

*Estimated
Source: Thailand, Ministry of Education, Educational Planning
Division, Statistics for Educational Planning (Bangkok, 1969), p. 50.

school system in preparing the population for a modern
society in which new ideas are constantly being introduced and existing beliefs challenged became readily
apparent.   It was evident that education would have to
become a lifelong process extending beyond the narrow
span of childhood.

The concept of adult education, therefore, has undergone a transformation.   It is now recognized that the
adult education programs serve two functions.   First,
they supplement the formal system efforts in developing
a more qualified working force, vital to the economic
development of the country.   Second, by supplying necessary
information, correcting ingrown misconceptions, and providing training in skills, they help the people solve
the problems which are obstacles to their attempts to
improve their standard of living.

While adult education was only briefly mentioned in
the Second Educational Plan (1967-1971), it is one of the
main concerns in the Third Educational Plan (1972-1976).
During these five years, the government plans to promote
all adult education programs with special emphasis on
continuing education, use of audiovisual equipment, and
provision of reading materials to the out-of-school population.

Although the budget allocated to adult education is
only 0.52 percent of the educational budget in 1972, there
has been a regular annual increase from less than 8 million
baht in 1967 to a projected 55 million baht in 1974.
Furthermore, although the Adult Education Division is the

official organization responsible for education for the
out-of-school population, in the last twenty years numerous private and government programs have come into existence all over the country. Aiming at common goals, on
the whole they operate independently, each one serving
specific objectives and specific target groups.

In 1970 the government revived the National Committee
on Adult Education, first formed in 1940, with twelve
Under-Secretaries and Director-Generals from governmental
agencies and the Minister of Education as chairman, to be
responsible for the formulation of national policy and
the planning and coordination of adult education programs
in Thailand. However, the 1971 coup d'état dissolved the
cabinet, and a new Advisory Committee of Nonformal Education was set up. In making recommendations based on the
National Committee's earlier survey, the Advisory Committee classified nonformal education in three categories:
1) education equivalent to the formal system, 2) education
and training in specific skills, and 3) mass education
through mass communication.

Education equivalent to the formal system is accomplished by several organizations in evening classes for
the out-of-school population, from the literacy level
to the university level, and is rewarded by certificates
equivalent to the formal system certificates. The Adult
Education Division supervises the administration, curriculum development, and coordination of programs through
the upper secondary level. There is no coordinating body
in charge of the increasingly popular university level
programs.

Specific skills are taught in short courses ranging
from five hours to several months. Although the certificates issued to the students do not carry the same
credit as those of the formal system, there are a large
number of programs operated by both private and governmental agencies. There is no central coordinating body
and the programs, suffering accordingly, cannot make the
best use of limited budget and personnel.

Mass education, requiring smaller budgets, reaches
a large segment of the population through library and
reading centers, youth centers, panel discussions, lectures, mass media, museums, and exhibitions.

Appendix 8.1 lists various educational activities
under the above categories undertaken by the government
agencies in Thailand.

The Advisory Committee has made a number of recommendations in 1972 to guide the future development of
nonformal education. Briefly, the recommendations are:

1. The existing National Committee on Adult Educa-
    tion should be the planning and coordinating
    body for nonformal and adult education activities
    and, to avoid misunderstanding, should be called
    the National Committee on Nonformal Education.

2. The Adult Education Division in the Ministry of Education should continue to coordinate nonformal academic programs up to the upper secondary level.
3. A separate body under the Bureau of Universities should be established, or the Adult Education Division should be expanded for guiding post-secondary continuing education.
4. The Ministry of Education should be in charge of nonformal vocational training, working in cooperation with agencies that have the need for such a program.
5. The Department of Labor should survey the demands of the industry and inform the training agencies so that training programs can be developed accordingly.
6. Special consideration should be given to support the public libraries and newspaper reading centers, which have proved to be highly valuable in developing human resources.
7. Other nonformal activities in connection with mass media, youth centers, and printed matter which have been successful in reaching a large number of the population at lower cost should be supported and improved, and subcommittees appointed to study each program.

Although nonformal education programs of various types abound in Thailand in terms of numbers served and resources invested, more significant work has been done in the first category of nonformal education--nonformal program for general education and courses equivalent to the formal system. The remainder of this study will be devoted to two such programs: a functional literacy and family life educational program, and an upper primary and secondary level equivalency program.

FUNCTIONAL LITERACY AND FAMILY LIFE EDUCATION

Historical Background

The first literacy evening classes were established by the Adult Education Division in 1940 when a law was promulgated requiring all Thais to possess literacy skills at least up to pratom 2 level. The early literacy program was generally known as the "fundamental education program," since it was intended to provide fundamental education to the out-of-school population, particularly in the rural areas. Although these evening classes were established for illiterates over the age of fifteen, the

academic curricula were similar to the primary school
curricula, with no account taken of the interests or the
psychology of adult learning. They were taught Thai,
mathematics, civic responsibility, geography, history,
health education, and basic vocational training, with 70
percent of the time spent on academic subjects and 30
percent on vocational. The vocational content of the
curriculum, however, was too simple to be of any practical
use to the adult learners, and the supplementary reading
materials were merely reading exercises. On the whole the
fundamental education program was equipped to teach only
literacy.

The program was divided into two six-month courses,
with an examination at the end of each course, for which
passing students received pratom 2 and pratom 4 certificates. These certificates, however, were merely indications that the students had been through literacy
courses at pratom 2 and pratom 4 levels and could not be
used as formal school diplomas. It was reported that
within three years of the program's operation the total
number of illiterates was reduced by 1,409,686.

However, economic instability forced the government
to abolish the compulsory provision. Although the literacy
classes remained operating on a voluntary basis, enrollment dropped sharply and the program came to a standstill.
Postwar prosperity allowed the government to renew interest
in education for the out-of-school population. But the
literacy program elicited little response from the public.
Because of its high cost, lack of motivation among adult
illiterates to attend classes, and the fact that the
government favored other adult education programs, it
gradually became the least significant of all adult
education programs.

It was not until 1963, when the national census revealed that 23 percent of the population over 15 years
old were still illiterate, that the government was forced
to institute a literacy program again, keeping the original fundamental education program as the literacy
program for the rural population, and developing a more
academic curriculum to attract urban illiterates. The
new program also consisted of two six-month courses leading respectively to pratom 2 and pratom 4 equivalency
certificates, though these did not permit students, entry
into the formal system.

Although the newly introduced curricula were successful in attracting illiterates who needed formal credentials, the program still suffered from high dropout rates
and high failing rates. In 1963, for example, only 6,922
students out of an enrollment of 11,208 actually completed
the course. In 1963, as we have noted, 23 percent of the
population over 15 years old were found illiterate, 4
percent of school age children failed to enter school,
and approximately 33 percent of primary school graduates

reverted to illiteracy each year. The total number of illiterates, therefore, was increasing every year. It was obvious that the existing literacy program was far from adequate to cope with illiteracy. Not only did the curriculum have to be revised, but a new approach towards literacy had to be adopted.

In 1965, the United Nations, Educational, Scientific and Cultural Organization (UNESCO) sponsored an international seminar on literacy, attended by the Minister of Education and the Chief of the Adult Education Division where the concept of "functional literacy" was introduced. Literacy alone was recognized as insufficient for development or for motivating adult illiterates to attend class. Therefore, UNESCO programs combined literacy with the teaching of occupational skills directly relevant to adult illiterates.

In 1968 an experimental functional literacy program was set up in Lampang, a province in the north of Thailand, and was later expanded to other provinces by 1970. The core of the curriculum was two reading primers and supplementary reading materials, based on a UNESCO survey of the target population and similar in presentation to the textbooks used in regular classes--with functional materials on health care, nutrition, and agriculture added. After the learners passed a certain reading level, general information about occupational skills was provided.

The program was not without problems. A final evaluation showed that the program had failed to motivate the students to attend classes regularly and the attrition rate was very high. A large number of students dropped out of the program before the functional aspect of the curriculum was introduced. On the whole the students performed well in the literacy area, but learned little of the functional aspects of the curriculum. Although initially the program had planned to employ health officials, doctors, and other extension workers to demonstrate how to apply newly learned information, it did not take into account the shortage of these workers and the lack of transportation facilities to and from classes held at night. Hence primary teachers without specialized training were called on to supply both general information and practical knowledge of occupational skills. Often they did not know more about the occupational skills than the students. The teachers' lack of confidence made them ignore the functional aspects of the curriculum and concentrate on teaching reading and writing for which they were trained and experienced.

These problems led the Adult Education Division to revise its program in 1970. In June of that year, World Education, a voluntary agency based in the United States, invited a group of Thai educators and health officials to an interregional workshop on functional literacy and family life planning held in India where the entire approach to

functional literacy was examined and a new design for
integrating family life planning and functional literacy
was suggested. With technical and financial assistance
provided through World Education and the United States
Operations Mission to Thailand (USOM), revision of the
functional literacy curriculum began in 1970. Fundamental
education and academic literacy curricula are still used
in literacy classes all over the country, but since they
have proved to be unsuccessful with the illiterate population they are being replaced gradually by the functional
literacy and family life education program.

Objectives and Content

The ultimate goal of the Thai functional literacy and
family life education program is to help illiterates cope
with the problems of their environment by providing
necessary and useful information, correcting misconceptions,
and encouraging the application of acquired knowledge.
In support of these objectives curriculum development
begins with identifying the problems in the daily life of
the rural communities. First, a baseline survey of the
target population is conducted, observing their beliefs,
habits, living conditions, needs and language patterns.
Then representatives from various ministries, such as the
Ministry of Interior, the Ministry of Public Health, and
the Ministry of Agriculture, describe the problems they
have met in rural areas. From these sources come a list
of problems focused on the interrelated needs of the
family unit, in four aspects of life: 1) earning a living;
2) family economics and consumer education; 3) health and
family planning; and 4) civic responsibility. The curriculum is then developed in an attempt to solve these problems by teaching right concepts.
Students are provided with information and facts to
enable them to understand why existing conditions are
problems and how these problems affect their lives. Alternatives are explored and the implications of adopting
these alternatives examined. When necessary, outside
persons are invited to provide further information on the
application of acquired knowledge. For example, if farmers
leave their fields uncultivated after the harvesting
season, there is a loss of possible income and the field
grows infertile. Farmers are, therefore, taught the
concept of rotation.
Concepts are taught through group discussion which
takes advantage of the natural learning environment of Thai
adults, who often gather in the evenings to chat about
family and village problems. Learners are urged to participate actively by presenting their own experiences and
comparing them with alternatives. They must also listen

and consider conflicting ideas from others. This discussion technique has proved effective in making the
learner more rational and practical in deciding how to
improve existing conditions.

Accompanying the teaching of concepts is the teaching
of literacy skills. Although mastery of literacy skills
alone is no longer regarded as the end product of the
educational process, it serves as a means to increase
knowledge and to gain access to useful information. Adult
students are given to read and memorize complete sentences
about concepts that they have discussed thoroughly and
are phrased in everyday language. As students begin to
associate sounds, symbols, and meaning, reading ability
increases. The rationale for this method is anthropological
studies which show that illiterates tend to compensate for
lack of literacy symbols by developing their memories,
and relying on word-of-mouth information.

The text consists of individual cards ultimately bound
together in a looseleaf cover. During the first class,
students receive an empty file and the cards for the first
lesson. In each consecutive class they receive only those
cards that they will study that night. Each card consists
of two parts: a photograph depicting the concepts of the
lessons with key words printed underneath to stimulate
discussion and a summary text to be used as both reading
exercise and after-class reference material. Reading,
writing, and arithmetic exercises are provided in separate
volumes.

The design of the text as a group of cards is based
on past experiences in the literacy program that have
shown that illiterates tend to be discouraged by thick
volume texts. Moreover, as the program expands to other
regions, the looseleaf feature of the text makes it easily
adaptable to them by inserting new cards or taking out
irrelevant ones. The accumulation of cards as the learner
progresses through the course provides a ready measure of
accomplishment and psychological incentive.

Instructional Personnel and Administration

Like the earlier literacy programs, functional literacy
classes rely on school teachers, selected by local educational officers on the basis of their familiarity with
the problems in the area, their personality, and their
academic credentials.

Since most of these teachers have no previous experience working with adult illiterates, they are given a one-
week precourse training stressing adult education, curriculum, psychology, teaching techniques, and evaluation.
Illiterates are hired to serve as students for practice
teaching. Resource persons such as health workers, agri-

culturalists, and district officers, are invited to give
the teachers background information on the topics included in the syllabus. Two teachers' manuals have been
developed with detailed lesson plans and additional information. Twice during the course supervisors and administrators conduct follow-up meetings in which video-taped
classroom performances are evaluated and teaching problems discussed.

The use of primary schoolteachers in functional
classes has certain advantages: the additional salary
supplements teachers' earnings in the rural areas, and
the experience with adults often helps them teach children
better. One disadvantage lies in the primary teachers'
adherence to the lecturing technique, when group discussion
should be promoted in functional classes; another is that
able teachers of literacy are often too concerned with
literacy skills to convey concepts and to encourage changes
of attitude.

Beginning in 1973, the program plans to use local
leaders or resource persons with at least a pratom 7
education to teach in functional classes. They are to be
selected on the basis of their understanding of the local
problems, their experience with community development, and
their prestige in the village, and are to include youth
leaders, who received training at the UNESCO Fundamental
Education Center at Ubolrajchathani (no longer in operation), village headmen, monks, and respected villagers.

Supervisors play an important role in the functional
literacy and family life education program, particularly
in curriculum development and teaching materials production, teacher training, classroom supervision, and
evaluation. Since the curriculum and teaching techniques
employed in the program differ from most educational programs, the supervisors have to attend workshops before the
program begins in their districts. The adult education
supervisors, evaluation supervisors, chiefs of provincial
supervisory units, provincial education officers, and
district education officers from 12 provinces, trained
up to 1972 to work in the program, are expected to take
over from the Division of Adult Education staff in Bangkok
the main responsibility for implementing the program.
Provincial education officers are already in charge of
the administration of functional literacy classes, with
technical assistance from supervisors. The opening of
each new class, however, has to be approved by the Department of General Education upon recommendation of the
regional officer. As the program expands, the Adult
Education Division will try to decentralize in order to
achieve greater flexibility and to give regional and local
officers a greater sense of responsibility.

Although the policy of the government is gradually to
replace all traditional literacy classes with functional
literacy and family life education classes, expansion to

new areas requires new curriculum training of teachers and supervisors, a countrywide task that cannot be completed before 1977. (See Table 8.6.)

TABLE 8.6

Expansion Plan of Functional Literacy and
Family Life Education Program

Year	No. of Regions	No. of Provinces	No. of Classes	No. of Students
1971	1	2	20	427
1972	2	12	102	2,120
1973	6	32	280	5,600
1974	8	44	400	8,000
1975	9	51	600	12,000
1976	10	60	800	16,000
1977	12	71	950	19,000

Source: Thailand, Ministry of Education, Division of Adult Education.

Clientele

The clientele for functional literacy and family life education program varies by age, sex, marital status, and academic backgrounds, although most are engaged in agriculture. It includes adults who have never attended schools, dropouts from the formal system, and primary school graduates who have reverted to illiteracy.

Approximately two-thirds of the students in the samples of 1971 and 1972 were males, a not surprisingly high proportion considering the males' more compelling desire to earn certificates leading to jobs and the females' preoccupation in the home. Whatever the reasons, the program is attempting to correct any inhibiting factors, so that more women will become enrolled in the program.

Officials are considering ways and means of increasing the attendance rate of the 20-34-year-old group, inasmuch as in the past two years there have been three times as many students over 30 years old than under. (See Table 8.7.) The fact that most are married and have children suggests that the family life education part of the curriculum should foster population awareness, help prepare the minority who are still single for married life, and assist families with large numbers of children to solve their problems.

   Although the program aims at illiterates who have
never attended school, more than 50 percent of the students
in two sample groups admitted to having received some
schooling, but only 15 percent of the sample had had more
than pratom 2 education. The number of those who have
attended school may in fact be even more, since many
adults do not want to admit a reversion to illiteracy.

TABLE 8.7

Sample of Students in Functional Literacy Program
Classified by Age, 1971-1972

Age Group Yrs.	Sample in 1971	Sample from 5 Southern Provinces in 1972	Total %
Under 15	5	–	1
15-19	66	21	25
20-24	23	8	9
25-29	16	7	6
30-34	38	8	13
35-39	49	16	19
Over 40	55	40	27
Total	252	100	100

   Source: Thailand, Ministry of Education, Division of Adult
Education.

   The survey data suggest that the students in functional classes are representative of most rural illiterates. For although they come from varying backgrounds,
over 80 percent were engaged in agriculture (see Table 8.8).
Since only 4 percent were in civil service, a career that
requires academic credentials for job promotion, there
seem to be other motivating factors to attract adults in
occupations that do not require academic credentials.

Other Programs

   Attempts have been made to coordinate the functional
literacy program with other adult education programs.
Audiovisual units visit all functional classes to show
educational films and, when possible, extension workers
from the adult education vocational section and other

TABLE 8.8

Educational Background of Two Samples of Students

Highest Level Completed	Sample of Students in 1971	Sample from 5 Southern Provinces in 1972
Never attend school	110 (44%)	30
Primary grade 1	57 (23%)	5
Primary grade 2	47 (18%)	15
Primary grade 3	21 (8%)	28
Primary grade 4	8 (3%)	11
Unspecified	9 (4%)	11
Total	252 (100%)	100

Source: Thailand, Ministry of Education, Division of Adult Education.

organizations are invited to provide detailed information to the students. In addition, public libraries and reading centers are established to supply the new literates with reading materials at provincial and district levels.

To provide further follow-up materials at the village level, a newspaper reading center project has been initiated; since it requires a relatively small budget, it is planned to be expanded to selected villages in all 71 provinces in 1973. It appears to be promising in creating a desire for literacy skills at the village level, helping literates to retain their reading abilities, promoting reading habits generally, fostering an awareness of what is happening in other parts of the nation, and encouraging villagers to become actively involved in community projects. The Division is also encouraging outside organizations to publish reading materials geared to rural readers with pratom 4 reading ability.

Since functional literacy classes are conducted in elementary schools or other existing facilities in the area, there is no capital cost. The government must provide for all of the following, as there are no tuition or textbook costs to the students.

1. teachers' remuneration (20 baht per hour for 200 hours, or 4,000 baht for each class of 25 students)
2. expenses for classroom materials (approximately 600 baht per 200 hour course)
3. supervisors' remuneration and traveling expenses (a total of 424 baht to supervise one class)

   4. teachers' preservice and inservice training (an
       average of 800 baht per teacher)
   5. printing costs (about 1,207 baht for each class)

Hence the cost of one class of 25 students for the six-
month course is 7,031 baht, or roughly 281 baht per
student.

Evaluation

     Evaluations of functional literacy and family life
education programs are conducted by the Adult Education
Division in cooperation with supervisors in the provinces
to assess the implementation of program policies and to
measure the student's performance. Three methods are
used:

   1. precourse and postcourse tests to evaluate the
       effectiveness of the program in reaching speci-
       fied goals:
       a. reading test which measures reading abili-
           ties on a scale of one to nine, ranging from
           ability to recognize the alphabet to the
           ability to read complex sentences (these
           scales do not correspond to the grades in
           the formal schools)
       b. mathematics test which is similarly graduated
           from the ability to recognize math symbols
           to the ability to solve complex problems on
           a scale of one to nine
       c. questionnaire to assess attitudinal change
           by multiple-choice questions designed to
           determine attitudes towards concepts taught
           in class
   2. classroom evaluation by the supervisors through-
       out the program
   3. periodic tests to measure student progress after
       completion of every three lessons in the program
       (ninety percent of tests are multiple-choice
       questions while remaining 10 percent are open-
       ended questions, covering both literacy and the
       concepts introduced in the three lessons)

     These three methods have been employed up to 1972 to
measure both the implementation of the program and the
performance of the students. From 1973 onwards, however,
the supervisors in the provinces will take over the
responsibility of measuring the performance of the
students. Students with more than a 70 percent attendance
rate will automatically receive a certificate that is
equivalent to a pratom 4 certificate in the formal system.

Students with less than 70 percent attendance rate will have to make up for the time missed and pass an examination in literacy and arithmatic skill administered by the provincial supervisors, while an oral examination and a teacher's evaluation will measure their understanding of concepts.

The decision to grant the completers of the six-month course of functional literacy and family life education certificates equivalent to the four-year program of lower primary education is based on many reasons. Although the program is shorter and different in content than the primary school curriculum, adults are recognized to have a wider experience and knowledge than children. Their larger oral vocabulary and more highly developed memory are expected to lead them to read and write more quickly than children, particularly when the text is based on familiar vocabulary. Since most adult illiterates have mastered some mathematical concepts from their experience, they can presumably progress faster here too. The explanation and exercises in the mathematics lessons are chosen to apply to their lives: an example in graphs, for instance, might be a graph showing the increase in the productivity of the soil after the use of fertilizer.

Although the two curricula are not identical, the syllabus of functional literacy and family life covers a wider scope, by providing factual information on specific topics and training in special skills, on the basis of which personal problems are more easily solved. Despite the fact that most completers are not expected to continue their education in the formal system and that they will remain in rural areas, academic credentials remain essential keys to employment and education.

Outcome of the Program

Creating Interest and Motivation

In the beginning, the program encountered difficulties in trying to convince adult illiterates to enroll, particularly those who had no occupational need for formal credits. Many associated the new functional classes with the rigid traditional literacy and primary classes; some felt they did not need literacy; and still others felt they were too old. However, community leaders, such as village headmen, monks, and respected villagers, helped the educational officers to convince potential students of the differences between functional literacy and literacy programs in the past. The provision of follow-up materials at the village level, involvement of local leaders, and success of previous literacy classes in the area are expected to motivate more adult illiterates to become enrolled.

A baseline survey and other studies of past experience in community development indicate that the program has been relatively successful in developing a curriculum to serve the needs of society as well as of the individual. But although the curriculum has come closer to being relevant to the daily lives of the people than most educational curricula, it still does not cover many major problems in the rural areas. Therefore, educational officers in each region in the program are conducting intensive studies to make recommendations for curriculum improvement. Furthermore, in the future, the Division will not develop a "complete" curriculum, but will train teachers to work with the students in identifying special community problems and finding their solutions.

As we have seen, teachers' inadequate qualifications hinder the effectiveness of the program. With more intensive training, closer supervision, further development of teachers' manuals, and employment of some outside experts, the problems are expected to be less severe.

One of the major problems in all literacy programs is the high dropout rate. The functional literacy program is trying to be as flexible as possible in meeting the conditions and needs of the learners. Apart from the disciplines that are exerted by unique curricula and learning materials, classes are more relaxed than formal primary classes. In order to make the illiterates feel less restricted and inhibited, some classes are conducted outside the primary classroom, often in the temple grounds or at the teacher's house. Clothing rules are minimal. In some cases, the learners are allowed to bring their children to class. Class hours and the timing of the courses are set at the convenience of the students. For example, in villages where the farmers leave their land to work in other areas after harvesting season, the program is suspended during that period.

Teachers are encouraged to be actively interested in their students. They often invite them to stay on after class for informal gatherings. Group activities are organized. On the whole the program attempts to maintain regular attendance, not only by making classroom activities relevant and interesting, but also by transforming the class into a friendly social gathering to create a sense of belonging.

In the last two years of the pilot project, the program has succeeded in achieving a relatively low dropout rate. The dropout rate in 1971, for instance, was 12.6 percent, or 55 students out of a total enrollment of 452. Almost all of the dropouts were forced to abandon the program for justifiable reasons, such as poor health, migration, occupational engagement, and death.

In the second year of implementation in the northern provinces, the dropout rate was estimated at less than 10 percent; in the south where the program was under way for the first year, the dropout rate was quite high at 37

percent. A close examination of the southern program
reveals that dropout rates tend to differ strikingly from
one class to another. At Surasthani, where the functional
literacy program class seems to be closest to the ideal,
there were no dropouts at all, while in other less successful classes, the rates ranged from nearly 20 percent to
50 percent.

Achievements

In the first year of the program, the reading ability
of a sample group that was administered tests before and
after the course was found to increase substantially
(from an average of 3.94 level to 6.43 level on the evaluation scale described above). The group also recorded gains
in arithmetic skill (from 3.79 level to 6.53 level). In
both cases the students in functional classes made more
progress than the students in the control group. The
available data on students in region 3 suggest that the
progress of the students in the second year program was
equally satisfactory.

Up to the present time (1972) there have been no
studies comparing the literacy skills of primary graduates
and functional literacy graduates. Furthermore, since
there are no graduates from the first year program enrolled
in higher levels of education, there are no data on how
well the functional literacy program has prepared the
students for higher education. Plans are being made,
however, to conduct a follow-up evaluation of the functional literacy graduates in order to measure how well
they retain the knowledge gained from the courses.

Information collected through questionnaires suggests
that students in general are learning the material conveyed
in the classes and are developing more positive attitudes
toward the concepts in the program. These questionnaires
are not, however, clear indications of changes of attitudes and are being revised so that a more accurate assessment can be made. In addition, plans are being made to
see what practical application is made of knowledge acquired
in the program.

Concluding Comments

In conclusion, it can be said that, although the
functional literacy program is still operating on a small
scale, it has already made an impact on the Thai educational system. In spite of its problems, it has introduced a new approach to education for the out-of-school
population and to the eradication of illiteracy. It has
also demonstrated that the two objectives of education,
preparing students for further education and training them
to become responsible members of society, can be reconciled.

The functional literacy program within two years of
its existence has demonstrated other areas of promise:

1. A discussion technique and learner involvement
    can be used to cover the entire curriculum within
    the time limit.
2. With careful planning, unique teaching materials
    suitable for adults can be developed to serve as
    both reading texts and reference materials.
3. Flexible examinations and measures of achievement
    can be designed without sacrificing educational
    standards.
4. Classroom regulations can be relaxed to suit the
    needs of the learners without causing chaos.
5. Through development of individual courses, im-
    provement of teaching techniques, and greater
    involvement of community leaders, literacy pro-
    grams can attract many adult illiterates from
    varying backgrounds.
6. Careful planning of the curriculum for adult
    illiterates and inclusion of more relevant topics
    can significantly reduce the duration of lower
    primary education.
7. Nonformal approach can in this case reduce the
    cost of education, since the functional literacy
    course is shorter and makes use of existing faci-
    lities.

In taking a broad view of educational objectives, the
nonformal functional literacy and family life education
program is expected to affect formal primary education
and the role of education in the community. It is certain
that the program has led to greater recognition of the
necessity to incorporate the specific learning needs of
the student in the curriculum. Supervisors and elementary
school teachers who have been trained in functional literacy programs will be qualified to introduce new techniques
into primary education, avoiding heavy reliance on the
"lecture method." Further, employment of qualified outsiders to work as teachers in functional literacy classes
will lead to a change in the concept of the teacher from
one who simply teaches traditional literacy skills and
provides information on specific topics to one who helps
students solve problems in their daily lives. Finally,
the involvement of local leaders in the program will
create a greater general interest in education within the
community. It will help make education an integral part
of daily life in the rural community.

POSTLITERACY ACADEMIC EQUIVALENCY PROGRAM

Origin and Content

Private institutions had been offering for a long time tutorial classes to prepare the out-of-school population for the formal examination at upper primary and lower secondary levels. In order to accommodate this rising demand and to control the standard of education, the Adult Education Division decided in 1949 to expand nonformal academic programs beyond the literacy level. The operation of these classes, however, remained in the hands of the private institutions. The role of the Division was limited to supporting the classes financially by remunerating the teachers and academically by providing classroom supervision. Except for their being taught in evening class hours, these adult classes were similar to formal classes with identical curricula, teaching methods, and formal examinations, and they led to the award of similar academic credentials.

In 1960 the postliteracy academic program was revised, so that adult students could complete the course in one year, rather than the three years required to complete either upper primary and lower secondary education. This adapted curriculum attracted many of the out-of-school population, but inasmuch as course content was identical to the formal curriculum, the program had to proceed so rapidly that many students could not keep up and they failed the examination for which regular school students had three full years to prepare.

In 1965, the postliteracy academic program underwent a drastic revision to become what is known today as Academic Level 3 (equivalent to three years of upper primary education) and Academic Level 4 (equivalent to three years of lower secondary education). The duration of the courses was extended to one and a half years and the subjects were divided into three sets of pairs, which the students were now allowed to take in any order as long as all three pairs were completed in five years.

In Academic Level 3 the pairs are: mathematics (160 hours) and health education (40 hours) for a total of 200 hours; Thai language (80 hours) and English (120 hours) for a total of 200 hours; and social science (80 hours) and science (120 hours), also for a total of 200 hours. Classes meet five days a week, two hours per day in two semesters beginning in November and May.

In Academic Level 4 the pairs are: mathematics and health education (300 hours); Thai language and social science (300 hours); and English and science (also 300 hours). The classes meet five days a week, two and a half hours a day.

This pairing of subjects allows adult students to
concentrate on a few subjects, rather than cram all the
subjects into the same time. Since they are allowed to
accumulate their credits over a period of five years,
they can drop out of the program if necessary and become
enrolled again at their convenience. Reorganization of
the curriculum means that topics covered several times
at different depths and at greater length in formal education are here consolidated into one semester. It also
takes into account the larger repertoire of knowledge and
experience of adult learners.

In 1970 an experimental Academic Level 5, equivalent
to two years of upper secondary education, was started.
The new curriculum has not yet been developed from its
formal prototype, but preparations are being made to
develop curricula similar in character to Academic Levels
3 and 4.

Since 1970, the Adult Education Division has issued
certificates carrying the same credits as formal certificates to students who pass the examination for Levels 3
and 4. Two types of examinations determine the student
performance: a periodic test given at least twice a
semester on each subject, and a final examination for all
students with at least an 80 percent attendance rate,
similar to examinations for formal upper primary and
lower secondary classes--without being identical to them.
Since the revised curriculum means that the students take
only two subjects at a time, they are tested only on these
subjects, allowing them more time to prepare for the
examination. Within the five-year limit (after which the
credits are annulled) they can accumulate credits until
all six subjects are completed. Unlike the regular school
examination in which an average score of 50 percent is
considered as a passing grade, Level 3 and 4 tests require
a score of at least 50 percent on each subject.

Level 5, operating under the formal curriculum, uses
the formal examinations prepared by the schools in which
they enroll at the end of the first year; at the end of
the second year they have to take Mawsaw 5 examinations
with the students from the regular schools. Those who
pass receive the regular school diploma. When the Level
5 curriculum is developed along the lines of Level 3 and
4, it will have a new examination system as well.

Administration and Personnel

The Adult Education Division operates postliteracy
classes through public and private schools which make a
request to set up classes for 20-40 students. As the
requests for Level 3 and 4 have been well beyond the
budget of the program, only about 60 percent can be

approved each year. Hence, the schools' applications must be submitted through provincial education officers six months in advance to give the Division time to consider such factors as the number of adult schools in the same locality, the qualifications of the teachers, the number of potential students, the recommendations from provincial officers, and, if the classes have been in operation before, the past achievement of the students.

After a class has been approved, local education officers and supervisors under the Division are placed in charge of its administration, supervision, and examinations. Unless the class becomes a complete failure (when no students pass the examination, for example) the initial approval is valid for as long as there is a required number of students. At the end of each year, the Division sends out a questionnaire to all classes to determine if they expect to continue operation.

The teachers in all postliteracy nonformal academic classes must have at least lower teaching certificates, but since the curricula of the teacher training courses do not include adult education, most teachers know very little about teaching adults, and tend to teach them as if they were children. The Adult Education Division has attempted to remedy this situation by providing seminars and inservice training to some teachers, but a tremendous increase in the budget would be necessary to provide training for all teachers. Plans are being made, however, to set up training centers in different regions of the country, and in the future only teachers who have been through training courses will be allowed to teach in the program. Since the allowance for teaching in the program supplements teachers' regular earnings, it is expected that they will be willing to pay for the training themselves, and the government will not have to invest large funds to support training centers. Since a large number of these teachers are regular school teachers, formal teaching will be the better for the nonformal teacher training.

Supervisors must somehow compensate for the lack of well-qualified teachers, and in so doing they play a crucial role in maintaining the standards of the nonformal academic program. But, for at least three reasons, effective supervision will be difficult until current corrective measures prove successful. In the first place, while the program has been expanded to cover approximately 69 provinces of the country, only 43 provinces have supervisors in adult education. Therefore the program in 26 provinces must rely on neighboring supervisors who are already burdened with their own work. Second, the existing supervisors are not very well qualified--almost three-quarters of them have only a teaching certificate. Most supervisors with high academic credentials have been trained in other fields, as no adult education programs for supervisors are offered. The Division has organized

a number of seminars and workshops in which supervisors
have discussed new techniques and shared their experiences;
it is also working in cooperation with several universities
to set up appropriate courses in adult education for
supervisors.   Third, since adult classes are at night and
often in remote areas, the supervisors have to be very
devoted and conscientious to visit these classes regularly,
particularly since many provinces lack the vehicles needed
for trips and money for traveling expenses.

Clientele

Attempts have been made to keep enrollment regulations
in the program at a minimum. The selection criteria are
that the students must:

1. be over 15 years old, so that compulsory age
    students will not leave regular school to become
    enrolled in these nonformal classes
2. not be enrolled in a similar course in regular
    school
3. be free from a contagious disease
4. have Pratom 4 credits to enroll in Level 3 and
    Pratom 7 credits to enroll in Level 4

If there are more students enrolled for the course
than there are available spaces, the school may have to
select the students according to the time of application,
age, results of entrance examinations, or previous educational accomplishment.
     Since attempts have been made to decentralize the
administration of the program, very little record of the
students is kept by the Division. However, questionnaires
returned by schools operating equivalency classes provide
interesting information on the clientele during the first
semester of the 1972/73 academic year.
     The clientele is both rural and urban: in 1972 there
were 26 adult schools in metropolitan Bangkok and 234
adult schools in 69 provinces. The students were younger
in this academically-oriented program than in the functional literacy and family life education program, with
almost 60 percent from the 16-20 year old group, which
stands in particular need of academic credentials. They
came from varied backgrounds, with monks forming half the
group. For example, there were 191 monk classes and 469
ordinary adult classes. While there are attempts to
attract students from other occupations it is the Division's
policy to support and promote education for monks who
can provide spiritual and moral guidance and also work
as teachers in adult classes in rural areas often lacking
qualified teachers. The reason students most frequently

gave to explain their attendance was "to acquire further knowledge," which of course can be interpreted in many ways. However, the next most popular reason was to continue further education, which is certainly akin to the first. Less than 10 percent cited occupational factors.

Costs and Finance

Students in postliteracy programs are required to pay for tuition, texts, registration, and an examination, spending a total of 480 baht for Level 3, 895 baht for Level 4, and 1,165 for Level 5. (See Table 8.9.) Of these amounts tuition is, of course, by far the largest expense. Approximately 25 percent of the tuition is put in the education trust fund to improve the adult classes and the remaining 75 percent pays for about 78 percent of the cost of remuneration of the teachers, with the government supplying the remaining 22 percent.

TABLE 8.9

Average Cost for 18-month Equivalency Courses in 1972

			(in bahts)		
Level	Gov't Cost for Teachers per 5 Class-rooms	Gov't Cost for Head-master, Admin. Asst., Janitor per 5 Classrooms	Total Gov't Cost per 200 Students in 5 Classes	Gov't Cost per Student	Fees from each Student
3	13,200	16,200	29,200	147	480
4	36,600	10,200	52,800	477	895
5*	79,200	21,600	100,800	504	1,165

*Level 5 course duration is two years.
Source: Thailand, Ministry of Education, Division of Adult Education.

The government also pays the salaries of the headmaster, administrative assistants, teachers, and janitors. In principle, the government pays for inservice training and supervision of teachers. However, this expenditure is modest, since a very small proportion of teachers and supervisors now receive such training. There are no capital costs, because the continuing education programs utilize formal school facilities.

Since nonteaching staff serve several classes at the same time, the government cost per student can be estimated by dividing the total governmental expenditure in support of five classes by the number of students in five classes. Per student cost to the government on this basis was 147 baht for Level 3, 477 baht for Level 4, and 504 baht for Level 5.

In the first semester of 1972/73 there were approximately 1,187 government-supported classes. The requests for classes have exceeded this number limited by the budget, and some schools, known as the self-supported schools, have agreed to operate temporarily without government support, so that they would have first priority in the next semester for government support. In these schools the headmasters, the administrative assistants, and the janitors receive no remuneration, and often the teachers' salaries are lower than scale, coming entirely from tuition fees. In the first semester of 1972-73, there were approximately 894 self-supported classes.

Performance of Equivalency Program

The postliteracy nonformal academic program is popular with the public. The enrollment of students in Level 3 and 4 rose from 7,105 in 1969 to 48,158 in 1972. The Level 5 course, operating on an experimental basis, had 17 classes with 680 students in 1972. If the present trend continues, it is likely that the number of students will far exceed the enrollment of 151,200 projected for 1976 in the Third Educational Plan. Be it noted that in 1972 the actual number of classes exceeded projection by 655 and the actual number of students exceeded projection by 20,158. In order to accommodate the future demand, the Division is studying the possibility of organizing radio correspondence programs as alternatives to regular classes.

There are several plausible explanations for the high interest of the public. First, there is a widespread belief that formal academic credentials are important for future success and that the nonformal academic program can provide these credentials. Second, the cost to the students in the nonformal academic program, particularly at the secondary level, is lower than in the formal system. Moreover, it is possible to complete the course more quickly. Third, the curriculum has been developed to suit the needs of the adult learners by allowing them to concentrate more on each subject. An attractive feature of the program is the fact that students can accumulate their credits over a period of five years. Under this arrangement, if students abandon classes early, they do not have to start all over again, but can continue where they leave off. In addition, since the program now operates throughout the country, if students have to move to a new province they can transfer their credits and continue their courses. This flexible arrangement is most suitable for adult students who are often troubled by financial matters, job reassignment, and change of working hours.

At present the postliteracy academic program is very academically oriented. The content of the curriculum is similar to the formal curriculum and the teaching methods are based on the formal school model. As a result, the program attracts mainly young adults under 20 years of age who wish to obtain academic credentials.

In order to attract a larger and a more varied group and to achieve the second objective of nonformal education, namely to help people solve the problems in their daily life, the Division plans to revise the curriculum along the lines of the functional literacy and family life education program.

Lack of qualified and experienced teachers has been a major obstacle in improving the quality of nonformal academic programs. In the future, teachers will have to take preservice training from adult education centers to be qualified to teach.

Since the administration of Level 3 has been decentralized, and local officers often fail to submit reports to the central officer, there are insufficient data on the dropout rate at this Level. For Level 4, however, the Division is in charge of the examination and calculates the dropout rate from the number of enrolled students who fail to register for the final examination.

On the whole, the dropout rate in Level 4 is quite low (7 percent in 1972, down from 12 percent in 1966), especially if all factors inhibiting regular attendance of working adults are considered. In addition, as many as 48 percent of those who dropped out did so because they had moved, a fact which means that they might continue their education in other schools. Other reasons given for dropout were travel difficulties, job change, poor health, lack of funds, and academic failure.

But if the dropout rate is low, the failure rate in Level 4 is relatively high--21 percent in 1972. This rate is averaged from the failing rates in each subject. For example, the failing rate for 1972 is the average of the failing rates in Thai (37.9 percent), social science (11.7 percent), mathematics (23.3 percent), health education (8.9 percent), English (14.5 percent), and science (34.8 percent).

The failure rates of the program cannot be directly compared to formal education rates. Although the students in the nonformal academic program have more time to study each subject for the examination, the passing grade in the nonformal program is more rigid than in the formal system, since 50 percent is required on each subject

rather than an average of 50 percent. Furthermore,
unlike the students in the formal system who have to study
the entire curriculum again if they fail, the students in
the nonformal academic program can make up the credits for
the single subjects that they have failed. The failing
rate, therefore, is not as costly to the educational budget as the failing rate in the formal system.

In order to reduce the failing rate, the Division
is revising the curriculum, particularly in Thai, mathematics, and science, which had the highest failing rates
in 1972. It is expected that curricular revision and
better trained teachers will bring about a lower failing
rate.

Theoretically, the students can complete the entire
curriculum of Level 3 or Level 4 in one and a half years.
In practice, however, many students take time off after
completing a semester. There are no available records on
the number of students who have completed Level 3 (under
the administration of the provincial officers), but because
the Division is in charge of the examination for Level 4,
it is known that in 1970/71, 2,104 students received
Level 4 certificates and 1,554 in the first semester of
1971/72--a sharp rise from 148 in 1966/67. (See Table
8.10.)

TABLE 8.10

Performance of the Nonformal Academic Program, Level 4, 1966-72

Year	Number completing course	Average % of failure	% Dropout
1966/67	—	41	12
1967/68	148	16	10
1968/69	282	21	10
1969/70	698	16	7
1970/71	1,237	16	5
1971/72	2,104	19	5
1972/73	1,154*	21	7

*Data for the first semester only

Source: Thailand, Ministry of Education, Division of Adult
Education.

Concluding Comments

At present the postliteracy nonformal academic program has many shortcomings and the curriculum must be revised along the lines of the functional literacy program. However, the program has been highly popular with the public and has demonstrated some of the same strengths as the functional literacy program.

There remains a tremendous demand for academic credentials among the out-of-school population. Although attempts are being made to minimize the importance of these credentials, many governmental and private agencies still demand them. In the meantime, this strong motivating factor should be employed to attract students to educational programs that may not otherwise appear useful to them. Reorganization of the curriculum can cut down the amount of time required, but even without complete revision, the program caters to the needs of many adult students merely by changing class hours and relaxing regulations.

The program demonstrates that an educational equivalent to the formal system can be developed at a lower cost for the student. As we have noted, at present the costs to the students in the equivalency program range from 480 baht to 1,165 baht, while student costs in the formal private school system, range from 1,800 baht to 3,600 baht.

The postliteracy program has affected the formal system directly in a variety of ways. It has helped the formal system to satisfy the demand for secondary education and lessened the dual problems of reliance on private schools and migration of rural students into the cities. Since the program has been expanded to cover all but three provinces in the country, it has opened up new educational opportunities in remote areas. It is also expected that employment of formal school teachers and supervisors in adult classes will help improve the performance of these teachers in regular classes.

NOTES

1. Thailand, Ministry of Education, Prawat Krasuang Suksa Thikan 2435-2507 [History of the Ministry of Education 1892-1964] (Bangkok: Kurusabha Press, 1964), pp. 270-272.

2. Aree Sanhachewee, "Evolution in Curriculum and Teaching," in Education in Thailand: A Century of Experience, comp. Thailand, Ministry of Education, Department of Elementary and Adult Education (Bangkok, 1970).

3. Thailand, Ministry of Education, Department of Elementary and Adult Education, "Report on the Research on Literacy of Pratom 4 Graduates," [in Thai], mimeographed (Bangkok, 1968).

4. It takes more than four years for one student to complete
elementary education. The estimated cost for educating repeaters
is approximately 300 million baht per year or more than 5 percent
of the total budget.

APPENDIX 8.1

List of Nonformal Programs in Thailand Compiled in the Preliminary
Survey of National Committee on Adult Education, 1972

Category I

·   Education Equivalent to the Formal System

Responsible Organizations   Activities

Office of the Prime Minister
    Chulalongkorn University   twilight course for degrees;
                                         certificates issued by uni-
                                         versity
    Thammasart University   higher certification course
                                         operated by the university

Ministry of Education
    Department of General Education   general education courses for
                                         adults organized by Adult
                                         Education Division

Ministry of Interior
    Department of Public Welfare   courses for women in rehabili-
                                         tation centers in cooperation
                                         with the Adult Education Divi-
                                         sion
    Department of Corrections   courses for prisoners in coopera-
                                         tion with Adult Education
                                         Division
    Department of Local Administration   general education course for
                                         youths and volunteers in
                                         cooperation with Adult Educa-
                                         tion Division

Ministry of Justice
    The Dika Court of Child and Youth   general education courses for
                                         youths in rehabilitation in
                                         cooperation with Adult Educa-
                                         tion Division

Public Enterprises
    State Railway Organization   electric engineering course;
                                         certificates issued by organi-
                                         zing bodies
    Metropolitan Electric Authority   aerial engineering trainees;
                                         certificates issued by organi-
                                         zing bodies

Responsible Organizations	Activities
Local Administration	
Metropolitan Municipality, Division of Education and Social Welfare	general education courses in cooperation with Adult Education Division
Association and Philanthropic Foundation	
National Council of Women	general education courses in cooperation with Adult Education Division
War-Veteran Organization	general education courses in cooperation with Adult Educa-Division

Category II

Training in Specific Skills

Responsible Organizations	Activities
Office of the Prime Minister	
Internal Security Command	vocational training for youth in cooperation with the Adult Education Division
National Statistical Office	course in statistics
Department of Public Relation	training course in mass communication
Meteorological Department	training required for promotion, primarily for officers in the department
Chulalongkorn University	special education course for administrators
Public Service Division, under the Office of the National Youth Development	National Youth Training Project
Community Development Department	skill training
Ministry of Education	
General Education	adult vocational school and mobile education unit in cooperation with Adult Education Division
Vocational Education	mobile vocational training school
Fine Arts Department	summer courses
Department of Religious Affairs	religious education
Teacher's Association	summer courses
Thammasart University	summer courses in social welfare, anthropology, mathematics, and statistics; certificates issued by university

Responsible Organizations	Activities
Ministry of Interior	
Department of Public Welfare	training in barbering, handicrafts for youths and handicapped, in cooperation with the Adult Education Division
Ministry of Justice	
The Dika Court of Child	vocational training for youths in reformatory institutions in coordination with the Adult Education Division
Ministry of National Development	
Office of the Under-Secretary of State	courses in cooperative organization operated by the ministry itself
Department of Technical and Economic Cooperation	English course for officers
Ministry of Agriculture	
Department of the Agricultural Extension	training in agriculture and economics
Department of Agriculture	experimental projects on mulberry nurturing, cotton planting and harvesting, mechanical training and rubber industrial analysis
Ministry of Industry	
Department of Industry Promotion	experimental projects on cotton and silk filament, needlework, lacquerware
Ministry of Economic Affairs	
Department of Economics	training course on the administration of small industry
Ministry of Public Health	
Department of Health	health education course
Ministry of Communication	
Department of Land Transport	training course in transportation for conductors and fare collectors
Public Enterprises	
Thailand Tobacco Monopoly	course in tobacco processing procedure
Export and Transport Organization	training course for officers
Thailand Aviation Company	training course for aviators
Association and Philanthropic Foundation	
Thailand Social Welfare	skill training course
Sports Promotion Organization	sports training course
Thai Woman Society	skill training course in cooperation with the Adult Education Division
War-Veteran Organization	course for guards and janitors

Category III

Mass Communication Programs

Responsible Organizations	Activities
Office of the Prime Minister	
Central Security Organization	public library service in cooperation with the Adult Education Division
Public Service Division under the office of the National Youth Development	library service in cooperation with the Adult Education Division
Community Development	community development library exhibition
Ministry of Education	
General Education Department	library, village newspaper, reading center, public library, youth center, educational radio broadcasting, museum, and panel discussion in cooperation with the Adult Education Division
Fine Arts Department	museums and exhibitions
National Library	library service
The College of Education	library service to college students
Thai Youth Club	Youth Center
University of Fine Arts	library and museum service in university
Thammasart University	library service in each department, discussion groups, sociological and anthropological information service, exhibitions
Ministry of Interior	
Department of Public Welfare	youth center service, library service
Department of Corrections	library and youth center services for prisoners
Ministry of Agriculture	
Department of the Agricultural Extension	discussion groups and seminars
Ministry of Industry	library service
Ministry of Public Health	
Department of Health	library service in health centers
Public Enterprises	
State Railway Organization	library service in schools
Metropolitan Electric Authority	discussion groups, seminars
Local Administration	
Metropolitan Municipality, Division of Education and Social Welfare	library service, discussion and seminars in cooperation with the Adult Education Division

Responsible Organizations	Activities
Public Health Service Unit Association and Philanthropic Foundation	discussion and interest groups
Thailand Social Welfare	youth center, discussion, radio and TV programs, publications
Anti-Tuberculosis Association	library service
Thailand Kindergarten Education Association	publications radio and TV programs

In this preliminary survey, the data were gathered through questionnaires which were sent out to 127 governmental agencies. Nonformal activities conducted by private organizations were to be included in a second survey.

UPPER VOLTA:
A RURAL ALTERNATIVE
TO PRIMARY SCHOOLS
Prepared by the Editors
on the Basis of Reports
by IEDES and Sven Grabe

In 1971, following a short visit and an examination of the available documentation and earlier studies, Sven Grabe of the ICED staff carried out a brief review of the Rural Education Centers (Centres d'Education Rurale) in Upper Volta. It soon became apparent that with a more specific investigation the Voltaique experience could probably shed light on a number of significant rural education issues: 1) How can a poor country endowed with meager resources and with only a thin spread of schools provide basic learning for all its children and youth? 2) What are the advantages and disadvantages, both pedagogically and financially, of delaying schooling from the age of childhood to an older age? 3) What impact can a "ruralized" school have on the development of the local area in which it is situated?

To glean what evidence was available on these questions ICED commissioned L'Institut d'Étude du Développement Économique et Social (IEDES) of the University of Paris to carry out an investigation. The study was conducted by Mlle. I. Deblé, assisted by Y. Lefèbvre, M. Lefèbvre, and L. T. N. Trân of IEDES in November-December 1972. Limitation of both time and funds required the scope of the field investigation to be confined to 11 villages in two districts, Yatenga and Koudougou, in which the operations of typical RECs were observed, performance testing was carried out, and interviews conducted. This chapter is based on the findings of the IEDES study, (l'Éducation Rurale et la Diffusion des Nouvelles Techniques Agricoles en Haute-Volte, Paris, 1973), and the earlier ICED review. Since the completion of the study, there have been new developments in respect of the REC program and the overall educational system, which are not reflected in this study, although efforts have been made to note some of the changes.

INTRODUCTION

Upper Volta is one of the poorest among the poor countries of the world. Whatever measure is applied in

determining levels of development, the country's name invariably appears near the bottom of the list.[1] The total
population of the country was estimated at around 5 million
in 1970. This population is divided among a great number
of ethnic and linguistic groups, of which the Mossi and
assimilated groups are dominant with some 3.5 million
people.[2] The total land area is approximately 400,000
square kilometers (about the size of Italy). Population
density varies in different parts of the country. The
average is 13 inhabitants per square kilometer, but it is
only 2 per square kilometer in some parts and reaches
over 50 in the more densely populated regions of Mossi
country in the center and north.

Outside of a few limited areas, agricultural practices
applied by the farmers of Upper Volta are primitive. Draft
animals are rare; most agricultural work is done with simple
hand implements, and the average yields are among the lowest in Africa. A major part of the harvest is consumed by
the individual farm families, and only a small proportion
of the products are sold. The cash income of a typical
farm family, even in good years, amounts to a few thousand
CFA (Communauté Financière Africaine) francs (CFAF 250=
US$1 in 1970)--little more than the absolute minimum for
paying the poll taxes and buying salt and cloth. Local
famines are not uncommon.

The climate is hot, and the conditions for agriculture
are delicate. Temperatures--which vary little over the
year--reach a daytime maximum of some 40° to 45° centigrade during the hottest season in the warmest areas.
Temperatures below 10° centigrade are rare even on the
coolest nights. The rainy season is short in most parts
of the country. The north, on the Sahelian fringe of the
Sahara, has a total rainfall in July, August, and September of no more than 400 millimeters. This is the area in
which a majority of the Voltaiques, and particularly the
Mossi, live. The south has more rain and a longer rainy
season: up to 1,000 millimeters between June and September
in the areas bordering the Ivory Coast and Ghana. But
the risk of disease makes people shun these regions.

Almost 95 percent of the population are engaged in
agriculture, most of them in smallholder subsistence
farming on lands of communal ownership. Employment opportunities outside the agricultural sector are few. Most
paid jobs are in government services and the rate of growth
in these is low. The education system is the largest
single source of paid employment in the country. There
is little industry and, as yet, very limited mining or
other extracting, trading, or manufacturing activity in
what may be considered as a modern sector.

Many young Voltaiques take short-term employment
in neighboring countries to earn cash before they settle
down in their home villages. According to one study made
in 1960-61, more than 26 percent of the active male

population of Upper Volta were working in other countries,
notably in Ghana and the Ivory Coast, at the time of the
enquiry.[3] Seventy percent of the emigrants were between
20 and 30 years old and went abroad for periods of more
than six months.

Rural development efforts of the government include
promotion of commercial production of cash crops, such as
groundnut and sesame, and of overall agricultural output
by changing primitive farming practices, using fertilizers
and pesticides, opening facilities for distributing the
farm supplies, and buying the surplus products from farmers.
The main mechanism for implementing these actions is the
Regional Development Organization (RDO), an arm of the
Ministry of Agriculture set up for each of the 11 districts
(circonscriptions). Both of the districts that IEDES
visited have such an organization and are receiving external assistance: the RDO in Yatenga is being aided by the
European Development Fund (FED) and the Koudougou RDO is
assisted by the World Bank. The district RDOs are directed
by a district organizer and carry out extension, sale of
supplies, and produce-marketing with the help of a number
of sector administrators and supervisors within the district. In principle, RDOs are expected to assist in
developing Rural Education Centers (RECs) and in dove-
tailing REC work with local development, for instance,
by advising teachers of new farming techniques, helping
in REC farm management, organizing cooperatives with REC
trainees, and marketing REC farm produce. In actual practice, close cooperation with the REC, an organ of the
Ministry of Education, is not common.

The formal school system, modeled on the French pattern, is embryonic and spread thinly, even though enrollments have doubled over the past ten years. Primary
schooling is available to only 1 in 10 of the age-group
concerned and only a third of the intake consists of
girls. There is a heavy urban bias: in towns about 65
percent of the children between 6 and 12 years attend
primary school; in rural areas less than 8 percent of the
age-group are enrolled. In addition, national dropout
rates and repeater rates are high and only a half of those
who begin school are likely to complete the six-year
primary cycle. Yet in 1972 the government was spending
over 20 percent of its national budget on education alone.
The official national language--and hence the language of
instruction in the schools--is French, although only 6
percent of the male population over 15 years understand
it and far fewer can use it effectively. For those who
actually get to school, half the time at the primary
level is spent learning French and becoming literate in it.

The educational dilemma facing newly independent
Upper Volta in 1960 was seen to be acute. By the time of
the UNESCO Addis Ababa Conference (1961), which established the regional goal of universal primary education,

it was already clear to Voltaique authorities that such
a goal was not a feasible option in the foreseeable future.
In 1961 the government attempted to face up to the realities of the situation and decided to experiment with an
alternative approach, embodied in a law that gave birth
to the Rural Education Centers.

RURAL EDUCATION CENTERS IN OPERATION

Origin and Purpose

The initiative for launching an experimental scheme
of rural education as a basic form of primary education
combined with vocational training seems to have grown out
of discussions in the late 1950s among educational planners in the Ministry of Education at Ouagadougou, when
Upper Volta was still a French colony.[4] The first plan
was formulated by Medard and Christol, two Frenchmen
working in the Ministry, and is generally referred to as
"Plan Christol." The plan was approved by the Legislative
Assembly in late 1959.[5]
The Plan Christol suggested that, given the low
level of economic development of the country, it would be
impossible to allocate the funds necessary to provide
universal primary schooling for all children and adolescents in Upper Volta for many years. Although more than
600,000 children were of primary school age, the capacity
of the school system was only 50,000 pupils at that time.
Dropout rates were high, and only a handful of those who
entered the first year of primary school could expect to
reach secondary and higher levels of education. As noted
earlier, educational opportunity heavily favored the urban
population, particularly that of the larger agglomerations
in Ouagadougou and Bobo-Dioulasso.
The Plan Christol advocated a sharp deviation from
previous policies of educational development. Universal
primary schooling should no longer be the first objective
to be pursued. Instead, the primary schools should be
given the principal role of providing basic training and
education for the few who would be most likely to enter
secondary schools and ultimately to form the nation's
elite. For the masses of the rural population, an education focusing on rural life should be provided, with three
years of agricultural vocational training combined with
instruction in basic literacy in French and numeracy
sufficient for effective work in agriculture and for a
literate adult life. This broad, vocationally-oriented
education should be geared primarily to the learning
needs and capacity of the average youth. The plan proposed
that for some time the intake of children in rural areas

should normally be once every three years at age 14 or 15
(no longer at age six) and the school leaving age should
be 16 or 17.

A great number of advantages were envisaged in this
radical change in the policy of educational development.
Since the higher age-group for the rural education program is smaller than that of the normal primary school
age-group (the population increases by about 2 percent
each year and child mortality is high), it would obviously
cost less to provide teaching and other facilities for
older children than for all children. Furthermore, older
children could be expected to be better motivated, better
disciplined, and better able to learn than children at
age six. More material could be taught in a shorter
period of time than would be needed in a conventional
primary school.[6] While learning to work, the students
in rural education would also be producing. More important
still, by using modern methods in the fields, those in the
rural education center would set an example for others.
Thus rural education would have an immediate impact on
the production of the whole village.

The principal aims and assumptions of the project
may be summarized as follows:

1. to provide opportunities for all rural youth
   to receive at least a minimum of literacy
   and numeracy by attending a full-time school
   during adolescence
2. to inject an element of modernization into
   the villages by training all young people
   in the basic principles and methods of
   modern agriculture
3. to lower the total cost of education for the
   masses by combining education with practical
   farm work and by shortening the total period
   of education during the first decades of
   expansion of the educational system
4. to reduce wastage in education by concentrating the teaching on a more receptive and
   better motivated age-group than that normally
   taken into the primary schools

The Plan Christol envisaged that the expansion of
primary education, which had been slow but steady during
the 1950s, would be slowed down. Most of the funds anticipated for further development of the total education
school system could, therefore, be used to expand the
rural education system. It was estimated that by 1970
approximately 76 percent of all boys and 24 percent of
the girls would have an opportunity to go through a
course of rural education. After 1970 the rural education
system would be gradually expanded to take in both boys
and girls outside the formal school system until,

ultimately (before 1985, it was hoped), the whole youth
population could be given some kind of elementary education. Only then would further expansion of primary
education be permitted, mainly by an extension of the
rural education system to lower age-groups.

Implementation of the Plan

Implementation of the scheme began in 1961 when the
first group of teacher candidates was recruited and trained
in a short course of five months. The first centers were
constructed in 180 villages, and 8,100 students were
selected to participate. Most of these centers were built
with local materials, using the same techniques as those
employed in building rural homes in the country.

Expansion of the program has been rapid since the
first years of experimentation and search for a methodology.
Following are the most important early accomplishments:

  . A directorate of rural education was established
    in Ouagadougou in 1960 consisting of an adminis-
    trative group, including the director, his
    assistant, and a technical bureau for planning
    and programming of rural education.

  . A teacher training institute was set up, also
    in 1960, at Kamboincé--12 kilometers outside
    Ouagadougou--with a capacity of training 120
    teacher-trainees per year in ten-month courses.

  . A second teacher training institute for boys
    at Farako-Ba in the southwestern part of the
    country, also with a capacity of 120 students,
    was ready to receive its first trainees in 1968.

  . Teacher training courses in rural education
    were arranged for girls in Ouagadougou.

  . A system of inspection by "rural education
    counsellors" was set up with nine counsellors
    serving in an equal number of districts.

  . By the end of the 1970/71 school year, 759 centers
    were in operation; of these, 680 centers were for
    boys and 79 centers, for girls. They had a total
    of 21,598 students recorded in attendance at the
    end of the school year.[7] Students in rural
    education represented about one-fifth of the
    total school population in Upper Volta (as
    102,000 pupils were attending primary and
    secondary schools).

Between 1966 and 1968 RECs expanded at a rate of more than 10 percent a year. Since 1968, however, the rate of REC expansion has dropped and formal schools are still the dominant type of rural learning institution. Although their numbers were to have been frozen, primary schools actually expanded by 4 percent a year from 1966 to 1968. Between 1965/66 and 1969/70, REC enrollments rose from 21,000 to 26,000, and then dropped by about 20 percent in 1970/71. At the same time, enrollments in primary schools rose from 93,000 to 102,000. However, compared with the primary school, the RECs had lower dropout rates and fewer students per teacher. Moreover, there were no problems of repeating levels, since individual repeating was barred in the REC. (The REC system does allow for entire classes to repeat, but this policy has rarely been resorted to.) Although completion rates have been relatively high, in recent years they have tended to worsen: in the period 1966-70, for every 1,000 starters, 878 completed the course; during the overall period 1966-72, for every 1,000 starters, 760 completed full courses.

Quantitative expansion of the REC system, however, has fallen far short of the original goals. By 1972/73, there was actually a drop in the number of RECs to 737, although enrollment increased to 24,000 youths (84 of these centers enrolled 2,500 girls), which is no more than one-sixth of what had been projected. Meanwhile, regular primary schools have continued to expand steadily and, in fact, to get the lion's share of the education budget.

Assistance was sought for the program from the European Economic Community-sponsored European Development Fund (FED), which agreed, in 1961, to finance 225 centers to be established for 11,250 boys. (The first centers built with funds from the FED, however, were not completed until 1966.) The FED also agreed to equip the central administrative services and five regional inspectorates. Further contributions to the implementation of the scheme were later received from FED for establishing teacher training institutions. Smaller contributions were received from UNICEF--mainly tools and equipment; from the Food and Agriculture Organization (FAO)--seeds, fertilizers, and gardening tools; from French bilateral aid--books and documents mainly for language teaching, and resources for printing basic agricultural education manuals used in the schools; and from bilateral and private American sources--various teaching aids and some food to help feed students during the months before the harvest.

Personnel

Rural education constitutes a separate and independent part of the educational system in Upper Volta. The director of rural education has the same status in the ministry as the directors of primary and secondary education and competes with them for priority in the preparation of long-term plans and annual budgets. As for the planning and development of rural education, the Minister of Education is advised by an interministerial committee composed of representatives of the Ministries of Planning and Health and of persons delegated from the various technical services that have an interest in rural and agricultural education and development.

Teaching staff is trained in three centers located in Kambcincé and Farako-Ba (for boys) and Ouagadougou (for girls). The first two centers have permanent facilities; the center for girl teacher-trainees as of 1972 was housed in temporary quarters.

Candidates for teacher training should be at least 18 years old and have an education corresponding to at least ten years of primary and secondary school. The educational level of the candidates has risen over the years. There are no special requirements relating to practical experience, but the Ouagadougou center gives some preference to girls who have acquired the certificate of home economics training in one of the technical middle schools.

Teacher training takes 10 months and covers a wide range of subjects. The latest syllabus for teacher training, prepared by an interministerial committee of experts in April 1967, includes the following content:

General education
    French
    Arithmetic
    History and civics
    Physical education
Agriculture
    General agriculture
    Applied agriculture
    Breeding
    Rural infrastructure
    Water and forests
Agricultural fieldwork
Workshop (use of hand tools and simple construction)

The girls follow the same program as the boys in all subjects other than practical work. The agricultural activities for girls are limited mainly to garden crops and household animals, the preparation of seeds and soil for garden and household crops, and the storage of food.

The program for the girls also includes theoretical and practical initiation into the care of children, basic elements of nutrition and preparation of food, economics of the home, and simple sewing.

Both boys and girls take a two-hour per week course in pedagogy and teaching methods; they undergo practice teaching for one week each month under the supervision of their teachers in the school of applied teaching attached to the training center.

The teacher training center at Kamboincé occupies a total area of 29 hectares. It has buildings for administration and classrooms, housing for the director and faculty members, an ample supply of water, sheds for draft animals and poultry, manure pits, ensilage arrangements, and large fields for demonstration and training.[8] The demonstration fields are divided into plots of .12 hectares, which are distributed to the staff of the center and to the classes of trainees. Each class of trainees has separate fields for cotton, groundnuts, millet, rice, and vegetables. Each trainee is given a small plot on which he can grow what he wants. Trainees take turns in attending to the chicken shed. The production activities of the center are run as a cooperative, and the trainees participate directly in all business and accounting operations.

In workshops the trainees learn basic operations in work on wood and metals and learn simple construction work. By the time a young teacher has completed his training he is supposed to be able to make a school bench, repair a chair, construct a barn, and weave a basket for the harvest. He learns to handle hammers, saws, files, and other basic tools for maintenance and repair of simple equipment.

After the first three months in the teacher training center all trainees spend one month in a rural training center to get a clear idea of the work that lies ahead. During the first week they observe the teacher of the center; they then spend a week taking turns at assuming the role of the teacher. All trainees prepare a description of the village in which they are practising and submit this to the teachers of the institute on their return.

Proceeds from marketed products are used for purchasing seeds and fertilizers for the next class in the center and for pocket money given to the departing students. An amount of cash is set aside each year as working capital for the cooperative. Sufficient foodstuffs and fodder are to be in the barns when a class is terminated, so that the animals may be fed during the period remaining until the next harvest. Natural manure is prepared for fertilizing the fields.

Preservice training is supposed to equip the teacher for his multiple duties in the village, because supervision with only one counsellor for each 100 centers is

inadequate, to say the least. The lone teacher in the
village REC is expected to supervise and carry out instruction, manage a profitable school farm, account for
the produce, organize school cooperatives, act as local
animateur, form a liaison with the village leaders--both
to gain their assistance in running and maintaining the
school and its equipment and to reciprocate by providing
services to the village. In return for this variety of
heavy duties he would be paid only half the salary of his
counterpart in the primary school, have a more limited
security of job tenure, and almost certainly have inferior
housing. These conditions have made it difficult to
recruit and hold good quality staff, and the poor morale
in the REC structure and teaching services has led at its
worst to fraud and absenteeism, and at its best to an
unending uphill struggle for the rural teacher whose
enthusiasm is difficult to sustain.

Facilities

The nature and quality of the buildings and fields
vary greatly in the several centers. Some centers built
with assistance from the FED were designed by an archi-
tectural firm and constructed on a metal frame, with
brick walls, cemented floor, corrugated aluminum roofing,
and an insulating inner ceiling. The classrooms measure
55 square meters and a small room for storing teaching
materials is attached. The teacher's house is 40 square
meters and contains a living room and two bedrooms; an
attached kitchen and "bath" area is covered by the roof
of the building. There is also a small veranda in front,
covered by the roof. The FED centers are equipped with
movable furniture.
     The other centers, built mostly by villagers, are
much more primitive. Most of them have walls constructed
of mixed clay and straw or locally manufactured unburnt
bricks, thatched roofs, and school benches shaped from
wet clay.
     The size and quality of the fields provided by the
villagers for the centers also vary greatly. Most of the
first centers had small fields. A sample taken in 1965/66
of 101 centers showed an average of 1.05 hectares per
center. The averages have since increased considerably
to 1.38 (179 centers) in 1967/68 and to 1.64 (347 centers
in 1969/70.[9] The hectarage allocated to each center is
generally considered too small; newer rules provide for
a minimum of three hectares to be allocated to newly
established centers. Many experts, however, consider even
this too small for adequate occupation and training of
the 45 trainees that each center should have according to
the rules.

Observers who have visited a large number of centers and the counsellors of rural education are unanimous in their comments on the quality of the soil: too many villages have given the worst possible fields to the rural education center, a dubious benefit that probably explains the mediocre harvests recorded at many of them.

Normally the centers are built on the fields allocated to them, well outside the village. In villages where there are centers for both boys and girls, the centers are generally located on the same site, close to each other. But they are distinct establishments and coeducation does not take place in any of them.

The centers are for the most part inadequately equipped. Among the ten centers visited by the IEDES team, only three possessed adequate agricultural implements to allow the center's normal functioning according to the recommendations of the RDO. The others had only some of the basic implements, and some did not have even the improved "manga" hoe, not to speak of a plough or animals to draw the plough. Some had a donkey cart without a donkey. Only one of the ten centers possessed all three indispensable elements for recommended "harnessed cultivation" (as opposed to the traditional digging of the field with a hoe)--the "manga" hoe, a trained donkey, and a ploughshare weeder.

Daily Center Activities

Daily work in a center normally starts at seven o'clock in the fields, so that most of the day's practical work and instruction may be done during the cooler part of the day. After two hours of field work the class moves into the classroom for related agricultural instruction and general education until 11:30 a.m. The class meets again from 3 to 5:30 p.m.; after classroom work the students go out to the fields again to finish the day with an hour or two of practical work.

The curriculum of agricultural work follows the seasons--beginning with the turning of the soil when the rains come in June or July and finishing with the harvest in October or November. If the center has a sufficient water supply for irrigation, the teacher can prolong agricultural instruction in the school garden, but not all centers offer such possibilities. Practical work during the dry season is devoted mostly to crafts, using elementary tools and local materials or whatever the teacher and the students can find in and around a poor village in a country where wood is scarce.

Classroom lessons during a major part of the first two years are devoted to the teaching of basic French. The target in the first year is to teach the students at

least 600 words, with an equal number of words added in
the second year for the basic needs of conversation. The
methods and the textbooks are, in most cases, the same
as those used in the primary schools. Two factors make
this first period of teaching extremely difficult: the
absence of French in the environment--as indicated, few
villagers know any French--and the fact that the students
and teachers sometimes speak different indigenous languages.

The young people often learn the texts without really
understanding their meaning. It usually takes a long time
before French becomes an effective medium of instruction in
the schools. Because of this factor, the teaching of agricultural science, civics, and related instruction is often
put off until the third year, a postponement that greatly
diminishes the effectiveness of the educational program.

In principle no male student should be less than 15
years old and the median age should be 17.[10] In fact,
the median age is lower, with some students as young as
11 years. Reports from 382 centers in 1970/71 indicated
that 14 percent were between 11 and 13, 81 percent were
between 14 and 18, and 5 percent were 19 years or older.
The median age (19 percent of the students enrolled) was
16.[11]

The age level of students has proved to be an important determinant of the efficiency of rural education.
In general it has been found that the younger students
are less well motivated and have greater difficulties in
outdoor activities than the older ones.[12] On the other
hand absenteeism is higher among the older students,
particularly during the planting, weeding, and harvesting
seasons.[13]

REC Performance

The IEDES study team attempted to assess the performance of RECs by conducting field investigation in
two of the 11 districts--Yatenga (principal town,
Ouahigouya), 180 kilometers north from the capital city
of Ouagadougou, and Koudougou, 80 kilometers west from
Ouagadougou on the main thoroughfare to Abidjan. The
team visited 11 villages with RECs, seven in Yatenga and
four in Koudougou; and six villages, four in Yatenga and
two in Koudougou, that had no RECs but where some of the
children went to primary schools. (The team actually saw
nine centers in operation, because the teacher and students in one Yatenga center had gone away to collect
wood and in one center in Koudougou the teacher had been
absent for six months.) The team gave written performance
tests or interviewed 256 final year REC students, 114
former REC students, and 81 former students of primary
schools in the two districts. The team also interviewed

village chiefs, heads of family holdings, village notables, parents of REC students, REC teachers, REC counsellors, and rural development organizers about various aspects of REC operations.

The written test was on French, computation, and agricultural knowledge. The French test called for giving written answers to simple questions about personal information (name, age, address, and so on), filling out a form of the type required by government departments, answering reading comprehension questions after silent reading of a simple text on cooperatives, and writing a letter to the agricultural monitor requesting insecticide and instruction on how to use it. The computation test consisted of everyday problems that required the use of the four basic operations at an elementary level. The agricultural knowledge test included twenty questions on the major crops of the area and the innovations advocated in REC lessons in raising these crops.

TABLE 9.1

Average Score of Third Year Students in 10 RECs
in the IEDES Written Performance Test

Center Code (Y=Yatenga K=Koudougou)	Average Total Center Score		No. of students taking tests
	French, Computation, Max. possible 116	Agricultural Tests Range of Scores	
Y1	64.6	5-103	25
Y2	67.1	20-86	18
Y3	55.4	15-89	21
Y4	61.8	10-86	28
Y5	60.1	27-78	36
Y6	48.4	14-76	26
K1	43.2	15-69	40
K2	7.2*	-----	16
K3	44.1	8-65	15
K4	48.1	29-67	26
Total/Average for Yatenga	59.3	5-103	154
Total/Average for Koudougou	45.0	8-69	81
Total/Average for both districts	54.4	5-103	235

*Score is for only French and Computation test out of a maximum possible of 76 points.

Source: IEDES.

The test results indicate that about half of the
third year students in the selected RECs acquired the
basic mechanisms of reading, writing, and computation at
an elementary level, and presumably this limited knowledge could be applied outside the school context in
solving practical problems of life. However, practical
application depended largely on whether students would
have the opportunity to build on the foundations laid in
REC and to improve further their level of facility in the
basic skills. According to the test results, the majority
of the rest did not learn to read and write or to do basic
calculation. Some who acquired rudiments of basic skills
probably did not learn enough to make use of these skills
functionally outside the school context. On the whole,
students in the Yatenga district performed better than
those in Koudougou. The significance of the regional
variables is discussed later.

The results of the agriculture test were not any
more promising than the French and computation test scores,
even though supplementary explanation in Moré, the local
language, was added to the original questionnaire in
French. The average score in agriculture for the whole
group was 17 out of a maximum possible score of 40. In
the agriculture test the Yatenga centers also scored
better than the centers in Koudougou. Incidentally, the
teachers of nine RECs in the sample were invited to
answer the agriculture questionnaire, and some of these
responses (for some questions, eight responses out of
nine) were found to be incorrect.

The literacy test was given to 42 former REC students
and the computation test was given to 21 former students.
The scores collected from such a small sampling do not
permit valid conclusions; however, the test data supplemented by impressions gathered from interviews suggest
that of the small proportion of REC students who acquire
the basic reading, writing, and computation skills, a
still smaller proportion retain these skills and make
use of them in practical life. Comparison of the two
districts in this respect is definitely favorable to
Yatenga, where organized follow-up activities in the form
of postschool groups have been an important factor in the
retention, use, and further improvement of the basic
skills of those who originally acquired them in REC.

By way of comparison, 34 former students of primary
schools aged 17 years or more were given the literacy and
computation tests. The test results, though based on a
very limited sampling, established the former primary
students as a group ahead of the REC students in both
literacy and computation skills. The former primary students were clearly at ease with all the items--reading,
filling out a form, writing a letter, making use of the
four arithmetic operations--and, unlike the REC students,
did not have any trouble in understanding the test

questions or following instructions. It should be mentioned that most of the former primary students in the
sample had completed the six-year primary cycle; **furthermore** they were a self-selected group taking the test
voluntarily. A more representative sample, including an
appropriate proportion of dropouts and rejects of the
primary school, might well have produced a less favorable
result.

The results obtained in agricultural production have
been studied on three occasions by the counsellors of the
rural education system. In all three cases only partial
data were received from the districts, and the figures
obtained cannot therefore be considered as fully representative.

In 1966/67, 101 centers reported an average income
from agricultural production of CFAF 43,254 (US$180).
In the following year, reports were obtained from a total
of 184 centers that showed an average income of CFAF
25,216 (about US$100), from the main crops--groundnuts,
cotton, sorghum, and rice.[14] In 1969/70, 337 centers
reported a slightly increased income of CFAF 26,492
(US$105), but the hectarage had also increased (by 19
percent).[15]

The span between the low and high productivity in the
centers was very wide. The 25 centers producing least had
an average income in 1969/70 of only CFAF 3,529 (US$14)
while the 25 highest-producing centers earned an average
of CFAF 84,000 (US$340).

In line with general agricultural policies in Upper
Volta, the largest single crop in 1969/70 was cotton with
a total production by 329 centers of 166 metric tons on
278 hectares. Groundnuts were grown by 293 centers on 110
hectares for a total crop of 67 tons; sorghum, by 268
centers on 121 hectares yielding 68 tons; and rice, by
137 centers on 48 hectares with a yield of 56 tons. Thus,
a majority of the 337 centers included in the enquiry had
at least three crops, many of them four, on an average of
1.64 hectares. This would suggest that most trainees in
the centers have an opportunity to participate in all
stages of cultivating most major food and cash crops
grown in Upper Volta.

While the scope of cultivation, that is, the number
of different crops grown at each center, might be considered satisfactory, the methods used in many centers
were not. Only one out of every three centers in 1969/70
put fertilizer into their groundnut fields, a recommended
practice. The cotton fields received fertilizer in 182
centers (out of 319), and 187 centers made one or more
sprayings during the growing season. Three to four sprayings are recommended by the extension service. The main
reason for not following the advice appears to be the
uncertainty of rainfall (which may turn the investment
into an expensive loss), lack of the necessary implements,
and shortage of operating funds.

The net result is that many centers do not give their
pupils adequate training in the application of modern
agricultural methods, and less than 50 percent of the
centers reporting yields are able to show higher production figures per hectare for various crops than the
average farmer can obtain in his own fields.

IEDES's observation lends support to the conclusion
that agricultural production of the centers is largely
dependent on weather conditions and how hard the teacher
is willing to drive the students in physical labor in
the field, sometimes for the teacher's personal profit.
The IEDES team also notes that the production figures
reported by teachers are not likely to be very accurate,
because many of them cannot measure accurately the land
under cultivation for different crops and the yields for
each crop per unit of land.

As for the attitudes of the graduates of the RECs
compared with those of early dropouts and failures of the
formal schools, the IEDES study concluded that REC graduates were better emotionally equipped to face challenges
in their home environment, while the formal school dropouts felt isolated and guilty of failure and thought
only of fleeing the village. The rural education student,
on leaving the center, had no such discouragement, particularly if there was a postschool group in existence.
But this probably is more a function of different expectations of parents and students in respect to primary schools
and RECs than the performance of these institutions. The
primary school is seen as the means of escape from the
village; when this does not materialize, students feel
a sense of frustration. While some rural people want to
view the REC as a substitute for primary schools, the REC
definitely aims at preparing its students for a livelihood in the rural milieu.

Rural Postschool Groups

One major recent modification of the system deserves
special mention and is explored in the ICED/IEDES study,
because it offers important clues to providing essential
follow-up to any scheme of basic education and training.
This innovation was first introduced by a particularly
imaginative rural education counsellor in the district of
Yatenga. He recognized a need for reenforcing supplementary and continuation activity to preserve and build
on what had been achieved in the REC, and he saw a potential answer in the existing traditional indigenous youth
associations and forms of mutual assistance of the Mossi
people.

The main indigenous elements that have been harnessed
to the RECs include nam, a traditional localized association of young people with cultural, social, and economic

functions; sosoga, a form of mutual assistance between
neighboring families during periods of important work;
and songsongtaba, a long-term association of family groups
who agree to cultivate their lands in common.

Out of these institutions REC graduates have developed
a small but growing system of post-REC groups. In a number of instances groups have formed cooperative farms on
which to put into practice the farming lessons acquired
at the REC. Profits from farming have led to the use of
banking facilities, including borrowing to assist other
group economic activities. Continuation learning programs have been introduced in conjunction with RECs to
improve literacy skills, to add to agricultural knowledge,
and to supplement such other necessary learning requirements as simple accounting and bookkeeping. A number of
groups have begun taking correspondence lessons on agricultural modernization. (The "Agri-Service-Afrique"
correspondence courses offered in several African countries by the Institut africain pour le développement
économique et social [INADES] are a case in point.)
Some postschool groups which were initially oriented
solely toward farming are beginning to diversify their
activities. New activities include, for instance,
commerce, handicraft, transportation, and agricultural
implement repair work.

An incidental though crucial benefit of the postschool group has been its effect on the RECs themselves.
A successful group effectively demonstrates by example
the usefulness of rural education; it can put pressure on
the village chief to see to the REC's good functioning;
it can help motivate the teacher who is the main pivot of
the system; and it can exercise surveillance over former
students through the development of an esprit de corps.

The IEDES team concluded that, although retention of
learning among former students of rural education three
to six years after their leaving the center is on the
whole poor, there was sufficient evidence that, where
postschool groups existed, the situation was showing marked
improvement. The mere fact of belonging to a postschool
group appeared to be of fundamental importance for a former student. IEDES found that the only students of rural
education to have maintained or even enriched their
knowledge were those who were members of these groups,
managed by former students in conjunction with the teacher
and village notables. Moreover, they were the only ones
who took the initiative to organize themselves and participate collectively in the supplementary courses. These
young adults displayed an extraordinary sense of dynamism
and a spirit of invention.

In 1968 a government decree recognized the formation
of postschool groups as an integral part of the new rural
education system and by 1972 approximately 60 groups were
active, though mostly in the Yatenga district.

Regional Variables

The difference in performance between the centers in Yatenga and Koudougou with respect to learning achievements and overall impact of the program, as illustrated by the formation of postschool groups, calls for explanation. The IEDES team noted several points in this regard.

There is no significant difference between the two districts insofar as soil fertility and the availability of water are concerned. Nor is there any important cultural difference between them: the inhabitants in both districts are members of the Mossi tribe, sharing a common history and tradition. The significant variable is probably to be found in the administrative organization and personnel of the two districts.

Yatenga district has an area of 12,300 square kilometers and 70 RECs, whereas Koudougou is a much larger district with an area of 26,300 square kilometers and 121 centers. However, because both districts have one rural education counsellor each and the same number of RDO staff it is manifestly impossible to offer the same level of supervision and guidance to the centers in Koudougou as in Yatenga. Moreover, the counsellor in Yatenga is an exceptionally dynamic and devoted man, who saw the need for follow-up activities, took the initiative to form postschool groups, and established ties with the local RDO. The RDO also seems to have responded in kind. The effect of all this, as the IEDES team noted, was a more favorable attitude among villagers to RECs, greater willingness of parents to send relatively older children to RECs at some cost to the economy of family farms, relatively less absenteeism, and, ultimately, better learning results.

Costs and Resources

The rural education system was deliberately designed as a low-cost operation. At practically every point in the buildup of the system, efforts were made to cut the costs to the lowest possible figure and to make classes as large as possible. As a consequence the per capita annual current cost of rural education is no more than 40 or 45 percent of that of general primary education.[16] The investment costs for the government in the average self-help school building, excluding the contributions in kind from the local population, amounted to less than US$1,000 for each center and for the most part were in the form of tools and equipment for work in the fields and for wood- and metal-work activities.

The cost of a center built with assistance from the European Development Fund according to standard design and better equipped is much higher. The average cost of these centers, including furniture but not equipment, amounted to US$10,000 in round figures.

The major current cost of the centers is the salary of the teacher.[17] Little money, if any, is spent on repair and maintenance of equipment. Only a few centers have draft animals, and those that have them normally do not have any direct cost for feeding them. They graze with other animals of the village. Investments in seeds, fertilizers, insecticides, and other agriculture materials are low on the average--far too low, in most cases--for efficient utilization of the fields. Only a handful of schools are adequately equipped with books, teaching aids, and tools and materials for the craft work to be done by the pupils. The low figures for per capita current costs, therefore, are not indicative of what the operation of a rural education system should really cost.

The overhead costs for running the system can be summarized in a few figures relating to the activities of the teacher training institutes and the directorate. The directorate itself had a staff consisting of only four professional employees in 1971. To this should be added the eight regional counsellors in post in the same year. (One post has been vacant for several years.)

The operating cost of training a total of 115 students in the three teacher training institutes was estimated at CFAF 16,000,000 (US$64,000) in 1971/72, excluding the cost of expatriate staff and without taking income from agriculture into account.[18] However, the output of the teacher training schools being considerably lower than the total enrollment, the real per capita current cost for graduates is higher than what these figures suggest. In 1970/71, total intake in the three institutes was 90; 10 dropped out of the course and only 49 graduated.[19] Assuming a similar wastage in the following year, per capita cost for each graduate would be in the neighborhood of CFAF 300,000 (US$1,250).

Little is known about the opportunity cost of students in the rural education centers. No study has been made of the sacrifices made by parents in letting their adolescent children go to school for 35 hours a week for some 40 weeks a year for three years. There is every reason to believe that families find this opportunity cost rather high. It is well known from other parts of Africa, and elsewhere in the developing world, that seasonal labor shortages at the peak of farming activities constitute important limiting factors in the expansion and development of agriculture or in the introduction of improved practices such as systematic advance preparation of the soil, correct planting and weeding, and adequate storage of the produce. One or more sons usually make an important contribution

to the standard of living of the family, for a boy of 16
or 17 years is expected to contribute a man's work effort
on the family farm.

ISSUES IN RURAL EDUCATION

The experience of the REC program brings to the surface several important issues which probably would arise
in one form or another in carrying out a rural education
program in any poor country with limited opportunities
for formal education. The issues that have significantly
affected the performance and effectiveness of the Upper
Volta program relate to the clarity and acceptance by the
government and the rural people of the main objectives,
the overall rural development effort and the place of the
educational program in this effort, the general political
climate and the degree of government commitment to the
program, and the sensitivity and ingenuity applied in
solving various operational problems that inevitably arise.

Question of Objectives

The program began as an experiment in providing
elementary education and teaching practical agricultural
skills to the 90 percent of youths who had no chance of
going to the primary school. The original intention was
that the expansion of the traditional primary school would
be halted and ultimately the two kinds of institutions
would merge into a unified national system of basic education for all children--the primary schools taking on
some characteristics of the REC and both institutions
enjoying "parity of esteem."
What really happened was, of course, very different
from intention. The number of new RECs remained well
below the number planned and became almost frozen after
1968, while primary schools continued to be expanded in
the cities and towns at a steady pace, although it was an
accepted fact that the blessings of the primary school
could be extended to only a small fraction of the children. Indeed, it remained a highly selective institution,
ruthlessly pruning the number of participants, granting
a small proportion the privilege of completing the six-
year course, and opening up for them the prospects of
further educational opportunities and the rewards of
white-collar occupations. A student in the REC, on the
other hand, irrespective of his talents and ambitions,
had little chance of transferring to the formal system
and claiming a stake in the perquisites associated with
it. Moreover, the proclaimed objectives of the REC, in

most cases, were not fully achieved. Parents of rural youths and the youths themselves, of course, clearly saw what was happening and regarded the REC, at best, as a temporary expedient that should be replaced by the real thing, the primary school, and at worst, a symbol of discrimination against the rural people. In fact, as the IEDES investigation has revealed, parents continued to hope that the REC would be converted to a regular primary school and tried to send primary school age children to the REC. But when after a three-year cycle the REC was not converted into a primary school, the villagers' hopes were shattered and new REC recruitment efforts faced increasing resistance from the villagers.

The ambivalent attitude of the government towards the objectives to be served by the program and the lack of comprehension of its aims by its clientele (or perhaps their shrewd reading of government ambivalence) obviously do not augur well for the program. It is doubtful that the program can be effectively expanded and that meaningful results can be achieved from it unless the stigma of blatant discrimination is removed from it and ways are found to restore its original purpose, that is, to serve as a precursor to a unified and realistic system of basic education for all children and youths. This is not to say that such a system should be without variations and modifications to fit different conditions.

Links with Other Rural Activities

A rural education program, especially one of a practical nature and designed to bring about improvement in rural living conditions, cannot be viewed in isolation from the overall rural development effort. The Upper Volta farmers, burdened with poor farm land, entirely dependent on the vagaries of the weather for their next harvest, and always concerned about producing enough food for survival before taking chances with untried methods, need far more help than just knowledge of new agricultural techniques. In a situation where the animal-drawn plough is virtually an agricultural revolution not because the farmer does not know its value, but because he cannot afford the price of the plough and the animal, the villagers can be justifiably skeptical about a program to teach better farming practices unless the program is linked to an overall attack on the obstacles to poor farming.

In principle, the RDOs could provide the framework for tying the educational functions of the REC to other efforts aimed at raising agricultural production and improving rural living conditions. In practice, the RDO neither takes such a comprehensive view of its functions,

nor does it have the human and physical resources to
carry out this mission. It is generally not remarkable
for its effectiveness even in its limited tasks of distributing chemical inputs, promoting cash crop production,
and marketing the farmers' surplus. Moreover, no definite
organizational link has been established between the RDO
and the REC, the latter being under the control of the
Ministry of Education. Where a working relationship between the two has evolved, as it has in the Yatenga
district, it is the result of initiatives by imaginative
individuals from either side.

When the RDO has functioned in a relatively effective
manner and its organizer and the rural education counsellor have established even limited cooperation--for example,
by using the center as a model farm and by supporting the
formation of postschool groups--the positive results have
been amply manifested in better performance of the REC
students, greater acceptance of the REC as a useful institution by the villagers, and a higher degree of adoption
of change in farming practices in the locality. Although
these positive elements do not amount to a radical improvement in the situation of the villagers, they mark a contrast to the frustration and skepticism found in other
districts where these positive signs do not exist, and
they underscore the importance of integrating as well as
reinforcing the educational components with other rural
development efforts.

Indeed, IEDES interviews with villagers have revealed
that they associate various development services and institutions (such as health clinics, transportation facilities, stores for agricultural supplies, and market centers), not with the REC, but with the primary school. It
may not have been planned that way, but the location of
the primary school coincides with the location of these
services, and at least some villagers believe that once
a primary school is opened, the other institutions will
follow, whereas the REC can apparently offer no such
prospect. This belief may be unfounded, but it reflects
a perception of the REC role in rural development.

                    Support and Commitment

Establishing a proper role for a rural education
program and making it a key element in a national endeavor to provide basic learning opportunities to all
children and youth call for a national commitment by
political leaders, the administrative personnel, and the
general public. Similarly, making a rural educational
program an essential ingredient in a rural development
thrust requires an environment of willing and constructive support. Without attempting to pass judgment on

the Upper Volta rural development activities and the total educational system, it may safely be said that the REC does not enjoy the unequivocal support of the government. The objectives and rationale of the program, which was originally conceived in colonial days mostly by expatriates, have always been the subject of debate and the program still remains officially labeled "experimental" even after more than ten years of existence.

A comparison of the primary school and the REC in respect of the teachers' remuneration, physical facilities, and provisions for equipment and supplies immediately tells where the government priority lies. It is true that the RECs were intended to be community-supported institutions, and one reason for their existence is that they are low-cost alternatives to the primary school. But a comparable cost-saving effort has not been applied to the primary schools, even though the educational task assigned to the REC is considerably more complicated than that of the primary school. Low cost by itself is meaningless unless it is associated with the results achieved. Obviously, costs can be too low when very little achievement can be shown for them.

While any realistic program for rural education must take advantage of all cost-saving opportunities and make efficient use of available and new sources of support, it obviously must have basic resources that are commensurate to the tasks it is expected to perform. If the program can engender community support, the financial burden on the government can be partially reduced. In the case of REC, government financing has been inadequate and community support has lagged, in part because of a lack of popular enthusiasm for the program, but also because of the crushing poverty of the Voltaique rural families.

Operational Problems

The operational problems that have affected the satisfactory performance of the Rural Education Centers include questions about the medium of instruction, instructional and supervisory personnel, renewal and adaptation of the content, provisions for supplies and equipment, and follow-up activities for the trainees.

The choice of the medium of instruction poses a difficult problem in French-speaking Africa. French is the medium in RECs, presumably because it is the language of government and business and it is also used in the primary school. Contacts with government personnel and people from outside the region, as well as business transactions in the market town, demand a knowledge of French. It would be difficult for the more ambitious rural youth to

get ahead in life without a knowledge of French. On the
other hand, a disproportionate amount of the students'
time and energy during the three years is spent on what
for most students amounts to a smattering of spoken French
and an even more limited functional facility in reading
and writing. IEDES researchers have noted that much is
lost in the process of communicating technical agricultural information to the REC students and, subsequently,
to the villagers because French is used in the centers.
An alternative that might have been given at least a
trial is Moré, the language of the Mossi people that is
spoken and understood by more than half of the people of
Volta. It also has a written form in the Roman script
and printed publications, including the Bible. While
teaching in Moré would have been more efficient, it is
possible that it might have reinforced rural people's
perception of REC as a symbol of discrimination, since
official and commercial transactions could not be carried
out in this language.

The multiple roles and responsibilities of the REC
instructor and his relatively meager rewards compared to
those of the primary teacher have been noted. The main
capital for his trade is his 10-month preservice training.
He is left virtually alone to fend for himself in an
essentially unpromising atmosphere without much supervisory and technical backstopping or opportunity for
professional growth. Supervision is so lax in some districts that, according to IEDES, one center has not been
open to students for six months, yet the instructor has
collected his salary regularly every month. Supervisory
and technical help to the field personnel in a rural
education program is more important than in a traditional
primary school where the teacher's role and the instructional content is more well defined.

Another essential kind of backstopping lies in the
area of selecting and adapting the content of instruction.
The experience of agricultural extension in general shows
that the extension service can be effective only when
there is a systematic provision for responding to the
changing needs and problems of farmers by validating the
extension message and adapting it to the specific
situation. The same lesson applies to the REC, but both
the Ministry of Education and the Rural Development
Organization appear to be unequal to the task. The REC,
therefore, continues routinely to propagate certain stock
practices and attempts to implement them in the center
farm within the limits of its meager resources, even
though the villagers are forced to cling to their own
time-tested methods as the best insurance for survival
in the face of climatic vagaries.

The RECs find themselves operationally in an unten-
able position, because they are expected to manage model
farms where improved farming techniques are practised for

the benefit of the students and the village people, yet
none of them have been provided with even a modest complement of agricultural tools considered essential for
their operation, and most have received as donation the
poorest of the poor village land for their farms.   While
the REC farm should not set standards of cost and investment totally out of line with those of the village farms,
it needs to be provided with the resources to carry out
initial experiments and demonstrations, especially since
it is not designed to be a self-financing operation.   A
scarcity of essential supplies, such as books and paper,
also persists.   It was not part of the REC plan that
these scarcities could or would be met by the poverty-
stricken rural communities of Upper Volta.   However,
failure in meeting such scarcities is probably another
indication of lukewarm government enthusiasm for the
program.

The REC experience clearly demonstrates the vital
role of follow-up activities for the trainees of a rural
education program.   Two comments on follow-up are in
order.   RECs and similar occupationally-oriented programs
by themselves cannot carry on effective follow-up activities.   First, while the REC teachers, and especially
the rural education counsellor of a district, have played
a catalytic role, it was the relatively effective RDO
activities and RDO support for the postschool groups that
have made the difference in the district where these
groups have emerged.   Second, the factors that are helpful to the follow-up activities--the overall rural development milieu and the imagination and dedication of the
educational program managers--are also the factors that
contribute to the good performance of the program itself.
There is a positive correlation and a high degree of
mutual reinforcement between program performance and
effective follow-up activities.   It should be noted,
however, that the post-REC groups have taken root in one
district only through individual initiative and are yet
to spread to other areas, although they have met with
government approval and their importance is now well
recognized by REC authorities.

[Recognizing the contradictions in the REC program,
the government has instituted some major changes in the
program in 1974.   The RECs have been taken out of the
Ministry of Education and placed under the Ministry of
Planning and Rural Development.   They have been renamed
as the Young Farmer Training Centers (Centres de Formation
de Jeunes Agriculteurs, or CFJAs), emphasizing their role
in training rural youths for farming.   A plan is underway,
with assistance from the World Bank and the European
Development Fund, to strengthen the Rural Development
Organizations in five districts.   It is expected that the
RDOs and the centers, now being under the same national
ministry, would work closely with each other in serving

their rural clienteles. The plan provides that the
trainees from the centers are to be encouraged to form
cooperative postschool groups and are to receive assistance from RDOs in establishing farming and other economic
enterprises. The results of these changes are yet to be
seen.]

CONCLUSIONS

    The ICED/IEDES study was not designed to evaluate
the overall REC system or to make a judgment on its
viability. It is apparent, however, that the original
plan which laid out the operating base has in important
respects not been adhered to. It may reasonably be
argued that the system as it was originally conceived has
been given something less than a fair trial. What was
intended to have been the major national educational
thrust has from the outset been only the "poor relation"
of the formal schools.
    Nevertheless, it is evident that for poor countries
with scanty resource endowment and only a thin spread of
conventional schools, an REC-type system offers a way of
spreading learning opportunities more widely than can be
afforded by conventional approaches. There is evidence,
too, that there are advantages to be gained by an older
age-group from the shorter time exposure to institution-
alized learning than by the younger age-group in primary
schools. Despite all the difficulties, the better centers
have proved that the mechanisms of reading, writing,
ordinary conversation, and computation connected with
everyday life have been acquired (and in a foreign language too) by a sizable number of students. The students
undoubtedly also acquire new agricultural knowledge, even
though they do not have the opportunity to apply all of
it either in the center or in the village. Indeed,
considering the limitations of resources, the briefer
time span, the nonselective nature of the clientele, and
the broader scope of the objectives, any comparison of
the REC with the primary schools only on the grounds of
literacy and arithmetic is unfair.
    The "technical" feasibility of the REC program and
its ability to achieve some results in spite of all the
difficulties, do not, however, ensure its future viability
and effectiveness at least in Upper Volta. The RECs,
even in conjunction with RDOs where cooperation between
the two institutions exists, do not constitute a real
attack on the main problems of rural Upper Volta--absolute
poverty, poor soil, drought, and inability of farmers to
use farming techniques that they know can produce better
results--either because the farmers cannot afford to buy
the supplies or because they cannot afford to risk their

family subsistence. The main necessity in this situation does not seem to be the dissemination of new technical knowledge, but provision for the means of utilizing already known improved techniques. It is not the REC's business to do so, nor are the RDOs' resources and capabilities equal to the task. While the REC program remains incapable of contributing as much as it was originally expected to making life better for the future farmers and rural residents, it also fails to open the door to the city and the modern sector of the economy, a promise that the primary school fulfills for at least a segment of those who succeed in staying in school long enough.

It is the conclusion of the IEDES observers that after ten years of operation the program of rural education in Upper Volta with its 737 centers and 24,164 students--still labeled as an experimental program, because the government cannot make up its mind about its future--has reached a state of stagnation, if not degeneration.

The program had seen a happier time when it was first initiatied. The new buildings were constructed either with outside assistance or by the villagers themselves, the first batch of students was recruited, and the villagers and the teachers were full of enthusiasm and anticipation. But three to six years later, as the IEDES team described the situation, there were frustration and low morale all around. All the authority of the commander of the cercle was now needed to recruit and to ensure attendance of students who, much younger in age, were more like the primary school children and less in conformity with the "profile" foreseen by the experts. If the roof of the center gave way or blew away, nobody wanted to repair it; if the pedagogical and agricultural equipment needed to be replaced or repaired, as they were worn out by usage or for lack of maintenance, the needed resources were not available from anywhere. The parents began to doubt the literacy ability of former students and would not mind revoking their children's right of access to what was billed as an adequate educational equivalent to the primary school cycle. The teacher lost faith and asked to be relieved, or he tried to quit rural education once his contract for six years was over.

The lesson of the Upper Volta experience is that a rural education program cannot be effective as long as it stands as a symbol of discrimination and fails to get the acceptance of the rural people. The stigma of discrimination can be removed and the confidence of the rural people in the program regained if there is a government commitment supported by necessary action to build a unified national system of basic education, or at least to remove the more pernicious elements of a dual system, and to provide the needed support for the program to

succeed. This is a political choice that Upper Volta and
all other countries seriously interested in rural education must make.

Furthermore, in extremely poor rural areas with poor
soil, uncertain weather, and little natural resources,
where the people's main concern is to raise a subsistence
crop to stave off starvation, general and vocational
education by itself is of little help. In such a situation concerted and systematic efforts are needed to attack
the basic obstacles to improvement in the condition of
people's lives. A commitment to rural education in this
situation entails a commitment to a major systematic
rural development thrust of which educational activities
would be integral parts. Even then, effective rural
education for the poorest regions will be a long and
uphill task.

It should be noted that the Upper Volta program was
conceived when the country was not fully independent and
its leaders not fully in control of their own affairs.
It was not a program that originated and developed
indigenously, although, since independence, many people
in government and education must have considered it worthy
of support and substantial budgetary allocations. Then
the program faced the common problems in newly independent,
poor, developing countries--the thin layer of administrative competence, the elitist power structure of society,
the rising expectations of students and parents, the
tradition-bound outlook of rural people, and so on.
The fact that the program has survived for so long and
has expanded is no mean achievement. In a sense, the
program might have come too early, when the political
climate and the professional educational opinion were
not ready; and the need for a rural development thrust
that could create a conducive atmosphere for such a
program had not yet become widely accepted.

In any event, the Upper Volta experience should not
become an excuse for advancing the point of view that
there cannot be any radical departure from the conventional
primary schools in the effort to spread basic and relevant
educational opportunities in a poor country. With the
changes initiated in 1974 in order to overcome some of its
major shortcomings, the program may yet demonstrate, as
its advocates have all along proclaimed, that the
approach and concepts underlying the program constitute
a sound basis of a strategy for meeting important learning needs in a poor country.

NOTES

1. For example, per capita income is estimated at less than US$50 per annum. Andrew M. Kamarck in The Economics of African Development, rev. ed. (New York: Praeger Publishers, 1971), p. 56, lists Upper Volta as one of the three African countries (together with Burundi and Somalia) with the lowest per capita GNP.

2. The figures vary greatly between sources, as different ethnic definitions are used by different authors.

3. J. C. Rouch quoted in J. Christol, "L'Enfance et la Jeunesses dans le Developpement National de la Haute-Volta," mimeographed (Paris: Société d'études pour le développement économique et social [SEDES], 1966), p. 45.

4. Decree No. 237 of July 14, 1957 is the first official document issued on the subject. It requires the establishment of a rural education system within two years.

5. SEDES, Scolarisation en Haute-Volta (Paris, 1959). The report was adopted by Resolution No. 37/59 AL of the Legislative Assembly on November 26, 1959.

6. In plain figures: 20,500 classes of 40 would be needed to provide six years of schooling for the 820,000 children aged six to twelve by 1975, if no account is taken of repeaters and dropouts. The rural education system would need only 9,000 classes for the 360,000 adolescents aged 14 to 16 going through a three-year program.

7. Upper Volta, Ministry of National Education, Rapport de Fin de l'Année 1970-71 (Ouagadougou, 1971). There were in all 788 centers at the beginning of the 1971-72 school year. Enrollment figures had not yet been tabulated in October 1971.

8. Some of these facilities have been built by the students as a part of their training.

9. Jean Folliero de Luna, "Étude sur la Production Agricole de 337 Centres d'Éducation Rurale au cours de la Campagne 1969-1970," mimeographed (Ouagadougou: Ministry of National Education, Director of Services for Rural Education, June 8, 1971), p. 3.

10. Upper Volta, Director of Services for Rural Education, Instructions No. 46/DER (Ouagadougou, March 20, 1968).

11. Data on the age of students should generally be accepted with some caution. Birth registration is not common in Upper Volta, and parents eager to get their children to school early may often misinform the authorities about the real age of the child. Several observers have noted that the lack of physical maturity of many pupils in the RECs would suggest that the age levels are systematically overestimated. The Instructions No. 46 suggest that "in case of doubt, look how tall the boy is."

12. A Mostafaoui and J. Ader, "Haute-Volta: Evaluation du systeme d'éducation rurale," mimeographed, 560/BMS. RD/EDM (Paris: UNESCO, April 1968), p. 31.

13. Information received from rural education counsellors. Instructions No. 46 makes the point that work in the village fields should be encouraged but emphasizes that this should not mean "the temporary closure of the school."

14. An average traditional farmer in Upper Volta has a gross income which may be estimated at a cash value of CFAF 10,000 to

15,000 (US$50 to $60) per hectare. A family without oxen seldom
cultivates more than two to five hectares, depending upon the number of adults in the family. Livestock grazing on communal lands
may provide some additional income.

15. The figures on yield and income have been taken from J.
Folliero de Luna, op. cit. The total income for each center was
calculated on the basis of reported yields evaluated at CFAF 21 per
kg. groundnuts, CFAF 32 per kg. cotton, CFAF 13 per kg. sorghum, and
CFAF 23 per kg. paddy rice. The revenues reported do not include
fruit trees and garden crops and other minor production commodities,
which in some of the better-run centers provide additional income
or are used to improve the food of the pupils in the center.

There is no explanation for large drop in income per center
between 1966/67 and the following years despite increases in the
acreage. The income reported for 1966/67 appears exceedingly high
in view of the small hectarage reported to be under crops. The
1968/69 averages do not appear unrealistic--they suggest an average
yield which is some 10 to 20 percent above the yields of traditional
agriculture.

16. The recommendation of the Executive Director to the UNICEF
Board in 1970 (Doc. E/ICEF/P/L 1343) estimated the charge to the
national budget at CFAF 4,500 per pupil per year, equivalent to
about US$18. Estimates vary greatly between different reports
depending upon how the cost of central services, teacher training,
and equipment received through foreign aid are handled in the
calculations. Whatever methods are used, the basic fact of rural
education having considerably lower costs than ordinary primary
education remains undisputed. A recent report (1970) uses standard
cost figures of CFAF 12,200 for primary education and 5,500 for
rural education for its projections.

17. During the first years rural education teachers were
employed as temporary staff with salaries amounting to about half of
those paid to primary school teachers. The difference is no longer
as great, as the salaries of rural education staff were raised a
few years ago.

18. Upper Volta, Ministry of National Education, Cout de
Formation d'une Élève-Maître et d'une Élève-Monitrice Année 1971-72
(Ouagadougou, n.d.). The calculation was prepared by the Rural
Education division.

19. Upper Volta, Ministry of National Education, Rapport de Fin
de l'Année 1970-71, op. cit., p. 4.

10

AFGHANISTAN:
EDUCATION IN
AN INTEGRATED
AGRICULTURAL PROGRAM
Manzoor Ahmed
and Philip H. Coombs

ICED chose PACCA for a case study to learn how educational elements fitted into the rest of the "integrated package." Another reason was to discover how such an integrated approach would work out in a nation that is among the world's poorest. Fieldwork for the study was done in December 1971 when an ICED team visited the project. The field visit was supplemented by numerous documentation provided by the headquarters staff of SIDA (Swedish International Development Authority) and FAO (Food and Agriculture Organization) as well as the directors and staff of PACCA. The Program Manager of PACCA also commented on a draft of the study and reported on later developments in late 1972. What is said in this report, however, is entirely the responsibility of the authors.

INTRODUCTION

The Program of Agricultural Credit and Cooperation in Afghanistan (PACCA) is an attempt to apply the concept of an integrated approach to agricultural development. PACCA was designed to combine and coordinate the provision of various services--such as credit, cooperatives, extension, training, marketing, and the supply of physical inputs-- necessary for increased agricultural production.

PACCA was planned for one of the least developed countries. More than 90 percent of the Afghan population are illiterate. Per capita income in 1970 at current prices was about US$70. The society is highly tradition-bound, and institutions that might serve as modernizing influences are underdeveloped. Trade of both goods and ideas has been difficult for this landlocked, rugged country. More than 80 percent of the population are engaged in agriculture, but mostly on a subsistence basis. Farming methods are generally primitive and yields are low.

There are, however, some positive features. With 14 million hectares of arable land and 14 million population, there is not the great pressure on land that exists in several other Asian countries. The soil north of the Hindu Kush mountains is generally fertile and about 70 percent of the cultivated land is already under irrigation. The climate and soil condition offer the potential of a diversified agriculture, including commercial crops, though the growing season is relatively short. About half of the farmers own their land. Recent development efforts have gone into the building of major highways that have opened up some of the remote regions of the country to modern transportation.

The PACCA plans were prepared in 1968, when negotiations were completed for the Swedish International Development Authority (SIDA) to provide financial assistance, the FAO to offer technical assistance, and the Ministry of Agriculture and Irrigation of the Government of Afghanistan to execute the program. The program became operational in early 1969. The major components of the program are:

1. two development centers, which are the basis for organizing cooperatives and improving agriculture in two separate pilot areas, one with about 5,000 multiple-crop farmers and the other with 10,000 grape farmers

2. an institute for training extension agents, extension supervisors, cooperative advisors,and credit supervisors for the program as well as for the national system

3. a functional literacy component, added to the program in 1970, with technical assistance from UNESCO

THE PACCA PLAN

In July 1966, FAO with financial support from the Swedish International Development Authority (SIDA) set up an international exploratory mission of four members with background in cooperation, agricultural development, and international assistance. The mission's assignment was to:

1. discuss the nature and objectives of integrated agricultural development activities through credit and cooperative measures with Afghan authorities

2. appraise the existing institutional structure of agricultural services and the feasibility of strengthening them

3. assess the problems of fitting and tying in the proposed approach with the overall agricultural policy and institutional structure of the country
4. evaluate the existing facilities for training agricultural service personnel, estimate the training needs of local personnel, and examine the possibility of attaching the training program envisaged for a pilot project to local institutions
5. identify a sufficiently large and representative area in which to locate a pilot project for a trial of an integrated approach
6. assess the prospects of farmers' active participation in the proposed program through farmers' associations and saving schemes
7. design a system for periodic evaluation of progress and modification of the program
8. judge whether launching a pilot project in Afghanistan was feasible and, if so, to prepare a plan of operation[1]

The mission completed its assignment in about three months, including six weeks in Afghanistan. It met groups of farmers and individuals in five meetings arranged in different parts of the country; held interviews and discussions with officials in the Ministries of Agriculture, Finance, Planning, Agricultural Bank, provincial administration; sugar, cotton, and fruit industries; and a number of nongovernmental and international organizations in Kabul; and made field trips to prospective sites for the proposed pilot project.

Concept of an Integrated Approach

From the beginning, the focus of the exploratory mission and the program was on the role of credit and cooperatives in agricultural development. It was recognized that credit facilities and cooperative societies were not the only components that needed to be integrated, but the provision of credit and the setting up of cooperatives would, the mission and the program sponsors assumed, make it possible to bring together other necessary elements--such as extension, supply of inputs--and build a common strategy of agricultural development.

Institutional credit was considered a necessary condition for enabling the farmer to buy the various inputs needed for efficient nonsubsistence production. Moreover, the provision of credit would allow the farmer the option to wait for better prices, to invest in processing, or to explore better markets, which require some

working capital. But the availability of credit would
not guarantee the supply of the inputs or the creation
of a favorable market situation, nor would it mean proper
utilization of the supplies or the marketing channels by
farmers. The cooperative structure, besides being a
credit union, could itself undertake or work closely with
the extension service, could arrange for purchase and
delivery of seeds, fertilizer, pesticides, and equipment,
could take over or assist and coordinate processing,
storage, transportation and exploration of markets for
the agricultural products, and could also become the
channel for technical and educational inputs.

The mission placed special importance on not isolating
such a pilot program from the total administrative and
institutional structure of the country. The continued
viability of the pilot project and its expansion beyond
the pilot areas after the withdrawal of foreign technical
and financial assistance would depend on the acceptance
of the new approach by the national administrative and
institutional system and the competence of national personnel. This is why a training component not just for
the pilot project personnel but for personnel of the
national extension credit and cooperative services was
considered essential.

The two dimensions of integration in the pilot program, therefore, were 1) concerted provisions for credit,
production prerequisites, extension, storage, processing,
and marketing for achieving agricultural improvement in
the pilot project area through the development center and
ultimately through a cooperative structure; and 2) strengthening the national training facilities for agricultural
personnel and working closely with the existing national
agricultural agencies to ensure the continuation of the
integrated approach and its dissemination outside the
project areas after the withdrawal of foreign assistance.

As the preceding discussion indicates, a number of
fundamental principles for agricultural development were
accepted by the sponsors of PACCA--FAO, SIDA, and the
Afghan government--as the basis for initiating the program
and as guidelines for implementing it:

1. To achieve agricultural development and improve-
    ment of farmers' lives, an integrated and coor-
    dinated combination of services should be pro-
    vided to farmers.
2. Cooperatives of farmers can be the key organiza-
    tional means for integrating and coordinating
    the services.
3. Provisions for training, credit, and other
    aspects of the program should be integrated
    with the national system of agricultural insti-
    tutions and services so as not to isolate the
    program from the national agricultural production
    and development system.

4. The program should include ample training opportunities for local personnel within the program and for other agricultural personnel in the country.
5. Built-in evaluation procedures should be included in the program, underscoring its experimental nature.

The implicit underlying assumptions were that the private benefits to farmers and the social benefits to the country would outweigh the costs to the farmers, the government, and the international agencies. Apparently, it was assumed that the markets and prices for farm products would provide the incentives for farmers to work for agricultural improvement.

Factors Affecting the Plan

The mission considered factors that would have a direct bearing on the operation of the pilot project, including the existing credit situation of cooperative activities, extension service, training of agricultural personnel, and the agricultural policies of the government.

Selection of Pilot Areas

Two districts in different parts of the country were proposed as sites for the program because of their relatively favorable agricultural situation and because they represented two different crop patterns.

One site is in Baghlan province--one of the most productive agricultural areas in Afghanistan. The area has about 5,000 farmers and 15,000 hectares of land. The land in the province is fertile and 80 percent of it is under irrigation. A wide range of crops ensures a degree of stability for farmers' earnings. The highway between Kabul and the Russian border passes through the province, providing access to markets. The introduction of sugar beets and cotton in the 1930s and 1940s had helped many of the farmers in the area make the transition from subsistence to commercial farming. The fruit market had also opened recently because of improved transport. The land tenure situation, with owner-farmers as the dominant group, was not considered by the mission to be a major obstacle to agricultural development in the area.

The second project area, the Koh-i-Daman Valley, is about 30 kilometers north of Kabul along the highway to the Russian border. A large share of the total grape production of Afghanistan comes from about 10,000 farmers in this region (an area of about 450 square kilometers).

Four-fifths of the irrigated land in Koh-i-Daman is
occupied by vineyards. Some fruits and cereals are
grown, mostly in nonirrigated areas. Essential agricultural data about the area were unavailable; the mission,
however, made the following estimates: number of vines
per jerib (about 1/5 hectare)--300, of which 250 are in
production; average size of farm--3 jeribs, or 900 vines
of which 750 are in production; average yield per plant
in production--1.5 ser (10.5 kg.); total production in
the area--about 80,000 tons (more than 40 percent of
national production, 1966). The major agricultural problems of the area, as identified by the mission, were
water management, unavailability of production supplies
and credit, and limitations on grape and raisin marketing.

Credit and Cooperation

Institutional facilities for agricultural credit were
almost nonexistent in Afghanistan   and   quantitative
information about the indebtedness of farmers was very
inadequate.[2] There were, however, a number of traditional
forms of lending operations in existence. Short-term
loans, generally used for nonproductive purposes, were
available in the bazaar at interest rates ranging from
20 to 50 percent or higher per year. The salaam system,
by which a merchant or moneylender buys a farmer's crop
before the harvest at a discount price, was widely practised. A mortgage system (ghrawi) that allowed the
lender the use of mortgaged land until the debt was repaid provided some long-term credit.

In 1954 the Ministry of Agriculture established an
agricultural bank as a national institutional source for
agricultural credit. But the bank's impact on the
country's agriculture was negligible. After heavy
initial losses, the bank in recent years had been limited
to the financing of large irrigation works with Ministry
of Agriculture guarantee, the sale of small quantities
of fertilizer and sulphur, and loans for purchasing
tractors. At the time of the mission's visit, a World
Bank team was studying the prospects of extending the
bank's scope of operation and improving its services.

In Baghlan, some credit was available to farmers from
the cotton and sugar companies, which granted limited
interest-free advances against later delivery of crops.
Absence of institutional credit in the Koh-i-Daman area
was considered to be a serious constraint to increased
yield.

There was no government agency in the country with
overall responsibility for promoting, supervising, and
regulating cooperative societies. The question of enacting cooperative legislation had been under consideration
since the early 1960s and a draft law had been pending
for the National Assembly's consideration since 1965.

There were, however, a number of marketing cooperatives of Karakul sheep owners in operation since 1964 and 1965 in the northern provinces. These functioned under bylaws drafted by the Ministry of Agriculture and provided representation of sheep farmers in London and New York export markets. The mission was not able to assess their effectiveness because up-to-date financial statements were unavailable.

Extension and Inputs

An organizational structure for the extension service was adopted in 1957, with an extension director, supervisors, and extension agents in each of the 29 provinces. The total system was to have 1,500 extension agents and 150 supervisors. By 1967, the pattern was completed in six provinces and a start was made in four others. The province of Baghlan, with 30 extension workers, was one of the six that had an extension service. There was no extension service in the province that included Koh-i-Daman.

Provincial directors and supervisors in the extension service were in principle required to have a university degree. Extension agents were recruited from the graduates of agricultural high schools in Kabul and Baghlan. There were no facilities for specialized extension training. Two new agricultural high schools were being planned in 1967.

The mission considered the training and preparation of the extension personnel weak and their performance ineffective, but did not specify which aspects of the university and high school agricultural preparation of extension workers were deficient, and in what ways personnel were ineffective (except for the mention of a specific problem in the Baghlan area).

Farmers in both project areas knew about chemical fertilizer. According to the mission, Koh-i-Daman farmers knew that the application of fertilizer would increase grape yields by 50 percent. However, no research facility was in existence to provide correct technical answers about the utilization of inputs and production techniques. For instance, the ICED team was informed in Koh-i-Daman that a phosphate deficiency of the soil impaired the quality of the grapes, but the problem was never recognized and it was assumed that the soil was rich in phosphate.

Two processing firms in Baghlan, the Spinzer Company (cotton ginning) and the Sugar Company, gave free insecticides, free or subsidized fertilizer in limited amounts, and free seeds of rather poor quality to the farmers who supplied them with raw materials. In Koh-i-Daman, fertilizer and sulphur were occasionally sold in small quantities by the Agricultural Bank or the Ministry of Agriculture.

Water supply was a major obstacle to increased productivity, particularly in Koh-i-Daman. The water was
supplied primarily from <u>kurez</u>--unlined tunnels in the
hillside which bring water <u>by</u> free flow from underground
aquifers for surface irrigation. A kurez may be many
kilometers in length, and the number of farmers using
one kurez varies from 10 to 100 or more. Usually a few
farmers join together to construct and use a kurez, each
paying a share of the investment and receiving proportionate amounts of water. Grape yields were low for those
farmers who did not have shares in a kurez and yields
dropped for those who did not maintain it properly for
lack of funds.

Agricultural Prices and Government Policies

The agricultural price situation did not provide
strong incentives for farmers to increase production. A
controlled price structure for agriculture was a major
source of government revenue. For instance, the government set the price of sugar beets and cotton and required
farmers in the main producing areas to plant the crops in
certain proportions--sugar beets on 20 percent of land,
and cotton on 25 percent of land. The government also
set a high price for domestically produced sugar to cover
production costs and imported sugar at a much lower price
but resold at the high domestic price, retaining the difference for the treasury. For the main agricultural
export items, exporters were obliged to convert their
foreign earnings into Afghan currency at low and variable
rates (US$1 was worth 45 Afghanis (Af) for pelt export-
ers, Af38   for wool exporters, and   Af32 for cotton
exporters, compared with a free market rate of Af76).
In Koh-i-Daman the farmer's problems in marketing
grapes were threefold. His relationship with middlemen
was usually unfavorable to him; the backyard or rooftop
processing of raisins (and the consequent lack of quality
control and grading standards) limited the export market
potential for the product; and the uncertainty of the export market due to the perishability of grapes, dependence
on transit facilities in Pakistan, and import restrictions
imposed by Pakistan and India were disincentives to investments for raising production.
The mission noted that though agriculture was the
predominant sector of the economy and the major provider
of export earnings, the sector had a low priority in the
government development and investment plans. In the
second five-year plan, which expired in 1967, only 23
percent of development expenditure was allocated to agriculture and only about half that amount was actually
spent in agriculture. Much of the agricultural investment was concentrated in a few large irrigation projects.
There were no indications that development priorities and

the allocation of resources would substantially change in the third five-year plan.

Components of the Plan

The planners of PACCA were faced with a situation where the tradition of a cooperative movement, an understanding of the cooperative principles and methods, and even a legal framework for organizing cooperatives did not exist. Their task was, therefore, not only to build a cooperative movement but also to establish agricultural services almost from scratch and drastically reorganize those that existed. In addition, a way had to be found to make agricultural services operate with a measure of unity and consistency; in effect, a temporary substitute for the cooperative structure had to be devised. The solution to this problem was seen in the establishment of two Development Centers, one in each project area.

Development Centers

A development center, modeled after the Thana Training and Development Center in the Comilla project in East Pakistan (now Bangladesh), was to be the nucleus of all agricultural development activities for each project area.
Established as part of the Ministry of Agriculture organization in the two provinces and staffed by both international and Ministry of Agriculture personnel, the centers were assigned four primary functions:

1. planning, initiating, organizing, guiding and evaluating development activities in the field of agriculture
2. promoting a cooperative organization among the farmers for carrying out different activities such as credit, supply, and marketing
3. providing advisory service to the farmers through the extension agents
4. training farmers and officials for the above purposes[3]

The two main departments in the centers were for extension and cooperatives. (See PACCA Organization Chart, Fig. 10.1.)
The extension services' department, located in the center, would devise the content of extension, and agents would carry out the plan in the field. The center in Baghlan would work closely with a research station operated by the Ministry of Agriculture. The Koh-i-Daman center would set up its own research station. The centers would also take trainees for practical experience from the

FIGURE 10.1

PACCA Organization Chart

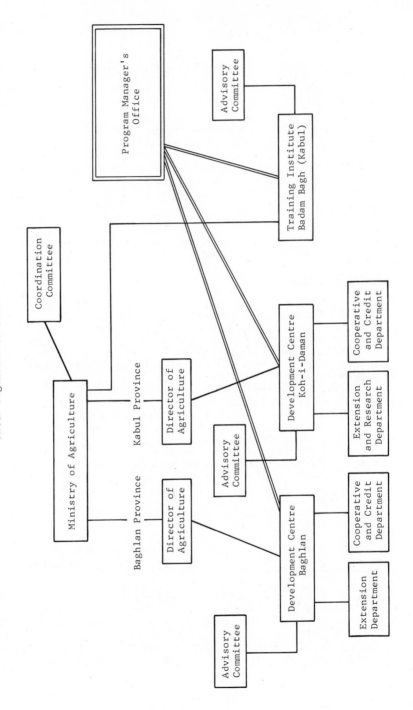

proposed Training Institute (see below), organize educational experiences for members and officers of cooperative societies, and arrange training for "model farmers" and other farm leaders.

Through its Cooperative Department, each center would actively propagate the principles and methods of cooperatives and would organize farmers' cooperatives. Other services that are often performed by multipurpose cooperatives, such as provisions for production supplies, marketing, storage, and processing, would be undertaken by this department as the need arose and circumstances permitted. The department would also secure credit for farmers who became members of cooperatives from the Agricultural Bank or from a revolving fund provided by the government. Other activities, such as youth clubs, family improvement, and women's programs, would be undertaken under the auspices of the Development Center, as a means of promoting all-round development of the area.

Because the concepts and methods of modern cooperatives were unknown in the project areas, the plan indicated uncertainty about the best means of propagating cooperatives. It was suggested, therefore, that a socioeconomic survey of the Koh-i-Daman area be undertaken at the initial stage of the project and that the establishment of cooperatives should proceed gradually and in phases, permitting the center to modify its activities in the light of experience.

The plan did not suggest any action in respect of marketing of the two major commercial crops in Baghlan. In Koh-i-Daman, it was envisaged that cooperatives would gradually develop an important role in marketing of grapes and raisins, and the possibilities of a raisin-processing plant in the area would be considered.

Training Institute

The Institute of Cooperative, Credit and Extension Training, included in the project plan, was seen as the means not only for training project personnel but also for developing a national training facility for agricultural personnel which would pave the way for the ultimate spreading of the project techniques outside the pilot areas.

The trainees for positions as extension agents were to be recruited from among graduates of agricultural high schools. Trainees for supervisory extension work were to be recruited from the university's Faculty of Agriculture. Both groups would be trained after they had been appointed by the Ministry of Agriculture as extension agents, cooperative advisors, or extension supervisors. Trainees for the credit course would be employees of the Agricultural Bank. The courses planned were:

1. eighteen-month preservice course for extension agents
2. eighteen-month course for cooperative supervisors and credit officials of the Agricultural Bank
3. six-month preservice course for graduates from the Faculty of Agriculture, who would serve as extension supervisors
4. one to two months inservice training for extension agents and supervisors
5. other refresher courses for personnel at different levels

The Institute was to be established near Kabul but parts of its courses were to be held in the Development Centers in the project areas. Other aspects of personnel development in the project would be the experience acquired by counterpart staff and other personnel in the project in working closely with the international staff, and the fellowships for study abroad to be awarded to selected project staff.

Altogether, 25 internationally recruited staff were to spend about 800 man-months in the program over a period of three years. The planned national staff was to consist of 20 counterpart personnel, at least 27 other professional staff, and 30 to 60 extension agents who were to devote a total of about 2,000 man-months to the project over the first three years. Fellowships in 12 subjects for 168 man-months of study were provided for in the plan.

A functional literacy component was added to the program in October 1970 with technical assistance from UNESCO. The functional literacy activity was seen as a part of UNESCO's Experimental World Literacy Program (an experimental program to develop the concepts and methods of functional literacy and to test their effectiveness). The plan under PACCA provided for a total coverage of the 15,000 families in the two project areas within a period of four years. (The target was revised in 1971 to cover 9,000 people instead of 15,000 "families.")

Integration with the National Administrative Structure

Several measures, in addition to the sharing of training facilities with the Ministry of Agriculture, were proposed for integrating the program operations with the national administrative structure for agriculture and other development activities.

1. The Development Centers were placed under the supervision of the provincial director of agriculture, and all of the national personnel were the employees of the Ministry of Agriculture or the Agricultural Bank. The extension agents working in the Development Centers were members of the national extension service, though they were under

the authority of the center head as far as daily
duties were concerned.
2. The credit and cooperative activities were, insofar as possible, to be carried out within the framework of a national legal structure, rather than under
any special provision for the program, so that the
methods and approaches followed in the program could
be utilized elsewhere.
3. The detailed planning, coordination, administration, and execution of the program were proposed to
be shared by the program manager, appointed by FAO,
and the co-manager, appointed by the Ministry of
Agriculture. In addition, provision was made for a
coordination committee, with the Deputy Minister of
Agriculture, the President of the Research, Training
and Extension Division, the Director General of Extension Services and the President of the Agricultural
Bank as members. This committee should concern itself,
among other things, with ways and means of relating the
program operations to the development activities in
the country and for coordinating the actions of various
government agencies with those of the program. Advisory committees were to be set up for the two pilot
areas and the Training Institute. The committee for
each pilot area was to include the provincial governor or the district subgovernors concerned, the
Director of Agriculture, representatives of local
industries and the Agricultural Bank, three representatives of farmers, and the project manager and co-
manager. The advisory committee for the Training
Institute was to consist of representatives of the
university, various departments in the ministries of
agriculture, education, and interior, and the two
managers of the project areas.

Costs

A picture of the overall costs and cost breakdowns and
of the sources of support for the first three years of the
PACCA program was provided by the operational plan (though
this picture may well differ from actual expenditures).
Total costs for this three-year period were estimated at
about US$2.4 million, derived from the following sources:

> Allocation from SIDA through FAO Freedom From
>   Hunger Campaign--US$1,791,600
> Counterpart contribution by Afghan government
>   in kind and through personnel--US$598,600
> Cash contribution by the Afghan government--
>   US$13,000

More than half the total (US$1.3 million) was allo-
cated for internationally recruited staff and consultants.

Recurrent expenditure for local personnel and other current items to be paid by the Afghan government, was calculated to be US$133,000 (see Table 10.1).

Capital expenditures to be incurred by the Afghan
government for land, buildings, equipment, and furniture
for the Training Institute, the two Development Centers
and the Program Manager's office, were to be the equivalent of US$466,000. Additional capital expenditures from
SIDA funds for equipment and supplies were expected to
total US$151,000.

TABLE 10.1

Planned Costs of PACCA for First Three Years
(in US$)

	Total for Three Years	Third Year
From International Source		
International staff	$1,249,330	$549,690
Consultants	59,090	12,250
Fellowships	74,000	27,000
Equipment and supplies	150,915	22,190
Miscellaneous	66,265	26,870
Service charge to FAO	192,000	76,000
TOTAL	$1,791,600	$714,000
From National Source		
Capital Cost		
Land and building	412,000	35,000
Equipment and furniture	54,000	15,000
Recurrent Cost		
Professional staff	64,840	34,260
Other staff	30,760	12,120
Trainees allowances	25,000	9,000
Transportation and handling of equipment	5,500	2,000
Records and information	1,500	500
Miscellaneous	5,000	2,000
Local costs for the international staff	13,000	--
TOTAL	$ 611,600	$109,880
GRAND TOTAL	$2,403,200	$823,880

Source: FAO, Plan of Operations, Program on Agricultural
Credit and Related Services through Cooperatives in Afghanistan
(Rome, November 1967).

The major activities to be carried out during the
first three years of the program in the two pilot areas
and Training Institute are shown in Table 10.2.

TABLE 10.2

Schedule of Major Activities Planned for the First Three Years of PACCA, 1969–71

	Koh-i-Daman	Baghlan
At Training Institute	**First Year**	Program not yet started
1. An 18-month course for 25 extension agents 2. An 18-month course for 10 cooperative supervisors and a 9-month course for 6 to 10 trainees from the Agricultural Bank 3. A 6-month course for 10 students from the Faculty of Agriculture for training extension supervisors 4. A preparatory course for officials involved in the two pilot projects	1. Definition of the pilot area, its size and distribution; mapping 2. Economic and social survey of the area as described in the program 3. Starting extension activities for part of the pilot area; outlining a research program 4. Approaching some 500 farmers for grouping into cooperatives; collection of raisins for building up member's share capital; starting marketing operations on a limited scale; providing short-term credit in kind for the next cultivation season	1. Definition of the pilot area, its size and distribution; establishment of the center 2. Starting intensified extension activities for part of the pilot area; concentrating on one crop (wheat) 3. Survey of potentialities for starting cooperatives; examination of group behavior and leadership in villages; consideration of location of societies; approaching 200 farmers for creating the first local cooperatives 4. Providing credit to farmers through the first established cooperative societies.
1. Completion of the first two 18-month courses; starting two new ones 2. A 6-month course for students from the Faculty of Agriculture 3. A 1-month course for in-service training for extension agents and supervisors 4. Short courses for cooperative personnel from the pilot area	**Second Year** 1. Expanding extension activities to reach other farmers; taking up new cultivation problems to be solved by the research program 2. Approaching 1,500 other farmers for creating local cooperatives 3. Providing credit to farmers, making use of the best consolidated cooperatives; otherwise, still individual credits 4. Starting regular training courses for "model farmers" and cooperative leaders	

379

Table 10.2 continued

See previous year	Third Year

1. See previous year

Third Year

1. Expanding extension, credit, and marketing activities; approaching additional 2,000 farmers
2. Starting provision of medium-term credit for farmers who joined the project the first year
3. Starting a saving scheme among the farmers
4. Extending training and education activities to farm women

1. Expanding extension activities to other farmers and also other crops; concentration on wheat and sugar beets
2. Approaching 400 additional farmers for creation of more local credit societies
3. Providing credit to farmers through the first established cooperative societies
4. Starting regular training courses for "model farmers" and cooperative societies

Source: FAO, Plan of Operations, Program on Agricultural Credit and Related Services through Cooperatives in Afghanistan (Rome, November 1967).

IMPLEMENTATION OF THE PLAN

The three major components of the program became operational on different dates. The Koh-i-Daman Development Center began in February 1969. The Training Institute began the first courses in April 1969. The Baghlan project activities were started in February 1970. Recruitment of all international and local personnel attached to the three locations had not yet been completed by these dates. A brief description of the major activities and achievements of the program by late 1971 is presented below.

Cooperatives, Credit, and Extension

No progress had yet been made on enacting a cooperative law, the draft of which was still pending, as of March 1972, before the National Assembly. However, about 170 farmers in Koh-i-Daman area had joined an "informal" cooperative formed under the auspices of the Development Center. The target had been to have 1,500 farmers in cooperatives during the first two years. [Since the time of ICED's visit to the project in 1971 a Cooperative Law was drawn up within the framework of the Afghan commercial code. The Cooperative Societies Regulations of Afghanistan which were the result became law in September 1972.] In Baghlan, discussion and education on cooperative methods had been undertaken with about 200 farmers, but no society had been yet organized. A consultant was invited in mid-1969 to undertake a socioeconomic survey of the Koh-i-Daman area. There is no indication in the semiannual progress reports of what the findings were or if they were taken into account in the plan of activities of the Koh-i-Daman Center.

A line of credit was established by the Koh-i-Daman Development Center with the Agricultural Bank, and limited credit was made available to the farmers. In 1969, 22 loans were made for an average amount of about Af1,000; 215 loans averaging about Af2,000 were made in 1970. In Baghlan, loans were made in kind--in the form of fertilizers, insecticides, and seeds--to a small number of farmers. Repayment rates in both areas have been outstanding. Limitation of funds available to the centers prevented provision of credit to more farmers.

Extension activities in both project areas had thus far involved only a relatively small number of farmers. In early 1970, 28 extension agents and international advisors were working in Koh-i-Daman with 150 pilot farmers. Four extension agents were working with 29 pilot farmers in Baghlan.

By 1971 a total of about 600 farmers had received direct assistance from the extension service in the Koh-i-Daman area. The 1971 plan for the Baghlan area called for working with about 180 farmers, with substantial addition to the extension staff.

Arrangements for land and facilities for demonstration and research in Koh-i-Daman were not completed until March 1971. At an early stage, however, and by good fortune, the international specialists in the center were able to identify and cure fungal diseases of grapes (Anthraenosis and Downey Mildew), thereby promptly heightening farmers' confidence in the center's activities. In Baghlan, the center has cooperated in demonstration and trial activities of the Ministry of Agriculture's Research Station.

Agricultural Production and Marketing

By following the techniques and practices suggested by the extension agents--mainly using fertilizer, pruning and trellising--farmers participating in the Koh-i-Daman center's program achieved yields averaging between 11.9 to 16.5 kilograms per vine in 1970 compared to an average of 7.5 kilograms in the area. In Baghlan's demonstration plots in 1970, cotton yields were up to 50 percent higher and sugar beet yields up to 300 percent higher than yields elsewhere.[4]

Educational activities in the centers included periodic group meetings of farmers, planning and technical meetings of extension and cooperative agents conducted by the specialists, and practical training of the students in the Training Institute.

The Development Center in Koh-i-Daman entered into grape marketing quite early in its operation. In the 1969 season, 65.5 tons of fresh grapes and 2.6 tons of raisins produced by the farmers participating in the center's program were marketed by the center in Kabul and exported to Pakistan and India. The center sustained a 5.5 percent loss from this venture, mainly because it overestimated the market prospects and paid farmers about 20 percent more than the prices paid by local merchants. The center collected a modest revenue, however, in the following year after paying the farmers what they considered a fair price.

During the 1971 grape season a marketing problem arose because the increased production from Koh-i-Daman saturated the limited grape market in Pakistan and India and forced the price down. This situation highlighted the importance of exploring the market prospects of less perishable raisins.

In 1970 an FAO consultant arranged a demonstration of proper drying techniques and produced raisins of greatly improved quality. Samples of these raisins were sent to Germany, Denmark, Sweden, and England. Afghan exporters have also shown interest in the products from the center.

As noted earlier, no marketing services were provided in the Baghlan area.

Training Institute and Staff

The Training Institute combined the four regular courses originally planned into two courses: an 18-month course for extension agents and cooperative advisers, and a six-month course for extension supervisors and bank employees. After two years, 31 extension agents and cooperative advisers, 10 bank officials, and 4 extension supervisors had completed the training. Twenty-eight extension agents, 4 extension supervisors, and 12 bank officials were in training in late 1971.

In the extension agents' course, six months are spent in the Development Centers for practical experience. Under the supervision of the specialists in the center and extension supervisors, trainees participate in field work with farmers, attend farmers' meetings in the center, and plan and prepare for extension activities in the project area. Trainees, in fact, constitute the major proportion of the extension field staff in the project. Trainees in the other course are also periodically taken to the Development Centers.

According to the project manager's report,[5] the original syllabi for the courses were not sufficiently coordinated with one another or with the activities of the Development Centers. Nor were extension agents prepared for their role in the functional literacy program. Review and modification of the curriculum were therefore undertaken.

The personnel development activities--the appointment of counterpart staff and the fellowship program--have functioned as planned. Shown below are the various professional staff positions as of September 1970.[6]

<u>International Staff</u> (27)   <u>National Staff</u> (55)

A. <u>Program Manager's Office</u> (4)

Program manager   Program co-manager
Administrative officers (2)

B. <u>Training Institute for Agricultural</u>
<u>Cooperation, Credit and Extension</u> (24)

Head of institute   Co-head of institute
Extension specialist   Agronomy officer
Cooperative and credit specialist
Agronomist   Extension officers (2)
       Extension and rural
       youth officer

International Staff	National Staff
Rural sociologist	Rural sociology officer
Agricultural economists (2)	Counterpart of institute head
Cooperative management specialist	Cooperative management officer
Extension and rural youth specialist	Equipment officer
Equipment superintendent	Agricultural economics officer
Administrative assistant	Administrative officer
Consultant on socioeconomic survey	
Consultant on audiovisual aid	

C. Koh-i-Daman Development Center (43)

Project manager	Co-head
Marketing specialist	Extension supervisors (4)
Grape-growing specialist	Grape-growing officer
Instructor in cooperative marketing	Marketing officers (2)
Administrative assistant	Extension agents (18)
Consultant of grape and raisin handling	Cooperative advisors (10)
Consultant of plant diseases	

D. Baghlan Development Center (11)

Project manager	Co-manager
Farm management specialist	Extension officer
Extension specialist	Extension agents (3)
Functional literacy specialist	Cooperative advisor
	Farm management officer

Functional Literacy

Though a functional literacy program became formally a part of PACCA in late 1970, a UNESCO expert attached to the Ministry of Education had already started a general literacy course in December 1969 in the Koh-i-Daman area. More than 300 villagers, in 18 classes, attended the four-month part-time course, and 250 completed it. A similar course with more than 400 participants was organized in the winter of 1970-71 and an equally high proportion completed the course. The high retention rate was reported to be partly due to the support of religious leaders for the course as a means of learning to read the Koran.

It was the opinion of the functional literacy specialist of the program that much was needed before the literacy education became truly functional. The greatest problems, in his view, were the lack of content dealing with practical agricultural topics and the absence of trained instructors for functional literacy courses. Most of the instructors so far had been primary school teachers, though extension agents and literate farmers were considered more desirable for the task. Some progress had been made toward developing functional reading material with the assistance of an instructional materials expert.

Semiannual progress reports presenting a concise account of PACCA activities have served as one of the evaluation tools. In addition, more systematic evaluation efforts were undertaken by a three-man SIDA team in October 1970 and by two professors of Kabul University in 1971. The results of the last two evaluations, however, were not available to ICED in written form, and it is not clear whether they resulted in any modification of PACCA's plan or activities.

A joint Afghan government-FAO-SIDA team reviewed PACCA operations in Spring 1970 and made some proposals concerned largely with practical and organizational matters. A similar team visited PACCA for over two weeks in May 1971 in connection with plans for the second phase of PACCA, covering five years beginning March 1972. Although the team's main function was not to evaluate but to prepare a plan of operation for the next phase, it did note some factors that had hampered PACCA's program. These included: the absence of a cooperative law, weaknesses in the Agricultural Bank operations, problems regarding the physical facilities in the Training Institute and the centers, unattractive conditions of service for counterpart field personnel, and the delayed start of PACCA after the Plan of Operation was signed. Despite these difficulties, however, the team emerged with the positive conclusion that--"the integrated PACCA approach had produced encouraging results and had, at the same time, instilled great hopes and expectations among farmers ... PACCA activities should be continued and strengthened during a second phase."[7]

The coordination arrangements included in the plan of operation have apparently worked well; no significant coordination problem had been mentioned in progress reports through 1971. The high-level coordination committee and advisory committees mentioned earlier had each met formally three times during the first three years to review the periodic progress reports of the program manager and to discuss operational and policy matters regarding PACCA activities.

[The PACCA Project Adviser informed us in May 1973 that:

Phase 1 came to an end on 20 March 1972.
External funding for the Phase II of PACCA
had not been approved as of August 1972,
six months after it was scheduled to start,
because the passage of the Cooperative Law
was a prerequisite required by SIDA before
they would agree to finance Phase II. The
Project was carried by bridging finance
provided by SIDA until 20 March 1973.
This allowed time for the preparation and
passage of the prerequisite Cooperative
Law. The Plan of Operation for Phase II
was signed on 21 March 1973, following
the adoption of a cooperative law. During
the period of bridging finance, recruitment
of new and replacement staff was stopped
and the Project suffered a loss in development momentum, especially with regard to
cooperative development in the field.]

APPRAISAL OF PACCA'S EARLY YEARS

Even before PACCA was launched the exploratory
mission had observed that:

. . . although it should be possible to
assess the quantitative impact of the
program on agricultural production, trade,
prices, farm income, etc., its success or
failure should not be judged exclusively
in terms of immediate and measurable
results. The educational influence of
the program in changing traditional
attitudes hampering agricultural development, in creating an interest in new
techniques and in encouraging farmers
to participate actively in the running
of cooperatives and other organizations
concerned with the economic and social
welfare of the rural population must
not be underestimated . . . Second, the
program extends over several years and
while it is reasonable to expect some
tangible benefits at a fairly early stage
of operation, the effects of the various
projects will not be fully felt until
much later.[8]

The project, indeed, has been in existence for too
short a time to permit a thorough appraisal of its
effects. Moreover, the evidence available to the ICED

team on which to base even a limited appraisal is confined to the facts and judgments contained in the PACCA
progress reports and other relevant documentation and to
what could be learned additionally from interviews and
observations during a brief visit to Afghanistan in December 1971. Unfortunately, although the initial plan
stressed the need for careful and continuing evaluation,
there does not seem to have been the time or means thus
far to conduct systematic economic and social analyses
necessary to obtain reliable answers to a number of
critical questions about the project and to test some of
its basic assumptions.

Despite these limitations, however, several potentially useful observations can be made at this stage
about PACCA's early experience and, more important, about
several issues that will crucially influence its future
success. Some of these issues directly involve the
educational components of the PACCA program while others,
mainly economic in character, will indirectly affect the
productivity of the educational efforts.

The Record of Implementation

To translate a relatively complex development plan
into practical action, especially in a poor nation like
Afghanistan, presents formidable difficulties. Even the
best-conceived plan is bound to encounter delays and
unforeseen problems, and the PACCA Plan is no exception.
As noted earlier, there were delays in staffing and in
securing a legislative base for cooperatives; there were
also limitations on credit. Marketing problems, especially for grapes, were encountered sooner than expected.
The functional literacy component was a late addition to
PACCA and was still not well integrated with the rest of
the program by the end of 1971.

Still, the impressive fact remains that in less than
three years after its official launching PACCA was a going concern, accomplishing much of what it had set out
to do in its initial phase. By the end of 1971 the
central Training Institute and the Development Centers
in the two pilot areas had been established, were largely
staffed, and were rendering substantial services. A
good number of people had already received training and
were on the job. Extension workers and the Development
Centers were providing a variety of types of aid to
participating farmers, and the farmers, though limited
in number, had boosted their yields substantially. No
major hitches seemed to have developed within the program's own organizational structure or in its coordination with related organizations such as the Ministry of
Agriculture.

Thus the main question at the end of 1971 was not
whether the program had gotten off to a reasonably good
start but whether in the next phase it would be able to
cope successfully with certain critical problems that
were by then more visible than when the initial plan was
made. Specifically these problems concern 1) markets
and incentives; 2) the institutional structure, including
the question of cooperatives; 3) the viability of the
extension approach being used; 4) the recruitment and
training of extension personnel; and 5) future research
needs.

Even the best agricultural extension service can
have little prospect of success if farmers are financially unable to apply its recommended technologies, or
if market conditions and cost-price relationships are
unfavorable as seen by the farmers. PACCA could well
find itself confronted by such circumstances in its next
phase.

The architects of the PACCA plan had noted the price
and marketing problems that might arise but had made no
specific provisions for averting them, except for the
suggestion that attention should eventually be given to
increasing raisin production as a means of expanding the
export market for grapes. No solutions were prescribed,
however, for the processing bottlenecks and pricing
arrangements that adversely affected the incentives and
incomes of cotton and sugar beet farmers.

These were problems, of course, that could hardly be
dealt with adequately within the limited framework of a
program involving only two pilot areas. They were essentially national problems that could be handled effectively
only at the highest level of national agricultural, trade,
and fiscal policy. But unless these fundamental problems
were resolved, the more successful the PACCA program became in boosting production in the pilot areas, the
sooner it would run into serious trouble on the price and
marketing front.

The sponsors of PACCA are currently well aware of
the price and marketing difficulties that jeopardize the
success of the program and have taken steps to provide
an expert marketing advisor to the government. (No
marketing expert was originally provided for; the two
agricultural economists on the PACCA staff have apparently
been too fully absorbed in training duties to undertake
research and analysis on the practical economic problems
facing the program.)

A related but perhaps more easily solvable problem
concerns production credits for small farmers, which was
seen at the outset as one of the critical needs. Thus
far, it appears, farmer demand for credit in the pilot
areas has exceeded the supply available through the
Development Centers. Perhaps this shortage was only a
marginal constraint on production in the early period,

but if the marketing and price incentive problems should be satisfactorily solved in the future and if a much larger number of farmers consider it worthwhile to adopt the PACCA practices, credit could rapidly become a critical bottleneck to the whole program. Again the sponsors are aware of this difficulty and are endeavoring to overcome it.

The foregoing economic factors could prove to be the Achilles' heel of the PACCA program. Unless they are effectively dealt with, agricultural extension efforts and all the other efforts being invested in the program could prove to be of little avail. To handle them effectively will surely require more investment in research, not simply agricultural research but economic and other social science research. Much more needs to be learned not only about markets and price behavior but about the motivations and responses of Afghani farmers, and about how the economics of PACCA looks through their eyes.

The Institutional Framework and
the Extension Approach

From the outset the planners of PACCA sought to integrate the new program into the existing national structure in order to prevent it from becoming an isolated hothouse plant that later on would be difficult to incorporate into the regular structure and to spread to other areas. Moreover, it was felt that the PACCA training program could infuse new ideas, personnel, and practices into the national extension service, even while PACCA was still in a pilot stage. The further aim was to build a new infrastructure of cooperatives that would give farmers a larger voice in their own affairs and serve as a more efficient and equitable mechanism for securing their inputs and marketing their products.

Good progress seems to have been made toward integrating PACCA into the national extension service, but much less progress has been made toward developing a cooperative movement. However, it is still an open question whether Western-style cooperatives will find hospitable soil in Afghanistan. There are, to be sure, a few encouraging precedents--particularly the traditional arrangement by which farmers join together to construct and maintain a kurez and to share the resulting water supply (though the possibility of building on this indigenous base is not dealt with either in the PACCA plan or in the progress reports). The Development Centers in their surrogate role are gradually building a base for possible cooperatives in the future, but whether the centers will eventually evolve into authentic, self-governing cooperatives remains to be seen. At best it is

likely to require considerable time and, judging from the
experiences of many other developing countries where
attempts have been made to implant alien cooperative
models, the prospects for success should be estimated
with caution.

In any event, as desirable as cooperatives might be
in Afghanistan, it seems evident that they are not indispensable to the effective functioning of other aspects of
the PACCA plan. Afghani farmers have shown a willingness
to get help on credit and input supplies, technical advice, and marketing, whether these services come through
a cooperative or through some alternative type of farmer
association or other channel.

Understandably, the growth of PACCA's extension activities was slow in the first three years. But the question arises whether Afghanistan can afford the extension
approach now being used on a wider scale, and whether the
existing system of recruiting and training extension personnel will get the desired results.

The present extension method involves a highly intensive, individual-to-individual approach. During the
first two years in Koh-i-Daman and the first year in
Baghlan a ratio of five to seven participant farmers
per extension worker was maintained. In the plan of
operation a ratio of 70 farmers to one extension agent
during later years of the program was indicated. While
no ideal ratio can be prescribed, and a concentrated
effort at the initial stage is justifiable, the ratios
foreseen by the PACCA plan would appear to be of doubtful economic feasibility for much broader scale application in the long run.

It seems fair to ask why such high ratios of extension agents to farmers were considered necessary,
especially with farmers who are experienced in commercial
farming, who are already aware of the advantages of
fertilizer, and who, at least for the present, are not
required to make drastic changes in their customary
practices in order to achieve significant increases
in yields. A closer examination of farmer attitudes,
motivations, and incentives, and of possible alternative
approaches to meeting extension needs in a more efficient
way, would seem to be warranted.

Training and Research

Apart from the high cost of the extension methods
being employed, there is serious question about the
practicability of the present PACCA procedures for
recruiting and training extension personnel. The current
practice is to recruit future extension workers from the
existing agricultural high schools and supervisors from

the agricultural faculty of the university, and give them special preservice training in extension at the PACCA Training Institute followed eventually by occasional short-term refresher courses.

The programs of the agricultural high schools and university agricultural faculty are described as being highly theoretical, with little practical work, and offering no real preparation for extension work. What is more serious, however, is that their students are largely from urban areas and basically aspire to careers in the modern urban sector. Most have little familiarity with agriculture or rural life and little taste for a permanent career involving living and working in the countryside. These factors seem bound to create eventual problems of low staff morale and high turnover, resulting in exorbitant costs and reduced effectiveness.

It is doubtful whether a nation as poor as Afghanistan, where relatively few young people get beyond primary school and most of those who do come from urban backgrounds, can build an effective extension service on the basis of formal secondary and university-level education. While a substantial formal educational base (of the right kind) is essential for the higher-level officers of the service, it is doubtful that in such circumstances a large enough cadre of competent field-level workers can be supplied by urban-oriented secondary schools and universities.

In this respect, Afghanistan faces the same problem as many other developing nations. The solution may lie in the direction of recruiting bright and motivated rural young people who have achieved an effective level of literacy and maturity, and giving them a sustained period of training and initiation that combines appropriate theoretical knowledge with a large amount of practical apprenticeship experience, then following this later, once they have assumed full responsibilities, with frequent short-term refresher courses and career development studies. Such an approach would not be easy or cheap, but it is difficult to believe that its cost-effectiveness would not in the long run greatly exceed that of the relatively conventional approach presently being followed.

PACCA has not depended upon new "miracle" varieties to boost agricultural yields; production has been increased largely by more intensive and better balanced applications of fertilizer plus more extensive use of insecticides. Hence the need thus far for sophisticated research capabilities has not been great. The Ministry of Agriculture's research facilities in Baghlan have been available to PACCA as needed, but the proposed new research facility for Koh-i-Daman has not yet been established.

In the future, however, a much stronger and more dynamic agricultural research process may be needed in

Afghanistan if agricultural productivity is to keep
rising. The existing technologies now being propagated
through the extension service can carry production to a
new and significantly higher level (provided incentives
and input supplies are adequate), but once its potentialities are exhausted the curve will flatten. To keep
agriculture growing thereafter will require steady in-
fusions of new research findings through the extension
services.

Even before then, substantial research capabilities
will be needed to adapt present technologies to the special conditions of various areas and to answer the growing number of questions that farmers will have as agriculture quickens its pace. Changes in market conditions,
both domestically and internationally, are likely to make
it desirable for many farmers to shift into new crops and
to move toward mixed farming, and this will further increase the need for fresh research.

The same factors that are likely to compound the
requirements for research will also compound the tasks
of the extension system, whatever form it takes. The
relatively simple technical "messages" now being conveyed through PACCA's extension channels will not long
suffice if Afghanistan's farmers really get on the move.
Given a favorable combination of circumstances, this can
sometimes happen with surprising speed, as happened with
many of India's wheat and rice farmers in the late 1960s
as a consequence of research breakthroughs. Unless the
extension system is equipped to meet the challenge, it
can become a serious bottleneck to progress. These are
the possible longer-term needs that must be kept in view
as PACCA moves toward helping Afghanistan build viable
and efficient rural extension services. Viewed in this
longer-range perspective, it seems very doubtful that the
present approach to extension will suffice.

Functional Literacy

Another vital long-term requirement is to spread
literacy, in its broadest meaning, throughout the rural
areas of Afghanistan. There appears to be a great deal
of interest in and support for literacy among the farmers
as the high rate of completion in the first courses indicate. Evaluation of the level of achievement of those
who so far completed the courses was, however, not
available.

Experts attached to the literacy program in PACCA
emphasize the difficulties of designing and implementing
on a large scale a truly functional literacy program.
They have confidence that with the development of new
reading materials well adapted to local agriculture and
to other topics of genuine interest to rural people, and

with the establishment of closer working relations with
the extension and cooperative staff of the program,
literacy teaching can be made more functional. But
they also point out that literacy is not achieved by a
one-time course. It is a process that once started must
be continued, and for this there must be a steady flow
of new reading materials that are relevant to the interests and lives of new literates.

The original targets have been trimmed toward more
realistic levels, but it still appears that an excessively
wide audience coverage is being sought at too fast a pace
for a program that is thinly staffed and is supposed to
be experimental in nature. The inclusion of as many
people as possible in the early courses, without regard
to their motivations, practical needs, potential uses
of literacy, and the continuous availability of relevant
reading materials is an invitation to poor quality and
low effectiveness.

Though it would be premature to try to derive definitive conclusions from the limited experience in PACCA
there is strong reason to suppose that concentrating
functional literacy efforts on selected people who have
a strong need for literacy and a strong motivation to
attain it--such as cooperative leaders, managers of
marketing operations, and others who must be able to
read, write, and keep accounts to play their development
roles effectively--would be a more effective way to lay
the foundations for a wider functional literacy movement
over time.

Costs and Benefits

It is much too soon to apply any systematic cost-
benefit tests to the PACCA program, even if adequate
data were available for the purpose. PACCA is still in
the early developmental stage when starting costs are
high and when the main benefits still lie at a considerable distance. But it is not too early to begin to look
critically at costs and benefits and establish benchmarks
and methods that will facilitate such evaluations later
on. This does not appear to have been done as yet.

It should be possible, for instance, to create some
simple costing models to project the resource requirements for the program as it expands, allowing for various
alternative assumptions and possible program modifications. This would be particularly important to do with
respect to training and operating costs of the extension
service. Unfortunately, however, neither the data nor
the time available to the ICED team permitted such an
exercise. It would be extremely useful to examine the
economics of farm operation from an individual farm
household point of view, which would indicate the

profitability of different inputs. It would also be
desirable to identify a series of indicators of benefits,
both economic and noneconomic, from which it would be
feasible to collect at least rough evidence in the future
on which to base later appraisals of social and individual
benefits.

So far as individual farmers are concerned, their
benefit-cost ratio is not merely a long-term question
but a matter of immediate and vital concern. Small and
poor farmers can ill afford to make a serious miscalcu-
lation of this ratio even for a single crop season. By
the same token, unless many farmers in the years immediately ahead envisage a quite favorable benefit-cost
ratio through adoption of PACCA's recommended practices,
the program will not succeed in its broader and longer-
term objectives.

This is why it is so important to keep close tabs on
the costs and receipts of a cross-section sample of
farmers in the pilot areas. As far as the ICED team
could ascertain, however, such data are not yet being
collected.

Lessons of the PACCA Experience

Even at this early stage, PACCA's experience suggests a number of important lessons for other developing
countries.

First, PACCA's achievements, although with a small
number of farmers, in increasing yields, providing
credit and inputs, training extension staff, offering
technical assistance to farmers, and establishing a
local institutional structure for coordinated agricultural services indicate the desirability and feasibility
of moving from a piecemeal approach to a broader and
more integrated approach to agricultural development.
Whatever shortcomings there may be in the extension
approach used by PACCA, it does have the decided merit
of tying the extension function intimately to the other
essential farmer support services involving, for example,
credit and input supplies, marketing and research. PACCA
also demonstrates the importance of creating a local
institutional base, in this case a development center,
which can link the various ingredients of agricultural
development together into a consistent set of policies
and actions at the local level.

Second, the PACCA experience demonstrates that it
is not enough for a pilot program to be well integrated
internally; the planning and operation of such a scheme
must also take careful account of factors on the larger
national and even international scene that are bound to
have a vital influence upon its success or failure.
Above all it is important to consider a) the market

behavior and prospects for the particular agricultural commodities involved; b) the implications for the project of prevailing national policies and priorities with regard to agricultural development, prices, subsidies, imports and exports; and c) the compatibility--short-run and long-run--of the project's staffing requirements and training provisions to the existing educational establishment and government personnel policies.

Third, more specifically with respect to staff recruitment and training, PACCA's experience hints at problems that may occur in all poor, agrarian nations--with grossly underdeveloped educational systems--that rely on urban-oriented students and urban-oriented formal educational institutions to provide the basic staff needed for rendering essential rural development services. Serious consideration should be given to alternative recruitment and training arrangements that enlist a larger number of able and motivated rural young people into the critically important enterprise of rural transformation.

Fourth, the PACCA program sets a good example in its effort to relate a pilot program closely to the national structure of agricultural and rural services, so as to avoid becoming isolated from the national system (whatever its deficiencies may be) while at the same time perhaps contributing to the improvement of it.

Finally, the PACCA experience underscores once again the absolute importance of building adequate evaluation measures and processes into any major pilot program, both to monitor and improve its performance in the short run and to steadily test its feasibility for the long run. Periodic progress reports and visits by outside observers are helpful, but they are no substitutes for well-aimed operational research and analysis as an integral and continuous activity within the program.

NOTES

1. Food and Agriculture Organization (FAO), Report of the Agricultural Credit Mission to Afghanistan (Rome, 1967), pp. 8-9.

2. A French consulting firm, Société Grenobloise d'Études et d'Applications Hydraliques (Sogreah), made a survey in 1966 of the Kunduz river basin where one of the project districts (Baghlan) was located. The survey reported that farmers' indebtedness in the area had been steadily increasing over the past few years and more than half the farmers were in debt at any given moment.

3. FAO, Plan of Operation, Program on Agricultural Credit and Related Services through Cooperatives in Afghanistan (Rome, November 1967), p. 3.

4. Gote V. Gronevik, Farm Management, Marketing, Cooperation and Credit Work in the Baghlan Region (Kabul: Program of Agricultural Credit and Cooperation in Afghanistan [PACCA], 1971).

    5. PACCA, Semi-Annual Progress Report, no. 6 (Kabul, Septem-
ber 1971), p. 5.
    6. _____, Semi-Annual Progress Report, no. 4 (Kabul, Septem-
ber 1970).
    7. FAO, "Plan of Operation, Program on Agricultural Credit and
Related Services through Cooperatives in Afghanistan," mimeographed
draft (Rome, March 1972).
    8. _____, Report of the Agricultural Credit Mission to
Afghanistan, op. cit., p. 55.

COLOMBIA: A MOBILE
SKILL TRAINING PROGRAM
FOR RURAL AREAS
Stephan F. Brumberg

ICED was interested in examining Promoción Profesional Popular-Rural (PPP-R), a special rural program of Colombia's National Apprenticeship Service (SENA), in large part because the PPP-R represents an alternative approach to meeting some important rural skill needs --a mobile approach that brings training opportunities directly to rural people where they live.

Field work for the study was done in late 1971. The study team consisted of, Dr. Stephan F. Brumberg, a member of ICED staff; Dr. Tomás Nieto Arteta, former Director of Agricultural Extension in the Colombian Ministry of Agriculture; Rafael Diaz, agricultural engineer; Humberto Ruiz, sociologist; Jeffrey Puryear, a University of Chicago graduate student doing research in Colombia at the time; and Paul Martin, another ICED staff member. Dr. José Castañón-Pasquel, an FAO agricultural extension expert in Colombia, served as an advisor to the team. Considerable time was spent by the team at SENA's headquarters in Bogotá in discussions with officials and in examining documents and records. The team also visited several selected rural districts and systematically interviewed former trainees, local leaders, and SENA instructors. At the conclusion of the field trips, the team held a seminar in Bogotá at which there was a full and candid exchange of views between SENA officials and team members on the team's findings and conclusions, on which there proved to be a high measure of agreement.

INTRODUCTION

Colombia's National Apprenticeship Service (Servicio Nacional de Aprendizaje, SENA), founded in 1957, is charged with the task of training the skilled manpower needed for an expanding and modernizing economy.

SENA's initial orientation was primarily urban and industrial. In the mid-sixties, however, SENA broadened its training activities in the rural-agricultural sector.

In 1967 it began a program called Promocion Profesional
Popular-Rural (PPP-R), which provides short-term low-cost
skill training to farmers, farm laborers, rural artisans,
and small entrepreneurs within their own communities.
Training is offered at "mobile units" which, in theory,
can deliver a variety of prestructured training courses
to any area in rural Colombia. By 1970 more than 115,500
of SENA's 280,500 trainees (41.2 percent) were enrolled in
agricultural courses and an additional 10,000 (3.6 percent)
were enrolled in courses for rural nonagricultural workers.

SENA training programs range from three-year formal
apprenticeship programs to 20-hour courses for migrant
agricultural workers. Most trainees, especially in rural-
agricultural programs, complete their instruction in less
than one year.

About half of Colombia's total population of 20
million live in rural areas, and most of the rural population are poor. In large part due to its mountainous terrain, land communications are difficult in Colombia, and
many campesinos are physically isolated from urban centers.
Even with difficult living conditions in the mountains,
most of Colombia's population lives at higher elevations
and especially along the major mountain chains. This is
so even though there exists considerable underdeveloped,
sparsely populated plains land in the south of the country
(the llanos).

As shown in Table 11.1, of 1,370,000 farm families,
12.8 percent hold no land and 55.8 percent work on

TABLE 11.1

Distribution of Colombian Farm Families
Shown by Class of Farm, 1960

| | Families | |
Class of Farm	#(000)	%
Large multifamily farms	15	1.1
Multifamily farms	54	3.9
Family farms	361	26.4
Subfamily farms	765	55.8
Landless	175	12.8
TOTAL	1,370	100.0

NOTE: "Large multifamily farms" can employ 12 or more persons
at prevailing levels of technology; multifamily, 4 persons; family,
2 persons; and subfamily, less than 2 persons.

Source: International Labour Office, Towards Full Employment:
A Programme for Colombia (Geneva, 1970), p. 67.

subfamily farms (farms that cannot productively employ
two persons). In 1960 approximately 45 percent of the
cultivated and pasture lands were held by 1.2 percent
of the people, and 65 percent of the rural population
(58 percent farmers or sharecroppers and 7 percent
landless) were on 5.5 percent of the land.[1] A full
range of agricultural products is produced in the
country, including cotton as well as staple crop pro-
duction--wheat, maize, potatoes, and yams. The leading
cash crop is coffee, which accounts for approximately
70 percent of export earnings.

Many members of farm families living on subfamily
farms, as well as the landless, find full-time employment on large estates or seasonal employment as
migrant laborers in the coffee, cotton, and rice
harvests. Others try to supplement their meager
farm income by off-season migration to towns and
cities in search of unskilled jobs.

In large part due to low rural incomes and population pressures on the land, there has been considerable
migration to cities. The country's major cities are
growing rapidly (6 to 7 percent a year) with concomitant high unemployment, poor housing for many, and
overburdened public services. One of the hopes for
the PPP-R program is that it will help in the effort
to slow down the rural-to-urban migration.

Educational development in rural Colombia lags
far behind urban areas. The average length of schooling of the rural population in 1964 was only 1.7
years compared to 5.1 years for urban dwellers.[2] In
part, this is due to selective migration. The better-
educated rural inhabitants are more likely to migrate
to cities than those with little or no education.
But the low average level of schooling also reflects
the condition of rural schools. Fifty-eight percent
of all primary students were enrolled in rural schools
in 1964, but few schools provided a full five-year
primary course: 64 percent provided only one or two
years of schooling under poorly trained and often
unqualified teachers. Only 3 percent of those who
enter rural primary schools complete the five-year
course compared to 46 percent of urban children.[3]

Further primary and secondary education are virtually
nonexistent in rural areas. Most children must commute
or move to towns if they wish to continue their education beyond the first few years of primary school.

The level of reported illiteracy (of those over
15) in rural areas in the 1964 census was 41.3 percent;[4] in urban areas the illiteracy rate was 15
percent.

AN OVERVIEW OF SENA

Structure and Scope

SENA was established by government decree in 1957 to provide skill training for employed adults and apprenticeship training for adolescents (aged 14-20). Administratively, it is part of the Ministry of Labor but it enjoys considerable autonomy, with its director appointed directly by the President of the Republic. SENA's governing council has representatives from the Ministries of Education and Labor, the National Planning Office, the Catholic Church, and management and labor organizations. It is now responsible for the major part of manpower training in all sectors of the economy, with an enrollment of 280,500 young people and adults in a wide range of courses.

Much of SENA's autonomy, as well as its ability to expand its programs rapidly, derives from the nature of its financing which is largely based on a payroll tax. In 1971, anticipated SENA income (and expenditures) was expected to reach 500 million pesos--equivalent to 1/4 of the Ministry of Education's budget in the same year.

Most of the training offered by SENA in its early years was directed to the industrial, commercial, and services sectors. Since 1967, agricultural training has become an important element in SENA's activities. SENA has now taken on the responsibility for providing skill training to the unemployed. In 1970 the government authorized SENA to devote 10 percent of its budget for such courses. Some of SENA's unemployed trainees are in PPP-R courses and many others are in the PPP-urban courses (devoted to basic industrial commercial/service skill training in short-term courses, usually offered in temporary locations in urban centers).

SENA now trains more skilled workers than does the formal vocational school system. SENA had a total of 280,500 trainees enrolled in 1970 compared to 126,700 enrolled in 1968 in vocational programs (excluding teacher training) in formal schools.[5] However, SENA courses normally last for less than a year (up to three years for apprentices, who make up 7.3 percent of total enrollment), while formal vocational secondary school courses may last up to six years.

In addition to its new role in training the unemployed, SENA now offers technical assistance to small industries for upgrading the skills of their staffs, and offers semiprofessional training for staff of larger businesses.

Ties to Rural Development Agencies

SENA provides training services for many of the public and private agencies in Colombia that are working to promote rural development.

SENA is working with the Coffee Growers Federation (Federación de Cafeteros) to improve farm practices in coffee growing zones as well as in a program to help these farmers diversify their farm businesses. It has also worked with the Cotton Growers Association (Federación de Algodoneres) in the training of migrant workers. This program is described more fully below.

SENA also works with INCORA (Instituto Colombiano para Reforma Agraria), the national land reform agency, in training the agency's own staff and by seconding SENA instructors to teach courses organized by INCORA for recipients of redistributed land (aparceros).

SENA has an agreement with the Agricultural Bank (Caja Agraria) to promote a program called "Operación Telar," designed to upgrade the skills of workers in the woolen handicrafts industry. SENA, along with the Bank, INCORA, and the armed forces, also provides training in rural skills for military personnel about to leave the service.

The Colombian Agricultural Institute (Instituto Colombiano Agropecuario--ICA), the government agency responsible for agricultural research and extension, and SENA are seeking to improve coordination of their field activities. At present, official collaboration is limited to minor programs such as promoting the raising of improved strains of sheep.

The Applied Integrated Nutrition Program (Programa Integrado de Nutrición Aplicada) is an interministerial effort (Labor, Agriculture, and Health) designed to improve the nutritional practices of rural inhabitants. SENA is a party to this convention, whose activities include educational programs and the distribution of foodstuffs. The PPP-R has made use of the food program as an incentive to participation in its courses in some communities, especially those in more remote areas.

SENA is working with the Artisans of Colombia (Artesanias de Colombia), a government-run program to promote traditional handicrafts production (much of it rural-based) and to strengthen the marketing of products.

The Popular Cultural Action (Acción Cultural Popular --ACPO), a private nonprofit educational institution, provides basic education to rural Colombians by means of mass communication (radio and newspaper) coordinated with local (mainly volunteer) personnel.[6] SENA has made its training materials available to ACPO, which in turn offers the use of its national radio network to SENA to promote its training activities among the rural audience.

Although SENA has no formal relations with the
school system, the Ministry of Education is represented
on SENA's governing board so that some interchange between these two educational agencies can be expected.

Organization and Facilities

SENA is organized into three operational divisions:
Agricultural, Industrial, and Commercial/Services. Administratively, the PPP-R is located within the Agricultural
Division and is headed by a coordinator in the director's
office.

SENA has constructed substantial training facilities,
especially for its regular training programs in urban
areas. But it also uses outside and temporary facilities,
especially in the PPP-R program. (See Table 11.2.)
Approximately 63 percent of SENA students receive training outside of fixed SENA training centers. SENA operates
eleven agricultural training centers serving all sections
of the country. These centers offer formal apprenticeship
training in rural occupations as well as short courses at
the skilled and semiskilled level. All these centers have
boarding facilities for the trainees in addition to classroom workshops and demonstration fields.

The PPP-R program itself is decentralized to 14
regional offices which cover all sections of the country.
PPP-R offices are usually housed at a SENA training center, if such a center is within one of the 14 PPP-R
regions. However, PPP-R instruction is not offered at
these centers but in temporary facilities in rural
communities.

SENA's Training Programs

SENA offers a wide variety of vocational and some
general courses to meet the needs of clienteles ranging
from unskilled adolescents and adults to skilled workers,
technicians, and professionals responsible for personnel
training. Courses in 651 subject-matter fields were
offered in 1970. (A full training in a given occupation,
however, may include several courses.)

A breakdown of the major forms of training in SENA's
total program is shown in Table 11.3.

The largest group of trainees are enrolled in
courses offering "complementary" instruction. This form
of training is designed to complement and upgrade knowledge and skills already possessed by (mostly employed)
workers. The theory behind complementary training is
that with a relatively short training course a worker

TABLE 11.2

SENA Enrollments, Courses and Classes, Instructional and Student Hours, 1970
Shown by Location of Training Program

	Students Enrolled #	%	Courses #	%	Classes into which courses are divided #	%	Instructional Hours #	%	Student Hours #	%
PPP-R program Temporary locations in rural communities	104,948	37.4	2,622	29.7	3,937	32.0	223,490	10.8	4,618,944	13.5
PPP-U program Temporary locations in urban areas	18,749	6.7	516	5.8	755	6.1	92,757	4.5	1,870,708	5.5
Regular training programs In SENA centers	102,781	36.6	3,566	40.5	5,056	41.1	1,501,836	72.5	23,540,155	69.0
Outside SENA centers	33,456	11.9	1,222	13.9	1,537	12.5	181,157	8.8	2,966,757	8.7
Advisory services to firms	14,766	5.3	642	7.3	734	5.9	45,971	2.2	733,551	2.1
Internal training of SENA staff. Usually in SENA installations	1,103	0.4	58	0.7	59	0.5	2,163	0.1	33,653	0.1
Other programs (various locations)	4,718	1.7	189	2.1	233	1.9	23,800	1.1	376,706	1.1
TOTAL	280,521	100.0	8,815	100.0	12,311	100.0	2,071,174	100.0	34,140,474	100.0

Source: SENA, Análisis Cuantitativo de la Labor de Formación Profesional en el Año 1970, doc. no. 33-48 (Bogotá, June 1970).

TABLE 11.3

SENA Vocational Training Programs: Forms of Training, Objectives, Target Groups, and Enrollment 1970

Form of Training	Target Group	Objective	Average hrs/ student	Number enrolled #	Percentage of total enrolled %
1. Apprenticeship	Adolescents 14-20 years	Train skilled workers	695.0[a]	20,443	7.3
2. Elementary training ("Habilitacion")	Working adolescents or adults who need preparation in a semi-skilled occupation	Train semiskilled workers	117.4	53,055	18.9
3. Complementary training ("Complementacion")	Adult semiskilled workers or supervisors who are insufficiently prepared for their jobs	Correct skill deficiencies in workers at the semiskilled, skilled and supervisory level	78.9	127,598	45.5
4. Upgrading	Semiskilled, skilled and highly skilled workers	Train workers for promotion to higher level job, including supervisory positions	329.6	2,742	1.0
5. Specialized training	Skilled or highly skilled workers, technicians	Train specialized workers	120.8	682	0.2
6. Accelerated training	Adults without occupational skills	Train semiskilled workers	20.3[b]	47,077	16.7

Table 11.3 continued

7.	Technical cooperation (offered to firms for the training of their own personnel)	Professionals, technicians, supervisors or highly skilled workers who are responsible for personnel training within the firm	Promote and improve training within firms	37.6	280	0.1
8.	Prevocational training ("Nivelacion Previa")	Workers whose basic education is deficient	Remedial education to prepare workers to take skill training within firms	107.3	6,716	2.4
9.	Information and promotion	All employees and employers	Promote interest in training	27.2	20,916	7.5
10.	Instructor training	Potential SENA instructors	Preparation of instructional staff	384.0	1,018	0.4
	TOTAL			121.7	280,527	100.0

a. Instructional hours for one year. Does not include time on the job (six months out of the year). The total program may last up to three years and total 1,750 hours of instruction off-the-job.

b. In 1970 migrant worker training (for cotton harvesting) was classified as accelerated training and made up nearly all enrollments in this training mode. The average number of hours of instruction for migrant workers was 19.7.

Sources: SENA, Campo de Accion y Modos de Formacion (Bogotá, n.d.) and Analisís Cuantitativo de la Labor de Formación Profesional en el Año 1970, doc. no. 33-408 (Bogotá, June 1970).

will be able to improve his skills and productivity in an occupation in which he already has had work experience. Most PPP-R agricultural courses are of this type.

The second most common type of instruction is "elementary" training to provide basic skills for semi-skilled occupations to adolescents and adults working in unskilled jobs. Unemployed workers may also be expected to take elementary courses. Several PPP-R courses are classified as "elementary," primarily those that treat industrial (artisanal) and commercial occupations.

Accelerated training for the development of basic skills is another important instructional mode, which is directed primarily to adults and is more concentrated (and of shorter duration) than elementary training. In 1970, however, nearly all trainees enrolled in accelerated training courses took part in very short courses for migrant cotton harvesters; therefore, though training was intensive it was not utilized for a new semiskilled occupation. Since the migrant workers' program is included within the PPP-R, nearly all those enrolled in accelerated training courses were also classified as part of the PPP-R.

Apprenticeship training in industry, services, and agriculture sectors is also offered by SENA. This is the longest and most costly form of training, with apprentices alternately spending six months at a SENA training center and six months in a firm.

In addition to skill training in specific occupations, SENA also offers more general courses, such as agricultural credit, work safety, and human relations. In terms of total enrollments, these types of courses are not very significant. The PPP-R program offers several general courses.

Enrollments

In 1970, 24.6 percent of the total enrollment (280,500) were in the industrial sector, 34.2 percent in commercial/services and 41.2 percent in agriculture.

In tabulating enrollments, PPP-R students are classified by appropriate economic sector, and not all are within the Agricultural Division. Approximately 90 percent of PPP-R trainees, however, were classified in the Agricultural Division, which represented about 82 percent of that sector's enrollment in 1970 (115,674 trainees). Less than 3 percent of agricultural enrollments are accounted for by apprentices (3,269) who receive long-term training (two to three years) in such fields as rural mechanics, tractor operation and repairs, field crops, cattle raising, and commercial fishing.

Most of the remaining agricultural trainees receive instruction at one of the eleven SENA agricultural centers throughout the country in courses generally lasting from three to six months. Apprentices also spend half their time at these centers where they receive both practical and theoretical instruction.

The PPP-R is the largest program (in terms of total enrollments): in 1970, it accounted for 37.4 percent of all students enrolled in SENA. This figure, however, must be read with caution. First, it includes nearly 47,000 migrant workers enrolled in a special course in cotton picking. The course was only 20 hours, with nearly 40 workers per class. This special program alone accounts for 16.7 percent of total SENA enrollments and 44.6 percent of PPP-R enrollments.

Second, enrollment figures for the PPP-R program are compiled by the program's instructors in the field, and no checks are made by SENA to verify these figures. This may result in some error in final program totals.

Even though the PPP-R accounts for well over a third of SENA's enrollments, it represents only 10.8 percent of instructional hours and 13.5 percent of student hours. PPP-R courses are shorter than the average SENA course (PPP-R courses average 63.6 hours of instruction per student exclusive of those for migrants, 44.0 hours including migrants; SENA courses average 121.7 hours). Also the average PPP-R class is generally larger than SENA's (26.7 per PPP-R class compared with 22.8, SENA).[7]

The migrant workers program began in 1970, was repeated in 1971, and is expected to continue as a regular PPP-R activity. This program has greatly increased the number of student hours in the PPP-R program (see Table 11.4). An hour of instruction in the migrant program

TABLE 11.4

Instructional Hours and Student Hours in the PPP-R
1970

	Instructional Hours		Student Hours	
	#	%	#	%
PPP-R (Exclusive of migrants)	199,825	89.4	3,696,600	80.0
Migrant workers	23,665	10.6	922,344	20.0
TOTAL	223,490	100.0	4,618,944	100.0

Source: SENA, *Analisís Cuantitativo de la Labor de Formación Profesional en el Año 1970*, doc. no. 33-048 (Bogotá, June 1970).

yields more than twice the number of student hours[8] than
in other PPP-R courses because 1) migrant classes are
nearly twice the size of other PPP-R classes, 2) dropout
rate for migrant courses is considered nil, while it is
12.5 percent in other PPP-R courses, and 3) it is assumed
that there are no absences in the migrant courses, while
absences are recorded in other PPP-R courses.

Including migrant workers, PPP-R graduates in 1970
represented 84.6 percent of agricultural sector graduates
and nearly 44 percent of all SENA graduates (Table 11.5).

TABLE 11.5

Graduates of PPP-R and Other SENA Training Programs, 1970
Shown by Economic Sector

| | TOTAL | | ECONOMIC SECTOR | | | | | |
| | | | Agricultural | | Industrial | | Commercial & Services | |
	#	%	#	%	#	%	#	%
PPP-R	98,483	43.9	88,509*	84.6	2,901	5.9	7,073	10.0
Other	126,022	56.1	16,097	15.4	45,926	94.1	63,999	90.0
TOTAL	224,505	100.0	104,606	100.0	48,827	100.0	71,072	100.0

*Includes 46,846 in migrant cotton workers program or 20.9%
of all graduates and 52.9% of PPP-R agricultural graduates.

Source: SENA, Analisís Cuantitativo de la Labor de Formación
Profesional en el Año, doc. no. 33-048 (Bogotá, June 1970).

But while the PPP-R is now SENA's largest program, it is
of relatively minor importance financially. It accounts
for an estimated 7.0 percent of total expenditures in
1971.

THE PPP-R: AN EDUCATIONAL DELIVERY SYSTEM

The PPP-R program, offering basic skill training to
Colombia's rural population, has shown impressive growth:
by its third year (1969) the PPP-R enrolled over 52,000
trainees. This figure more than doubled in 1970, and in
1971 it was expected to expand by an additional 60 percent.

Objectives and Clientele

As officially described, the PPP-R "seeks to bring the benefits of vocational training to the most distant regions of the country, improving the skills of workers in the different jobs in the industrial, commercial, and agricultural sectors, by means of mobile centers and in accordance with the specific necessities of each region." The program's stated objectives are:

1. to provide underemployed and unemployed persons with the skills required for improving their productive capacity, whatever their educational level, and

2. to train semiskilled workers in order to facilitate access to employment and consequently their integration into the processes of production and consumption.[9]

PPP-R courses are directed to almost the entire rural population, adults and adolescents, men and women, agricultural and nonagricultural workers. The agricultural workers enrolled include those with land (owners, share-croppers and aparceros--those who recently received land in the land redistribution program), and without (those employed on large estates and migrants), but not large landholders. There are no educational requirements for entry into courses; literate and illiterate follow the same program of training.

Many PPP-R courses enroll both men and women, especially in artisanal and commercial courses and in agricultural courses dealing with family gardens and the raising of certain kinds of livestock (rabbits, sheep, goats, chickens) and beekeeping. In addition other courses in more traditional home economics subjects are now being offered to women.[10] Women account for 27.7 percent of SENA's overall enrollment. Unfortunately data for economic sectors and the PPP-R program are not recorded by sex. In the ICED study's sample of 145 PPP-R participants, 23 percent were women, which is close to the overall proportion of women in SENA courses.

Methods, Materials, and Content

The PPP-R program uses "mobile units" to bring training to rural communities. A unit may be a single instructor, or an instructor with a fully equipped instructional vehicle, plus a prefabricated classroom-living unit. In most cases, an instructor has access to a truck or jeep and brings to the teaching site instructional materials, including tools and audiovisual equipment and, if necessary, an electric generator. In most communities, an attempt is made to use existing facilities as classrooms, although there has been some experimentation with prefabricated classroom buildings which can be rapidly assembled at the teaching site.

Nine of the fourteen instructors interviewed by the ICED study team had their own vehicles--usually a truck equipped with necessary audiovisual equipment. None made use of prefabricated classroom units.

As the PPP-R courses are designed either to improve a rural worker's ability to perform in his present job (as in the case of most farmers) or to teach him new skills, instruction is practical rather than theoretical and there is little classroom work. Instructors rely heavily on demonstrations and trainees are expected to duplicate and practice the lesson. Wherever possible instructors make use of locally available tools and equipment so that what is learned can be practised by trainees after finishing the course.

Instructors work from detailed training syllabuses prepared by the SENA Documentation Center and use visual materials also provided by the center. It is up to the individual instructor to alter the content to fit particular local conditions. By and large, trainees do not receive printed instructional materials though they may receive promotional literature. According to SENA officials the production of such materials is not yet warranted because of the high rate of rural illiteracy, the high cost of producing didactic materials for use directly by students, and the need to alter content to suit the vast variety of local conditions.

The course offerings in the PPP-R program are extremely varied. Most can be classified under the following headings:

> Agriculture (crop production)
> Livestock
> Poultry, rabbits, bees (minor
>   farm industries)
> Tractor operation and maintenance
> Agricultural machinery repair
> Rural mechanics
> Rural construction
> Cooperatives (administration)
> Rural administration
> Handicrafts
> First aid and practical nursing
> Breadmaking/baking
> Human relations

Most courses are in the categories of agriculture, livestock, minor farm industries, and handicrafts.

Each course is viewed as a self-contained unit which includes only as much learning material as can be conveniently taught in the time allotted. A course may last from 40 to 120 hours; the average course length in 1970 (excluding migrant courses) was about 63 hours. Most courses last less than a month and none exceeds three months. Classes last from 2 to 6 hours a day.

The tendency of late has been to shorten rather than lengthen courses, according to SENA, because of the difficulty in maintaining interest and commitment on the part of trainees in courses lasting more than a month. In order to shorten courses, subject matter has been divided into smaller units. For example, a single course on chicken raising has been divided into three: hatching, rearing, laying. The problem is that this three-unit sequence may not be offered in the same village to the same trainees. SENA argues, however, that each individual unit in the sequence has sufficient value to justify its being offered separately.

PPP-R courses are provided without charge and are offered at a time of the year and hours of the day considered most convenient to local inhabitants. Most class sessions are held during daylight hours since instruction relies heavily on field demonstration.

Planning of Courses

SENA has recognized the need to base its planning for the PPP-R program on field investigations aimed at determining rural manpower needs and defining the rural milieu within which training is offered.[11] As envisaged by SENA, such studies should take into account:

1. the training needs of a given region, quantitatively and substantively
2. existing programs of agricultural development in a region, such as those undertaken by INCORA, ICA (agricultural extension) and supervised credit programs (such as those of the Caja Agraria), and the training needs generated by these activities
3. programs within a region designed to diversify agricultural production or bring new land under cultivation
4. the possibility of coordination of the PPP-R program with other groups working in agricultural development
5. Possibilities for exploiting nonfarm rural employment in artisanal trades

The location, quantity, and type of training needed could be determined in large part from the above.

In addition to determining training needs, the studies to be conducted should also determine the principal activities of a given region and the times of the year most favorable for training. The PPP-R must also adapt its program to the socioeconomic characteristics of each community, taking into account patterns of land tenure, occupational structure, and ecological conditions.

In large part due to the difficulties of conducting research in rural Colombia, little work has been done by SENA or other agencies in defining rural manpower needs. Nor has the rural context been adequately defined. Planning of courses in terms of numbers and types of training, therefore, must be undertaken in the absence of research data.

Production targets for the PPP-R program (numbers of students to be enrolled, courses to be offered) are set at the national level in conjunction with the determination of SENA's overall targets, its total budget, and the availability of trained instructional staff. It appears that the national production target for the PPP-R is distributed among the 14 PPP-R regions roughly in proportion to the size of the population covered by each region. The regional supervisor then distributes courses throughout his region based on his general assessment of the training needs of each community. He arrives at such an assessment through interviews with local leaders, parish priests, and local representatives of development agencies.

SENA has recognized the limitations of its present planning procedures, and the Division of Human Resources is now conducting an evaluative study of the PPP-R which may shed much needed light on the planning of rural manpower training. In a recent publication it was made clear that the PPP-R must seek to improve the fit between its courses and the particular characteristics of a given community.[12]

In some sections of the country the SENA PPP-R program has collaborated with other development agencies such as INCORA and the agricultural extension service of ICA. In many areas, however, there is either lack of cooperation or the PPP-R is the only agency at work in the community. In such cases the instructor must arrive several days before a course is scheduled to begin and attempt to generate interest and enroll the quota of 20 students. It is sometimes impossible to enroll a sufficient number of participants or it may be found that the intended course is, in fact, inappropriate for the community. But since the instructor's teaching manual and equipment are for the intended course, he may find it impossible to switch to a more suitable subject.

In some sections of the country where there are large estates, a PPP-R course may be given to an estate's farm laborers directly on the estate grounds. Such courses are offered on the request of the owner or manager. In other sections of the country where there is considerable land reform activity, INCORA organizes new land recipients into classes and requests that SENA provide courses through its PPP-R program. In such cases course selection is largely in the hands of INCORA.

Once a course is completed the PPP-R instructor leaves the community, perhaps to return at a later date to offer another course which may or may not be related to the earlier course.

Personnel

More than 300 full-time instructors are assigned to the PPP-R program. Also, instructors from the 11 SENA agricultural training centers are sometimes seconded to the PPP-R in order to teach one or more courses.

In principle instructors are required to have a secondary technical diploma or teacher's certificate in agriculture, with one year of specialization and two years of practical experience. In practice some instructors have less than the full academic preparation. All instructors take a three- to six-month course at SENA's National Training Center. In addition to pedagogical instruction and technical specialization, the course focuses on the special role of PPP-R instructors as agents of social change in isolated rural communities. It is the PPP-R instructor, acting on his own initiative, who is expected to adjust a national normative curriculum to the specific needs of a community. Such a task involves social understanding and awareness as much as technical expertise.

The 14 instructors who were interviewed by the ICED study team had all received the SENA instructors' course. None had more years of education than required by SENA for its instructors and some had general secondary school (bachiller) rather than agricultural/technical secondary education. All claimed that job security was good but that there was a lack of promotional opportunity within the PPP-R program. They received an annual salary of approximately US$1,775.

Special Activities of the PPP-R:
Migrant Workers Program

The training program for migrant cotton-pickers is
a good example of the PPP-R program's ability to rapidly
meet a need for training, once it has been clearly identified. In 1969, after difficulties in the 1968-1969 cotton
harvest, the national government through the Ministry of
Labor created a National Committee on Rural Migrant
Workers. The committee was to organize, channel, and
mobilize migrant cotton-pickers required for the year's
harvest. SENA (through its PPP-R program) presented a
plan to this committee for the accelerated training of
50,000 migrant workers. The plan encompassed training
not only in basic techniques of cotton-picking but also
in basic health and nutrition, work safety, and job ethics.
The course lasted for 20 hours and classes were held in
the migrant camps.
     This massive training program was conducted in 1970-
71 in the cotton growing region of Colombia's Northern
Coastal region. The area was divided into nine zones,
with a leader and instructors assigned to each. The program's general coordinator and nine zone leaders first
worked to gain local cooperation, especially among cotton-
growers. A month later the instructors arrived with six
mobile units, each outfitted with projector, slides, tape
recorder, public address system, and electric generator.
     Instructors worked directly in the fields, giving
practical demonstrations complemented by audiovisual
presentations. Additional lessons were given while workers were preparing meals and in the evening.
     Within eight weeks SENA enrolled nearly 47,000
migrants in this special PPP-R course. The program covered
approximately 88 percent of all cotton growing estates.
While most of the participants were male, 7.3 percent of
those enrolled were female.[13]

COSTS AND FINANCING

     SENA has secure and independent sources of financing,
the most important of which is a 2 percent payroll tax
levied on enterprises above a certain size. · SENA receives
its income from:

     1. a tax of 0.5 percent on wages and salaries
         paid by the central government
     2. a payroll tax of 2 percent levied on all public
         and private enterprises with capital exceeding
         50,000 pesos (approximately US$2,500) or
         with at least 10 employees

    3.   certain fines related to labor practices, imposed by government
    4.   contracts for services to other organizations
    5.   sale of products at its training centers
    6.   returns on investment

By 1971 SENA's revenues had increased to approximately 500 million pesos (an increase of 51 percent since 1968), in large part because of a 1969 increase in the payroll tax levied on firms from 1 percent to the present 2 percent. Expenditures had increased even more dramatically; they were anticipated to equal revenues in 1971 (an increase of 127.6 percent between 1968 and 1971). Most of the increase in expenditures can be accounted for by rapid program expansion, especially in the number of trainees enrolled. In part, however, it reflects the high rate of inflation Colombia experienced during this period.

PPP-R Budget

In 1971 the Agricultural Division accounted for 95.3 million pesos or 19.1 percent of SENA's budgeted expenditures. Within the Agricultural Division's budget the PPP-R program represented less than 37 percent of budgeted expenditures (Table 11.6). Thus the PPP-R budget allocation is

TABLE 11.6

Estimated SENA Agricultural Division Budget for 1971
(000's of current Colombian pesos)

		Budgeted Expenditures (in 000's Col. pesos)	%
1)	Recurrent expenses for fixed centers	50,400	
	Investment	8,000	
	Subtotal	58,400	61.3
2)	PPP-R recurrent	32,200	
	PPP-R investment	2,700	
	Subtotal	34,900	36.6
3)	Central administration	2,000	2,000	2.1
	TOTAL		95,300	100.0

Source: Estimates provided by SENA Agricultural Division

substantially less than its share of agricultural sector enrollments (over 80 percent), and the Agricultural Division as a whole receives proportionately less than its share of total SENA enrollment (over 40 percent) would suggest.

In 1970 the PPP-R budget was nearly 26 million pesos. The distribution of budgeted expenditures in that year among the fourteen PPP-R regions is shown in Table 11.7. There has been little capital investment in the PPP-R program, with this item accounting for only 7.3 percent of total expenditures.

TABLE 11.7

PPP-R Budget for 1970
(in 000's of Colombian pesos)
Shown by Region

Regional Center	Recurrent Expenditures	Capital Investment	Total	%
Medellín	4,687	466	5,153	19.8
Barranquilla	1,513	355	1,868	7.2
Cartagena	967	-	967	3.7
Boyaca	1,181	-	1,181	4.5
Manizales	982	23	1,005	3.9
Popayan	1,028	53	1,081	4.2
Bogotá	4,301	410	4,711	18.1
Neiva	1,480	30	1,510	5.8
Santa Marta	1,707	452	2,159	8.3
Pasto	461	-	461	1.8
Cucuta*	800	-	800	3.1
Bucaramanga	956	-	956	3.7
Cali	1,811	51	1,862	7.2
Pereira*	568	59	627	2.4
General administration	377	-	377	1.4
Subtotal	22,819	1,899	24,718	95.1
Migrant workers			1,269	4.9
TOTAL			25,987	100.0

*The PPP-R budget for this region includes costs for other undefined programs which cannot be separated out. While believed to be small, these additional costs raise PPP-R costs for this region.

Source: SENA, Promocion Profesional Popular Rural, doc. no. 23-030 (Bogotá, September 1970).

The regional PPP-R centers of Bogotá and Medellín (both of which include geographic divisions larger than their home department) together account for nearly 38 percent of expenditures. The distribution of expenditures by regions, however, is roughly proportionate to the regional distribution of enrollments and graduates (Table 11.8) if migrant worker enrollments and graduates are discounted. However, the variation in expenditures/enrollment ratios can be seen more clearly when viewed in terms of unit costs at each of these centers.

TABLE 11.8

PPP-R Enrollments and Graduates, 1970
Shown by Region

Region	Enrollments		Graduates	
	#	%	#	%
Medellín	11,016	10.5	9,983	10.1
Bogotá	9,426	9.0	8,272	8.4
Cali	5,234	5.0	4,586	4.7
Neiva	5,148	5.0	4,686	4.8
Cartagena	4,961	4.7	4,136	4.2
Bucaramanga	4,028	3.8	3,822	3.9
Boyaca	3,683	3.5	3,293	3.3
Cucuta	2,905	2.8	2,718	2.8
Santa Marta	2,777	2.6	2,519	2.6
Manizales	2,756	2.6	2,244	2.3
Barranquilla	2,512	2.4	2,039	2.1
Popayan	2,066	2.0	1,898	1.9
Pasto	999	0.9	922	0.9
Pereira	589	0.6	517	0.5
Subtotal	58,100	55.4	51,635	52.4
Migrant workers program	46,848	44.6	46,848	47.6
TOTAL	104,948	100.0	98,483	100.0

Source: SENA, Analisís Cuantitativo de la Labor de Formación Profesional en el Año 1970, doc. no. 33-048 (Bogotá, June 1970), p.5; graduate data provided by SENA to ICED.

Table 11.9 presents the average cost per student, per graduate, per hour of instruction, and per student hour for each region and for the special migrant workers program. Discounting costs in the Pereira region (which include costs unrelated to PPP-R program), cost per student varies from a high of 789 pesos in Santa Marta to a low of 197 in Cartagena with an average unit cost of 425 pesos per student per course (excluding the migrant workers course which must be treated separately from other PPP-R activities). Cost per graduate is somewhat higher in each center and for the PPP-R as a whole due to dropouts (Table 11.9). The variation in unit costs among regions may be explained largely by differences in the average size of classes in

TABLE 11.9

PPP-R Unit Costs and Cost-Related Factors, 1970
(in current Colombian pesos)
Shown by Region

	Unit Costs				Cost-Related Factors		
	Cost per Student	Cost per Graduate	Cost per Instruc- tional Hr.	Cost per Student Hr.	Average Class Size	Average Hrs. Instruction per Student	Dropout Rates
Region							
Santa Marta	789	870	173	12.5	16.6	63.2	9.3
Barranquilla	755	931	152	8.7	18.3	86.8	14.1
Popayan	531	578	136	8.6	17.3	61.8	3.3
Bogotá	507	578	146	7.5	22.6	67.7	12.3
Medellín	475	524	145	7.4	22.5	64.1	9.4
Pasto	469	508	411	24.1	19.6	19.4	13.9
Manizales	370	455	110	7.4	17.7	50.1	18.6
Cali	361	412	122	6.5	22.4	55.3	12.4
Boyaca	326	364	76	3.8	22.7	85.4	5.0
Neiva	298	327	86	5.4	18.2	55.1	12.7
Bucaramanga	241	254	97	4.0	30.0	60.7	5.1
Cartagena	197	237	72	3.5	25.3	57.0	16.3
Pereira*	1,081	1,232	227	14.6	17.8	73.9	5.1
Cucuta*	280	299	66	3.7	18.3	74.4	5.3
Average excluding Migrant workers	425	479	123	6.7	21.2	63.6	12.5
Migrant workers	27	27	53	1.4	39.0	19.7	0.0
Average all PPP-R courses	248	264	116	5.6	26.7	44.0	6.0

Note: In calculating unit costs, the amount budgeted for general administration was proportionately distributed among regions according to their share of the total budget.

*The PPP-R budget for this region includes costs for other undefined programs which cannot be separated out. While believed to be small, these additional costs raise PPP-R unit costs for this region.

Source: SENA documents and information provided by SENA.

each center and in the average number of instructional hours.

The range in costs per instructional hour is harder to explain. In part it appears to be related to the average course length; in regions with shorter courses (on the average) the cost per instructional hour is higher. Possibly the time between courses and start-up time is proportionately greater when a number of short courses are mounted than the time required to set up a few long courses. Perhaps more important, the pay scales for instructors vary by region and, as personnel costs represent the major recurrent cost item, would strongly influence the regional cost per instructional hour.

Costs for Migrant Workers Courses

The unit cost for the migrant worker courses was only 27 pesos per student, which is accounted for by the large classes (39.0 average enrollment), short course duration (19.7 hours) and no recorded dropouts. This low cost reduces the unit costs for the PPP-R program as a whole to 248 pesos per trainee.

ICED made use of available information to calculate the average PPP-R program cost per enrolled student in 1971. With total estimated PPP-R expenditures of 34.9 million pesos and estimated PPP-R enrollments of 166,000 (including roughly the same proportion of enrolled migrant workers as in 1970), the average cost per student is 210 pesos compared to 248 pesos in 1970. This represents a 15.3 percent drop in costs compared to 1970.

If 210 pesos approximates the actual unit cost per student for 1971, this drop in costs may reflect SENA's decision to increase average PPP-R class size and shorten the average number of hours of instruction per course. Such moves simultaneously reduce costs per student and increase total enrollments. It is presumed, however, that there would be a reduction in the amount of instruction offered per student as well.

PPP-R courses are inexpensive compared to other, more extensive forms of SENA training. SENA's apprenticeship courses last up to three years and can cost as much as 29,000 pesos (1970) per graduate. Most apprenticeship courses, however, cost about 18,000 pesos on the average, with considerable variation by occupation and by region.

IMPACT OF THE PPP-R PROGRAM

In the absence of evaluative material on the PPP-R, the ICED study team conducted a field survey to gain some impression of the local impact of the PPP-R.

The Survey Sample

Since the PPP-R training is geared to the different agricultural activities in the major ecological zones of the country,[14] ICED conducted its survey in three departments of two representative regions. Within the two regions, interviews were obtained in nine rural municipalities that were reasonably accessible in terms of land communications. Several PPP-R courses had been offered in each community. The distribution of interviews by department and municipality is shown in Table 11.10.

One set of interviews was conducted in the northern coastal Departments of Atlantico and Bolivar. This region has a tropical climate and generally flat land; its main products are tropical crops and cotton. Much of the land in this area is concentrated in large estates although there are numerous small landholdings as well.

TABLE 11.10

Distribution of Interviews in the ICED
Study of the PPP-R
by Department and Municipality

Department	Municipality	Completed Interviews with Former PPP-R Trainees	
Atlantico	Sabanalarga	26	
	Santo Tomás	17	
	Santa Lucia	13	56
Bolivar	Maria la Baja	14	
	Mahates	10	
	El Carmen	6	30
Antioquia	Yarumal	17	
	Peñol	31	
	Carmen de Viboral	11	59
TOTAL			145

Note: An additional 25 interviews were conducted but are not shown because it was determined that the interviewee had not taken a PPP-R course.

A second set of interviews was conducted in the central Department of Antioquia. This is a mountainous region with cattle raising the main activity in the communities in the sample. The climate ranges from temperate to cold and most of the land is dispersed among numerous smallholders. Ecologically this area is quite

typical of Andean regions of Colombia where the majority
of the population is to be found.

SENA regional offices supplied the names of PPP-R
graduates in 1970 in the selected communities. It was
impossible, however, to randomly select names from these
lists because many of them could not be located, some could
not be reached in the time available (13 days) and others
had presumably left their communities since the end of the
course. All interviews were conducted by the two team
members during the last week of November and first week of
December 1971. The team tried to interview as many persons
on the list as possible in the available time. The resulting sample represented approximately one in seven to one in
eight of the PPP-R graduates in the respective municipalities.

It cannot be claimed, therefore, that the results of
this study are representative. Rather they should be regarded as only suggestive of the actual impact the PPP-R
has had in rural Colombia. One of the obvious shortcomings of the study is that only those who remained in their
communities could be interviewed. The number of former
trainees who may have left, presumably for urban areas, is
unknown, although SENA claims that the number is relatively
small.

The age-sex distribution of the sample was as follows:

	North	Antioquia
Average Age (in years)	37.1	32.5
Sex	%	%
Male	74.5	82.0
Female	25.5	18.0

All interviewees in the North had been enrolled in
beginning level courses, mainly in agriculture, whereas in
Antioquia several interviewees had participated in more
specialized agricultural/husbandry courses as well as
courses in rural administration, handicrafts, nursing, and
social relations. The length of these courses varied from
one week to three months. Most interviewees were enrolled
in courses lasting less than one month.

Table 11.11 presents the distribution of the sample
in terms of land tenancy. Over half the Antioquia sample
is composed of landowners (mostly with small holdings)
whereas in the northern region most interviewees were
either renters/sharecroppers or agricultural laborers,
most of whom were permanently employed on estates.

TABLE 11.11

Distribution of Sample by
Type of Landholding

	North		Antioquia	
	#	%	#	%
Landowners	4	4.7	31	52.6
Tenants and aparceros*	38	44.2	4	6.8
Landless agricultural laborers	29	33.7	11	18.6
Nonagricultural occupations	15	17.4	13	22.0
TOTAL	86	100.0	59	100.0

*Those who received land under the land redistribution
program of INCORA.

Source: ICED Study Team Report.

Findings

        The first measure of impact that the study sought to
determine was whether participants had applied what they
had learned (Table 11.12).
        Over 86 percent of the northern sample claimed to
have practiced what they learned in the course, compared
with 59 percent in Antioquia. In the North nearly all
agricultural laborers claimed to have applied what they
learned in the PPP-R course, probably because they worked
for estate owners or managers who had arranged to have the
PPP-R courses given to their workers and then sought to
put the training into practice.
        A smaller proportion of nonagricultural workers said
they had applied what they had learned than did agricultural sector workers. Within the agricultural sector there
was a higher rate of application among tenants and aparceros
than among landowners and landless laborers (see Table
11.12).
        There is an almost complete lack of correlation be-
tween the amount of formal education and application of
PPP-R training (see Table 11.13). Application was highest
among those with no formal schooling but many of those
with no education were among the agricultural laborers who
worked on estates in the North where the estate managers
encouraged application.
        The 109 interviewees who had applied their new train-
ing were asked what enabled them to do so. More than 20
percent claimed it was due to the availability of credit,
more than 18 percent to the availability of additional
technical advice (from agencies other than SENA); more

TABLE 11.12

Application of Training
Shown by Type of Landholding

	Total Sample					
	Total		Applied Training		Did Not Apply Training	
	#	%	#	%	#	%
TOTAL	145	100	109	75.2	36	24.8
Landowners	35	100	24	68.6	11	31.4
Tenants and aparceros*	42	100	40	95.2	2	4.8
Landless agricultural laborers	40	100	29	72.5	11	27.5
Nonagricultural occupations	28	100	16	57.1	12	42.9
	North					
TOTAL	86	100	74	86.0	12	14.0
Landowners	4	100	3	75.0	1	25.0
Tenants and aparceros*	38	100	37	97.4	1	2.6
Landless agricultural laborers	29	100	27	93.1	2	6.9
Nonagricultural occupations	15	100	7	46.7	8	53.3
	Antioquia					
TOTAL	59	100	35	59.3	24	40.7
Landowners	31	100	21	67.7	10	32.3
Tenants and aparceros*	4	100	3	75.0	1	25.0
Landless agricultural laborers	11	100	2	18.2	9	81.8
Nonagricultural occupations	13	100	9	69.2	4	30.8

*Those who received land under the land redistribution program of INCORA.

Source: ICED Study Team Report.

TABLE 11.13

Application of Training
Shown by Level of Formal Schooling

Amount of Schooling	Total		Applied Training		Did Not Apply Training	
	#	%	#	%	#	%
None	29	100	26	89.7	3	10.3
1 yr. primary	44	100	32	70.1	12	29.9
2-3 yrs. primary	27	100	20	70.4	7	29.6
More than 3 yrs. primary	45	100	31	66.6	14	33.3
TOTAL	145	100	109	75.2	36	24.8

Source: ICED Study Team Report.

than 60 percent mentioned no further outside assistance.

Interviewees were also asked if participation in a PPP-R course had had any effect on their income. Many interviewees had difficulty in perceiving increases in income in other than money terms (more sales of their product). For example, cattle raisers who had participated in a course on disease diagnosis and animal vaccination did not necessarily perceive that there was increased income from an animal that had been saved through proper diagnosis or prevention of illness. Moreover such benefits were difficult to estimate in monetary terms. Taking this into consideration, 34.5 percent of the interviewees claimed that their income had increased as a result of their participation in a PPP-R course. (No attempt was made to calculate the amount of increase.) There was considerable variation between the two regions: in the North nearly 46 percent claimed their incomes had increased compared with 20 percent in Antioquia. In the entire sample less than 10 percent of landless agricultural laborers claimed their incomes had increased. Approximately 60 percent of the nonagricultural workers in the sample said that their incomes had increased as a result of their taking a PPP-R course.

Interviewees were asked if they had changed occupations as a result of their course participation. Only 4 percent claimed to have done so. This result is clearly in line with the types of courses offered in the PPP-R program which are largely intended to upgrade the occupational skills of workers rather than teach them new occupational skills.

Table 11.14 shows the number of PPP-R courses taken by interviewees. While nearly 65 percent had only taken one course, 35 percent had taken more than one. The proportion taking several courses was greater in the North, where nearly 14 percent had taken more than three courses.

TABLE 11.14

Number of Different PPP-R Courses
Taken by Interviewee

Number of Courses	Northern Region	Antioquia
1 course	50	44
2 courses	14	9
3 courses	11	5
More than 3 courses	11	1
TOTAL	86	59

Source: ICED Study Team Report.

Of those taking more than one course, however, only 10
percent took courses that were interrelated.

In order to determine if the PPP-R program had any
training impact on others besides those enrolled in a
course, interviewees were asked if they had passed on
information they had learned in a course to others in
their community. More than 46 percent of the interviewees
claimed they had done so; 59 percent in the North compared
with 27 percent in Antioquia. The study team also attempted to assess the interviewees' opinions about the desirability of courses for women. Most interviewees said
there should be courses for women, particularly in domestic
sciences and in agricultural subjects.

The ICED team also looked into the degree of participation of the interviewees in the preplanning and selection of courses for their community. Only 14.5 percent
claimed to have participated, slightly more in the North
than in Antioquia. However, when asked if their community
leaders had been consulted by SENA prior to setting up a
course, 81 percent in the North said this was done compared with only 37 percent in Antioquia. Informal interviews conducted by the ICED study team with PPP-R instructors and community leaders in both regions confirm these
results. More community leaders and instructors in the
North mentioned PPP-R's cooperation with other rural
development agencies, such as ICA, than did those in
Antioquia. Instructors and local leaders in the North
also believed that local participation was regularly
sought out; this was less frequently reported in Antioquia.

While the results of the study team's field investigation are not conclusive, they suggest that the PPP-R is
having an impact on the economic lives of its participants.
The strength of this impact, however, could not be
adequately measured in the short time available for this
study.

Field Study Conclusions

The generally greater impact of the PPP-R in the
North compared with that in Antioquia appears to be
related to the degree to which the program in the North
effectively integrated itself into the area. The team
members concluded that the involvement of clientele in
preplanning and course selection was crucial to success,
as was collaboration and cooperation with other rural
service agencies.

One important element of preplanning in the view of
the team members--the assessment of markets for those
products being encouraged by the training programs--was
lacking in both areas. In the North, for example, participants in a citrus fruit course reported that they were
unable to market the citrus fruit they had been taught to
grow.

The lack of necessary physical inputs, credit, and
information about how to obtain these inputs was also
cited by participants as limiting the application of their
training. In Antioquia, for example, cattle raisers could
not improve their herds (as they had learned to do in
their PPP-R course) because they did not have the required
funds. Credit was available, but the participants mis-
takenly believed that the terms of credit were disadvan-
tageous (when in fact the opposite was true). This faulty
information was not corrected by the PPP-R instructor (as
credit information was not part of the course content).

The lack of credit itself appeared to be especially
serious for participants in courses that sought to introduce new farm enterprises such as rabbit raising, egg
production, and beekeeping. Without credit many participants could not practice what they had learned.

PROGRAM APPRAISAL

The PPP-R experience suggests certain improvements
that can be made in the cost-effectiveness and benefit-
cost ratios of short-term rural training programs of
similar design. Obviously SENA itself is far better
qualified to decide on the specific changes needed in
the PPP-R and on how these can be implemented.

The cost-effectiveness of a training program reflects
its internal efficiency--the relationship of outputs
(educational results) to inputs (the human and physical
resources employed). The benefit-cost ratio relates the
cost of inputs to the ultimate benefits attributable to
the training program. Obviously, both of these ratios
are extremely difficult to calculate and are affected by
many factors.

Aspects Related to Cost-Effectiveness

Trainee selection and retention. PPP-R trainees are
drawn from the adult rural population and most have previous experience in the occupation for which they are to
receive training, although few have formal schooling and
a considerable proportion are illiterates.

SENA, having concluded on the basis of experience
that trainee interest cannot be sustained over a long
period of time (the longer the course, SENA maintains,
the higher the dropout rate), has shortened PPP-R courses
to an average of less than one month. SENA claims that
this has resulted in higher retention, although at the
cost of an abridged curriculum. Since training is relevant to the work experience of trainees, however, SENA
claims that a significant amount of subject matter can
be imparted in the short courses.

Shortening the courses has required that a given subject field be divided into parts (poultry raising is
now presented in three courses rather than one). Unless a
complete series of courses is offered in the same community, participants will not have the opportunity to learn
all the new skills relevant to a given field.

Course content. The experience of the PPP-R program,
as indicated in ICED's field study and in conversations
with SENA personnel, strongly suggests that the content
of rural training courses must go beyond knowledge of
production if the course is to be relevant to trainee
needs and if trainee interest is to be sustained. Basic
knowledge of farm business management is important to the
farmer if he is to put his newly gained technical knowledge of farm production to profitable use. He needs to
know how to use available technical services, how to
obtain credit when needed, and how to secure the required
physical inputs. Finally, he needs to know how to market
his product successfully. The same is true for small
businessmen who receive industrial or commercial/service
training.

At present PPP-R courses make limited use of printed
instructional material. However, literacy in rural
Colombia (despite the low schooling rate) appears to be
sufficiently widespread, which suggests that most farm
families have at least one literate member. Printed
material (which could rely heavily on illustrations)
could help to reinforce the oral presentation of teachers
and serve as a reference once the instructor has left the
community. Such material could also be designed as a
source book which would list the appropriate local agencies
the farmer may need to rely on to satisfy new demands for
information, services, and physical inputs which training
generates.

Personnel. While SENA PPP-R instructors are well
paid, there is a problem of recruiting qualified staff
who must work under difficult conditions, often in isolated rural communities. This is a worldwide problem in
the recruitment of rural staff. SENA, however, has suggested a procedure to improve conditions of service by
rotating staff from field positions to posts in fixed
agricultural training centers. This is now done to a
limited extent with some instructors seconded from centers to give specific courses in the PPP-R program. A
side benefit derived from such a procedure is that it
provides invaluable knowledge for center staff from their
direct contact with rural inhabitants and their practical
problems.

Instructional facilities. The PPP-R program has
significant cost-saving features. It has demonstrated
that training can be brought to the participants and
that temporary facilities can be used as training sites.
With little additional capital expenditure, SENA has
trained many rural inhabitants.

Communications. In its attempt to reach all of rural
Colombia, including isolated areas, the PPP-R program suffers from overextended lines of communication. There are
reports of instructors not receiving salaries on schedule
and of supplies not arriving on time.[15] Instructors work
by themselves in the field without sustained contact with
other instructors or their supervisors. Mistakes and poor
planning often go unnoticed.

Program evaluation. To determine the cost-effectiveness of a training program a measure, however rough, is
needed of educational results as well as benefits (such
as income increases) attributable to that program.

At present the PPP-R program has not attempted to
measure the educational results of the training program:
there are no examinations given at the end of each PPP-R
course, for example. Admittedly this is a difficult
problem when dealing with a trainee population which contains a significant number of illiterates. But knowledge
of the number completing courses and the number dropping
out is insufficient for the curriculum planner to determine how courses ought to be altered to increase learning
on the part of participants. An evaluation of trainee
performance is required to determine the cost-effectiveness of the training program and to indicate in what
respects the program should be revised.

Factors Affecting Benefit-Cost Ratio

To attain a favorable benefit-cost ratio, benefits
can be realized only if the content of a program is relevant to participants' needs, and if the program itself has
strong links to the local socioeconomic context.

Planning and coordination. A program such as PPP-R, which does not embrace a full range of rural development services (such as follow-up mechanisms, physical inputs, credit or sustained technical services), must seek to cooperate and collaborate with local development agencies to enhance benefits from the training offered. To a considerable extent, therefore, program planning should be envisaged as a collaborative effort among rural development agencies.

Ideally the PPP-R would like to function in a community which has a local development plan and within which specific training tasks have been identified. This is usually the case with PPP-R courses offered in collaboration with INCORA or ICA. In most communities, however, there is no development plan. SENA uses the national plan as a guide to its local action, but its interpretation of the plan and its decision as to what training should be offered may differ considerably from the interpretation of other development agencies at work in the field. SENA representatives who attended an ICED-sponsored seminar cited the limited nature of local and regional planning activities and stressed the need for SENA to coordinate its efforts with other development agencies, especially at the field level.

Before the planning of training activities begins, an assessment of skill needs (quantitatively and substantively) is required. In addition a market analysis is necessary to determine whether there is an actual market for the goods or services being promoted through training.

The PPP-R experience suggests that a rural-based training program must seek the support and involvement of its client population and of local community leaders so that it does not offer courses for which there is neither need nor interest on the part of the community. This also suggests that at times the training organization must mount a special promotional effort for types of training for which there is effective demand but no perceived need or interest in the community.

The issue of employment creation again makes clear the need for coordinated research and planning. Given the national goals of increasing rural employment opportunities and simultaneously slowing down migration to cities, the PPP-R undoubtedly has a significant potential role to play, but the full exercise of that role requires working in concert with other government and private agencies 1) in order to determine priority training needs within each section of the country and 2) in order to ensure that the training offered will be supported by other development services (credit, physical inputs).

The importance of coordination at the local level is indicated by the ICED field study: the findings suggest, for example, that training was more successful in the North than in Antioquia because SENA benefited from

collaboration with ICA, a view also held by officials at
SENA headquarters. Whether it be ICA's extension agents
or other local development workers, someone is needed
within the community to assist in "needs" assessments, to
promote the training course that has been selected for the
community, and to recruit participants.

Follow-up to training. If training is effective
(participants have learned new skills), one may expect that new demands will be generated by participants,
including demands for additional training, technical services (soil testing, veterinarians), credit, physical
inputs, and marketing facilities. SENA is capable of meeting only one of these needs directly--additional training.
A program such as the PPP-R needs to pay greater attention
to the total programming of courses in a given locality.
As most PPP-R training is short, a single subject may be
divided into several courses. The PPP-R should attempt
to offer all courses in a sequence within a given community.

While SENA cannot provide follow-up technical services, credit or required physical inputs, it has occasionally included information in courses on how these can
be obtained. It has invited representatives of agencies
in the community that deal with these services to attend
class sessions where they can explain how these services
or products can be secured. This procedure is now practiced in some courses in several communities and could be
expanded.

As has been suggested above, further benefits may be
realized from training efforts if additional information
on marketing and farm (or small industry/service) business
practices is included as a part of the training curriculum.

Training and land tenure. The ICED study suggests
that those with land rights can and do put their learning
into practice, especially if follow-up services are available.

Agricultural workers without land, however, are not
in a position to decide whether or not their new skills
can be applied. On large estates where owners and managers
were convinced of the relevance of the training, the farm
laborers put their training into practice. But this may
not be the case if employers see little merit in the training. This suggests that if SENA offers training to landless laborers, SENA must convince their employers (preferably before the training course is offered) of the importance of the training. If employers are opposed to the
introduction of new skills and practices, there seems to
be little benefit to be derived from training their workers.

Evaluation. At present it is impossible to calculate
a benefit-cost ratio for the PPP-R program since benefits
attributable to the program have not yet been measured.
There is a crucial need to determine whether or not PPP-R
training is being put into practice and whether it has
had any effect on production and income of rural participants. The PPP-R evaluation study now being conducted

by SENA may answer some of these questions. The ICED field study does suggest that the PPP-R program has had some impact in rural Colombia.

LESSONS OF THE PPP-R EXPERIENCE

1. The PPP-R program demonstrates that it is possible to operate a large-scale mobile training program that reaches isolated rural areas at relatively low cost. However, other countries looking at the PPP-R experience need to note some of its special features. PPP-R has developed out of a securely established, well-financed national organization with considerable experience in providing vocational-occupational training. SENA provided, and still provides, strong administrative and technical backstopping to the PPP-R program and lends this program some of the prestige SENA has gained throughout Colombia.

2. SENA's experience with the PPP-R suggests the feasibility of adding such a program to a pre-existing organizational base and expanding coverage (in terms of geographical spread and number of trainees) quite rapidly. Starting a PPP-R program from scratch, without an established base, however, would undoubtedly take longer to implement and cost relatively more.

3. Any country attempting to establish a short-term rural training program such as the PPP-R may expect to derive greater benefits for its training efforts if:

a) training courses are tailored to diagnosed needs
b) local leaders and potential participants are drawn into the planning and course selection process at the local level
c) training efforts are keyed to the larger development plans for an area
d) inputs complementary to training are available to participants
e) there is a market for the product or service being promoted by training and such a market is known and accessible to participants

4. A training agency cannot be expected to undertake all planning efforts at the national, regional, and local levels. It can benefit, however, from the planning conducted by other development agencies.

5. Evaluation and follow-up procedures must be established in order to judge current performance and to identify aspects of the training program that must be adjusted.

6. One of the most difficult staffing problems is to find qualified people to work full-time in rural areas. The experience of the PPP-R suggests that rotating staff

between field assignments and posts at permanent training
centers may be a means of ameliorating this difficulty.
     7. The PPP-R experience suggests that farmers (and
rural artisans/entrepreneurs) require business knowledge
(including marketing and management practices) in addition
to knowledge of new or improved production practices. Such
business knowledge should be an integral part of course
content.
     8. Agricultural training is more likely to yield posi-
tive results when participants own (or effectively control)
their own land. Such individuals enjoy greater freedom and
incentive to apply their new knowledge than do landless
agricultural workers. However, such landholders (generally
smallholders) may not be able to apply new practices if
they do not have access to required inputs (credit and fertilizers). This again underscores the need to coordinate
training efforts with the activities of other agencies
providing development inputs and services.
     9. The PPP-R experience demonstrates the crucial im-
portance of the context within which training is placed.
If the local context is properly structured, the training
expertise of SENA can be brought rapidly into the scene and,
with the adaptation to local conditions, can supply an
important service at relatively low cost. If the context
is inadequate (lack of credit facilities, inputs, technical
services, marketing channels), however, a short-term training input such as a PPP-R program can be expected to make
only a minimal impact.

NOTES

     1. International Labour Office, Towards Full Employment: A Pro-
gramme for Colombia, prepared by an interagency team organized by the
International Labour Office (Geneva: ILO, 1970),p. 67.
     2. Dragoslav Avramovic, Economic Growth of Colombia: Problems and
Prospects, World Bank Country Economic Report (Baltimore and London:
The Johns Hopkins University Press, 1972), chapter 22, p. 408.
     3. Ibid.
     4. With the average level of formal schooling in rural areas at
less than two years, it is hard to understand how the level of reported
literacy is so high (59 percent). Possibly literacy was gained in only
two years of schooling or was acquired through other agents outside the
school. Assuming the data are correct, this is a question which merits
further investigation.
     5. Secondary vocational school enrollment figures for 1970 were
unavailable. But as secondary school enrollments are estimated to be
growing at 11 percent, on the basis of the 1968 figure of 126,700, a
probable calculation for 1970 might be 156,000--or well below SENA's
280,500.
     6. See Chapter 1.
     7. Based on information in SENA, Analisís Cuantitativo de la
Labor de Formación Profesional en al Año 1970, doc. no. 33-048
(Bogotá, June 1970).

8. Student hours are calculated on the basis of the number of students in attendance per instructional hour. Thus class size, dropout rate, and attendance record all affect the number of student hours generated by each instructional hour.

9. SENA, Promoción Profesional Popular Rural, doc. no. 23-030 (Bogotá, September 1970), p. 2.

10. SENA, Guía Para la Acción de Formación Profesional de la Mujer del Medio Rural, doc. no. 23-025 (Bogotá, July 1970).

11. SENA, Promoción Profesional Popular Rural, op. cit.

12. SENA, Analisís de los Objetivos del PPP-R e Importancia de la Unificación de Conceptos, doc. no. 23-074 (Bogotá, July 1974), p. 6.

13. SENA, Informe Final Programa Migraciones Campesinas 1970-1971, doc. no. 23-065 (Bogotá, May 1971).

14. In the Agricultural Division of SENA there is distinct training for the occupational classification "skilled agricultural worker" in the three major climatic zones--hot, temperate, and cold.

15. SENA, Analisís de los Objetivos del PPP-R e Importancia de la Unificación de Conceptos, op. cit., p. 8.

**INDIA: NONFORMAL
EDUCATION IN THE
DEVELOPMENT OF
SMALL ENTERPRISE**
John C. de Wilde

*One major way in which nonformal education can contribute to
rural development is through training and extension services for
small, nonfarm entrepreneurs and their employees. Since India has
had a longer and broader experience in this field than any other
developing nation, ICED asked John C. deWilde, who had just retired
from the World Bank as an economist and had done a large study for
the Bank on the training and promotion of small entrepreneurs in
several African nations, to review the Indian experience in this
field and seek the lessons that might benefit other nations. Field
visits for the study were done by the author in company with
Harkishan Singh, a former Indian official with long experience in
small industries, in fall 1971 and the report was completed in
early 1972.*

INTRODUCTION

The objective of this study was to analyze India's
"experience with nonformal education aimed at the development of small entrepreneurs and small industries with
particular reference to rural areas." The scope of the
study was to include "the Rural Industries Project Program; various training, extension and service programs
and institutes under the direction of the Development
Commissioner for Small-Scale Industry; the recently
initiated entrepreneurship development program...; and
such other related activities as are pertinent to the
subject."

Among the developing countries India has had the
largest and most diverse experience in stimulating the
development of small-scale industry in both urban and rural
areas. A study of its experience is therefore of particular relevance to other countries facing similar problems
and dedicated to similar objectives. It is important to
analyze the methods it has employed and the results it

has achieved, not only to illuminate what can be accomplished, but also to point up the problems and difficulties that have been encountered and that might at least be partly avoided or overcome.

The material for this study was gathered during a month's visit to India extending from early November to early December 1971. A substantial amount of documentation was collected. Numerous conversations were held with central and state government personnel concerned with the relevant programs. Apart from New Delhi, visits were paid to several cities and rural areas in Punjab and Hariyana States and to Ahmedabad (Gujerat State), Bombay (Maharashtra State), Bangalore (Mysore State), Hyderabad and Nalgonda (Andhra Pradesh State), Agra, Meerut and Deoband (Uttar Pradesh State) and Jaipur (Rajasthan State). Most of the time was devoted to an examination of the activities of the Small Industries Service Institutes and Extension Centers. It proved possible to visit only two of the forty-nine Rural Industries Project areas, owing to limitations of time and the remoteness of these areas from the cities. However, these visits--to the Nalgonda and Deoband projects in Hyderabad and Uttar Pradesh States respectively--were supplemented by an extensive study of documentation and discussions of the program at central and state government levels.

Since this study is concerned with "nonformal" education in "small-scale industry," some definition of both these terms is necessary. The concept of "nonformal" education has been interpreted as embracing virtually all means of imparting knowledge and developing human resources outside the formal educational system extending from primary schools up to and including higher educational institutions. Thus in the industrial field it includes all types of advice and guidance to existing and potential entrepreneurs on technical and managerial problems, industrial opportunities, sources of finance, government regulations, and any other matters relevant to the establishment and operation of industrial enterprises. While essentially "nonformal," it comprises also more formal training courses for adults who have already completed their formal schooling (whether academic, or technical and vocational) and who are entrepreneurs or would-be entrepreneurs or are already engaged as workers or employees in small enterprises.

"Small-scale industry" has been defined by the Indian Government as embracing all manufacturing enterprises with an investment in plant and machinery not exceeding RS750,000 (or RS1,000,000 for certain types of industry, including particularly those making components and parts for large-scale industry). Since "manufacturing" is the critical qualifying adjective, service industries such as those concentrating on repairs and maintenance and the construction and contracting industry

are both excluded in principle. However, in practice
repair establishments have been included when they produce some spares and components ancillary to their
activities.

This study is concerned with entrepreneurial training and development in the context of three principal
programs: the general program for the promotion of
small-scale industry carried out through the Small
Industries Service Institutes (SISIs) and Extension
Centres (ECs); a more specific program for rural industrial development comprising 49 "pilot" Rural Industries
Project areas; and a special program for training and
assisting unemployed engineers and technicians to undertake small-scale industrial units.

The first two programs have been motivated principally
by a desire 1) to create and multiply employment opportunities at a relatively low cost in terms of capital
investment on the premise that capital-output ratios are
much lower in small-scale industry than in large-scale
industry, and 2) to increase the dispersion of industry
in terms of both its ownership and geographic location
in order to bring about a wide and "democratic" ownership
of the means of production and to reduce regional disparities in industrial development. The rural industries
program has had the additional objectives of enhancing
rural incomes and employment opportunities and of reducing
rural migration to the cities. The third program was
designed to cope with the problem of increasing unemployment among young engineers and technicians that is estimated to total at least 40,000.

All three of these programs fall currently under the
jurisdiction of the Small-Scale Industrial Development
Organization (SSIDO), which in turn is directed by the
Development Commissioner (Small-Scale Industries) of the
Central Government's Ministry of Industrial Development,
Company Affairs and Internal Trade. However, it should
be stressed that the promotion of small-scale industry,
or, indeed, of industry as a whole, is by no means an
exclusive responsibility of the central government.
Industry is an important state subject as well, and the
States' Directorates of Industries play a significant role
in the regulation and promotion of industrial activities.
While the SISIs and ECs are exclusively central government
institutions, they are expected to work closely with and
for the state governments. The Rural Industrial Program
(RIP) was initiated and has been almost wholly financed
by the central government, but its actual administration
has been entrusted to the states.

GENERAL SMALL-SCALE INDUSTRY PROGRAM

The general small-scale industry program in India was launched in the fifties. It owed much of its initial inspiration to the findings of a Ford Foundation team which visited India in 1953-54, drew attention to the importance of stimulating the development of small industries, and made a number of specific recommendations of an organizational and policy nature that were subsequently translated into action. The objectives of this program, as laid down in the Industrial Policy Resolution of 1956, were

1.   to create immediate and substantial employment opportunities at relatively small capital cost
2.   to facilitate mobilization of capital and skills that might otherwise remain inadequately utilized
3.   to bring about integration of small-scale industries with the rural economy on the one hand and large-scale industry on the other hand
4.   to improve the productivity of workers and the quality of small-scale industry products and
5.   to ensure equitable distribution of national income and balanced industrial development in different regions in order to provide the basis for a "decentralized" society

Organization and Staffing

The Small-Scale Industrial Development Organization carries out its extension and training activities primarily through a network of 16 Small Industry Service Institutes (one in each state and in the Union Territory of Delhi), 5 branch institutes, 60 extension centers, two centers for training in footwear manufacturing, two production-cum-training centers, and one shoe-last factory. The SISIs are supposed to service virtually the entire range of small-scale industries existing within their geographic areas. On the other hand, the ECs, which operate under the supervision of the SISIs, provide more limited facilities for one or more industries.

In 1970 the number of professional posts in the SSIDO totaled 849, including vacancies, of which 118 were at headquarters and 731 in the field. Apart from the Development Commissioner, the Joint Development Commissioner, and two industrial advisers, the table of organization provided for a total of 368 posts at the

upper levels--directors, deputy directors and assistant
directors, industrial designers and assistant designers--
for 293 positions at the level of Small Industry Promotion
Officer, and for 136 "Investigators" posts at the lowest
level. In terms of substantive competence, the 849 positions were distributed as follows:

Technical officers for specific industries or industrial processes	604
Economic investigators and statisticians	143
Industrial Management and training experts	73
Experts and advisors for:	
1. Ancillary development[1]	38
2. Administration and coordination	29
3. Industrial designing	9
4. Export promotion	7
5. Rural industries development	7
6. Civil engineering	5
7. Publications	7

The overwhelming predominance of technical posts reflects
the great emphasis put by the SSIDO on technical extension and training services.[2]

SSIDO Activities and Growth
of Small-Scale Industry

The SSIDO has engaged in a wide and ever broadening
range of activities. Extension (that is, advisory) and
training services play a very important and, indeed,
vital role. However, these are only part of a larger,
integrated program through which the SSIDO also 1) provides common facilities for production and testing,
2) assists industry in improving the design of its products, 3) assesses industrial opportunities and markets,
and 4) advises financial institutions on the feasibility
of projects submitted for financing. In addition the
SSIDO carries on special programs for 1) the development
of ancillary production, that is, the manufacture of parts
and components by small-scale industry for larger industrial establishments, 2) the qualification of small-scale
units for government contracts, 3) the assessment of
small-scale industrial capacity with a view to more
equitable allocation of scarce raw materials, and 4) the
promotion of small-scale industrial exports.

Technical Advice and Training

There is little doubt that advice on technical
problems has been the most useful activity of the SSIDO.
There are several reasons for this. The technical

officers constitute the largest and probably the best qualified group among the personnel available to the SISIs and their ECs. A large majority of small-scale industrialists are still in need of technical assistance, even though a proportion of them have progressed to a stage where their need is no longer so acute or the SSIDO is no longer capable of furnishing the more sophisticated advice needed. Small-scale entrepreneurs are also more appreciative of technical advice because it is concrete and its impact can readily be assessed. Both the detailed instances of advice contained in the annual SISI reports and the testimony of a considerable number of small-scale industrialists are a convincing demonstration of the continued usefulness of the SSIDO's work in this field. The counseling covers a wide range of problems: the installation, realignment, resetting and repair of machinery and equipment; selection of proper equipment; product specifications; design and adoption of proper tools, jigs, fixtures and gauges; machinery layout; improvements in machining, melting and casting, heat treatment and electroplating; adoption of appropriate manufacturing methods and processes; and so forth. The annual reports of the SISIs usually provide some detailed information on the nature and effect of the advice given in some 40 to 60 specific instances.

As a complement to this type of technical assistance, the SSIDO also does considerable work in industrial design. A central design cell attached to the SISI in Delhi is engaged in designing industrial products for small-scale industry and the development of prototypes. In addition the individual SISIs supply a large number of drawings, blueprints, and designs for small units. The number so furnished rose from 3,425 in 1964/65 to a peak of 10,000 in 1967/68, but has since dropped back to a total of 4,100 in 1969/70. The contribution of this type of work is difficult to assess, but it has presumably been useful in improving the quality of products and in introducing more uniform specifications.

For the most part small-scale industrial units employ very few technicians and skilled workers trained in formal vocational and technical institutions. They rely almost entirely on personnel trained on the job. While this type of training has the advantage of being highly practical, the personnel of small-scale industry is still characterized by many technical deficiencies, particularly but not exclusively in terms of theoretical grounding, ability to work from blueprints, and so forth. The many technical training courses organized at the SISIs and ECs were thus primarily designed to upgrade the skills of people already employed in small-scale industry. For most of the courses, usually ranging in duration from three months to one year, the trainees accordingly had to be sponsored by their employers and a small monthly

stipend paid to enable participants to maintain themselves
during the training period. Outside the framework of
these "sponsored" courses, nonstipendary training has
also been given in blueprint reading and special subjects.
The number of people trained at SISIs and ECs rose from
752 in 1960/61 to 3,500 in 1965/66 and has since fluctuated around the latter total. In addition, training
courses are carried to small towns and rural areas by
the mobile vans of the SISIs. Over the decade 1960/61
to 1969/70 these vans gave an average of 4,496 demonstrations per year and provided short-term courses for 5,881
rural artisans per year.

Whatever may be the value of this training, it is
clear that the whole concept of sponsored training has not
worked out in accordance with the original plans. Many
employers have in fact been reluctant to sponsor their own
workers for training, and in many cases they "sponsor"
trainees who have actually never worked for them. Employers are disinclined to spare their own workers during an
extended period for training, all the more since only a
small percentage of the truly sponsored have in practice
come back to work for them. Employers have apparently
been unwilling to pay the higher wages to which workers
considered themselves entitled after training. In part
this reluctance may be due to a skepticism, whether justified or not, of the value of the training. Perhaps a more
important factor is the method of promoting workers
primarily by seniority rather than merit, a practice
which has become prevalent in private industry as well as
in government. Thus trouble is likely to be created if a
young worker with relatively little seniority in the plant
is given a higher wage than more senior workers after he
has upgraded his skills by taking a training course. On
the other hand, if he applies for a job with higher technical qualifications in another enterprise, he apparently
encounters less difficulty in getting a higher wage. On
the whole, it appears that the concept of "sponsored"
training and the factors which have made both employers
and workers reluctant to take full advantage of the training facilities should be thoroughly examined.

The number of participants in management training
courses, which are given in the evening, increased from
1,687 in 1960/61 to 3,860 in 1968/69. In 1969/70 the
total was 3,572, including 1,567 in the so-called "general
industrial management appreciation" course, 1,032 in
specialized courses, and 973 in ad hoc courses. The
duration of these courses is usually 80 hours (40 days),
50 hours (25 days), and 20-25 hours (10-12 days) respectively. In general it appears to have been somewhat
difficult to give the general management course the
practical relevance that appeals to entrepreneurs. There
has accordingly been a growing interest in specialized
and ad hoc courses which generally have a more specific,

concrete focus; and a few SISIs have virtually abandoned
or certainly de-emphasized the general course in favor of
the special and ad hoc courses, although in principle
participation in the latter is conditioned on previous
attendance at the general course. Examples of specialized
and ad hoc courses are those in financial management, cost
control, inventory management, export marketing and general
marketing, quality control, and industrial relations.

The management personnel of the SISIs also do consultancy work of two types--problem-oriented consultancy,
and comprehensive in-plant studies. Over the three-year
period 1967/68 to 1969/70 the SSIDO claims to have given
advice on specific management problems in no less than
15,581 instances of which, however, only about one-half
were given on the spot, that is, in the enterprise itself.
The range of problems on which advice is given is apparently
quite broad and covers such subjects as production management, inventory control, financial management and control,
and marketing. Another type of service is the comprehensive in-plant studies which are carried out by a team
of technical, management, and economic experts. Because
such studies entail considerable time and personnel, the
SSIDO's capacity to provide this service is very limited.
From 1962/63 to 1969/70 SSIDO was able to make only 276
of these in-plant studies, including 57 in 1969/70.
Their aggregate impact has accordingly been small.

The author of this study gained the impression that
the SSIDO is much weaker in this field than in technical
advice and training. This disparity is probably due in
part to the fact that nearly all the people engaged in
management consultancy and training have little or no
practical experience in industry. While this deficiency
is compensated in part by their experience and training
in pedagogical methods, it does detract from their ability
to give practical and concrete advice. The quality of the
personnel concerned with industrial management also appears
to vary quite markedly. Finally, small-scale entrepreneurs
find it difficult to appreciate the need for improved
management, which to many of them is a somewhat abstract
concept; and the SSIDO itself has not done enough to make
employers conscious of the management problems that in
many ways are more acute than their technical problems.[3]

Assessment of Industrial Opportunities and Markets

Assessing industrial opportunities and markets is
primarily the task of the SSIDO's economic staff in the
various SISIs. This staff prepares industrial outlook
reports, industrial prospect sheets on specific industrial
possibilities, market surveys, and area studies designed
to inventory the resources of a particular area and to
give indications of its industrial development potential.
Most of its time, however, is apparently spent in answering

all sorts of ad hoc inquiries on such subjects as sources
of supply for equipment and raw materials, sources of
finance, markets, government regulations pertaining to
industry, and availability of various services. This
type of information service is presumably quite useful
and does appear to be utilized to a considerable extent.
Undoubtedly many would-be entrepreneurs obtain some guidance on the types of industries or plants they might
establish.

    While SSIDO can provide useful information, its
capacity to assess the market for specific products in
specific areas appears to be rather limited, mostly because the data on already existing productive capacity
and actual consumption, although improving in reliability,
are still seriously deficient. In fact, many of the entrepreneurs interviewed by the author considered the lack of
reliable information on markets as one of the most serious
handicaps of small-scale business.

    In the past it has been the general practice of
financial institutions, particularly the commercial banks,
to seek the advice of SISIs on projects submitted to them
for financing. True, the SISIs have not been the sole or
even primary source of such advice. The State Directorates of Industry are usually asked also for an advisory
opinion, and financing institutions have in recent years
relied increasingly on their own staff and on special
panels of consultants to appraise the technical feasibility
of projects. In view of the growing volume of small-scale
industry financing, the SISIs have found it increasingly
difficult to cope with their responsibility of advising
financial institutions. To illustrate the magnitude of
the task, it is sufficient to point out that in the 14-
month period from June 1969 to August 1970 more than
15,000 new loans were made by commercial banks to small-
scale industry.

Encouragement of Ancillary Production

    In recent years the SISIs have devoted increasing
attention to encouraging large-scale units to subcontract
the production of parts and components and to assisting
small-scale industry to manufacture such products according to required specifications of quality and volume of
output and of delivery schedules.

    The encouragement of ancillary production in India
has taken a variety of forms. The SISIs have organized
a substantial number of seminars and conferences to
acquaint small-scale industries with the problems involved.
Assistance has been given in producing parts and components
of uniform and higher quality. Large-scale units have been
canvassed in an effort to get them to specify the types
and quantities of components, the manufacture of which
they might be prepared to subcontract. The SISIs at

Madras and Bombay have established special subcontract exchanges in which it is possible to match the requirements of large-scale enterprises for components and parts with the capacity for various types of machining jobs and other production operations available in small-scale industry. A number of large-scale plants, including Hindusthan Machine Tools and Bharat Electronics at Bangalore, Heavy Electricals (India) at Bhopal and the Heavy Engineering Corporation at Ranchi, have set up special "ancillary industrial estates" in which small-scale units are located for the purpose of producing and supplying components to their plants under close supervision. One of the earliest pioneers in this field was Hindusthan Machine Tools, a government corporation, which established an ancillary estate in which eventually 51 small units were set up. A few of these units in turn provide common facilities for others, including casting, forging, and heat treatment. Hindusthan Machine Tools initially provided assistance in the procurement of raw materials; in the supply of appropriate tools, jigs, and fixtures; in the training of workers; and, to some extent, even in the mobilization of finance. Careful inspection of products to insure proper quality was, of course, also carried out. In view of the many difficult problems involving ancillary production, it is not surprising that progress has been slow. In 1970 it was estimated that some 10,000 units were supplying components to about 200 large-scale establishments valued at Rs228 million. While this still represents an infinitesimal percentage of total small-scale industrial output, it is reasonable to expect that the current efforts will bear increasing fruit in the future.

The provision of production and testing facilities has also been very helpful to many small-scale industrialists who often cannot afford the equipment to carry out certain processing and machining operations or to test their products and raw materials for conformity to desired specifications. In many cases the machine shops also produce spare parts, special components, dies, jigs, and fixtures for small-scale units. The common facilities provided by the SSIDO at various SISIs and ECs include machine shops, electroplating, heat treatment and foundry shops, and laboratories. The number of parties assisted through these facilities rose from 13,911 in 1962/63 to 31,355 in 1969/70, although the increase has shown some tendency to level off in recent years. In contrast to the other services provided by the SSIDO, payments are required for the use of common facilities, although the rates charged are apparently well below cost.

Other Activities

As small-scale industry has become more competitive and developed some capacity to compete in foreign markets,

the need for effective counseling on export marketing has
increased. While the SSIDO has sought to meet the need,
its capacity to do so still appears to be extremely
limited. Another one of its tasks has been to assist
small-scale enterprises in qualifying and registering
for government contracts. The value of contracts placed
by the Director General of Supplies and Disposals with
small-scale units did indeed increase sharply from
Rs6.2 million in 1957/58 to a peak of Rs341.8 million in
1963/64, but it has since stabilized at a lower annual
level of around Rs200 million. In the last year or two,
in cooperation with the State Directorates of Industries,
a considerable number of the staff of SISIs has been
engaged in making assessment of the capacity available in
small-scale industries for the purpose of providing
guidance in the allocation of scarce raw materials. An
increasing amount of effort has also been devoted to
espousing the claims of small-scale industries for larger
allocations of such materials. These efforts highlight
one of the most persistent and acute problems of small-
scale industry--the chronic shortage of raw materials
that in many cases prevents full capacity production.

                    Extension Training and Methods

     Before turning to a discussion of the principal
problems and deficiencies of the SSIDO, a brief consideration of the training of SSIDO staff and the extension
methods used by this organization is appropriate.

Small Industries Extension Training Institute (SIET)

     Special facilities for training personnel concerned
with the development of small-scale industry are provided
at the Small Industry Extension Training Institute (SIET),
which was established in 1962, and is now organized in
Hyderabad as an autonomous "registered society." This
institute was originally designed to provide personnel
from SSIDO and the State Directorates of Industry with
training in industrial management, extension methods, and
techniques for area development analysis. For this purpose two basic three-months' courses were devised--one
dealing with industrial management, and the other with
area development. The management course covers such
topics as production, marketing, finance, accounting,
human relations, extension, communications, and organization. A feature of the course is the assignment of small
groups of participants for three weeks to a selected
industrial enterprise, after which they are expected to
produce an analysis of its operations and recommendations
for its improvement. The area development course was

intended to train participants, particularly the District
Industries Officers of the states, in analyzing the industrial potential of an area and drawing up an appropriate
development program for such an area. Three weeks of this
course were devoted to a practical field exercise. However, this course has developed in recent years into a
more general "Small Industry Development and Promotion"
course.

In addition, SIET gives a considerable number of
short special courses--for bank personnel concerned with
the financing of small-scale industry, for entrepreneurs,
and for small industries personnel from abroad.

Altogether SIET trained 1,807 people in the nine-
year period 1962/63-1970/71. Of these people 471 were
from SSIDO and 364 from state governments. Of the remaining 935, there were 259 from banks and 581 from other
institutions and enterprises, while 132 were foreigners.
Over the last four years the number of SSIDO and state
government trainees has been smaller than previously, but
this has been more than compensated for by trainees from
other sources, particularly from banking institutions
that have become progressively more involved in the financing of small-scale industry. The total number of trainees
rose from a low point of 156 in 1968/69 to 302 in 1969/70
and 313 in 1970/71.

Apart from training, SIET was originally expected to
undertake research on subject matter, teaching methods,
and communications materials required for development of
small-scale industry. In this field its accomplishments
have been less impressive. In part this shortcoming is
probably due to the attitude of the central government
and the SSIDO which apparently wanted to limit SIET's
activities outside of the narrow field of training. If
SIET had been enabled to embark on a research program
focusing on the study and evaluation of problems and on
measures and policies relating to small-scale industry,
the findings of such research could undoubtedly have been
usefully employed in its training courses. A two-man
team that evaluated the performance of SIET did recommend
in its report of March 1967 that the Institute should
function as an intellectual clearinghouse for ideas on
small industries development and as a place for study of
past performance and trying out new experiences in the
small industries sector, but the central government, which
provides about 75 percent of SIET's operating expenditures,
has never acted on this recommendation. While SIET has
produced some useful studies, it has never had the resources to carry out a comprehensive and well-integrated
research program.

Extension Approach

In general the most effective extension work, whether
on technical or on managerial problems, is accomplished in

the course of plant visits, particularly if they are not
so brief as to preclude an adequate consideration of the
concrete difficulties experienced by the enterprises.
However, limitations of staff and the shortage of transport have always severely limited the scope for this type
of extension work; and the difficulties have increased
with the rapid expansion in the number of small units.
Moreover, there never has been adequate capacity to provide continuing technical and managerial advice to enterprises located at a considerable distance from the
major cities in which the SISIs and the ECs are themselves
located. Perhaps partly for these reasons there appears
to have developed a progressively greater emphasis on what
might be styled "group" methods of extension. One of these
takes the form of seminars and "open-house" discussions to
which industrialists are invited and in which guest
experts, representatives of the State Directorate of
Industries and financial institutions often participate.
The subjects are themes which the SISI is anxious to
propagate and which are deemed of interest to a considerable number of entrepreneurs. For example, to cull a few
illustrations from the 1969/70 reports of the SISIs,
seminars or open-house discussions were held on such
diverse topics as market opportunities for small-scale
industry, productivity in small-scale industries, quality
control in specific industries, subcontracting, latest
developments in plastic industry, forging techniques, heat
treatment of steel, machinery for the leather industry,
and export possibilities to Japan. In this way a large
number of entrepreneurs can be reached at the same time.
Another "group" extension method is the "intensive campaign," which is utilized particularly for the purpose of
stimulating development in outlying areas or districts
that are not regularly reached by the SISIs and ECs.
The objective is to convoke in one place representatives
of all the authorities and institutions concerned with
industrial development, including not only a team of
officers from the SISI, but also representatives from the
State Directorate of Industries, the financing institutions and local bodies, and the district industrial
officer and collector. To lend glamor to the occasion
and enlist interest, a leading political personality is
often invited to open the meeting. Before the meeting a
hasty survey of industrial possibilities in the area is
usually made, existing and potential entrepreneurs are
contacted, and arrangements are made for advance publicity.
At the meeting itself the SISI technical officers discuss
specific industrial possibilities with interested entrepreneurs; state industrial officers explain the formali-
ties for registration of enterprises, the procurement of
raw materials and other facilities; and the representatives of financial institutions clarify the conditions of
financing and assist in such matters as filling out

applications for financing. In these ways at least the preliminary steps toward the formulation of projects and the mobilization of all the facilities essential for their implementation can in principle be taken in a coordinated fashion. The "intensive campaign," however, represents a rather summary way of dealing with a set of rather complex problems. While it may be possible to identify prospective entrepreneurs by the degree of enthusiasm and interest they display, these qualities are hardly an adequate test of their potential capacity as entrepreneurs. It is evident at any rate that considerable follow-up is necessary to ensure that new projects are in fact launched and carried out successfully. Unfortunately the capacity to follow up is frequently lacking on the part of both the entrepreneurs and the authorities and institutions concerned.

Accomplishments and Prospects

It is by no means easy to appraise the effectiveness of either the whole of the SSIDO program or of its separate components. Statistics contained in the annual reports of the SISIs appear on their face quite impressive. For example, the reports for 1969/70 record 84,968 instances of advice on technical questions, 35,641 "advices" on starting new enterprises, 99,072 "advices" of a "general nature," and 69,562 visits to enterprises, ostensibly for giving on-the-spot advice. These statistics, however, give no indication of the usefulness of the advice rendered. They also make no distinction between casual observations in brief visits and conversations on the one hand, and in-depth advice of a more substantive character entailing considerable expenditure of time on the other hand. Under these circumstances, an appraisal of SSIDO's various activities must be based primarily on "impressionistic" evidence obtained from a careful reading of its annual reports and those of the SISIs, from discussions with SSIDO personnel both at headquarters and in the field, and, above all, from the testimony of the beneficiaries of SSIDO assistance, both small-scale entrepreneurs and banking institutions. Thus the observations offered on SSIDO's activities and the subsequent discussion of this organization's key problems are primarily based on this evidence.

It should be noted also that SSIDO's operations are only part of a broader program for the promotion of small-scale industry. Other elements in this program are 1) the extension of financing facilities to small enterprises, 2) the establishment of industrial estates with provision for infrastructure and worksheds, and 3) reservation of the manufacture of a considerable number of products to small-scale industry, complemented by the grant of a price

preference in the awarding of government contracts. The
latter has helped to shield small-scale industry to some
extent against competition from larger units. The second
element has been of primary benefit to urban small-scale
industries, although it is well to remember that the number of worksheds--5,413 in all--provided on the 303
government industrial estates functioning at the end of
1969/70 was very small in relation to the total number of
small-scale enterprises. The availability of financing
has unquestionably been the most important of these three
elements. Small-scale industry has been able to draw on
many sources for financing: public funds made available
by state governments under the State Aid to Industries
Act and extended for the most part directly to entrepreneurs through the various State Directories for Industries,
but also in part indirectly through the State Finance
Corporations; the state-owned Finance Corporations existing in every state and operating under the general supervision of the Reserve Bank of India; some special state
corporations, such as the Gujerat Industrial Investment
Corporation and the Maharashtra Small-Scale Industries
Development Corporation, which provides equipment and
machinery on hire-purchase; and the commercial banks.

The total amount of credit disbursed to small-scale
industries under the State Aid to Industries Act and by
the State Finance Corporations and the government-owned
commercial banks rose from Rs223.12 million at the end
of March 1962 to Rs2,635.7 million at the end of March
1969. Government-owned commercial banks have played an
increasingly important role in this financing, with their
share in the above-mentioned totals rising from 53 percent
to 76 percent. With the encouragement of government, the
commercial banks have remained in the forefront in the
expansion of credit to small-scale industry. All the
banks have progressively liberalized their credit terms,
particularly with respect to the security demanded from
borrowers and the requirements for "margin money," that
is, the proportion of investment which entrepreneurs have
to furnish from their own resources. The expansion of
bank lending has been considerably encouraged by a credit
guarantee system initiated by the Reserve Bank of India
that now automatically insures credits extended to small-
scale industry against loss up to 75 percent of the
principal.

The progress made by small-scale industry over the
last decade might be cited as evidence of the effectiveness of all these measures. This progress has unquestionably been substantial, although deficiencies in the data
on production make any accurate measurement difficult.
The number of small-scale units registered increased from
36,109 in 1960/61 to 190,727 in 1969/70, although this
somewhat overstates the rate of development since many
existing but previously unregistered units have found it

advantageous to register as a necessary qualification for
government assistance. In the period 1960/61 to 1969/70
employment in the small-scale factory sector is estimated
to have increased from 3.60 million to 4.53 million, and
its share in total factory employment from 38.7 percent
to 41 percent. At the end of March 1970 employment in
small-scale industry, including the nonfactory sector,
was put at 6.3 million, gross annual output at Rs36,700
million, and investment at Rs4,500 million.

While this progress can hardly be attributed entirely
to government efforts, the availability of government
assistance and SSIDO activities were undoubtedly encouraging factors.

A number of problems have impaired SSIDO accomplishments and continue to set limits on its contribution to
small-scale industrial development.

Staffing Difficulties

Staffing is probably the most critical of the problems confronting the SISIs and ECs. In numbers the
staff has not grown in relation to the expansion of
small-scale industry and the ever-growing number of tasks
imposed on it. The work load has increased tremendously
as the SISIs have striven to meet the rising demand,
emanating at least in part from headquarters, for such
additional activities as more training courses, seminars,
conferences, raw material assessments, advisory opinions
on projects, and additional work in outlying areas. In-
plant consultancy on technical and managerial problems
has apparently suffered in consequence.

There is a great need today to increase the number
and diversify and raise the qualifications of the staff.
Some attempts have been made to invoke the assistance of
outside experts through the organization of panels of
industrial consultants. While a few of the SISI staff
appear to have taken part on such panels, they have done
so rarely because resources to pay the consultants have
been lacking. Occasionally the staff has sought advice
on equipment and industrial processes from such government research organizations as the National Council for
Scientific and Industrial Research and the various
National Laboratories, but these confine themselves to
written reports and have no capacity for in-plant consultancy and there is doubt in some quarters that their
research is sufficiently adapted to practical requirements.

One of the most disturbing aspects of the increasing
disparity between SSIDO's capacity and the growing requirements is its inability to discharge effectively its
task of advising financing institutions on new projects
and of providing the necessary follow-up technical and
managerial assistance that the host of new entrepreneurs
need if they are to become truly successful. On the part

of the financing institutions there has been some loss
of confidence in the quality and timeliness of the services they receive from the SSIDO. This is reflected in
the recommendations made in 1971 by The Committee on
Banks' Credit Schemes with Reference to Employment Potential. This committee stressed that the need for a larger
flow of bank credit had to be accompanied by arrangements
that would enable borrowers to obtain technical guidance,
machinery, land and buildings, raw materials, and advice
on finance, marketing and management. It criticized the
SISIs for being excessively slow in certifying the technical feasibility of projects and recommended that banks
should develop their own capacity for assessing project
feasibility and for "follow-up by way of maintaining
close contact with the activities of the borrower and
keeping themselves informed about the difficulties, if
any, experienced by him and offering suitable guidance,
where required." The committee suggested that such
arrangements could best be made if the banks were to
cooperate in setting up their own "multi-service agencies."
    In the last analysis the only way in which SSIDO can
obviate the necessity of establishing other organizations
with largely similar responsibilities is to develop a
staff sufficient in calibre and numbers to cope effectively
with the tasks it is supposed to handle. It is unlikely
that this can be done without converting SSIDO into an
autonomous organization, largely independent of the government, and with sufficient freedom to determine its own
staffing patterns, its own priorities, and its own salary
scales and conditions of service. However, organizational
autonomy alone will not be enough as long as it depends
almost wholly on the government for its financing and is
therefore presumably subject to considerable government
supervision and control. While the SSIDO may be able in
time to earn some income by initiating charges for some
of its services that are now with a few exceptions given
free, it will undoubtedly remain dependent on substantial
outside subsidies. It is desirable, however, to examine
carefully whether or not it would be possible to obtain
this outside financing on more ample and liberal terms
from both the financing institutions and the small-scale
industries that together are supposed to be the primary
beneficiaries of the SSIDO's services.
    Organizational and financial autonomy would also
eliminate the hamstringing effect on SSIDO of other government regulations and procedures. Though expected by headquarters constantly to extend the geographic scope of
their operations, virtually all the SISIs are seriously
hampered by lack of transport. Even one of the largest
of the SISIs has only two vehicles available for the field
work of its staff. Travel allowances are usually inadequate. The need to recruit professional personnel
through the all-India Civil Service Commission often

leads to inordinate delays in filling vacancies. Cumbersome government procurement regulations make the purchase of urgently needed supplies in the local market excessively difficult even when only small outlays are involved.

Need for Modernization of Common Facilities

There is also a great need for the modification of the common facilities which the SISIs can offer to industry. The original workshops, laboratories, and testing equipment were undoubtedly very useful in the earlier period and continue in part to be serviceable. However, here again pace has not been kept with the evolving requirements of small-scale industry. Many small-scale industrialists no longer need the common facilities of an ordinary machine workshop, but want access to special purpose machines capable of doing more specialized work. The need for more modern and sophisticated testing equipment is also often expressed. Above all, there is a growing demand for up-to-date, well-equipped tool rooms that can design and produce the special dies, tools, jigs, and fixtures that small-scale industrial units cannot readily manufacture themselves.

Choice of Industries and Technology

Among the continuing problems that have not been satisfactorily resolved are the choice of industries which are suitable for small-scale operation and the corresponding choice of the technology that is appropriate to small-scale industry. Not enough research has so far been devoted to the selection of industries that will in the long run be really capable of competing at reasonable costs with plants operating on a larger scale. Economies of scale need to be investigated more carefully. The promotion of all types of small-scale industry without adequate attention to economies of scale appears to be rather indiscriminate. Sight is often lost of the fact that small-scale units that do not produce for a very localized market often experience serious and, in some cases, insuperable handicaps in finding or devising effective distribution channels for the sale of their products. The selection of technologies appropriate to small-scale industry and the relative cost of labor and capital in India undoubtedly pose difficult problems. In a country like India where population pressure is severe, unemployment high, and capital short, there are undoubted advantages in promoting labor-intensive technologies. Small-scale industry tends to be favored because it does employ far more labor in relation to capital than large-scale industry. However, this fact should not be used to justify undiscriminating encouragement of small-scale industries or opposition to improvement of their technology even at the cost of greater

capital investment. In large part the low capital-output
ratio in small-scale industry is simply due to the inability of the latter to engage in types of production
and processes which by their very nature require heavy
investment, such as the production of iron and steel,
basic chemicals, cement and fertilizers, heavy engineering, and the refinement of petroleum. The low capital-
output ratio prevailing in small-scale industry does not
necessarily demonstrate that this type of industry makes
the most efficient use of its capital or that a more
efficient use of capital could not be achieved if its
products were produced on a larger scale or with better
technology.

An Appropriate Technology Cell has now been set up
within the SSIDO in New Delhi to direct more systematic
research in this field. Its initial efforts are focused
on the technologies for leather and tanning, ceramics
and pottery, food processing and preservation, agricultural tools and equipment, road building, and general
construction. In addition it is examining the possibility
of devising technologies that will make it possible to
scale down the manufacture of such products as sugar,
paper, and cement in a manner that will not seriously
affect the costs of the large-scale plants that have
so far largely monopolized the output of these products.

Factors Discouraging Small-Scale Industry

While government has encouraged small-scale industry
through the SSIDO, a number of its policies and procedures
have in fact discouraged small-scale industry. One of the
most acute problems faced by most small-scale entrepreneurs is the chronic shortage of raw materials--
supplies that are considered inadequate in quantity and
quality and are excessively high in price. Not all materials, of course, are in short supply. The shortage is
most serious in certain key items of iron and steel and
nonferrous metals and in some materials that are largely
imported. Many small-scale enterprises operate far
below capacity because of lack of raw materials. The
proliferation of new enterprises has made it necessary
to distribute limited supplies over an ever larger number of units with attendant low-capacity operation and
a wasteful use of capital investment. Government policies do not appear well conceived to increase the available supply of industrial materials. The shortages are
probably aggravated by an unwillingness to permit
significant expansion of large-scale private enterprises
capable of adding to the supply and by government concentration on the establishment and development of
government plants that in many respects have not been
able to achieve adequate production. Too large a proportion of India's limited resources appears to have

been allocated to capital investment, leaving too little
for the raw materials required to utilize available productive capacity. Production probably could be substantially increased by selective, but significant, cuts in
capital investment. Policies governing the pricing of
industrial materials appear also to have been at fault.
While the government has in recent years "decontrolled"
a number of industrial materials (in the sense that
government distribution controls in the form of quotas
have been abandoned), it has not permitted prices to
rise to a level where effective supply and demand would
be in equilibrium.[4]

Small industry is also handicapped by the many
government controls and the slowness of the procedures
involved in administering them. Government action is
required for registering an enterprise and for obtaining
such necessities as power, land, raw materials, and
import permits. While the need for considerable government intervention can be appreciated, the number of
regulations appears excessive. The time required to get
all the requisite sanctions for starting an enterprise
seems unduly long, all the more so because they cannot
usually be obtained simultaneously, but only in sequence.
Many entrepreneurs complain bitterly about excessive
"red tape."[5]

While it must be recognized that the government has
assisted small-scale enterprise in many ways, the time
has now come, not only for a careful review of the past
performance and future role of the SSIDO, but also for
an overall reconsideration of all programs and policies
affecting the development of small enterprises.

RURAL INDUSTRIES PROJECTS PROGRAM

The pilot program of Rural Industries Projects (RIP)
was launched in April 1962 when the Central Government's
Planning Commission established a Rural Industries Planning Committee together with a Standing Committee to
provide day-to-day guidance. The program was started in
45 pilot areas, later increased to 49, each of which on
the average comprised three to five of the old "community
development blocks" and had a population ranging between
300,000 and 500,000.

Prior Efforts to Promote Rural Industrialization

Khadi and Village Industries Program

The RIP was by no means the first effort to stimulate
rural industrialization. In 1952/53 five all-India Boards
were established to foster the production of Khadi (hand-
spinning) and Village Industries, Handlooms, Coir, Silk,
and Handicrafts; and these continue to this day. They were
all oriented toward the rural areas (except for the Handicrafts Board which has concentrated on urban as well as
rural handicrafts) and were designed to revitalize and
redevelop basically manual crafts and trades that had long
been traditionally carried on in rural communities but had
languished under the impact of modern factory production.
Their activities were largely inspired by the Gandhian
concept of village self-reliance and self-sufficiency as
well as that of creative work as a form of self-discipline
and a means of enhancing human dignity.

The most important of these Boards has been the one
which is concerned with khadi and traditional village industries and which was re-named in 1957 the Khadi and
Village Industries Commission. The competence of this
Commission extends to khadi (both hand-spinning and weaving)
and 14 other village industries, including hand-pounding
of rice and processing of other cereals; beekeeping; the
production of edible and nonedible oils and of soap; the
manufacture of handmade paper, matches, pottery, leather,
and products from fibres other than coir; blacksmithing
and carpentry; and the production of various types of
sugar from cane (gur and khandsari) and palm (gur), of
lime from limestone, and of manure and methane gas from
cow dung. The Commission has for the most part retained
direct responsibility for the promotion of khadi, but has
entrusted the stimulation of other village industries
primarily to State Khadi and Village Industries Boards.

The Commission and State Boards carry on a wide range
of activities. Training facilities are provided both for
artisans and supervisory personnel. A field staff fur-
nishes technical extension services. Production is organized principally by nonprofitmaking "registered societies"
and through cooperatives. There is an extensive program
of loans and grants, including loans at low rates of
interest and subsidies. Assistance is given for the
procurement of raw materials and the marketing of products, and the sale of khadi is facilitated by a 20
percent subsidy. Finally, the Commission conducts a
research program focusing largely on improving the technology of traditional village industries.

There has been a substantial though declining training component in this program. For example, during the
first three Five-Year Plans (up to the end of 1968/69),

nearly 565,000 artisans were trained in khadi and almost 92,000 in other village industries. About 90 percent of these were sponsored by registered societies and cooperatives. In addition, 26,784 production managers and supervisors were trained--25,181 for khadi and 1,603 for other village industries. Stipends and traveling expenses have been paid to encourage trainees to take advantage of these training facilities. However, the demand for training has dropped off rather sharply in recent years; in one institution visited, for example, only half of the training capacity was being utilized. The need for such training has been largely satisfied, particularly now that the expansion of village industries has for the most part leveled out. While the training provided has undoubtedly done much to improve artisan skills, it has apparently not contributed much to an improvement in the management of cooperatives. Thus the Report of the Khadi and Village Industries Committee, which was published in February 1968 and was designed to evaluate the Commission's whole program, concluded that only 30-35 percent of the cooperative societies were functioning effectively.

The entire program has unquestionably been useful in developing and maintaining employment opportunities, particularly in rural areas where more attractive and, especially, more remunerative alternative employment has not been available. Khadi has made the most important contribution in this respect, employing 1,100,000 workers in 1969/70, of whom 973,000 were part-time, producing goods to a value of Rs256.4 million and paying out wages totaling Rs149.3 million. However, both production and employment in 1969/70 were considerably below the peaks reached in the mid-sixties. Despite the increases in wages and prices paid, the very low level of cash income attainable in this cottage industry has tended to become progressively less attractive by comparison with the rising expectations of the rural population and, in many cases, the improvement of other opportunities. Moreover, despite subsidies, it has become increasingly difficult to sell khadi, since many consumers are reluctant to buy khadi cloth that generally wears less well than machine-made cloth and is less uniform in the quality of its yarn and its weaving. While many traditional village industries other than khadi--particularly the cottage match, soap, leather, pottery, and fibre industries, as well as blacksmithery and carpentry--have continued to make some progress, largely because they offer a somewhat better return than khadi. All told they occupied only 900,000 part-time and full-time workers in 1969/70, and their total wage disbursements amounted to but Rs122.1 million.

One of the drawbacks of the khadi and traditional village industries program has been its cost. Thus in 1968/69 and 1969/70 respectively the Khadi and Village Industries Commission spent Rs66.8 million and Rs62.2

million on the promotion of khadi in the form of rebates
and subsidies, establishment expenditures, training and
research; and these amounts, which make no allowance for
the cost of concessional interest rates or losses due to
defaults on loans (the amount in default at the end of
1969/70 stood at Rs24.2 million), represented no less than
53 and 42 percent respectively of the total wages earned
in khadi production during each of these two years. For
other village industries net grants and subsidies paid
out were somewhat less in relation to total wage income--
namely, about 11 percent in 1968/69 and 9 percent in
1969/70.

The Khadi and Village Industries Commission has tried
to increase the productivity and income of the industries
under its jurisdiction through the development of improved
technologies. In some measure it has been successful--for
example, in developing better rope-making machines and
improved potters wheels equipped with ball-bearings to
ensure more rapid and smoother operation. For spinning
it has devised, in replacement of the traditional spinning
wheel and the two-spindle ambar charkha, six-spindle and
even twelve-spindle equipment. However, this more modern
equipment accounted in 1969/70 for only 5.3 percent of
the total output of hand-spun cotton yarn. Adoption of
this newer equipment has been slow because most of the
spinning is done by women at home as a part-time activity.
Spinning on the new equipment in general requires a work-
shop-type of operation, since power is needed for the
preparatory processes of carding and roving. In general
one is inclined to agree with the judgment of the special
Khadi and Village Industries Committee which concluded
in its February 1968 report that while khadi would continue to have a recognized role as one of the rural
industries and although it may be the most important rural
industry in some areas, with the development of scientific
agriculture and advance of rural electrification, khadi
may be replaced by other more paying rural industries such
as agricultural processing and manufacture of agricultural
inputs.

Industrial Extension in Community
Development Program

Attempts were also made to include rural industrialization within the scope of the Community Development Program, which was initiated in the early fifties and was
designed to assist and stimulate rural self-help efforts
on a broad front. The accomplishments and limitations
of this program, which was long carried out by a special
ministry but has now been deemphasized and entrusted to
the Ministry for Food and Agriculture, will not be examined here. It should be noted, however, that the all-
purpose block development officer or village worker was

progressively replaced by a more specialized staff, including a block-level extension officer for industries known as the BLEO (I). This extension worker, operating under the general direction of the head block development officer, was supposed to be responsible, not only for supplementing the activities of the Khadi and Village Industries Commission and the corresponding State Boards, but also for stimulating the development of more modern small-scale industries with power-driven equipment. To fit him for this dual responsibility his training was initially divided between the SSIDO and the Khadi and Village Industries Commission, with the former providing four months and the latter eight months of the training required. Later, however, two specialized and integrated institutions were established--one at Hyderabad, which was closed in October 1970, the other at Nilokheri. Up to the end of 1969/70 these two institutions had trained 466 extension workers. In addition refresher courses have been given for those who have already served in the field.

These two institutions have provided training in industrial development and extension work, industrial technology, program planning, and cooperatives. The content of the courses appears on the whole to be well conceived. About 60 percent of the time is devoted to practical training and to observation and study visits to rural industrial units and institutions. Trainees are taught how to operate the equipment used in the khadi and traditional village industries and installed at the Nilokheri center, and they are also given, at the Haryana Polytechnic at Nilokheri, some practical knowledge of the eight trades (blacksmithery, machine shop practice, fitting, foundry work, sheet-metal work, welding, internal combustion engines and hydraulics) more commonly employed in rural small-scale industry. However, the relative emphasis on these two types of practical training appears to vary with the predilections of the principal.

Although in principle it appears desirable to train industrial extension workers and post them to community development blocks, the effectiveness of such workers has in practice been seriously circumscribed. Since the training of these extension officers is of necessity rather general, they often do not have the requisite skills to assess specific industrial possibilities and to provide technical advice. At the same time they have little facility for commanding the services of more qualified personnel in case of need. They usually occupy a rather anomalous and ill-defined position in the state service, with extremely low rates of pay and few opportunities for promotion. In terms of both their physical location and their lowly position in the hierarchy, they are so remote from the centers of decision that they have little influence in obtaining for rural industrial units

the financing, raw materials, power, and other facilities
needed. Falling at least partly under the administrative
control of the principal block development officer, the
industrial extension workers are often diverted by this
officer to nonindustrial tasks. Thus their morale is
often very low. In general it cannot be said that this
extension service has been very effective, except in a
few states; and at least one state has entirely abolished
the service. This experience illustrates the oft-observed
principle that training, no matter how intelligently conceived with respect to content, is unlikely to be useful
unless those who have received it can be employed under
conditions that make it possible for them to work
effectively.

State Promotion of Rural Industrialization

Apart from the establishment of the block-level
industrial extension service and the work of the Khadi
and Village Industries Commission and its associated State
Boards, the state governments in many cases also initiated
and have continued various other activities for the promotion of rural industry prior to, and independent of,
the RIP Program launched in 1962. For example, the author
of this study noted that the state governments of Punjab
and Haryana had established and were operating industrial
estates, common facilities, and rural artisan training
centers. Often these have taken the form of rural industrial centers that provide at a single place training in
certain rural crafts, workshops for the location of small
producing units, and common production facilities that
individual artisans cannot themselves afford. Some
comment on these will be made in connection with an
examination of similar facilities made available under
the RIP program.

Nature and Financing of RIP Program

All of the measures and activities outlined above
suffered to some degree from a lack of focus and an
excessive diffusion of effort. In large part the RIP
program was designed to overcome these disadvantages by
concentrating on a specific number of relatively small
pilot areas all the resources that were regarded necessary
to make a significant impact on rural industry. These
included staff for appraisal of industrial opportunities
and the provision of extension services, financing for
individual and cooperative enterprises, training of artisans, common production facilities, rural industrial
workshops, and the like. Even so, the size of the program,
embracing 49 project areas and a total population of around

20 million in 34,073 villages and 234 community development blocks, was by no means insignificant.

The RIP program has been financed by the central
government, which has also laid down its general principles and guidelines with the advice of a Rural Industries Planning Committee. The actual implementation as
well as the determination of the detailed content of the
program was left to the state governments, which have
discharged their obligations through a network of committees operating usually under the general supervision
of the State Directorate of Industries. At the area
project level there was to be a staff consisting as a
minimum of a technical officer, a planning-cum-survey
officer, and two technical officers, assisted at times
by the BLEO (I)s. At the central government level
responsibility for the program was exercised at first by
the Planning Commission. At the beginning of 1968 the
program was transferred to the Ministry of Industrial
Development, where it was first entrusted to the Commissioner (Industrial Cooperatives). Still later, in April
1970, responsibility for the program was assigned to the
Development Commissioner (Small-Scale Industries) apparently in an effort to secure better coordination between
the small-scale industry effort as a whole and the RIP
program.

Up to the end of 1970/71 the central government had
provided financing for the program to a total of approximately Rs137.5 million, of which a little less than half
had been provided in the form of grants for staffing,
training, and so forth and the balance in the form of
loan funds (to be utilized by the states, under the procedures of their State Aid to Industries legislation)
for the financing of rural industrial enterprises.
Beginning in the first year of the fourth Five-Year Plan
(1969/70), the central government's financial support was
sharply slashed, particularly that for industrial loans
which, it was decided, should henceforth be provided
principally by banking institutions. By the end of the
current Five-Year Plan (that is, after 1973/74), the
states are expected to take over all of the financing of
the existing 49 projects, while the central government
will launch and finance 50 new pilot projects.

RIP Accomplishments

It is extremely difficult to assess the effectiveness
of the RIP Program. To date there have been only two
evaluations, and both of these were published in 1968 and
covered approximately the same period. The first was
done by an Evaluation Study Group of the Rural Industries
Planning Committee that visited six project areas; its

report appeared in April 1968. The second was carried out
by the Programme Evaluation Organisation of the Planning
Commission; and its report, covering eight projects in
detail, was published in December 1968. In addition there
has appeared a report giving a very brief summary of the
activities in all of the 49 project areas up to and including 1969/70, but this does not purport to make a
critical evaluation of the program. Finally, the Ministry
of Industrial Development has published a statistical
record of the progress said to have been achieved up to
the end of 1970/71.

On the face of it, this statistical record appears
impressive. They key "progress indicators" for the seven-
year period are given in Table 12.1. While these figures

TABLE 12.1

Progress of the RIP Program

	1964/65	1967/68	1970/71	Total for period
Training facilities				
No. of centers at end of year (cumulative)	261	418	250	-
No. of artisans trained (cumulative)	5,963	27,268	39,575	39,575
Common facilities				
No. of centers at end of year (cumulative)	124	137	118	-
No. of industrial units assisted (each year)	1,487	18,392	20,215	-
No. of industrial units financed*	3,033	4,435	1,530	30,171
Existing	1,575	2,681	972	16,294
New	1,458	1,754	558	1,530
Value of new industrial investments (Rs millions)	11.88	23.17	19.02	185.83
Value of industrial output (Rs millions)	8.87	70.00	264.17	739.59
No. of people employed in industry (cumulative)	32,090	79,705	133,343	133,343
Pattern of new industrial investment				
Total (Rs millions)	-	-	-	185.08
From project loan funds	-	-	-	69.40
From banking institutions	-	-	-	47.50
From entrepreneurs	-	-	-	68.90

*Excluding those financed by banks

Source: India, Ministry of Industrial Development.

confirm that something has been accomplished, they do not
provide very satisfactory information on the exact extent
and quality of these accomplishments. The data on employment and production may well be subject to some discount,
since it is notoriously difficult to obtain reliable information of this sort from rural artisanal and small-
scale enterprises.[6] Furthermore, the personnel available
for the collection of such data has been very limited.

Unfortunately very little information is available
on the degree of success that new industrial enterprises
have enjoyed. Data on loan defaults could provide some
criterion of success or lack of success, but these are
unfortunately not readily available. The two evaluation
reports, the summary report on progress to the end of
1969/70 and the "statistical indicators" of progress cited
above, do not provide any information on defaults. Some
estimates cited to the author are not altogether reassur-
ing on this score. In two states it was indicated that
between 30 and 40 percent of the loans extended to rural
industry under State Aid to Industry Acts were in default;
and in still another the proportion of defaults was said
to fluctuate around 50 percent. In one rural industrial
project area visited by the author it was estimated that
only 10 percent of the loans were being regularly and
fully repaid. In this same area 28 percent of the new
units brought into being, accounting for 36 percent of
the total investment, had closed down. However, the repayment record on loans made by banks that have taken over
virtually all of the financing in the last few years
appears to be much better. Improvement is due largely,
no doubt, to more effective and objective screening of
loan applicants and projects as well as to more adequate
control over the disbursement of the loan proceeds.

RIP Training and Extension Services

In examining the RIP program, the nonformal educational components, consisting of training and extension,
will be considered first.

Training Services and Centers

Training has been provided for both 1) traditional
rural artisans and their sons and 2) new entrants into
the labor force. This has been supplemented in many
states by the provision of tool kits to artisans with a
75 percent subsidy and by loans enabling those who finished
their training to set up enterprises of their own. Training has been made available in a variety of ways. The
great majority of states set up special training centers
for this purpose, but a number relied exclusively or
primarily on sending candidates for training to already

existing training institutions either inside or outside
the state or arranged with larger enterprises for in-plant
training.

The number of new training centers reached a peak of
428 at the end of 1966/67. By the end of 1970/71 the number had dropped to 250 and was still declining. This
reduction was due, not only to a curtailment of financial
support, but to a realization that the number of centers
had grown out of all proportion to the demand for training. For example, considering the fact that the period
of training was about one year, the training centers
existing at the end of 1966/67 apparently trained during
the following year an average of only 11 people per center. During the first three years 22,410 persons were
trained, or an average of 7,200 per year, but in the
last four years the average has fallen to around 4,000.

Demand for training was disappointing for several
reasons. The traditional rural artisans had only a
limited interest in extended training. They are nearly
all "hereditary" artisans, passing on their craft from
father to son. They have always relied on "on-the-job"
training, have been rather set in their ways and little
disposed to innovate. Most of these artisans could not
afford to spare the time for training and were even
reluctant to spare their sons for training because they
needed the help of their sons in practising their trade.
Each training center was generally able to draw its
trainees from a limited radius of about 10 miles. Eli-
gibility standards often had to be dropped in an effort
to fill up existing places, and in many cases people who
otherwise had nothing to do attended principally for the
purpose of drawing the training stipend, which generally
ranged from Rs20 to Rs30 per month. Under these circumstances the training centers proved to be rather expensive.
Moreover, the quality of the training they have imparted
has apparently left much to be desired. Most of the instructors have been of low calibre, largely because the
pay offered was insufficient to attract capable talent.
Many of them apparently had long ago graduated from one
of the numerous Industrial Training Institutes in India
and had not been successful in their previous occupations.
It seems in retrospect that it would probably have been
advisable to recruit instructors among skilled practising
craftsmen employed in industry. In that event, however,
pay scales would have had to be more attractive.

Although training in newly established centers has
been by far the most prevalent practice, a few states
have followed the practice of paying stipends to candidates despatched for training to already existing institutions, and other states have increasingly followed suit
as they closed down the special RIP centers. This form
of training has certainly been more economical owing to
the savings in investment costs. To a still lesser extent

facilities have been provided for in-plant training.
Maharashtra has apparently been the state which has
utilized this method of training to the largest extent.
While it has had to pay larger stipends for this purpose,
Rs75-100 per month, it appears that this additional current expenditure has been more than compensated for by
the higher quality and more practical nature of the training thus obtained.

Information on the subsequent employment of trainees
is not very reliable. The Evaluation Study Group of the
Rural Industries Planning Committee noted in its 1968
report that there were no data on the fate of about half
of the 17,500 people who had been trained in the first
few years. On the other hand, in the summary review of
progress in all of the RIP areas up to the end of 1969/70,
claims are generally made that the vast majority of
trainees have found employment and usually in the trades
for which they had been trained. Some oral testimony,
however, casts at least some doubt on these claims and
indicates that many may have found only temporary employment. Moreover, the staff available in the RIP areas has
hardly been adequate to follow up on the trainees and
determine whether they have been effectively integrated
into the rural economy. Traditional artisans in the rural
areas are generally averse to the employment of nonfamily
labor and are therefore unlikely to have provided many
employment opportunities to trainees other than their sons.
Small-scale industrial entrepreneurs have usually been
disposed to train their own personnel, although it is not
improbable that many of the new units brought into being
by the RIP program have given employment to trainees.
Those who have received in-plant training have probably
been most successful in finding permanent and remunerative
employment. For example, a study of the 466 persons
given in-plant training by Maharashtra State over the
six-year period ended 1969/70 indicated that only 53, or
a little over 10 percent, had remained unemployed. Moreover, 38 of them started industries of their own and
received loans for this purpose.[7] Undoubtedly it would be
desirable to undertake some thorough sample studies to
determine how useful the various methods of training have
been in generating both paid employment and self-employment. Such studies should, among other things, focus on
possible means of adapting training programs more effectively to the requirements for various skills. There is
some reason to believe, for example, that little or no
attention has been paid to the need for upgrading skills
in the rural building trades.

Extension Services

By and large the extension services provided to
existing and new enterprises in the form of advice on
technical, managerial, and marketing problems have been

on a very limited scale. This has been primarily due to
inadequacies in staffing. Although the number of personnel assigned to the RIPs has increased significantly in
recent years, the latest summary review of progress up to
the end of March 1970 indicates that 31 out of the 49
project areas still lacked sufficient staff. Moreover,
the quality of the staff, while varying markedly from
state to state, is often not good enough. Pay scales and
other conditions of service have not been in many cases
sufficient to attract capable personnel to what are, after
all, rather remote rural areas that frequently cannot provide adequate housing for personnel of the requisite
calibre or educational facilities for their children.
Frequently shifts in personnel have also impeded the
effectiveness of the extension work.

Since the beginning of 1970, when the Small-Scale
Industrial Development Organisation of the Ministry of
Industrial Development was put in charge of the RIP program, efforts have been made to have existing SISIs and
ECs provide more assistance to the local project staff.
Directors and personnel of these institutions have been
asked to pay more frequent visits to the RIP areas. Somewhat more technical assistance has been provided in this
way; the number of "intensive campaigns" of the type
already outlined has apparently also increased; and the
personnel of SISIs have completed new or re-surveys of
the industrial development possibilities of some of the
RIP areas. However, the limited number of personnel
available to the SISIs and ECs, as well as the acute
shortage of transport, have made this assistance rather
discontinuous and occasional in character. Thus the
provision of extension services remains a weak point in
the RIP program.

Other Contributing Elements

Financing for Rural Industry

The greatest impact of the RIP program has undoubtedly
been through the provision of financing for existing and
new enterprises. For the first time financing has been
made available for rural industry on a more adequate scale
and on liberal, concessional terms. As already noted,
financing was initially provided entirely from public
funds made available under State Aid to Industry Rules.
Up to the end of March 1971 no less than 30,171 units had
received assistance from this source to a total amount of
Rs116.9 million. This type of financing, however, has
undoubtedly been rather wasteful, owing to inadequate
screening of projects and borrowers and deficient controls
over disbursement. In recent years there has been a

salutary transition to institutional or bank financing
that has been provided on a more business-like basis.
Thus the State Bank of India, which has been the principal institution engaged in this type of finance, had
extended, up to the end of March 1971, credits to 7,114
RIP enterprises for a total amount of Rs47.5 million.
Financing from both government and bank funds has been
made available on rather liberal terms with respect to
interest rates and security. Under State Aid to Industry
Rules, loans were generally provided at about 3 percent;
those up to Rs1,000 or Rs2,000 were usually granted without security; while larger loans up to Rs5,000 required
only a surety by a third party. Bank loans have been
available at a much higher interest rate. However, conditions respecting security were greatly relaxed under a
special liberalized scheme introduced by the State Bank of
India in January 1970. Under this scheme loans up to
Rs5,000 have been provided without any security on the
recommendation of the RIP project officer. There has
been criticism, however, that this amount has been sufficient to finance only artisans and not small-scale industrial enterprises that need more capital investment.

Common Production Facilities

Originally it was intended that the provision of
common production facilities would be one of the most
important services to rural artisans and entrepreneurs.
However, the contribution of these facilities has been
rather disappointing. By the end of 1965/66 a maximum of
161 common facility centers had been established, but
since that time the number has steadily declined to 118
at the end of 1970/71; and of the remaining ones many are
not being fully utilized. The centers provided facilities for a wide range of activities, such as machining
and welding, carpentry, tanning, textile dyeing, wool
carding, milk chilling, fruit preservation, pottery making,
stone crushing, and concrete mixing. In a number of cases
RIP areas also set up their own production units, such as
general engineering workshops and enterprises for manufacturing paints and varnishes, sprayers and dusters, footwear, woolens, and chalk. Less frequently attempts were
made to provide workshop space on small rural industrial
estates.

The common facilities established within the RIP
areas have proved much less useful than those operated by
the SISIs and ECs, undoubtedly because of their poor
location. However, even at best it was difficult to find
in the rural areas a concentration of artisanal and
industrial enterprises sufficient to ensure adequate
utilization of the common facilities. Most of them have
therefore operated at a considerable loss. The production
units operated by various RIP areas have also for the most

part been conspicuously unsuccessful and have again demonstrated the unsuitability of government departments for
operating commercial enterprises. The small industrial
estates or workshop clusters have seldom attracted sufficient occupants, largely because most rural entrepreneurs
prefer to locate their workshops in or near their places
of residence or in close proximity to the customers they
serve. This is borne out by similar experiences in rural
areas outside the RIP program. For example, out of some
75 worksheds provided in rural areas by the States of Punjab, Haryana,and Himachal Pradesh, only 17 were found to
be occupied by operating private enterprises. Similarly,
the experience of Punjab and Haryana States with the so-
called "rural industrial centers," which have previously
been mentioned, has also been disappointing. Here too,
the percentage of occupation of the workshops provided
has been very low.

Problem of Industrial Opportunities

Undoubtedly the most serious difficulty that confronted the RIP areas was to find a sufficient number of
potentially profitable industrial opportunities. This
difficulty was greatly aggravated by the restrictive
criteria used in the selection of the pilot areas and
also by the original decision to exclude from these areas
all towns with a population of 15,000 and over. Both the
central and state governments were understandably concerned
that so many areas in India had lagged far behind others in
progress. The RIP program was conceived primarily as a
means of helping these lagging areas. Thus the decision
was made to include in the program principally areas
1) where agriculture was being carried on mainly under un-
irrigated conditions and there was therefore considerable
unemployment, 2) where there was considerable unemployment
owing to unfavorable natural conditions and lack of potential resources, 3) where there were tribal or otherwise
backward populations, and 4) where agricultural conditions
were favorable and some agricultural progress had been
achieved but where there was heavy population pressure on
available resources. Except perhaps for those in the last
category, the project areas that were chosen were virtually
all backward in varying degrees. Therefore, they had no
large surpluses of agricultural raw materials available
for processing, the purchasing power for industrial products was very limited, and the possibility of supplying
agriculturists with facilities for servicing agricultural
implements and machinery and for supplying inputs required
for production was also seriously circumscribed. The
decision to exclude towns with a population of 15,000 and
over, prompted by a desire to keep the program "rural" in
character, made these limitations even more serious.
Small-scale industries located in the larger local towns

within the district would have been able to draw on a
bigger area for raw materials and to serve a wider market.
Moreover, such towns were more adequately provided with
the necessary infrastructure--transport, power and water
supply, facilities which most of the poorer villages lack.
Finally, the industries located in these towns would
probably have attracted a considerable number of workers
from the nearby rural areas. Although proposals made in
recent years to include towns with a population up to
30,000 and even 50,000 in the project areas have found
widespread endorsement, the central government has so far
failed to act on them.

Area Surveys

Originally surveys were made of all the RIP areas to
inventory their resources and to determine their potentialities for industrial development. Since then new
surveys have occasionally been undertaken, usually by
personnel made available by the SISIs. The quality of
these surveys has understandably varied considerably. In
many cases they were not very specific in their recommendations on industrial possibilities. In any event many
of the suggestions made in the survey reports have not been
carried out for a variety of reasons: lack of continuity
in project staff, inadequate information on resources,
impracticability of the proposals, insufficient technical
know-how on certain industries, and lack of entrepreneurs.[8]
Sometimes project officers have ignored the survey reports
entirely, perhaps justifiably. In one project area
visited by the author of this report the project officer
had apparently never consulted a comparatively recent
survey report, either because he was ignorant of its
existence or because he was convinced it would not in any
event give him any practical guidance.

Constraints on Rural Small-Scale Industry

Experience has demonstrated that industries relying
for raw material supplies and markets outside the RIP
area and immediately adjoining areas have encountered
the most difficulty. Yet to a considerable extent efforts
have been made to foster such industries, simply because
the limitations of local markets and sources of supply
severely restricted other possibilities. The problems
faced by these industries have been formidable. Even for
small-scale industrial enterprises located in or for large
urban areas marketing is in most cases the severest constraint. For small-scale industries located in rural
areas far from their markets this difficulty is much
greater. They cannot readily find regular customers, and
their prices, burdened by the costs of "importing" raw
materials and transporting their finished goods to rather

distant markets, are often not competitive. Industries
in the rural areas not working with locally available
materials tend to have far more difficulty than their
urban counterparts in obtaining access to scarce raw
materials, even though the authorities during recent years
have made special efforts to meet their needs in this
respect. It is appropriate to point out that the numerous
government regulations and controls militate against the
location of industries in remote rural areas and small
towns. The management of business in India today requires
frequent contacts with government and at a level where
decisions can be made, or at least decisively influenced,
with respect to such questions as the registration of
factories, the sanctioning of power connections, the
allocation of raw materials, the procurement of import
licenses, and the approval of financing. Given these
conditions, small-scale industries in rural areas not
working for local markets or utilizing locally available
raw materials are at a considerable disadvantage. In one
area, for instance, it was found that two out of three
small radio assembly shops for which there was obviously
an inadequate local market had closed. In another area
a small wire-drawing plant and a small shop designed to
produce automobile parts and components were virtually
idle owing to lack of raw materials and markets; and a
larger factory making and printing tinplate containers
was working at less than half capacity because of inability to obtain tinplate. Examples of this nature can
undoubtedly be multiplied many times.

Conclusions

In the enthusiasm and concern for promoting development in the more remote and backward areas, efforts to
encourage rural industrialization have tended toward
excessive dispersion in terms of both the range of industries and units and the entrepreneurs that have been
assisted. There has been insufficient discrimination in
the selection of entrepreneurs and the types of industries.
Inadequate attention has been paid to staffing constraints
and the limitations governing rural industry. In retrospect the judgments made in April 1963 by R. P. Lynton
and J. E. Stepanek have been only too prophetic. These
two experts on small-scale industries pointed out that
"present government practices, whether official policy or
not, favour distribution of raw materials, funds and other
assistance to the largest possible number of receivers
. . .," aggravating the problem of raw materials for
existing enterprises in efforts to ensure minimal supplies
to new units. They criticized the tendency to evaluate
technical advice "in number of units visited and people
seen, not in terms of results," and advocated the

concentration of outside assistance "on a few promising
groups in a locality and, within these groups, on those
people who have the motivation and other characteristics
which are usually found in successful managers." They
expressed concern "over the tendency to carry industrialization to villages and the very small towns before an
industrial base has been established in the rural towns
of 20,000 to 100,000 population" and recommended that
industrialization in rural areas should first concentrate
on these larger towns and then link such industry with
new industries in adjoining rural areas.[9]

In some respects the lessons of past experience are
being taken into account in future planning. Thus in the
50 new RIPS which the central government expects to
finance, the intention is apparently to concentrate efforts
on towns that are already comparatively well endowed with
infrastructure and can become "development growth points"
for the surrounding area; and this planning is proceeding
on the tentative assumption, not yet confirmed by a formal government decision, that towns up to 50,000 in
population will be included in the RIP areas. Elsewhere
there is to be a "thin" program focusing primarily on the
upgrading of rural artisans. Banks involved in the
financing of rural artisans are to concentrate their
efforts initially on areas within a 10-15-mile radius
of their branches, so that they can more effectively
supervise their borrowers.

In other respects, however, the dispersion of effort
may be even greater in the future. The central government is initiating a program of 50 new RIPs at a time
when there is serious question that the state governments
will have sufficient resources to finance and improve the
already existing RIP areas as well as other schemes for
which the central government is transferring responsibility
to the States. In 1971 the decision was taken to broaden
the scope of existing RIP areas, hitherto confined to
three to five community development blocks, to the entire
district (except for towns of 15,000 and over), even
though existing staffs were barely able to cope with the
tasks confronting them in the more limited areas.[10] In
addition, the central government, in cooperation with
the States, has launched an entirely new program--the so-
called "backward districts" program. The elements of
this program were worked out by two working groups established in 1968 and charged respectively with the responsibility of identifying backward districts and recommend-
ing fiscal and financial incentives that would encourage
the establishment of small and medium industries in such
districts. In this plan large numbers of districts (210)
have been declared "backward." Institutions, such as the
Industrial Development Bank of India, the Industrial Finance
Corporation of India, the Industrial Credit and Investment
Corporation of India, have been induced to offer more lib-

eral financing terms to new industries in these districts,
namely concessional interest rates, longer periods of
grace before the repayment of loans, more extended schedules of repayment, reductions in commitment charges, reductions in the owners' equity capital required, and
possible participation in risk capital. In a more limited
number of districts--around 40--the central government has
undertaken to defray by an outright grant   10 percent of
the cost of fixed capital investment in new units, provided such total investment per enterprise does not exceed
Rs5 million. Fiscal concessions have also been made.
While this program puts primary emphasis on financial and
fiscal incentives, it also involves increasing burdens in
terms of technical assistance, screening and supervision
of projects, allocation of scarce materials and other
facilities that are likely to put additional strains on
the already overextended staffs of financial institutions,
SISIs, and other government agencies.

It must be conceded that the gravity and extent of
India's economic problems are such as to demand urgent
action and put severe pressures on both the central and
state governments to initiate new approaches and to multiply programs. Geographical disparities in economic
progress have produced a legitimate concern with the
creation of employment opportunities in economically lagging or backward areas. The allocation of considerable
resources for the purpose of developing employment opportunities in such areas is in principle justified when
there are significant sociological and linguistic obstacles
to internal migration and where it is desirable in any
event to prevent massive emigration to large urban centers.

At the same time limitations of financial resources
and of available personnel of the right calibre obviously
make it necessary to avoid excessive dispersal of effort
and to concentrate on the formulation and execution of
programs that will really produce significant results.
Past and projected programs fall significantly short of
this requirement. The objectives of the RIP program,
while achieved in a modest measure, have been to a considerable extent frustrated. Industrial development where
the agricultural production base has not previously been
expanded has proved predictably difficult. Under these
conditions there has been an excessive preoccupation with
the industrialization of purely rural areas and a somewhat obstinate unwillingness to recognize ·that industrialization in the larger towns and cities serving these areas
might be far more productive. The reliance on small-scale
industries as the vehicle for industrialization of the
backward areas also seems largely misplaced. Severe constraints on the supply of locally available raw materials
and on the purchasing power of local markets severely
limit the opportunities for such industries. Small-scale
industries that do not work within the framework of local

markets and local raw material supplies are singularly
ill-suited to cope with the problem of procuring raw
materials from more distant sources of supply and of
selling their products in wider and more distant markets.
It seems necessary to find ways and means of attracting
medium- and large-scale industries to the backward areas.
Such industries would have far greater capacity for dealing with the attendant locational disadvantages. They
have the resources for developing at least part of the
infrastructure required and for training their own labor.
Apart from the direct employment they could generate,
they would tend to create more opportunities for small-
scale industries that could cater to the market afforded
by the labor force of the larger-scale plants and engage
in the manufacture of parts and components for such plants.
The new "backward districts" program appears in fact to be
more oriented toward the attraction of larger-scale industries, although the central government's investment subsidy
is still limited to enterprises whose fixed investment does
not exceed the relatively modest sum of Rs5 million. It
would be desirable to study in depth the cost and content
of a program, including the provision of infrastructure
and direct subsidies, which would induce more large-scale
industry to locate in economically backward regions by
effectively overcoming the disadvantages that now prevent
them from doing this.

TRAINING FOR ENTREPRENEURSHIP

In many less developed countries, particularly those
in sub-Saharan Africa, there are as yet relatively few
indigenous entrepreneurs. Those governments that are
interested in developing locally owned and managed enterprise are faced with the need of devising effective ways
and means of assisting people without any previous entrepreneurial experience--new school graduates and employees
of government or foreign business concerns--to launch and
conduct their own business. To do this they must know
how to motivate people to go into business and how to
impart through training the practical substantive business skills the new entrepreneurs will require.
India has been the scene of some experiments in this
field that are of relevance. Some pilot programs in
achievement motivation training were carried out in 1963,
1964, and 1965, and some experimentation with these techniques has continued. In April 1970 three Gujerat State
public corporations--the Gujerat Industrial Investment
Corporation, the Gujerat Finance Corporation, and the
Gujerat Industrial Development Corporation, all located
at Ahmedabad, sponsored for the first time an entrepreneurship development course designed to train would-be

industrial entrepreneurs in the selection of an industrial
enterprise and the business skills requisite to operate
it.   Four courses of this type have since been conducted.
Finally, later in 1970, the Government of India decided to
sponsor similar entrepreneurship development courses to be
given by 21 selected institutions, but tailored specifically to enable unemployed engineers and technicians, for
the most part fresh graduates, to start industrial enterprises. By the end of 1971 most of the participating
institutions had conducted three or four of such courses.
The nature and results of these types of training will now
be reviewed.

Achievement Motivation Training

        In his book, The Achieving Society,[11] Professor
David C. McClelland of Harvard University marshaled
evidence tending to show that a particular motive, the
need for achievement, promotes entrepreneurship and that
societies that emphasized this need for achievement in
their culture made more rapid economic progress than
others. At first this motivation to achieve was believed
to be entirely the product of early childhood training
and environmental influences, including early schooling,
but later a number of psychologists, including Professor
McClelland, came to the conclusion that minimum motivation
could be strengthened even in adults through appropriate
training. This has led to considerable experimentation
with achievement motivation training of entrepreneurs and
business executives in the United States, Spain, Mexico,
India, and other countries.[12]
        The techniques for identifying and developing achieve-
ment motivation are not easy to describe briefly, particularly for one who, like the author of this study, has
himself no first-hand experience of them. Achievement
motivation training might be characterized broadly as
"stimulated self-analysis." The first step is usually to
test the degree to which a person, looking at situations
in which he and others may be involved, thinks and reacts
to "achievement terms," by which are meant concern with
achieving certain goals; the specific acts required to
attain these goals; the recognition of obstacles, either
personal or external, to reaching the objectives; and the
emotional reactions to success or failure. He is then
encouraged, through self-analysis, personal counseling,
group discussions, consideration of "business success
stories," and the like to examine his own motivations,
his sense of values, and his objectives in life; to set
himself realistic and attainable goals involving calculated risks; to think clearly about the means of attaining
these goals; and to develop a personal commitment to their
achievement.

The first achievement motivation courses were given early in 1963 in Bombay by the Center for Research in Personality of Harvard University under the auspices of the Bombay Management Association. A total of 29 businessmen participated in three courses that were organized in the form of 11 evening sessions. Later, in 1964 and 1965, residential courses lasting 10 days were conducted at SIET Institute for 52 businessmen from the town of Kakinada and 26 businessmen from the town of Vellore. While the program was subsequently suspended, principally for want of financing, the interest in achievement motivation training has been maintained by the Behavioral Science Center (BSC) in Delhi, and elements of this type of training have been incorporated in the more comprehensive entrepreneurial development courses given by SIET and by the Gujerat development corporations at Ahmedabad.

The usefulness of such training is difficult to assess. Success in business depends not merely on entrepreneurial talent, but also on the grasp of substantive business skills and on the availability of opportunities which in varying degrees may be limited by factors over which the businessman has little or no control. The impact that these factors have on success or lack of success cannot readily be assessed separately. Moreover, the results of achievement motivation courses depend considerably on the quality and skill of the personnel conducting them. The techniques are not easy to master. Conductors of the courses can easily sink into a morass of psychological jargon and leave the participants more baffled than enlightened.

However, some success has been achieved in devising rough measures of the subsequent performance of course participants in "achievement-related" activities, and in comparing this performance, not only with their own pre-course activities, but also with those over the same time period of "control groups" of nonparticipants similar in composition, background, and activities. In any event the experience with motivation training in India appears to have been sufficiently promising to warrant further experimentation.

Entrepreneurship Development Courses at Ahmedabad

The basic objective of the entrepreneurship development program started by the three Gujerat development corporations in April 1970 was to train people for starting and operating an industrial enterprise through a 12-week course focusing on the preparation of an industrial project that could be submitted to some institution for financing. To get admitted to the course applicants had to have a fairly definite idea of a product or products they wanted to manufacture. There were no specific

requirements with respect to previous education and experience. In fact, the educational qualifications among
the 55 participants in the first course varied widely; 21
(39 percent) had a secondary education or less, and of
these 7 had gone only to primary school; 6 (11 percent)
had some form of undergraduate education; 25 (45 percent)
were degree-holders in arts, science, commerce, engineering, or pharmacy; and 3 (5 percent) had technical diplomas.
Efforts were made to include participants with different
backgrounds and varying degrees of experience. All of them
had some work experience--18 with one to three years and 27
with six or more years of experience. Their occupational
backgrounds were extremely diverse; 30 (54 percent) were
people who had acquired considerable technical know-how
working in industry; 15 (27 percent) were merchants with
little technical know-how, but a good knowledge of marketing; 2 (4 percent) had been employed as salesmen/store-
keepers; and 8 (15 percent) were engineers or technicians
with a good theoretical technical education but little
experience. In the first group there were 5 people who
had actually been active as industrial entrepreneurs.

The formal part of the curriculum was covered in
evening sessions. The first week was devoted to analysis
of the basic concepts of an entrepreneur, a project, an
enterprise, and the factors conditioning success or
failure. In succeeding weeks the course dealt with basic
management, financial management, sources of financing,
management organization and techniques; production planning and techniques; raw materials and purchasing;
accounting and accounting ratios; depreciation, costing
and taxation; marketing, sales techniques and advertising;
and employment procedures, personnel management, and labor
legislation. In the third and fourth courses, a brief
period of achievement motivation training was also introduced with the assistance of the Behavioral Science Center.
In the last six weeks participants were organized into
groups based on their interests in particular products,
and facilities were given to each group to visit enterprises in their field, to talk with successful entrepreneurs, and to have discussions with specialists from
government and financial institutions. During this period
the emphasis was on the preparation of specific projects
and the relevant technical and marketing analysis, as well
as the determination of the investment and working capital
required and the sources of their financing.

While a small faculty under a project director was
provided, great reliance was placed on outside lecturers
from trade, industry, government, universities, and
management institutes. In each case considerable care was
taken to ensure the planning of such lectures in such a
way as to ensure their relevance to specific subjects in
the curriculum.

The course participants themselves contributed much to each other's learning experience. This interplay was made possible, above all, by the inclusion of people with varying occupational backgrounds and practical experience. The engineers and technicians among the participants helped to give others a better theoretical grasp of technical problems, but in turn profited from the practical knowledge of those who had considerable work experience in industry. Merchants benefited from the technical advice of others, but could themselves provide practical advice on marketing. The few industrial entrepreneurs who participated profited from a systematic view of all the problems pertaining to enterprise development and could simultaneously give others the benefit of their practical experience. Apparently this considerable exchange of knowledge and experience proved quite fruitful.

By no means were all of the participants able to complete their projects before the end of the course. After completion of the course participants were called together periodically for group discussions and reviews, and continued counseling on project preparation was also made available. As of October 1971, 47 out of the original 55 participants in the first course had completed project reports, and 20 out of the 42 participants in the second course had likewise done so. However, only 21 projects had actually been submitted to financing institutions, and loans had been granted to only 13. Part of the delay in financing was apparently due to management problems in the Gujerat Industrial Investment Corporation, which was originally expected to finance a considerable number of the projects. Nevertheless 31 of the participants had actually started their factories, most of them without outside financial assistance.

The coordinator of this training scheme has made an interesting attempt to compare 35 of the course participants who had set up factories, or were likely to do so, with 18 participants who appeared unlikely to do so. From this comparison he has tentatively drawn the conclusions that 1) people in the middle age bracket, ranging from 26 to 40 years old, are more disposed to go into business for themselves than those who are younger or older, 2) the level of a person's education is not a decisive factor in starting an enterprise, and 3) those with three years or less of practical experience tend to be least successful, and those with 4 to 15 years of experience most successful.

A final word should be said on the achievement motivation training that was incorporated experimentally in the third and fourth courses. The coordinator of the training program was evidently not altogether happy with experimentation in the third course. Apparently quite a few of the participants found it difficult to grasp the rationale and methods of the achievement motivation training and considered the illustrative material used

in this part of the course rather remote from their experience and irrelevant to the more substantive part of the
course. Perhaps the personnel of the Behavioral Science
Center were not sufficiently skillful in their explanation
of the training methods involved or in eliciting responses.
The psychological jargon employed also seemed to have confused many participants. For the fourth course efforts
were to be made to use more practical and relevant examples
in this type of training.

The pioneering work of the entrepreneurship development program at Ahmedabad has stimulated other training of
this kind. The Government of Maharashtra started a similar
program at five centers, drawing heavily on the Ahmedabad
Center for advice and guidance on the curriculum and teaching methods. However, the most important program largely
inspired by the Ahmedabad Center is the one launched by
the Government of India for the training of unemployed
technicians and engineers as entrepreneurs. It is that
program which will now be examined.

Central Government Program for Engineers and Technicians

Two factors were instrumental in the adoption of this
program for engineers and technicians. One was the "over-
production" of such people by engineering schools and
polytechnics. The number receiving degrees or diplomas
in engineering and technical fields had apparently risen
from 4,000 in 1960 to 50,000 in recent years. Employment
opportunities had failed to keep pace, so that by 1970
there were estimated to be 40,000 unemployed engineers
alone. The other factor was a serious deficiency in the
education of engineers and technicians. Not only has this
education been excessively theoretical in the technical
field, but it has not been effectively complemented by any
training that would motivate engineers and technicians to
become entrepreneurs or enable them to assume managerial
responsibilities.

The program launched by the central government in the
fall of 1970 was designed solely to train unemployed engineering graduates and diploma holders, although in
exceptional cases science graduates with a minimum of
three years' production experience in industry could
become eligible. In each state a committee headed by
the Director of Industries and including, as a minimum,
a representative of the SISI as well as someone from
industry,was established to screen candidates for training and to select those with an adequate motivation and
commitment to start some industrial project. To carry out
the requisite training the government designated, the two
prototype Production-cum-Training Centers of the National
Small-Scale Industries Corporation, the SIET Institute,

and the Gujerat Industrial Investment Corporation. The
government undertook to pay each institution Rs1500 per
trainee to cover the cost of training and a monthly stipend of Rs250, which was to be paid to every trainee in
lieu of board and lodging. The duration of the course
was first fixed at four months, but was then reduced to
three; and the number to be admitted to each course was
fixed at approximately 30. On this basis it was expected
that some 6,000 engineers and technicians would be trained
to become entrepreneurs during the remainder of the fourth
Five-Year Plan, that is, up to the end of March 1973.

As a further encouragement to "engineer-technician
entrepreneurs," the central government undertook to sub-
sidize the normal lending rates of financing institutions,
so that the interest on loans to such entrepreneurs would
be reduced to 5 percent for an initial period of three
years, or five years when the enterprise was located in
an area designated as "backward." Previously a few
banking institutions had already arranged special financing
terms for new "technician-entrepreneurs." Thus, in mid-
1967, the State Bank of India had inaugurated a new scheme
to finance enterprises started by experienced craftsmen or
newly graduated engineers and technicians. Under this
scheme new entrepreneurs were able to obtain loans up to
Rs100,000 (Rs200,000 in case of partnerships) to cover
all the capital requirements of the enterprise without
any obligation to put up any capital of their own or to
furnish security other than the fixed capital assets
created by the loan. However, the number of loans extended
by the end of 1970--somewhat less than 500, of which only a
little over 100 had been granted to unemployed engineers--
had proved disappointing. In July 1969 the Gujerat Industrial Investment Corporation (GIIC) had also launched a
"Technicians' Scheme" for people with similar qualifications. For these types of borrowers the GIIC had reduced
its normal lending rate of 9.5 percent to 5 percent in
the first two years, provided an initial period of two
years of grace on the repayment of principal, and fixed
the subsequent period for amortization at eight years.
New entrepreneurs had been relieved of the obligation to
contribute any capital of their own in case of loans up
to Rs200,000 for individuals and up to Rs300,000 for
partnerships. Moreover, the GIIC had made arrangements
with the Gujerat Industrial Development Corporation to
make land and worksheds available on the basis of deferred payments and with the commercial banks to provide
necessary working capital, with the GIIC guaranteeing that
portion of working capital that entrepreneurs were normally expected to furnish from their own resources. The
number of loans under this scheme had risen somewhat more
rapidly than those extended throughout India by the State
Bank of India, for by November 1971 some 553 of such
"technician" loans had been sanctioned for a total amount

of Rs42.23 million. Yet only Rs4.42 million had actually
been disbursed, and apparently only a small proportion of
the borrowers had been fresh graduates of engineering and
technical schools. In a sense the entrepreneur   development program sponsored by the three Gujerat development
corporations and the broader entrepreneur   training program launched by the Government of India might be said to
represent attempts to qualify more inexperienced engineers
and technicians for the benefits of these special financing
schemes.

Curriculum

The institutions providing the training received from
the SSIDO in the Ministry for Industrial Development general guidelines about the content of the curriculum and
the subjects to be covered, but were left considerable
freedom in planning the details of the curriculum and
choosing or devising appropriate instructional materials.
The actual curriculum followed has been generally similar
to that developed by the Ahmedabad Center. The first part
of the course is general in character, devoted to the concept and problems of entrepreneurship, management, production, marketing, financing, taxation, and government
legislation and regulations, as well as a general survey
of industrial opportunities. The second part is more
specific, oriented toward the problems and opportunities
of special industries, particular groups of interested
participants, and the elaboration of individual industrial
projects. The final focus on project preparation is
undoubtedly sound, for it should force the prospective
entrepreneur to face up to all the practical problems
involved in launching and operating an enterprise.

Preliminary Evaluation

Experience with the program is as yet too brief to
warrant definitive judgments about the quality of the
training and its effectiveness in "producing" successful
entrepreneurs. Discussions with those responsible for
the training indicate that the quality inevitably varies
considerably with the capacity, imagination, and degree
of commitment of the training personnel involved. For
many of the SISIs the inauguration of these courses has
entailed still another task for personnel who considered
themselves already overburdened; and this extra burden
has had its impact on the degree of enthusiasm they have
displayed in this new assignment. Often not enough
training personnel has been available to give the trainees
effective individual counseling on their projects; and
some of the personnel have evidently not had sufficient
industrial experience themselves to provide realistic
and practical advice on projects. An examination of some

of the projects prepared by the trainees raises at least
some doubts about the quality of the training program.
Only a small proportion of these projects appears to have
been elaborated in sufficient detail to warrant a proper
judgment of their merit by a financing institution. Quite
a few contain only a cursory examination of market prospects. Many rather unrealistically assume that full
production can be achieved almost immediately after the
factory workshop has been established, although practical
experience indicates that it usually takes a considerable
time before capacity operations can be achieved because
of the need to iron out initial production problems and
to establish the product in the market. Requirements for
working capital seem generally to be underestimated, because they tend to ignore that much of this capital will
be used up in the initial "running-in" period.

It is as yet difficult to say how large a proportion
of the participants in the entrepreneur   training courses
will actually succeed in launching an enterprise. A few
tend to drop out before the course is finished, and some
apparently take the course only to benefit from the stipend and entertain no serious commitment to start an
enterprise of their own. The great majority do complete
some sort of a project, although some of these, of course,
fail to get the necessary financing or to meet all the
other requirements that must be fulfilled in order to start
an enterprise. According to preliminary indications, perhaps 15 to 30 percent of the course participants may
succeed in launching a business, although in some cases
the percentage may be higher. However, only time will
tell how many of these will survive the rigors of competition.

Key Problems in Training for Entrepreneurship

One critical problem encountered in these programs is
that of identifying potential entrepreneur   talent. This
problem arises first in screening applicants for admission
to the course and again during the course. For the purpose
of optimizing the number of successful entrepreneurs, it
is obviously desirable both to avoid the rejection of
candidates with entrepreneur   talent and to single out
those likely to be successful.

In general the number of applicants far exceeds the
limited number that can be admitted. The GIIC at Ahmedabad had 700, 550, 465, and 265 applicants respectively
for its first four courses conducted for the Government
of India. The SISI at Bombay reported that it had 600-
900 applicants for each course; the SISI at Bangalore had
1,800 applications for its first two courses; and the
other training institutions have had a minimum of 250
applicants for each course. A first screening takes place

on the basis of the written applications in which the
candidates provide information on their educational qualifications, their experience (if any), and the industrial
or business background of their relatives, and they provide a brief description of the type of enterprise they
want to start. In this screening those who have a definite "project idea" and come from a family background of
business are reported to be favored. A much more limited,
but still considerable, number of applicants are then
interviewed by a panel either individually or in groups.
However, the interview appears to be extremely cursory
and brief, averaging only about five minutes per candidate,
except in the case of the SISI at Ludhiana where it was
reported to average 20 minutes. One is doubtful whether
a sound and objective judgment of the candidates was
possible on the basis of such brief interviews.

A few experiments have been made with more refined
selection techniques. The director of the training program at Ludhiana, who had had some training in psychology,
devised an aptitude test in which applicants were asked
to 1) characterize the qualities which in their opinion
they possessed that would make them successful entrepreneurs, 2) engage in an exercise of self-analysis by
listing at least 15 of their "strong" and "weak" points,
and 3) describe how they would deal with a given situation
that was briefly outlined to them and that involved a test
of their ability to think in terms of organization, leadership, and initiative. Unfortunately it was not possible
for the author of this study to examine the responses and
appraise the usefulness of this approach to selection.

The Entrepreneurship Development Center at Ahmedabad
invoked the assistance of the Behavioral Science Center
in screening its applicants for the third and fourth
courses. The BSC administered a number of tests designed
to bring out the applicants' motivation to achieve and
their thinking in terms of concrete goals and means of
accomplishing them. On the basis of these tests and subsequent "discussion" interviews the qualifications of the
applicants for admission to the course were assessed.
However, those in charge of the course were evidently not
fully satisfied with these ratings, which involved a considerable amount of subjective judgment on the part of
those administering the tests, and accordingly they
modified them to a significant extent in making the
final decisions respecting admission. In general both
the experts of the BSC and many of the training institutions frankly admit the inadequacy of existing selection
procedures. Proposals have been made to request the
United Nations Industrial Development Organization (UNIDO)
to study this entire subject, but no action had been taken
by the end of 1971.

Two special problems arise from the rather narrow
education and lack of experience of the unemployed
engineers and technicians on whose training as

entrepreneurs the Government of India program is focused. The concern about the high degree of unemployment among newly graduated engineers and technicians is entirely understandable. Yet it may be questioned whether it is really advisable to restrict admission to the training courses entirely to such people. Engineers and technicians of this type are not ideally qualified to become entrepreneurs. Their education has been primarily oriented toward jobs rather than toward entrepreneur activity. Moreover, even granting their ability to deal with the technical production problems of manufacturing, it must be emphasized that their success as entrepreneurs will depend primarily on their capacity to deal with problems of marketing, procurement of raw materials, accounting and costing, and to handle effectively their relations with government authorities. The objective should be to identify and develop persons with entrepreneur talent and reasonable prospects of success. Whether the entrepreneurs are themselves engineers and technicians or give employment to persons with an engineering or technical education does not greatly matter.

The lack of practical experience, even in technical matters, among unemployed engineers and technicians is generally acknowledged to be a problem. It is recognized that some way must be found to supplement the standard three-month course with practical training in small-scale industry before any enterprise is launched. At the Ahmedabad Center, a link has been established between its old continuing entrepreneur development program and the courses it is conducting for the Government of India. Participants in the Government of India program are given their more formal training in the evening together with the participants in the original type of course. During the day they are sent to work in factories in order to learn the practical aspects of machine operation. The SISI at Bangalore has made informal arrangements to provide those who have completed the course with opportunities to get practical training in various industries over a period of three to six months, and it has proposed to qualify such people eventually for stipendiary training under the Government of India program for apprenticeship in industry. The Indian Institute of Technology in Delhi has made proposals to the Government of India to incorporate in-plant training in its program for engineers and technicians. These initiatives give evidence of a praiseworthy effort to remedy a serious deficiency. However, a more comprehensive approach is evidently needed.

A final problem remains to be noted. This involves the organization of an effective follow-up on the trainees who manage to start industrial enterprises. Because most of these have little or no experience, they are likely to experience considerable difficulties. Unless they are given continuing help and guidance in surmounting their problems, their failure rate may well be unduly high.

Some of the SISIs frankly acknowledged that they had either
no capacity or no plan to provide such follow-up services,
although a few others hoped that they would be able to do
so. While only a small percentage of the trainees have so
far launched their enterprises, it is important to plan
now for the extension of adequate advisory assistance to
the growing number who will be embarking on business
ventures. In the last analysis, however, this problem can
probably not be effectively tackled without remedying some
of the SISI staffing deficiencies that have already been
mentioned.

LESSONS FROM INDIA'S EXPERIENCE

In the preceding sections we have described and
analyzed the significant efforts made in India to promote
small-scale industry in the urban and rural areas and to
train and develop new entrepreneurs, with special emphasis
on the training and extension services provided. In the
course of analysis a number of suggestions for improvements
in India's program have been made. These will not be
repeated here. It is necessary, however, to sum up and
set forth briefly the lessons of India's experience which
may be relevant to other developing countries.

1. India has demonstrated that it is feasible to
organize and staff reasonably effective training and
advisory services for the development of industrial enterprise.

2. Such services should be furnished only as an
integral part of a coherent sound and comprehensive program
for the promotion of small-scale industry. Such a program
should include provision for adequate financing of new
and expanding industries and well-planned common production
and testing facilities that individual enterprises cannot
afford; it should also ensure the climate and the incentives essential for the growth of industry under competitive conditions. Care should be taken to avoid a multiplication of government regulations and cumbersome government procedures which create far greater difficulties for
small-scale industry than for large-scale industry.

3. Training and extension services for small-scale
industry can obviously be effective only in proportion to
the opportunities for profitable investment available to
such industry. The problem of selecting types of industries that can operate profitably and competitively on a
small scale has not yet been fully resolved. Nor have
adequate efforts been made to devise technologies appropriate to small-scale industries in which the availability
of capital and labor skills is varied. In rural areas
profitable opportunities for the expansion of traditional
industries or the introduction of new and more modern

industries are likely to be severely limited unless there
has been a significant prior development of basic agricultural and livestock production that can provide the
raw materials for processing or the markets for service
and consumer goods industries. There is little justification, too, for efforts to improve the training of
traditional village artisans, unless they can be made
more receptive to changes in working methods and can find
a larger remunerative market for their services. Attempts
to promote some measure of rural industrialization are
likely to prove more effective if they focus on the large
rural towns which can command a considerable area in terms
of markets and supplies and can become focal points of
growth for the surrounding rural area.

    4. Adequate staffing is a key problem. The person-
nel concerned with extension and training must have
practical experience in industry, supplemented by training in extension methods. Conditions of service generally
competitive with those in private industry must accordingly
be offered. As small industries develop, diversify and
experience the need for a more sophisticated technology,
the staffing patterns of advisory services must be changed
to provide for more specialized personnel, and opportunities should be given to the existing staff to upgrade
their experience and skills.

    5. The tendency toward an excessive dispersal of
activities must be resisted. Emphasis should not be on
the number of services provided but on the quality and
impact of such services. Means should be devised to focus
assistance on those entrepreneurs with a real capacity for
development. An entrepreneur should be helped, not simply
because he is "small," but because he has evidenced a
capacity to become "bigger." Small-scale enterprise should
to a significant extent become the nursery for the development of medium-scale and even large-scale enterprise.

    6. Extension and training should not be allowed to
degenerate into a routine government service. They should
be dynamic and innovative. It is unlikely that these
characteristics can be maintained unless advisory and
training services are assured a large measure of organizational and financial autonomy that makes it possible to
recruit and retain competent personnel and to resist
political pressures for an excessive dispersal of activities.

    7. Small-scale entrepreneurs are most receptive of
advice on technical problems because they can readily see
the concrete results. They are less conscious of management problems, even though these may be serious by any
objective standard of measurement, largely because management to them is a rather abstract concept. Experience has
shown that it is difficult to give general management
courses the concrete content which entrepreneurs will find
relevant to the operation of their own enterprises. A

greater disposition to profit from management training
is likely to develop only if the extension services have
sufficiently experienced personnel to give advice specially tailored to the requirements and problems of
specific enterprises.

8.   Experience has shown that there is usually a
need to upgrade the skills and productivity of the labor
force in small-scale industry. However, progress in this
field is difficult to achieve, unless small employers
appreciate the value of this training and are willing to
pay higher wages for properly trained labor, and unless
the training can be provided in the evening so that
employers do not have to release their workers and the
workers themselves do not have to forgo remunerative
employment.

9.   The training and development of new entrepreneurs
is a critical need in many developing countries. India's
pioneering efforts in this field have demonstrated that
the training of people for entrepreneurship is by no means
easy, particularly when the trainees have had no previous
practical experience in industry or any other business.
However, the project-oriented training initiated in India
appears to be sound in principle. It must, however, be
complemented by practical in-plant training for those
without previous experience in industry. Better results
are likely to be achieved if people of various occupational backgrounds and types of experience are associated
with fresh graduates from engineering and technical
schools in the training process. In order to avoid an
excessive failure rate among people selected for training,
the problem of identifying and developing entrepreneur
talent and motivation must be resolved. There is presump-
tive evidence that the achievement motivating training
techniques first developed at Harvard University and
tested on a modest scale in India may help to solve this
problem. However, further experimentation with these and
other techniques appears to be necessary.

NOTES

1.   "Ancillary development" refers to the development of manufacture of parts and components for supply to large-scale industry.

2.   The figures on personnel cited in this paragraph are taken
from India, Ministry of Industrial Development and Internal Trade,
Development Commissioner, Small Scale Industries, Small Scale Industries (New Delhi, 1971), p. 343. The 1969-1970 report on small-scale
industries emanating from the same office gives somewhat different
data, showing a total of 627 posts, excluding those of "investigators,"
as compared with 713 in Small Scale Industries.

3.   For example, small-scale entrepreneurs seldom use accounting
as a management tool. A survey of the small-scale machine tool industry in Punjab disclosed that 68 percent of the entrepreneurs

sampled did have some form of accounting, but only to satisfy government agencies, particularly the tax authorities. Accounting was seldom used for the purpose of determining costs or as an aid to cost
reduction. See Bhagwan Prasad, "Machine Tool Industry in the Small
Scale Sector of Punjab," mimeographed (Hyderabad, India: Small
Industry Extension Training Institute, October 1971).

4. It might be contended that if prices were allowed to rise to
a level where market demand and supply would be in equilibrium, many
producers and importers would earn unjustifiable "windfall profits."
However, such profits could be taxed away by appropriate excise duties
and import surcharges that would incidentally enable the government
to mobilize considerably more revenue.

5. See K. J. Christopher, "Socio-Psychological Factors Influencing the Starting of a Small Industry Unit," ICSSR Abstracts [of the
Indian Council of Social Science Research], no. 1 (December 1970).

6. "It has . . . to be recognised that it is extremely difficult
to obtain correct information in regard to the gross value of production, sale, etc. On our visits to the six projects we found it very
difficult to rely upon the figures of gross value of production furnished to us for various reasons . . . " India, Ministry of Industrial Development and Company Affairs, Rural Industries Planning Committee, Report of the Evaluation Study Group on Rural Industrial
Projects Programme (New Delhi, April 1968), p. 34.

7. See B. N. Rangaramu, "The Role of Rural Industries Projects
in the Rural Industrialization of Maharashtra," Industrial Bulletin
[of the Government of Maharashtra, Directorate of Industries]
(October 1971).

8. India, Ministry of Industrial Development and Company Affairs,
Rural Industries Planning Committee, op. cit., p. 14.

9. R. P. Lynton and J. E. Stepanek, "Industrialization Beyond
the Metropolis: A New Look at India," mimeographed (Hyderabad, India:
Small Industry Extension Training Institute, April 1963).

10. It might be mentioned also that the Union Ministry of Food
and Agriculture launched in 1970 still another rural artisan training
and promotion program within the framework of "Pilot Projects for
Small Farmers, Marginal Farmers and Agricultural Labour" which it is
setting up. This program will not only provide training, but assist
artisans in installing workshops and in the procurement of equipment,
tools, and power.

11. David C. McClelland, The Achieving Society (Princeton, New
Jersey: D. Van Nostrand Co., 1961).

12. The nature of this training and an analysis of the results
achieved are set forth in David C. McClelland and David G. Winter,
Motivating Economic Achievement (New York: The Free Press, 1971).

REPUBLIC OF KOREA:
A MULTIPURPOSE FARMER
EDUCATION PROGRAM
Manzoor Ahmed

The ICED had several reasons for deciding to study the Office of Rural Development (ORD)--a semiautonomous operating arm of the Republic of Korea's Ministry of Agriculture. ORD seemed unusually well conceived as an integrated nonformal educational "system" designed to serve the learning needs of small farmers and other rural people who must be the main engineers of rural development. ORD's aims, clients, and operational methods appeared conspicuously broader and more diversified than those of the usual agricultural extension service. Though its central purpose is to help today's farmers improve their practices and productivity, ORD is also concerned with helping rural young people acquire a variety of useful skills to become tomorrow's progressive farmers. Beyond this, it has helped farm families to supplement their incomes with sideline jobs during the long winter season and to improve their nutritional and homemaking practices.

A further reason for choosing the ORD for special study was that South Korea has been undergoing a dynamic and rapid transition from a predominantly agrarian economy to a modernized one in which the relative importance of agriculture and industry is being reversed. This provided an opportunity to test the hypothesis that in such dynamic circumstances all types of rural extension services would be obliged to "reprogram" themselves steadily and rapidly if they were to be fully effective.

Finally, there were promising opportunities in South Korea for the ICED staff to work in close partnership with competent Korean researchers, particularly through the Central Educational Research Institute (CERI) which had already displayed an interest in nonformal education.

A preliminary study plan was made in the spring of 1971. Members of CERI began gathering basic data and they were later joined by two ICED staff members who visited South Korea in October 1971 for extensive interviews and visits to various program sites. This case study, therefore, reflects the situation through 1971, although information has been updated till late 1972 on the basis of comments from readers of the unpublished draft study.

BACKGROUND AND SETTING OF ORD PROGRAM

Economic Transition

The economy of the Republic of Korea (South Korea) has been undergoing rapid transformation in recent years. In the mid-1950s, South Korea was a predominantly agricultural and impoverished country--cut off from the more industrialized north and ravaged by war. By the end of the 1960s, however, the South Korean economy reached a stage where only about one-quarter of the GNP was derived from agriculture. A little less than half of the population depended on agriculture for a livelihood, and the booming industrial and service sectors were quickly drawing the labor force into nonagricultural occupations. The population growth rate dropped to 1.8 percent per year and the decline is expected to continue. (The population in 1970 was 32 million.) A rapid process of urbanization raised the proportion of urban population to about 43 percent from less than 30 percent a decade earlier. Per capita income rose sharply from US$115 in 1965 to more than US$250 in 1971 at current prices. This economic dynamism has made Korea an atypical country in Asia.

Agriculture, however, has been less than an equal partner in the economic growth of the 1960s; the average annual growth rate for agriculture has been about 4 percent compared to about 16 percent for the industrial sector.[1]

Urban-Rural Economic Gap

Data are lacking on the distribution of economic gains during the last decade and the relative economic positions of different segments of the population. The uneven rates of growth for agriculture and industry have clearly resulted in uneven gains for farm and nonfarm population. The indices of prices received and paid by farmers for their sales and purchases from 1965 to 1970 show that the prices of farm supplies increased more rapidly than the prices of grains. (See Appendix 13.1.)

Data on sectoral shares in national income indicate that agriculture's share fell from about 40 percent in 1960 to about 26 percent in 1969. The share of the nonfarm wage-earning employees rose from 31 to 39 percent during the same period. The agricultural sector has traditionally sustained a proportionately larger labor force than its share of national income and this trend continued during the decade. The decline in agricultural employment (from about 60 percent to a little less than 50 percent) has been less than the decline in its share in the national

income, thus further lowering the relative level of
per capita income for the farm population derived from
agricultural sources. As a result of general economic
growth, the income of farm population from nonfarm sources
may have increased during the decade (about 25 percent of
the farm population income is currently estimated to be
from nonfarm sources). It can be estimated that the income disparity between the farming population (including
nonfarm earnings) and the nonfarm population is of the
order of 1:2.[2]

The Agricultural Situation

Despite the relative lag of agriculture within the
Korean economy, progress during the decade of the 1960s
was above the norm for developing nations. The overall
annual agricultural growth rate of 4.2 percent was considerably ahead of the population growth. Production of
food grains increased by 44 percent (see Table 13.1) with
significant contribution to this increase by minor crops.
Increase in rice production, the major food grain, was
about 30 percent between 1959 and 1969 (both relatively
good years). A sizable portion of the increase in agricultural production may be ascribed to the expansion, by
about 15 percent, of cultivated land, but the bulk of the
increase resulted from increased productivity of existing
land, as shown in Table 13.2.

TABLE 13.1

Growth in Agricultural Production, 1959-1969

	1959	1969	Net Increase 1959-1969 (%)
Agricultural product (thousand million won at 1965 prices)	225.11	328.35	45.9
Food grains (thousand metric tons)	5,359	7,737	44.4
Rice	3,150	4,090	29.8
Barley	1,666	2,459	47.6
Potatoes	299	778	160.2
Beans	158	273	72.8
Other grains	86	137	59.3

Source: Korea, The Third Five-Year Economic Development Plan,
1972-76 (Seoul, n.d.), p. 139.

TABLE 13.2

Yields per Hectare--1937-1969
by Crop (Rough Grains)

Crop	(metric tons per hectare)					
	1937-38	1945-49	1950-54	1955-59	1960-64	1965-69
Rice (rough)	3.0	2.5	2.6	3.7	4.1	4.2
Common barley	1.5	0.9	1.0	2.0	2.2	2.3
Naked barley	1.6	1.0	1.1	1.6	1.7	2.5
Wheat	1.1	0.8	1.0	2.4	2.8	2.9
Italian millet	1.4	0.5	0.8	0.6	0.7	0.9

Source: Ministry of Agriculture and Forestry, Yearbook (Seoul, 1969).

One of the factors that provided incentives for higher agricultural productivity during the last decade was land reform. A vigorous land reform program began during the late fifties and created an atmosphere conducive to agricultural growth. As a result of land reform, 69 percent of all farm families in 1970 were full owner-operators, 24 percent were part-owners, and only 17 percent were tenants. Only 1.6 percent of the farms are now more than three hectares in size; the larger farmers own only 7.1 percent of total farmland. The average size of a Korean farm is less than a hectare.[3]

Diversification of agriculture gradually gained momentum in the 1960s and contributed to the total value of agricultural product and to some extent to increases in farmers' income. Of the total product value in the agricultural sector, including forestry and fishery, major grains accounted for 69 percent in 1960 but shrunk to 46 percent by 1969. Labor-intensive commodities such as fruits, vegetables, livestock, and tobacco increased their share of the agricultural product during these years. The farmland utilization pattern for 1965-1968 indicates that just over one-third of planted area (counting multiple-cropping) was used for rice; one-third for barley and wheat; 21 percent for various grains, pulses, and potatoes; 6 percent for fruits and vegetables; and 5 percent for sericulture, tobacco, and other crops. As a result of diversification and improved water facilities, a considerable amount of multicropping has been possible. The total cultivable area currently produces more than 1.5

crops in a year, a significant feat considering the relatively short growing season in Korea.[4]

Despite diversification, the agricultural policy in
recent years has been dominated by the objective of achieving self-sufficiency in rice. Rice occupies about 55 percent of total arable land (not counting multiple-cropping)
and rice production has already extended into marginal
land that could possibly be put to better economic use.

Various government measures, including a 75 percent
increase in the rice procurement price between 1968 and
1970, concentrated research efforts, preferential provisions for chemical inputs and irrigation facilities, have
been taken to reach the goal of self-sufficiency in rice.
A major share of ORD resources and personnel is devoted
to rice. But the goal continues to elude achievement and
Korea is forced to import increasing amounts of rice each
year.[5] Meanwhile, the improvement of rice production remains the highest priority in the ORD farmer education program.

FUNCTIONS AND ORGANIZATION OF ORD

Origin and Functions

Agricultural extension and research work in Korea were
initiated and continued sporadically under Japanese rule
between 1910 and 1945, the motivation being to exploit
Korea as a source of food and raw materials. Many of the
current practices and much of the agricultural technology
of Korean farmers were introduced under the Japanese.[6]

The beginning of agricultural extension as it exists
today in Korea may be traced back to 1957, when the Agricultural Extension Law was promulgated and the Institute
of Agriculture was created. The functions of the extension service specified in the Act were as follows:

1. research and experimentation for the improvement
    and development of agriculture (farming, foresta-
    tion, animal husbandry, horticulture, and other
    farming activities) and teaching and dissemina-
    ting knowledge and techniques thereof
2. research, experimentation, and guidance related
    to methods of improvement and conservation of
    farmland and soils
3. guidance related to the method of operation of
    agricultural cooperative organizations
4. guidance and education of rural youth
5. guidance for the advancement of rural life
6. education and training of officials who are to
    engage in the activities prescribed above

    7. other operations directly related to the activities described above[7]

The Institute of Agriculture began pilot projects for agricultural improvement and supported activities of young farmer groups such as 4-H Clubs. Meanwhile, in 1958 a Community Development program was initiated with the placement of multipurpose extension workers in pilot villages. Both these pilot programs continued to operate with varying success in selected areas throughout the country. In 1962 a comprehensive Rural Development Law was enacted to combine the activities of different agencies into a unified rural development program under the Office of Rural Development (ORD).

The purpose of "rural guidance" activities of the Office was seen as "conducting experimentation and research, rendering enlightenment and guidance service, diffusing techniques, and training workers, as necessary for rural development."[8]

The Rural Development Law also specified the content of ORD's "rural guidance" activities:

1. dissemination of new techniques and information on agriculture and home improvement
2. dissemination of new knowledge and information on farm side-jobs and part-time jobs for rural population
3. promoting farmers' understanding of preservation and utilization of natural resources as necessary for agricultural development and improvement of rural life
4. developing rural organizations in order to promote agricultural and home improvement
5. assisting and supporting farmers in undertaking pilot rural development projects
6. securing and training volunteer leaders who can lead in community development activities[9]

The functions of the Office of Rural Development and those of the old extension service appear to differ in three major ways: the agricultural cooperative activities have been taken out of the extension service and entrusted to a separate organization, the National Agricultural Cooperative Federation; ORD uses "volunteer leaders" from the villages for achieving extension aims, in contrast to the former exclusive reliance on agent-to-farmer contacts; and community development functions in rural areas have been assigned to ORD.

The broad and general nature of the functions of ORD and the inclination towards pilot projects are probably derived from one of its predecessors, the Community Development program. ORD's activities as of 1972 may be grouped under the following categories:

1. dissemination of farming technology
2. agricultural research and experimentation
3. family, home, and general rural improvement acti-
    vities
4. rural youth programs
5. training and information support for its activi-
    ties through farmer training and agricultural
    information

The main focus of ORD operations is on the dissemination of farming technology through guidance workers in the
field and a network of offices and farmer training centers.
Other activities such as agricultural research, training,
and information support are subsidiary to the main operation. The rural youth program is also designed to promote agricultural skills among youths through 4-H Clubs.
Only a small fraction of ORD resources and personnel is
devoted to family, home, and rural improvement--activities
that are not directly related to dissemination of farming
technology.

Organization

ORD is organized with a national office located at
Suwon, about 40 kilometers south of the capital city of
Seoul; 9 provincial offices; 172 county and city offices;
and 618 branch offices at the subcounty level. Though
attached to the Ministry of Agriculture and Forestry, ORD
is run more or less autonomously by its administrator,
who is directly responsible to the Minister of Agriculture.
At both the national and provincial levels, ORD is
divided into two major bureaus, one for research, the
other for guidance (that is, extension). Each bureau has
a number of divisions (see ORD Organization Chart, Fig.
13.1). In the Rural Guidance Bureau are located the divisions of Programming and Evaluation, Community Development, Home Improvement, Rural Youth, and Agricultural
Information. In addition, one Technical Dissemination
Officer and one Applied Nutrition Officer are attached
to the bureau. In the Research Bureau, there are two
divisions for Research Management and Research Publication,
two research coordinators, and one agricultural economics
coordinator. Outside the two bureaus, there is a General
Affairs Division with responsibility for general administrative matters.
At the provincial offices, the organizational structure is basically a smaller version of the national structure. The two bureaus of research and guidance are again
divided into several divisions. Under the Research Bureau,
there are usually two divisions for crops and plant environment. The divisions in the Rural Guidance Bureau

FIGURE 13.1

ORD Organization Chart

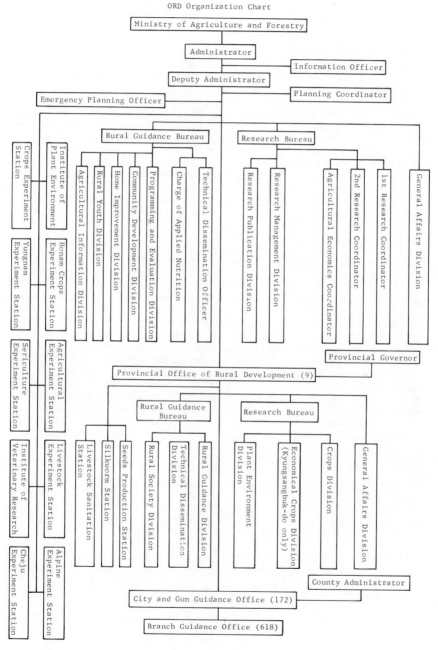

are usually Rural Guidance, Technical Dissemination, and
the Rural Society. Each provincial office also maintains
a seed production station, a silkworm station, and a livestock sanitation station, serving farmers of the whole
province.

At the provincial and county levels, training centers
are attached to the ORDs, where short-term training of
farmers take place. The provincial training centers also
offer short inservice training courses for ORD guidance
workers.

Administrative Coordination. It is noteworthy that the
provincial and county ORD offices are under the general
administrative and supervisory control of the provincial
governors and county chiefs, civilian administrators
appointed by the government. Local ORD offices are responsible for implementing both the national programs ori-
ginating from national ORD and local agricultural programs
formulated by the provincial and the county administrators.
The major portions of budget for provincial and county
ORD activities come from the respective civil administrative offices.

It is difficult to judge how effectively the administrators have performed their coordinating role in the
various provinces and counties. An administrator who
gives high priority to agriculture can indeed help remove bottlenecks, facilitate cooperation of various government and nongovernment agencies in achieving rural development objectives, and lend the prestige and support of
his office to agricultural programs. In general a politically appointed administrator would be sensitive to
national priorities in development policies and programs
and would be in a position to adapt national policies
and decisions to reflect local needs and problems. The
ICED team heard complaints, however, particularly at
several county ORD offices, that local administrators
were insensitive to the needs and problems of the extension program and sometimes used the extension staff for
activities that were not related to agricultural extension.

Research. Under its national research program, the office
also operates ten national research institutes, listed
below, with a total staff of 513 research workers (in
1971). Additional research stations are also operated by
the provincial offices of rural development.

1. The Institute of Plant Environment, Suwon
2. Crop Experiment Station, Suwon, with four branch
   stations
3. Honam Crop Experiment Station with one branch
   station
4. Youngnam Crop Experiment Station

5. Horticulture Experiment Station, Suwon, with five branch stations
6. Sericulture Experiment Station, Suwon
7. Livestock Experiment Station, Suwon
8. Veterinary Research Laboratory
9. Alpine Experiment Station
10. Cheju Experiment Station[10]

Major research activities currently under way are: the elimination of undesirable characteristics of the new rice variety IR-667, improvement of insect and disease control, improvement of cultural practices for increased yields, development and improvement of exportable and import-substitute commercial crops, improvement of pasture utilization and forage development, and design and adaptation of farm machinery.

IR-667 rice variety was developed in a cooperative project with the International Rice Research Institute (Philippines) and the Agricultural College of Seoul National University. Trial cultivation of the variety in 1970 produced a maximum of about 500 kg. per 1/10 hectare or about one-third higher than the best regular varieties. The government plans to spread the variety to 200,000 hectares by 1972, though the performance of this strain under diverse farming conditions in Korea is yet unknown.

ORD research activities organized at the national level as described above are supplemented by considerable adaptive research undertaken by the provincial offices of Rural Development.

Personnel and Staffing

ORD employs about 6,000 rural guidance workers, about 800 research workers in the national and provincial research institutions, and another 900 administrative and professional workers in the national and provincial offices.

Of the 6,000 guidance workers, about one-third are located in the Gun (county) guidance offices and the rest are attached to the branch offices. Both of these groups maintain direct contacts with the farmers, though those at branch offices devote more time to village-level activities than do those at the guidance offices, who have additional responsibility for conducting the farmer training courses at the center. Taking all the guidance workers at the Gun and branch levels into account (excluding the national and provincial-level employees and research workers), the average number of farm households served by one guidance worker is about 425.[11]

When ORD began, most of its guidance workers were agricultural college graduates. More recently, it has become increasingly difficult to attract agriculture graduates to the guidance service because of widening job opportunities in agriculture-related industries and businesses and the relatively poor salary and promotion prospects in ORD. For instance, an agricultural high school teacher with the same qualifications as a guidance worker receives up to 50 percent higher salary.

Low salaries, the harsh living conditions, long working hours, and the isolation of rural life have resulted in a high rate of staff turnover. ORD has become for many a convenient entry point to other civil service positions. At present only about a quarter of the guidance workers are agriculture graduates; the rest are mostly agricultural high school and junior college graduates, and a small proportion are general college graduates.

Guidance workers may be third-, fourth-, and fifth-grade civil servants. The civil service requirements for the three categories are as follows:

Third-Grade Civil Servants:
    1. graduation from agricultural college, or
    2. graduation from agricultural high school and work experience in ORD for more than two years

Fourth-Grade Civil Servants:
    1. graduation from a four-year college, or
    2. graduation from junior agricultural college and work experience in an agricultural research institution for more than two years, or
    3. graduation from agricultural high school and work experience in agricultural research for more than four years

Fifth-Grade Civil Servants:
    1. graduation from high school and at least one year of experience in agricultural research or extension organization within the previous three years

Besides the regular staff of ORD, 116,000 volunteer leaders, recruited from among the farmers, serve as a further link between the guidance program and the villagers. The volunteer leaders, who are periodically brought into the Gun farmer training centers for orientation and training, take leadership in various village-level activities sponsored by the guidance program. The major activities currently promoted with the help of the volunteer leaders are Farm Improvement Clubs, Home Improvement Clubs, and 4-H Clubs.

OVERVIEW OF ORD EDUCATIONAL ACTIVITIES

Within the framework of national priorities and policies in agricultural and rural development reflected in the five-year development plan and Ministry of Agriculture decisions, the Office of Rural Development determines its educational activities and sets national targets each year. On the basis of the priorities and targets of the national ORD, each provincial and county ORD prepares a plan of action, sets targets with the concurrence and approval of the provincial and the county administration, and assumes the responsibility of carrying out these plans.

An overview of the main farmer education activities undertaken by ORD is presented in the following pages.

Farmer Training Centers and Farmers' Clubs

Farmer training centers, attached to the provincial and county offices, and farmers' groups or clubs organized in the villages with the help of the volunteer leaders, are the major vehicles for providing farmers with needed information and knowledge, helping change their traditional practices and ideas where necessary, and mobilizing their support for fulfilling the plans and targets for each area.

There are 11 provincial-level farmer training centers where, according to ORD, about 20,000 selected farmers from the counties were given short (6 to 13 days) training courses in 1971. Similarly, in 1971, about 180,000 volunteer leaders and other selected farmers were reported to have been given two to six days of training in 113 farmer training centers attached to the county ORDs.

The Farm Improvement, Home Improvement, and 4-H Clubs, with a total enrollment exceeding a million persons, are the focal points of guidance efforts in the field by guidance workers and volunteer leaders (see Table 13.3).

In 1971, the farmer training center courses and the field activities of guidance workers covered, with varying emphases, improved rice production, upland crop production, fruit and vegetable production, improvement of soil fertility, plant protection, improvement of sericulture, livestock, farm management, and agricultural marketing. A closer view of the training centers and field activities in a province and in a county is presented in this chapter.

TABLE 13.3

Number of Clubs, Members, and Volunteer Leaders--1970

Clubs	Number of Clubs	Membership	Number of Volunteer Leaders Active in Club
Farm Improvement Clubs	28,949	356,140	32,582
Home Improvement Clubs	18,189	266,648	19,962
4-H Clubs	29,803	633,481	63,208
TOTAL	76,941	1,256,269	115,752

Source: Office of Rural Development

Youth Activities

Organizing rural youth activities through 4-H Clubs
is one of the major functions of the ORD rural guidance
workers. Training tomorrow's farmers is an essential part
of ORD farmer education program. The 4-H movement, which
started in 1947 with U.S. inspiration, gradually expanded
into one of the largest 4-H organizations anywhere and,
after the end of the Korean war, became an integral part
of the national government's rural development program.
By 1970, the 4-H movement claimed a membership of 633,481
youths in 29,803 clubs throughout the country, though
these figures must be accepted with caution as some clubs
are inactive.
The 4-H Club program is now administered through the
Rural Youth Section in the Rural Guidance Bureau of the
national ORD. Policy and guidance for the program is
determined at the national office and transmitted to the
nine provincial and the 172 county and city ORDs which are
responsible for executing the program. The rural guidance
workers in the counties are assisted in organizing 4-H
activities by about 56,000 volunteer leaders from the
villages who take the initiative and provide guidance in
the formation and continued functioning of the local 4-H
Clubs in their respective villages.
Boys and girls between the ages of 13 to 24 can become members of the 4-H Club; about 44 percent of the
members in 1970 were between 16 and 18 years of age.
About one-third of the members are girls. A large major-

ity of the members had completed primary or middle school education.[12] Half of the members continue their membership in the movement for at least two to three years. (See Appendix 13.2.)

Several types of educational and training activities are undertaken by 4-H Clubs, including individual and group projects, on-the-farm training, farm engineering training, farm machinery training, specialized farm training, community assistance activities, regional and national competitions, and international farm youth exchanges.

Individual and group projects involve crop-growing, livestock, horticultural, or other agricultural activities for which the individual or the group is responsible for planning, making decisions, maintaining records and accounts, and managing the project as a business operation. Volunteer leaders and guidance workers advise and help the individual or the group in implementing the project.

The on-the-farm training project provides for three months of work experience for 500 members every year in 68 advanced farms throughout the country. Somewhat along the line of on-the-farm training, 50 selected 4-H members are brought at a time to a training farm for specialized farming experiences of varying duration. Seven such training farms have been established since 1969 in five provinces, and two more have been planned.

Another type of training provided by 4-H Clubs relates to farm engineering and farm machinery. In 23 4-H Farm Engineering Training Centers, about 2,000 members per year in three-week courses are taught fundamental skills in carpentry, earth block making, and operations of hand tillers and other small equipment. A longer and more sophisticated course to train farm machinery operators is offered in the National 4-H Farm Machinery Training Center.

The volunteer leaders who assist the guidance workers in organizing and promoting 4-H Club activities are given special training of two days to a week's duration in the provincial and county farmer training centers. The subject matters include general agriculture, home economics, 4-H Club organization and leadership, and citizenship.

A credit fund has been created by ORD to assist promising individual and group projects of 4-H members. In 1970, about 15,000 members in 5,000 clubs received a total of 138 million won (W370 = US$1) in loans from this fund.[13]

Community Improvement Activities

The total effort and resources of ORD directed toward community improvement activities have been limited. More than 18,000 Home Improvement Clubs (with about

267,000 members and 20,000 volunteer leaders), which could
serve as the vehicle for organizing home improvement activities, were listed in 1970, but the total number of guidance workers with special responsibility for home and
community improvement activities in 1971 was only 360, an
average of two guidance workers per county compared to an
overall average of 35 guidance workers per county. The
two workers in the county were posted in Gun offices;
none were located in the branch offices or in the villages.
Regular guidance workers spent a minimal amount of time
in home and community improvement activities.

Three main activities are undertaken under the community improvement program: promotion of part-time and
off-season occupations for farmers; improvement of the
sources of domestic fuel in rural areas through the installation of methane gas facilities; and applied nutrition projects.

Sideline jobs. The aim of the projects for promoting sideline jobs for farmers is to increase the total
number of days they are engaged in gainful activities,
thus raising their total earnings. This is of special
significance in Korea because of the long winter season
when crop production is impossible.

Between 1967 and 1970, a total of 231 localities in
the country were chosen for sideline job promotion. Technical advice and training in simple manufacturing, handicrafts, and agricultural processing were provided, and the
formation of cooperatives for marketing and procurement
of raw materials was encouraged by ORD.

About 39,000 farm households were reported to have
participated in the sideline job projects and by 1970
about 10,000 villagers had been given technical training.
The projects were to be expanded to 31 new areas in 1971,
bringing the total to 261 localities in the country.

Domestic fuel. The pilot project for use of methane
gas as domestic fuel was launched in 1969. According to
an ORD analysis of rural fuel costs, use of methane gas
produced from animal wastes could result in up to 75 percent savings in fuel costs for cooking, in addition to
the preservation of depleting forest resources and the
production of composts for farmland.[14]

ORD activities in the pilot project included advising farmers about the benefits of the new source of fuel,
instructing on how the facilities could be installed, and
installing demonstration facilities. In 1969, with the
guidance and assistance of ORD workers, 444 facilities
were installed; 740 more were set up in 1970; and 3,000
were planned for 1971. Data about the adoption of the
new method by farmers or the number of facilities installed independently by farmers were unavailable, but
the ICED team was informed that adoption was minimal.

Applied nutrition projects. Details about the magnitude and scope of activities of ORD in the nutrition

field were not available to ICED researchers. In one
province (North Kyong Sang) such activities were limited
to selected population in 39 villages. Presumably in
other provinces, too, a limited number of selected villages and people were directly affected by the applied
nutrition projects. The main project activities were a
survey of the status of nutrition and diet in rural areas;
guidance on food preservation and preparation of balanced
meal; the establishment and management of pilot nutrition
centers in rural areas; and guidance on sanitary well
construction.

Special Projects
for Increasing Farmers' Incomes

Special projects designed to stimulate production of
cash crops of high marketability such as silk cocoons,
livestock, mushrooms, asparagus, grapes, and forest and
marine products have been in operation since 1968 in 90
rural regions throughout the country. To stimulate production, concentrated efforts in the form of subsidized
farm inputs, extension services, and credit along with
price supports and guaranteed market outlets are channeled
to the designated regions, which already possess certain
natural advantages. About 450,000 farm households participated in these projects between 1968 and 1971, resulting in an estimated (by ORD) 10 percent increase in the
participating farmers' income.
The special projects are planned to continue during
the Third Plan period, during which time another 100
rural zones will be selected for concentrated services,
allowing 300,000 farm households to participate in the
projects for increasing farmers' income. It is evident
that the burden on extension and other services will be
heavy if the projects are to accomplish their objectives.

Communication and Information Support

Communication and information support activities for
rural guidance are directed from the Agricultural Information Division of the national ORD located at Suwon.
Built up with generous assistance from the U.S.
Agency for International Development (AID), mainly in the
form of hardware, the division is equipped with a sizable
printing shop, and means of making still black-and-white
photographs, color slides, and filmstrips with synchronized sound, black-and-white and color motion pictures,
a large quantity of diagrams, posters, wallcharts, flip
charts, and other visual materials.

The division produces <u>Agricultural Techniques</u>, a farmers' journal published twice a month, and weekly radio programs for farmers and rural audiences; holds audiovisual presentations in villages by mobile information units; distributes charts, diagrams, and occasional publications such as pamphlets and leaflets among farmers, and supplies communication materials to the provincial and county ORDs to support their specific activities.

<u>Agricultural Techniques</u> is said to have a print run of 800,000 copies. It is distributed among farmers by hand; each county and branch guidance office is responsible for distributing about a thousand copies, and one in every three farm households is supposed to receive a copy. The journal, printed in Korean, includes an abundance of charts, graphs, tables, and national output figures.

Talent for graphic displays appears to be well developed in Korea. A visitor to the ORD office is impressed by the elaborate audiovisual representation of the ORD operations. In fact, a visitor to any of the provincial or even a county rural guidance office is also greeted with an impressive display of visual materials, containing statistics of past performance, future plans, and work in progress.

The ICED team was not in a position to assess fully the effectiveness of ORD communication support activities, but found the following general impressions during brief observation visits to the national ORD and several provincial and county offices.

The basic concept of integrating messages delivered via radio, films, and printed materials with the current program objectives of ORD and with the day-to-day efforts of guidance workers was sound and imaginative, but the practical application of this concept left much to be desired. Budget stringencies had seriously curtailed the production of up-to-date films, for example; hence the messages still being delivered were likely to be in some measure obsolete. There had been few if any systematic audience studies to evaluate the effectiveness of radio programs, films, and other materials or to guide producers in fitting future programs to the primary needs and interests of the intended audience. The technical quality appeared to vary considerably, with some of it distinctly inferior. For instance, some 8-mm. films made for a mobile unit for presentation to villagers contained out-of-focus shots, were badly scratched, and suffered from poor sound quality.

The overall impression of the ICED research team was that the audiovisual operations were not sufficiently integrated with other ORD educational and information efforts and that they had suffered a decline in priority and support since their heyday when they enjoyed strong support from AID.

Notwithstanding these deficiencies, however, the audiovisual components are still significant in the ORD system and can undoubtedly be made more valuable if in the future they receive adequate support and are well-tailored to fit complementary communications efforts and changing program goals and strategies.

ORD Staff Training

Preservice training of newly recruited ORD employees as well as inservice training is provided in the Training Institute for Agriculture and Forestry Public Officials, located in Suwon and operated by ORD. The general pattern of preservice and inservice training planned for the institute was as follows:

1. preservice training for newly appointed employees in grade-4 position in rural guidance, home improvement, research, and administration for 8-12 weeks
2. inservice training, providing refresher courses in general and specific subject matter fields to employees below grade-4 position, for four weeks, every four years
3. inservice training, providing refresher courses for subject matter specialists in ORD and provincial ORDs, for 4-12 months
4. inservice training, providing advanced refresher courses in agriculture subjects to employees in grade-3 positions, for two weeks[15]

In recent years, the duration and frequency of various training programs have been somewhat curtailed, according to ORD, because of budgetary constraints. A newly recruited guidance worker is now generally given three weeks of preservice training before he is assigned to a county guidance office, where he goes through a brief orientation period. In 1971, a total of 500 rural guidance workers and 50 home improvement workers were in preservice training.

A guidance worker becomes eligible for an inservice training course after working four years in the field. This implies that 25 percent of the guidance workers or about 1,500 should be brought in for inservice training every year. Actually, in 1971, only 515 guidance workers were brought back to the Institute in separate groups for two to three week courses in increased food production, horticulture practices, livestock development, sericulture practices, agricultural engineering, mushroom growing, and inland fish farms.

The other program currently offered is a special 10-
month training for outstanding guidance workers in five
subjects (a 10-month course for each subject): rice, upland crops, plant protection, sericulture, and agricultural
engineering. A total of 50 persons, 10 in each subject,
went through this program in 1971.

A VIEW FROM THE LOCAL LEVEL: FARMER EDUCATION IN
NORTH KYONG SANG PROVINCE AND IN YONG CHUN COUNTY

Education and training of farmers undertaken by the
Provincial Office of Rural Development (PORD) in the North
Kyong Sang Province and the County Office of Rural Development in Yong Chun County in the same province are described here to illustrate the nature, scope, and methods
of such activities in all nine provinces and 172 counties
in Korea.
The educational activities in each province and its
counties may be grouped into two broad categories: guidance and extension activities in the field, and short
residential training in the provincial and county farmer
training centers. The two categories of activities are
closely related, carried out essentially by the same group
of people, except in the provincial training centers, and
designed to serve the same basic objectives of disseminating information and securing farmers' support in fulfilling the agricultural goals and targets for the year.

PORD Educational Role

The role of the PORD in field extension activities is
mainly to plan the provincial program and to support and
guide the counties in carrying it out. The plan is
broken down into specific tasks for each county.   The
PORD operates a separate residential training center in
the province. Training is also carried out in the county
farmer training centers. In the following discussion,
therefore, we will consider the field extension activities
for the whole province and then look separately at the
residential training courses in the provincial center and
in one county center in Yong Chun.
The North Kyong Sang Province, located in the east-
central part of South Korea along the Sea of Japan, has
an area of about 20,000 square kilometers and a population of about 4.5 million. There are 29 counties and
5,700 villages in the province. The farming population
is about 2.7 million and the total arable land area is
about 370,000 hectares, of which about 200,000 hectares
are paddy land. Agriculture is dominated by rice and

barley cultivation. Diversification into soybean, livestock, sericulture, vegetables, sweet potatoes, and or-
chard fruits has grown in recent years. The number of
farm households in the province is about 441,000. The
number of total ORD personnel in the province was 1,151
in 1971. The breakdown of the staff is: 1,065 guidance
workers in county guidance offices, 40 research and veterinary staff in the provincial office and research stations,
39 guidance specialists in the provincial office, and 7
guidance workers in the provincial training center.

There are 19,974 volunteer leaders in the province
who assist the guidance workers at the village level. In
1971 there were 5,503 Farm Improvement Clubs with 71,200
members; 4,000 Home Improvement Clubs with 59,400 members;
5,674 4-H Clubs with 112,000 members.

Field Activities in Farm Improvement

Field activities in North Kyong Sang, as in the nationwide program, can be grouped into three types: farm
improvement activities, home improvement activities, and
rural youth activities. Most of such activities are organized by the guidance worker and the volunteer leaders
in the villages around the clubs, but participation is
also open to nonmembers.

The major activities for farm improvement undertaken
in the province in 1971 are briefly described below.

Cooperative rice cultivation zones. About one-quarter
(46,000 hectares) of the total rice land in 3,738 locations in the province has been selected for concentrated
attention by ORD for producing higher rice yields. These
locations are known as the cooperative rice cultivation
zones. The role of ORD is to emphasize and propagate the
use of improved seed varieties, improved transplantation
practices, better fertilizer treatment, soil improvement
measures, and disease and insect control measures, by
means of training (in county centers)   volunteer leaders
and selected participants in the cooperative program,
group sessions in the villages, demonstration farms, and
individual advice. The guidance workers also help in securing the necessary inputs for the cooperative zone farmers, and government policy accords preferential treatment to these farmers in the supply of inputs from the
National Agricultural Cooperative Federation, the supplier
of fertilizer, chemicals, and credit.

The 1971 target for the cooperative zones was a yield
of 4.3 tons per hectare compared with the provincial average of 3.6 tons. This target had been achieved in the
cooperative zones in the previous year.

Disease and insect control. Guidance workers, with
the help of volunteer leaders, watch for the signs of insect attack on crops and forecast and issue warnings about
such dangers. The provincial and county agencies as well

as farmers are accordingly informed and arrangements are
made for spraying insecticides.

Special projects for increasing farmers' income.
Projects for improvement of livestock and commercial crops
have been carried out in selected areas of the province.
ORD provided technical advice to participant farmers in
the special projects. The number of farmers involved in
the project was not available.

Calendars. PORD prepares printed work calendars for
preparing seed beds, transplanting, weeding, applying
fertilizer, harvesting, and so forth. These are widely
distributed among farmers.

Farm efficiency and mechanization. Through county
offices PORD operates 12 farm equipment centers and 20
farm mechanization demonstration centers in the province.
The equipment centers are primarily for the training of
the cooperative zone farmer in the handling, operation,
and maintenance of various farm equipment. The demonstration centers show how efficiency can be raised by the use
of tractors, combines, binders, automatic threshers, mechanical sickles, driers, and amplifiers. For this purpose,
tracts of land in selected counties are cultivated and
managed under the direct supervision of a guidance worker.

Farmers' training during winter. Short group training sessions, usually for one day, are arranged in the
villages. Volunteer leaders, supervised by guidance workers, conduct these sessions. Typical topics for such sessions are specific problems regarding increased rice
yields, use of methane gas as a source of fuel, use of
vinyl covers against frost, and explanation of government
agricultural programs and policies. In 1971, a total of
460,000 man-days were spent in such training sessions in
the province.

Home Improvement Activities

Though about 4,000 Home Improvement Clubs with about
60,000 members are claimed to be in existence, most of the
time and efforts of guidance workers at the county level
were devoted to agricultural improvement rather than the
community development activities. The home, family, and
community improvement activities in the province in 1971
involved a concentrated effort in 53 selected areas in
the province.

The list of projects included nutrition improvement,
methane gas use, and the promotion of sideline jobs. The
nutrition improvement project involved 39 villages, where
farmers were educated on the importance of proper nutrition and nutrient content of food. In the methane gas
utilization project, the method of building methane gas
units was taught, and 500 units were installed in 1971.
The sideline job project, intended to supplement farmers'
incomes and keep them gainfully occupied when not farming,

in 1971 involved about 1,000 people in seven locations. These people were given training and technical advice, through group and individual contacts, on livestock raising, handicrafts, processing of farm products, and making farm tools.

4-H Club Activities

The scope and nature of the nationwide 4-H movement have already been described. In the province, besides individual and group club projects involving over 100,000 members, activities included farm engineering training and on-the-farm work and training.

There are four 4-H farm engineering centers in the province, in which a total of 360 young people in 1971 were trained in 20-day courses in simple rural construction activities, carpentry, and farm tool use and maintenance.

In the provincial 4-H training farm 50 youths were trained for six months in practical farming with special emphasis on livestock and commercial crops. In addition, 95 youths in seven locations went through a month-long "technical exchange" training course, with emphasis again on practical farming experience.

Farmer Training in the Provincial Center

The provincial farmer training center has two classrooms, dormitory, dining hall, barnhouse, and offices-- altogether about 1,500 square yards of floor space. It has a regular instructional staff; a number of people from the provincial guidance staff also help in conducting the training courses.

The main function of this center is to offer short training courses to upgrade the knowledge and skill of volunteer leaders and other farmers selected from the counties. About 2,000 trainees attended 13 three-day courses in eight subjects in 1971. Each course had 150 to 175 trainees at a time. The subjects and the approximate number of trainees are listed below:

1. Vegetable production: 150 trainees
2. improved rice cultivation: 150 trainees
3. use of methane gas: 150 trainees
4. sericulture: 150 trainees
5. livestock raising: 150 trainees
6. farm machinery: 450 trainees in three groups
7. 4-H Club organization and management: 450 trainees in three groups
8. child care and nursery management: 350 trainees in two groups

Farmer Training
in the Yong Chun County Center

Most residential farmer training takes place in the
29 county centers in the province. The 1971 program for
the Yong Chun County farmer training center described below is typical of training activities in the county farmer centers.

At the county level, farmer training is the direct
responsibility of the guidance personnel. Plans for field
activities and residential training are prepared and implemented by the same staff; equipment and facilities are
shared for both activities; and funds for both are drawn
from the common county ORD budget.

Yong Chun County, located in the southeastern part
of the province, has an area of 908 square kilometers
and a population of 198,000 (in 1968). About 21 percent
of the land area or about 19,400 hectares are arable, of
which 11,300 hectares are rice land. There are 24,000
farm households (152,000 persons). About 75 percent of
the farms are less than one hectare and 37 percent are
less than a half-hectare in size.

Yong Chun County is now at an initial stage of farm
mechanization. In 1971 the farm machines used in the
county were 55 tillers, 444 sprayers, 438 automatic
threshers, and 136 dusters.

The county center in 1971 offered nine courses: wet
paddy farming, dry field farming, greenhouse farming,
livestock, sericulture, agricultural machinery, rural
development, village-life improvement, and youth activities. Each course is approximately 14 hours or two days
long. The contents of each course are summarized below.

Course	Contents of Training
Wet Paddy–Cooperative Cultivation	1. the meaning and purpose of cooperative farming 2. the effects of cooperative farming 3. practical principles of cooperative farming 4. rice cultivation 5. controlling disease damage to rice 6. soil testing 7. principles of soil improvement
Dry Field Farming	1. wheat and barley 2. potatoes 3. corn (maize) 4. sweet potatoes 5. sesame

	6.	garlic
	7.	strawberries
	8.	onions
	9.	peanuts
	10.	cabbage
Greenhouse Farming	1.	vinyl house construction and greenhouse cultivation
Livestock	1.	preparing pasture land
	2.	final crops and fodder cultivation
	3.	raising and breeding cattle
	4.	raising chickens
	5.	raising hogs
Sericulture	1.	cultivating mulberry trees
	2.	raising silkworms
	3.	preventing silkworm diseases
Village-life Improvement	1.	construction of methane gas facilities
Agricultural Machinery	1.	motors
	2.	mechanical hand plow
	3.	sprayer
Youth Activities	1.	4-H Club organization
	2.	4-H Club activities and record keeping
Rural Development	1.	problems of rural development

The total number of participants in 1971 was 1,028. The largest number of trainees were elementary school graduates, followed by middle school graduates. These two groups made up about 80 percent of the trainees.

The majority of trainees was over 25 years of age. Participation in youth activity courses is limited to those below the age of 25, since this training is aimed at 4-H Club members.

There are no full-time instructors for farmer training; courses are taught by the county guidance staff. In Yong Chun County, for example, 15 county guidance office staff members and one farm equipment technician are involved in actual farmer training. Of these, 3 are graduates of agricultural colleges, 2 are graduates of general colleges, and the remaining 10 are graduates of agricultural high school.

For all of the courses, except agricultural machinery, classroom instruction takes up the largest part of the time--90 percent--with 10 percent of the time for practice. In the agricultural machinery course classroom instruction takes up 30 percent of the time, and practice involves 70 percent.

Planning for each year's training is completed by the end of the previous year. Before the plans are established, guidelines for training are given by the PORD. These guidelines regulate the content of the training program and the number of trainees who are to participate. County guidance office staff members draw up actual plans for training, taking into account PORD guidelines and local county policies. Training plans and the budget for the training program are approved by the county executive. Through this process, those subjects emphasized in national, provincial, or   local policy are given the greatest attention. The time schedule of training activities is drawn up independently by the county guidance office staff members.

Trainees are selected by each county guidance office, which also decides on the specific number of trainees to be selected from each township or town in the county. At this point the recommendations of town or township chiefs are solicited, but final selection is by the branch of the county guidance office.

Persons recommended by the agricultural cooperatives or the Farmland Improvement Associations are automatically selected for training, but in 1971 no such recommendations were made.

FACTORS INFLUENCING ORD'S EFFICIENCY AND EFFECTIVENESS

ORD farmer education activities are components of a larger knowledge-generation and dissemination system in agriculture, and its operations form part of an agricultural and rural development system. Therefore, ORD's efficiency in terms of the quality and quantity of its educational services is affected by such elements as the formal agricultural education system which provides initial preparation for ORD personnel, inservice training to promote staff competence, agricultural research which generates educational content for ORD, and the mass media which reinforce and facilitate ORD's educational effort.

Other factors in part define ORD's educational tasks and create the conditions for meeting the ultimate objectives of agricultural and rural development. These factors include the provision of credit and supply of inputs, without which many educational precepts cannot be practiced; agricultural price and production policies, which determine the incentives for investment and efforts by farmers; and changing market demands and diversification of agriculture, which impose new educational requirements.

Inservice training of ORD staff and the communication support activities have already been discussed. In the following pages other major influences on the internal efficiency and the external effectiveness of ORD educational activities will be discussed.

The Formal Agricultural Education System

A descriptive note on the formal agricultural education system is included in Appendix 13.4. In brief, the formal agricultural education system is characterized by the following weaknesses:

1. Entry into agricultural education at the secondary and postsecondary level is at best a second choice for many of the students; their first preference would be to gain admission to a general academic high school or to a more prestigious sector of the university.
2. The academic character of the examinations and requirements for admission for agricultural colleges heavily favor the graduates of academic high schools--most of whom are young people reared in urban areas who know little about rural life and are likely to develop later an aversion to an agricultural career.
3. Positions in agriculture are at a strong competitive disadvantage--in salary, opportunity for advancement, prestige, and personal conveniences and comfort--relative to positions in the modern urban sector or elsewhere in the national civil service.

No less serious is the excessively abstract character and the low quality of most agricultural schools and colleges, according to witnesses who have examined them closely. Little or no conscious attention is given to preparing practical extension workers, by including work in the social sciences as well as agriculture and a good balance between classroom instruction and practical work in the field. Although some institutions are doing excellent work--most notably the prestigious Seoul National University College of Agriculture at Suwon--overall these formal agricultural educational institutions are not making a collective contribution to staffing and strengthening the nation's agricultural sector and advancing rural development commensurate with their prime mission or with the substantial resources they consume.

Evaluation of roles and functions in the total agricultural research and extension effort of the nation is
needed. Such an evaluation would include: 1) an examination of the manpower requirements for strengthening
agricultural and rural development; 2) a clear definition
of the roles and priorities of agricultural schools and
colleges in relation to meeting these requirements; and
3) broad adjustment in admission procedures, curriculum
content, and training strategies designed to meet these
requirements most effectively. If all this were done, it
seems likely that Korea could meet its needs for well-
trained agricultural and rural manpower with fewer institutions and at no higher total cost.

Agricultural Research

Although agricultural research in South Korea is
primarily the responsibility of the Office of Rural Development, the agricultural faculties of the universities
carry out agricultural research. A general complaint is
that the colleges of agriculture are starved for resources
and facilities for research and that there is not enough
cooperation and coordination between the research activities of ORD and the colleges. (According to the Director
of ORD, various measures have been taken recently to promote cooperation between the colleges and ORD. Specifically, Presidential Decree no. 5889 of December 28, 1971,
established a cooperative research program in agriculture
which provided for a joint coordinating committee, joint
participation in research, exchange of personnel, and a
12 million won research grant for colleges of agriculture
from ORD.)
Korean agricultural policymakers have recognized the
importance of adaptive research in agricultural development and have built up considerable research capability
in the ORD research institutes, experiment stations, and
provincial offices. It is impossible to make a precise
assessment of the contribution of the research efforts
to agricultural growth. There has been no dramatic dis-
covery of "miracle" varieties, but it seems plausible to
assume that the extensive research activities of ORD
have contributed to steady incremental increases in the
productivity of Korean agriculture. It appears likely
that research efforts can be even more productive in the
future if: 1) there is more attention given to the economic implications of recommended technical practices
based on new research findings; 2) there is more feedback
from farmers about practical problems requiring research;
3) there is more adaptive research on farmers' own plots
and more study of practical obstacles to farmers' adoption of new practices; and 4) there is closer planning

and collaboration between researchers at ORD and those
in agricultural colleges.

Agricultural Credit and Supply of Inputs

Because of the large number of small owner-operators
in Korean agriculture, an institutional source of farm
credit is vitally important for the growth of progressive
agriculture. The National Agricultural Cooperative Federation (NACF) is the agricultural supply and marketing
organization and the main source of institutional credit
for farmers in Korea.

The cooperative organization has a three-tier structure. At the base is the Ri or Dong (village) cooperatives which are affiliated with the Gun or county cooperatives; the latter, in turn, are affiliated with the NACF.
In 1970, there were 6,740 Ri or Dong cooperatives and 140
Gun cooperatives with a membership extending to more than
90 percent of the estimated 2.6 million farm households.
There were also 148 special cooperatives, organized for
specific agricultural commodities, affiliated directly
with NACF. The NACF employs about 10,000 persons including 1,500 in the national and provincial offices and
the rest at the county level.

In 1970, the funds available for NACF operations
were 224,000 million won (about US$700 million), but the
major portion of the loan fund was used by NACF as working capital for the purchase and distribution of fertilizer, pesticides, and farm machinery. In 1969, only 11
percent of all loans went for short- and medium-term agricultural production loans.

Knowledgeable persons with whom ICED researchers discussed the credit situation thought that the proportion
of small owner-operators reached by some form of institutional credit needed to be substantially enlarged. Many
farmers still depend on high-interest noninstitutional
credit or operate without any source of production loans.
The lack of widespread credit has limited agricultural
growth and is likely to limit it even more in the future
unless institutional credit facilities expand and improve
substantially.[16]

The NACF has a monopoly on fertilizer distribution
and is also the major supplier of pesticides and farm
machinery. Korea has made relatively slow progress in
increasing the amounts of chemical fertilizer used, compared with amounts used by other temperate zone farmers.
However, compared with usage in other developing countries,
its usage is high. Fertilizer used per hectare increased
from 110 kilograms in 1965 to 148 kilograms in 1969.
There was little use of pesticides and lime during 1966-
1969. (See Appendix 13.3.)

A gradually decreasing supply of farm labor and
shortages during peak farm activity are making agricultural mechanization profitable for Korea. Mechanization,
though yet at a low level, has rapidly increased since
its introduction in 1960. (See Appendix 13.3.) The
mechanization program will be considerably intensified
during the Third Plan period with the objective of bringing 450,000 hectares under mechanized farming. Operation, repair, and maintenance of farm machinery and the
farmers' ability to pay for mechanized services may prove
to be bottlenecks unless present efforts in farm machinery
training and better access to credit by various forms of
institutional support for small farmers are substantially
strengthened during the coming years.

There appears to be little coordination and communication, particularly at the field level, between the activities of the NACF and ORD. Both organizations have hier-
archies of national, provincial, and local officials and
large numbers of field staff. Both are serving a largely
overlapping group of clients and both are supposed to
work toward the achievement of complementary objectives
in agricultural and rural development. Yet the field
staff as well as the national and provincial offices of
the two organizations apparently operate quite independently, without sufficient functional linkages between the
educational and advisory activities of ORD and the supply
of production inputs and credit by NACF.

Land Policy

The overall responsibility for development of land
and water resources is vested in the Agricultural Development Corporation (ADC)--a semiautonomous public entity
within the Ministry of Agriculture. Besides managing capital projects, the ADC tries to ensure proper utilization and
maintenance of improved facilities by organizing the beneficiary farmers into Land Improvement Associations.

There are three major facets relating to the use of
land for agriculture which have affected agricultural
growth in Korea: 1) extending total cultivable area by
bringing into cultivation previously nonarable land, such
as reclaiming upland areas and tidal land; 2) consolidating small holdings of land into large contiguous tracts
in order to extend farm mechanization and other economies
of scale; and 3) irrigation and water management in order
to provide a regulated supply of water for farmland.

Of a total land area of 9.9 million hectares in
Korea, only about 2.3 million hectares are at present
cultivable. About 15 percent of this farmland (on a net
basis, deducting about 1 percent farmland lost to industrial uses per year) has been made cultivable between the

years 1960 and 1970. There is, however, some scope for
further reclamation of upland and subwatershed area. Upland development would involve bench terraining, small-
scale irrigation facilities, pasture development in the
higher areas, and fruit growing along the piedmont.

Very few landholdings in Korea are more than three
hectares in size and even those are often fragmented.
This situation has given rise to a policy of consolidating
land for efficient water management, use of mechanical
farm equipment, and increased farm labor efficiency. A
total of 600,000 hectares or about half of all rice paddies in Korea are planned to be ultimately brought under
the consolidation program. By the end of 1970, about
158,000 hectares had been consolidated. The target for
the Third Plan is to consolidate a total of 450,000 hectares or 75 percent of land considered suitable for such
a measure.[17]

Korea possesses a relatively developed irrigation
system, particularly for rice land. About 50 percent of
all rice paddies are considered fully irrigated and another 20 percent are partially irrigated. The Third Plan
objectives are to increase the proportion of fully irrigated land and to improve overall water resources through
comprehensive development of four major river basin areas.
The river basins (of the Kum, Yongsan, Nakdong, and Han
rivers) make up 1.2 million hectares or 54 percent of all
land under cultivation. The plan, to be completed by
1981, includes projects for erosion control, construction
of multipurpose dams, modification of river facilities
and industrial waterworks, and extensive irrigation and
drainage facilities. Of 12 multipurpose dams in the plan,
eight are scheduled to be completed during the Third Plan
period.

Because land reform, improvement in agricultural
services, and growth in agricultural production coincided
during the 1960s, it cannot be proved that better agricultural services would not have raised production under
the old tenure system. It can be argued, however, that
the large increase in the number of small owner-farmers
as a result of land reform created the conditions and
the need for expansion of agricultural services, which,
in turn, contributed to increased productivity.

Different aspects of land development policy, viz.,
reclaiming upland and piedmont areas, consolidating small
paddies, and improving river basin water management, have
wide implications for the nature and scope of extension
activities. So far a relatively small share of ORD efforts has been devoted to the diversified agricultural
uses of the hill slopes compared to a much larger effort
that has gone to rice cultivation including consolidation of small rice paddies. Extension activities in the
future, it appears, should move in the direction of a
greater emphasis on terrace cultivation, orchards, pas-

ture development, and other forms of farming appropriate
for hill slopes as well as intensive multiple-crop utilization of the river basin land developed with high capital
investment. These, it would appear, are the frontiers
where farmers can benefit most from knowledge of new
technologies and other support services.

Diversification of Agriculture

Progress towards diversification and the emphasis in
government agricultural policy on rice self-sufficiency
have been noted. Many reports on Korean agricultural
development, although supporting the efforts to increase
rice productivity per unit of land, question the almost
exclusive pursuit of rice self-sufficiency at any cost
and the neglect of possible economic advantages for farmers in other crops, given the necessary infusion of
technology and inputs. For instance, there has been
relatively limited research, extension efforts, and inputs for the production of barley, the second major grain
in the country.
Improved economic conditions for the Korean people
have created an unfulfilled demand for meat, poultry, and
dairy products. Per capita demand for meat is projected
to increase 60 percent between 1970 and 1976; the demand
for eggs is expected to rise 50 percent; and for milk and
milk products, more than 100 percent during the same
period.[18] The demand for agricultural products offers an
opportunity for higher agricultural income which can be
exploited only with greater emphasis on diverse agricultural activities, both in government policy and in farmer
education services.

Price and Market Incentives

The real income of farmers was unfavorably affected
during the mid-1960s by the unequal rise in prices of
farm products and goods purchased by farm families.
Government price stabilization, through sales and purchase of grains, has been designed to reduce seasonal
variations of prices to benefit both consumers and producers. In practice, according to knowledgeable observers, the policy has generally benefited urban consumers
more than the farmer. The government has checked high
prices in the scarcity months of July and August by importing grains, but has not offered a high enough price
to farmers during the period after harvest. The situation improved for farmers, however, when their produce
prices were raised substantially between 1968 and 1970.

In any case, the price situation generally has offered
enough incentive for farmers to permit a continuous increase in agricultural productivity, though it may not
have been sufficient incentive for realizing the full
potentialities of Korean agriculture.

A greater problem than the general level of agricultural prices will probably be the agricultural marketing
facilities. Unless remedial measures are planned, the
increasing volume of agricultural production and the
greater commercialization and diversification of products
are likely to create a marketing bottleneck, which can
become a disincentive for agricultural improvement and a
major obstacle to agricultural extension and education
efforts. The total volume of commercial marketing in
agriculture is expected to increase during the Third Five
Year Plan (1972-1976) 40 percent over the level of 1969.
But certain products are projected to show much higher
increase: vegetables about 50 percent, fruits 70 percent,
eggs 75 percent, meat over 90 percent, and milk nearly
200 percent.[19] According to a joint study of the U.S.
Department of Agriculture and AID, the required improvements in agricultural marketing will call for substantial
investment in physical infrastructure (rural roads, central markets, storage and processing facilities, and so
forth); marketing research, information services; training
in marketing and agribusiness; and capital funds for
marketing enterprises.[20]

COSTS AND FINANCES OF ORD OPERATIONS

The funds for ORD activities at the national, provincial, and local levels are drawn from government budget allocations at the three levels. The national ORD
is financed by the national government; funds for the
provincial ORDs come from both national and provincial
governments; and at the county level, about a quarter of
the funds, including salaries of guidance workers, come
from national and provincial sources, and the rest from
the county administration.

National Expenditure

In 1971 the total amount budgeted at the three levels
of government for all ORD extension activities (excluding
expenses for research) was 2,074 million won or about
US$5 million. (See Table 13.4.) This amount is equal to
about 0.3 percent of the contribution of the agriculture
sector to GNP in 1970, which was 728,000 million won in
current prices.[21] Average per farm expenditure for the

TABLE 13.4

Office of Rural Development Budget, 1971

	(in million won)

A. Total ORD Expenditure · 3,864

1.	Research	1,382
2.	General Administration	408
3.	Rural Guidance	2,074
a)	National ORD guidance expenditure including salaries at all levels	525
b)	Cash grants to provincial and county offices	272
c)	Contribution from provinces	378
d)	Contribution from counties	899

B. Distribution of National Expenditure for Rural Guidance (items 3a and 3b above) [a]

	797.4
General Administration (equipment and transportation)	179.3
Increase in food production	122.0
Allowance for selected volunteer leaders	119.2
Information support	94.3
Rural youths (4-H Clubs)	93.6
Home improvement projects	81.4
Community development	74.8
Cash crops and livestock	18.5
Farm management and farm machinery	14.3

Source: National Office of Rural Development

[a]Distribution of province and county expenditures was not available. For examples of budget breakdown for one province and one country see Tables 13.5 and 13.7.

2.5 million farm households was approximately 800 won or a little over US$2. By comparison, the average annual expenditure by farmers for agricultural inputs per farm household for 1969 was reported to be 47,000 won.[22]

Provincial Expenditure

Information on budgets and costs for the total province-level activities in the nine provinces was not available. Budget figures for one province are shown in Table 13.5 to illustrate the level and composition of provincial expenditures.

TABLE 13.5

Major Expenditures in
the Provincial Office of Rural Development,
North Kyong Sang--1971

	(in thousand won)
Total Budgeted Expenditure	316,490
General administration	111,000
Guidance service	106,000
Livestock, sericulture and seed stations	52,000
Research	38,000
Provincial farmer training center	9,490

Source: Kyong Sang Puk DO Office of Rural Development.

The total budgeted expenditure for the North Kyong Sang Province in 1971 was 316 million won. This amount was almost equally divided among expenditures for: guidance activities; research, experimentation, and breeding and veterinary stations; and general administration. The expenditure for the provincial farmer training centers was 9.5 million won.

The large expenditure for general administration is presumably because the provincial office provides administrative support to the county offices.

The budget for the provincial farmer training center shows the following distribution of expenditure:

Total provincial farmer training
  center expenditure in 1971   9,490,000 won

  Administration   4,001,000
  Salaries   2,858,000
  Trainees' boarding   1,544,000
  Travel   895,000
  Resource persons   192,000

    An explanation for the large amount for administra-
tion of the center was not available from documents provided by the PORD.
    Assuming that the above figures represent the opera-
ting costs for the center for 1971, the average recurrent
unit cost per course of three-day duration for 2,000
trainees was about 4,700 won (about US$12).

County Expenditure

    The financial and budget details for the Yong Chun
county rural guidance activities collected by the Central
Education Research Institute (CERI) are again presented
as a sample of a county budget.
    The value of the capital assets for the county gui-
dance center including land, buildings, and equipment was
about 130 million won (see Table 13.6).
    The operating budget of the county office of rural
development in 1971 was 8.5 million won (see Table 13.7).
Salaries constituted about 15 percent of the operating
budget, a relatively low percentage in a labor-intensive
operation. The general administration cost appears to
be high, but it presumably includes some of the personnel
costs such as travel expenses.
    The additional recurrent costs for operating the
training courses were 454,000 won in 1971 or just over
400 won (US$1) per trainee for a two-day course for
approximately 1,000 trainees. About half of the expenditure was for trainees' boarding and the rest was for
teaching and practice materials, and observation and
field trips. The training cost constituted about 5 percent of the county operating budget. The difference in
the training costs at the provincial and county centers
is explained by the fact that salaries of instructors
are included in the provincial cost figures, and the
travel costs paid by the provincial center for its trainees were higher. (The ICED team was not able to probe
costs and finances beyond the readily available data.)

TABLE 13.6

Capital Assets of the Yong Chun County Office of Rural Development

I.	Land (1971 estimated value)	<u>W75,140,000</u>
	Office site (2,400 pyungs)*	60,000,000
	Demonstration farm (600 pyungs)	15,000,000
	Branch office site (70 pyungs)	140,000
II.	Buildings (1971 estimated value)	<u>W29,295,000</u>
	Office building	17,800,000
	Warehouse for machinery	1,275,000
	Storage and silo for	
	demonstration farm	7,235,000
	Dormitory and dining room	1,125,000
	Night-duty room	480,000
	Branch office	1,350,000
	Methane gas production	
	facility	30,000
III.	Equipment (purchase price)	<u>W25,080,000</u>
	Tractors (6)	14,700,000
	Farm tools and machinery	1,250,000
	Auto-cycles and bicycles	
	(9 + 27)	1,530,000
	Carpentry and mechanical tools	2,000,000
	Audio-visual equipment and	
	instructional materials	1,000,000
	Furniture and office equipment	1,000,000
	Others	3,600,000

*1 pyung = 3.3 sq. meters.

Source: Central Education Research Institute, Seoul.

IMPACT ON FARMERS

The ultimate test of the effectiveness of ORD's guidance and educational activities will be the changes effected in the farming practices in Korean villages and the consequent economic and other benefits both for the villagers and for the nation. Evaluative evidence of the ORD's impact at the village level was scarce. ICED, therefore, made arrangements with the Central Education Research Institute (CERI) in Seoul to undertake a study of the effects of ORD activities in the villages of one representative county.

CERI conducted a survey of 300 farmers in 30 villages in Yong Chun county.[23] A total of 230 questionnaires, 175 from participants in farmer training courses and 55 from nonparticipants, were obtained (see Table 13.8). The participants, most of whom also were volunteer leaders, attended two-day training courses on different farming techniques and rural development in the county farmer training center. The responses provide data on the extent of adoption of the agricultural practices taught at the county training centers and about differences in income of course participants and nonparticipants.

TABLE 13.7

Operating Budget of the
Yong Chun County Office of Rural Development--1971

		Sources of Funds (In thousand won)		
Items	Amount	National	Provincial	County
General administration	2,295	–	–	2,295
Salaries	1,380	1,380	–	–
Training center	454	–	–	454
Programs in food crops	2,764	555	167	2,042
Programs in livestock and commercial crops	564	33	–	531
Programs in village improvement	357	125	–	232
Youth activities	347	73	31	243
Soil testing	247	6	–	241
Programs in rural life improvement	151	27	–	124
Community development	41	–	–	41
Public information	36	–	–	36
Total	8,636	2,199	198	6,239

Source: Central Education Research Institute, Seoul.

TABLE 13.8

Respondents in CERI Survey of Farmers
in Yong Chun County

	#
Participants in farmer training courses	175
Courses:	
Wet paddy cultivation (rice farming)	78
Dry field cultivation (barley, wheat)	39
Sericulture	17
Agricultural machinery	13
Livestock	12
Greenhouse farming (special crops)	8
Youth activities	4
Rural development	2
Village-life improvement	2
Nonparticipants	55
TOTAL	230

Adoption of Practices

The results of the survey of adoption practices
(Tables 13.9 - 13.10) show the following:

1. a high adoption rate, ranging from over 70 to
   100 percent, of a number of recommended practices
   in rice, barley, and wheat farming by all farmers
   including those who did not participate in any
   of the training courses
2. little overall difference in adoption rate between participants of courses where the respective practices were taught and participants in
   other courses
3. a relatively higher adoption rate for the participants as a group compared to nonparticipants,
   though nonparticipants also had an absolute high
   rate for some practices along with the participants
4. a consistently low rate of adoption for a number
   of practices in rice, barley, and wheat farming
   for all three groups of farmers--nonparticipants,
   participants in courses where a specific practice was taught, and participants in other courses

5. an overall low rate of adoption by all farmers
    of recommended practices in livestock raising
    and special crops

Sources of Information and Help

In responses to questions about the sources of information on recommended agricultural practices and
sources of help and advice in employing new practices,
the guidance worker was the most frequently mentioned
source by all three groups of farmers (see Tables 13.11,
13.12). Volunteer leaders were considered next in importance to guidance workers as the source of help in
employing new practices, whereas agricultural high school
teachers and students were not regarded as sources of
help. The farmer training courses were not specifically
mentioned in the CERI questionnaire but presumably courses
were included under "contacts" with guidance workers.

Interestingly, radio and bulletin boards were more
frequently credited with being important sources of information on new farming practices than the magazine
published by ORD and other reading materials (even though
literacy is fairly high in South Korean rural areas).

TABLE 13.9

Adoption of Recommended Practices in Rice Farming
in Yong Chun County, 1971

	Adoption of practices by:		
Practices:	Participants in rice farm-ing course (100% = 78)	Participants in other courses (100% = 97)	Nonparti-cipants (100% = 55)
	%	%	%
Adoption of recommended seed varieties	87	85	78
Seed sterilization	95	97	82
Improved seeding bed	3	3	4
Soil testing	58	52	24
Addition of fresh earth	66	68	47
Application of weed-killer	87	95	73
Control of disease and insects	97	95	91
Group cultivation	50	41	46
Balanced fertilizing	14	9	4

Source: CERI Survey.

TABLE 13.10

Adoption of Recommended Practices in Barley and Wheat Farming
in Yong Chun County, 1971

	Adoption of Practices by:		
	Participants in barley and wheat farming course	Participants in other courses	Nonparti- cipants
Practices:	(100% = 39)	(100% = 136)	(100% = 55)
	%	%	%
Adoption of recommended seed varieties	81	78	73
Seed sterilization	100	87	82
Wide drilling culture	59	52	25
Application of weed killer	94	92	76
Transplantation	21	17	15

Source: CERI Survey.

Problems in Adoption of Practices

In response to a question about reasons for not adopting recommended practices, the following answers were given (in order of frequency of mention, indicated in parentheses):

1. shortage of labor additionally needed to employ the recommended practices (31)
2. unavailability of funds (17)
3. lack of practical experience in applying new practices (12)
4. inconsistency perceived by farmers between theoretical instruction and practical experience (11)
5. lack of skill in the operation of farm machines required in utilizing new techniques (10)
6. opposition of family to adoption of new practices (10)
7. inadequate understanding and knowledge of the new technique (6)
8. poor results produced by the application of new practice (6)

In response to questions about training courses that would benefit farmers most and are desired most by them, only six courses out of a list of 15 were selected by 11

percent or more of the farmers as desired courses. These
were, in order of preference: vegetables, livestock,
special crops, farm machines, improvement of seeds, and
food crops. It appears that the respondents were uncertain about the value and utility of most of the courses
(Table 13.13).

Income Differences of
Participants and Nonparticipants

CERI compared farm incomes of course participants
with income of nonparticipants. The net average earnings
of participants per one-tenth hectare was 40 percent higher than that of nonparticipants, with 13 percent higher
input and management costs for participants (Table 13.14).
The CERI investigations did not provide any information
about the differences in the use of physical and management inputs by the two groups or about the comparability
of the two groups with respect to other variables that
might affect farming efficiency. It is very doubtful that
the training courses per se, which are very short in dura-

TABLE 13.11

Sources of Information About
Recommended Practices in Agriculture

	Frequency of mention of source by groups of farmers			
	Participants			Non-Participants
	Rice Farming Course (100%=78)	Dry Field Course (100%=39)	Other Courses (100%=58)	(100%=55)
	%	%	%	%
Contact with guidance workers	85	80	75	73
Reading bulletin boards	45	69	55	56
Listening to radio	35	44	33	33
Friends	14	15	16	29
Reading Agricultural Technique	24	18	21	18
Other reading materials	15	15	29	18

Source: CERI Survey.

TABLE 13.12

Sources of Help to Farmers in Employing New Practices

Sources:	Frequency of mention of source by groups of farmers			
	Participants			
	Rice Farming Course (100%=78)	Dry Field Course (100%=39)	Other Courses (100%=58)	Non-Participants (100%=55)
Guidance workers	97	84	86	87
Volunteer leaders	36	59	38	51
Friends	23	23	21	31
Teachers of agriculture high school	0	0	3	0
Students of agriculture high school	0	0	0	0

Source: CERI Survey.

tion, seriously influenced the income differences. Possibly the most important factor is that most of the course participants were volunteer leaders, selected in part because they were more progressive farmers to begin with.

On the basis of evidence presented above on the relatively high adoption rate of recommended practices by all farmers in rice, barley, and wheat cultivation (but a higher adoption rate for all participants of training courses irrespective of the courses attended) and the high frequency of mention of the guidance worker by all farmers as the source of information and help with respect to new practices, it can be concluded that the guidance activities at the village level are effective in introducing certain improved practices of farming for rice, barley, and wheat. The contribution of the farmer training courses to the effectiveness of the guidance program is not clear. The training courses are of course an essential element of the guidance program and it is probably useless to attempt to isolate their effects. But the short residential courses represent considerable capital investment and require a substantial amount of the county guidance offices' personnel and financial resources, which could be devoted to increased field activities or other uses. Evidence and data available to ICED did not provide a basis for judging whether the training courses represent a proper utilization of resources nor did they offer gui-

TABLE 13.13

Training Courses Desired by Farmers in Yong Chun County

| | Courses Desired by Percentages of Farmers in Different Categories: | | | | |
| | Participants | | | | |
Courses:	Rice cultivation course (100%=78) %	Dry field culti- vation course (100%=39) %	Other courses (100%=58) %	Non- Participants (100%=55) %	Total (100%=230) %
Food crops	6	3	19	16	11
Vegetables	24	23	34	24	27
Fruits	9	8	0	5	6
Farm machines	22	15	9	4	13
Special crops	17	10	21	9	15
Livestock	18	20	34	11	21
Improvement of seeds	11	20	16	2	12
Farm management	4	8	3	9	6
New seed varieties	3	10	2	0	3
Bee culture	4	3	3	0	3
Fertilizers	3	0	0	0	1
Methane gas	1	3	9	0	3
Sericulture	0	5	3	0	2
Rural life improvement	0	5	2	0	1
Sideline jobs	1	0	0	0	0

Source: CERI Survey.

Note: Respondents were asked to indicate courses desired. Some indicated multiple choices while others did not make any choice. The percentage figures represent frequency of mention by farmers of each course.

dance regarding the relative emphasis and appropriate combination of training courses and field activities at the present stage of Korean agricultural development.

Impact of the Farmers' Clubs

A large number of farmer groups or clubs are reported to have been organized and more than 100,000 volunteer leaders recruited to assist the guidance workers. The clubs and the volunteer leaders, if effectively utilized, could be the means for translating technical information disseminated by ORD into educational activities relevant for agricultural and general development of individual villages.

The real impact of the clubs and the volunteer leaders is, however, unclear. The Office of Rural Development has attempted to evaluate the 4-H Clubs and their activities and classified them into three categories.

1. Class A: The club holds regular monthly meetings; at least 80 percent of the members in the club participate in at least one 4-H project; and at least 80 percent of these participants complete their projects. A total of 8,459 or 28 percent of the clubs are in this category.
2. Class B: The club holds regular monthly meetings; at least 50 percent of the members participate in

TABLE 13.14

Comparison of Farm Earnings for Participants and
Nonparticipants of Farmer Training Courses

	Participants	Nonparticipants
Number of farm households[a]	28	25
Average gross earning (won per 0.1 hectare)	28,157	21,818
Average management and input costs (won per 0.1 hectare)	10,348	9,125
Average net earnings (won per 0.1 hectare)	17,809	12,693

Source: CERI Survey.

[a]Information on farm earnings was obtained for two sub-samples and not for total sample.

projects; and at least 50 percent complete their
projects. There are 10,503 clubs, or 35 percent
of the total, in this category.

3. Class C: The club does not hold monthly meetings
and few members participate in projects. Over
36 percent or 10,843 clubs are in this category.

The above classification shows that less than a third
of the clubs are fully active and are performing the regular functions of a 4-H Club, and over a third of clubs
are inactive and might as well be taken off the roll of
4-H Clubs. Yet the responsibilities of about 50 percent
of the volunteer leaders are supposed to be primarily in
youth activities.

Apparently no attempt has been made to evaluate the
performance of other clubs and volunteer leaders. It is,
however, unlikely that the performance of these would be
better than for the youth program. In fact, the extremely
limited number of guidance workers employed to work with
volunteer leaders and clubs in the field of home and family
improvement projects suggests that there is not a high
level of activity and performance in this area.

Limited Focus of ORD Operations

Though the short training courses in the provincial
and county training centers cover a fairly wide range of
subjects, the field activities of guidance workers have
concentrated heavily on rice cultivation. The cooperative
rice cultivation zones in each province, singled out for
concentrated attention by ORD and preferential treatment
for supply of inputs, receive a major share of guidance
workers' time and energy. Other field guidance activities
such as those dealing with plant disease and insect control,
use of farm machinery, group training sessions for farmers,
and dissemination of information through the media are
also largely oriented to rice production.

ORD activities in community and home improvement,
youth projects, income-generation, sideline jobs, and so
forth, appear, in terms of total personnel time, research
efforts, and resources devoted to them, as mere appendices
to the main activity of promoting agricultural production
increases, particularly in rice.

This disproportionate emphasis on rice production in
ORD guidance activities contradicts the broadness of vision
and concepts regarding ORD objectives and functions, though
it does reflect the government's priority on achieving
self-sufficiency in rice. Moreover, such emphasis raises
basic questions about the role of ORD at the present stage
of agricultural and economic development of Korea. It has
been mentioned earlier that the government agricultural

policy may be pushing rice cultivation to land areas where
the relative economic advantage probably lies in other
crops. It has also been noted that agricultural diversification is likely to accelerate as an individual farmer
attempts to run his farm in an economically optimal manner
and as the fruits of economic development spread more
equitably in both urban and rural areas. The question,
therefore, is whether ORD, not only in order to live up to
its conceptual design but also to meet needs of all-round
rural development, should not put greater emphasis on a
broader range of activities designed to promote diversified
farming and general improvement of rural life.

LESSONS FROM ORD EXPERIENCE

The ORD guidance program, in operation for a decade
as a broadly designed agricultural and rural extension
service, offers some useful lessons that may be relevant
to farmer education programs in other developing nations.

Operational Linkages and Coordination

First, even when an agricultural extension service is
conceived broadly with the objective of improving farmers'
lives, besides increasing crop yields, and is designed to
function as an element in the total effort toward agricultural and rural development (as was the case with ORD),
there are many practical difficulties in establishing
operational linkages and coordination among the different
parts of the development system and in maintaining a broad
view of extension objectives.
     In South Korea, the four major agencies responsible
for clusters of components--viz., credit, chemical inputs,
and marketing; physical infrastructure development; formal
agricultural education; and research and extension--have
not established a mechanism for systematically coordinating their policies, objectives, and actions in order to
serve the common goal of agricultural and rural development. The reliance on the provincial and county administration for forging a consistent and complementary set
of actions and policies for the respective areas has
apparently produced varying results depending on the personality, sense of priority, and style of operation of the
local administrator.
     Although coordination of actions and policies at the
regional and field levels is essential--in fact, one important measure of success would be the extent of coordination achieved in field operations--the inspiration and
the guidance on the substance and mode of coordination

must come from the national level, especially when national organizations exist for different functions. Organizations cannot cooperate at different levels and serve
common objectives of rural and agricultural development
unless they are partners in a common strategy to achieve
commonly accepted goals.

Incentives for Improved Field Operation

Second, a dilemma for any education or service agency
with extensive field operations is that whereas success or
failure is determined by the impact made in the field, the
personnel structures usually do not permit the most competent and experienced staff to be retained at the field
level. In Korea, this problem has been compounded by
unattractive salaries and working conditions for the field
workers compared with those of the central staff of ORD
and with those of employees with comparable qualifications
in other organizations.

The general problem of incentives and competence of
field staff is intractable because of the cost implications of any conceivable solution. Within the limits of
available resources, however, there are options: for
example, raising the status and rewards of the field staff
compared with those of office staff, or providing for a
smaller, well-prepared, adequately remunerated, and motivated field staff rather than a large, less competent,
dissatisfied, and unmotivated field staff. The particular
method would depend on the defined role and function of
extension agents in a particular situation at a particular
stage of agricultural and rural development. The important thing is to achieve a realistic matching of tasks
assigned to agents and the resources and personnel required to accomplish those tasks.

Inservice Training

Third, another issue with respect to the performance
of extension agents is the relative emphasis on the initial preparation of personnel and the opportunities for
improving their knowledge and competence on the job. ORD
recognized the inadequacy of the formal agricultural preparation for extension work and made provisions for
special preservice and inservice training as well as a
supervisory structure through the county and the provincial offices. The importance of inservice training, however, has been minimized over the years as the shorter
duration and lessened frequency of such training at different levels indicate. At the same time, the level of

initial formal preparation of the new recruits of ORD
has also gone down.

Whatever the level of formal agricultural education
of extension workers, the importance of inservice training cannot be overstressed if only because research
generates new knowledge and the informational and technical needs of farmers change. The downgrading of inservice training would certainly affect the productivity
of extension workers, especially if the emphasis of extension work widens beyond one crop and includes diversified and relatively new types of farming activities.

Changing Extension Functions and Messages

Fourth, the functions and messages of the extension
agency must continue to change as the agricultural situation itself changes. In fact, the more effective an
extension service is, the greater the need for its adaptation to change. The recent growth, diversity, and dynamism of Korean agriculture, for instance, suggest some
needed changes in the country's extension service. A
national extension agency, operating in a dynamic agricultural and economic situation, needs to pay increasing
attention to:

1. building a specialized, more qualified (not
    necessarily with higher degrees), and probably
    smaller field staff which can cope with the in-
    creasingly complicated, sophisticated, and
    diverse technical information needs of farmers
2. more effective "backstopping" of the field staff
    by using competent specialists as supervisors in
    frequent contact with field staff, supporting
    frequent and specialized inservice training, and
    promoting close ties and two-way communication
    between research institutions and field staff
3. greater and systematic reliance on mass media,
    such as radio, films, journals, and bulletins,
    with emphasis on specialized and practical con-
    tent
4. more systematic use of local volunteer leaders
    for the simpler, routine, well-defined types of
    extension activities which are now performed by
    extension agents. Setting up a demonstration
    plot, advising individual farmers on simpler
    technical questions, and distributing literature
    and certain supplies are the types of activities
    that volunteer leaders or model farmers can take
    over if they are recruited with care and given
    more training at the farmer training centers on
    specific technical topics.

Role of the Farmer Training Center

Fifth, the residential farmer training center needs
to be seen as a part of the agricultural extension system
and its appropriate role determined by the level of agricultural development and the organization and functions of
the extension service.

During the winter months the farmer training centers
attached to the county and provincial ORDs offer short
courses--much shorter than courses in farmer training
centers in other countries--to adult farmers, who are mostly the volunteer leaders. The courses, particularly in
the county centers, probably should be considered as brief-
ing sessions and opportunities for group contact of guidance workers and volunteer leaders rather than as training
sessions. Viewing the training courses in this light makes
it impossible and unnecessary to consider the costs and
effectiveness of the courses separately from the total extension program in the field. There is probably very
little that Korean adult farmers need to be taught in prolonged residential farmer training (as in East Africa) that
they cannot be taught through periodic field contacts with
extension agents.

One clientele that probably could profit most from
somewhat prolonged and systematic farm training is the
rural youth. The training centers only indirectly and marginally serve the rural youth through contacts with the
volunteer leaders who are supposed to assist in organizing
4-H clubs. A more active role of the county centers in
offering systematic training in farm practices to selected
rural youths who are likely to stay in agricultural occupations and in providing the support of the guidance service in launching them as progressive farmers would be
more effective in promoting agricultural development than
are the existing vocational agricultural high schools.
This would also make the proposed farmer training centers
of the Ministry of Agriculture largely redundant (see
Appendix 13.4).

In an extension service more attuned to the needs of
the dynamic Korean agriculture, the county training center,
as noted earlier, might offer training on specific and
well-defined technical content to volunteer leaders who
may take over some of the functions of the present extension agents. The center still can serve as the home-base
for the guidance workers and as a point of group and individual contacts among the guidance workers, volunteer
leaders, and farmers as well as a training facility for
young farmers.

Review of the
Total Agricultural Education System

Sixth, the Korean experience lends support to the idea of the continuous monitoring and periodic reviewing of the tasks and performances of the total agricultural education system including its various components. This is especially important in a dynamic agricultural and economic situation. It appears that no basic appraisal of agricultural education, research, and extension has been undertaken in Korea since the establishment of ORD, though the agricultural and general economic situation has changed substantially.

The process of reviewing the total agricultural education system would include critical examination of such matters as the preparation and competence of the personnel, scope and relevance of research efforts, the relative emphases on different projects and operations, and the priority objectives and tasks of the different components of the system. The goal would be to make formal agricultural education, agricultural research, and the extension service responsive to the changing needs and conditions of agricultural and rural development. Such evaluation is also the precondition for improving efficiency and productivity of the total agricultural education system as well as the extension service.

Organizational Features

Finally, among the noteworthy features of ORD are its relatively autonomous organizational character (as it is not directly a part of the Ministry of Agriculture and Forestry) and the use of volunteer leaders from villages in the extension process. It has not been possible in this study to examine the effects of this autonomy on ORD operations or to evaluate how efficiently the volunteer leaders have been utilized. Nevertheless, the implications and prospective advantages of these features would be worth considering in any large-scale farmer education program.

NOTES

1. Republic of Korea, The Third Five-Year Economic Development Plan, 1972-76 (Seoul, Korea, 1971), p. 135.

2. Estimated on the basis of data from different sources including the Bank of Korea, Economic Statistics Yearbook 1971 (Seoul, Korea 1971) and the Third Five-Year Plan.

3. Robert R. Morrow and Kenneth H. Sharper, Land Reform in South Korea, Spring Review Country Paper (Washington, D.C.: U.S. Agency for International Development, June 1970).

4. Statistical information collected from Ministry of Agriculture sources.

5. 139,999 metric tons in 1967, 247,000 metric tons in 1968, 631,000 metric tons in 1969, and 777,000 metric tons in 1970. Bank of Korea, Economic Statistics Yearbook, Table 151.

6. Office of Rural Development (ORD), "The Outline of Agricultural Guidance Work in Korea," mimeographed (Suwon, Korea, 1972).

7. U.S. Operations Mission (USOM) in Korea, Rural Development Program Evaluation Report (n.p., 1967), p. 235.

8. ORD, "The Outline."

9. Byung Choon Lee, "Agricultural Development and Rural Guidance Work in Korea," mimeographed (Suwon, Korea: ORD, 1971).

10. ORD, Agricultural Research in Korea (Suwon, 1971).

11. Estimated by ICED on the basis of data on guidance workers and total farm households provided by ORD.

12. The middle school is a postprimary and presecondary three-year program.

13. ORD, A Brief Description of Rural Youth Work in Korea (Suwon, Korea, n.d.), pp. 14-15.

14. ORD, Rural Guidance Work in Korea (Suwon, Korea, 1971), p. 19.

15. USOM/Korea, Rural Development Program, p. 245.

16. See David C. Cole and Princeton N. Lyman, Korean Development: The Interplay of Politics and Economics (Cambridge, Mass.: Harvard University Press, 1971), and National Agricultural Cooperative Federation, Annual Report 1969.

17. Korea, The Third Five-Year Plan, p. 37.

18. U.S., Department of Agriculture, Planning Korea's Agricultural Development, Foreign Economic Development Series Field Report No. 5 (Washington, D.C., August 1970).

19. Ibid., p. 4.

20. Ibid., p. 39.

21. Bank of Korea, Economic Statistics Yearbook 1971, Table 5.

22. Ibid., Table 97.

23. The original agreement between ICED and CERI was that CERI would undertake a survey and personal interview of farmers in selected villages of a county to collect data about the impact and relative effectiveness of ORD guidance and educational activities and educational influences from other sources. For various reasons, CERI could not carry out this plan and used instead a printed questionnaire to farmers distributed and collected through guidance workers and volunteer leaders.

APPENDIX 13.1

Index of Prices Received and Paid by Farmers--1965-1970

	Prices Received				Prices Paid			
	All Items	Grains	Fruits and Vegetables	Livestock, Sericulture and Poultry	All Items	Farm Supplies	Household Goods	Wages and Charges
Weight	(1,000) [a]	(635.95)	(62.16)	(232.43)	(1,000)	(245.86)	(631.36)	(122.78)
Year								
1965	100.0	100.0	100.0	100.0	100.0	100.0	100.0	100.0
1966	106.0	105.1	123.3	108.8	112.2	111.7	112.1	114.3
1967	121.5	117.8	109.4	140.5	127.0	124.8	126.4	133.8
1968	142.3	133.6	116.7	182.4	152.2	160.1	145.7	163.4
1969	162.4	162.5	135.2	178.5	167.2	173.7	158.2	200.0
1970	191.5	182.7	248.8	211.1	193.1	194.9	181.5	248.6

Source: Research Department, National Agricultural Cooperative Federation. Reported in Economic Statistics Yearbook 1971, Table 162.

[a] This total for prices received includes a residual category with a weight of 69.46, not shown in this table.

APPENDIX 13.2

Age and Education of 4-H Club Members, 1970

AGE		
Years	Members	
	#	%
13-15	162,877	25.7
16-18	274,186	43.6
19-24	196,618	30.7
Total	633,681	100.0

Educational Background

Educational Level Completed	Members	
	#	%
No education	18,084	2.8
Primary education (6 yrs.)	265,883	42.0
Middle School (9 yrs.)	232,018	36.6
High school (12 yrs.)	114,536	18.1
Unknown	3,160	0.5
Total	633,681	100.0

Source: ORD, "A Brief Description of Rural Youth Work in Korea" (Suwon, 1971).

APPENDIX 13.3

Supply of Major Agricultural Inputs in Korea,
1960 and 1966-69

	1960	1966	1967	1968	1969	1970*
Fertilizer ('000 tons)	279	423	486	478	533	563
Pesticides and insecticides ('000 tons)	5.9	12.5	10.0	10.0	18.0	–
Lime ('000 tons)	5.7	175	192	155	284	398
Farm machinery** (nos.)	40+	8,588	12,720	20,193	34,316++	–

*Approximate figures.
**Excluding those supplied directly to farmers by private enterprise.
+Supplied in 1961.
++Includes 25,192 power sprayers, 8,941 power tillers, 133 bulldozers and 60 tractors.

Source: Ministry of Agriculture and Forestry.

APPENDIX 13.4

A Note on the Formal Agricultural Education System

The formal agricultural education system in South Korea consists of 17 university faculties or independent colleges of agriculture, 7 junior colleges of agriculture, and 115 secondary-level vocational agricultural schools. All of these institutions fall within the jurisdiction of the Ministry of Education.

The college-level courses leading to the B.S. degree require four years to complete after 12th grade and include the following fields of specialization: agronomy, forestry, zootechny, agricultural chemistry, horticulture, agricultural economics, agricultural engineering, sericulture, agricultural biology, agricultural education, and food technology. A course in agricultural extension was being planned in 1971 for the College of Agriculture of the Seoul National University.

The junior technical colleges offer, among other courses, agricultural subjects in a five-year program covering 10th to 14th grades. In the vocational high

schools, the courses are three years long at the 10-12
grade level. The curriculum includes a general education
content of 30 to 40 percent in the junior colleges and
about a half in the vocational schools.[1]

Vocational Agricultural High Schools

Vocational agricultural high schools were established
in the 1950s when agriculture was the predominant economic
sector and these schools were viewed as the means for
modernizing agriculture and solving the problem of finding
productive employment for the output of the secondary-
level institution. These expectations, by and large, have
not been fulfilled.

A survey of one agricultural school in Suwon in 1968
showed that only 25 percent of graduates were engaged in
some agriculture-related occupation; another 25 percent
were employed in other occupations; and the remaining 50
percent were either unemployed or enrolled in higher educational institutions.[2] It is believed, however, that
many students go back to their farms after graduation only
to bide time till employment opportunities open up in the
city; therefore, the actual employment in agriculture is
probably lower than 25 percent. Enrollment in the agricultural schools has remained constant at around 40,000
with an annual graduation rate of about 10,000 throughout
the 1960s.

Evidence of the success of vocational agricultural
schools in inducing young people to become modern progressive farmers is rather scarce. In Korea the rapid
growth of the nonagricultural sector, the high rate of
urbanization, and the relative lag of rural and agricultural development coupled with the lack of practical
orientation of agricultural school instruction have made
the agricultural school an alternative means of formal education leading to some form of urban employment.

The wisdom of continuing a large program of formal
agricultural education at the secondary level is, therefore, doubtful. The number of people actually needed with
secondary-level training for agricultural services should
be examined, and a more efficient way of training needs
to be devised.[3]

---

[1]UNESCO, *Agricultural Education in Asia*. A Regional Survey
(Bangkok, Thailand, 1971), pp. 141-49.

[2]UNESCO, *Agricultural Education in Asia*.

[3]The Ministry of Agriculture and Forestry is currently considering a plan for opening a network of farmer training centers
throughout the country to train young people for farm occupations.
In view of the already existing network of farmer training centers
under the Office of Rural Development and the poor performance of

Formal Agricultural Education System in Korea, 1971

Type of Institution	Grade Level	No. of Institutions	Enroll- ment	Gradu- ates
Vocational agri- cultural high school	10-12	115	39,788	10,877
Junior technical college (agri- cultural section)	10-14	21	5,554	981
Agricultural faculty in univ- ersity or agri- cultural college	13-16	17	10,689	2,113
Graduate Courses (Masters and Doctorate)	17+	11	267	82

Source: Ministry of Education, Statistic Yearbook of Education, 1971.

Higher Agricultural Education

Higher agricultural education is the province of 17 university faculties and colleges and 21 junior technical colleges. A sizable number of institutions in both of these categories are privately managed. It is generally believed by knowledgeable people in Korean agricultural education that the existence of such a large number of separate agricultural programs has resulted in deficien- cies in equipment, staff, and facilities in all the insti- tutions. The standards of training are considered low in most institutions, with the exception of the presti- gious Seoul National University(SNU) College of Agricul- ture. There are questions about the relevance of the course content to Korean agricultural problems, particul- arly with respect to the preparation of graduates for agricultural extension service.

---

vocational agricultural schools, it would seem to be very important to identify clearly the overall agricultural training needs and to assess the strengths and weaknesses of existing institutions in meet- ing these needs before launching another set of institutions, and thereby possibly dissipating limited resources through a multipli- city of overlapping programs.

An annual output of more than 2,000 college graduates
and 1,000 junior college graduates in agriculture appears
to be high relative to the personnel requirements of
agricultural service and supply organizations. In Korea's
booming economy, graduates appear to find some kind of
employment readily, but many are not employed in agriculture or even in related activities. The Ministry of
Education estimates that of the 2,600 graduates of agriculture and fishery courses for the year 1969, only about
300 were employed in jobs related to agriculture and
fishery; 1,300 were employed in other wage-earning activities, mainly public services, and the rest went either
to postgraduate education or to the military service, with
a small number unemployed. Even among graduates of the
SNU College of Agriculture, who usually receive preferential treatment in employment, more than half are estimated
to be employed in occupations unrelated or only marginally
related to agriculture. Of the 3,288 graduates of this
institution in ten years from 1956-66, in 1967 only 1,463
or 44.5 percent were employed in jobs that could be considered connected with agriculture (see Table below).

Employment Record of Graduates of
Seoul National University, College of Agriculture 1956-66

Employing Organizations	No. Employed as of 1967	Percent Employed
Agricultural Employment:	1,463	44.5
Office of Rural Development	500	15.2
Private Companies	268	8.2
Agricultural High Schools	199	6.1
National Agricultural Cooperative Federation	116	3.5
Colleges and Universities	113	3.4
Provincial Governments	82	2.5
Ministry of Agriculture and Forestry	66	2.0
County Government	44	1.3
Foreign Agencies in Korea	44	1.3
Grain Inspection Office	31	0.9
Nonagricultural Employment	1,825	55.5
TOTAL GRADUATES	3,288	100.0

Source: School Affairs Section, Seoul National University,
College of Agriculture, cited in USOM/Korea, Rural Development Program Evaluation Report, 1967.

The trend is, presumably, for an even lower percentage to be employed in agriculture, as the employment pattern of 1969 graduates from all institutions showed.

The Office of Rural Development, which came into existence in 1962, was in its early years the largest single employer of the SNU College of Agriculture graduates. Although recent statistics are unavailable, it is believed that ORD is no longer a large employer of agricultural graduates. New recruits in ORD staff are now mostly graduates of agricultural high schools, junior colleges, and even general colleges.

14

NIGERIA:
PROGRAMS FOR SMALL
INDUSTRY ENTREPRENEURS
AND JOURNEYMEN
Clifford Gilpin
and Sven Grabe

The Industrial Development Centre (IDC) and the Vocational Improvement Centres (VICs) in northern Nigeria were selected by the ICED for special investigation as part of its study of Nonformal Education for Rural Development for three main reasons: 1) the programs have been operating for several years, and sufficient experience has been acquired with different approaches to make an evaluation meaningful; 2) the total number of persons trained is large in comparison with most similar programs in other countries; 3) the VICs in particular constitute an original approach to the problem of upgrading the skills of workers in small-scale undertakings.

After a review of available literature, ICED commissioned Victor Diejomaoh, of the University of Lagos, to arrange for comprehensive interviews of entrepreneurs in the Kano area who had received help from the IDC and of former students of the VIC courses at Zaria and Maiduguri. These interviews were held in September and October 1971 and provided some of the evaluative material presented in this paper. The data from the literature and the interviews were supplemented by direct observations by ICED staff during visits in November 1971 to Zaria, Kaduna, and Kano.

INTRODUCTION

As a part of the attempt to diminish the gap in rates of economic development between the North and South of Nigeria, three programs were introduced in the sixties to promote the development of indigenous small-scale industry in the Northern Region. Lag in development was due in part to lack of capital for expansion and modernization, lack of skills needed to produce goods and services for the modern sector, and (in the late sixties) an exodus out of the North of entrepreneurs and skilled workers, causing shortages in the technical departments of the government, in large- and middle-sized business undertakings, and in small industry and services.

The plan for development of small industry and services represents a three-pronged attack: 1) provision by
the states through the Small Industry Credit Scheme (SIC)
for loans to small-scale manufacturers for the purchase
of equipment, 2) establishment by the government of a
management and technical advisory service for entrepreneurs
wanting to improve their knowledge of business practices
and of machines through the Industrial Development Centre
(IDC), and 3) trade training in state Vocational Improvement Centres (VIC) for self-employed craftsmen or manufacturers and their employees wishing to acquire government certification in their trade. Administratively
separate, the three programs contribute to the same broad
objectives. Informal ties between the loan schemes of the
states and the IDC involve the latter in feasibility
studies and recommendations to the loan board; there are
no direct connections between the SICs or the IDC and the
VICs of the states.

Nigeria has one of the largest land areas in sub-
Saharan Africa (356,669 square miles) and the largest population (about 60 million). Eighty percent of the labor
force are employed in agriculture, which provides 56 percent of the GNP. The per capita income (US$80 in 1969)
represents a median position for black Africa, but conceals
wide differences in regional development, particularly
between North and South.

Nonfarm rural enterprise, more developed in Nigeria
than elsewhere in black Africa, is an important activity
in both northern and southern Nigeria. While trading has
been a traditional occupation throughout Nigeria, a large
number of Nigerians are also engaged in some form of
cottage or small-scale manufacturing industry. A rural
economic survey conducted by the Federal Office of Statistics in 1964 estimated that 900,000 households were
involved in cottage industry enterprises, the vast majority
of which used hand tools only and relied entirely on their
own financial resources. Many of the employees were
apprentices; in the Western and Midwestern states they
accounted for 80 percent of the total number employed in
nonfarm enterprises.[1]

While small businesses are a prominent feature throughout most of Nigeria, there are important differences of
scale between those in the North and in the South. In
1964, Archibald Callaway recorded 3,135 small businesses
with 14,500 employees in the city of Ibadan in the Western
State. In 1961, five cities in the North--Zaria, Kaduna,
Kano, Jos, and Maiduguri--with a combined population two
to three times that of Ibadan were estimated to have had
1,701 small industries with 4,869 employees. Only 2 percent of the northern businesses had ten or more employees,
and the average number of employees was less than three.[2]

The northern states are commonly regarded as much
less developed.[3] Many areas are thinly populated and

transportation is a major problem. Provision for formal
education is much less than in the south; in Kano State,
for example, 9 percent of the relevant age-group go to
primary school. This is partly a consequence of the greater
resistance of the Islamic north to western influence and
institutions.

Although there has been relatively less government
investment in development in the North, the region contains
important centers of indigenous development and growth.
Kano has retained its traditional importance as a West
African center of manufacture and trade. Jos has unusually
large high-level manpower resources, with a significant
concentration of small- and medium-sized industry and a
per capita income three times the national average.

Large- and medium-scale industry is in the hands of
expatriate firms or expatriate-and-government partnerships.
To a large extent distribution is also controlled by non-
Nigerians. Nigerians are prominent in trade, transport,
construction, services, and a wide range of small-scale
manufacturing activities.

While it has been the general policy of the federal
government to increase Nigerian participation in all
aspects of trade and industrial development, little action
was taken in the 1960s to promote specifically the development of small-scale industry. Although the 1962-68
National Development Plan proposed the establishment of a
National Development Bank to promote large- and medium-
scale industry,[4] the regions were left to formulate individual policies for small-scale industrial development.

Since 1968 the economic and political climate for
small businesses has improved. The federal government set
up a National Committee on Small-Scale Industries in 1969
and devoted special attention to this sector in the
1970-74 National Development Plan.[5] The new plan is critical of the previous plan (1962-1968) for its failure to
match its goals with "well-articulated projects and closely-
defined policies geared towards their achievement" and for
permitting overlapping projects in the different regions.[6]

The 1970-74 Plan has proposed preinvestment surveys
to be carried out by the states and the establishment of
an Industrial Training Fund. To increase rapidly indigenous ownership and participation in manufacturing, the
plan proposes federal support for the Industrial Development Centres in Zaria and Owerri and a new Centre in the
Western State, to be assisted by a federal advisory
committee. The Plan calls for each IDC to specialize in
its zone's priorities for small-scale industries and a
matching fund of ₦600,000 (US$1,680,000) to be allocated
to the state Small Industry Credit Funds.[7] The expansion
of small industry credit schemes in the northern states
has also generated new interest in the private sector;
in 1970, Barclays Bank became an integral part of the
SIC program in the North-Western State with the provision
of US$280,000 for state-approved loans.[8]

Recent political changes in Nigeria have had an important effect on overall development in northern Nigeria. At independence in 1960, the Federation of Nigeria was divided into three large, semiautonomous regions, each with its own government and legislature. The Northern Region was made up of the present six northern states. Because it lagged behind the Eastern and Western Regions in development and formal education, wage employment in both the government and private sectors was dominated by Nigerians from the other regions, who also dominated much of the commercial and manufacturing business. The resentment felt by "northerners" at this dominance was an important cause for the outbreak of civil war in 1967 between the federal government and the former Eastern Region. One result of the political disturbances was the flight of the majority of Ibos from their businesses and jobs in the Northern Region. An economic and employment vacuum was created from mid-1966 onwards, at precisely the same time that both the VIC and IDC programs were being established and their operations expanded. After the war a period of scarcity was followed by an economic boom and a growth of the manufacturing industry. As a result, both the IDC and VIC programs have developed in a period characterized by special and temporary economic circumstances. Therefore, conclusions drawn from their performance and achievements may be of limited applicability.

The division of Nigeria into twelve states in 1968 was designed to provide greater autonomy to a larger number of ethnic groups, not the least those who felt that development of their areas had received comparatively little attention. Among the responsibilities delegated to the new states were those for education, trade, and industry. Although the state governments were considered best equipped to assess local potential and requirements and to encourage local development, many of the northern state governments, lacked trained manpower to evaluate development needs. Moreover, decentralization of authority, therefore, has significantly affected the organization and focus of both the IDCs and the VICs.

ORIGINS OF THE IDC AND VIC PROGRAMS

The economic importance of self-employed craftsmen and small-scale industry throughout Nigeria, including the northern states, is documented in a number of government and private surveys[9] and in studies of individual indigenous industries.[10] Nevertheless little is known about the precise nature and organization of training within different crafts and skills, particularly in the north. Archibald Callaway has written of a large and organized

traditional apprenticeship system within indigenous crafts
and small-scale industry in Ibidan.[11] His description of
apprenticeship in western Nigeria has been carried further
by case studies of blacksmithing and auto repair that add
to our knowledge of the apprenticeship system.[12] While
apprentices were traditionally related to their masters,
the modern trades employ many who are not related. An
apprentice learns by doing, frequently over three to five
years, under fixed conditions. He may become a journeyman
or set up his own business after a formal freeing ceremony,
which may include a trade test and the presentation of
simple hand tools. Many of the masters in the modern
trades learned their skills in government employment or
expatriate firms, but an increasing number are now learning modern as well as traditional crafts and trades through
the apprenticeship system. Be that as it may, the IDC
and VIC programs had available little previous research
done in the North on which to base their training hypothe-
ses. The precise needs and possibilities for development
of small-scale industry were only vaguely defined.

However, both the VIC and IDC programs identified an
urgent need for training of entrepreneurs and their
employees in small-scale industry. Their essential hypothesis was that this type of indigenous enterprise
could be improved through additional training of those
who had already acquired some skills in small-scale industries. The VIC was designed to provide trade training;
the IDC, to provide training in business management and
the use of new techniques and machinery. Neither program
was centrally concerned with the provision of credit.

Establishment of the IDC

The initiative for the establishment of the Industrial
Development Centre in Zaria came from the Ministry of Trade
and Industry of the former Northern Region Government; one
function of the Ministry was to encourage and regulate the
growth of what were called "small-scale" industries.[13]

The assistance provided by the ministry was limited
mainly to directing such industries through appropriate
channels for obtaining the information, documents, and
licenses required for their operation. Little technical
advice could be made available even on request. In the
early 1960s a rapid increase in the number of requests
from a variety of entrepreneurs encouraged the ministry
to reappraise its approach.[14] Additional reasons for this
reappraisal may have been 1) a growing disillusionment
with the economic effectiveness of large state-run enterprises, and 2) growing political pressure to allocate
industrial development more evenly among the states, to
emphasize industries that favored the rural population,

and to provide Nigerians with a larger share of the ownership of the industrial sector.

Up to 1962, government financial assistance for industry was made available through the Northern Region
Development Corporation, financed by grants from the
Marketing Board. However, the corporation's activities
were widely spread over the commercial, industrial, and
agricultural fields and not reinforced by technical
assistance. In the 1962-68 Northern Region Development
Plan it was proposed to split up the Northern Region
Development Corporation and to establish an Industrial
Development Corporation that would operate on a profit-
making basis, prepare and execute schemes by itself or
"in cooperation with a technical partner," and "maintain
a high standard of investigation and analysis of projects."[15] The Northern Region Development Plan also
expressed the government's desire to encourage local
entrepreneurs to undertake "increasingly large industrial
projects."

In 1963 the Northern Ministry of Trade and Industry
entered into an agreement with U.S. Agency for International Development (AID) for the establishment of an
Industrial Development Centre to "provide training in
commercial and industrial techniques to private businessmen together with credit for the purchase of modern
equipment."[16]

Implementation of the IDC program began in 1964, with
AID technical personnel and equipment. Two IDCs were
established: one at Owerri in the Eastern Region and one
at Zaria in the Northern Region.

The only available statement of objectives of the
IDC at Zaria lists the following functions:

1. to provide technical and management assistance
    to owners, managers, and supervisors of small-
    scale industries
2. to improve management and organization of the
    small industries in order that, through improved
    productivity, these enterprises could become
    more viable and prosperous
3. to identify opportunities, encourage entrepreneur-
    ship, and to aid in the establishment and imple-
    mentation of industrial projects
4. to evaluate applications for private and govern-
    mental loans for the establishment or expansion
    of small industries
5. to adopt and adapt indigenous materials for the
    design and production of new products by the
    local manufacturers
6. to provide technical library services and informa-
    tion on specific industries[17]

Both IDCs focused on two main activities: visits to
businessmen to give technical and management advice; and,

for selected groups of entrepreneurs, short seminars and workshops at the Centre, dealing with new production techniques, new machinery, bookkeeping, and the management of small industry. The five major small industries chosen for concentration were woodworking, metalworking, auto repair, textiles, and leatherworking.[18]

The original selection of entrepreneurs to be assisted was apparently random. The Owerri Centre depended on missionaries and other knowledgeable people in the locality to identify entrepreneurs for the IDC staff.[19] The Owerri Centre developed mainly on a trial-and-error basis, and action taken at the Zaria Centre was partly determined by this experience.[20]

Establishment of the VICs

Nigeria inherited its pattern of trade training from Great Britain: government recognition of a craftsman's skills was based on his passing trade tests and examinations that met strictly British requirements (often unsuitable to the needs of Nigeria). Broadly speaking, there were two possible ways to become a certified craftsman. One was through on-the-job training in either a government department or a large (usually expatriate) firm. For example, a worker might acquire recognized qualifications by passing a Ministry of Labour Trade Test or by sitting for a City and Guilds of London Examination. The other possibility was by gaining admission to a government trade training school and completing a three-year course. Entry requirements included a primary school certificate and three years' postprimary education. Only three such institutions existed in all six northern states of Nigeria.

In a study sponsored by the Ford Foundation in 1962, Adam S. Skapski criticized the traditional, unregulated (by government) pattern of trade training and recommended more simplified realistic, shorter courses that would produce more employable trainees.[21] He further recommended that the Trade Training Centres be used to upgrade apprentices from small industries by giving them a broad theoretical background of their trade in evening or day-release courses and to enable craftsmen (with the possibility of obtaining aid from a loan fund) to manage small private enterprises successfully. He felt that these "improvement courses" could provide a satisfactory level of accomplishment in ten months and even suggested the use of mobile vans to reach apprentices living at a distance. Noting a lack of provision, particularly in the Northern Region, for upgrading the traditional apprenticeship training system and for linking it to other governmental vocational and technical training efforts, the Ford Foundation worked in concert with the Ministry of Trade and Industry of

the Northern Region (in cooperation with the Ministry of
Education) and developed a program to meet these needs.
The first of the VICs, known as the Business Apprenticeship Training Centre (BATC) at Kaduna was established in
1964 as a two-year pilot project.

Automobile service and repair, building and carpentry,
and furniture making were identified as the trades on
which to concentrate training in the Centre. It was
believed that the skills of apprentices in these trades
could be improved at least to the level of the Grade III
trade test by evening instruction four times a week over
ten months. To improve the general educational level
among apprentices in all the trades selected, one session
per week was to be devoted to such subjects as English,
practical mathematics, and elements of operating a small
business enterprise.

In order to encourage apprentices to set up their
own businesses a credit and business management consultant
would visit the improvement courses regularly to advise
on the crucial role of credit in developing small businesses.[22] The achievement of a trade test certificate
offered the potential inducements of entry into the
government wage scale (or equivalent) and greater chance
of receiving a government contract.

IMPLEMENTATION OF VIC PROGRAM

The Pilot Project (BATC)

The first VIC--the Business Apprenticeship Training
Centre (BATC) commenced courses on February 1, 1965 at
Kaduna, the seat of the regional government and also the
site of the Ford Foundation-assisted Small Industry Credit
scheme.

Facilities and Students

The Ministry of Education provided classroom and workshop space free of charge at the Kaduna Technical Institute, although building alterations were later necessary.
The equipment purchased at the outset was mainly simple
hand tools.

The Ford Foundation employed William Gardner, a
British expatriate with twenty years' experience in technical education in Nigeria, and previously acting principal
of the Technical College, Ibadan, to direct the project.
The teaching staff were all Nigerians. All teachers of
general subjects, recruited for part-time employment from
the Commercial Department of the Technical Institute and
the Federal Administration Training School, were required

to hold at least a Grade I teaching certificate and to
be able to teach in Hausa and English. In 1971 six of
the eight technical instructors and all six general subject teachers were employed part-time, because of shortages
in qualified personnel.

Persuasion and eventual recruitment of trainees involved visits to entrepreneurs in Kaduna, advertisements
in the newspapers, and assessment of general ability and
commitment in interviews. Although formal school education was not a requirement, a condition of acceptance was
that the applicant be indigenous to the former Northern
Region. The courses were given free of charge.

Initially, provision was made for four classes of
16, chosen in the first year from 28 applicants in carpentry, 52 in auto repair, 110 in bricklaying, and 35 in
electrical installation. By 1970 the number admitted
had increased to 130, and the number of applications had
risen to more than 1,000.

Courses and Methods

The course, originally 10 months long, was later
extended to 12 months. Trade instruction was given for
three hours, three evenings a week. At the beginning
of each course, a practical test was given in the particular skill to discover the capabilities of each trainee.
In the conviction that the trainees had little theoretical
knowledge or understanding of the principles of technology,
it was decided to teach basic arithmetic and English as
part of a general education.

Certain observations convinced Gardner to modify
the design of the courses. As a rule young men worked as
apprentices for two years or less and set up businesses
of their own when they thought they had sufficient skills.
However, on the basis of a carpentry test, he concluded
that most had not learned more than practical manual
operations at a semiskilled level and that the quality of
their work did not improve with the years. He saw that
the majority of apprentice motor mechanics carried out
"most operations without knowledge of the reasons for
doing so" and that apprentice masons could lay bricks
only after the leading bricklayer had set up profile lines
and corner blocks. Supported by data collected later for
the Maiduguri VIC by the School of Social Studies in
Lagos, Gardner realized that apprentice electricians
(75 percent of whom had a minimum of six years of primary
education) and motor mechanics were better educationally
fitted than masons and, in particular, carpenters and
furniture makers, most of whom "could not read or write
Hausa or English."

Initially, attendance was compulsory at one evening
session devoted to English, simple mathematics, and
general studies (including general knowledge, simple

storekeeping and simple elements of operating a small
business enterprise). The trainees were split into two
groups, according to whether they had any formal educational background or not. Instruction began in Hausa.
An attempt was made to make the learning functional, as
seen from Gardner's description:

> The aim is to make them capable to conversing,
> read and write in simple English, to add up
> and keep diaries and transact business with
> bankers and other enterprises with ease. The
> General Studies . . . topics at present include
> those on geography, banking, taxes, anything
> to increase their general awareness of their
> business and general surroundings.

After the completion of the first course, Gardner
decided that the trainees initially needed more intensive
general education as well as a longer period of technical training. The length of the technical course was
extended to 12 months and was preceded by a three-month
course in general subjects. It is not known how successful this experiment was, but the procedure was not adopted
by other VICs.

The BATC offered some additional training features.
Attendance was optional on the fifth evening at a class
in first aid. Credit advice was made available on a
rather informal basis to the trainees, and Gardner provided a form of consultant service during his visits to
small industries in the Kaduna area. The BATC was also
responsible at this stage for advising the SIC scheme
on all technical matters in respect of applications for
loans for buildings and equipment. The integration of
these two schemes does not seem to have been carried
beyond this.

Arrangements were made with the Ministry of Labour
for trainees to take the appropriate grade of trade test
at the end of the course. The main financial inducement
was the prospect of an increased wage or a contract that
accompanied the receipt of a trade test certificate. In
addition, tool awards were made to the best two or three
trainees. These awards were valued at between US$45 and
US$80.

The dropout rate for the BATC, one-sixth in the first
year, was nearer one-third in the three years following
1968. Examples of pass rates in the trade test examinations in Kaduna were 44 out of 54 in 1966 and 71 out of
78 in 1971. Unfortunately, because the BATC has no
system for following up its trainees, there is inadequate
information on the subsequent employment of its trainees
to permit even an approximate calculation of benefits.

Financing and Costs

The costs of the pilot project were higher than for each VIC under the expanded program (which will be dealt with separately). The Ford Foundation made an initial grant, over a two-year period, of US$156,000 for the establishment and running costs of the Kaduna BATC. At the end of two years, responsibility for the BATC was entirely assumed by the Ministry of Trade and Industry. The actual costs of the project were US$56,000 less than anticipated because of the employment of part-time staff and the provision of free classroom and equipment facilities. The largest single annual cost, the salary for the director, has been spread over an increasing number of Centres as the program has expanded. Costs per student for 1965-66 are estimated at US$170, in terms of the total enrollment of 64 students, or US$250, in terms of those successful in the trade test (44 students). These do not include costs to the Ministry of Education for maintenance and utilization of plant and equipment.

Expansion of VIC

By the end of its first two years, the BATC was considered to have made "visible impact on the small business community in Kaduna," in recognition of which the Council of Vocational and Technical Training recommended extension of the program to other parts of Nigeria. The Centres were to be renamed Vocational Improvement Centres and the first VIC was ready to open in Kano in January 1967. Other VICs were quickly established and a further grant of US$56,000 in 1969 from the Ford Foundation was made to complete the establishment of a total of 12 VICs in the six northern states of Nigeria.[23]
The impact of the pilot project was assessed on the basis of the impressions formed by staff and others involved with the project and not as the result of any formal evaluation. One inducement to expansion was the savings from the initial Ford grant, which contributed to the costs of opening four additional VICs by 1968. The Ford Foundation observed in 1969 that "it is quickly evident that this project met a need for which there was wide demand, both among artisans and in the Ministry of Education" and that the project was regarded "as one of the most successful developments assisted by the Foundation in West Africa."
It was intended that the VICs follow the pattern of the Kaduna BATC. Gardner remained director and, with an expatriate assistant, supervised the establishment of the new VICs. The state governments assumed responsibility for their administration from the beginning and full

financial responsibility after one year. Most Centres
were under the state ministries of education; the Kaduna
and Maiduguri centers were under the state ministries of
Trade and Industry.

All VICs have a common pattern for supply of plant
and equipment and for employment of staff; all use existing buildings and equipment, although the latter usually
has to be supplemented. The Maiduguri VIC, for instance,
uses a primary school for teaching general subjects and
the Bornu Local Authority Workshops for practical work.
No rent is paid, but the center has had to install electricity and buy its working tools and equipment.

Almost all the staff at the VICs are employed part-
time. The VIC supervisor in Maiduguri, for instance, is
the chief commercial officer in the Ministry of Trade and
Industry. There are seven other instructors, all of
whom are employed in government ministries or schools.
There is no administrative staff. Staff training is not
included in the operation of the program.

VIC in Operation

To assess the effects of the VIC operation, ICED asked
the Director of the School of Social Studies at the University of Lagos to arrange for the collection of data on
trainees at the Maiduguri VIC. Maiduguri, a typical Centre,
was selected because it had been in operation for four
years and would therefore yield sufficient information
for a survey.

Information was obtained from both the class registers
from 1969-71 and interviews with 45 ex-trainees of the
Centre. Because interviews had to be limited to ex-
trainees whose whereabouts were known to the school's
director, the responses may represent the bias of those
employed in government departments or large firms who had
remained in the Maiduguri area following their training
course at the VIC. However, the respondents included 14
persons who had dropped out of the course or had failed
the examinations.

The ex-trainees, interviewed by students of the
School of Social Studies, were asked questions about their
type of employment before and after the VIC course, wage
increases since the course, and their general background
(age, education, father's occupation, initial training in
their skill). The information in the following sections
on the Maiduguri VIC is based on these data. (See Table
14.1.)

Participants and Their Selection

Although the declared target population of the VICs
is the self-employed artisan or the apprentice of a small-
scale entrepreneur, this aim is far from being achieved.
Less than one-third of the trainees were self-employed;

TABLE 14.1

Information About Trainees at Maiduguri VIC

I. Total Enrollment 1968/69 - 1971/72					
Subject	1968/69	1969/70	1970/71	1971/72	Total
Motor mechanic	24	48	19	40	131
Electrical installation	24	34	49	33	140
Carpentry	24	30	14	13	81
Bricklaying and masonry	24	21	7	14	66
Painting and decoration	–	–	6	9	15
TOTAL	96	133	95	109	433

II. Performance of Trainees 1968/69 - 1970/71

No. admitted	324
No. presented for examination	180 (52%)
No. of passes in examination	72 (22%)

III. Information from Class Registers 1969, 1970, and 1971
(incomplete)

A. Age	1969	1970	1971	Total	%
Under 20 (rarely under 18)	6	5	–	20	14
20 - 29	47	5	43	95	65
30 - 39	12	2	15	29	20
Over 40	1	–	1	2	1
TOTAL				146	100

B. Geographical Origin					
Maiduguri area	38	8	42	88	63
Elsewhere in north	21	3	17	41	29
Outside the north	5	1	6	12	8
TOTAL				141	100

C. Employment					
Government	25	7	34	66	53
Large (expatriate) firm	4	2	4	10	8
Small (indigenous) firm	2	2	10	14	11
Self-employed	21	–	14	35	28
TOTAL				125	100

D. Education					
None	12	1	16	29	23
Some primary	35	10	34	79	62
Postprimary	3	–	3	6	5
Adult education (literacy)	8	–	5	13	10
TOTAL				127	100

Source: Records at Maiduguri Vocational Improvement Centre.

more than half came from government departments or large
firms. Of the 45 ex-trainees interviewed in Maiduguri,
only three were self-employed before taking the VIC course,
although 13 mentioned previous apprenticeship training in
a small indigenous firm.

John de Wilde has confirmed that training for small-
scale industry is not wholly realized in other Centres
as well. Of 180 trainees surveyed at the Kano VIC in
1970, only 10 came from this sector.[24] This may be con-
trasted with recruitment for the BATC which by special
effort did attract many of its trainees from small-scale
industry.

Since few apprentices from small businesses are
trained at Maiduguri, the information obtained about the
background characteristics of such apprentices is spotty.
The predominant age-group for Maiduguri VIC trainees is
20 to 30 years. Trainees are rarely under 18 years old.

Of the ex-trainees interviewed and of those not interviewed for whom information was available on the class
registers, 60 percent or more had had at least some primary education. In addition, a number made reference to
"adult education" or literacy training. The proportion
of those with no literacy in both groups was less than
30 percent.[25] Of the 45 artisans interviewed, only 7
claimed to have fathers in business or trade and 21 said
their fathers were farmers.

Applicants for the VICs are selected on the basis of
the information contained in their application forms.
In addition to requirements related to geographical origin and type of employer, the only condition for acceptance
is that the applicant must have been actively engaged in
the trade he wishes to train in for at least two years.
There is no educational requirement. Once admitted, it
is possible to take the trade tests for Grade III, Grade
II, and even Grade I in consecutive years.

Organization and Content of Course

The training program lasts ten months and is organized
in much the same way as was the pilot project. It does,
however, devote more time to related instruction. The
timetable for Maiduguri shows that of ten hours a week of
instruction only four are devoted to practical work in the
particular trade; the amount of English and arithmetic
given varies from course to course and trainees in electrical installation receive only half as much instruction
in English and arithmetic together as those in the other
courses. Trainees are divided into two groups for instruction in the general subjects, one for literates and one
for illiterates. Other subjects taught are bookkeeping
and business methods. Instruction is given in Hausa if
necessary.

Arrangements are made with the Federal Ministry of Labour to test trainees at the end of the course. The basic four trades in which courses are offered at nearly all the VICs are motor mechanics, carpentry and furniture making, bricklaying and concreting, and electrical installation. In Maiduguri there has been a marked drop in numbers enrolled in carpentry and bricklaying. While adding courses in painting and decorating, Kaduna has dropped bricklaying and concreting, possibly because masonry as a trade is particularly subject to seasonal fluctuation and unemployment.

Of the total number admitted to courses at the Maiduguri VIC since its inception, 48 percent dropped out and 30 percent failed the examination. It is clear from the interviews that conflicts with employment hours contribute in large part to poor attendance at classes and absence from the final examination.

Financing and Costs

The Ford Foundation contributed US$5,600 to each new VIC as the capital cost necessary for the adaptation of buildings and purchase of initial equipment. At all centers, the recurrent costs are significantly lowered by the use of existing facilities and equipment and, of course, the employment of part-time staff. Instructors are paid 30 shillings (US$4.20) per hour. The annual recurrent cost at Maiduguri VIC is about US$8,400, which excludes the cost of the services of the director and his assistant, who administer the program as part of their civil service duties. If the average enrollment over the four-year period is taken, the cost per student enrolled is US$104, and the cost per student successful in the examination is US$467. For purposes of comparison, it may be noted that the cost of training a student for one year in a trade school is estimated at US$930, or US$2,790 for the three-year course (excluding dropout costs).

Assessment

There is no firm evidence available to show that success in a VIC course has encouraged an artisan to set up his own business on a full-time basis. The VICs do not maintain a system for follow-up of their trainees.

However, information from the interviews conducted in Maiduguri gives some indication of the impact of the VIC course on the trainee, whose only cost is the opportunity cost, transport costs, and a small examination fee for the trade test. As most trainees are in wage employment, the greatest potential benefit, of course, is a wage increase. Of the 25 "successful" trainees in wage employment interviewed, 15 had received an increment,

often representing more than 30 percent of the former
wage. None of the respondents in wage employment had
moved to full-time self-employment within a few months
after training. However, four of the wage earners had
an established part-time business with their own employees
or apprentices, and nine did contract for casual work on
a sporadic basis. A number expressed the hope of eventually setting themselves up in their own businesses.

SMALL INDUSTRIES CREDIT SCHEME

The Small Industry Credit scheme (SIC) was established in October 1965 under the Northern Region Ministry
of Trade and Industry with a grant of US$380,000 from
the Ford Foundation. The object was to serve small
industrial enterprises that were labor-intensive in order
to relieve unemployment, and to support small productive
units. Credit services were to be provided on a commercial basis, with thorough continuous supervision and
training for both lending staff and loan applicants.
The scheme was to be insulated from political interference
and loans were to be made on the basis of individual
economic merit.

In practice, most of the Ford grant was spent on
the salaries and housing of the three expatriate credit
advisors. Few guidelines in the project plan were
adhered to. The loan limit was set at £N5,000 at 5 percent interest, instead of the recommended £N2,000 at 10
percent. The SIC staff were not qualified to give technical advice and this task was passed on, to a limited
extent, to the Kaduna BATC and subsequently to the IDC,
which was only partially operational until the end of
1968. Follow-up advice on management and bookkeeping and
a training program for lending staff were not effectively
supplied.

There was strong criticism of the SIC loan policy
before 1969: only 75 loans had been made up to that time;
and of these, 32 were small agricultural processing loans
for businesses with "meagre growth potential without any
particular plan in mind."[26] The number of staff was so
small and the distribution of loans so geographically
wide that it was impossible to carry out any effective
follow-up. In an analysis of the loans, Gerald Faust
found that the use of loan funds was best in mechanical
workshops, fair in leather and wood, and poor in agricultural processing. He also found a high correlation
between successful projects and projects located in towns
which had an adequate economic infrastructure.[27] Robinson
and Turner criticized the scheme for trying "to do something for everywhere" and concluded that it had failed
because of the lack of a "well-timed, coordinated and

integrated series of activities designed to meet all problems of the small industry manager . . . ."28

It is clear that insufficient thought had been given
to the training requirements for the successful operation
of the scheme. However, the program was also a victim of
the political events of the time. Faust has written that
the rationale for supporting agricultural processing was
social and political.[29] It seems reasonable to assume
that political events affected most types of small industry and that the main achievement of the credit scheme
has been to contribute to filling the vacuum resulting
from the emigration from the north of many in small industry because of the war.

SIC made no further loans from April 1968 to April
1969. During that period the old scheme was divided into
six separate loan schemes for the six northern states.
In 1969, each state made an initial contribution, varying
from ₤N10,000 to ₤N25,000, toward a revolving fund of
₤N50,000 (US$140,000) planned for each state. A further
₤N 170,000 was contributed by the states for the year
1970/71.

Although the adoption of the Small Industry Credit
scheme by all of the northern states indicated their
support for this kind of investment, it has posed also
a number of problems. In most states the scheme is
administered by a single loan officer who often lacks the
qualifications to make an adequate technical evaluation.
Thus, supervision and follow-up of loans made is weak at
the state level. Increased political autonomy for the
states has also brought the SIC schemes under new political pressures. For example, the North-East State has
insisted that loans should be distributed as widely as
possible and has excluded the policy of requiring a
borrower's contribution to the loan, with the result that
the proportion of delinquent payments in the state has
risen to 30 percent.

INDUSTRIAL DEVELOPMENT CENTRE, ZARIA

Changes in the development of SIC and the problems
it has encountered have significantly affected the operation of the IDC. The original IDC emphasis on short
training courses at the center and on-site consultation,
with a rather random system of identifying the target
population, has been modified. For a number of reasons,
it was decided to change the emphasis to one of support
for the SIC scheme. Originally, the IDC was a companion
program to the SIC and the VICs under the Northern Region
Ministry of Trade and Industry, although the three schemes
were never formally integrated. In 1968, when the other
two programs became the responsibility of the various

northern states, control of the IDC passed to the federal
government. The IDC has remained a single federal institution, although now tied to six separate state credit
schemes.

Facilities and Administration

The actual site of the IDC is in Samaru, opposite
Ahmadu Bello University and five miles from the outskirts
of Zaria city. Thus far, the IDC has developed 80 of the
160 acres allocated to it. By 1969 about 20 modern buildings had been constructed. These include staff offices,
dormitory and other facilities for those attending courses,
and four large workshops for woodwork, metal work, auto
repair, and leathercraft. The courses themselves, ranging
from five days to two weeks, introduce the participants
to new management and workshop techniques, new tools and
equipment. Each course, dealing with a specific trade,
is restricted to those actually engaged in it.
     A recent part of the IDC operation is the development
of product prototypes, mainly consumer goods or agricultural tools, designed to meet the requirements of intermediate technology. A large quantity of sophisticated
and expensive modern machinery has also been purchased.
This equipment is evidently unsuitable for local use and
is poorly utilized.
     From the outset, the administration of the IDC has
been under a Nigerian director. There were four expatriate
technical experts in October 1971, of which the two U.S. AID
personnel were to leave in December 1971 with the termi-
nation of United States assistance. Twelve Nigerian technical staff are responsible for running the workshops
and seminars and providing on-site consultations. Although
U.S. AID originally sought highly trained technical counterparts, these could not be obtained and trade school graduates have been employed instead. This appears to have
worked successfully, for the turnover of apparently competent Nigerian staff is low. Staff training includes
on-the-job training with the expatriate advisors, and 15
weeks of weekly seminars using background papers and including the preparation of trial preinvestment proposals.[30]

Loan Policy and Procedures

In April 1969 when the state SIC committees recom--
mended that loan operations be resumed, the emphasis of
the IDC project changed from training and advice to include undertaking feasibility studies for the SIC schemes.
An advantage of this shift, presumably, would be that

concrete indications of performance would compensate for
IDC's abstract if not uncertain measurements of training
effectiveness; furthermore, the IDC could reinforce random
methods of trainee selection by using SIC identification
of entrepreneurs needing assistance.

In processing loans, the state SIC sifts initial loan
applications and those that satisfy the basic requirements
are forwarded to IDC for further investigation and recommendations. The IDC prepares a preinvestment proposal on
the basis of a feasibility study of the project. Applicants who have participated in IDC courses have a good
chance of being recommended for a loan, and if a loan is
recommended it is generally granted. The IDC preinvestment proposal sets forth such details as the appropriate
allocation of capital, number of workers to be employed,
raw materials and equipment to be procured, and a calculation of expected sales, costs and incomes, and percentage
returns.

Once a loan is approved by the state SIC and the
conditions accepted by the applicant, IDC provides comprehensive supervision and assistance. The loan is
usually disbursed in the form of local purchase orders for
machinery and equipment, which the IDC obtains for the
loan applicant. This is accompanied by a series of workshop visits and training in both the technical and management aspects of the business. The IDC even trains employees
and apprentices, assists in the installation of new
machines, and helps to secure contracts and market outlets
for the entrepreneur.

From August 1969 to August 1971, 153 loan applications
were recommended for approval by the IDC from a total of
400 applications referred to it by the state SICs. This
compares with a total of 73 loans made before April 1968.
In 1970, the average loan was approximately US$7,280,
ranging from US$700 to US$28,000. The emphasis has changed
somewhat. After loan operations were resumed in 1969,
corn mills were no longer eligible. Other categories, such
as building contracting, continued to be excluded. Loans
for agricultural processing, which made up 47 percent of
the loans before 1968, constituted only 5 percent of 104
loans approved since 1969. Since 1969 auto repair, metal
work, carpentry, and concrete blockmaking have accounted
for 65 percent of the loans. Certain other conditions also
apply: the business must usually be owned by a northerner,
but may not be owned by a government official; a business
already in existence is preferred to one not yet operational.

It has been noted that the IDC has really accomplished
little "in the way of identifying investment opportunities,
establishing investment priorities and general techno-eco-
nomic analysis."[31] In fact, the IDC has come to play a
somewhat passive role in small-scale industrial development.
Market assessments, if any, are undertaken by the state

SIC staff. Normally there is only one loan officer, whose knowledge of individual industry is perforce limited. Initial identification of applicants is made by the states, and the political pressures on IDC include rivalry between the states for its services. Moreover, the activities of IDC are spread over an extremely large area (78 percent of the total area of Nigeria). In 1971, "IDC appeared to be rather overwhelmed by the volume of project work it had been requested to do" and the processing of a loan application now requires a minimum of one year.[32]

Analysis of feasibility studies of 53 IDC-assisted businesses revealed that before the loan 41 percent had no employees, 45 percent had five or less. Although 34 businesses gave no information, 16 had one to ten apprentices, only eight of whom were said to be related to the owners. Employment increases recommended by IDC could not be verified.

Of the 53 owners, mostly between 30 and 50 years of age, 30 percent had some primary education, 15 percent had postprimary technical education. Literacy levels, badly reported, revealed 19 percent of the respondents have had either adult education or literacy in Hausa. Fourteen of the respondents indicated that their basic trade training was received through small firm apprenticeships. Eleven of the owners were partners, 13 had some other business or employment. No written partnership deeds existed. The large assets of a number of owners suggest that lack of training rather than lack of capital was the main problem.

Costs

The total capital cost of IDC to date, exclusive of certain donations, is estimated at US$425,600 with a projected expenditure of US$47,600 for the purchase of further machinery and equipment. Recurrent costs are difficult to calculate, because staff cost figures are not available. However, the IDC employs 38 staff, including four expatriates, and other annual running costs are at least US$10,000. It must be remembered that services are free to participants in IDC activities, not counting food and travel for course participants.

These costs must be set against effectiveness of the training provided and the results of feasibility studies. Even allowing for a slow start in 1969, the figure of 60 loan applications processed annually, representing 5 for each technical officer, indicates a fairly high cost. Time and expense of travel are factors; and the benefits in increased employment may be substantial but they cannot be accurately calculated.

An analysis of the sales of 47 businesses over the period since they first received IDC assistance shows an

average annual gross income increase of 253 percent.[33]
However, because these businesses have benefited from
IDC support not only in technical and management advice
but also in obtaining raw materials and equipment and in
securing government contracts and market outlets, it is
difficult to assess their performance as independent
enterprises. It is also difficult to assess their long-
term potential in the present special circumstances
created by political events and in the absence of studies
clarifying investment opportunities and priorities.

CONCLUSIONS: LESSONS FROM NIGERIAN EXPERIENCE

The three programs, conceived separately, administratively independent, have basically the same objectives:
to improve the quality of middle-level manpower in small
industrial operations and to improve small industry itself. They operate on basically the same four assumptions:

1. Small-scale manufacturing has an important role
    to play in the industrial development process;
    properly coached, guided and assisted, small
    entrepreneurs will step into this role.
2. Development of the economy called for priority
    support in the fields of agricultural products
    and food processing, leather preparation, and
    the metal and electrical trades.
3. In terms of small industry's need, the best
    contributions are in capital, advice on managerial
    and technical problems, and upgrading of skilled
    workers.
4. Although indigenous apprenticeship and other on-
    the-job training are adequate for work in small
    industry, they need to be complemented by special
    upgrading at the journeyman level if small in-
    dustry is to develop properly.

On the first assumption no conclusion can be drawn
from the Nigerian experience. The large number of applicants clearly shows that small businessmen in Northern
Nigeria have the will to develop or expand a business of
their own. The high rate of repayment and the high rates
of increase in turnover in most of the business undertakings that have received loans may be used as indicators
to conclude that both entrepreneurship motivation and
management ability can be found among small manufacturers
in the area.
    As for the second assumption, the high rate of
failure in the maize and rice processing field calls for
caution and suggests the need for careful market research
and planning as backstop action for loan schemes and

management advisory services. Opportunities for expansion obviously exist in the other fields, although present practices preclude knowing when limits are reached.

Study of the third assumption regarding the types of contribution is hampered by lack of data on new businesses. Feasibility studies suggest that most if not all entrepreneurs need help with both managerial and technical consultancy and training. Their marketing knowledge is generally limited, their accounts unreliable and badly organized for adequate control of operations, their organization of work often wasteful, and their concepts of quality often below what is needed for successful competition with larger undertakings.

But helping small industry is costly. The high cost suggests that an individual enterprise-by-enterprise approach may not be economically feasible except in special circumstances such as those existing in Northern Nigeria at the time when the operation was started. The void left by the southern Nigerian entrepreneurs who moved out when the emergency began had to be filled to avoid serious damage to the economy. In such circumstances concentration of effort on a few hundred enterprises with proven potential is probably warranted, although such attention will not be possible in the future as the economy grows. The perspective for any cost-benefit analysis is a long one in such situations because the task is essentially to create a business culture, not just to put a few undertakings on their feet.

The fact that a number of trainees in the VIC upgrading courses have passed the trade tests and thereby acquired recognized qualifications in their trade after only a short course of complementary training would seem sufficient evidence for the fourth assumption that indigenous apprenticeship and other on-the-job training does constitute a reasonable basis for training to upgrade skilled worker level. As was noted earlier, the high dropout rates from the courses are partly explained by organizational shortcomings.

The high rate of failure in the examinations may have two explanations. One is that the trade tests are essentially geared to the needs of the larger government departments, not to small industry and services whose workers have acquired skills other than those for which the tests were designed. Another is probably that the training period is too short for those whose educational background is insufficient for them to keep the pace.

Another justification for the efforts in upgrading skills lies in the over-subscription of most of the courses. That many employers, particularly in government departments, appreciate the effort is shown by the fair number of workers receiving higher pay after their passing the tests.

Two practices in the Nigerian pattern of small industry development services are unusual. One is the

flexible use of facilities and staff of the VICs: extensive use is made of existing schools, workshops, and training centers at times when they would otherwise be idle;
the use of part-time staff has made it possible to adjust
training offerings to meet demand. The other is the
successful use of trade school graduates as staff members,
conducting advisory services and feasibility studies in the
IDC scheme.

The greatest weakness in all the activities described
appears to be overall lack of plan in terms of needs and
potentialities and relying on "intuitive" planning based
on uninformed demand (leading to overinvestment in corn
and rice mills). There is no machinery for identifying
underinvestments in fields that have not caught the imagination of would-be entrepreneurs or young skilled workers.

It was hoped that a study in depth of the performance
of trainees in the VIC courses and of entrepreneurs who
had received loans would give some clues to essential
shortcomings in the indigenous training process, but this
did not prove possible. The VICs--partly because of their
"light" organizational structure and the part-time character
of their management--do not have adequate records for
follow-up studies and research on problems encountered by
trainees during courses and when sitting for the trade
tests. The feasibility study reports and other records
on advice given to undertakings do not include sufficient
data from which a reasonably clear picture could be constructed.

This is to be regretted: such data could be of great
help for evaluating the advisory and training system and
for suggesting alternative lines of action for lowering
cost or increasing effectiveness. It would be of particular value to learn the background and training of the
entrepreneurs, with a view to determining whether it would
be possible to reinforce and improve their training at
an earlier stage, before they have established a business
of their own. Training more people better might lead to
increasing the number of successful entrepreneurs and to
cutting cost by diminishing the need for enterprise-by-
enterprise advisory services.

The experience in Nigeria--as in many other countries--
shows that indigenous apprenticeship and other on-the-job
training can provide much of the learning required for
indigenous enterprises to grow, if the economic climate is
right. But data are insufficient for determining properly
what additional training may yield the greatest benefits
at the lowest cost; who should receive additional training;
at what stage or stages additional training efforts may be
most beneficial to future entrepreneurs in industry and
independent craftsmen in the trades.

NOTES

1. John C. de Wilde, The Development of African Private Enterprise, Report no. AW-31, 2 vols. (Washington, D.C.: The International
Bank for Reconstruction and Development, December 10, 1971), vol. 2,
chap. VIII, pp. 3-4.
2. Ibid.
3. In 1968 the Northern Region was divided into six states:
Kwara, Benue Plateau, North-East, North-Central, Kano, and North-West
states--which make up 78 percent of the total area and roughly half
of the population of Nigeria.
4. Federation of Nigeria, National Development Plan 1962-1968
(Lagos: Federal Ministry of Economic Planning, 1961).
5. Federal Republic of Nigeria, Second National Development
Plan 1970-1974 (Lagos: Federal Ministry of Information, 1970).
6. Ibid., pp. 10; 140-141.
7. Ibid., pp. 145-146; 151.
8. U.S. Agency for International Development, "Industrial
Development Centre, Zaria," mimeographed (Washington, D.C., n.d.), p. 3.
9. For example: Nigeria, Federal Ministry of Industries,
Industrial Analysis Division, "Report on the Development of Small
Industries in Northern Nigeria," mimeographed (Lagos, April 1968);
Nigeria, Ministry of Trade and Industry, Interim Common Services
Agency, "List of Existing Industries in the Northern States," mimeographed (Kaduna, January 1968); Peter Kilby, "Nigerian Industry in
the Northern Region," mimeographed (Lagos, April 19, 1961); and Robert
R. Nathan Associates, Inc., "Indigenous Industry in Nigeria," mimeographed (Washington, D.C., March 1964).
10. For example, Peter Kilby, African Enterprise: The Nigerian
Bread Industry, Hoover Institution Studies no. 8 (Stanford, California:
Stanford University, Hoover Institution on War, Revolution and Peace,
1965); and E. Wayne Nafziger, "Nigerian Entrepreneurship: A Study
of Indigenous Business in the Footwear Industry" (Ph.D. diss., University of Illinois, 1966).
11. Archibald Callaway, "From Technical Crafts to Modern Industries," ODU, University of Ife Journal of African Studies 2, no. 1
(July 1965).
12. N.A. Faminu and B.T. Koch, "The Rural Blacksmith--Case
Studies in Nigeria," CIRF, Training for Progress 6, no. 1 (1967):
3-9;   and M. Koll and Y. Lajunji, "Auto Repair--Full Service
Through Cooperation," CIRF, Training for Progress 6, no. 1 (1967):
10-18.
13. "Small-scale" in the context of Nigerian industrial development has been defined in different ways. Kilby defined it in terms
of production methods, as an industry of artisans employing pre-
industrial methods to produce low-quality goods (African Enterprise,
op. cit., p. 2). The Nigerian Factory Act defined it as an industry
of 10 employees or less. The Ford Foundation Small Industry Credit
scheme used the definition of less than 50 employees (H.E. Robinson
and F.L. Turner, Consulting Report: Review of Program of the Northern
States of Nigeria to Promote Indigenous Small Industry, with Recommendations [Lagos, Nigeria: Ford Foundation, West African Regional
Office, September 1968], p. 9). The extent to which the IDC uses

these definitions is unclear, but it recently added a further definition of a small-scale industry as one which has a total capitalization of less than ₦N30,000 (US$84,000) (U.S. AID, op. cit., p. 1).

14. Requests included those of leather-workers, rice-millers,
weavers, tin miners, boat-builders, carpenters, cabinet makers, metal
workers, corn-millers, woodworkers, bakers, tailors, printers, saw-
millers, soapmakers, concrete-block makers, blacksmiths, tanners, and
mechanics.

15. Federation of Nigeria, op. cit., pp. 142-3.

16. Ibid., pp. 138, 141.

17. Industrial Development Centre, "Technical and Management
Assistance for Small Scale Industries," mimeographed (Zaria, n.d.).

18. Ibid., pp. 4-5.

19. Interview with Mr. G. Hawbaker, August 16, 1971.

20. The Owerri Centre closed with the onset of the Nigerian
Civil War.

21. Adam S. Skapski, The Development of Technical Education and
its Relation to the Educational System in Western Nigeria, 1962-1970
(Ibadan: Western Nigeria Government Printer, May 1962).

22. The introduction of credit advice was part of a plan to
link the VICs with another Ford program, to be described later, to
provide supervised credit for small-scale industry.

23. Locations, based on the availability of technical training
facilities and the proximity of small-scale industry were as follows:
North-East, Sokoto and Minna; North-West, Maiduguri and Bauchi; North-
Central, Katsina and Kaduna; Kano, two centers; Bauchi Plateau,
Makurdi and Jos; and Kwara, Ilorin and Lokoja.

24. de Wilde, op. cit., p. 19.

25. Literacy may be in either Hausa or English, in Roman or
Arabic script, although this is not clearly separated in the interviewee responses.

26. Robinson and Turner, op. cit., p. 37.

27. Gerald Faust, "Small Industries Credit Scheme in Northern
Nigeria: An Analysis of Operational and Lending Patterns," The
Nigerian Journal of Economic and Social Studies, 2, no. 2 (July 1969):
216-219.

28. Robinson and Turner, op. cit., p. 18.

29. Faust, op. cit., p. 222.

30. Interview with Mr. Turner, IDC Zaria, November 18, 1971.

31. Faust, op. cit., pp. 207-209.

32. de Wilde, op. cit., p. 15.

33. This figure is taken from a chart prepared by Mr. Hawbaker
of the IDC staff in September 1971.

15

**PHILIPPINES:
TRAINING EXTENSION
LEADERS FOR
PROMOTING NEW
RICE VARIETIES**
Manzoor Ahmed
and Philip H. Coombs

A study of the training program of the International Rice Research Institute (IRRI) is of particular interest because it deals with some important issues in respect of training programs for extension workers and reveals some of the ways in which such programs can be evaluated with a view to improving their productivity. Field visits for the study were done in fall 1971 and the writing was completed in June 1972.

INTRODUCTION

Agricultural research has taken great strides in recent years and has made significant contributions to the achievement of higher yields. The International Center for Maize and Wheat Improvement in Mexico (CIMMYT) and the International Rice Research Institute (IRRI) in the Philippines have done much to launch the Green Revolution through the development of high-yielding varieties, often referred to as "miracle seeds." As agricultural research capacity grows in the developing countries, it is becoming evident that research is of little value unless the research findings are made available to farmers in ways they can understand and evaluate for themselves.

Though the initial spread of the genetic discoveries has been rapid and wide enough to initiate the Green Revolution, further dissemination of new technology-- particularly among the small farmers, the disadvantaged majority of world peasantry--is proving difficult; so is the sustained growth of agriculture after relatively progressive farmers and well-endowed farmlands are brought into the realm of new technology. For rice, particularly, average yields in the tropical region have a long way to go: the present yield level is about 1,500 kg. per hectare compared to over 5,000 kg. per hectare in leading rice-producing countries of the temperate zone.

Both CIMMYT and IRRI have found it necessary to pay attention to the problems of translating research results into operational practices and transmitting the messages about appropriate practices and behavior to farmers. CIMMYT's effort in this respect has taken shape in Plan Puebla, a pilot project for improving farmers' productivity and income. IRRI has worked with the extension services-- the intermediary between the research institute and the farmer--by operating a rice production course for trainers and supervisors of extension agents.

IRRI, established in 1960 by the Ford and Rockefeller Foundations with the cooperation of the Republic of the Philippines, is situated at Los Baños, Laguna, 40 miles south of Manila, near the College of Agriculture of the University of the Philippines. The program of the institute is devoted primarily to conducting basic and applied research on the rice plant to improve its productivity and quality. The institute also has a training program for research scientists.

The rice production training program of the International Rice Research Institute is of significance in a study of nonformal rural education for several reasons: a) the program highlights weaknesses in the conventional training and preparation of agricultural extension personnel in numerous countries and illustrates pedagogical approaches and techniques to help remedy some of these weaknesses; b) the program suggests a special role for agricultural research institutions in various countries in strengthening extension services; c) despite the small size of the program, IRRI's status as an international research institution and its cooperative relations with the countries in Asia suggest a potential for influencing the training programs and performance of extension services in various rice-growing countries; and d) it illustrates the importance of regularly subjecting training programs to cost-effectiveness and cost-benefit tests in order to improve their performance.

This report examines exclusively the regular six-month training program for extension leaders and does not cover other training activities of IRRI, such as ad hoc short training courses for extension personnel, the multiple-crop production course, or the training of research scientists.

RATIONALE AND HISTORY OF THE PROGRAM

The success in the efforts of rice-growing countries to increase their rice yields depends on the interplay of several factors, including the use of new varieties capable of responding to increased amounts of nitrogen and a wide assortment of new practices in rice culture. Another crucial element in the process is the farmer's knowledge, skill, and attitude regarding the new techniques and practices. It is obvious that the necessary knowledge and skill have to be acquired and the appropriate attitudes developed among farmers before they can contribute to increased rice production.

It is common practice to rely on some kind of an extension service and extension agents to disseminate the new knowledge and skills and to encourage favorable attitudes on the part of farmers. This assumes that the extension workers are knowledgeable in the arts and science of rice production, are capable of identifying the individual farmer's problems of growing rice, and are able to find solutions to these problems in most instances. IRRI has discovered, though, that these assumptions are often unfounded.

Tests of diagnostic ability were given to several thousand extension workers as well as advisers on tropical rice-growing with advanced degrees in agriculture. These examinations consisted of such items as the identification of common diseases of the rice plant; pests and insects and the damage caused by them; nutritional problems of the rice plant; and the chemicals commonly needed in improved rice production. Extension workers answered only about 25 percent of the questions correctly; the rice specialists did no better. The institute concluded that:

> Whatever the reasons, and these vary with situations, the typical extension worker in most southeast Asian countries lacks background knowledge of rice culture and has had little or no first-hand paddy experience. Moreover, when he lacks the necessary diagnostic skills, he cannot identify the problems in the farmer's field and thus cannot advise him on appropriate action. Consequently, he is reluctant even to approach the farmer to show him how things might be done.[1]

A relatively short period of specialized training dramatically improved the diagnostic skills of the trainees, which was not surprising because the training undoubtedly concentrated on the test items. A high test score also does not necessarily indicate how well the skills would be retained and utilized. It was concluded, therefore, that an appropriate training program should include not only needed theoretical knowledge but also the practical experience of actually producing a crop.

By early 1964, when the new cross-bred dwarf varieties of rice began to show great promise in IRRI and other experiment stations in the Philippines, IRRI's scientists began discussing ways of shortening the usual lag between research and application by making the new technology available to farmers as quickly as possible. Filipino

agricultural officials who were watching the progress of
research work in IRRI were also anxious to put the results
into practice. Agreements were soon reached between IRRI
and the Philippine Agricultural Productivity Commission
(APC), the national extension agency, that IRRI would
train some of APC's extension workers in the application
of the new technology for rice cultivation.

The program of training in rice production began in
June 1964. The first trainees were five farm management
technicians whose appointments as rice extension specialists had been proposed by the Philippine Agricultural
Productivity Commission. Five more barrio (village) farm
management agents from APC joined the course six months
later and had intensive training for six months, while the
earlier group had training for a period of 12 months. The
design of the course and its implementation were developed
during the initial six months.

The aim of the training course for barrio technicians
was to prepare them for the role of rice production specialist in each of nine regions in the Philippines chosen for
accelerated development of rice production. The function
of these specialists was described as follows:

> Each man was to become proficient in all phases
> of rice production (soils, entomology, weed con-
> trol, pathology, etc.), and be responsible for
> all APC rice activities within his region. He
> would provide the barrio technicians with techni-
> cal guidance, trouble-shooting assistance, and
> periodic refresher training on rice subjects.
> New information on rice culture would flow
> through him to the barrio agents in his region;
> problems beyond resolution at the barrio or the
> rice specialist level would flow through him to
> research workers.[2]

After completing their course, nine of the ten
trainees from APC were each assigned to train five farm
management technicians in each of the nine regions; the
tenth trainee was attached to the APC office.

The second group of trainees in 1966 consisted of 28
members: 25 were from the various agricultural agencies
in the Philippines; the others were from the United States,
the Sudan, and Nigeria. This and all subsequent courses
were six months long. The third course, started in June
1967, had the first truly international group of trainees.
Since then about 35 trainees from various rice-growing
countries have been taken each year into the six-month
course (only one course is given per year). By 1971,
over 200 trainees from 24 countries had gone through the
training course. (See Table 15.1.)

Though no set standards or requirements are applied
in the selection of trainees, normally those admitted have

TABLE 15.1

Trainees of the Rice Production Training Course
Shown by Country of Origin
1964-1971

Country	No. of Trainees
Philippines	66
India	23
Sri Lanka	22
Indonesia	19
Pakistan	13
South Vietnam	10
Thailand	9
U.S.A.	9
Laos	8
Burma	6
Fiji	5
Malaysia	3
Others*	18
TOTAL	211

*Includes the following countries with one or two trainees in the rice production training course: Afghanistan, Cambodia, Ghana, Iraq, Japan, Kenya, Korea, Nepal, Nigeria, Sierra Leone, Sudan, Tanzania.

Source: International Rice Research Institute.

had at least an agricultural diploma and experience in the extension field. It is IRRI's expectation that the graduates of the course would go back to their countries to train other extension agents, applying the methods and approach of the IRRI course in their own training courses. In this manner, IRRI's training effort would have a broad multiplier effect on upgrading national rice extension programs, thereby justifying the investment involved in the program.

MAIN FEATURES OF THE PROGRAM

The IRRI training program stresses rice production technology and diagnostic skills, fundamentals of communication and extension, and applied research methodology. Its important characteristics are briefly described below.

Learning by Doing

Approximately half of the total training time is spent in rice production. Trainees, individually or in small task forces, actually cultivate plots of rice. The schedule of lectures, discussions, and other classroom instruction is flexibly adapted to the training requirements of the field work. Classroom sessions are often recessed in order to take the group to the field so that the trainees can identify and resolve the problems on the spot.

Responding to the criticism that extension workers themselves do not often go through the experiences of a rice farmer, the training program is synchronized with the normal wet or dry rice-growing season. The trainees perform every operation necessary to produce the crop, from preparing the land to harvesting, thus gaining practical experience in production steps. At the same time the trainees experiment with and demonstrate the effectiveness of alternative techniques or inputs. As one of IRRI's training experts stated, "Field experience with different varieties and practices gives the worker conviction and credibility when he talks to farmers. If he cannot grow rice, he finds it difficult to win and maintain the farmers' confidence. It is difficult to teach what one does not know."[3]

The training program is characterized by what the institute terms the <u>communication approach</u>. All elements of training concentrate on methods and inputs necessary to change the behavior of farmers through communicating with them in a way that will effect desirable changes in their practices. The identification of the desired learning outcomes in terms of skills, knowledge, and behavior and the specific instructional techniques and content needed for achieving these objectives is emphasized in the training.

As a part of the course, each trainee, individually or in groups, is required to develop, plan, and organize a two-week training program in rice production. The emphasis of this exercise is on giving the trainees practice in the arts of building motivation for learning, breaking down key points of the learning content into appropriate cognitive units for the specific learner group, organizing practical experiences for learners, and evaluating the training activity. The IRRI trainee actually teaches the two-week course he has designed. Participants in such short courses are trainees from agricultural agencies in the Philippines and other countries. Thus the trainees can put their theories and learning to practical use, while they are still participants in the training.

Authoritative Knowledge and Information

IRRI's training program, based as it is at the foremost research center in the world for rice production,
draws upon the specialized knowledge of about two dozen
scientists and specialists on various aspects of rice
production. Scientists and specialists are regularly
invited as resource persons and they prepare instructional
materials specifically for the trainees. The specialists,
in turn, consider the issues of dissemination of their
knowledge through extension activities. Rice production
trainees also attend weekly seminars held in IRRI on
various aspects of rice production throughout the year.

New seeds and other technical solutions found through
research can affect production only when the knowledge is
made available to farmers in an appropriate "package of
practices" suitable for a region of the country. Before
this new knowledge can be disseminated there must be extensive experimentation to adapt it to local circumstances.
Extension agents need to work closely with experiment
stations in setting up field trials, possibly on plots of
farmers' land, to make the trial as close to actual farming conditions as possible and to make the farmers partners in such adaptation. Extension agents are also the
channel for feedback to research institutions and have
to signal them about the problems of farmers that should
become subjects of research.

Experimental methodology and practical experience
in applied research form an important part of the course
content. Each trainee, individually or in small teams,
is required to design, implement, and assess the results
of one or more applied research projects. Research projects in which the trainees of the 1970 course participated were the following:

1. Granular Herbicide (Applied Research Trial)
2. Spacing x Variety Interaction Experiment
3. IR22 Production Plot (Transplant and Broadcast)
4. Farmers Evaluation of New Selections (Applied
   Research Trial)
5. Insect Control Display Plot
6. IR20 Production Plot (Row Sown and Broadcast)
7. Stand Establishment (Applied Research Trial)
8. IR127 Production Plot (Transplant and Broadcast)
9. International Rice Variety Display Plot
10. Insect Control (Applied Research Trial)
11. Mini-Kit Rice Variety Trial
12. C4-63 Production Plot (Transplant and Broadcast)
13. Fertilizer (Applied Research Trial)
14. Fertilizer Display Plot
15. IR127 Production Plot (Broadcast)[4]

Development of Teaching Materials and Methods

The training staff of the program consisted of seven full-time members in 1971, but a large number of experts from IRRI and other institutions regularly participate as lecturers in specific topics. In cooperation with these lecturers, the training staff has attempted to develop the specific behavioral objectives for each topic, to compile the lecture materials in writing, and to develop a detailed syllabus.

Much attention has been given to providing the trainees with instructional materials for their own use in conducting training courses. The lectures of the course have been compiled into a two-volume "resource syllabus" for similar training elsewhere. In addition, a <u>Training Manual in Rice Production</u>, containing lessons on the skills of rice production, has been prepared. Tapes of many of the lectures are available and the possibilities are being explored of using color videotapes of the training activities of IRRI in courses given in other countries. There is, however, no indication whether training materials from IRRI are being used in courses in other countries.

IMPACT OF THE PROGRAM

The basic aim of the IRRI rice production training program, as we have seen, is to strengthen the capacity of the extension services of cooperating nations to promote the adoption of new rice varieties and the general improvement of rice production. ICED was able to obtain only limited evidence of how great this impact has been, partly because the program is still relatively young but also because IRRI itself has made only limited efforts to ascertain the impact.

Philippines

The evidence of impact in the Philippines itself, though limited, is relatively better than for most other countries. The program was launched in 1964 with Filipino rice production workers and until 1967 remained confined mostly to extension workers for that country. By that time about 40 rice production workers had been trained and these became the "change-agents" in selected priority regions throughout the country. It appears that all or most of these trainees were subsequently utilized in a manner that would put their IRRI training to effective use where it could have a multiplier effect on the improvement of extension and rice production. A number of them were made responsible for organizing training programs patterned after the IRRI approach in their own regions. In 1965, for instance, nine IRRI trainees were allotted plots of land and each was charged with the training of five extension workers. After a year, in May-June 1966, the 45 new trainees were brought to the institute for two weeks of special testing and refresher training.

The production performance of ten teams of Filipino trainees growing a new variety (IR8) under practical field conditions demonstrated that the training had enabled these extension workers to produce as good a crop as a farmer would produce under ideal circumstances. As reported by IRRI, the trainees made all the management decisions needed for growing the crop, supervised the work, directed the laborers, and kept records. All ten teams produced high yields and returned substantial net profits on their investment. Four teams, for whom comparable figures were available, achieved yield increases ranging from over 50 percent to over 300 percent in their plots.[5]

It is difficult to say what the new training approach for a limited number of Filipino extension workers did for rice production in the country. It is reasonable to assume that the training made some contribution to the marked increase in rice production in the country starting from 1966. The participants in the training program were undoubtedly equipped to render practical advice and assistance to the general run of rice farmers.

Sri Lanka

The impact of the training program on the extension services of other rice-growing countries is difficult to judge because accurate information about the placement and utilization of the trainees on their return is not available. Rather surprisingly, as of late 1971 IRRI had made no systematic effort to trace what had happened to its former trainees and how they had been utilized to improve the training of rice extension workers in their respective countries. The IRRI training program office claimed, however, that training courses modeled after the IRRI course were being operated or planned by national extension or other agricultural agencies in a number of countries, including the Philippines, Malaysia, Laos, South Vietnam, Pakistan, India, Sri Lanka, Thailand, Indonesia, and the United States.[6] On the other hand, a top IRRI officer estimated that less than 30 percent of the more than 200 IRRI trainees to date were engaged in extension training and supervisory work that could effectively utilize their IRRI training.

Sri Lanka, however, stood out as an exceptional case. Sri Lanka had sent a large number of trainees to IRRI and by 1971, with the former head of the IRRI training program as resident adviser, it was rapidly building a broad rice extension training program based on the IRRI model.

The training courses in Sri Lanka began in 1968, soon after four Sri Lanka graduates from the IRRI course returned home. The Inservice Training Institute at Peradeniya began the program in the form of one-week and two-week courses for extension agents, farmers, and other agricultural personnel. Two of the IRRI graduates also organized a mobile training team which traveled to the villages, "bringing new technology to some 50,000 farmers."[7]

Short courses of the type now used in Sri Lanka had first been developed by two rice specialists from IRRI in 1966 when a series of two-week training courses for extension agents were given in Bangladesh (then East Pakistan). Many of the essential features of the full-length IRRI course are maintained in the shorter course. It is, of course, impossible to take the trainees through the steps of a complete crop production cycle or to involve them intimately with applied research projects in the short course. But this deficiency is partially overcome by arranging activitues for small teams of trainees in a series of plots. Some of the plots are prepared and planted in advance, on a staggered schedule, to permit trainees to observe and participate in activities related to later stages of the crop. This way, in a week a trainee can gain a few hours of experience in each of the successive operations involved in crop production. The short courses are considered highly useful in reaching a large number of extension agents and other agricultural personnel with new technology within limited time and resources.

In early 1970 plans were being implemented to cover the 22 districts of Sri Lanka with District Extension Training Centers which would regularly offer short rice production courses to village-level extension agents, farmers, and rural youth. As a first step toward this goal, 22 extension officers were given a two-month intensive training course in Sri Lanka to prepare them for the role of the District Extension Rice Production Specialist.[8]

With the implementation of large-scale irrigation schemes (such as the Walawe Scheme in southern Sri Lanka, where 30,000 acres of fully irrigated riceland have been reclaimed from the jungle, and the Mahaveli Irrigation Scheme in central Sri Lanka, involving about 900,000 acres of land), Sri Lanka will need a larger number of extension agents trained in new production techniques if the full potentialities of the newly reclaimed land are to be realized. The nationwide rice production training courses are expected to meet this demand.[9]

Other Countries

As noted above, IRRI had provided direct help to organize short training courses for extension agents at the Comilla Academy for Rural Development in Bangladesh (then East Pakistan). In 1970, IRRI specialists worked with local staff to train 361 extension agents. A rice research institute with a production training center is now being developed in Bangladesh with technical assistance from IRRI and financial help from the Ford Foundation.

As of late 1971 IRRI was arranging collaboration with the Indonesian government in building an extensive rice research and training program, with financial support from a combination of bilateral assistance agencies. Increasingly effective use may thus be made of Indonesian personnel trained at IRRI.

IRRI collaborated extensively with India in building what by late 1971 had become a strong national rice research system. By contrast, however, it appears that IRRI's training program has had at best only a minimal impact on India's extension system.

A survey of the utilization of 14 trainees from India indicated that the trainees were not systematically used for extension training.[10]

The 14 trainees had been selected from seven state agricultural organizations and from the Central Rice Research Institute. They had not been primarily concerned with the training of extension workers before they went for training, and on their return from IRRI they were again placed in positions where their primary responsibility was not training.

As of July 1970--about two years after the return of the first group of 10 and one year after return of the second group of four--eight returnees in four states were involved on an ad hoc basis in a total of 22 short training courses. The courses involved 497 persons including farmers, village-level workers, other extension personnel and research workers. The eight returnees devoted a total of 247 man-days to the short courses.

The significant point is that there was no systematic plan for using the returnees for training on a continuous basis, and in three states the returnees did not conduct training even on an ad hoc basis.

Donald G. Green reported that plans were being prepared in Andhra Pradesh in 1970 to establish a rice training center to serve the extension workers in the delta area of the state on a continuous basis. The Central Rice Research Institute in Mysore, which had sent two trainees to IRRI in 1968, also submitted a proposal to the government to start a "train-the-trainer" program in rice production patterned after the IRRI course. The trainees

of the Central Institute would presumably conduct similar
training at the state level. If these two plans are
implemented, the utilization of IRRI rice extension
trainees in India would improve. [We have been informed
in July 1972 that the Andhra Pradesh center did get
started in late 1970 and by mid-1972 several groups of
extension workers have been trained using a two-week
short course format modeled after the IRRI course. The
proposal of the Mysore Institute was yet to be approved.]

COSTS AND FINANCE

     The rice production training program's costs are
difficult to estimate with any degree of precision for
several reasons. It is a relatively marginal aspect of
IRRI's total program: it shares certain staff, services
and facilities with the main research program; the training staff itself spends only six months per year on this
activity and performs other duties during the rest of
the year; the training program is not separately costed
and budgeted in IRRI's own regular accounts; some of the
costs are financed by other agencies; and finally, IRRI
itself has made no special analysis of the overall total
or unit costs of this particular activity.
     Nevertheless it was possible, with the help of IRRI's
Treasurer's office, for the ICED team to construct a
reasonable approximation of these costs as of 1971, shown
on Table 15.2. The annual cost for maintaining the small
training staff was US$72,000 in 1971, of which a minimum
of 50 percent (six months) should be charged against the
rice production training program. IRRI allocates US$7,000
overhead (administration, general supplies and services,
and so forth) against the program. Initial capital cost
of the training building plus furniture and equipment is
carried at US$77,000. If amortized arbitrarily over 10
years, this amounts to US$7,700 per annum. General
support of trainees (travel, board and room, allowance
for personal expenditures, and so on, including US$500
for estimated intercountry travel cost) totals roughly
US$1,800 per six months (defrayed by fellowships and
grants from national governments, aid agencies, and others).
Added together and divided by an average of 35 trainees
in the program, the unit cost for the six-month period
works out to US$3,249.
     This estimate, which is essentially of budgetary
costs, is unquestionably on the low side; it makes no
allowance for the part-time contribution of members of
the research staff to the training program, and the allocation of overhead costs seems very modest. It is clear
in any event that the costs would be considerably higher
for a comparable training program that was operated
separately and not as a marginal adjunct of a major research activity.

TABLE 15.2

Estimate of Costs for the IRRI Rice Production
Training Program, 1971

Cost to IRRI	US$	
Fixed Assets:		
Rice production training program building	65,000	
Furniture and equipment	12,000	
	77,000	
Unit cost (assuming 35 trainees per year		
and 10 percent average annual depreciation)		US$ 220
Recurrent instructional costs (per six-month		
course):		
Instructional staff	36,000	
Overhead costs, including administrative		
and supplies	7,000	
	43,000	
Unit cost (with 35 trainees per course)		US$1,229

Maintenance and Support per Trainee (per six-month course)		
Board and lodging	780	
Books, medical expenses, and travel within		
country	220	
Stipend for personal expenses	300	
Total per trainee	1,300	1,300
Travel between home-country and IRRI per		
trainee (estimated average)		500
Total cost per trainee per course		US$3,249

Source: Based on data provided by the International Rice Research Institute, Treasurer's Office, October 1971.

The real costs of the IRRI training program, of course,
are much higher than the budgetary costs shown above, for
they include the opportunity costs involved in diverting
the trainees from their regular work. A proxy measure
of this opportunity cost would be one-half of their regular annual salary back home.

Even excluding these opportunity costs, however, the
cost per IRRI trainee who actually applies this training
in the intended manner after returning home would be on
the order of three to four times the US$3,249 unit cost
estimate shown above, if the full costs of the program
are allocated entirely to these "success" cases.

APPRAISAL AND LESSONS

It would be presumptuous to attempt a full-scale
appraisal of IRRI's training program, including a cost-
benefit test, on the limited evidence that was available
to the ICED team at the time of its investigation and analysis. Nevertheless, the evidence is sufficient to illustrate some basic points that ought to enter into such an
appraisal, to illuminate useful lessons for others, and to
suggest possible ways in which the benefits of such a
program might be further enhanced in relation to the costs.

Pedagogical Effectiveness

There can be little doubt that the combination of the
lecture-discussion method, direct field practice, and practical experience with research and experimentation in the
field--all geared to the various stages of the growth of
a crop--constitutes a highly effective pedagogical approach
compared to more conventional ways of training extension
personnel.

IRRI's unique performance tests have revealed dramatically that most extension officials and even highly trained
researchers are ill-prepared to demonstrate rice production
techniques to the farmer and to help him identify and
remedy such problems as plant diseases. IRRI has also
demonstrated that some of these knowledge deficiencies can
be remedied rather quickly (even in a week or two) for
persons already possessing substantial education, specialized training, and experience.

Its six-month program, however, seeks to achieve much
more than this. It endeavors to develop a deeper understanding of the newer technologies of rice production and
of the techniques for training extension workers who can
communicate such informtion effectively to ordinary farmers.
Direct observation of the program in action leaves little
doubt that the IRRI program is highly effective in achieving these objectives.

The IRRI method of gearing the training content and
experiences to the stages of development of a crop is one
that other extension training programs in the tropics and
subtropics could well heed. It appears, from the experience with short courses in different countries and in IRRI
itself, that a course need not necessarily last the full
duration of a crop cycle. It may be possible in many
situations to stagger the planting of adjacent plots so
that trainees can observe the essential operations required at each stage from land preparation and seeding to
harvest.

The question then arises whether even more of value
might not be accomplished within the relatively long six-

month period of the IRRI training program to strengthen
extension services of the cooperating nations. The content of the program at present concentrates largely on
the techniques of rice production and gives marginal attention at best to such matters as individual farm planning and management, processing and marketing, the economics of rice production as seen by the individual farmer,
and his problems of choosing between straight rice production and mixed cropping. These appear to be important
matters on which many Asian farmers need help, along with
technical advice on production itself.

The ICED researchers found indications (though the
point warrants much fuller investigation) that some of
the IRRI trainees felt that six months was unnecessarily
long for the substance covered. Conceivably, therefore,
though this would need careful consideration, the curriculum might be somewhat broadened and enriched to cover
other important topics, including some of those mentioned
above, on which conventional extension training has been
notoriously weak. If the complaints of the participants
are valid and if it proved feasible to broaden the scope
of the program without prejudice to the present objectives,
IRRI graduates could return home even better equipped to
help strengthen their respective national extension services.

IRRI is in a unique position, because of its special
research capabilities and its involvement in training, to
create and disseminate rich, authoritative, and up-to-date
instructional and informational materials. When properly
adapted to special local conditions, these could be of
great educational value to vast numbers of extension
workers and rice farmers in many countries. IRRI is in
fact engaged in such efforts, for example by preparing
staff lecture notes, films, and other learning materials
for its own trainees which they are encouraged to take
home and apply. With relatively modest additional effort
and cost, IRRI might be able to enlarge its educational
impact by developing a larger flow and wider distribution
of well-designed self-instructional materials on rice
production. The point applies equally to major national
agricultural research institutions with which IRRI is
cooperating.

Improving Benefit-Cost Ratio

IRRI was initially conceived of as a rice research
institute in quest of scientific breakthroughs which, if
achieved, could greatly benefit the poor and huntry masses
of Asia and perhaps other regions as well. As such it was
a classic example of the use of private philanthropic
funds as venture capital in the service of humanity.

Happily this scientific gamble succeeded and in a surprisingly short time touched off a green revolution in rice, parallel to the green revolution in wheat (the result of a similar gamble on research). No one needs to bother trying to calculate the rate-of-return on the investment in IRRI's rice research; it would obviously be an astronomical figure.

But what of the benefit-cost ratio of IRRI's training program, which was added later to the initial research program? Presumably the training program was to enhance the benefit-cost ratio of the research itself, by helping to build a stronger bridge between useful research findings and their practical application by millions of farmers. The potential benefits of such application are so enormous that the unit costs of training may be a minor consideration. The issue hinges mainly on 1) whether the training process itself is relevant, of good quality, and pedagogically effective and 2) whether those who are trained exert strong leverage on the improvement of their agricultural extension services after returning home.

On the first point, as has been stated, the IRRI training program clearly ranks high, though possibly it could be even further improved by broadening its coverage (if time permitted) to give additional attention to concerns of rice farmers other than production technologies and techniques. Conceivably IRRI could also broaden and strengthen the impact of its educational efforts by generating and disseminating many more top-quality training materials.

On the second point (how IRRI graduates utilize their special training after returning home), findings are mixed. It seems ironic that such a distinguished biological research organization would not have undertaken the very modest social science research effort required to keep track of its former trainees when so much was at stake. Somehow the cost-benefit style of thinking that may have entered into the decision to add extension training activity to the research program seems not to have carried over into an assessment of the training program's performance.

If the hunch expressed by IRRI officials in late 1971 was anywhere near correct--that fewer than one-third of the more than 200 former IRRI trainees were actually putting their training to effective use--then clearly there exists a wide margin for improving the benefit-cost ratio of the program. This should not be taken, however, as evidence that the overall benefit-cost ratio thus far has been unfavorable. There is no evidence for making such a judgment. Available evidence does suggest that the IRRI training investment has probably had poor returns thus far in India, but with respect to Sri Lanka and perhaps Indonesia the reverse is probably true. Clearly, a modest investment in a tracer study of IRRI graduates would be warranted.

It should be noted that IRRI officials, particularly
those directly involved in the training program, have all
along been aware of the "wastage" described above. As
early as 1967 an IRRI publication noted that the

> . . . experiences of the early graduates reflect
> problems which must be overcome if an extension
> service is to be fully effective in a developing
> country. A major issue has been the lack of
> finances in the national agencies, making it
> difficult to increase the salaries of the special-
> ists trained, or to provide them with the sup-
> plies, equipment, and travel funds necessary to
> carry out their work. Some graduates have been
> borrowed from their intended assignments to staff
> emergency programs, while others have had dif-
> ficulty gaining acceptance from co-workers and
> supervisors of the kinds of activities in which
> rice extension specialists should engage. When
> their ability to perform was handicapped by a
> lack of logistic or administrative support,
> critics of the training have been quick to point
> out that their behavior or performance hardly
> differed from those who had not been trained.[11]

The "wastage" problem is further underscored by the
results of an ICED questionnaire administered to participants of the IRRI training program in 1971 concerning
their training and employment background and their expectations. (See Table 15.3.) Only 14 of 34 trainees had
been devoting more than 50 percent of their time to extension or extension training in the jobs they held just
prior to coming to IRRI; 15 had been devoting less than
half their time to these activities while 5 had had no
responsibility in the extension field. Moreover, half
of these trainees did not expect to be employed in extension or extension training in the future. Significantly,
more than two-thirds expressed the desire to work in the
extension field after they completed the IRRI course, yet
half did not expect to be assigned to such work.
    In admitting new trainees, IRRI has tried to consider
the functions they would perform on returning home and
has sought commitments from sponsoring governments and
organizations to ensure their appropriate placement and
utilization, but these measures have obviously not been
very effective. The solution clearly lies much less in
IRRI's hands than with the sending governments and employing organizations and their personnel systems. Only when
a government gives priority to overhauling and strengthening its extension services and takes steps toward this end
can IRRI have reasonable assurance that its training
efforts will not be wasted. This is now the situation in
Sri Lanka and Indonesia and may become increasingly the
case in other nations that IRRI is seeking to assist.

TABLE 15.3

Profile of 34 Rice Production Trainees
in the 1971 Course

	Less than 12 years		12 years or more
1. Formal general educational background	5		29
	Less than 2 years	2-4 years	Over 4 years
2. Formal agricultural education background	1	17	16
	No training	1 year or less	Over 1 year
3. Inservice extension training	5	27	2
	Nil	Less than 50%	Over 50%
4. Time devoted to extension and training activities in the last job assignment	5	15	14
	Extension or Extension Training	Rice Research	Other
5. Jobs to which trainees are expected to go back	17	10	7
	Extension or Extension Training	Rice Research	Other
6. Jobs to which trainees desire to go back	23	7	4

Source: Anonymous response to ICED questionnaire.

Opportunities for Research Institutions

Anyone acquainted with the serious shortcomings and often disheartening struggles of most extension services to improve their performance can only be encouraged by the initiative taken by IRRI to assist them. Not only IRRI but other important agricultural research centers,

such as those now well-established in India, are in a
unique position to use their prestige and capabilities
to help build more effective connections between research
and application. In most situations it is neither feasible
nor appropriate for these research institutions to assume
full responsibility for the extension function. But
through cooperation with those who do bear such responsibilities, research institutes can help increase the ultimate effectiveness of their own research efforts. They
can help in various ways (as IRRI is doing) to improve the
preservice and inservice training of extension agents;
they can help greatly to improve the transmission of useful
and timely technical messages to practicing farmers; and,
with proper feedback channels and by bringing research
closer to the farmers themselves they can contribute more
fully to solving the current and emergent problems of
farmers. This in the last analysis is the raison d'être
of agricultural research.

Research organizations that have concentrated their
efforts with considerable success on a single commercial
crop, however, may soon find themselves obliged to broaden
their focus to take account of alternative crops. Rice
is a striking case in point. Almost all of the Asian
nations not already self-sufficient in rice are striving
to become so as quickly as possible, and most are making
rapid progress. This is bound to bring about major adjustments in supply-demand and price relationships in both
internal and external markets, and hence in the incentive
structures of rice farmers. Their interest lies not in
maximizing their rice yields per se but in maximizing
their net income, and as marketing conditions change, many
farmers may find that the best way to do this is by shifting or diversifying their crops. At that stage (which is
already upon some Asian farmers) they will need new kinds
of help from research and extension services. Unless
these services are dynamic and adaptable, the practical
value of their help to farmers and to the whole nation
will diminish. Aware of these prospects, IRRI was already experimenting in 1971 with short-term courses on
mixed cropping.

There is another way in which a research institution
such as IRRI might contribute to the improvement of extension services. On several occasions IRRI has hosted
regional meetings to discuss agricultural research
questions of mutual concern. If the appropriate authorities and experts in a few countries concerned with
strengthening extension services were interested in a
similar exchange, IRRI, in cooperation with national research institutions and agricultural universities, might
be an effective convener of occasional, informal get-
togethers for this purpose.

NOTES

1.   Francis C. Byrnes and William G. Golden, Jr., <u>Changing the</u>
<u>"Change Agent"--A Step Toward Increased Rice Yields</u> (Manila: The
International Rice Research Institute, September 30, 1967), p. 2.

2.   Vernon E. Ross, "The Evolution of the IRRI Rice Production
Training Program" (Paper delivered at the Annual Rice Research Con-
ference at the International Rice Research Institute, Los Baños,
Laguna, Philippines, April 19-23, 1974), p. 2.

3.   Byrnes and Golden, op. cit.

4.   International Rice Research Institute (IRRI), Office of Rice
Production Training and Research, "Project Review," mimeographed (Los
Baños, Laguna, Philippines, February 9, 1971).

5.   Byrnes and Golden, op. cit.

6.   Ross, op. cit., p. 3.

7.   William G. Golden, Jr., "Rice Production (And Other) Training
Programs in Ceylon" (Paper delivered at the Annual Rice Research
Conference at the International Rice Research Institute, Los Baños,
Laguna, Philippines, April 20-24, 1970), p. 2.

8.   Ibid.

9.   Ibid.

10.   Donald G. Green, "Rice Production Training--The Experience
of Fourteen Returnees from the International Rice Research Institute,"
mimeographed (New Delhi: Ford Foundation, September 1970).

11.   Byrnes and Golden, op. cit., p. 7.

**TANZANIA:
AN EDUCATIONAL
PROGRAM FOR
COOPERATIVES**
Sven Grabe

*Support and encouragement of the development of cooperatives is
the declared policy of many governments of developing countries.
The cooperative educational system of Tanzania was included as a
case study in the ICED research on nonformal education for rural
development for two reasons. First, Tanzania has built up a comprehensive system of cooperative education which is now providing information and new educational opportunities for the rank and file, the
elected officers, and the staff of the movement. Second, cooperatives have been accorded a central place in the national development process of Tanzania. For instance, the entire agricultural
production system is ultimately to be run by producers' cooperatives
handling all the managerial and commercial needs of agricultural
production outside the subsistence sector and also the distribution
and sale of consumer goods.*

*This paper is primarily based on an analysis of a great number
of reports, studies, and other papers which have been produced by the
Cooperative Education Centre and the Cooperative College in Tanzania
over the past few years. This analysis was supplemented by direct
observation during a field mission by an ICED team in October and
November 1971.*

INTRODUCTION

The system of cooperative education in Tanzania,
managed jointly by the National Government (primarily the
Ministry of Agriculture, Food and Cooperatives) and the
cooperative movement (represented by the Cooperative Union
of Tanganyika and its affiliated organizations), constitutes a comprehensive approach to the total training requirements of the system of cooperatives in mainland Tanzania.

In brief outline the cooperative movement in Tanzania
is composed of what are termed <u>primary societies</u>--which

may be producers', marketing, savings and credit, or consumers' societies. These are members of regional unions,
which in turn are affiliated to the Cooperative Union of
Tanganyika (CUT), which is at the organizational apex of
the movement. Unions and societies are registered with,
and controlled by, a Commissioner for Cooperative Development in the Ministry of Agriculture, Food and Cooperatives.

The Ministry, the CUT, and the unions employ a large
number of professional staff. The individual societies
normally employ at least one staff member, a secretary.
In a marketing society the secretary's main functions
are to receive, weigh, and record the products delivered
to the society's godowns (storehouses), to keep books on
the produce received, stored, and sold by the society,
and to make payments to the members. In larger societies
he may have assistant secretaries to help him, and members
may also do some voluntary or paid work for the society.
Management responsibility is vested in the chairman of
the society and the committee, normally consisting of ten
members (committeemen) elected by the general meeting of
the society.

The cooperative education system is composed of three
major parts: 1) the Cooperative College, which performs
staff college functions for personnel employed in the
movement and in the government administrative services
which control and supervise the cooperatives in the country; 2) the Cooperative Education Centre (CEC), which is
concerned mainly with the initial training of cooperative
functionaries, with the training of chairmen, committeemen, and members of primary societies, and with the dissemination to them of information on cooperative principles and practices; 3) the cooperative education wings,
union education secretaries, and zonal education secretaries,[1] who carry out the principal field operations in
the system.

The Cooperative College sponsors a wide range of
courses--ranging from a few weeks of full-time instruction to over two years of combined college and on-the-job
training--for the initial and further training of senior-
and middle-level staff in the Cooperative Department of
the Ministry and in the national and regional unions.
The college also provides courses for the advanced training of cooperative secretaries and other full-time staff
employed by the primary societies. All these courses are
residential. The college has complete classroom and dormitory facilities at Moshi, in the Kilimanjaro area of
Northern Tanzania.

The Cooperative Education Centre--also located at
Moshi in buildings shared with the college--runs a comprehensive correspondence course program covering the
basic elements of cooperative activities. These correspondence courses are designed primarily for the initial

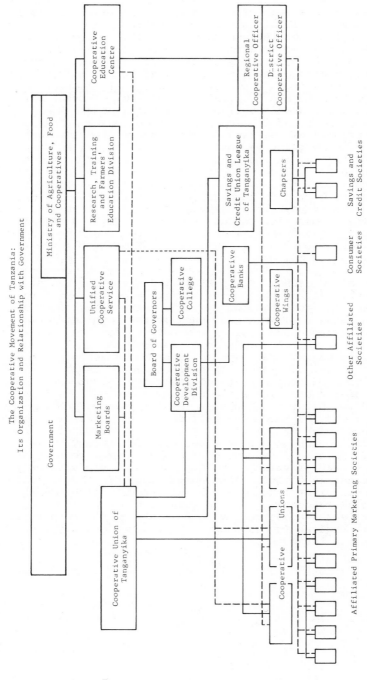

FIGURE 16.1

The Cooperative Movement of Tanzania:
Its Organization and Relationship with Government

*The services provided by the National Co-op Bank are to be taken over by the National Bank of Commerce.

———— Lines of Organization

‑‑‑‑‑‑‑ Lines of Jurisdiction

training, education, and information of the staff, committeemen, and members of primary societies. CEC activities are closely linked with the activities of the Cooperative College since successful completion of correspondence courses is an entry requirement in several residential courses. The CEC staff also designs radio programs and supporting printed material, and it participates in the broadcasting; it provides educational material for the journal of the cooperative movement and other printed material for use in various educational programs.

The Boards of Governors of the college and the center are composed of the same persons, drawn from the government, the cooperative movement, and political and educational circles in the country. The director is the same for both the college and the center--a senior official seconded from the Division of Cooperative Development. The staff of the college and the center, although employed on different payrolls, help in the work of both.

The cooperative education wings, eleven in number in 1971, are the decentralized regional arms of the Cooperative Education Centre. They cooperate with the unions and help the union education secretaries develop cooperative education in their member societies; they organize regional courses in which staff and elected officials from several unions and their affiliated societies participate; and they take on specific tasks in a number of adult education campaigns, such as the combined radio-correspondence group program preparing for the 10th anniversary of the independence of Tanganyika.

This educational program is being implemented in a country that has around 12 million people inhabiting an area of more than 360,000 square miles (about twice the size of France) with a per capita income of less than US$100. More than 90 percent of the population are living off the land, and half the GNP derives from agriculture, with 60 percent of agricultural production belonging to the subsistence sector. Illiteracy rates are high: around 90 percent of the adult rural population cannot read or write. The population is predominantly Bantu but is divided among a multitude of tribal groups with different languages. Swahili and English are the official languages. In the rural areas Swahili is spoken, or at least understood, by a majority of the male population. English is known by a small minority only, mostly living in the towns.

AN OVERVIEW OF
THE COOPERATIVE EDUCATION SYSTEM

Historical Background

The beginnings of a cooperative movement in Tanzania
date back to the mid-1920s when native planters' associations were formed in the Kilimanjaro and West Lake
areas by smallholder coffee growers. There was no legislation on cooperatives in the territory at the time.
From a hesitant start with only a few scores of members
in each primary society, the planters' associations grew
with some government support during the following two
decades; by 1952 the number of registered primary societies had reached 172 and unions had been formed in several
regions. The growth rate further increased during the
1950s, and on the eve of independence in 1961 there were
857 societies grouped together in 34 unions.
Most of these societies and unions were primarily
concerned with the processing and marketing of export
crops--notably coffee, cotton, and tobacco. Many of them
also carried out bulk purchasing of seeds, fertilizers,
and other commodities needed by the growers. The societies and unions worked in competition with private traders
and processors and, although they enjoyed considerable
government support, did not have a trade monopoly. The
vast majority of their members were smallholders with
only a few acres of land planted in export crops; the
larger plantation owners were normally not members of
these unions.
After independence the government embarked upon a
crash program for expanding the membership and functions
of the existing cooperatives and for extending the cooperative movement into regions where it had not yet taken
root. The number of cooperative societies increased
dramatically from 857 in 1961, to 1,362 in 1964, to 1,518
in 1965, reaching 1,737 by 1969.
The marketing of agricultural commodities was brought
under the complete control of marketing boards. The most
important of these was the National Agricultural Products
Board, which started operations in 1963 and appointed the
regional unions as its sole agents. A "single channel
marketing system" had thus been created with the unions
and societies as regional and local organs displacing
the private traders.
The sudden transition meant that there was not enough
time for careful training of staff, committee chairmen,
and members, whose duties and responsibilities had been
profoundly changed and substantially broadened almost
overnight. The system soon began to crack under these
new burdens. A government committee, reviewing the situa-

tion in early 1966, listed a number of defects in the
functioning of the unions and societies, resulting mainly
from insufficient training of staff and members, and
recommended that steps be taken rapidly to remedy the
situation.

The recommendations of the committee led to two important decisions relating to the staffing of the cooperative movement: a Unified Cooperative Service Commission
was established to deal with all personnel and career
questions of the staff of both unions and societies; and
steps were taken to improve the training of all staff employed by or concerned with cooperative societies and
unions.

The facilities for cooperative training existing at
the time of independence were clearly insufficient for
the rapid expansion of the cooperative structure. Cooperative inspectors of the government had been trained mainly at the East African School of Cooperation at Nairobi,
Kenya, an institution created by the colonial government
in 1931. The school (really a college) also trained staff
for the unions, but had no facilities for training lower-
level staff for the societies.

A school of cooperation designed mainly to provide
training for primary society secretaries had been set up
in 1957 at Mzumbe. This school had provided training for
350 secretaries in the five-year period between 1957 and
1962 but it was not large enough to cope with the new
needs and increased demands for staff training at the
level of the societies.

A first step toward consolidation and development of
the cooperative education system was taken in 1964 when
the Cooperative College was set up at Moshi. The Mzumbe
school was incorporated into this new institution.

The Cooperative College Act of 1964 is one of the
foundations on which the whole system of cooperative education in Tanzania was built. A second foundation stone
was the 1966 report of the above-mentioned special committee, which formulated some of the immediate objectives
of cooperative education. The Arusha Declaration of 1967
provided the long-term perspective for cooperative education in the country.

The cooperative education system in Tanzania as it
stood in 1971 had three principal tasks to perform in
close cooperation with the government cooperative service,
the cooperative movement, and the main political party of
the country, the Tanzanian African National Union (TANU):

1. to train staff for employment in the societies,
   the unions, and the government department concerned
2. to inform, educate, and train chairmen, committeemen, and members of the primary societies
3. to assist in changing the pattern of the coopera-

tive movement along the lines set out in the
Arusha Declaration--notably to speed cooperative
organization of production in Ujamaa villages.[2]

Educational Programs

The objectives and policies of cooperative education
have thus been determined in light of the specific Tanzanian situation and the long-term policies of transforming the society on the basis of socialist self-reliance.
The programs and techniques applied in cooperative education, however, have borrowed heavily from British pre-
cedents and Scandinavian educational patterns and practices. From its inception, the Cooperative College received much assistance from the Loughborough Cooperation
College in the United Kingdom and many of its staff went
there for training. In 1966 the Government of Tanzania
requested assistance from the Nordic countries (Denmark,
Finland, Norway, and Sweden) for reinforcing the existing
institutions of cooperative training and for developing
their programs. A Swedish expert was put in charge of
the cooperative college; Scandinavian personnel participated in both the college and the Cooperative Education
Centre in the development of new training courses. Scandinavian experts also shared the work of the cooperative
education wings with their Tanzanian colleagues and contributed to the various member education campaigns launched
through the wings and the radio stations in Tanzania.
All levels of staff and participants in cooperatives
are covered in the cooperative education program:

1. The Cooperative College provides long-term training for new entrants into the Government Cooperative Service and into full-time employment in the
   unions and the societies.
2. The college also provides fuller short-term training and upgrading for other professional staff
   in the government and the movement.
3. The Cooperative Education Centre provides initial
   training for full-time and part-time employees
   in the movement and for committee chairmen and
   committeemen in primary societies.
4. The Cooperative Education Centre also provides
   material and courses for the continuing information and education of staff, elected officers,
   and members of the societies.

MEMBER EDUCATION AND BASIC TRAINING FOR STAFF

The main target of the Cooperative Education Centre
is the active membership of the primary societies. The
center provides syllabi and materials for one-day meetings for the rank and file members, radio broadcasts and
correspondence courses for the more active members and
committeemen; five-day study sessions for working committeemen and chairmen; and longer study programs for
cooperative secretaries and other full-time staff employed
by the societies. These, briefly characterized, are the
principal means by which the Cooperative Education Centre
tries to consolidate and improve the cooperative movement.
However, the center does not run the courses; its principal role is to design the program, furnish the models and
the materials, and monitor the activities. Course management is in the hands of the regional wings and the union
education secretaries; and group study is controlled by
the secretaries and elected officers of the societies.
The cooperative education wings, noted above as decentralized regional arms of the CEC, are normally made
up of two professional staff (with offices in or near the
cooperative union in the main town of the region) who
travel some 20,000 miles a year into the remotest villages
of Tanzania with a Landrover or Landcruiser, a tape recorder, and a film projector.
The description below does not attempt a complete
coverage of all activities of the Cooperative Education
Centre and the wings. Emphasis is placed on programs
that have been developed in the past few years and that
may be considered representative of recent developments,
or as innovations in approach that have more than a local
interest.

Educating the Rank and File

A member education campaign was started on 1 September 1970, and continued for three months until the end of
November. It was the first of its kind and made use of
one-day meetings as the principal means of spreading the
message, reinforced by radio broadcasts, newspaper and
magazine articles, posters and other illustrated materials. An estimated 25,000 members, selected for their
active interest in the work of their society, participated
in one or more of the sessions held in their villages or
in the neighboring marketplace.
The plan to launch a major campaign for members was
developed after President Nyerere declared 1970 as "Adult
Education Year" and asked all educational and political
organizations in Tanzania to undertake mass education

campaigns for adults during that year. Lack of field
staff necessitated limiting the campaign to the regions
in which wings were already functioning. For the same
reason a large number of outside collaborators were
drafted to help with the campaign: 13 union education
secretaries, 14 zonal education secretaries, 48 TANU
officials, cooperative officers of the government, and
cooperative inspectors of the unions. The campaign
centered on three main subjects:

1. the marketing of agricultural produce
2. ujamaa (socialist) villages
3. the meaning and responsibilities of membership
   in a cooperative society

A comprehensive guide for these subjects was prepared for
the use of regional campaign organizers and those secretaries in the various unions and societies who would be
directly involved. This syllabus arranged the subject
material in three stages to be taught in September, October, and November respectively. Each subject was to be
covered in part at each session. There was to be one
session each month in each society chosen to participate
in the campaign.

Each wing was asked to select 20 societies for participation. Each committeeman (normally there are ten
committeemen in each society) was to bring five members
to the meeting; thus the meeting in each society would
ideally consist of 60 persons. The committeemen were
instructed to bring the same members to all three
sessions.

Both these ideas--arranging monthly meetings in a
series and charging committeemen with selecting partici-
pants--were new and untried in Tanzania. They were
adopted to help rejuvenate interest in the cooperative
society meetings and to change their nature. Such meetings in the past had often degenerated to complaint
sessions where the same problems were aired year after
year and follow-up action seldom taken.

The radio was mobilized both to spur interest and to
provide part of the information to the members and committeemen. Local meetings were announced in the broadcasts, and 22 programs were produced that reinforced the
main topics of the campaign. The programs also gave
progress reports on how the campaign was developing in
various parts of the country. These campaign broadcasts
went on the air for 15 minutes each Thursday afternoon
and were repeated on Saturday afternoon.

Print was also utilized for the campaign. Five
campaign articles were planned and published in Gazeti
la Ushirika, a monthly magazine published by the Cooperative Union of Tanganyika and distributed to all member
unions and societies. An introductory article appeared

in August, three articles dealing with the main topics during the campaign, and one follow-up article in December summing up results and experience from the campaign. A three-color poster and a one-page picture-story were also used to publicize the campaign.

In the first month of the campaign 12,249 members of cooperative societies attended 169 one-day courses and got the campaign off to a promising start; in several regions participation was well above what had been hoped for. The following months brought some disappointment: in October only 7,681 members participated in 112 courses, and in November participation fell to 4,679 in 91 courses.

The wings were asked to make a detailed report of their observations of the campaign, especially of difficulties encountered, and a poll was taken with 19 zonal secretaries replying to a wide range of evaluatory questions. The information received suggested some do's and don'ts in organizing mass education campaigns in a predominantly traditional, rural country.

The low participation for November was explained mainly by three factors. The Ramadan fast kept many Moslem members away from meetings. So did the political activities of many committeemen and members during the pre-election campaigns which went on during the same period. Finally, spending a whole day away from their farms was impractical for many smallholders during the harvesting season in October and November. Harvesting coffee, which begins earlier, probably influenced participation in September in the coffee growing areas. It proved difficult to get the information to all members that the meeting would take place. Moreover, the rule that each committeeman should select five participants to take part in all three meetings met with silent opposition; many of them brought different people to each of the three meetings. Local events had some impact on attendance and weddings and funerals in which village leaders were involved reduced attendance to zero in some cases.

The field organizers answering the opinion poll were generally positive about the planning and preparatory work for the campaign done by the center. They agreed on the importance of such campaigns and on the choice of key topics. Although they found the poster difficult to explain to the members because of its abstract language, they did like it and found in the very need to explain it a positive contribution to the campaign. The picture story on the other hand had been easy to understand, according to most of those returning the questionnaire, and had served a useful purpose. Few of the respondents had listened to more than a third of the radio programs-- which nearly all of them said were interesting. But they were not so sure that the radio programs had contributed much to the campaign. They were also rather doubtful about the value of the articles in Gazeti la Ushirika:

nine out of nineteen said the impact was "reasonable,"
six termed it "very little," and four had no comment.

Training the Member Elite and Staff

If the large-scale campaign is the preferred means of
the CEC for reaching large numbers with a basic message
in a short time, the correspondence courses constitute a
fundamental part of all long-term educational action and
are expected to have the most solid impact on the efficiency and overall effectiveness of the societies. The
potential clientele for the broadly aimed, basic correspondence courses is the total membership of all cooperative societies, but the target population is that group
of active members (about 20 to 30 persons in each society,
including the 10 committeemen) called the member elite.

The courses are the link between the training of active members (who are invited to take the courses on a
voluntary basis) and the functionaries of the societies
and unions (who must complete several courses to qualify
for training at the Cooperative College). The staff
study these courses individually, while the members, many
of whom are illiterate, read the "letters" and formulate
the answers in group study. A group normally consists of
10 to 15 members, many of whom are chairmen and committeemen.

Eight correspondence courses had been produced by the
end of 1970, entitled as follows:

- Duties of the Committee of a Primary Society
- Primary Societies
- Basic Economics
- Ujamaa Villages and Principles
- Consumer Cooperation: the Members, the Committee
  and the Society
- Elementary Bookkeeping and Cooperative's Account-
  ancy
- Bookkeeping for a Consumer Cooperative Society with
  One Shop
- Savings and Credit Societies

A complete correspondence course from the CEC is made
up of a varying number of "letters," plus a general introduction and a how-to-study guide for students. The letters are mimeographed or printed and contain between 24
and 72 pages of (in most cases) single-spaced text, illustrated by occasional drawings and a few photographs.
Each letter ends with a set of questions to be answered
by the individual student or the study group.

The text of all courses for both members and staff is
down-to-earth and practical; it repeatedly invites the

reader/student to reflect on the operation of his own
primary society and on how he could improve it. In other
words, the text is action-oriented; the objective is to
improve the ability of both members and staff to control
the business of the society. A related objective is to
improve the basis for mutual confidence within the society,
particularly between members who are not engaged in the
daily activities and the staff and committeemen who manage
the operations. Correspondence courses may be taken in
individual or group study. Most chairmen and committeemen, many of whom are illiterate, take the courses in
group study. A group normally consists of 10 to 15 members, who select their own leader, and another member to
take down the answers as formulated by the group.

The Major Correspondence Courses

    "Duties of the Committee of a Primary Society" course.
This is designed primarily for the training of chairmen
and committeemen in the societies. These and the active
members would normally begin by studying the four letters
of the course on the duties of the committee and of the
primary society. In this course letter one explains how
the groups are to study and what is meant by group action.
It goes on to give a brief history of the cooperative
movement and explains the basic rules applying to the work
of the cooperative society. Letter two explains the respective roles of members, committeemen, and staff of a
cooperative society. Letter three explains in more detail what are the responsibilities of a committee and how
it should organize its work and exercise control over the
society. Letter four, finally, explains the legislation
on cooperatives in Tanzania.
    "Basic Economics" course. The Basic Economics course
consists of eight letters. Letter one begins by describing the economic situation of a small farm family, the
materials they are likely to buy for their business, and
their income from selling the produce. This example is
applicable to a number of elementary mathematical operations relating to a small farmer's household and farm
accounts. Letter two discusses the use of agricultural
proceeds for buying clothes in the family, paying for
children's education, buying various consumer goods, and
paying taxes. Letters three and four are devoted to
various ways in which a farm family may improve its way
of life by using its money judiciously. Letter five discusses relationships between buyers and sellers in a free
market and explains the role of the middleman, the cost
of credit, and the hazards of bargaining as compared to
a system of fixed prices. Letter six explains the role
of banks in a society and why they can pay interest on
savings. Letter seven deals with the cooperative banks
and cooperative savings and credit societies. Letter
eight is devoted to consumers' stores.

"Ujamaa Villages and Principles" course. This course begins by explaining the importance to the country and the individual of having everyone work and work together. It explains the principle of self-reliance in an Ujamaa (socialist) society. In the second letter these principles are applied to the establishment and development of the Ujamaa collective villages--the producer's cooperatives. The subsequent three letters discuss the leadership and organization of village work, the establishment and implementation of the program and work plan of the village, and the use of the proceeds from products sold by the village. The last of these letters concludes with a discussion on the importance of gradually building up the capital of the village so that it can buy the vehicles and other collectively owned equipment it needs.

"Primary Societies" course. The Primary Societies course, which is designed mainly for staff training purposes, is longer and more demanding. It begins with a 29-page letter describing the basic principles of cooperation, various types of societies, and the national cooperative structure. At the end of the letter students are asked to formulate written answers to questions on the text.

The second letter (21 pages) considers a society's funds, explaining the nature of revenues, expenditure, and capital, budgeting and accounting, and invites the student to study his own society's record over the past few years. Letter three (42 pages) discusses in some detail the meaning of membership in a society and explains the share certificate, the membership register, the purpose of meetings, the voting rights and procedure, the standard agenda items (including provisions for education and training of staff and members), and how the minutes of meetings are prepared and what they should contain. Letter four (18 pages) provides information on how a committee should work, and the role of the chairman, the subcommittees, and committeemen in charge of particular aspects of the society's activities.

Letter five (36 pages) describes various procedures for planning the work of the society and handling the produce: receiving, weighing, grading, filling out the receipts and making advance payments, storing and controlling stock, and handling transport and sales. Letters six to nine cover the various bookkeeping and accounts operations of a primary society, explaining the procedure for the annual accounts and establishing a balance sheet. These four letters together make up a text of more than 170 pages with numerous examples and exercises. Letter ten (66 pages), the last, explains the handling of funds and capital in a society and ends with several questions relating to the management of the paid-in capital.

Enrollment in the Courses

Up to 1969, total enrollment in the correspondence courses had increased steadily since the first courses were published in 1965. During 1969 alone there were 1,882 new enrollees in 469 new groups. In 1970 the total number of individual students enrolled was 2,228--a normal increase over the previous year--but the number of new groups dropped to 355, a decrease of 114 from the 1969 enrollments of new students and groups.

The reasons for this decrease in group enrollments are not altogether clear. There was speculation that a saturation point had been reached in the societies--the cumulative total of 1,338 study groups indicates that more than the half of all societies and nearly all the marketing societies had had members enrolled in a study group. Approximately half of the societies were not touched by the activities of the wings until very recently and thus had less incentive than the others to encourage and promote enrollment and supervise studies. There are other reasons too. Several wings preferred to concentrate on getting the existing study groups to finish their courses--most groups take over a year to complete their first course, the Committeeman's course of four letters. Moreover, no new courses were launched between 1968 and December 1970 (when the Ujamaa course was published), and many groups and individual students had already completed all the courses of interest to them.

Staff of the CEC and the wings were unanimous in stating there was no lessening in member interest for studies. If a saturation point had been reached, it was temporary in their view, and preliminary to a new spurt in the enrollment.

Visits to societies at work give a general impression that the active members are eagerly seeking more knowledge and improved skill, but they are experiences difficult to describe. There are likely to be ten or fifteen men and women, young and old, seated in the small, dark office of the society or in the shadow of a tree on a farm, letter in hand, the group organizer reading sentence by sentence from the letter. Their clothes may be dirty and torn. The language may be difficult to understand and each sentence may need to be translated, discussed, and repeated several times before its meaning is fully understood by all group members or even a majority of them. Each question to be sent back to the CEC with an answer may have to be discussed, rephrased, and examined from different points of view for hours before the group is satisfied that the correct answer has been found. It is a slow process that explains many of the delays in determining completion rates. What impresses the observer is the thoroughness, the application, and the quest for knowledge that characterize the work of the group. The

observer is submitted to serious questioning about what
cooperatives are like in his country. How many are members? How are they organized? Do members come to their
meetings? Are they producers' or marketing cooperatives?
Are fraud and corruption a current problem? Such are the
endless questions that members in cooperative study groups
on the slopes of Kilimanjaro or on the sunbaked plains
of the Dodoma plateau ask the casual visitor.

Dropout rates for individual students are low compared to those generally found in commercial correspondence courses, many of which have a dropout rate as high
as 80 to 90 percent. Only about half of the Tanzanian
cooperative students give up before completing the last
lesson. But many individuals and groups are at this
writing only half-way through their courses, so the present recorded dropout rate may be little more than an
estimate. Between 1965 and 1969, only 1,748 individual
students of nearly 6,100 enrolled (about 28 percent)
actually finished a course and received their certificate.
Even if 50 percent (or 3,000) had in fact dropped out,
there would still be 1,300 students working on a course
that they began more than one year earlier. The completion rates are about the same for the groups: 1,338
groups have enrolled since 1966, and 297 (22 percent) had
received their certificate by the end of 1970.

Curiously, the completion rates for the cooperative
inspector trainees are not much better. They should be
the best educated and the best motivated among the correspondence students, as they qualify for the Cooperative
College course only after they have completed two (four
since 1969) correspondence courses. Only 206 inspector
trainees (of 437 enrolled) had completed the "Primary
Societies" course by the end of 1970; 165 had completed
the "Elementary Bookkeeping" course; and only three, of
112 enrolled in 1970, had managed to finish the "Consumer
Cooperation" course.

In absolute figures, the Cooperative Education Centre
hoped to enroll in their course offerings some 25 persons (the member elite) for each of 1,737 societies or,
in round numbers, between 40,000 and 45,000 persons. The
total numbers participating so far cannot be computed on
the basis of existing information, since group participation numbers vary and many groups have not finished
their courses, and dropout rates cannot be calculated.
It may be said, however, that the 1,338 groups that enrolled between 1 January 1965 and 31 December 1970 represent more than 15,000 active members in the cooperative societies, or about one-third of the target population for all courses. It may further be said that the
234 groups that had completed the basic course of four
letters by the end of 1970 represented some 3,000 active
members, most of whom were actual or potential committeemen, that is some 15 percent of all committeemen in the
cooperative movement of Tanzania.

Trends and Policies for the Future

The ambitious, comprehensive campaigns addressed to
the rank and file and the slow, grinding study-in-depth
correspondence courses for the more active members and
committeemen have become the central programs of the CEC
as far as member education is concerned. They are gradually replacing the less organized problem-oriented day
sessions for members (which the campaigns were designed
to do) as well as the shorter oral courses for committeemen and chairmen which the CEC and the unions organized
in the societies in previous years.

The trend away from an ad hoc approach has been reinforced by the adoption of longer-term educational
policies within the movement and by the government to help
develop a comprehensive approach to adult education
throughout the country. The informational job is largely
completed; members of most societies are now well aware
of the aims and objectives of the educational drive of
the movement. The situation differs somewhat between the
areas in which the wings have had a direct influence,
where long-term objectives can be pursued more systematically, and the peripheral ones, where the level of educational awareness may not yet have been raised sufficiently. Still, the general trend seems clear, and the initial
period of promotion is over for the most part.

There is also a trend toward building up a permanent
structure for the societies and unions themselves to take
care of the education of members and committeemen. All
unions have their own education secretaries; many societies
have nominated a committeeman or an assistant secretary
to take special responsibility for educational activities;
and all unions and many societies are setting aside a
proportion of the proceeds for educational purposes.
Gradually a structural basis for long-term educational
action is being established.

The education policy relating to members and elected
officers of the cooperative movement has been formulated
recently in the second Five-Year Development Plan of
Tanzania (1969 to 1974) and is further explained in the
Cooperative Education Five-Year Plan and the Handbook on
Cooperative Education, which was distributed to most
societies in 1970. The National Development Plan stresses
that the current plan period is a transitional one, during
which members and officers of cooperative societies need
to be made aware of and to understand the implications of
the shift made in economic and social policy: cooperative
education should continue to improve the marketing services
of the cooperatives; however, new growth of the movement--
and hence the thrust of cooperative education--should be
shifted in the direction of production societies and multipurpose cooperatives.

The Cooperative Education Plan (1969-1974) distinguishes three groups within the society: the majority of members, the member elite, and the committeemen. The plan provides for action relating to nonmembers and future members. As for nonmembers the CEC should supply basic educational and information material to political leaders, the national service, and government officials so that all can contribute to enrolling all farmers in the cooperatives. Young people are to be prepared as future members of a society of cooperative action at school.

Education of the majority of members will continue to take place primarily through campaigns consisting of one-day meetings, cooperative film shows, and weekly cooperative broadcasts. The member elite--defined as those who keep themselves informed, who attend meetings, who read papers (if they can), and who participate in study groups--are to be served mainly through brief courses organized by the unions and through long-term educational activities, mainly correspondence studies.

ADVANCED STAFF TRAINING

Staff training for the primary societies and the unions--and to a certain extent for the government service-- is a joint function of the Cooperative Education Centre and the Cooperative College. The division of responsibility between the two is essentially that education and training at home and in the field is done under the supervision and with the support of the center while residential courses are organized by the college.

The staff training function of the two educational institutions serves the whole range of staff employed by the primary societies, the unions, and the Cooperative Division. The center and the college together function as a training department of the cooperative system--understood in its widest sense as comprising all societies at all levels--and of the public controlling machinery.

The program of education and training for cooperative staff is gradually being developed to meet the requirements of a career service, in which the course for secretaries of primary societies and the trainee cooperative inspector program are base programs with the remaining courses designed as upgrading training for career purposes.

Training of Primary Society Secretaries

The course for secretaries in primary societies has evolved over the years from an essentially academic course

at the Cooperative College into a comprehensive training
program with many components. Since 1 January 1969 all
candidates wishing to enroll at the college first have to
qualify at home by completing the Primary Societies and
Basic Economics correspondence courses described in the
previous section. They are also taken into a two-week
orientation course before enrollment in the college course.

The college course lasts for eight weeks. It covers
in more depth the various subjects included in the Primary
Societies course and offers opportunities for participants
to apply the principles taught to a wide range of selected
cases and problems. The studies are largely based on
group work and case-study methods, applying principles
to working out solutions to problems that secretaries have
actually met in their societies.

The potential clientele consisting of primary society
staff is estimated by the director of the college to be
between 3,000 and 6,000 persons, depending upon how the
clientele is defined and how many assistant secretaries
and part-time employees of the societies will ultimately
be included. As seen from the numbers of individual students taking correspondence courses (a total of 6,100)--
most of whom are employees of the societies--total enrollment has already exceeded the estimate. Even when dropout rates and the fact that some students have taken
multiple courses are taken into account, it is likely
that at the level of society secretary the center is
rapidly approaching full coverage of its potential clientele with at least one course.

Data are not available from 1970 or later on the
actual enrollments, dropouts, and completions at this
level. F. Dubell, in a study of the training of secretaries, gives the following figures for the period 1 January 1965 to 22 July 1969 relating to the Primary Societies
correspondence course:[3]

Total number of students enrolled to date	3,487
Estimated number of active students	1,475
Students who have completed the course	376

By the end of 1970 the total number of completions
had risen to 820 for the Primary Societies course. The
rapid rise in the number of completions in the previous
one and a half years is explained by two main factors:
the larger number of enrollments in the 1968-1970 period
and the fact that completing the course was made a prerequisite for acceptance as student at the college on
1 January 1969.

Data available at the college indicate that by the
end of 1970 the center and the college in combination had
achieved the following: more than half of all secretaries
of marketing societies had completed a full cycle of train-

ing consisting of one correspondence course, a two-week
regional course, and an eight-week course at the college.
A few hundred more had completed more than one correspondence course. Moreover, the short courses for secretaries
organized by the wings had covered most of the secretaries
of primary societies in their respective regions. In
addition union education secretaries and many secretaries
in primary societies had been trained as study leaders or
had gone through other courses designed to help them serve
the membership better. Almost all secretaries and their
assistants had at least begun studying the basic correspondence course for secretaries.

Training for Union and Government Staff

The two basic courses provided by the center for new
employees in the unions and the government Division of
Cooperative Development are the Basic Inspectors course
and the Management and Administration course. Most other
courses are provided for promotion and updating purposes
or constitute updating training in new requirements or
procedures in the unions or in the educational field organization. Also, the College serves as the home for seminars
and meetings on questions concerning cooperative education
and the cooperative movement. Participants from other
countries often join such discussions.

The Basic Inspectors course serves to illustrate
the contents and methods applied in the initial training
of cooperative staff at professional level.

Total duration of inspector training is a minimum of
two years, and the minimum educational level for recruitment is completion of Form 4. The method of training is
basically an apprenticeship, with block release periods
of study interrupting practical experience and training
on the job. Study by correspondence reinforces field
experience and college training.

During the first six months after recruitment, the
trainee inspector is attached to an experienced field inspector whom he follows and assists in his work. Parallel
correspondence studies are added to the workload of the
students during this first period in order to impress upon
them the importance of education in the sound functioning
of the cooperative movement.

Two courses must be completed by all trainee inspectors during the first six-month period--the Primary
Societies course and the Elementary Bookkeeping course,
which includes double-entry accounting, establishment of
balance sheets, and other elements of basic business
economics. Completion of the two courses is a prerequisite for continued training and admission to the
college.

After the first six months in the field, the trainee
inspectors are brought to the college at Moshi for a 10-
week course. The lectures and seminars held during this
period and the individual study required of the students
cover such topics as the role, functions, and techniques
of inspection; the cooperative movement and the work of
the cooperative department; bookkeeping, accounting and
auditing techniques; application of society bylaws; cooperative principles; the organization and control of societies for marketing, savings and credit, and consumers and
multipurpose societies; and cooperative education. The
students are also given a basic course in mathematics
applied to commercial operations and basic political education relating to Tanzanian political institutions, their
role in society, and their ideological principles.

Returning to the field, trainee inspectors have before them a nine months period of "intermediate programmed
field training." The objective is to provide each trainee
with a reasonable amount of practical experience in all
the functions of an inspector in collaboration with an
experienced inspector. His experience during this period
includes inspecting different types of cooperative societies, living in and participating in the work of an
Ujamaa village, and organizing one-day courses for society
members.

Trainees who are successful in their 18 months of
basic training are permitted to enter the final phase of
the course--another six months at the college, covering in
greater depth such topics as inspection and auditing techniques, bookkeeping and accounting, business and personnel
management applied to cooperative unions and societies,
office administration and organization, financial management, production and farm management, agricultural credits,
marketing, wholesale distribution, consumer cooperatives
and retail shop management, savings and credit societies,
and political education. A large number of case studies
used in seminars are drawn from the recent practical
experience of the student inspectors in the field and
supplemented with inspection reports and court cases. The
students take turns running the consumers' cooperative
store owned by the college and make inspection trips to
neighboring societies and unions.

The CEC and the college provide a wide range of other
courses for staff in both primary societies and unions
and for the government staff concerned with the development of cooperatives and establishment of Ujamaa villages.
Some of these courses are short and are arranged for highly
specialized purposes, such as one- to five-day meetings
to tutor correspondence students who find it difficult to
finish their courses, and special problem-solving sessions
of one day or more with secretaries in societies that have
encountered new problems.

Other courses are longer and constitute contributions to the establishment of a career system within the movement. For example, there is an advanced course for secretaries who have completed their initial Cooperative College training plus an additional year of practical experience. There is a Cashiers' and Bookkeepers' course, a Storekeepers and Produce Clerks' course. There are also specialized courses for shop managers in consumers' societies (at beginners' and advanced training levels), and a Wholesale and Distribution course.

For the union, the college arranges training in the techniques of management and administration for senior staff. It arranges specialized courses for storekeepers, produce clerks, and other middle-level management staff. There are also courses for senior management staff and a diploma course for inspectors who want to qualify for more responsible work. All these staff courses last between 2 and 10 weeks and are residential. Most of them require practical experience and correspondence study before admission.

COST AND BENEFITS OF THE COOPERATIVE EDUCATION SYSTEM

Costs

The cost of capital investments in the central establishment at Moshi to date amounts to some T Sh4.5 million (Tanzanian shillings) or about US$650,000, financed by a long-term loan from the Scandinavian countries.[4] This covers the present installations, including the offices for the staff of the college and the center, dormitories and catering facilities for 150 students at any given time, and library, lecture hall, and seminar room facilities for the educational program. The existing facilities are considered too small for the needs of the sponsoring organizations and plans have been made to extend them to include boarding facilities for a total of 200 students, with a simultaneous expansion of educational and office facilities. The cost of additional investment has been calculated at close to T Sh2 million (about US$300,000).

Investments in the field structure are comparatively modest. The unions take care of the housing problems of the wings; the equipment of the wings consists mainly of one Landrover or Landcruiser and some audiovisual equipment. Frequent replacement of equipment is necessary: it is estimated that the car must be replaced in three years; projectors and tape recorders do not last much longer.

The current cost of the college in 1969/70 amounted to T Sh1.12 million (US$150,000). This included the

cost of eight Tanzanian teachers at the college, but not
the payment of salaries and emoluments for five expatriate
teachers nor the salaries of the expatriate administrative
officer. The current costs are rapidly rising as the
number of Tanzanian staff is being increased--the Five-Year
Plan foresees an increase from 8 to 20 Tanzanian teachers
during the first years of the Plan. This would increase
the annual current cost of operating the college to about
T Sh2 million (US$300,000).

In 1970 the total cost of running the Cooperative
Education Centre and the wings amounted to just under T Sh
1 million   (US$150,000), with about two-thirds relating
to the activities of the center (including the cost of one
wing stationed at Moshi) and one-third, to those of the
wings. In that year only seven wings were in operation
as compared to 11 at the end of 1971. One wing in full
operation costs some T Sh60,000 per annum to operate with
one Tanzanian official, not including equipment cost.
Salary costs for expatriate staff are not included in any
of the figures given above or in the table. By the end of
1970 the center had 13 professional staff (including the
director of the center and the college), and the wings
had 13 professional staff. Of this total of 26 professional staff, 9 were expatriates. If all staff were Tanzanian, the center's expenditures for salaries would increase by some 40 percent.

The activities of the college are financed largely by
a government subvention (which in 1969/70 corresponded to
25 percent of the budget) and course fees paid by the
government, the unions, and the societies. Other incomes
amounted to an insignificant share of the budget (T Sh
7,000). Thus practically all the costs for the college
were paid out of Tanzanian resources. The financing of
the center on the other hand, was largely taken care of
through agreements of technical cooperation with the
Scandinavian countries. In the agreement which ended in
December 1971, the total net costs of the center and 6
wings existing in 1969, plus 4 new wings to be set up in
1970 and 1971, were estimated as follows (all amounts are
in Tanzanian shillings):

Year	CEC	Wings	Total	Tanzanian contribution
1969	500,000	532,000	1,032,000	103,000
1970	500,000	816,000	1,316,000	244,000
1971	500,000	700,000	1,200,000	396,000

Total net cost corresponds to gross expenditure after
income from course fees and other income have been deducted.
Such income, which should be considered an additional
source of Tanzanian financing, amounted to T Sh187,000 in
1970, or 13 percent of total budget turnover. Again, cost
of expatriate staff is not included. On the other hand,

cost of equipment and vehicles is included in the expenditure figures, a fact that partly explains the variations from one year to another in the cost of the wings,
which are the great consumers of such items.

In summary, including shadow prices for Tanzanian
replacements for expatriate staff, the expenditure pattern
in the next few years--during the plan period at least--
would shape up like this for one year:

Cost of building at Moshi;
  investment T Sh6,500,000

    Annual depreciation 3 percent   195,000

Current cost of operation, including
  amortization of vehicles and
  teaching equipment:

College	2,000,000
Cooperative Education Centre	500,000
Wings	700,000
Added cost for Tanzanian staff where expatriates are now employed	200,000
Total expenditure budget	3,595,000

With the increased capacity of both the center and
the college, income from course fees and other sources
would be likely to increase somewhat and amount to at
least T Sh1.2 million.

Quantitative Benefits

For the estimated annual expenditure of T Sh3,595,000,
the cooperative movement and the government can
theoretically buy a total of some 9,000 trainee-weeks at
the college (with an estimated active period of 45 weeks
per annum). Actually the courses budgeted for in the
Five-Year Plan would require between 7,000 and 7,500
trainee-weeks, leaving some reserve capacity for other
activities such as seminars and conferences. The 7,000
to 7,500 trainee-weeks would allow for some college education each year of more than 1,500 staff of the movement
and the government division. This would correspond roughly
to one training opportunity at the college for every five
staff members.

The "contact surface" of the wings is more difficult
to calculate as is the potential prime clientele for its
activities. The total membership of the movement should
gradually approach 1,800,000 persons, which corresponds
to the number of farm families in Tanzania. If both

husband and wife are included--and there are good reasons
to do so in view of the objectives to be reached and
the fundamental change in attitude sought--then the total
target population would be more than 3.5 million individuals. How many of these need to be reached in order to
make an impact on the attitudes and behavior of the population? To this question there is no hard and fast reply.
The assumption on which the cooperative education system
is at present working is that mass contact in general is
neither necessary nor feasible; in any case that reaching
the member elite, which may serve as an intermediary agent,
must be placed first on the list of priorities.

Of course the cooperative education system is not
alone in organizing mass action and seeking to influence
the farm population as a whole. Its activities form a
part of a larger adult education complex composed of the
mass media, political party's educational activities, and
large-scale educational campaigns organized by the adult
education bodies--such as the "Wakati wa Furaha" (Time for
Rejoicing) radio and discussion group campaign, launched
by the adult education group to celebrate the 10th anniversary of Tanganyika's independence. Many adult education activities of these various bodies and organizations
have broadly the same objectives as the cooperative mass
education action--namely, to make the people understand
the basic rules of cooperative socialism as a basis for
Tanzanian development.

There is no way of estimating at present what the
total impact of these various activities may be. The
same applies to the role played by cooperative education
action in the total drive. What can be said is that the
film shows have been seen by some 100,000 spectators at
200 showings by the wings during 1970. The education
secretaries of the union have organized other shows, but
the size of the audience is unknown. The number of
listeners to the radio programs is unknown. It will be
remembered that the member campaign in 1970--with only
seven wings in operation--took in more than 12,000 participants in the first meetings during the month of September. An estimated 140 societies, or more than 10 percent
of all marketing societies, participated.

The potential reach of each wing was extensively
discussed with the officers concerned during the ICED
team's visit to Moshi and Dodoma. The following are some
of the determinants. Traveling 20,000 miles per annum in
Tanzanian dirt roads into the villages takes well over
600 hours of hard driving (calculated on the basis of 30
miles an hour, a high speed on most of those roads). The
two officers have a total of some 500 work-days at their
disposal. For the most part they travel together--often
visiting different societies--and the time they spend on
the road (roughly 160 days for the two officers together)
thus accounts for a third of their work time. Another

150 to 180 man-days are consumed by courses at the center, making reports, and doing other office work. Thus 170 man-days remain for visits to the societies within their respective regions. The eleven wings serve about 125 societies each. This means that the two officers together can make one or two visits to each society during a one-year period, hardly sufficient for societies with inexperienced secretaries and members.[5]

The extensive use of correspondence studies at all levels has undoubtedly cut the cost below what would otherwise have been required for achieving the same results. But study by correspondence also means high drop-out rates and frustration among nonsuccessful students, both of which must be considered when evaluating cost and benefits within the system. Results have undoubtedly been slower than hoped for when the courses were begun. Even the secretaries in the societies (many of whom have completed primary education and thus constitute the more educated group in the clientele for mass education) have taken from 10 to 14 months to complete a single course of ten letters. In a sample of 100 students taking the Primary Societies course, selected at random by Dubell, 30 students had needed less than 9 months to complete the course; 32 had needed 10 to 14 months; 24 had needed between 15 and 24 months; 14 were still working on their letters two years after they enrolled.[6] Groups take even more time to complete their courses, although they are much shorter and much less demanding than the Primary Societies course required of the secretaries.

[Since the completion of the case study, we have received the following information about the program:

> By mid-1972, a total of 4,616 persons had attended courses at the Cooperative College in Moshi; of these 855 were primary society staff, 526 union staff, and 934 government staff attending regular courses. Another 2,301 had participated in short courses and seminars, including 182 participants from other countries. The number of participants in courses and seminars in 1971-72 academic year was 762. A total of 10,244 individuals and 1,593 groups have enrolled for correspondence studies during 1965-1972. Of these, 2,750 individuals and 408 groups have received certificates after successful completion of their studies. An estimated 60 percent of the correspondence students dropped out during these years. About 70,000 people attended film shows presented by the CEC wings and 12,800 attended one-day meetings in 1971.][7]

CONCLUDING COMMENTS

Aside from the figures provided on enrollments, certificates granted, and courses discontinued, there are few
if any hard facts that can be used for evaluating the
system's performance. Leaders in the political and cooperative movements generally express great appreciation for
the work of the college and the CEC, but these judgments
are based mainly on impressions and unsystematic observation.

It is clear that the contents of the courses offered
and other educational materials need careful analysis.
For instance, it was observed that questions asked by
study group members were sometimes more sophisticated
than the level at which these questions were treated in
the letters. Some staff members of the Wings, however,
felt that courses designed for the members should be as
basic as they are now, since the courses are designed to
meet the requirements of the least educated and experienced
members of the primary societies. Increasing the difficulty of courses would lead to rising dropout rates.
According to this argument a high participation rate is
just as important as the level of learning attained. More
sophisticated members have the option of taking the longer
and more difficult courses. There is a fairly general
agreement that there are flaws in the pedagogical buildup. The curriculum of several courses had been produced
rapidly; expatriate staff, unfamiliar with the learning
levels of cooperative society members in Tanzania, had
written some of the text. As a result, the principle of
proceeding from the easy-to-understand to a more complex
learning experience was not always applied. Dubell has
illustrated this point in his study of the training of
secretaries. [8] In analyzing the number of repeaters for
each letter among the 376 secretaries who completed the
Primary Societies course, he found that the repeater rate
varied between a high of 25 percent (for letter one) and
a low of 3.9 percent (for letter six). Inadequate answers
had been received from more than 12 percent in the case of
three other letters.

More research and analysis of data available on
correspondence students control cards are now in order,
but perhaps more important for an effective evaluation
of the impact of the cooperative education system would
be the collection of a wide range of data from the primary
societies, the unions, and the Division of Cooperative
Development. Questions to be asked would be along these
lines: Are the accounts kept in societies with trained
secretaries markedly better than in societies with secretaries who have not yet had the benefit of full training?
Are there differences between the two groups of societies
with regard to irregularities, fraud, and corruption? Is
the performance of trained inspectors better or at least

as good as the performance of inspectors trained under the previous more costly system? Are the accounts produced more rapidly? After secretaries have been trained has reporting to unions been improved in any way? Are there any systematic errors in reporting or accounting that signal continuing deficiencies? Has inspection been facilitated by better order in the records of the societies? Is there a better control over stock and capital assets of the societies? Some observers have drawn attention to discrepancies between what is taught in the courses and practices recommended by the CUT and the Marketing Board.[9]

Search for indicators of effectiveness, however, should not be allowed to obscure what may be the most important role of cooperative education in Tanzania, that of helping to transform the country from a tribal society governed partly by chiefs and local leaders to a society founded on principles of self-reliance and democratic procedure. While advances made in this respect will be difficult to measure in quantitative terms, any evaluation of the cooperative education system should take this fundamental aspect into account.

Finally, it can be said with assurance that the establishment of a cooperative education system is an indispensable complement to the political decisions to introduce a single-channel distribution system. The need for staff training and cadre training among members has been heightened in Tanzania by the decisions to widen the application of the cooperative concept to include the producer function. As a result, cooperative action will become more complex and, at the same time, will increase in strategic importance as the social and economic functions of cooperatives are extended. The changeover from marketing societies to producers' societies will in itself require a considerable retraining of staff and an educational reorientation of a large number of members. In other words, a comprehensive and well-directed cooperative education effort is really a prerequisite for the implementation of governmental policy decisions.

NOTES

1. A zone is an organizational grouping of several unions; several zones are covered by a wing.

2. "Ujamaa" meaning "together" is the term used in Tanzania to describe new socialist policies of forming villages for collective production of goods.

3. Folke E. Dubell, "Statistical Study into Training of Secretaries," mimeographed (1970).

4. The figures contained in this chapter have mainly been computed on the basis of data contained in the Cooperative Union of Tanganyika and Cooperative Education Centre, "Cooperative Education

Plan for Tanzania 1969-1974," mimeographed (Moshi, Tanzania, n.d.),
p. 35 and Cooperative Education Centre, "Annual Report 1970," mimeographed (Moshi, Tanzania, 1971), p. 35. The two sources work with
different budget periods. It was not considered desirable to
adjust to one single budget period and thus deviate from the most
authoritative sources available. There is no reason to assume that
consolidation would substantially affect the calculations.

    5. Dubell, op. cit.

    6. Ibid., p. 8.

    7. Philip H. Coombs and Manzoor Ahmed, Attacking Rural Poverty
How Nonformal Education Can Help (Baltimore and London: The Johns
Hopkins University Press, 1974), p. 84.

    8. Dubell, op. cit., p. 11.

    9. See Herbert E. Kriesel, Charles K. Laurent, Carl Halpern,
and Henry E. Larzelere, Agricultural Marketing in Tanzania: Background Research and Policy Proposals (East Lansing, Mich.: Department of Agricultural Economics, Michigan State University, June 1970),
p. 79. Here the authors criticize the "insulation now existing
between the staff of the Cooperative College and the actual field
operation" and recommend operational research for feedback into the
College.

17

THAILAND:
MOBILE TRADE
TRAINING SCHOOLS
Manzoor Ahmed

This case study strikes at an important problem facing all developing nations: how best to generate artisan and craft skills as one of the prerequisites for balanced rural development. In preparing the study, two visits were made to Thailand in 1971 by the author (one of which was in company with Philip H. Coombs) to observe the program at first hand, to interview a variety of knowledgeable local people, and to gather further documentation and evidence. The information presented here represents the situation of the program as of late 1972.

INTRODUCTION

The Mobile Trade Training School (MTTS) program is an innovative effort by the Ministry of Education in Thailand to offer a short, low-cost, flexible training program in nonagricultural skills for rural out-of-school youth to alleviate rural unemployment. The MTTS program was initiated in 1960, and there are (as of 1972) 54 institutions, located in as many districts of Thailand, providing part-time training courses of five months' duration in a number of vocational skills to about 28,000 young people each year. The schools are called mobile because they are moved from one district to another at an interval of one to three years.

In the course of our study, it became apparent that a sizable training program of the MTTS type could not be properly assessed without viewing the underlying assumptions and objectives of the program in relation to the general economic situation in the country--relative growth in different sectors of the economy, shifts in the structure of production and employment, and distribution of income and incentives. All of these features determine the kinds of skills needed and the number of workers that can be effectively utilized in the economy.

It was also found that MTTS program raised certain
issues about the total middle-level skill development
arrangement in the country and that the program could not
be properly assessed in isolation from other major skill
training programs. While a general analysis of the economy
or an elaborate evaluation of the total skill training
system is not our intention, this report on the MTTS program begins with a description of the salient features of
the economic context of middle-level skill development and,
following a discussion of the program itself, concludes
with a broad sketch of skill development programs, including attention to issues relating to a skill development
strategy for the country.

                    The Economy of Thailand

     The Thai economy in 1971 was at a critical stage of
transition when the priorities and programs for the Third
Five Year Development Plan (1972-1976) were being formulated.[1] The concentrated and rapid growth of the industrial sectors in the metropolitan Bangkok area, the high
rate of population increase, and the decrease in the
amount of agricultural land available for reclamation had
intensified the economic disparity between urban and rural
areas. At the same time, the slump in the export market
for rice, the withdrawal of U.S. forces from Asia, and the
general reduction in the flow of capital from abroad had
forced the projected economic growth for the next five
years down to about 6 percent. The rate during the preceding decade had been over 8 percent. The growth of the
urban-industrial sector during the sixties had also
created skill shortages, resulting in the creation of
various training facilities, which drew their clientele
from both the urban and the rural areas. The current
slowing down of the economy is exacerbating the problem
of rural unemployment and raises questions about the
nature and scope of programs designed to promote skills
and employment in the rural areas.
     The manufacturing, mining, and construction sector
grew at the rate of about 10 percent during the period
1960-1969. This picture of dynamism was somewhat illusory.
The new consumer goods industries which grew during the
1960s relied very heavily on a policy of tariff-supported
import substitution pursued by the government. These
industries are generally characterized by low efficiency,
low productivity, low capacity utilization, and high cost.
As the easy import substitution opportunities became
exhausted, further industrial growth along the same line
could result only in more inefficiency and higher tariff
barriers, not to speak of poor overall import replacement
effect because of the imported capital and input require-

ments. There has been very little contribution to export
earning from the manufacturing sector.

The pattern of industrial development has resulted in
an extremely lopsided geographical distribution of industries in the country. About three-quarters of all
registered factories are situated in the Bankgok-Thonburi
area; the industries located outside the metropolitan
area are the primary processing industries, such as rice
mills, saw mills, and sugar mills. By design as well as
accident, both the market and sources of supply for industries, except for the processing industries, have been
concentrated in the Bangkok-Thonburi area. Attempts to
disperse industries have so far been ineffective.

The agglomeration of industries in one area has been
partly due to the lack of sufficient government concern
for small-scale industries that are less dependent on
external economies and economies of scale than are larger
industries. Traditional family workshops, which are
engaged in various service activities, simple manufacturing,
and even producing industrial supplies, constitute a
sizable segment of the industrial sector--at least in terms
of employment.[2] There has been, however, little concerted
effort to promote the labor-intensive, geographically
dispersed small-scale industries. The Ministry of Industries' credit operations have yet to make significant
contribution to small-scale industries, and the Small
Industries Service Institute has been a limited operation
within the Bangkok area.

Agriculture (including fishery and forestry) also
grew at a relatively high rate of 5.4 percent in the
decade of the 1960s. The growth rate for farm crops was
actually about 4 percent per annum during the sixties and
much of this growth may be attributed to expansion of
arable land, which increased from 56 to 66 million <u>rais</u>
between 1960 and 1967. It is estimated that the average
annual rate of increase for arable land is 1.6 percent
per year for the period 1962 to 1975, after which the
rate is expected to drop to an average of 0.5 percent.[3]
The scope for agricultural growth through land reclamation
is fast coming to an end.

Agriculture has so far provided about 90 percent of
export earnings for Thailand, with rice as the primary
export commodity. With the current slump in the international rice market, agricultural export can be maintained
at a high level only by diversification into various cash
crops with higher export potential. Because the limit to
further land expansion has been reached, successful diversification (while maintaining competitive prices) will
entail high productivity. A policy of high-yield farming
could, however, lead to rural unemployment or underemployment, unless the policy provides for high productivity
per unit of land with the application of labor-intensive
techniques.

During the 1960s, the share of agriculture in the
Gross Domestic Product (GDP) has dropped from about 40
to 30 percent and the shares for the industries and services have correspondingly increased. Employment patterns
have not, however, been reflected in this structural shift.
Between 1960 and 1969 total employment increased by about
3.3 million. Almost 2.2 million or 66 percent were employed in agriculture; 900,000 or 27 percent were employed
in services; and 232,000 or 7 percent were employed in
manufacturing and mining, although the nonagricultural
sector of the economy (in terms of value added) grew
twice as fast as the agricultural sector. The agricultural
sector (or the rural area) provides some sort of residual
employment, which is characterized by low productivity,
low efficiency, and low earning for the large segment of
the labor force not absorbed by industries and services
that are concentrated in urban areas. All signs indicate
that the residual employment function of the rural-agricultural sector will continue for the foreseeable future
(see Table 17.1).

The population in 1970 was estimated at 37 million
with a growth rate of about 3.3 percent per annum. About
85 percent of the population live outside the urban centers.
The population in Greater Bangkok constitutes about 85
percent of Thai urban population. Despite increasing
urbanization, the population in rural areas is likely to
be doubled by the end of the century. A relatively high
participation rate of the population in the labor force
is characteristic of Thailand, because many women are in
the labor force. The rate is higher in rural areas (about
84 percent compared to about 60 percent for urban areas
for persons of age 15 and over). Given the primacy of
agriculture in the economy, the high population growth
and high ratio of labor force participation imply underemployment, low productivity, and low earning in the rural
areas.

Urban-Rural Gap

The economic development policies pursued in the past
and the demographic factors have together created wide
economic disparity between the urban and rural areas.
According to the estimate of a working group of the
National Economic Development Board, the per capita GDP of
farm population in Thailand in 1970 was US$62 against
US$436 for the nonfarm population. The actual gap in
income levels may not be as wide because the cost of living
in rural areas is lower than that in the city. Nevertheless, according to the working group, "it would be very
optimistic to estimate that at present the average incomes
of the farm population reach 30 percent of the average

TABLE 17.1

Estimate of Employment Potential for the Third
Development Plan, 1972-1976

| Sector | Employment Potential | | | | Employment Increase 1971-1976 | |
| | 1971 | | 1976 | | | |
	No. of persons ('000) #	Per-cent %	No. of persons ('000) #	Per-cent %	No. of persons ('000) #	Per-cent %
1. Agriculture, forestry, hunting and fisheries	13,076	77.4	14,606	75.1	1,530	59.7
2. Mining and quarrying	51	0.3	66	0.3	15	0.6
3. Manufacturing	715	4.2	785	4.0	70	2.7
4. Construction, repair and demolition	150	0.9	191	1.0	41	1.6
5. Electricity and water supply	42	0.2	66	0.3	24	1.0
6. Commerce	1,278	7.6	1,688	8.7	410	16.0
7. Communication, storage and transportation	317	1.9	404	2.1	87	3.4
8. Services	1,273	7.5	1,658	8.5	385	15.0
TOTAL	16,902	100.0	19,464	100.0	2,562	100.0

Source: National Economic Development Board, Manpower Planning Division.

incomes of the nonfarm population. Moreover, it is very
likely that the relative income position of the farmers
will further deteriorate in the years to come."[4]
     There are also great regional variations in levels
of economic development. In 1966, per capita income in
the four regions in the country were as follows (in
current prices):[5]

Region	Per Capita Income
Central (including Bangkok-	
Thonburi)	4,700 bahts
South	3,077 bahts
North	2,808 bahts
Northeast	1,435 bahts

     The income differentials reflect the structural
differences in the GDP of the regions: the central region
possesses the bulk of the country's industries and much
of the services, whereas the other regions are predominantly agricultural. The urban-rural and regional income
disparities suggest that nonagricultural income-earning and
employment opportunities are very limited in all of the
rural regions; even more so in the North and Northeast
regions.
     The review of the economic situation brings out in
relief 1) that the absolute level of income in rural areas,
despite a substantial agricultural growth, is very low;
2) that nonagricultural income-earning and employment
potential is extremely low except in the central region;
and 3) that a high rate of population growth is exacerbating the rural development problem, particularly in relation
to employment.
     It should be noted, however, that the benefits of
industrial development and overall economic growth have
filtered down to the larger provincial towns, some of
which already had agricultural processing units. Increasing attention is also being paid to rural infrastructure development, particularly through the Accelerated
Rural Development (ARD) Program in 25 of the 71 provinces
in the country. The ARD activities, which were mainly
the construction of all-weather roads to villages, service
tracks, wells, and canals, were expanded in 1970 when
ARD launched a Comprehensive Rural Development Package
Program (COMPAC) with technical assistance from the Asian
Development Bank. The COMPAC program has so far been
extended to nine districts to provide coordinated services
in fish production, sericulture, livestock development,
and upland field crops.
     Increasing farm mechanization is also altering the
development and employment potential of the rural areas.
The importation of tractors into the country jumped from
1,487 in 1961 to 4,036 in 1967, and the prospects are

that tractor imports will rise by 5 to 10 percent per year. A variety of other farm equipment is also currently being imported and the trend shows rising import figures.[6]

The effects of farm mechanization on rural employment are complicated. In general, selective and well-planned mechanization in certain situations can raise employment on the farm and create supplementary employment in operation, repair, and maintenance of equipment.

During the 1960s the location of U.S. defense installations and air force bases throughout Thailand and "rest and recreation" visits by servicemen from the Southeast Asian countries have infused substantial foreign exchange into the Thai economy and have also generated income and employment in some remote regions of the country. This source is now fast drying up with the withdrawal of U.S. forces from Asia.

The demand for nonagricultural skills in rural areas should rise substantially during the coming years, if the Third Plan provides appropriately for 1) dispersal of industries and support to small-scale industries; 2) measures for diversification, increased productivity, and selective mechanization in agriculture; and 3) a larger outlay for rural infrastructure development, including housing construction and provision of special services.

Basic Educational Provisions

Thailand provides some form of primary education to almost all of its children. However, in 1970 about 700,000 of those who completed four-year primary education did not have the opportunity for any further education. This was the case too with about 50,000 children with seven years of primary education, 50,000 youths with ten years of schooling, and 20,000 youths with twelve years of education. These numbers represent respectively about 70 percent of those who completed four years of primary education, about one-quarter of those who finished seven years of primary education, and about one-half of lower secondary and upper secondary graduates. The vast majority of those who leave school at various stages, particularly after fourth grade, are rural children. For instance, in 1967, 85 percent of fourth grade students in Bangkok went on to fifth grade, but only 14 percent did so in the Northeast region.[7]

MOBILE TRADE TRAINING SCHOOL PROGRAM

The first Mobile Trade Training School (known as Mobile Trade Training Unit, or MTTU, until July 1970) was opened in Changwat Chumphon in Southern Thailand in 1960 by the Vocational Promotion Division in the Vocational Education Department of the Ministry of Education, giving effect to a Thai government decision to extend skill training to out-of-school youth with at least four years of education and no other opportunity to continue further education.[8] The second school was opened in 1964 in the Northeast province of Sakon Nakhon.

The program was rapidly expanded in 1966 when the Thai government sought and received assistance from the U.S. Agency for International Development (AID) in the form of equipment, technical advice, and foreign training of program staff. The purpose of AID assistance was to set up 52 more schools by 1972. Expansion has proceeded according to the original plan--five schools were established in 1967, eleven in 1968, and nine each year since 1969, making a total of 54 MTTS in 1972.

By the end of 1970, a total of about 51,000 trainees had enrolled in the MTTS courses and more than 30,000 had completed the five-month training course. According to the Vocational Educational Department's plans, more than 43,000 trainees are to be enrolled during 1972 and in each future year in the 54 schools. This number of trainees represents about 6 percent of the current out-of-school youths who have completed four years of primary education.

Objectives

As noted above, the program began with the government decision to provide skill training to out-of-school youth with four years of education and no opportunity for further education. This population is, of course, largely located in the rural areas. The formal objectives of the program are:

1. to set up mobile schools for the purpose of providing skill training to out-of-school youths and adults with only four years of compulsory schooling; training facilities are to be made available at the minimum possible expense and time for those who have had no previous skill training and for those who have some training but need further upgrading
2. to raise the standard of living of the less fortunate people living in rural areas and to help the individual to help himself
3. to supplement the training programs offered elsewhere in order to meet the ever-increasing demand for skilled and semiskilled manpower in accordance with the national economic development plan, and to prepare citizens for new job opportunities

4. to bring the Ministry of Education activities
    to the rural people so that they might, in turn,
    understand and support government aims[9]

The objectives listed above imply an intended supplementary character of the program--the schools would
supplement other training facilities supposedly available
to the rural population. The program is viewed as a
contributing factor in general economic development of the
rural areas, though not operationally identified as an
element in a broader rural development plan.

U.S. AID originally saw the program as a job-preparation activity benefiting the economically disadvantaged
and politically "sensitive" region of northeastern Thailand.
By 1971, however, these purposes had been modified. The
program had been extended throughout Thailand and was no
longer limited to the Northeast and its purpose was
widened beyond job-preparation, as indicated in the following description of project goals dated March 1971:

> To provide skill training to individuals with
> a minimum of four years of formal education
> and little or no opportunity to continue in
> the formal educational system to enable them
> to obtain employment, upgrade their employ-
> ment capability or improve their domestic
> situation.[10]

Inclusion in the program of skill training to "improve their domestic situation," which does not necessarily
lead to paid employment or earning, of course, substantially alters the character of the program and the criteria
for its evaluation.

Location and Clientele

The typical MTTS is located in one or more stationary
buildings rather than on wheels (only one mobile school is
actually on wheels, the shops being located on trailers).
The buildings are made available to MTTS either free of
charge or for rent. Typically, a school operates in one
location for one to three years and is then moved to
another district in the same or a different province. The
schools, according to the Vocational Promotion Division
(VPD), need to stay in one location for two or more
sessions, that is, one year or longer, to be able to serve
those who want the training. The distinguishing features
of the MTTS are the absence of capital expenditures on
permanent buildings and its ability to move out of one
district (once the demand for training is satisfied) and
go to another.

The selection of sites for the operation of the
schools and decisions about length of stay in one location
are made by the VPD on the basis of a number of factors:
"the urgent need of [politically] threatened provinces,"
interest of local people and potential enrollment, lack
of other vocational training facilities, employment and
economic condition of the area, and the availability
of physical facilities for the operation of the program.[11]

The usual procedure for determining the location is
to send one or more MTTS teachers to interview the government officials of the Changwad (province) and the Amphur
(district) regarding the interest of the local people and
the need for an MTTS in the locality. Often a location
is selected because Changwad officials request it. Non-
officials, such as businessmen, local leaders, prospective
employers, and so on, are usually not consulted.

So far as ICED researchers could ascertain, the
decision on location of a school is not preceded by an
economic survey of the district in terms of occupational
and employment structure of the area, present and potential employment demands, other skill development opportunities, and the economic development plans and potentials of
the area. Such an exercise, even in a relatively crude
fashion, would probably have highlighted the divergent
circumstances of different areas and the importance of
designing courses for the specific needs of the locality
rather than offering everywhere a selection of courses
from the same limited list. The implicit assumption of
the Vocational Promotion Division's program is that the
training needs of its clientele are fairly uniform throughout the country and the standard list serves these needs
adequately.

All the schools have been located in either a provincial or a district town, rather than in villages. The
reasons for this, as explained by VPD, are several:
1) a school can be located only where the supply of electric power is assured--even though most schools have
movable generators, they can be used only as a supplemental
source and cannot be relied upon for the entire power
requirement of a school; 2) the school must have a central
location with a sufficient concentration of people who
are interested in the training; and 3) the employment
market for many of the skills taught in the schools is
in the small as well as large towns rather than in the
villages.

The program is designed for out-of-school youths
who have completed at least four years of primary education. It is also intended to serve the rural areas. In
practice, however, "rural" is defined liberally to include all of Thailand outside metropolitan Bangkok.

Data about the geographical origin of trainees are
unavailable, but it is believed that most of the trainees
come from the district and provincial towns and their

environs because commuting from distant villages is unpracticable. The procedure for selecting trainees is simple and liberal. Few applicants are denied admission and, apparently, the schools stay in a location as long as there are sufficient candidates to fill a number of courses.

A survey of 613 trainees, 837 graduates, and 65 dropouts from eight MTTSs carried out in 1971 indicates the educational background and sex distribution of the trainees.[12]   (Table 17.2.)

TABLE 17.2

Educational Background of Trainees, Graduates,
and Dropouts from 8 MTTSs, 1971

	Pathom IV (Primary Grade IV)	Pathom V-VII (Primary Grades V-VII)	MS 1 or above (Secondary Grade 1 or above)
	%	%	%
Trainees	62.6	16.8	20.6
Graduates	49.7	21.0	29.3
Dropout	27.7	16.9	55.4

Source: National Research Council, Social Science Research Division, "Evaluation of the Mobile Trade Training Units and the Polytechnic Schools Project," mimeographed (Bangkok, 1971).

The program, of course, is designed for a clientele with a low level of formal education: more than 60 percent of the trainees and about 50 percent of the graduates in the sample had only a four-year primary education. According to the survey about 60 percent of the client population are girls. The survey also revealed that 238, or 39 percent, of the trainees were wage-earning employees and were presumably using the program to upgrade their skills and learn new skills in order to have greater employment options. About 85 percent of the trainees were over 17 years of age, with about two-thirds of them concentrated in the age-range of 17 to 24 years. It is interesting that, although the program is stated to be for out-of-school youths with only four years of schooling, the trainees do not come to the program till several years after completing four years of primary education.

Enrollment in the program has grown rapidly as the number of schools continued to increase since 1966. The estimated number of trainees[13] in the two sessions completed in 1971 was 23,000, although the Vocational Education Department target for the year was 36,000 in 45 schools. An estimated 14,00 trainees actually completed the courses and received certificates in 1971. With the existing trend in enrollment and graduation, the annual enrollment in the program would continue at the level reached in 1972 of about 28,000 in 54 schools against the VED target of 43,000; and the number actually completing the training would be about 18,000. The department's targets appear to be over-optimistic. The present enrollment works out to be a total of about 255 trainees in two daily shifts of three hours, each with an instructional staff of about 10 persons. Given the emphasis on practical experience and the personal attention of the instructor needed in many of the courses, it is difficult to see how larger numbers of trainees can be accommodated in a shift. More trainees can enroll in a school only if a third shift can be opened, which would mean some additional staff and consumable materials.

Content and Method

The distribution of enrollment in different courses during the first session of 1971 in 13 MTTSs is indicated in Table 17.3.

The repertoire of courses, listed in order of their popularity with trainees,[14] are: dressmaking, auto mechanics, tailoring, radio repair, electric wiring and installation, cosmetology and hairdressing, food preparation, welding, typing, bookkeeping, barbering, embroidery, and woodwork. Each school offers seven to ten courses from this list in one or two shifts for each course depending on the number of trainees.

The courses are offered on the basis of a uniform requirement of 300 hours of instruction and practice time for each skill, spread over a period of five months. Two shifts of three hours are offered (including one shift at night). Thus trainees can choose a convenient time of the day, and relatively high utilization of the facilities is ensured. Two five-month sessions are operated in a year.

Data in Table 17.3 also show that the rate of completion of the courses by those enrolled ranges from 50 to 80 percent in different courses; the overall rate is 65 percent. The average number of trainees per school in two shifts is 255, of whom 166 complete the training. An average school, therefore, enrolls more than 500 trainees per year and the annual output per school is about 330. More than 40 percent of the output is in auto-mechanics, radio repair, electricity, and welding.

The content of the courses is determined by and limited to a course-outline for each course prepared by

TABLE 17.3

Enrollment and Graduation in 13 MTTSs
for First Session in 1971

	Course	Enrollment #	Graduation #	Percentage of Enrolled who Graduated %
1.	Dressmaking	629	419	67
2.	Auto mechanics	522	371	71
3.	Tailoring	464	237	51
4.	Radio repair	331	213	64
5.	Electric wiring and installation	314	213	68
6.	Cosmetics and hairdressing	284	225	79
7.	Food preparation	251	177	70
8.	Welding	167	110	66
9.	Typing	142	70	49
10.	Bookkeeping	97	60	62
11.	Barbering	67	37	55
12.	Embroidery	30	24	80
13.	Woodwork	11	8	73
	TOTAL	3,309	2,164	65

Source: Vocational Promotion Division.

the VPD office in Bangkok. The standard outline and the
particular training of the teacher at the Bangkok Technical School or a comparable institution are the determinants
of what goes on in the courses. Virtually no other instructional materials are available, and little is being done
to develop general curriculum materials or to design MTTS
courses with the flexibility to adapt to a particular setting and need.

A materials development unit for the program has been
established in the Bangkok Polytechnic School with three
staff members. These people, however, have other administrative functions in the program and are at work on
instructional materials only part-time. As a result,
progress in this task has been slow. In 1971, three people
were undergoing training in the United States in curriculum
and materials development. The situation may improve somewhat if they are assigned full-time on the job on completion of their training.

The program is not subject to any formal external criteria of evaluation such as State Skill Tests or regulations. There is no provision for supervision or professional advice while the schools are in operation, except what can be offered by the principal of each MTTS. At the conclusion of each training session, a test is made up and administered by the instructor for his course, and a certificate is granted by the Vocational Education Department to those who pass. Most trainees who attend the course till the end of the session receive the certificate.

Instructional Personnel

A key element in the success of any skill training program, of course, is the capabilities of the instructors. The staff in each school usually includes a principal, a general assistant, and instructors. The teachers share some of the administrative and record-keeping tasks.

The qualifications specified for instructors include graduation from a postsecondary technical institute or a vocational teachers' college, which generally requires 15 years of schooling. This is followed, particularly for technical institute graduates, by a year of teacher training in Bangkok Technical School, specially designed for the MTTS program. A large number of teachers, however, come from vocational teacher training institutions with vocational teaching qualifications. In a sample of 101 MTTS teachers, it was found that 44 had been trained in technical institutes, while the rest had their training in vocational schools or vocational teacher preparation programs. Forty percent of the teachers in the sample were women. Following is the distribution of teachers by the subjects of their specialized training in the sample group.[15]

Home economics	29
General purpose vocational teacher training	22
Auto mechanics	12
Electricity	10
Metal trades	8
Commercial trades	6
Radio	4
Carpentry	4
Barbering	4
Machine shop	1
Industrial technology	1

A general problem in the vocational and training skill field is the difficulty in attracting and retaining quali-

fied instructors in the program, in competition with industry and business. The MTTS program also has difficulties in filling positions, particularly in industrial
skills and bookkeeping. It has the additional problem of
getting trained teachers who are willing to serve outside
the Bangkok area. Teacher shortages were sometimes met
in the past by assigning teachers full responsibility for
instruction without adequate supervision. According to
VPD, the problem has been eased somewhat as a result of
offering substantial financial incentives to MTTS teachers.
Teachers in the program are paid a per diem allowance for
their stay outside of Bangkok as well as overtime payments,
which together increase their income by more than 100 percent of that of regular secondary vocational school
teachers.[16]

ASSESSMENT OF THE MTTS PROGRAM

The assessment of costs and benefits of the MTTS
program is difficult; first, because quantitative data
are imprecise and inadequate; and second, because many
elements, particularly benefits, are not quantifiable.

The primary difficulty on cost data was that the
budget figures available from the Vocational Education
Department were in highly aggregated categories, often
including costs that were not exclusively for the MTTS
program. Moreover, there were considerable extra-budgetary
income and expenditure in the program, the full records
and breakdowns of which were not available. The ICED
investigators, therefore, had to rely on approximate
estimates of total operating and nonrecurrent costs for
the program from budgetary and nonbudgetary sources for
the financial years 1970, 1971, and 1972 that were provided by the Vocational Promotion Division.

On the other side of the cost-benefit equation, the
two major dimensions, not necessarily mutually exclusive,
are benefits derived from the program by individual
trainees and the contribution of the program to rural employment promotion and economic welfare, primary objectives of the program.[17] The main items under individual
benefits would be:

1. increased earnings as a result of the training
    for those who were employed before training
2. new employment opportunity as a result of
    training
3. increased options and flexibility in employment
    (resulting in monetary as well as nonmonetary
    utilities) due to training
4. increased efficiency and skill as housewife,
    mother, and homemaker (resulting in monetary
    savings for the family and other benefits)

The program's contribution to rural employment and welfare is difficult to gauge, partly because "rural," in the parlance of Thai bureaucracy, often means the entire country outside metropolitan Bangkok, including fairly large provincial towns. But 85 percent of Thai people live in small villages where agriculture is the main economic activity and there is neither the clustering of population nor the diverse socioeconomic services and activities typical of a town. These villages can be served by a nonagricultural skill development program like the MTTS if:

1. It offers training in such nonfarm skills as maintenance and repair of farm equipment; construction of rural housing, roads, irrigation channels, and so on; various artisan, craftsman, and commercial trades; and homemaking.
2. The trainees set up enterprises or take occupations in the villages as a result of the training.
3. The trainees coming from the village can utilize their training to take up gainful employment in the town, thus alleviating the rural employment problem.
4. The trainees, even if located in the town, produce services and goods for rural consumption that cannot be efficiently produced in the village.
5. The trainees, through their acquired skills, contribute to better home and family life and become more valuable members of the rural community.

Despite the statistical difficulties regarding part-time and full-time employment, voluntary withdrawal from the job-market and potential earnings if there had been no training program, it is possible to arrive at a monetary value of the training program in terms of increased earnings. It would, however, be very difficult to measure quantitatively increased employment options and the increased efficiencies of homemakers.

Numerical values can be derived easily enough on number of courses and trainees in different rural skills. It is also possible, if an adequate tracer system for trainees is worked out, to enumerate new rural enterprises and employment promoted by the training and the number of trainees finding employment outside the village. It would be much more difficult to quantify the goods and services produced by ex-trainees of the program for rural consumption; it would be impossible to express numerically the contribution to better home, family, and community.

While useful numerical data indicative of individual and social benefits of the MTTS program could be derived, these data, by themselves, would provide an incomplete picture of the program's benefits.

Although the program has been in existence for ten years and has expanded rapidly, there has been little effort to evaluate the program in terms of its costs, benefits, and effectiveness. The only serious evaluation attempt was one undertaken by the National Research Council in 1971. This evaluation provides some useful information about the students, dropouts, and graduates of eight sample MTTSs. It provides little information on benefits unrelated to employment and includes nothing on costs. There has been no systematic effort in the MTTS program to follow up the trainees, which could have illuminated many of the questions about the program's effectiveness. ICED investigators utilized the available information and relied on the impressions gathered from their observation of the program in operation.

Costs and Finance

The sources of funds for the program are the national budget allocation, U.S. AID contribution, counterpart funds in local currency created under United States PL 480, and tuition fees paid by trainees.[18] In addition, a considerable amount of materials and equipment have been made available to the schools from United States excess property and army surplus stocks in Thailand.

Between 1966 and 1970, when the number of schools rose from 2 to 36, total (capital and recurrent) expenditure for the program was US$6.40 million. Of this amount, $3.84 million was the U.S. contribution, used primarily for capital expenses, salaries for U.S. technical advisors, and advanced overseas training for staff. The national contribution has been used primarily for operating expenses. In addition, U.S. surplus properties estimated to be worth more than $4 million, were received by the program between 1966 and 1971.[19] A breakdown of the total estimated operating costs and the estimated capital expenditure and other nonrecurrent expenditures for the years 1970, 1971, and 1972 is presented in Table 17.4.

As the table indicates, roughly 45 percent of the operating costs are spent for personnel and another 30 percent for materials and supplies. The relatively large expenditure for materials and supplies is considered necessary to permit adequate practical experience for trainees, which means high use of consumable items. The remaining 25 percent go to various overhead costs and miscellaneous items. The largest amount of nonrecurrent expenditure is for equipment and materials. Other nonrecurrent expenses are for U.S. technical advisors and higher training for the staff; both items are expected to be phased out gradually.

The average annual costs for an individual school, as estimated by the Vocational Promotion Division and

TABLE 17.4

Estimated Costs of the MTTS Program
1970-1972
('000 US$)

Cost Category	FY 1970 36 schools	FY 1971 45 schools	FY 1972 54 schools
Operating Costs (National Contribution) Salaries for regular staff	360	450	540
General expenses	180	225	270
Overtime and personnel welfare	180	225	270
Supplies and materials	360	450	540
Miscellaneous	108	135	162
TOTAL	1,188	1,485	1,782
Nonrecurrent Costs[a] (U.S. Contribution) Commodities[b]	1,150	1,250	1,350
U.S. technical advisors	40	40	50
Participant training abroad	116	88	42.5
TOTAL	1,306	1,378	1,442.5
GRAND TOTAL	2,494	2,863	3,224.5

[a]The cost figures include allocation for two regional poly-technic schools under the Vocational Promotion Division.

[b]This item largely includes durable equipment. Assuming a capital cost of US$81,000 per MTTS and that nine schools were equipped each of the three years out of U.S. funds, this figure for the MTTS program would be about US$729,000 for each year.

Source: Vocational Promotion Division.

used by the division as standard cost figures, are as follows:

Recurrent costs

Salaries	US$10,000
General expenses	5,000
Overtime and personnel benefits	5,000
Supplies and materials	10,000
Miscellaneous	3,000
TOTAL	US$33,000

Capital costs (one time) US$81,000

The capital costs include tools and equipment for various skill areas and three vehicles--a jeep, a pickup truck, and a large flatbed truck.[20] This amount does not include costs for technical advisor and participant training. The recurrent cost figure includes such overhead items as central administration, storage, and transportation.

The recurrent unit cost for each trainee who completes the training and receives the certificate, calculated on the basis of average output of 166 trainees per session per school, is about US$100. The total cost per trainee, assuming an amortization period of eight years for capital items (as was done for cost estimates by VPD), is about US$130.

By comparison, the recurrent cost per student-year in the vocational secondary schools in Thailand is estimated to be about US$300 and, in the general secondary schools, over US$50.[21] These costs were calculated on the basis of total enrollment, and not for the output of the system, as was the case with MTTS. On the capital side, the costs for the vocational schools would of course be much higher than those for the MTTS.

The unit costs in MTTS can, of course, be reduced if the schools operate three shifts of three hours each, instead of the present two shifts and run a third short-duration but more intensive session during the summer months. A third shift and a third session were planned by the Vocational Promotion Division but were not put into practice. Another means of cutting costs would be to use locally recruited craftsmen and skilled workers as instructors instead of regular civil service employees.

Cost-Effectiveness of the Program

A primary objective of the program, as noted earlier, is to teach nonagricultural skills to out-of-school rural youths in order to facilitate their productive employment.

In the sample survey by the National Research Council mentioned earlier, it was found that 638 or 76 percent of 837 graduates were employed.[22] However, 434 or 52 percent of the graduates were already employed before their training and 80 percent of the previously employed were in their old jobs. Only 204 or 24 percent found fresh employment.

Of those who were not employed, about a quarter went on to further education and an undetermined number were not looking for jobs.

Of the 638 employed graduates, 304 or 48 percent "worked at home." This category included both the self-employed (cash earning) people and those who use their skills at home but not for the purpose of earning a livelihood--such as a housewife preparing food. This kind of "nonemployment" use of skills is more likely to occur in the cluster of skills associated with homemaking--food preparation, dressmaking, cosmetology, tailoring, embroidery, and so forth. Of 304 working at home, the number with homemaking skills training was 245, but some of these people certainly also have paid employment.

Among the employed, 449 or about 54 percent of the graduates could specify a definite income; presumably they were in full-time or part-time paid employment. (The survey, unfortunately did not make a distinction between full-time and part-time employment.) The proportion of people actually using their training to earn an income was, however, smaller. Of those who held jobs before training, 38 percent were employed after training in jobs where they could apply their newly earned skills. Of the newly employed, about 60 percent were employed in jobs requiring the use of their training. These statistics, of course, do not necessarily imply that the trainees would not later move to a job where the skills could be utilized or that there was no tertiary benefit of the training, even though the skills were not being used directly.

In summary, the employment effect of the training program, as indicated by the sample survey, is that a little over half of the graduates were holding some sort of full-time or part-time paid employment and less than half of this group were using in their jobs the skills learned in the MTTS.[23]

It is difficult, if not impossible, to judge the extent of the program's service to either the rural areas or the semi-urban population of the provincial and district towns. The location of the schools, as well as a description of the course offerings, indicates that the program's usefulness to rural people depends on the extent to which the towns serve as hubs of communication, transportation, and commercial activity for the surrounding areas. The program is not designed to include courses in improved agricultural and related techniques. Nor does it include such nonagricultural skills as the maintenance and repair of agricultural equipment and rural construction, both of which would create employment opportunities directly in the rural areas.

Although any estimate of return on the approximate investment of US$130 in giving a person skill training in the MTTS program would be highly speculative for reasons explained earlier, it may be pointed out that this amount is less than the national per capita annual income (about US$160 in 1970) and substantially less than the expense of equivalent training time in the vocational schools. The opportunity cost of the trainees' time in this program is also minimal, because the courses are part-time and offered in at least two shifts.

There is also room for improving the cost-efficiency
of the program, by making more intensive use of the
facilities and by using local craftsmen as part-time
instructors. The possibility of producing some salable
items by the schools could also be explored.

General Observations

Effectiveness in Employment Promotion. The MTTS program was intended to promote employment and general
economic welfare in the rural areas. As we have seen,
about one-half of the graduates are gainfully employed
and probably only one-quarter are using the skills for
earning an income. The effectiveness of the program in
promoting employment could be raised if the program were
linked with essential complementary services and the program design were to take into account the regional variations of the economy.

Although the nature of many of the skills taught and
the rural economic condition dictate that many of the
graduates should become self-employed entrepreneurs, no
element of entrepreneurial and managerial training is
included in the program. Neither is the program linked
to any public or private service facility that could offer
such training, or credit, technical supervision, and advice
for small rural enterprises. The Ministry of Education
need not and probably cannot operate all the necessary
follow-up services that would make a program of rural
employment generation a success. But a skill training
program of the ministry could be more effective if it is
conceived within a broader context of an employment and
skill promotion plan and when it is linked with the other
essential elements of the plan.

The program offers a uniform syllabus with a very
limited choice from the standard list of courses for the
whole country. There has been no attempt to discriminate
among the skill and occupational needs of the different
regions with wide economic variations. It has not been
possible for the investigators to compare the popularity,
performance, and results of the program between, for instance, the Central region and the Northeast. It is highly
probable that the employment potential for some of the
technical skills taught in the program would be much
greater in the more advanced Central region than in the
other regions. On the other hand, the occupational
structure and employment opportunities in the provincial
towns, where the schools are mostly located, may not vary
greatly regardless of the economic condition of the
surrounding rural area. The important variable may be
the size of the town rather than the economic condition
of the region. But the question that still arises is that

of the design and content of a program that can benefit
the rural population more directly than the MTTS and
that can address itself more appropriately to different
needs of the several levels of development of rural areas.
One is tempted to conclude that the high but geographically lopsided economic growth of the past decade has
created islands of relative prosperity in the provincial
towns and has generated a demand for various technical
skills, and that the MTTS program is catering to that
demand though only marginally benefiting the rural areas.

Relationship with Indigenous Training. There are no
evidences that the program has been planned to take into
account the already existing, indigenous ways of skill
development. The courses taught to girls and women will
illustrate the point. Many of the women clients of the
program presumably come to it to learn homemaking skills,
although a certain proportion use their training to earn
an income. The low private cost (to the trainee) for
the courses undoubtedly makes the program attractive to
the girls. (This may also be true for the boys.) While
the desirability of teaching girls how to be better homemakers is not disputed, no society is without a traditional mode of preparing its future wives and mothers.
The investigators believe that the program is not cogni-
zant of what existing traditional skill training the MTTS
courses are supplementing, reinforcing, modifying, or
replacing, or what the loss would have been if there were
no MTTS course. One indication of failure to recognize
traditional skill training opportunities is the program's
insistence on using instructors with formal teacher training rather than local craftsmen and skilled workers.

The question of relationship with the traditional
ways of skill development is not confined to homemaking
courses. Not all vocational skills in a society are
taught through organized training programs. A skill
training program, particularly in the rural areas, can
be more effective and efficient if it is designed to take
advantage of the already existing pattern of skill training: to strengthen it, to fill its gaps, and to modify
it when necessary. It is often ethnic, cultural, and
historical factors that determine who can learn and
perform the traditional skills.

Instructional Personnel for Skill Training. Although
the problem of MTTS teacher recruitment seems to have
been eased in a somewhat expensive way, the issue that
has not been resolved is whether the rigid requirements
of a long academic preparation and teacher certification
(as prescribed by Civil Service regulations) are necessary
or even helpful for achieving the objective of skill
training. The unanswered question is whether able practi-
tioners of specific trades in the locality, but without
14 years of formal education, might be used on a part-
time basis to teach their respective trades--possibly after

a brief pedagogical orientation. These people could be
less expensive than a full-time civil servant who must
be offered extra financial inducement to leave Bangkok.
It might well be that such master craftsmen and skilled
workers would make the courses more practice-oriented,
more flexible in content, and more relevant to local needs.

Methodological Aspects. The program has many interesting features from a methodological point of view. Dis-
pensing with a permanent physical structure contributes
to substantial savings in capital cost. The short duration and part-time character of the courses reduce their
opportunity costs for the trainees, who, particularly in
the rural areas, can continue to perform their normal
economic role. The mobility and short duration of the
courses also lend themselves to a greater flexibility
and adaptability in content and instructional method than
would otherwise be possible.

There are other potentialities of the relative
mobility and short duration of the program, although the
MTTS program has not been designed to take advantage of
all these. The courses could become modular units of
accelerated training in specific skills which could be
cumulatively built up and some of the trainees could come
back for higher courses, though the limited skill from
one course would still be useful. These possibilities
suggest that programs of the MTTS genre have great potential for being more effective and efficient for teaching
vocational skills than the predominant pattern of long-
duration, institution-based, and expensive training programs that are often devoid of practical experience in
the skills.

The MTTS program has grown as much out of an endo-
genous educational demand for providing further educational
opportunities to the out-of-school youths as out of the
demand for certain types of skill training. The Ministry
of Education has continued to expand the program apparently
without considering how the program may fit in the total
pattern of skill development in the country and how
various skill programs can complement one another. The
ministry is not, by any means, unique in this respect;
the questions regarding an overall policy and strategy
for middle-level skill development and the complementarity
of various programs need to be asked and resolved for all
skill training activities in the country. We turn next
to some of these questions.

VOCATIONAL SKILL TRAINING SCENE

A variety of vocational and skill development programs are operated by a large number of government and
private agencies. Such programs are found both within

the formal educational system (that is, having grade and
diploma equivalence with the general academic programs)
and outside; they provide training in the same or similar
skills as the MTTS and require an educational background
for entrants from middle to upper elementary level.

The Ministry of Education offers, besides the MTTS,
formal vocational education at the secondary level through
the vocational high schools, short-term vocational courses
in polytechnic schools, and short-term skill training for
adults and youths through mobile centers operated by the
Division of Adult Education. The Department of Labor and
the Department of Community Development, both under the
Ministry of Interior, have in recent years initiated short-
term skill training courses. The Department of Labor
established a skill training center in Bangkok in 1969
and plans to open several regional centers as a part of a
larger plan for industrial skill training and skill upgrading. The Community Development Department now operates
58 centers throughout the country offering vocational and
agricultural training to rural youth, usually through
full-time courses of four to six months. The Ministry of
Defense runs 10 centers offering two- to eight-month
courses in vocational skills for rural people living in
politically "sensitive" areas. There are at least 19
other governmental and paragovernmental organizations,
such as the Prison Department, certain municipalities,
State Railways, and the Post and Telecommunications Department, that operate preservice and inservice training
courses for their own workers and artisans. These latter
organizations had an enrollment of approximately 12,000
in 1968. A new organization set up in the office of the
Prime Minister--the National Youth Promotion Committee--
also plans to start out-of-school vocational training programs in both urban and rural areas. A partial list of
these training programs with entrance requirements of
primary level education or less is given in Table 17.5.

Two Major Programs

Two major skill programs with sizable foreign and
national investment are the Vocational Secondary Schools
under the Ministry of Education and the Skill Development
Program of the Department of Labor. The vocational
school program is one of the largest with a current
enrollment of about 40,000. The recently initiated Labor
Department program is potentially large if its plans are
fulfilled. The two programs represent two contrasting
approaches to intermediate level skill development,
although the stated objective of both programs is similar:
production of employable skilled workers.

TABLE 17.5

Nonagricultural Vocational Programs with Entrance
Requirements of Primary Level Education or Less

Agency	Enrollment	(Year of Data)	Course Duration
1. Adult Education Dept., Ministry of Education	15,309	(1969)	3-6 months
2. Bangkok-Thonburi Municipality, Youth Vocational Training Center	252	(1968)	1-3 years
3. Dept. of Labor, National Skill Development Institute	287	(1968)	6-12 months
4. Accelerated Rural Development Program, Office of the Prime Minister	383	(1968)	6-12 months
5. Vocational Secondary Schools, Ministry of Education	22,756	(1967)	3-6 years
6. Private Institutions	23,926	(1967)	1-12 months
7. Mobile Trade Training Schools, Ministry of Education	12,687	(1967)	5 months

Source: U.S. Operations Mission/Thailand, Education in Thailand,
A Sector Study (Bangkok, January 1971), pp. 39-42 and 51.

As the secondary schools began to produce more graduates than the system of higher education could absorb
during the fifties and early sixties, the less developed
countries sought to solve the problem by adding vocational
training courses in the secondary curriculum. So it was
decided in the First Development Plan, 1961-66, of
Thailand that "a more balanced growth between academic
and vocational stream is needed. Development of vocational
education has thus been rated top priority to meet skilled
manpower requirements."[24] Similarly the Second Development
Plan, 1967-1972, reaffirmed that "the secondary educational
system will be oriented toward satisfying occupational
requirements."[25]

As a result of the policy of promoting secondary
vocational education, the recurrent budget for this field
increased three-fold between 1966 and 1971 and came close

to catching up with the general secondary budget. In 1969,
there were 54 lower vocational schools (grades eight to
ten) and 121 higher vocational schools (grades eleven to
thirteen), 51 of which were combined with lower vocational
schools.

The three-year program of the lower vocational school
and the three years in the upper vocational school are
considered equivalent to general secondary education for
the purpose of entrance into higher-level general education. About one-half of the lower vocational and one-
third (45 percent for girls) of the upper vocational
curriculum is devoted to general education.

For the purpose of financing buildings and equipment
in 14 upper vocational schools (with an approximate 7,000
enrollment) a project costing US$14 million, including a
US$6 million loan (Loan for Improvement of Vocational
Education or LIVE) from the World Bank and additional
technical assistance from U.S. AID, was initiated in 1966.
The main emphasis of the LIVE program, in order to change
student goals from "being higher institution oriented to
immediate industrial employment," is on the following
fields:

1. automotive and diesel mechanics
2. welding and sheet-metal
3. machine shop
4. radio, television and electricity
5. industrial electricity
6. building construction[26]

The Department of Labor has an ambitious plan to
create a national organization that will initiate and
coordinate diverse types of intermediate-level industrial
skill development in the country. A National Council for
Skill Promotion has already been established for this
purpose. The assignments of the Council are:

1. to introduce new techniques for the promotion and
    development of apprenticeship, in-plant, and
    other training programs
2. to develop training standards, schedules, trade
    skill testing and certificate programs
3. to provide occupational information and career
    guidance services
4. to conduct research, develop and establish
    teaching materials, methods, and curricula
5. to train supervisors, instructors and specialists
    for skill promotion and job entry training pro-
    grams
6. to organize a network of Institutes for Skill
    Promotion and Job-entry Training for Industry
7. to utilize, wherever possible, existing training
    facilities or those to be established in the

future under the Ministry of Education and other
agencies that are suitable for the purpose and
that meet the standards of the National Service
by negotiated special arrangements with these
agencies [27]

Despite the broad responsibilities of the Council,
the emphasis so far seems to have been on establishing
institutes for skill development. One is now in operation
near Bangkok and offers courses in industrial skills at
different levels and durations ranging from a few weeks
to one year.
There are plans for opening four regional centers
that would offer training for maintaining and repairing
farm equipment and general construction skills in addition to teaching industrial skills. Progress on other
objectives of the Council has so far been minimal.
Funds totaling about US$6.6 million have been committed
from national and international (UNDP) sources. Technical assistance has been provided by the International
Labour Organisation (ILO) for the first phase of the project, which included the creation of the Council and a
national institute. The proposal for the second phase
includes the four regional centers.
Neither the vocational schools nor the Labor Department Skill Development program for nonagricultural skills
pays special attention to the needs of rural areas, although certain elements of the Labor Department's planned
regional institutes are to be aimed at the rural occupational needs.
Both the vocational schools and the MTTS program of
the Ministry of Education are training programs of relatively limited scope in terms of skills taught and teaching methods used, whereas the Labor Department project
envisages a national skill development program encompassing
a wide range of skills and various means of skill acquisition. Presumably, all of the Ministry of Education programs could be parts of a coordinated national action
anticipated by the Labor Department project. So far,
however, the different operations have developed in separate ways, with different approaches and assumptions regarding middle-level skill development.

Issues Relating to
a Comprehensive Skill Training Policy

Coordination. There is a great deal of overlap and
duplication in the content of the various training programs; one is left with the impression that there is a
lack of coordination among programs, although they are
aimed at achieving somewhat similar objectives. For

instance, auto mechanics courses of different duration and
presumably different levels of complexity are offered by
four agencies of the Ministry of Education, in addition to
courses given by Municipal Vocational Centers, the Department of Labor, and a sizable number of private institutions.
Conceivably, for these courses there could be standard
graded units of instruction with common instructional
materials and testing of achievements, thus improving the
efficiency and effectiveness of all of the courses.

Rural Skill Training. Despite a large variety of
programs, the total effort and resources directed to nonagricultural skill development in the rural areas have
been small. The MTTS is the largest of the programs with
a declared aim of serving the rural areas. The other
notable but smaller activities are those of the Department
of Community Development, Adult Education Division, the
Accelerated Rural Development Program and, in a limited
number of districts, the Ministry of Defense. The courses
in nonagricultural skills in all cases are essentially
replicas of similar courses in the cities with regard to
course content, specialization, and standards. Little or
no attention is paid, in designing courses, to the differences between urban and rural areas and to variations
within and between rural regions in employment structure,
degree of economic specialization, prices and incentives,
ethnic and cultural influences on occupations, and so
forth. It was noted earlier that little cognizance is
taken of the already existing traditional ways of meeting
essential skill needs in the villages. As a result of
these deficiencies, the skill programs, which are supposed
to serve the rural areas, end up at best catering to the
skill demands of the provincial towns and at worst proving
to be inappropriate activities serving nobody's interest.

It is true that providing skill training for the
provincial and district towns, besides being important in
its own right, is indirectly helpful to the rural population because many services and commodities for rural consumption can be economically supplied only from central
locations. But there are also certain goods and services
other than of farm origins that need to be, or can be,
profitably produced in the villages and for which skills
need to be developed. These categories include various
types of rural construction, agricultural processing,
operation and maintenance of farm equipment, crafts demanding multiple handyman skills, and various types of
artisanship for which certain villages offer a natural
advantage. The MTTS program does not cover these skills
and there is no evidence of a concerted effort to teach
them by the other agencies and programs.

Narrow View of Skill Development. A problem illustrated by the MTTS program is that skill programs and
policies are often very narrowly conceived. The programs
typically do not make adequate provisions for diagnosing

the skill needs in the specific socioeconomic context of
an area or for developing and designing the appropriate
content and method for the training program needed for the
specific clientele. The training as a rule does not extend beyond the mechanical skills to include equally important skills in management and entrepreneurship, even
though many of the trainees are expected to be self-
employed. Similarly, the provisions for necessary follow-
up services, such as technical supervision, credit facilities, and job-placement, are generally lacking in the
designs of the skill development programs.

Another aspect of the narrow conceptualization of
skill programs is an implicit assumption that the most
desirable form of skill training takes place through insti-
tutionalized formal courses. Typical manpower forecasting
exercises lend support to this inclination when shortages
in various aggregated skill categories are predicted and
plans are made to meet these shortages by expanding vocational schools. It is well-known that automechanics,
welders, sheet-metal workers, carpenters, and tailors are
being prepared in Thailand and elsewhere through informal
apprenticeship and on-the-job training, but planners of
skill programs rarely consider the possibilities of
exploiting and improving these already existing avenues
and choose the formal route even though the formal vocational schools usually are highly inefficient and expensive.

Resource Allocation. In the absence of an overall
strategy for skill development, there is a tendency for
various national agencies, sometimes several sections of
the same agency, and foreign aid organizations to push,
often successfully, the expansion of their own programs
irrespective of how these programs fit into the total
skill development pattern. A rational weighing of alternative uses of available national and foreign aid resources
does not occur, because of the absence of clearly defined
criteria of investment derived from a skill development
strategy.

Both at the National Economic Development Board (the
national planning agency), and the Department of Technical
and Economic Cooperation (the agency for coordinating
foreign assistance), considerable misgivings were expressed
to the investigators about the rapid expansion of the MTTS
program without adequate evaluation, and valid questions
were raised about the use of resources for the program in
terms of quality of training and the benefits derived by
the individuals or by the rural population at large. These
were necessary questions which should be asked about all
vocational and skill development activities. But the
proper approach to resource allocation and evaluation should
be in terms of a well-defined national policy, clearly
spelled-out strategy, and adequately specified criteria
of evaluation for the entire range of middle-level skill
development programs in the country. It may be parentheti-

cally noted that availability of foreign assistance for a
program is not sufficient justification for launching it,
because even an outright grant has an opportunity cost
for the recipient and invariably leads to tying up both
financial and human resources of the recipient country.

NOTES

1. Materials for this section have been drawn primarily from
a number of unpublished sources including the following: Manpower
Planning Division, National Economic Development Board (NEDB), "Report
of the Working Group on Rural Manpower and Employment," mimeographed
draft (Bangkok, Thailand, February 1971); drafts of sections of the
"Third Five Year Development Plan, 1972-1976" prepared by NEDB staff;
and working papers of the International Labour Organisation (ILO)
Asian Regional Team for Employment Promotion in Bangkok. For a
somewhat dated published source on the Thai economy see T.H. Silcock,
ed., Thailand: Social and Economic Studies in Development (Canberra,
Australia: Australian National University Press, 1967).
    2. In 1963, 16,707 registered firms with less than 10 employees
contributed about 10 percent of total industrial output and employed
about 30 percent of all industrial employees. National Statistical
Office, Report of the 1964 Industrial Census (Bangkok, 1967), Vol. I,
pp. 8-11.
    3. Food and Agriculture Organization, "Indicative World Plan
for Agricultural Development to 1975 and 1985: Asia and the Far
East Provisional Regional Study No. 4," mimeographed (Rome, 1968).
    4. NEDB, "Report of the Working Group," p. 9.
    5. Ibid.
    6. ILO, Asian Regional Team for Employment Promotion.
    7. Thailand, Ministry of Education, National Planning Office.
    8. The administration of the MTTS has been transferred in 1973
to the Division of Adult Education in the Department of General
Education.
    9. Thailand, Ministry of Education, Department of Vocational
Education, Vocational Promotion Division, Mobile Trade Training
Schools and Polytechnic Schools, 1970 Report (Bangkok, 1971).
    10. Alton Straughan and James Murray, "An Evaluation of the
Mobile Trade Training School Project," mimeographed (Bangkok:
United States Operations Mission (USOM)/Thailand, April 1971).
    11. Thailand, Vocational Promotion Division, op. cit., p. 38.
    12. National Research Council, Social Science Research Division,
"Evaluation of the Mobile Trade Training Units and the Polytechnic
Schools Project," mimeographed (Bangkok, 1971).
    13. Actual numbers of enrollment in the total MTTS program were
unavailable. The estimates of enrollment for 1971 and 1972 were made
by the writer by extrapolating actual enrollment in the first session
of 1971 in 13 MTTSs.
    14. The order was determined on the basis of enrollment in the
courses in 13 MTTSs during the first session of 1971.
    15. National Research Council, Social Science Research Division,
op. cit.

16. While the regular secondary general or vocational teacher salary is B1,000-1,200 per month, an MTTS teacher usually earns B2,100-2,500 per month. In addition, he usually gets a free residential accommodation. (A skilled industrial worker earns B2,500-3,000 per month.)

17. One may also raise the parallel question of social and private costs. The direct private cost is a tuition fee of 40 to 100 bahts for different subjects per course. The opportunity cost to trainees for lost time is considered negligible because the courses are offered on a part-time basis and trainees have the choice of two shifts in a day.

18. A fee ranging from 40 to 100 bahts per course is charged each trainee.

19. Straughan and Murray, op. cit., pp. 20-21.

20. The vehicles are used in many ways--to transport locally purchased consumable items, to transport equipment and materials from the central warehouse in Bangkok, to move the school from one location to another, and occasionally to provide a means of transportation for the school personnel.

21. T.M. Yusufu, "Education, Manpower and Employment in Thailand: A Preliminary Assessment," mimeographed (Bangkok: ILO, Asian Regional Team for Employment Promotion, June 1970), p. 38. Costs were estimated for 1967.

22. The report does not state how many graduates of the eight schools were not contacted in the survey. The definition of employment, although not explicitly stated, appears to have included all income earning activities, part-time and full-time, at home and in outside establishments. Also no breakdown for boys and girls was reported.

23. National Research Council, Social Science Research Division, op. cit.

24. NEDB, "Evaluation of the First Six-Year Plan, 1961-1966," mimeographed (Bangkok, 1967), p. 102.

25. NEDB, "The Second Economic and Social Development Plan, 1967- 1972," mimeographed (Bangkok, n.d.), Chapter XVI, para. 12.

26. Yusufu, op. cit., p. 39.

27. ILO Regional Office, Bangkok.

Bangkok, Thailand, 312,618,623, 626,629,631,632,643
Bangladesh, 578
Comilla Project, 373,579
Barranquilla, Colombia, 6,14,17
Benefit-cost ratio: IRRI, 583-86; SENA, 428-31; see also Costs and financing
Bernal-Alarcón, Hernando, 38,39
Bhopal, India, 443
Bobo-Dioulasso, Upper Volta, 338
Bogotá, Colombia, 6,14,17,28,52, 397,416
Bombay, India, 435,443,473,479
Bowles, Samuel, 63,68,99
Boyacá, Colombia, 38
Brumberg, Stephan F., 397
Buitrago, Rosa Esther, 1
Burma, 293

Cali, Colombia, 6,14,17
Callaway, Archibald, 545,547
Cambodia, 283
Campaigns, educational: ACPO, 25-7; Literacy Campaign, Cuba, 66,71-2; Literacy Campaign, Kenya, 207-9; mass educational campaign, Tanzania, 596-99
Canada, 134
Canadian Universities Service Overseas, 165
Castañon-Pasquel, José, 1,395
Castro, Fidel, 64-105 passim
Ceylon, 253; see also Sri Lanka
Christol, J., 338
Chulalongkorn, King of Thailand, 297
City University of New York, Queens College, 61
Colombia: Accion Comunal, 31,32; ACPO, 1-60,401; Antioquia department, 420; Artesanias de Colombia, 401; Association of Lenders, 31; Atlantico department, 420; Bolivar department, 420; Caja Agraria, 31,401,411; Cartagena region, 417; Editorial Andes, 6,8-22; Escuelas radiofonicas, 8-12,19,20,33,38, 43; Federacion de Cafetoros, 31, 401; general, 1-3, 396-97; Instituto Colombiano Agropecuaria, 401,411,412,413,425,429, 430; Instituto Colombiano para

Reforma Agraria, 401,411,412, 413; literacy rates, 2; Migrant Workers Program, 414; Ministry of Agriculture, 397, 401; Ministry of Education, 18, 52,400,402; Ministry of Health, 401; Ministry of Labor, 400,401, 414; National Committee on Rural Migrant Workers, 414; National Planning Office, 400; Programa Integrado de Nutricion Aplicada, 401; Promocion Profesional Popular-Rural, PPP-R, 398-432; SENA, 397-432
Colombo, Sri Lanka, 266-267,270, 276
Community development: Cuba, schools in the countryside, 98; Cuba, schools to the countryside, 82,98; India, RIP, 456-58; Kenya, NYS project, 200-1; Korea, 491; Korea, ORD, 499-501, 506-7; Sri Lanka, Shramadana Movement, 285-89
Condinamaica, Colombia, 38
Coombs, Philip H., 617
Cooperatives: Afghanistan, 370-76; Indonesia, 121; Korea, 491-505,513,514; Tanzania, Cooperative education, 593-615; Tanzania, Cooperative Movement, 589-92
Coordination of programs: ACPO, 31-3; Indonesia, Jombang project, 122-25; IRRI, 586-87; Jamaica, 151-53; 162-64; Kenya, 209-14; Korea, ORD, 494,531-532; Mali, 244-45; PACCA, 376-77; SENA, 399-400,429-30; Sri Lanka, 282-84; Thailand Functional Literacy Program, 314-15; Thailand, Vocational Programs, 643-44; Upper Volta, RECs, 350-56
Correspondence education: Agri-Service-Afrique courses, 351; Jamaica, 142-43; Kenya Correspondence Course Unit, 202-3; Kenya Literacy Program, 208; Tanzania Cooperative Education system, 600-5
Costs and financing: ACPO, 51-4; Cuba, schools in the countryside, 92-4; 102,106;

64,72-3,74,90,95,102,105;
Padrino system, 68-9; Partido
Comunista de Cuba, PCC, 74,76;
Peer group teaching, 68; Perez
Senior High School, 85; prerevolutionary Cuba, 61-62;
school in the countryside, 67,
86-94; school to the countryside, 67,72-86; secondary school
enrollment, 61-2,104; Seguidares
dé Camilo y Ché, 69; Sindicato
Nacional de Trabajadores de la
Educación y Cultura, CNC, 74;
Union of Communist Youth, UJC,
67,71,76

Dakar, Senegal, 218
Day care program: Cuba, 67
Deble, I., 335
Decentralization: ACPO, 30-33;
Jamaica YDA, 172
Dehesa, Miguel, 77,97
Delhi, India, 439,473,481
Denmark, 383,595
Deoband, India, 435
de Wilde, John C., 434,557
Dhamsakdimontri, Chao Phrya, 299
Diaz, Rafael, 397
Diejomaoh, Victor P., 544
Dougabougou, 219
Downey, mildew disease, 382
Dubell, Folke E., 613,641
Dulverton Trust, 205

East African School of Coopera-
tion, 594
East Pakistan. See Bangladesh
Editorial Andes: Biblioteca del
Campesino, 18,22,47; Cartillas,
18-19; see also ACPO; El
Campesino
Educación permanente. See Cuba
L'Education Rurale et la Diffusion
des Nouvelles Techniques Agri-
coles en Haute Volta, 335
Egerton, Kenya, 189
Ekala, Sri Lanka, 274
El Campesino, 11,18,19-22,27,28,
38,43,47,48; see also ACPO
Employment: Jamaica, 137; Jom-
bang, Indonesia, 114-15; Kenya,
176; Mali, 218-19; Sri Lanka,
250-52; Thailand, 295-96;
Upper Volta, 336-37.

England, 383
Enquesta Sobre Radiodifusion
Entre Los Campesinos, 16
Entrepreneurial development:
India, 436,471-82; Nigeria,
547-67
Equivalency programs: Jamaica,
142-43; Jamaica Youth Camps,
159-60; Kenya, 184-85, 204-6;
Thailand, 306,321-29; Upper
Volta, RECs, 338-62
Escuela radiofonicas, see ACPO
Ethiopia, 135
European Development Fund, FED,
227,230,239,241,337,341,344,
353,359
European Economic Community, 341
Evaluation, techniques and
problems: ACPO, 28-31; India,
RIP program, 459-61; Jamaica
Youth Camps, 160-61; Thailand
Literacy Program, 316-17

Facilities for Educational
Programs: India, RIP, 465-66;
India, SISI, 451; Jamaica,
Youth Centers, 161; Jombang,
Indonesia, 122; Kenya, NYS
program, 200; Mali, 226,228,
235,236; Nigeria, BATC, 551;
Nigeria, IDC, 561; schools in
the countryside, 90-92,102;
SENA, 400; Upper Volta, REC,
344-45
Family Life Education, Thailand,
307-20
Farako-Ba, Upper Volta, 340,342
Farmer Education: Korea, ORD,
497,507-10,521-29; Sri Lanka,
261,534; see also program
headings
Faust, Gerald, 559,560
Figueroa, Max, 64,65,88
Florida, 132
Food and Agriculture Organization (FAO), 1,165,341,365,366,
368,377,382,397
Ford Foundation, 437,550,551,
554,558,559,570
Formal education: agricultural,
511-12; Colombia rural areas,
399; combined with nonformal,
72-94; 100-3; dropouts from
112,115,182-183,223; Jamaica,

Department of Agriculture, 126;
Department of Cooperatives, 126;
Department of Health, 126;
Department of Manpower and
Internal Affairs, 113; Depart-
ment of Religion, 126; Depart-
ment of Transmigration, 126;
economic development, 111-13;
educational system, 115-16,
118-20; formal school system,
112-13; Inland Fisheries De-
partment, 121,126; Jombang
Youth Education Project,111-30;
Ministry of Agriculture, 112;
Ministry of Education and
Culture, 112,113,122,125;
Ministry of Religious Affairs,
112; Office of Educational
Development (BPP), 112; political upheaval, 116-18;
Pramuka, 113,121,123; Secondary Teacher Training College,
114,123;
Industrial extension service.
See India.
Informal education: definition
177; Thailand, 297-98,638;
see also Indigenous education
systems
Institut Africain pour le
Developpement Economique et
Social, 351;
L'Institut d'Etude du Developpement Economique et Social,
University of Paris, 335,337,
345,346,350,351,352,355,356,
358,360,361
Instructional materials and technology: ACPO, Colombia,
18-23; FLP, Mali, 231-32;
FLP, Thailand, 311; IRRI, 576;
literacy programme, Jamaica,
144; ORD, 501-3,597-99; schools
in the countryside, 102; SENA,
409-11; SISI, 451-52
Integration of programs: ACPO,
27-28, see also PACCA.
International Bank for Reconstruction and Development,
see World Bank.
International Council for Educational Development (ICED), 1,
34,37,42,111,131,175,217,293,
335,350,360,364,371,381,384,386,

395,397,409-34 passim,486,494,
500-27 passim,544,555,576,580,
583,589,612,626,631,633
International Labour Office, 146,
165,201,643
International Rice Research
Institute, 495, see also
Philippines
Isaacs, Fernando, 1
Ivory Coast, 336

Jaipur, Rajasthan State, India,
435
Jakarta, Indonesia, 116
Jamaica: agricultural development, 138-39; Boys' Brigade,
150,160; Boy Scouts, 150,161
Boys' Town organization, 147,
150; Bracco Training Center, 164;
Cape Clear, 155,156,157,164;
Chestervale Camp, 155,156,157,
164; Christiana Land Authority,
155,156,157; Citizen's Colleges,
152; Cobbla Camp, 155,156,157;
Community Training Center, 160;
Craft Development Agency, 154;
economic development, 135-39;
emigration, 137-38; formal
education system, 139-41,171;
Girls' Brigades, 150; Girl
Guides, 150; Girls' Town, 150;
Jamaica College of Arts, Science,
and Technology, 139; Jamaican
Certificate of Education, 139,
142,143,170,171; Jamaican
Federation of Women, 144,149;
Jamaican Labour party, 131;
Jamaica School of Agriculture,
139,149; Jamaica School of
Nursing, 139; Kenilworth, 155,
156,157,164; Literacy Program,
140-44; Lluida Vale, 155,156,
157,164; Ministry of Agriculture,
148,153,154; Ministry of Education, 131, 142,143,147,149,153,
168,170,171; Ministry of Health,
153; Ministry of Housing and
Welfare, 153; Ministry of Labour
and National Insurance, 145,
153, 162,163,171; Ministry of
Youth and Community Development,
144,151,153,162; National Council
of Jamaican Organizations,152;
National Industrial Training

Board, 145; National Literacy
Board, 172; National Volunteer
Organization, 152; National
Youth Service, 151; nonformal
education, 141-51, 171; Opera-
tion Friendship, 147; outside
influences, 134-35; People's
National Party, 131; plantation
system and slavery, 132-34;
Resource Development Unit, 164,
172; Rustafarian Movement , 135;
Social Development Commission,
147,149,150,152,153,162,163,
164,172; Sports Development
Agency, 154; Sugar Industry
Labour Welfare Board, 144,149,
150; YMCA, 144,150; Youth Camps,
153-161; Youth Community
Training Centers, 161, 167,
172; Youth Development Agency,
YDA, 150,153,160,161-66, 172;
YWCA, 150
Japan, 446
Jombang, Indonesia. See Indonesia
Jos, Nigeria, 545,546

Kabul, Afghanistan, 367,369,370,
376,382
Kabul University, 385
Kaduna, Nigeria, 545-549 passim
Kahl, Joseph, 82
Kakinada, India, 473
Kamboince, Upper Volta, 340,342
Kano, Nigeria, 544,545,546,557
Karima, Kenya, 191
Kati, Mali, 233
Katibougou, Mali, 244
Kenya: Adult Studies Center, 203;
Agricultural colleges, 186;
Agriculture Department, 199;
Agricultural Society of Kenya,
186,187; Alliance High School,
212; Board of Adult Education,
210-11; Boy Scouts, 184,185;
Busia district, 190; Capricorn
African Society, 203; Certi-
ficate of Primary Education,
179,180,206; Christian Indus-
trial Training Centres, 185;
clienteles, 205,206,214;
Correspondence Course Unit,
202-3; Correspondence courses,
185; Development Plans, 178,179;

economic development, 175-76;
East African Certificate of
Education, 181; Farmer and
Rural Training Centres, 185,199,
209; formal education system,
177-82; 4-K Clubs, 184,185,187-
89; general, 135,175-77; Girl
Guides, 184,185; Harambee
Schools, 183; Homecraft
Training Centres, 209; Insti-
tute of Adult Studies, Univer-
sity of Nairobi,201-4; Insti-
tute of Education, 202,206;
Jeanes School, 186,206;
Kakamega district, 175; Kenya
National Council of Social
Services, 210,213-14; Kenya
Polytechnic, 181-82,201; Kenya
provincial administrative
system, 190; Kenya Red Cross
Society, 184; Kenya Rural Youth
Program, 188; Kenya UN Student
Association, 213; Kenya Volun-
tary Development Association,
185; Kericho district, 205;
Kiambu district, 175; Kikuyu
district, 178,203,212; Kisinyaga
district, 178; Maendeleo ya
Wanawake, 185,209; Mau Mau
Emergency, 204,212; Ministry of
Agriculture and Animal Husbandry,
188; Ministry of Co-operatives
and Social Services, 190,205,206,
207; Ministry of Education, 202,
206-10 passim; Ministry of Labour,
205; Mombasa Polytechnic, 181;
Murang'a district, 178; National
Christian Council of Kenya, 189,
190,195,205,210,211,212-13,214;
National Development Plan, 178,
196; National Literacy Campaign,
207-9; National Youth Service,
185,189,196,197,201,204,206,214;
National Youth Service Act, 197;
nonformal programs, 184-215;
Ominde Commission of Inquiry,
177; Outward Bound Trust, 184;
Rift Valley, 191,192; Saint
John's Ambulance, 184; Special
Rural Development Project, 190;
Starehe Boys' Centre, 204;
Teachers' Training Colleges, 186;
Training Institute for Exten-
sion Workers, Embu, 187; Veteri-

44, 358-59; Vocational Train-
ing Development Institute, 146;
Voluntary, 8,23,55,86,164-65,266;
Women's movement, 239; Youth
Camps and Centres, 163
Philippines, 495,571,572,574,
576-77; College of Agriculture,
University of the Philippines,
170; Green Revolution, 569-70;
IRRI, 569-87; Philippines Agri-
cultural Productivity Com-
mission, 572
Plan Christol, see Upper Volta
Prevocational education: prevoca-
tional studies program, Sri
Lanka, 255
Primary education: Indonesia,
112,123,129; Kenya, 178-79;
Mali, 221-22,246; Thailand,
298-99,301,623; Upper Volta,
RECs. 338-62.
Primrose, Sister V., 40
Puryear, Jeffrey, 397

Ramos, Eduardo, 1
Ranchi, India, 443
Resources for education: Cuba,
schools in the countryside,
92-4; Indonesia, Jombang
Project, 120,125-26; Jamaica,
Youth Development Agency,
164-66; Sri Lanka, 274-75;
Upper Volta, RECs, 352-54
Rift Valley, Kenya, 191,192
Robinson, H. E., 559
Rockefeller Foundation, 570
Rono Arap, 205
Ruiz, Humberto, 397
Rural development: Sri Lanka,
280-82; Upper Volta, 337,
see also specific program
headings
Ruralization of schools
Mali, 224-26; Upper Volta,
354-60

Salcedo, Monseñor José Joaquín, 3
Sanakoraba, Mali, 239
Samuru, Nigeria, 561
Sangara, Mali, 242
Sanhachawee, Aree, 299
Santa Marta, Colombia, 417
Santardu, Colombia, 42
Santiago, Cuba, 62

Save the Children Fund, 205
Secondary education: Cuba,
schools in the countryside,
86-94, 100-3; Cuba, schools to
the countryside, 72-86,100-3;
Indonesia, Jombang, 129;
Kenya, 180-82; Thailand, 300-1,
303; Thailand, vocational
education high schools, 540;
Thailand, vocational programs,
639-42
Segou, Mali, 219,234,235,
Self-help movement: Indonesia,
Jombang Project, 118; Kenya,
176,190; Sri Lanka, 280-82
Seoul, Korea, 521
Side-Line Training, see Republic
of Korea
Singh, Harkishan, 434
Skapski, Adam S., 550
Skill training: India, 453-71;
Jamaica, 145-47,149-50; Kenya,
185; Nigeria, 544-67; SENA,
PPP-R, 397-432; Sri Lanka,
268-69,270-78
Small-scale Industry: India,
Small-scale Industry Program,
435-53,467-68; India, RIP pro-
gram, 453-71; Nigeria, 544-47;
Nigeria, IDC program, 547-50;
Nigeria, VICs, 550-59; Small In-
dustry Credit Scheme, 559-64
South Vietnam, 577
Soy, Kenya, 192
Spain, 132,472
Sports and recreation: Jamaica,
Youth Centers/Youth Clubs, 161-
63; Mali, 233-36, see also Cuba
Sri Lanka
Apprenticeship system, 270-71;
Brothers of Christian Schools
(Ceylon) Trust, 271; Department
of Agrarian Services, 261;
Department of Agriculture,
260,261,262; Department of
Health, 266,268; Department of
Labor, Vocational Training
Branch, 270; Department of
Rural Development, 268,280,282,
291; Department of Small Indus-
tries, 268,269,291; Divisional
Development Council, 279;
Diyagala Boys' Town, 259, 271-
75,277; economic development,

249-50; formal education, 252-59; general, 249-52; General Certificate of Education, Ordinary Level, 250,266,268,270, 271; Good Shepherd Congregation, 276; Hardy Institute, 271; Katubedda Technical College, 271; Land Commissioner's Department, 262; Lanka Jatika Sarvodaya Shramadana Sangamaya (Sarvodaya Movement), 259,285-89,291; Mahaveli Scheme, 578; Mala Hewessa Scheme, 263-64; Ministry of Agriculture, 279; Ministry of Education, 249,255, 257,258,279; Ministry of Planning and Employment, 278,279, 283; Ministry of Public Administration, Local Government, Home Affairs, and Justice, 280; Ministry of Small Industries, 279; Muther Iyan Kaddu Scheme, 263; National Certificate of General Education, 257; National Youth Service Council, 282-84, 291; Navajeevanam, 275,276-77; Practical Farm Schools, 261; prevocational studies, 255-59, 290; Regional Development Division, 278,279; Rural Development Societies, 291,280-82; School of Agriculture, 262; Settlement schemes, 262-64, 290; Sri Lanka Mahila Samiti, 259,265-68; Sri Lanka Technical Institute Project, 271; Walawe scheme, 578; Young Farmers Clubs, 260-62, 290; Yahapeth Endera Farm, 275, 276

Staffing, see Personnel
Stepanek, J. E., 468
Surabaya, Indonesia, 116
"Strategies of Development," 226
Sudan, 572
Surasthani, Thailand, 319
Suwon, Korea, 494,495,503,511
Sweden, 383,595
Swedish International Development Authority, SIDA, 365,366,368, 377,378,385,386

Tanzania: Arusha Declaration, 594; benefits of Cooperative Education, 611-13; Cooperative College, 589,590,595,599, 605-9,613,614; Cooperative Education Centres, 589,590,592, 595-615; Cooperative Education Plan, 605; Cooperative Union of Tanganyika, 589,590,597,615; Development Plan, 604,611; Dodoma plateau, 603,612; general, 592; Kilimanjaro area, 593,603; Marketing Boards, 615; mass media, 596-99; Ministry of Agriculture, Food, and Cooperatives, 589, 590; Moshi, 590,594,608-13 passim; National Agricultural Products Board, 593; Tanzanian African National Union, TANU, 594-95; Ujamaa, 597,601; West Lake area, 593

Teachers: Cuba, 63-4,68,98; Cuba, schools to the countryside, 103-5; Indonesia Jombang Project, 125; Mali, 225; Thailand, 300-3; Thailand, FLP, 311-13,318; Upper Volta, 340, 342-43

Thailand, 577; Accelerated Rural Development Program, ARD, 622, 644; Amphur district, 626; Bangkok Polytechnic School, 629; Bangkok Technical College, 629; Bangkok Technical School, 630; Bangkok-Thonburi area, 294,619; Bureau of Universities, 307; Changwat Chumphon, 624,626; Comprehensive Rural Development Package Program, COMPAC, 622; community development,640,644; Department of Elementary and Adult Education, 301; Department of Labor, 307; Department of Technical and Economic Cooperation, 645; Division of Adult Education, 293,304,305,307,309, 312,316,318,321-22,323,324,330, 640,644; economic development, 618-20; equivalency program, 321-29; Family Life Education, 307-20; formal education, 297-304; functional literacy, 307-

20; general, 293-96,617-23;
Ministry of Agriculture, 310;
Ministry of Defense, 640,644;
Ministry of Education, 293,298,
301,304,307,617,625,637,639,640,
643,644; Ministry of Interior,
293,298,310,640,644; Ministry of
Public Health, 310; National
Committee on Adult Education,
306; National Committee on
Nonformal Education, 306;
National Council for Skill Pro-
motion, 642-43; National Econo-
mic Development Board, 620,645;
National Research Council, 633,
635; National Youth Promotion
Committee, 640; nonformal pro-
grams, 304-7; Office of the
Prime Minister, 298; Post and
Telecommunications Department,
640; Prison Department, 640;
Second Educational Plan, 305;
Skill Development Program, 640,
643; Small Industries Service
Institute, 619; Third Educational
Plan, 305,326; Vocational
Promotion Division, 624-35 passim
Training Manual in Rice Produc-
tion, 576
Tran, L. T. N., 35
Turner, F. L., 559

Ubolrajchathani, Thailand, 312
Uganda, 176
United Kingdom, 135,139,186,595
United Nations, 165,172,239
United Nations Children's Fund,
111,165,226,239,293,341
United Nations Development Pro-
gram, 165,228,643
United Nations Educational,
Scientific, and Cultural
Organization, 18,73,165,226,
228,233,237,309,312,337,366,
376,384
UNESCO Addis Ababa Conference,
337
UNESCO Round Table of Special-
ists on Out-of-School Educa-
tion Programmes in Sub-
Saharan Africa, 226
United Nations Industrial Devel-
opment Organization, 480

United States, 132,134,135,148,
186,309,472,517,561,572,597,
618,623,629,633
U.S. Agency for International
Development, 200,501,502,517,
549,561,624,625,633,642
U.S. Operations Mission to
Thailand, 310
U.S. Peace Corps, 165
University of California,
School of Journalism, Los
Angeles, 1
University of Cambridge, 139
University of Chicago, 397
University of East Africa, 182
University of Lagos, 544
University of London, 139
University of Nairobi, 175,182,
201,203
Upper Volta: general, 335-38;
Ministry of Agriculture, 337;
Ministry of Education, 338,
356,358,359; Ministry of
Health, 342; Ministry of Plan-
ning, 342,359; Plan Christol,
338-39; Regional Development
Organization, 337,345,352,355,
356,358,359,360; Rural Educa-
tion Centers, RECs, 335-62;
Young Farmer Training Centers,
359

Vellore, India, 473
Vocational education and training:
Indonesia Jombang project, 113;
Jamaica Industrial Training
Centers, 145-47,171; Jamaica
Youth Camps, 158-59; Kenya NYS,
199; Kenya VPs, 189-97; Kenya
Youth Centres, 204-6; SENA,
397-423; Sri Lanka Mobile Skill
Training Centres, 270-71; Sri
Lanka Prevocational Studies
Program, 255-59; Thailand MTTS,
617-47; Thailand Vocational
Training Program, 639-43
Voluntary organizations, 150,152,
164-65
Vorapipatana, Kowit, 293
Voravarn, Kasama, 293

Welikala, G.H.F., 249
West German Volunteer Program, 165
Wijemanne, E.F., 249

MANZOOR AHMED is Associate Director of Educational Strategy Studies at the International Council for Educational Development (ICED), Essex, Connecticut, U.S.A. He previously taught for several years at the Institute of Education and Research, University of Dacca, Bangladesh and served briefly as the Chief of the Educational Reforms Unit of the Ministry of Education in Pakistan.

Dr. Ahmed was one of the principal researchers of the ICED non-formal education studies directed by Philip H. Coombs and sponsored by the World Bank and the United Nations Children's Fund. He is the co-author of two books emanating from these studies--New Paths to Learning for Rural Children and Youth and Attacking Rural Poverty-- How Nonformal Education Can Help.

Dr. Ahmed holds a B.A. from the American University of Beirut, M.Ed., from the University of Dacca, Ed.D. from the University of Northern Colorado, and has done postgraduate work at the Woodrow Wilson School of Public and International Affairs, Princeton University.

PHILIP H. COOMBS is Vice Chairman and Director of Educational Strategy Studies of the International Council for Educational Development (ICED). His previous positions include: Founding-Director of the International Institute for Educational Planning (IIEP) in Paris; Assistant Secretary of State for International Educational and Cultural Affairs in the Kennedy Administration; Program Director for Education in the Ford Foundation and Secretary of the Fund for Advancement of Education. He has served as consultant to several developing countries as well as the World Bank, UNESCO, UNICEF, and the FAO. He also served recently as a governor of the Institute of Development Studies in Sussex, England.

In his present capacity Mr. Coombs directed two major ICED studies of nonformal education for rural development commissioned by the World Bank and UNICEF, and was senior author of three resulting reports: New Paths to Learning, Attacking Rural Poverty, and New Educational Strategies. He is the author of several other works including The World Educational Crisis and (with Jacques Hallak) Managing Educational Costs.

Mr. Coombs attended Amherst College and did graduate work in economics at the University of Chicago and the Brookings Institution. He then served on the economics faculty at Williams College and at Amherst. More recently he has been a visiting professor at Harvard and Yale.

RELATED TITLES
Published by
Praeger Special Studies

COMPARATIVE HIGHER EDUCATION ABROAD:
Bibliography and Analysis
          edited by
          Philip G. Altbach

THE ECONOMICS OF NONFORMAL EDUCATION:
Resources, Costs, and Benefits
          Manzoor Ahmed

HIGHER EDUCATION IN DEVELOPING NATIONS:
A Selected Bibliography, 1969-1974
          Philip G. Altbach
          David H. Kelly

HIGHER EDUCATION AND SOCIAL CHANGE:
Promising Experiments in Developing Countries,
Volume 1:   Reports
          Kenneth W. Thompson
          Barbara R. Fogel

HIGHER EDUCATION AND SOCIAL CHANGE:
Promising Experiments in Developing Countries,
Volume 2:   Case Studies
          edited by
          Kenneth W. Thompson
          Barbara R. Fogel
          Helen E. Danner

INSTRUCTIONAL TECHNOLOGY IN DEVELOPING COUNTRIES:
Decision-Making Processes in Education
          Stuart Wells

METHODOLOGY FOR PLANNING TECHNICAL EDUCATION:
With a Case Study of Polytechnics in Bangladesh
          Jozef M. Ritzen
          Judith B. Balderston